ZAGAT®

New York City
Restaurants
2011

EDITORS
Curt Gathje and Carol Diuguid
COORDINATOR
Larry Cohn

Published and distributed by
Zagat Survey, LLC
4 Columbus Circle
New York, NY 10019
T: 212.977.6000
E: newyork@zagat.com
www.zagat.com

ACKNOWLEDGMENTS

We thank Jason Briker, Caren Weiner Campbell, Phil Carlucci, Leigh Crandall, Mikola De Roo, Randi Gollin, Lynn Hazlewood, Carolyn Koo, Bernard Onken, Steven Shukow, Kelly Stewart and Miranda Van Gelder, as well as the following members of our staff: Josh Rogers (senior associate editor), Danielle Borovoy (editorial assistant), Brian Albert, Sean Beachell, Maryanne Bertollo, Jane Chang, Sandy Cheng, Reni Chin, Bill Corsello, Caitlin Eichelberger, Alison Flick, Jeff Freier, Michelle Golden, Matthew Hamm, Justin Hartung, Karen Hudes, Cynthia Kilian, Natalie Lebert, Mike Liao, James Mulcahy, Becky Ruthenburg, Jacqueline Wasilczyk, Art Yaghci, Yoji Yamaguchi, Sharon Yates, Anna Zappia and Kyle Zolner.

This guide is based on public opinion surveys of regular restaurant-goers like you. The ratings reflect the average scores given by the survey participants who voted on each establishment. The text is based on quotes from, or paraphrasings of, the surveyors' comments. Phone numbers, addresses and other factual data were correct to the best of our knowledge when published in this guide.

JOIN IN: To improve this guide, **ZAGAT.com** or any other aspect of our performance, we need your comments. Just contact us at **nina-tim@zagat.com.** We also invite you to vote at **ZAGAT.com** – do so and you'll receive a choice of rewards.

© 2010 Zagat Survey, LLC
ISBN-13: 978-1-60478-306-3
ISBN-10: 1-60478-306-0
Printed in the
United States of America

Contents

Ratings & Symbols

Zagat Top Spot	Name	Symbols	Cuisine	Zagat Ratings

Zagat Ratings — FOOD | DECOR | SERVICE | COST

Area, Address & Contact

🅉 **Tim & Nina's** ◑ *Deli*   ▽ 23 | 9 | 13 | $15

W 50s | 4 Columbus Circle (8th Ave.) | 212-977-6000 | www.zagat.com

Review, surveyor comments in quotes

Nina's grandmother's "hobo stew" and Tim's mother's unfrozen casserole "à la cheap" make for "endless lines" at this "dismal dive" deep down in the Columbus Circle IRT station; service is about "what you'd expect from the MTA", and the tableware is of the "Dixie Cup" and "plastic utensils" variety.

Ratings

Food, Decor and **Service** are rated on the Zagat 0 to 30 scale.

0	–	9	poor to fair
10	–	15	fair to good
16	–	19	good to very good
20	–	25	very good to excellent
26	–	30	extraordinary to perfection

▽   low response | less reliable

Cost

Our surveyors' estimated price of a dinner with one drink and tip. Lunch is usually 25 to 30% less. For unrated **newcomers** or **write-ins,** the price range is shown as follows:

I	$25 and below	E	$41 to $65
M	$26 to $40	VE	$66 or above

Symbols

🅉   highest ratings, popularity and importance
◑   serves after 11 PM
🆂   closed on Sunday
🅼   closed on Monday
⊄   no credit cards accepted

Maps

Index maps show restaurants with the highest Food ratings in those areas.

About This Survey

- 2,115 restaurants rated and reviewed by 40,569 respondents
- 123 notable openings, 90 closings
- Meals out per week per surveyor: 3.0 (vs. 3.3 pre-recession)
- Average meal cost: $41.76 (down slightly from 2010's $41.81)
- Average meal cost at 20 most expensive restaurants: $154.82
- Winners: **Le Bernardin** (Food), **Asiate** (Decor), **Per Se** (Service), all rated 29 out of 30; **Gramercy Tavern** (Most Popular)
- No. 1 newcomer for Food: **Maialino** at 25

SURVEYOR STATS: Compared to six months ago, 27% are eating out less, 11% say more . . . Service is top complaint of 60% . . . Noise and crowds irked 33% pre-recession but only 23% this year . . . 36% avoid cash-only eateries . . . 61% think food should be locally sourced, organic or sustainably raised . . . 49% oppose a tax on sugary drinks, 44% approve . . . 26% say male diners are treated better, 9% say females, 65% say no difference . . . Celeb chefs: 29% in favor, 26% against . . . Average tip: 19.1% . . . One out of 11 use smartphones to photograph meals . . . Favorite cuisines: Italian (30%), French (15%), American (13%), Japanese (12%) . . . On 30-pt. scale, NYC rates 28 for culinary diversity, 24 for creativity, 17 for hospitality, 14 for table availability

NEW **NOTABLE DEVELOPMENTS:**

ABCs: NYC's Health Dept. adopted a letter-grade system requiring posting of inspection results (83% of surveyors approve); of the first 250 restaurants inspected, just over 48% earned A's, 31% B's, 12% C's and 8% were temporarily closed

BROOKLYN: No. 1 for BBQ (**Fette Sau**); Chinese (**Pacificana**); Deli (**Mile End**); Middle Eastern (**Tanoreen**); Pizza (**Di Fara**); Southern (**Egg**); Steak (**Peter Luger**); Turkish (**Taci's Beyti**)

NEWLY HOT NABES: Lincoln Center (**Atlantic Grill, Ed's Chowder House, Lincoln,** plus an upcoming Daniel Boulud venue and a **Café des Artistes** successor); NoLita area (**Kenmare, Travertine, Osteria Morini*, J&S Food Hall***); Madison Park area (**The Breslin, Eataly, Hurricane Club, SD26, Hill Country Chicken*, Millesime***) (*=to come)

BIG NAME OPENINGS: Batali-Bastianich (**Eataly**); Bloomfield (**The Breslin**); Chang (**Má Pêche**); Colicchio (**Colicchio & Sons**); Conant (**Faustina**); English (**Ça Va, Plaza Food Hall**); McNally (**Pulino's**); Meyer (**Maialino,** more **Shake Shack**s); Vongerichten (**ABC Kitchen, The Mark**); Zakarian (**Lambs Club**)

TRENDS: Korean fried chicken (new **Bon Chon Chicken** branches, **Kyochon**); Canadian touches (**Mile End, M. Wells**); sandwiches (**Meatball Shop, Mile End, No. 7 Sub, Saltie, Salumè, Tartinery, This Little Piggy, Torrisi Italian Specialties**)

TOUGH NEW TICKETS: The Breslin, The Lion, Torrisi

New York, NY
October 6, 2010

Nina and Tim

Nina and Tim Zagat

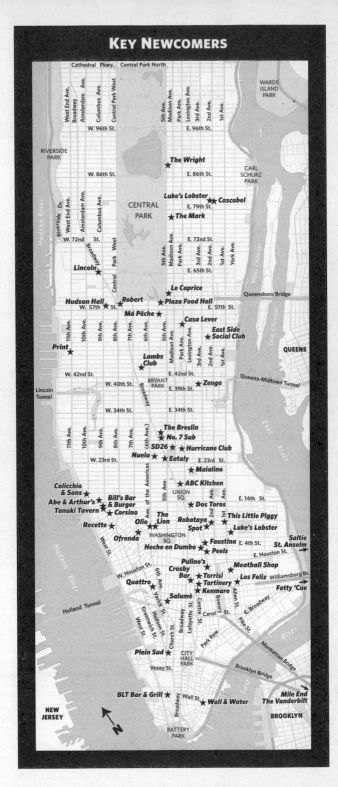

KEY NEWCOMERS

The Wright

Luke's Lobster ★ Cascabel
★ *The Mark*

Lincoln

Le Caprice
Hudson Hall ★ Robert ★ Plaza Food Hall
Má Pêche ★

Print

Casa Lever
East Side
★ Social Club

Lambs Club

★ *Zengo*

The Breslin
★ No. 7 Sub
SD26 ★ ★ Hurricane Club
Nuela ★ ★ Eataly

★ *Maialino*

★ ABC Kitchen

Colicchio & Sons ★ ★ Dos Toros
Abe & Arthur's ★ *Bill's Bar & Burger* ★ This Little Piggy
Tanuki Tavern ★ *Corsino* *The Lion* ★ Robataya ★ Luke's Lobster
Recette ★ *Olio* ★ Spot
Ofrenda ★ ★ Faustina *Saltie*
Hecho en Dumbo ★ Peels ★ St. Anselm
Pulino's ★ Meatball Shop
Crosby Bar ★ Los Feliz
Quattro ★ *Torrisi* *Tartinery* ★ Fatty 'Cue
★ Kenmare
Salumè ★

Plein Sud ★

BLT Bar & Grill ★ ★ Wall & Water ★ Mile End
The Vanderbilt

6   Menus, photos, voting and more – free at ZAGAT.com

Key Newcomers

Our editors' take on the year's top arrivals. See page 337 for a full list.

BIG NAMES
ABC Kitchen
Colicchio & Sons
Eataly
Maialino
Má Pêche
Mark
SD26

HOT SCENES
Abe & Arthur's
Breslin
Kenmare
Lion
Peels
Pulino's
Quattro Gastronomia
Torrisi Italian Specialties

STRIKING SPACES
Casa Lever
Hurricane Club
Lambs Club
Le Caprice
Lincoln
Lion
Plaza Food Hall
Robert
Wright

SMALL PLATES
Corsino
Recette
Robataya
Tanuki Tavern
Vanderbilt

SUPERIOR SANDWICHES
Meatball Shop
Mile End
No. 7 Sub
Saltie
Salumè
Tartinery
This Little Piggy

QUICK BITES
Bill's Bar & Burger
Fatty 'Cue
Luke's Lobster
Olio
Spot
St. Anselm

HOTEL HABITUÉS
BLT Bar & Grill
Crosby Bar
East Side Social
Faustina
Hudson Hall
Maialino
Plein Sud
Print
Wall & Water

LATIN HEAT
Cascabel
Dos Toros
Hecho en Dumbo
Los Feliz
Nuela
Ofrenda
Zengo

PROJECTS ON TAP (See page 338 for a complete list)

April Bloomfield – *John Dory Oyster Bar,* a seafooder in the Ace Hotel

Andrew Carmellini – American in SoHo's former Cub Room digs

Tom Colicchio – *Riverpark,* offering American food and East River views

Sara Jenkins – *Porsena,* an East Village pasta purveyor

Michael Psilakis – *Fish Tag,* a seafood reworking of Gus & Gabriel's

Marcus Samuelsson – *Red Rooster,* an American comfort fooder in Harlem

Gabe Stulman – *Jeffrey's,* a West Village market/oyster bar, and *Fedora,* a reworking of the longtime Villager

Michael White – *Osteria Morini,* an Emilia-Romagnan showcase in SoHo, and *Ai Fiori,* serving Italian coastal cuisine in Midtown

Top Food

Excludes places with low votes, unless otherwise indicated; * indicates a tie with restaurant above

23 Phoenix Garden
Philippe
Nice Green Bo

DELIS

25 Mile End (Bklyn)
24 Barney Greengrass
Katz's Deli
23 Ben's Best (Qns)
Ess-a-Bagel
22 2nd Ave Deli
Mill Basin Deli (Bklyn)
Liebman's (Bronx)

DESSERT

25 ChikaLicious
24 La Bergamote
Veniero's
Amy's Bread
Chocolate Room (Bklyn)
Bouchon Bakery
L & B Spumoni (Bklyn)
23 Ferrara

DIM SUM

25 Pacificana (Bklyn)
24 Oriental Garden
22 Chinatown Brasserie
Ping's Seafood
21 Shun Lee Cafe
Golden Unicorn
Red Egg
20 Excellent Dumpling

ECLECTIC

26 Carol's Cafe (SI)
25 Graffiti
Good Fork (Bklyn)
WD-50
24 Public
23 Stanton Social
Harry's Cafe/Steak
22 Soujourn

FRENCH

29 Le Bernardin
28 Per Se
Daniel
Jean Georges
Eleven Madison Park
27 Bouley
Degustation
L'Atelier/Joël Robuchon

FRENCH BISTRO

25 JoJo
DB Bistro Moderne

24 Capsouto Frères
Tournesol (Qns)
Le Gigot
Minetta Tavern
23 Bar Boulud
Raoul's

GREEK

27 Milos
26 Eliá (Bklyn)
Taverna Kyclades (Qns)
25 Pylos
Avra
24 Aegean Cove (Qns)
Anthos
Periyali

HOTEL DINING

28 Jean Georges (Trump Int'l)
27 L'Atelier/Joël (Four Seasons)
Café Boulud (Surrey)
26 Adour (St. Regis)
25 Maialino (Gramercy Park)
Benjamin Steak (Dylan)
DB Bistro Moderne (City Club)
Norma's (Le Parker Meridien)

INDIAN

26 Tamarind
25 Saravanaas
Tabla
Amma
24 Chola
23 Dawat
Vatan
Yuva

ITALIAN

27 Marea
Il Mulino
Babbo
Roberto (Bronx)
Trattoria L'incontro (Qns)
Al Di La (Bklyn)
Scalini Fedeli
26 Felidia

JAPANESE/SUSHI

29 Sasabune
28 Sushi Yasuda
27 Ushiwakamaru
Masa/Bar Masa
Soto
Gari/Sushi
Donguri
26 Nobu

KOREAN

- 24 HanGawi
- 23 Cho Dang Gol
  - Moim (Bklyn)
- 22 Bann
  - Woo Lae Oak
  - Kang Suh
- 21 Do Hwa
  - Kum Gang San

KOSHER

- 25 Azuri Cafe
- 23 Ben's Best (Qns)
- 22 2nd Ave Deli
  - Mill Basin Deli (Bklyn)
  - Prime Grill
  - Le Marais
  - Liebman's (Bronx)
  - Pongal

LOBSTER ROLLS

- 26 Pearl Oyster Bar
- 25 Luke's Lobster
  - Mary's Fish Camp
- 23 Brooklyn Fish (Bklyn)
  - Ed's Lobster Bar
- 21 Mermaid Inn
- 19 Ed's Chowder House
- 18 Ditch Plains

MEDITERRANEAN

- 27 Picholine
- 26 Convivium Osteria (Bklyn)
  - Il Buco
- 25 Little Owl
- 24 Alta
  - Red Cat
  - Savoy
- 23 Olives

MEXICAN

- 25 Cascabel
  - Molé
  - Calexico (Bklyn)
- 24 Fonda (Bklyn)
  - Pampano
  - Sueños
  - Dos Toros
  - Maya

MIDDLE EASTERN

- 27 Tanoreen (Bklyn)
- 26 Taïm
- 25 Azuri Cafe
- 24 Taboon
  - Taci's Beyti (Bklyn)
  - Ilili

Turkish Grill (Qns)
- 23 Gazala Place

NEWCOMERS

- 25 Maialino
  - Luke's Lobster
  - Mile End (Bklyn)
  - Cascabel
- 24 Recette
  - ABC Kitchen
  - Dos Toros
  - Mark

NOODLE SHOPS

- 25 Ippudo
- 24 Momofuku Noodle Bar
  - Soba-ya
- 23 Matsugen
  - Soba Nippon
- 22 Great NY Noodle
  - Bo-Ky
  - Pho Viet Huong

PIZZA

- 27 Di Fara (Bklyn)
- 26 Lucali (Bklyn)
  - Denino's (SI)
- 25 Zero Otto Nove (Bronx)
  - Amorina (Bklyn)
  - Keste Pizza e Vino
- 24 Franny's (Bklyn)
  - Posto

RAW BARS

- 26 Aquagrill
  - Pearl Oyster Bar
- 25 Esca
  - Blue Ribbon
- 24 Marlow & Sons (Bklyn)
  - Mark
- 23 Oceana
  - Faustina

SEAFOOD

- 29 Le Bernardin
- 27 Marea
  - Milos
- 26 Aquagrill
  - Pearl Oyster Bar
  - Taverna Kyclades (Qns)
- 25 Luke's Lobster
  - Avra

SMALL PLATES

- 27 Degustation
  - L'Atelier/Joël Robuchon
- 25 Graffiti

Zenkichi (Bklyn)
Kuma Inn
24 Sakagura
Frankies Spuntino
Recette

SOUTH AMERICAN

24 Caracas
23 Chimichurri Grill
Churrascaria
Buenos Aires
22 Empanada Mama
Pio Pio
21 Circus
Zebú Grill

SOUTHERN/SOUL

23 Egg (Bklyn)
22 Peaches∇
Char No. 4 (Bklyn)
20 Amy Ruth's
19 B. Smith's
Kitchenette
Sylvia's
18 Tipsy Parson

SOUTHWESTERN

23 Mesa Grill
21 Los Dos Molinos∇
20 Canyon Road
18 Agave
17 Cilantro
16 Cowgirl
15 Mary Ann's

SPANISH/TAPAS

26 Casa Mono
25 Tía Pol
24 Txikito
Las Ramblas
Socarrat Paella
22 Pipa
Sevilla
Boqueria

STEAKHOUSES

27 Peter Luger (Bklyn)
25 Sparks Steak

Wolfgang's Steakhouse
Strip House
Del Frisco's
BLT Prime
Keens
Benjamin Steak

THAI

26 Sripraphai (Qns)
25 Kuma Inn
23 Erawan (Qns)
Joya (Bklyn)
Pam Real Thai
Kittichai
Song (Bklyn)
Laut

TURKISH

24 Taci's Beyti (Bklyn)
Turkish Grill (Qns)
22 Sahara's Turkish Cuisine
Turkish Kitchen
Beyoglu
Hanci Turkish
Sahara (Bklyn)
21 Pera

VEGETARIAN

27 Dirt Candy
26 Taïm
25 Saravanaas
24 HanGawi
Candle 79
23 Candle Café
Vatan
Pure Food & Wine

VIETNAMESE

23 Omai
22 Má Pêche
Bo-Ky
Pho Viet Huong
Nam
Nha Trang
21 Le Colonial
Nicky's Viet.

BREAKFAST

27] Jean Georges' Nougatine
25] Maialino
Norma's
24] Locanda Verde
23] Balthazar
Egg (Bklyn)
21] Breslin
19] Regency∇

BRUNCH DOWNTOWN

24] Clinton St. Baking Co.
Blue Ribbon Bakery
Prune
Minetta Tavern
23] Balthazar
22] Five Points
20] Waverly Inn
18] Essex

BRUNCH MIDTOWN

23] Blue Water Grill
Artisanal
22] Cookshop
Penelope
Brasserie 8½
21] Water Club
20] Eatery
19] Cafeteria

BRUNCH UPTOWN

26] Telepan
24] David Burke Townhouse
Square Meal
Mark
23] Atlantic Grill
20] Sarabeth's
Nice Matin
19] Popover Cafe

CELEBRITY SCENES

24] Minetta Tavern
23] Balthazar
Spotted Pig
22] Rao's
21] Da Silvano
Standard Grill
20] Waverly Inn
17] Monkey Bar

CHILD-FRIENDLY

23] Shake Shack
22] Otto
21] Blue Smoke
20] Max Brenner

19] Peanut Butter & Co.
Serendipity 3
18] Bubby's
16] Cowgirl

DINING AT THE BAR

28] Gramercy Tavern
27] Picholine
26] Del Posto
25] Perry St.
24] Hearth
23] Colicchio & Sons
22] Oyster Bar
21] Centro Vinoteca

DRINKS DOWNTOWN

25] Bond Street
23] Spice Market
21] Freemans
Standard Grill
20] Double Crown
Employees Only
19] Hotel Griffou
17] P.J Clarke's/Hudson

DRINKS MIDTOWN

26] Modern
Nobu 57
25] Del Frisco's
24] Le Cirque
Piano Due
22] La Fonda del Sol
21] Michael Jordan's
17] Monkey Bar

DRINKS UPTOWN

24] Ouest
Mark
23] Bar Boulud
Geisha
Atlantic Grill
20] Cafe Luxembourg
Landmarc
18] Demarchelier

FOOD TRUCKS

(see ZAGAT.com for reviews)
24] Wafels & Dinges
Street Sweets∇
23] Van Leeuwen Ice Cream
22] Treats Truck∇
NYC Cravings∇
20] Schnitzel & Things∇
19] Rickshaw Dumpling Truck
Cupcake Stop

GROUP DINING

24	Buddakan
23	Stanton Social
	Churrascaria
22	Chinatown Brasserie
	Rosa Mexicano
	Hill Country
20	Carmine's
19	Ruby Foo's

HIPSTER HANGOUTS

25	Vinegar Hill Hse. (Bklyn)
24	Marlow & Sons (Bklyn)
23	Little Giant
	Spotted Pig
	Artichoke Basille's
22	La Esquina
21	Freemans
20	Double Crown

HISTORIC PLACES

27	Peter Luger (Bklyn)
25	Keens
24	Barney Greengrass
	Katz's Deli
22	Oyster Bar
20	Barbetta
	Waverly Inn
18	Walker's

HOT SPOTS

24	Minetta Tavern
22	DBGB
	Abe & Arthur's
21	Breslin
	Kenmare▽
19	Pulino's
-	Lion
-	Peels

LATE DINING

25	Blue Ribbon
24	Minetta Tavern
23	Spotted Pig
	Artichoke Basille's
22	La Esquina
	Joseph Leonard
21	Pastis
19	Pulino's

LOCAVORE

27	Blue Hill
	Mas
26	Telepan
25	Craft
24	ABC Kitchen
	Savoy

| | Farm on Adderley |
| 22 | Jimmy's No. 43 |

MILESTONES

75th	Monkey Bar
50th	Corner Bistro
25th	Chez Josephine
	Dawat
	Le Bernardin
20th	Shun Lee Palace

POWER LUNCH

27	Marea
26	Four Seasons (Grill Room)
24	Smith & Wollensky
23	Casa Lever
22	Patroon
	China Grill
	21 Club
21	Michael's

PRIVATE PARTIES

29	Le Bernardin
26	Four Seasons
25	Keens
24	Megu
	Le Cirque
	Buddakan
23	Spice Market
	Harry's Cafe

QUICK BITES

26	Num Pang
24	Caracas
	Amy's Bread
	Dos Toros
23	Porchetta
	No. 7 Sub
22	Meatball Shop
21	Bark Hot Dogs (Bklyn)

SENIOR APPEAL

26	Felidia
24	Pietro's
	Le Cirque
	Lusardi's
23	Mr. K's
21	Chez Napoléon
20	Barbetta
19	Russian Tea Room

SINGLES SCENES

23	Stanton Social
22	La Esquina
21	Tao
	Breslin
	Standard Grill
19	Kingswood

18 | Macao Trading
Bagatelle

SOCIETY WATCH

26 | Four Seasons (Pool Room)
24 | Elio's
23 | Casa Lever
22 | Ze Café
21 | Sant Ambroeus
Harry Cipriani
18 | Swifty's
17 | Le Caprice

24-HOUR

22 | Empanada Mama
Kang Suh
21 | Kum Gang San
20 | Sarge's Deli
19 | Veselka (2nd. Ave.)
Cafeteria
Maison
18 | L'Express

VISITORS ON EXPENSE ACCOUNT

29 | Le Bernardin
28 | Per Se

Daniel
Jean Georges
27 | Bouley
Marea
Masa
26 | Corton

WINE BARS

24 | Terroir∇
Peasant
23 | Bar Boulud
I Trulli
22 | 'Inoteca
21 | Felice
19 | Morrell Wine Bar
Accademia di Vino

WINNING WINE LISTS

28 | Daniel
26 | Alto
Veritas
Del Posto
22 | Bottega del Vino
Otto
Tribeca Grill
21 Club

BY LOCATION

CHELSEA

26 | Del Posto
Scarpetta
25 | Morimoto
Tía Pol
Da Umberto
24 | Txikito
La Bergamote
Sueños

CHINATOWN

24 | Oriental Garden
23 | Nice Green Bo
Peking Duck
22 | Great NY Noodle
Fuleen Seafood
Amazing 66
Big Wong
Ping's Seafood

EAST 40s

28 | Sushi Yasuda
26 | Convivio
25 | Sparks Steak
Avra
Benjamin Steak
Aburiya Kinnosuke

Sushiden
Hatsuhana

EAST 50s

28 | La Grenouille
27 | L'Atelier/Joël Robuchon
26 | Felidia
Alto
Four Seasons
Adour
25 | Wolfgang's Steakhouse
Caviar Russe

EAST 60s

28 | Daniel
26 | Sushi Seki
25 | JoJo
Park Avenue . . .
24 | David Burke Townhouse
Scalinatella
Post House
Maya

EAST 70s

29 | Sasabune
27 | Café Boulud
Gari/Sushi
24 | Campagnola

Candle 79
Lusardi's
Alloro
Mark

EAST 80s

27	Donguri
26	Sistina
25	Luke's Lobster
	Cascabel
	Erminia
	Spigolo
	Wa Jeal
	Poke

EAST 90s & 100s

24	Square Meal
23	Sfoglia
	Nick's
	El Paso Taqueria
22	Itzocan
	Pinocchio
	Paola's
	Pio Pio

EAST VILLAGE

27	Degustation
	Momofuku Ko
	Dirt Candy
26	Kyo Ya
	Kanoyama
	Jewel Bako
25	Pylos
	Ippudo

FINANCIAL DISTRICT

26	SHO Shaun Hergatt
24	Adrienne's Pizza
	MarkJoseph Steak
	Capital Grille
23	Delmonico's
	Harry's Cafe/Steak
22	Bobby Van's
	Bridge Cafe

FLATIRON/UNION SQ.

28	Gramercy Tavern
	Eleven Madison Park
26	Union Square Cafe
	Veritas
	Tamarind
25	Tocqueville
	15 East
	Aldea

GARMENT DISTRICT

25	Keens
23	Cho Dang Gol
	Frankie & Johnnie's
22	Szechuan Gourmet
	Uncle Jack's
	Kang Suh
21	Kati Roll Co.
	Lazzara's

GRAMERCY

26	Casa Mono
25	Maialino
	BLT Prime
24	Posto
	Novitá
	Yama
23	Pure Food & Wine
	Ess-a-Bagel

GREENWICH VILLAGE

27	Blue Hill
	Gotham B&G
	Ushiwakamaru
	Il Mulino
	Babbo
26	Num Pang
	Tomoe Sushi
25	Strip House

HARLEM

23	El Paso Taqueria
22	Dinosaur BBQ
	Chez Lucienne
	Covo
	Rao's
21	Hudson River Café
20	Patsy's Pizzeria

LITTLE ITALY

23	Ferrara
	Il Cortile
	Angelo's of Mulberry St.
	Pellegrino's
22	Bo-Ky
	La Esquina
	Wild Ginger
	Da Nico

LOWER EAST SIDE

25	Falai
	Molé
	Kuma Inn
	WD-50
24	Frankies Spuntino
	Clinton St. Baking Co.
	Ápizz
	Katz's Deli

MEATPACKING

- 25 Valbella
- 24 Old Homestead
- 23 Spice Market
  - STK
- 22 Macelleria
  - Abe & Arthur's
- 21 Paradou
  - Son Cubano

MURRAY HILL

- 25 Wolfgang's Steakhouse
  - Sushi Sen-nin
  - Saravanaas
- 24 Rossini's
  - HanGawi
  - Mishima
  - Primehouse NY
- 23 Vatan

NOHO

- 26 Il Buco
- 25 Bond Street
- 24 Bianca
- 23 Aroma
- 22 Chinatown Brasserie
  - Five Points
  - Sala
- 20 Mercat

NOLITA

- 24 Peasant
  - Public
- 23 Lombardi's
  - Ed's Lobster Bar
- 22 Café Habana
- 21 Emporio
  - Barmarché
- 20 Cafe Gitane

SOHO

- 26 Aquagrill
  - Blue Ribbon Sushi
- 25 Blue Ribbon
- 24 L'Ecole
  - Aurora
  - Giorgione
  - Savoy
- 23 Lure Fishbar

TRIBECA

- 27 Bouley
  - Scalini Fedeli
- 26 Nobu
  - Tamarind
  - Corton
- 25 Wolfgang's Steakhouse

Il Giglio
Pepolino

WEST 40s

- 27 Gari/Sushi
- 26 Aureole
- 25 Del Frisco's
  - Sushi Zen
  - Esca
  - Sushiden
  - DB Bistro Moderne
- 24 Sea Grill

WEST 50s

- 29 Le Bernardin
- 27 Marea
  - Milos
- 26 Modern
  - Nobu 57
  - Sugiyama
- 25 Seasonal
  - Azuri Cafe

WEST 60s

- 28 Per Se
  - Jean Georges
- 27 Picholine
  - Masa/Bar Masa
- 26 Telepan
- 24 Asiate
  - Porter House NY
  - A Voce

WEST 70s

- 27 Gari/Sushi
- 26 Dovetail
- 24 Salumeria Rosi
  - Ocean Grill
- 23 'Cesca
  - Shake Shack
- 22 Tenzan
  - Hummus Place

WEST 80s

- 24 Barney Greengrass
  - Ouest
  - Celeste
- 23 Spiga
  - La Mirabelle
- 22 Momoya
  - Land
  - Kefi

WEST 90s & UP

- 24 Gennaro
- 23 Pisticci
  - Indus Valley

22 El Malecon
Noche Mexicana
Hummus Place
Pio Pio
21 Terrace in the Sky

WEST VILLAGE

28 Annisa
27 Mas

Soto
26 Wallsé
Pearl Oyster Bar
Perilla
Taïm
25 I Sodi

BROOKLYN

BAY RIDGE

27 Tanoreen
26 Eliá
24 Tuscany Grill
Areo
23 Agnanti
Fushimi
Chadwick's
22 Pearl Room

BKLYN HTS/DUMBO

26 River Café
24 Noodle Pudding
Henry's End
Queen
Grimaldi's
22 Jack the Horse
20 Five Guys
Superfine

CARROLL GARDENS/
BOERUM & COBBLE HILLS

26 Saul
Grocery
Lucali
25 Mile End
Hibino
Calexico
24 Frankies Spuntino
Bocca Lupo

FORT GREENE/
PROSPECT HEIGHTS

25 Amorina
24 Franny's
James

Geido
23 No. 7
22 Café Habana/Outpost
Madiba
Smoke Joint

PARK SLOPE

27 Al Di La
26 Convivium Osteria
Blue Ribbon Sushi
25 Rose Water
Blue Ribbon
Stone Park Café
25 Palo Santo
Applewood

WILLIAMSBURG

27 Peter Luger
25 Fette Sau
Dressler
Zenkichi
24 Marlow & Sons
Caracas
Aurora
Motorino

OTHER AREAS

27 Di Fara (Midwood)
25 Vinegar Hill Hse. (Vinegar Hill)
Pacificana (Sunset Park)
Good Fork (Red Hook)
24 Tommaso (Dyker Heights)
Morton's (Downtown)
Taci's Beyti (Midwood)
L & B Spumoni (Bensonhurst)

BRONX

27 Roberto
25 Zero Otto Nove
24 Jake's
23 Dominick's
   Enzo's
22 El Malecon
   Patricia's
   Liebman's

QUEENS: ASTORIA/L.I.C.

27 Trattoria L'incontro
26 Taverna Kyclades
25 Piccola Venezia
24 Aegean Cove
   Tournesol
23 Elias Corner
   Agnanti
   Manducatis

QUEENS: OTHER AREAS

26 Sripraphai (Woodside)
   Danny Brown (Forest Hills)
   Don Peppe (Ozone Park)
24 Park Side (Corona)
   Turkish Grill (Sunnyside)
   Grimaldi's (Douglaston)
23 Sapori D'Ischia (Wooodside)
   Erawan (Bayside)

STATEN ISLAND

26 Carol's Cafe
   Denino's
25 Brioso
   Bocelli
24 Trattoria Romana
23 Joe & Pat's
   Fushimi
   Enoteca Maria

Top Decor

29	Asiate
28	La Grenouille
	Per Se
	Daniel
	Four Seasons
	River Café (Bklyn)
27	Eleven Madison Park
	Gilt
	Buddakan
	Le Bernardin
	Jean Georges
	SHO Shaun Hergatt
	One if by Land
	Adour
	Modern
	Bouley
	Carlyle
	Spice Market
26	Kittichai
	Del Posto

Park Avenue . . .
FireBird
Morimoto
Tao
Marea
Gramercy Tavern
Megu
Grand Tier
Le Cirque
Boathouse
Oak Room
Picholine

25	Gotham B&G
	EN Japanese
	Thalassa
	Valbella
	Terrace in the Sky
	Water's Edge (Qns)
	Casa Lever
	Public

PATIOS/GARDENS

Aurora (Bklyn)
Barbetta
Barolo
Battery Gardens
Boathouse
Brasserie Ruhlmann
Bryant Park
Cávo (Qns)

Convivio
Faustina
5 Ninth
I Coppi
Inside Park/St. Bart's
I Trulli
New Leaf
Pure Food & Wine

ROMANCE

August
Dressler (Bklyn)
Erminia
Gascogne
Il Buco
Lambs Club
Mas
One if by Land

Place
River Café (Bklyn)
Rye (Bklyn)
Taureau
Uva
Wallsé
Water's Edge (Qns)
Zenkichi (Bklyn)

VIEWS

Asiate
A Voce (W 60s)
Battery Gardens
Boathouse
Gigino Wagner Park
Lincoln
Metrazur
Modern

Per Se
River Café (Bklyn)
Robert
Sea Grill
Terrace in the Sky
View
Water Club
Water's Edge (Qns)

Top Service

29 Per Se	River Café (Bklyn)
28 Le Bernardin	25 Del Posto
La Grenouille	Marea
Daniel	Veritas
Jean Georges	Asiate
	Aureole
27 Eleven Madison Park	Degustation
Gramercy Tavern	Corton
Four Seasons	Modern
Adour	Carlyle
L'Atelier/Joël Robuchon	Valbella
Blue Hill	Dovetail
	One if by Land
26 Mas	Cru
Bouley	Saul (Bklyn)
Gotham B&G	Le Perigord
Picholine	Alto
Gilt	Babbo
Union Square Cafe	Piano Due
SHO Shaun Hergatt	Telepan
Café Boulud	
Masa/Bar Masa	

Best Buys

Everyone loves a bargain, and NYC offers plenty of them. Bear in mind: (1) lunch typically costs 25 to 30% less than dinner, (2) outer-borough dining is less costly than in Manhattan, (3) most Indian restaurants offer inexpensive prix fixe lunch buffets and (4) biannual Restaurant Weeks (in January and July) are big bargains.

ALL YOU CAN EAT

- [24] Chola
- [23] Becco
- Churrascaria Plataforma
- [22] Turkish Kitchen
- [21] Darbar
- La Baraka (Qns)
- Chennai Garden
- Utsav
- Sapphire Indian
- [20] Yuka

BYO

- [26] Lucali (Bklyn)
- [25] Kuma Inn
- Poke
- [24] Phoenix Garden
- [23] Peking Duck (Chinatown)
- [21] Tartine
- Angelica Kitchen
- [19] Tea & Sympathy

CHEAP DATES

- [24] Soba-ya
- [22] Snack
- Sala
- Sahara (Bklyn)
- 26 Seats
- [21] Holy Basil
- [20] La Paella
- Klong
- Turkuaz

EARLY-BIRD

- [25] Bocelli (SI)
- [24] Sueños
- Takahachi
- Italianissimo
- [23] Queen
- Kittichai
- [22] Jean Claude
- Uncle Jack's
- Kefi
- [19] Cucina di Pesce

FAMILY-STYLE

- [27] Roberto (Bronx)
- [26] Don Peppe (Qns)
- [25] Piccolo Angolo
- [24] Oriental Garden
- [23] Dominick's (Bronx)
- Pisticci
- Nick's
- Asia de Cuba
- [22] Patricia's (Bronx)
- Rao's

PRE-THEATER

- [27] Jean Georges' Nougatine
- [26] Telepan
- Sugiyama
- [25] Avra
- [24] Ocean Grill
- Anthos
- Ouest
- [23] Atlantic Grill
- Molyvos
- [21] Indochine

PRIX FIXE LUNCH

- [28] Sushi Yasuda ($23)
- [27] Gotham B&G ($31)
- Milos ($24)
- Jean Georges' Nougatine ($26)
- [26] Felidia ($30)
- Dovetail ($24)
- [25] 15 East ($24)
- Tía Pol ($18)
- Tabla ($24)
- [22] Maze ($26)

PRIX FIXE DINNER

- [28] Sushi Yasuda ($23)
- [27] Ushiwakamaru ($33)
- [25] Rose Water (Bklyn) ($26)
- JoJo ($38)
- [24] Capsouto Frères ($39)
- Ilili ($38)
- Hearth ($39)
- Geisha ($39)
- [23] Petrossian ($35)
- [21] Cafe Cluny ($30)

BEST BUYS: FULL MENU

Azuri Cafe | *Israeli*
Bereket | *Turkish*
Big Wong | *Chinese*
Bill's Bar & Burger | *Burgers*
Bo-Ky | *Noodle Shop*
Brennan & Carr (Bklyn) | *Sandwiches*
Café Habana | *Cuban/Mex.*
Café Henri | *French*
Calexico (Bklyn) | *Mexican*
Cascabel | *Mexican*
Chickpea | *Mideastern*
Dos Toros | *Mexican*
Egg (Bklyn) | *Southern*
El Malecon | *Dominican*
Energy Kitchen | *Health Food*
Excellent Dumpling | *Chinese*
Hummus Place | *Israeli/Veg.*
Ippudo | *Noodle Shop*
Joya (Bklyn) | *Thai*
La Bergamote | *French*
L & B Spumoni (Bklyn) | *Pizza*
La Taqueria (Bklyn) | *Mexican*
Maoz | *Mideastern/Vegetarian*
Mill Basin Deli (Bklyn) | *Deli*
Molly's | *Pub Food*

Nanoosh | *Mediterranean*
Nha Trang | *Vietnamese*
Nice Green Bo | *Chinese*
Noche | *Mexican*
Noodle Bar | *Asian*
Num Pang | *Cambodian*
Omonia Cafe (Bklyn/Qns) | *Greek*
Pacificana (Bklyn) | *Chinese*
Peacefood Café | *Vegan*
Peep | *Thai*
Penelope | *American*
Pho Bang | *Vietnamese*
Radegast Hall (Bklyn) | *European*
Rai Rai Ken | *Noodle Shop*
Ramen Setagaya | *Noodle Shop*
Rice | *Eclectic*
Saravanaas | *Indian*
Schnipper's | *American*
Shanghai Café | *Chinese*
Song (Bklyn) | *Thai*
Taïm | *Israeli*
Tiffin Wallah | *Indian*
Tom's (Bklyn) | *Diner*
Wild Ginger | *Asian*
Zaytoons (Bklyn) | *Mideastern*

BEST BUYS: SPECIALTY SHOPS

Amy's Bread | *baked goods*
Artichoke Basille's | *pizza*
Baoguette | *sandwiches*
BareBurger (Qns) | *burgers*
Bark (Bklyn) | *hot dogs*
Black Iron | *burgers*
Brgr | *burgers*
Burger Joint | *burgers*
Burger Shoppe | *burgers*
Caracas | *arepas*
Carl's | *cheesesteaks*
ChikaLicious | *dessert*
Chocolate Room (Bklyn) | *dessert*
Così | *sandwiches*
Defonte's | *sandwiches*
Denino's (SI) | *pizza*
Dishes | *sandwiches*
Dumpling Man | *dumplings*
Empanada Mama | *empanadas*
Ess-a-Bagel | *deli*
Five Guys | *burgers*
Goodburger | *burgers*
Gray's Papaya | *hot dogs*
Hale & Hearty | *soup*
Hampton Chutney | *Indian*

Hanco's (Bklyn) | *sandwiches*
Joe's Pizza | *pizza*
Kati Roll Co. | *Indian*
Kyochon | *chicken*
Lenny's | *sandwiches*
Luke's Lobster | *sandwiches*
Meatball Shop | *sandwiches*
Mile End (Bklyn) | *deli*
Momofuku Bakery | *dessert*
Nicky's Viet. | *sandwiches*
99 Miles to Philly | *cheesesteaks*
Once Upon a Tart | *baked goods*
Peanut Butter & Co. | *sandwiches*
Pizza 33 | *pizza*
Porchetta | *sandwiches*
Press 195 (Bklyn/Qns) | *sandwiches*
Pret A Manger | *sandwiches*
Roll-n-Roaster (Bklyn) | *sandwiches*
Shake Shack | *burgers*
S'MAC | *mac 'n' cheese*
sNice | *sandwiches*
Two Boots | *pizza*
Veniero's | *dessert*
Waldy's | *pizza*
'Wichcraft | *sandwiches*

Menus, photos, voting and more – free at ZAGAT.com

LUNCH: $35 OR LESS

Agua Dulce	$15	L'Ecole	28
A.J. Maxwell's	30	Le Perigord	32
Allegretti	24	Le Pescadeux	15
Almond	21	Le Relais de Venise	24
Angelo & Maxie's	21	Matsugen	26
Anthos	28	Maze	26
Armani Ristorante	30	Mercer Kitchen	26
Artisanal	24	Milos	24
Asiate	24	Molyvos	25
Atlantic Grill	24	Montenapo	23
Aureole	34	Mr. K's	28
Avra	29	Ocean Grill	24
Becco	18	Olives	24
Benoit	21	Orsay	25
Bobby Van's (W. 50s)	30	Osteria del Circo	28
Braai	15	Padre Figlio	22
Cafe Un Deux Trois	20	Pampano	28
Caviar Russe	20	Parlor Steakhouse	25
Centro Vinoteca	20	Patroon	27
Chiam	21	Periyali	26
Chinatown Brasserie	17	Pongal	8
Chin Chin	27	Remi	24
Cibo	25	Robert	29
Convivio	28	Rouge Tomate	29
David Burke Townhouse	24	Russian Tea Room	35
Del Frisco's	32	Sazon	25
Demarchelier	16	SD26	28
Dovetail	24	Seasonal	27
Duane Park	24	Serge	28
Fatty Crab	19	Shalezeh	20
Felidia	30	SHO Shaun Hergatt	30
15 East	24	Solera	29
FireBird	30	Spice Market	24
Five Points	26	Sushi Yasuda	23
Fulton	24	Tabla	24
Gallagher's Steak	28	Tamarind	24
Gascogne	21	Tao	27
Geisha	29	T-Bar Steak	24
Giorgio's/Gramercy	20	Telepan	22
Gotham B&G	31	Terrazza Toscana	15
HanGawi	20	Thalia	17
Il Bastardo	15	Tía Pol	18
Jean Georges' Nougatine	26	Tocqueville	24
JoJo	28	Tse Yang	28
Josephina	24	Turkish Kitchen	17
Kellari Taverna	26	21 Club	24
Kings' Carriage	19	Uskudar	14
La Boîte en Bois	27	ViceVersa	22
L'Absinthe	28	Wall & Water	29
La Mangeoire	20	West Bank Cafe	25
La Petite Auberge	20	Zarela	19

DINNER: $40 OR LESS

PT = pre-theater only; where two prices are listed, the first is pre-theater and the second for normal dinner hours.

Abboccato/PT	$35	La Bonne Soupe	24
Akdeniz	24	La Mangeoire	29
Aki	30	La Petite Auberge	29
Algonquin/PT	39	La Sirène/PT	29
Allegretti	39	Le Pescadeux/PT	24
Alouette/PT	25	Le Relais de Venise	24
Anthos/PT	38	Le Rivage/PT	37
Apiary	35	Le Singe Vert/PT	20
Artisanal	39	Maria Pia/PT	25
Atlantic Grill/PT	35	Marseille	35
Avra/PT	39	Matsugen	38
Bacchus (Bklyn)	25	McCormick & Schmick/PT	30
Bay Leaf/PT	21	Miranda	25
Becco	23	Molyvos/PT	37
Benoit	38	Ocean Grill/PT	25
Bombay Palace	30	Orsay	35
Braai	35	Osteria del Circo	38
Brasserie Cognac/PT	25	Ouest/PT	29
Brasserie Julien	22	Padre Figlio	39
B. Smith's/PT	29	Parea/PT	30
Cafe Cluny	30	Parlor Steakhouse/PT	35
Cafe Loup	28	Pascalou/PT	20
Cafe Un Deux Trois	28	Pasha/PT	24
Capsouto Frères	39	Patroon	39
Centro Vinoteca/PT	25	Pera/PT	35
Chez Napoléon	30	Periyali	35
Chin Chin	35	Petrossian	35
Cibo	35	Pomaire/PT	25
Cipriani Dolci	40	Quercy (Bklyn)	22
Compass	35	Remi	35
Demarchelier	26	Rose Water (Bklyn)	26
Docks Oyster Bar/PT	32	Seasonal/PT	38
Etcetera Etcetera	35	Serge	28
Fulton/PT	35	Shalezeh	25
Gascogne	27/29	Sueños/PT	30
Geisha	39	Sugiyama/PT	32
Gigino	28	Sushi Yasuda	23
HanGawi	40	Table d'Hôte	24/29
Hearth	39	Thalia/PT	35
Ilili	38	Tommaso (Bklyn)	25
Il Punto/PT	35	Tournesol (Qns)	25
Indochine/PT	35	Turkish Cuisine	27
Japonais/PT	35	21 Club	40
Jean Georges' Nougatine/PT	38	Ushiwakamaru	33
Jewel of India/PT	30	Vatan	31
JoJo	38	ViceVersa	35
Kefi/PT	17	Vincent's	28
Kellari Taverna/PT	33	Water Club	35
Kittichai/PT	35	West Bank Cafe	30

RESTAURANT DIRECTORY

	FOOD	DECOR	SERVICE	COST

Abboccato *Italian* | 21 | 19 | 20 | $57

W 50s | Blakely Hotel | 136 W. 55th St. (bet. 6th & 7th Aves.) |
212-265-4000 | www.abboccato.com

"Well-located" a "hop and a skip" from City Center and Carnegie Hall,
this "dependable" Midtowner plies "interesting" Italian food in an "attractive room" that's "less hectic" than others pre-curtain; but given
the "upscale" price point, regulars stick to the "great-value" prix fixe.

Z NEW ABC Kitchen *American* | 24 | 23 | 23 | $55

Flatiron | ABC Carpet & Home | 35 E. 18th St. (bet. B'way & Park Ave. S.) |
212-475-5829 | www.abckitchennyc.com

The "locavore concept" gets a "smart take" via Jean-Georges
Vongerichten at this Flatiron newcomer in ABC Carpet; it serves a
"super-fresh", "haute green" seasonal menu of "farm-to-table" New
American dishes, delivered by an "informed" team and set in a "whitewashed", "country-chic" room; cheap no, worth it yes.

NEW Abe & Arthur's *American* | 22 | 23 | 20 | $69

Meatpacking | 409 W. 14th St. (bet. 9th Ave. & Washington St.) |
646-289-3930 | www.abeandarthursrestaurant.com

An "instant success" with "pretty young things" and "famous" folk, this
über-"trendy" Meatpacking District debut in the former Lotus digs
splices an "energetic" buzz with "well-executed" New American steaks
and seafood; it's way "expensive", but no one cares given the "glitzy"
setting, "hot" staffers, "high hip factor" and "impressive" food.

Abigael's *Eclectic* | 20 | 16 | 19 | $51

Garment District | 1407 Broadway (bet. 38th & 39th Sts.) | 212-575-1407 |
www.abigaels.com

So "sophisticated" you "wouldn't know it was kosher", this Garment
District Eclectic plies an "unexpected variety" of "high-quality" dishes
from chef Jeff Nathan, plus sushi and Pan-Asian noshes upstairs; it's
all "served competently", though the decor is "showing its age."

Abistro Ⓜ *African* | ▽ 24 | 14 | 21 | $35

Fort Greene | 154 Carlton Ave. (bet. Myrtle Ave. & Willoughby St.) |
Brooklyn | 718-855-9455

"Fabulous" French-accented West African cooking draws huzzahs at
this "sweet" Fort Greene BYO, where "big flavors" and small tabs offset the "cramped", "bare-bones" setting; though "largely under the radar", it's a "neighborhood favorite" with "long waits" at prime times.

Aburiya Kinnosuke *Japanese* | 25 | 20 | 21 | $53

E 40s | 213 E. 45th St. (bet. 2nd & 3rd Aves.) | 212-867-5454 |
www.aburiyakinnosuke.com

"Less familiar" Japanese fare is a "real eye-opener" at this sushi-free
Midtowner where the "exotic" robata dishes and "must-have" housemade tofu are "genuine" enough to attract "expats"; although "not
cheap", it's "totally worth it" to be "transported to Tokyo."

Z Acappella Ⓢ *Italian* | 25 | 21 | 24 | $72

TriBeCa | 1 Hudson St. (Chambers St.) | 212-240-0163 |
www.acappella-restaurant.com

"Old-world" is the word on this TriBeCa Northern Italian offering "fantastic" traditional cuisine served in "formal" digs by "tuxedoed" wait-

ers who "can't do enough for you"; true, prices are on the "business-class" end of the scale, but at least there's "free after-dinner grappa."

A Casa Fox ⓜ Pan-Latin
20 | 20 | 19 | $35

LES | 173 Orchard St. (Stanton St.) | 212-253-1900 | www.acasafox.com
Known for her "personal touch", caterer Melissa Fox fashions "flavorful" Pan-Latin fare – from "mini" bites to clay pots – with "TLC" at this "small" but "homey" Lower Eastsider; service "may take some time", but on the other hand this "cozy" joint "won't dent your wallet."

Accademia di Vino Italian
19 | 19 | 18 | $50

E 60s | 1081 Third Ave. (bet. 63rd & 64th Sts.) | 212-888-6333
NEW W 80s | 2427 Broadway (bet. 89th & 90th Sts.) | 212-787-3070
www.accademiadivino.com
This "bustling" UES "staple" (and its much "needed" new UWS sibling) seems to have "found the right recipe", pairing "well-prepared" Italian fare with an "extensive" wine list and a "stylish" setting; despite "rushed" service and a "mass-produced feel", both attract "constant crowds."

Acqua Italian
19 | 17 | 19 | $40

W 90s | 710 Amsterdam Ave. (95th St.) | 212-222-2752 | www.acquanyc.com
It's "not fancy", but this UWS "local joint" dishes out "great thin-crust pizza" and other Italian staples with "no pretense"; the "nondescript" setting and "predictable" offerings may have "no wow" factor, but fans feel it delivers "good value."

ⓩ Adour French
26 | 27 | 27 | $123

E 50s | St. Regis Hotel | 2 E. 55th St. (bet. 5th & Madison Aves.) | 212-710-2277 | www.adour-stregis.com
"French cuisine in the grand style" earns adouration at Alain Ducasse's "top-tier" Midtowner, a vino-centric showcase pairing "sublime" food and wine with "out-of-this-world" service in a "transporting" David Rockwell setting; though some are "underwhelmed", overall this is "exceptional" dining – albeit at an "astronomical price."

Adrienne's Pizzabar ● Pizza
24 | 16 | 17 | $25

Financial District | 87 Pearl St. (bet. Coenties Slip & Hanover Sq.) | 212-248-3838 | www.adriennespizzabar.com
"Ever popular" with Wall Streeters seeking a "sit-down pizza experience", this casual Financial District Italian wins "top marks" for its "old-fashioned" pies; the "mob scene at lunch" spills out to coveted tables on "quaint" Stone Street, so "be prepared to wait."

Aegean Cove Greek
24 | 20 | 22 | $43

Astoria | 20-01 Steinway St. (20th Ave.) | Queens | 718-274-9800 | www.aegeancove.com
"More upscale" than the norm, this Astoria Greek purveys a "splendid menu" of Hellenic classics In "comfortable", "feel-right-at-home" quarters; regulars report it's "waiting to be discovered" (it's "a bit off the beaten path"), adding that "parking is easy."

Afghan Kebab House Afghan
20 | 11 | 17 | $26

E 70s | 1345 Second Ave. (bet. 70th & 71st Sts.) | 212-517-2776
W 50s | 764 Ninth Ave. (bet. 51st & 52nd Sts.) | 212-307-1612

(continued)

(continued)

Afghan Kebab House

Astoria | 25-89 Steinway St. (28th Ave.) | Queens | 718-777-7758 |
www.afghankebabs.com ☽
Jackson Heights | 74-16 37th Ave. (bet. 74th & 75th Sts.) | Queens |
718-565-0471
"Spicy kebabs" lead the "right-on" lineup at these Mideast "holes-in-
the-wall", "satisfying stops" for "economical" eats; "minimal" service
and "uninspiring" looks are trumped by the "excellent" BYO policy.

Agave *Southwestern*

18 | 18 | 17 | $39

W Village | 140 Seventh Ave. S. (bet. Charles & W. 10th Sts.) | 212-989-2100 |
www.agaveny.com
"Mind-zapping margaritas" are the draw at this Village Southwesterner
that's best if you're "young and pretty and have a loud voice"; though
the food and service are "average" and the whitewashed digs "could
use an update", the "excellent tequila list" is fine as is.

Aged *Steak*

17 | 20 | 17 | $48

NEW **W 80s** | 2398 Broadway (88th St.) | 212-712-0700
Forest Hills | 107-04 70th Rd. (Austin St.) | Queens | 718-544-2433
www.agednyc.com
As an "alternative" to higher-end chop shops, this Forest Hills steakhouse and its new UWS sibling deliver "decent" beef in "contemporary",
"Meatpacking-esque" settings; although they're "reasonably priced",
"inconsistent" kitchens and "spotty" service suggest "growing pains."

Agnanti *Greek*

23 | 14 | 19 | $36

Bay Ridge | 7802 Fifth Ave. (78th St.) | Brooklyn | 718-833-7033
Astoria | 19-06 Ditmars Blvd. (19th St.) | Queens | 718-545-4554
www.agnantimeze.com
"Like a mini-vacation", this Astoria and Bay Ridge duo excels at "true
Greek" cooking (notably "dockside fresh" grilled fish) served "with a
smile" for "affordable" dough; the taverna settings are "relaxed" but
often "packed", and the Queens branch offers popular "outdoor dining."

Agua Dulce ☽ *Pan-Latin*

22 | 24 | 22 | $42

W 50s | 802 Ninth Ave. (bet. 53rd & 54th Sts.) | 212-262-1299 |
www.aguadulceny.com
A "refreshing find" in Hell's Kitchen, this "contemporary" yearling
specializes in "innovative" Pan-Latin dishes served in a "Miami-style"
duplex that's "more Collins Avenue than Ninth Avenue"; though it may
be "under the radar", many say it's a "definite repeat."

Aja ☽ *Asian*

20 | 21 | 19 | $44

E 50s | 1068 First Ave. (58th St.) | 212-888-8008 | www.ajaasiancuisine.com
"Cooler" than the norm in Sutton Place, this "creative" Pan-Asian
vends "high-quality" sushi in an "attractive" room equipped with a "koi
pond" and a "great big Buddha"; it "can get pricey", but the "noisy"
"young" crowd seems to have "other interests."

A.J. Maxwell's Steakhouse *Steak*

22 | 20 | 21 | $66

W 40s | 57 W. 48th St. (bet. 5th & 6th Aves.) | 212-262-6200 |
www.ajmaxwells.com
This Rock Center steakhouse supplies "succulent, super-sized" cuts
along with "engaging" service, yet its best asset is an address "conve-

nient" to both Midtown and the Theater District; it's "quieter" than the big-name competition, but you should still expect to "pay a bunch."

Ajna Bar ◐ *Asian* | 20 | 25 | 18 | $60 |

Meatpacking | 25 Little W. 12th St. (bet. 9th Ave. & Washington St.) | 646-416-6002 | www.ajnabarnyc.com

It's "not just about food" at this "cavernous" Meatpacking scene – though the Asian fusion chow is "very good" – it's more about the "amazing", Eastern-themed setting; despite "slow" service and "expensive" tabs, it attracts a "loud" crowd primed for late-night hijinks.

Akdeniz ⧆ *Turkish* | 21 | 12 | 18 | $32 |

W 40s | 19 W. 46th St. (bet. 5th & 6th Aves.) | 212-575-2307 | www.akdenizturkishusa.com

"Cost-conscious" patrons plug this Theater District Turk for its "ample" helpings and "bargain" rates (e.g. the $24 prix fixe dinner); the "narrow", "uninspiring" space is manned by a "quick" team, so "don't plan to dawdle."

Aki *Japanese* | 25 | 15 | 21 | $45 |

W Village | 181 W. Fourth St. (bet. Barrow & Jones Sts.) | 212-989-5440

"Lilliputian" dimensions don't stop this West Village Japanese from turning out an "amazingly creative menu" of "sublime sushi" inflected with "clever" Caribbean twists; "courteous" service and "reasonable" tabs make for "rewarding" dining – "if you can fit in."

A La Turka *Turkish* | 18 | 14 | 17 | $36 |

E 70s | 1417 Second Ave. (74th St.) | 212-744-2424 | www.alaturkarestaurant.com

"Popular with the natives", this "everyday" Upper Eastsider provides a "flavorful" sampling of "basic Turkish" cooking for "good-value" prices; the interior's "a little drab" and "service can be spotty", so some opt for "takeout."

Alberto *Italian* | 23 | 19 | 22 | $52 |

Forest Hills | 98-31 Metropolitan Ave. (bet. 69th & 70th Aves.) | Queens | 718-268-7860 | www.albertorestaurant.com

On the scene since '73, this Forest Hills stalwart has "withstood the test of time" thanks to "outstanding" Northern Italian cuisine and "pro service"; although a bit "pricey for Queens", it's "great for a special occasion" and you will always be "well taken care of" here.

Al Bustan *Lebanese* | 19 | 19 | 20 | $46 |

E 50s | 319 E. 53rd St. (bet. 1st & 2nd Aves.) | 212-759-5933 | www.albustanny.com

"Reborn" in a "fancy" new location, this East Side Lebanese now plies its "distinctive" cooking in a "spacious" duplex setting; the "congenial staff" ensures "a warm welcome", but as of yet it's less than bustling.

Alchemy *American* | 19 | 18 | 19 | $30 |

Park Slope | 56 Fifth Ave. (bet. Bergen St. & St. Marks Pl.) | Brooklyn | 718-636-4385 | www.alchemybrooklyn.com

An "easy neighborhood" nexus in Park Slope, this American gastropub puts out "fancified" "bar grub" in an "inviting" tavern setting complete with a "fantastic garden"; even when the eating's "not memorable", the crowd of "friends and neighbors" conjures up "good times."

	FOOD	DECOR	SERVICE	COST

Aldea ⓩ *Portuguese* | 25 | 22 | 24 | $65 |

Flatiron | 31 W. 17th St. (bet. 5th & 6th Aves.) | 212-675-7223 |
www.aldearestaurant.com

"Believe the hype": this Flatiron "revelation" helmed by the "inspired"
George Mendes "elevates Portuguese cuisine", drawing "captivating
flavors" from "lovingly prepared" local ingredients in an "understated", "modern" setting; given the "deft" service and "remarkable"
quality, it's a bona fide "foodie experience" – especially if you sit by
the "open kitchen."

ⓩ Al Di La *Italian* | 27 | 19 | 23 | $47 |

Park Slope | 248 Fifth Ave. (Carroll St.) | Brooklyn | 718-783-4565 |
www.aldilatrattoria.com

Al di "locals" laud this Park Slope trattoria for its "hearty, complex"
Venetian specialties and "cordial" staff – "especially at these prices";
but while the cooking leaves most "blissed out", the "no-reservations
policy" translates into "brutal waits" and "tightly packed" tables, so
regulars "get there early" or "go for lunch."

Alfredo of Rome *Italian* | 19 | 19 | 19 | $49 |

W 40s | 4 W. 49th St. (bet. 5th & 6th Aves.) | 212-397-0100 |
www.alfredos.com

Disregard the "touristy feel" and this Rock Center Italian is "acceptable" for "filling" if "unoriginal" fare served "without fuss" in a big,
"busy" room adorned with Hirschfeld drawings; still, critics contend
the "quality could be better for the price."

Algonquin Hotel | 18 | 23 | 20 | $58 |
Round Table *American*

W 40s | Algonquin Hotel | 59 W. 44th St. (bet. 5th & 6th Aves.) |
212-840-6800 | www.algonquinhotel.com

Steeped in the "mystique" of bygone "literati", this circa-1902 Theater
District "landmark" retains enough "old-fashioned charm" for those
hoping to "channel Dorothy Parker"; but since the "routine", "overpriced" American food proves "you can't eat history", some go 'round
for just "drinks and conversation."

Alias Ⓜ *American* | ▽ 22 | 15 | 20 | $40 |

LES | 76 Clinton St. (Rivington St.) | 212-505-5011 |
www.aliasrestaurant.com

"Hip and low-key", this "unexpected" little LES "find" offers "sophisticated" twists on "homegrown" Americana served by "attentive" staffers; despite "funky" decor and "cramped" seating, it's a natural for
brunch and Sunday's $30 dinner prix fixe is a "steal."

Ali Baba *Turkish* | 21 | 15 | 18 | $34 |

E 40s | 862 Second Ave. (46th St.) | 212-888-8622 |
www.alibabasterrace.com
Murray Hill | 212 E. 34th St. (bet. 2nd & 3rd Aves.) | 212-683-9206 |
www.alibabaturkishcuisine.com

It's "worth a detour" for the "authentic" meals served at these
East Side "Turkish delights" where "you get your money's worth"
from an "extensive menu" of "exemplary" eats; a "prompt" staff
oversees the "modest" digs, and there's a "special" roof deck at the
Second Avenue location.

	FOOD	DECOR	SERVICE	COST

Alice's Tea Cup *Tearoom* — 19 | 21 | 18 | $26

E 60s | 156 E. 64th St. (Lexington Ave.) | 212-486-9200
E 80s | 220 E. 81st St. (bet. 2nd & 3rd Aves.) | 212-734-4832
W 70s | 102 W. 73rd St. (bet. Amsterdam & Columbus Aves.) |
212-799-3006
www.alicesteacup.com

"Cherished" by "mom-and-daughter" duos, these American tearooms
vend "super scones" and an "exhaustive list" of brews in "fanciful",
"Alice-in-Wonderland" settings; though they're perfect for "clamorous
birthdays" or "snacks with the girls", nonfans cite "sporadic service"
and "oppressive waits."

Allegretti Ⓩ *French* — 23 | 20 | 24 | $67

Flatiron | 46 W. 22nd St. (bet. 5th & 6th Aves.) | 212-206-0555 |
www.allegrettinyc.com

Chef Alain Allegretti's "refined" Flatiron "jewel" showcases the "essence of Nice" with "exciting", "upscale" French cooking delivered by
a "discreet" crew in "spare" yet "attractive" digs; still relatively "undiscovered", it caters to "discerning grown-ups" who don't regretti the
"big price tags."

Alloro *Italian* — 24 | 17 | 24 | $51

E 70s | 307 E. 77th St. (bet. 1st & 2nd Aves.) | 212-535-2866 |
www.alloronyc.com

UES "haute Italian" "sleeper" specializing in "inventive twists" on classic dishes that verge on the "experimental"; the "weird" green-and-
white color scheme may compromise the "cozy" ambiance, but the
"cheerful" servers (overseen by the chef's "perky wife") will "do
cartwheels for you."

Alma *Mexican* — 21 | 21 | 19 | $37

Carroll Gardens | 187 Columbia St., 2nd fl. (Degraw St.) | Brooklyn |
718-643-5400 | www.almarestaurant.com

"Fantastic Manhattan skyline views" from the open-air "rooftop
tables" are the secret weapon of this "small" Carroll Gardens
"hangout" where a "lively crowd" tucks into "delicious" Mexican
fare and deadly margaritas; as it's both "enjoyable" and "not expensive", it "fills up fast."

Almond *French* — 19 | 18 | 19 | $48

Flatiron | 12 E. 22nd St. (bet. B'way & Park Ave. S.) | 212-228-7557 |
www.almondnyc.com

With its "great big", "beachy" interior and "convivial" atmosphere,
this Flatiron spin-off of a "Bridgehampton favorite" is a "safe" bet for
"solid" French bistro standards served at an "acceptable price"; just
don't let the "din" from the "bustling" bar – and "pool table" –
drive you nuts.

Alouette *French* — 21 | 17 | 21 | $44

W 90s | 2588 Broadway (bet. 97th & 98th Sts.) | 212-222-6808 |
www.alouettenyc.com

"Gallic charm" pervades this "jaunty", "very French" UWS "standby"
where the "delightful" bistro fare is "easy on the wallet" if "nothing
overly fancy"; the "quaint", bi-level quarters could be "more roomy",
but "warm service" sets a *"gentil"* tone.

	FOOD	DECOR	SERVICE	COST

Alta *Mediterranean* | 24 | 23 | 19 | $46

G Village | 64 W. 10th St. (bet. 5th & 6th Aves.) | 212-505-7777 | www.altarestaurant.com

"Irresistible" Med tapas is the lure at this "intriguing" Village duplex set in a "candlelit" townhouse equipped with an "extra-big fireplace"; the "creative" small plates can "add up quickly", but if money's no object, order the "whole shebang" for $420; P.S. "try the Brussels sprouts."

☑ Alto ☒ *Italian* | 26 | 24 | 25 | $86

E 50s | 11 E. 53rd St. (bet. 5th & Madison Aves.) | 212-308-1099 | www.altorestaurant.com

A "world of sophistication" in Midtown, this "adult" class act is a showcase for chef Michael White's "flawlessly executed" Northern Italian cuisine, paired with "superb wines"; the "swanky", wine bottle-lined setting is a magnet for "power suits" unfazed by the "alto prices."

Amaranth ● *Mediterranean* | 20 | 19 | 20 | $60

E 60s | 21 E. 62nd St. (bet. 5th & Madison Aves.) | 212-980-6700 | www.amaranthrestaurant.com

Catering to the "thin", "chic" set, this "buzzy" UES bistro is better known for "swish" socializing than its "not-bad" Med menu; while Park Avenue regulars and "Euro" air-kissers can count on "solicitous service", outsiders may find it "snooty" and "overpriced."

Amazing 66 *Chinese* | 22 | 11 | 16 | $24

Chinatown | 66 Mott St. (bet. Bayard & Canal Sts.) | 212-334-0099

Folks "bored with the usual" tout the "extensive" menu at this C-town Cantonese that offers some "interesting spins"; maybe the "minimal" service and decor are "not so amazing", but the prices are a "steal."

Amber ● *Asian* | 19 | 19 | 18 | $37

E 80s | 1406 Third Ave. (80th St.) | 212-249-5020 | www.orderamberuppereast.com

G Village | 432 Sixth Ave. (bet. 9th & 10th Sts.) | 212-477-5880

Murray Hill | 381 Third Ave. (bet. 27th & 28th Sts.) | 212-686-6388 | www.ambergramercy.com

W 70s | 221 Columbus Ave. (70th St.) | 212-799-8100 | www.ambercolumbus.com

"Cooler than you'd think", this "popular" quartet satisfies with a "large menu" of "pleasing" Pan-Asian fare and "quality sushi" served in "stylish", "Buddha-ful" settings; "affordable" tabs and "local convenience" draw an "upbeat" "young crowd" that gets "super-loud" at times.

Amma *Indian* | 25 | 18 | 23 | $46

E 50s | 246 E. 51st St. (bet. 2nd & 3rd Aves.) | 212-644-8330 | www.ammanyc.com

"Brilliant", "subtly spiced" Northern Indian specialties and "exceptional" service make this "small", "tucked-away" East Midtowner an "unsung hero"; sure, the "gourmet" quality means "you'll pay more here", but the "amazing" $50 tasting menu is a bona fide "bargain."

Ammos ☒ *Greek* | 22 | 21 | 20 | $53

E 40s | 52 Vanderbilt Ave. (bet. 44th & 45th Sts.) | 212-922-9999 | www.ammosnewyork.com

Parked a "stone's throw from Grand Central", this "designer Greek" provides a "breezy", "open" backdrop for "upscale" Hellenica focused on an array of "fine" "fresh fish"; it's "busy" at lunchtime with "business" types, "quieter" at dinner and "expensive" all the time.

Amor Cubano *Cuban* ▽ 22 | 16 | 20 | $32

Harlem | 2018 Third Ave. (111th St.) | 212-996-1220 |
www.amorcubanorestaurant.com

Bringing "nights in Havana" to East Harlem, this "festive" Cuban transports diners to "the tropics" with "tasty, authentic" chow, "right-on" mojitos and a "live band" banging out "Latin classics"; given the "smiling" service and "reasonable" tabs, fans can't wait to "come back for more."

Amorina *Pizza* 25 | 15 | 19 | $26

Prospect Heights | 624 Vanderbilt Ave. (Prospect Pl.) | Brooklyn |
718-230-3030 | www.amorinapizza.com

Roman-style "pizzas with panache" are the trademark of this Prospect Heights "local favorite", turning out "spectacular" thin-crust pies with "unusual" toppings in a "casual", "red-checkered-tablecloth" room; "family-friendly vibes" and "sweet" staffers compensate for the "small", "crowded" conditions.

Amy Ruth's *Soul Food* 20 | 12 | 17 | $27

Harlem | 113 W. 116th St. (bet. Lenox & 7th Aves.) | 212-280-8779 |
www.amyruthsharlem.com

"Heaping" servings of "surefire" comfort staples make this "Harlem mainstay" a "real treat" for soul food fans who "don't think about calories"; there's "not a lot of atmosphere", but even so the "wait is crazy" for that "chicken-and-waffles" Sunday brunch.

Amy's Bread *Bakery/Sandwiches* 24 | 12 | 18 | $14

Chelsea | Chelsea Mkt. | 75 Ninth Ave. (bet. 15th & 16th Sts.) |
212-462-4338

W 40s | 672 Ninth Ave. (bet. 46th & 47th Sts.) | 212-977-2670

W Village | 250 Bleecker St. (Leroy St.) | 212-675-7802
www.amysbread.com

"Omnipresent queues" testify to the "superior quality" of the "boffo" artisanal breads, "top-notch" sandwiches and "addictive" desserts at these "well-worth-the-dough" bakery/cafes; aesthetes feeling less amiable about the "bare", "hectic" settings suggest "takeaway."

Anella Ⓜ⊄ *Italian* ▽ 26 | 23 | 25 | $37

Greenpoint | 222 Franklin St. (bet. Green & Huron Sts.) | Brooklyn |
718-389-8100 | www.anellabrooklyn.com

This "cheerful" Greenpoint yearling has a rep as a "local winner" for "spectacular" pizza and rustic Italiana, with "extra points" for the "bread baked in flower pots"; a "typically Brooklyn" outfit with a patio, knowingly "antique" decor and a cash-only policy, it also hosts an "excellent brunch."

Angelica Kitchen ⊄ *Vegan/Vegetarian* 21 | 16 | 18 | $26

E Village | 300 E. 12th St. (bet. 1st & 2nd Aves.) | 212-228-2909 |
www.angelicakitchen.com

Vegans "never tire" of this 35-year-old East Village "standard-bearer" that lures "organically minded" types with "creative" "crunchy" chow at "thrifty" prices; despite "confused service", "spartan" digs and a "cash-only" rule, purists leave "feeling better" about themselves.

| | FOOD | DECOR | SERVICE | COST |

Angelina's *Italian*   22 | 22 | 19 | $63
Staten Island | 399 Ellis St. (off Arthur Kill Rd.) | 718-227-2900 |
www.angelinasristorante.com
"Top-shelf for Staten Island", this Tottenville Italian "delivers in every regard" with "fabulous" classic cooking, "attentive" service and a "beautiful" setting (a three-story "mansion" "overlooking the water"); sure, it's "way expensive", but devotees declare "you get what you pay for."

Angelo & Maxie's *Steak*   21 | 19 | 20 | $55
Flatiron | 233 Park Ave. S. (19th St.) | 212-220-9200
Maxie's Bar & Grill ◑ *American*
Flatiron | 233 Park Ave. S. (19th St.) | 212-979-7800
www.angelo-maxies.com
"Partying bachelors" turn to this Flatiron chop shop for "gargantuan" steaks and "man-size" martinis "ably served" in a "loud" room with a "booming bar scene"; the "dependable" beef "won't break the bank", and the "grill next door" offers a more "casual" option for "burgers and beer."

Angelo's of Mulberry Street ⓜ *Italian*   23 | 15 | 20 | $47
Little Italy | 146 Mulberry St. (bet. Grand & Hester Sts.) | 212-966-1277 |
www.angelomulberry.com
It's "no wonder" this "been-around-forever" Little Italy "bastion" (since 1902) is still "thriving" given its reputation for "true old-style" Neapolitan food and "cordial" service; the "pretty ordinary" space is "bursting at the seams" on weekends with "old-timers and first-timers" alike.

Angelo's Pizzeria *Pizza*   20 | 13 | 16 | $26
E 50s | 1043 Second Ave. (55th St.) | 212-521-3600
W 50s | 117 W. 57th St. (bet. 6th & 7th Aves.) | 212-333-4333
W 50s | 1697 Broadway (bet. 53rd & 54th Sts.) | 212-245-8811
www.angelospizzany.com
These "no-fuss" Midtowners supply "crispy" coal-fired pizza accessorized with your "favorite toppings"; "service is haphazard" and "there's no atmosphere", but they're "convenient" for "low-cost refueling" with "work colleagues."

Angus McIndoe ◑ *American*   16 | 15 | 18 | $41
W 40s | 258 W. 44th St. (bet. B'way & 8th Ave.) | 212-221-9222 |
www.angusmcindoe.com
"Producers, agents and marquee names" rub elbows at this "show-bizzy" Times Square triplex that's naturally "convenient to the theaters"; the American grub may be pretty "ordinary", but no one cares when "Matthew Broderick" is at the next table; P.S. for "celeb spotting", try the third floor "post-curtain."

Ann & Tony's ⓜ *Italian*   20 | 16 | 20 | $35
Bronx | 2407 Arthur Ave. (bet. 187th & 188th Sts.) | 718-364-8250 |
www.annandtonysonline.com
"Red-sauce" fanciers tout this circa-1927 "Arthur Avenue standby" purveying "old-style" Neapolitan food priced for "value"; it's more "low-key" than its neighbors and "seems stuck in time", but at least "you won't leave hungry."

	FOOD	DECOR	SERVICE	COST

Annisa *American*

28 | 24 | 26 | $77

W Village | 13 Barrow St. (bet. 7th Ave. S. & W. 4th St.) | 212-741-6699 | www.annisarestaurant.com

Now fully "recovered" after a fire, this "intimate" West Villager showcases the "exquisite" New American cooking of "masterful" chef Anita Lo; "stylish" new decor and "terrific service" round out a "first-class" experience with prices to match.

Anthos 🗷 *Greek*

24 | 20 | 22 | $66

W 50s | 36 W. 52nd St. (bet. 5th & 6th Aves.) | 212-582-6900 | www.anthosnyc.com

Greek goes "high style" at this "refined" Midtowner from restaurateuse Donatella Arpaia, where the "imaginative" menu, "pro service" and "sophisticated" setting add up to a "consistent wow"; prices are predictably "upscale", though "less expensive" mezes are on offer upstairs; P.S. the big question is "will it be as good?" given the departure of original chef Michael Psilakis.

Antica Venezia *Italian*

22 | 20 | 25 | $52

W Village | 396 West St. (W. 10th St.) | 212-229-0606 | www.avnyc.com

Although "out of the way" on the West Village's "far edge", this Italian "secret" proffers "excellent" classic cuisine and "theatrical", "old-world" service; furnishing freebies from apps to after-dinner grappa, it makes for a "charming date" – and is "especially beautiful at sunset."

Antonucci *Italian*

22 | 16 | 19 | $53

E 80s | 170 E. 81st St. (bet. Lexington & 3rd Aves.) | 212-570-5100

A "top local" draw, this "side-street" Italian is "reliable" for "first-rate food" and "warm" service – and ergo, "always busy"; its "well-heeled" clientele considers the cost "reasonable for the UES", though the "loud", "close" quarters can recall a "packed subway car."

A.O.C. 🌒 *French*

19 | 18 | 17 | $40

W Village | 314 Bleecker St. (Grove St.) | 212-675-9463 | www.aocnyc.com

A.O.C. Bistro 🌒 *French*

Park Slope | 259 Fifth Ave. (Garfield Pl.) | Brooklyn | 718-788-1515 | www.aocbistro.com

"Informal" à la the "Left Bank", these "popular" West Village/Park Slope bistros proffer a "broad menu" of "basic", *"très bien"* French bites; "lackadaisical" service "comes with the territory", but the "price is right" and the Bleecker Street garden is just plain "adorable."

Aperitivo *Pizza*

21 | 19 | 18 | $35

E 40s | 780 Third Ave. (48th St.) | 212-758-9402 | www.aperitivonyc.com

The "pizza rocks" at this Midtown Italian set in a sleek duplex that works for a "reasonably priced business lunch" or an "after-work" get-together; a "cute outdoor" terrace makes the "haphazard" service easier to abide.

Apiary *American*

23 | 20 | 21 | $57

E Village | 60 Third Ave. (bet. 10th & 11th Sts.) | 212-254-0888 | www.apiarynyc.com

"Delighted" admirers of "innovative" chef Scott Bryan label this "chic" East Villager the "bee's knees" for its "first-class" New Americana, "caring service" and "smartly decorated" room; however, the "upbeat" crowd raises "quite a buzz" and you can expect a honey of a tab.

	FOOD	DECOR	SERVICE	COST

Ápizz *Italian*
24 | 21 | 21 | $49

LES | 217 Eldridge St. (bet. Rivington & Stanton Sts.) | 212-253-9199 |
www.apizz.com

A "surprise" in an "offbeat location", this LES "hideout" features a
"wood-burning oven" that produces "excellent" pizza and "robust"
Italian eats in "rustic" digs with "charm to spare"; though "somewhat
pricey", it's a "romantic" option for a "special date."

Applewood Ⓜ *American*
25 | 20 | 22 | $48

Park Slope | 501 11th St. (bet. 7th & 8th Aves.) | Brooklyn | 718-788-1810 |
www.applewoodny.com

"Locavores" love this Park Slope New American's "farmhouse-fresh",
"sustainable" ingredients prepared with "inventive flair"; "welcoming"
servers oversee the "snug" space, but it's "not cheap" and there may
be a "wait", especially for the "marvelous brunch."

AQ Kafé *Scandinavian*
20 | 17 | 17 | $24

W 50s | 1800 Broadway (bet. CPS & 58th St.) | 212-541-6801 |
www.aqkafe.com

Taking a cue from "casual" cafes, this "agreeable" Columbus Circle
"taste of Scandinavia" plies "Swedish comfort food" and "terrific"
baked goods in a "spare", "no-frills" setting; prices are "moderate" for
the area, while well-wishers wish it stayed open "beyond 9 PM."

☒ Aquagrill *Seafood*
26 | 19 | 23 | $60

SoHo | 210 Spring St. (6th Ave.) | 212-274-0505 | www.aquagrill.com

With its "wicked fresh" fish and "spectacular raw bar" stocked with
"more oysters than Narragansett Bay", this "genial", 15-year-old SoHo
enclave is "hard to beat" for "first-rate", "fairly priced" seafood; it's often
"crazy busy" with finatics who've fallen for it "hook, line and sinker."

Aquamarine ● *Asian*
21 | 21 | 20 | $37

Murray Hill | 713 Second Ave. (bet. 38th & 39th Sts.) | 212-297-1880 |
www.orderaquamarine.com

There's "never a dull moment" at this "near-hip" Murray Hill Pan-
Asian with reasonably priced, "tasty sushi" and sizzling platters
served in a bamboo-lined, "waterfall"-equipped space; after dark, it
morphs into a "scene" for "noisy twentysomethings."

☒ Aquavit *Scandinavian*
25 | 24 | 25 | $101

E 50s | 65 E. 55th St. (bet. Madison & Park Aves.) | 212-307-7311 |
www.aquavit.org

Though Marcus Samuelsson is no longer manning the stoves, this "quietly sophisticated" Midtowner is "still a standout" thanks to "delectable"
Scandinavian cuisine, "discreet" service and "striking" "stream-
lined" decor; you'll "pay dearly" for the prix fixe–only experience,
but the "low-key" adjoining cafe provides a preview for "a lot less."

Areo ●Ⓜ *Italian*
24 | 19 | 21 | $52

Bay Ridge | 8424 Third Ave. (bet. 84th & 85th Sts.) | Brooklyn | 718-238-0079

"Like walking into *Saturday Night Fever*", this Bay Ridge Italian is a
"lively", "loud" nexus for "delicious pastas" at "Manhattan prices"; if
the room's "nothing to look at", the mobs of "Snooki's cronies" and
"wannabe Sopranos" trying to impress their dates make for a great
"dinner *and* a show."

	FOOD	DECOR	SERVICE	COST

Arepas Café ⓂVenezuelan
▽ 24 | 12 | 21 | $19

Astoria | 33-07 36th Ave. (34th St.) | Queens | 718-937-3835 | www.arepascafe.com

"Outstanding" arepas (corn cakes stuffed with "*fantastico*" fillings) make this "authentic" Venezuelan worth the "trek to Astoria"; the storefront setting is strictly bare-bones, but devotees "can't get enough of" the flavor and "value" – you almost can't afford to miss it.

Arirang Hibachi Steakhouse Japanese
19 | 17 | 21 | $38

Bay Ridge | 8814 Fourth Ave. (bet. 88th & 89th Sts.) | Brooklyn | 718-238-9880

Staten Island | 23A Nelson Ave. (Locust Pl.) | 718-966-9600 www.partyonthegrill.com

"Family fun" abounds at this cross-borough brace of "Benihana wannabes" where "entertaining", "food-tossing" hibachi chefs grill "not-bad" Japanese steakhouse items amid choruses of "Happy Birthday"; it may be the "definition of corny", but after a few "exotic drinks" everyone "enjoys the show."

Armani Ristorante Italian
19 | 25 | 19 | $66

E 50s | Armani/5th Ave. | 717 Fifth Ave., 3rd fl. (56th St.) | 212-207-1902 | www.armanirestaurantny.com

The "fashionable look" is no surprise at this "pretty-people" place on the third floor of Midtown's Armani flagship, a "slick, ultramodern" haven that sets the tone for "chic" Italian cooking; "expensive" tabs and "bored" staffers may explain why it's always "easy to get a seat."

Arno ⓈItalian
19 | 17 | 20 | $52

Garment District | 141 W. 38th St. (bet. B'way & 7th Ave.) | 212-944-7420 | www.arnoristorante.com

"Rag-trade" types and "Penn Station commuters" tout this Garment District vet as a "safe bet" for "satisfying" Italian standards delivered with "no surprises" by "good-natured servers"; however, given the "old-fashioned" milieu, some suggest it's "a bit overpriced."

Aroma ●Italian
23 | 18 | 20 | $36

NoHo | 36 E. Fourth St. (bet. Bowery & Lafayette St.) | 212-375-0100 | www.aromanyc.com

For "macro tastes in a micro setting", sniff out this "teeny" NoHo "hideaway" that fills up fast thanks to "scrumptious" Italian food paired with an "amazing wine list" for an "appropriate" price; its basement is "great for intimate private parties."

Arté Italian
18 | 17 | 19 | $45

G Village | 21 E. Ninth St. (bet. 5th Ave. & University Pl.) | 212-473-0077 | www.arterestaurant.com

It's "not fancy", but this "old-style" Villager can be counted on for "moderately priced" Italiana served in a "quiet", cozily "fireplaced" setting; foes find it "pedestrian", citing "worn" decor and a "tired" crowd.

Arté Café Italian
18 | 17 | 17 | $36

W 70s | 106 W. 73rd St. (bet. Amsterdam & Columbus Aves.) | 212-501-7014 | www.artecafenyc.com

This "straightforward" UWS "stalwart" plates "consistently decent" versions of the "usual Italian suspects" at a "fair price"; naysayers knock the chow as "uninspired" and the service as "varying", but proximity to Lincoln Center can make it "a bit of a zoo" pre-curtain.

Artichoke Basille's Pizza ●⊄ *Pizza*

| 23 | 6 | 13 | $10 |

E Village | 328 E. 14th St. (bet. 1st & 2nd Aves.) | 212-228-2004 | www.artichokepizza.com

The signature slice "slathered with artichoke dip" is "ecstasy" at this East Village "hole-in-the-wall" where the "unique" pizza attracts "ridiculous lines" of "hipsters", even "at 4 AM"; service is "rough" and there's "no seating", so you'll have to "bring it home" or "eat while walking"; P.S. a larger West Chelsea sibling at 114 10th Avenue is in the works.

Artie's Deli *Deli*

| 18 | 10 | 15 | $24 |

W 80s | 2290 Broadway (bet. 82nd & 83rd Sts.) | 212-579-5959 | www.arties.com

A "popular" UWS "heartburn hotel", this "affordable", "kid-friendly" deli deals out "hefty" sandwiches and other "Jewish soul food" in an "ersatz authentic" setting with typically "cranky" service; while "not the Katz's meow", it "covers the bases" when you're in a pickle.

☑ Artisanal *French*

| 23 | 20 | 20 | $54 |

Murray Hill | 2 Park Ave. (enter on 32nd St., bet. Madison & Park Aves.) | 212-725-8585 | www.artisanalbistro.com

"Cheese lovers" say you can't beat the "phenomenal" fromages at Terrance Brennan's "aromatic" Murray Hill brasserie that's also "worth the money" for its "classic" French cooking and "fantastic fondues"; it's a "dandy" place to "indulge", though the "vibrant" crowd puts the "din" in dinner.

Arturo's Pizzeria ● *Pizza*

| 21 | 13 | 16 | $27 |

G Village | 106 W. Houston St. (Thompson St.) | 212-677-3820

"Old-school to the hilt", this 1957-vintage Village pizzeria "still rocks" with "crackling" thin-crust pies served in "funky" digs festooned with "amateur art"; "affordability" and live "jazz trios" make it a natural for "locals" and "college kids" alike.

Asia de Cuba *Asian/Cuban*

| 23 | 24 | 21 | $62 |

Murray Hill | Morgans Hotel | 237 Madison Ave. (bet. 37th & 38th Sts.) | 212-726-7755 | www.chinagrillmgt.com

"Cacophonous" and "frenetic", this Murray Hill Asian-Cuban still "packs 'em in" with its "exotic", "high-priced" fusion fare served in a "stylish" white room with a "happening" communal table ; sure, some snipe it's "moving toward mass market", but for the majority the "excitement in the air" "never gets old."

☑ Asiate *American/Asian*

| 24 | 29 | 25 | $111 |

W 60s | Mandarin Oriental Hotel | 80 Columbus Circle, 35th fl. (60th St. at B'way) | 212-805-8881 | www.mandarinoriental.com

You'll "feel on top of the world" at this "über-stylish" perch (voted No. 1 for Decor) in the Mandarin Oriental, where "mesmerizing" Central Park and UWS views provide the "perfect backdrop" for "delectable" Asian–New Americana and "pampering" service; it's made for "special occasions" with a "special someone", and though the prix fixe–only dinner tabs are "stratospheric", the $24 weekday lunch is "a steal."

	FOOD	DECOR	SERVICE	COST

Aspen Social Club ● *American*
18 | 23 | 18 | $42

W 40s | Stay Hotel | 157 W. 47th St. (bet. 6th & 7th Aves.) | 212-221-7200 | www.aspensocialclub.com

"Very cool" for Times Square, this "club"-like spot is done up in ski-chalet style with "birch trees", antler chandeliers and a "simulated roaring fire"; despite "decent" enough moderately priced New American grub and cocktails, critics find the atmosphere "more singles bar than serious restaurant."

Atlantic Grill *Seafood*
23 | 19 | 21 | $54

E 70s | 1341 Third Ave. (bet. 76th & 77th Sts.) | 212-988-9200
NEW **W 60s** | 49 W. 64th St. (bet. B'way & CPW) | 212-787-4663
www.brguestrestaurants.com

Upper Eastsiders label Steve Hanson's "solid" seafood "staple" a "consistent" "crowd-pleaser" owing to its "fabulous fish", "super brunch" and "jumping bar" scene; though everyone's "packed in like sardines" and "Giants Stadium is quieter", that's all part of the "hugely popular" deal; P.S. the new UWS spin-off in the former O'Neals' space opened post-Survey

At Vermilion *Indian/Nuevo Latino*
20 | 22 | 20 | $57

E 40s | 480 Lexington Ave. (46th St.) | 212-871-6600 | www.thevermilionrestaurant.com

The "stark but stunning" setting serves as a "calming backdrop" to the "fanciful" Indo-Latin fusion fare served at this "unique" duplex near Grand Central; it's fairly "undiscovered", and some say that's because it's "trying too hard" for a "trendy vibe."

August *European*
22 | 20 | 21 | $47

W Village | 359 Bleecker St. (bet. Charles & W. 10th Sts.) | 212-929-8727 | www.augustny.com

An "escape from the city", this "tucked-away" West Village European is a "good deal" for "uniformly fine" wood-oven dishes served in "rustic" "boho" digs; inside, there's "flattering lighting" for "date night", but regulars make a beeline for its "lovely enclosed garden."

Au Mandarin *Chinese*
20 | 15 | 20 | $33

Financial District | World Financial Ctr. | 200-250 Vesey St. (West St.) | 212-385-0313 | www.aumandarin.com

Long a "staple" for Battery Park City types, this World Financial Center Chinese is also favored by "late-working" Wall Streeters who can handle the "higher-than-necessary prices"; though the food's "well prepared", the "non-elegant" atmosphere helps explain the "thriving take-out" trade.

Ⓩ Aureole ● *American*
26 | 24 | 25 | $109

W 40s | Bank of America Tower | 135 W. 42nd St. (bet. B'way & 6th Ave.) | 212-319-1660 | www.charliepalmer.com

"Kudos to Charlie Palmer" for this "truly impressive" remake, now ensconced between Bryant Park and Times Square and showcasing "smashing" American cuisine via chef Christopher Lee, "top-shelf" service and a "spectacular", Adam Tihany–designed room; ok, you'll have to "open up your wallet" wide for the prix fixe–only dinner, but the "more informal", more "energetic" front cafe offers à la carte options.

	FOOD	DECOR	SERVICE	COST

Aurora *Italian*
24 | 20 | 20 | $47

SoHo | 510 Broome St. (bet. Thompson St. & W. B'way) | 212-334-9020
Williamsburg | 70 Grand St. (Wythe Ave.) | Brooklyn |
718-388-5100 ⊟
www.auroraristorante.com

"Such a find", these "cool" Williamsburg/SoHo "havens" really "hit
the mark" with "tantalizing" Italian cooking, "midrange prices" and
"charming" "farmhouse" settings; Brooklyn's garden is "quite special", though its "no-credit-cards policy" is not.

Austin's Steakhouse 🅂 *Steak*
22 | 19 | 21 | $53

Bay Ridge | 8915 Fifth Ave. (90th St.) | Brooklyn | 718-439-5000 |
www.austinssteakhouseny.com

"If steak's your thing", this "friendly" Bay Ridge "neighborhood joint"
delivers "large" portions of "surprisingly decent" beef and sides to a
"quiet, mature" clientele; still, some find it "overpriced" for an experience "several tiers below the big boys."

🅉 A Voce *Italian*
24 | 22 | 22 | $66

Flatiron | 41 Madison Ave. (26th St.) | 212-545-8555
W 60s | Time Warner Ctr. | 10 Columbus Circle, 3rd fl. (60th St. at B'way) |
212-823-2523
www.avocerestaurant.com

"Upscale charm" marks this Madison Square Park Italian (and its Time
Warner Center sibling "overlooking Columbus Circle") that offers
"splendid" seasonal cuisine from chef Missy Robbins, "solicitous service" and "sleek", "stylish" surroundings; expect "expense-account"
pricing and so much "buzz" it's hard to "hear your own voce."

Avra ❶ *Greek*
25 | 22 | 22 | $60

E 40s | 141 E. 48th St. (bet. Lexington & 3rd Aves.) | 212-759-8550 |
www.avrany.com

Like a "trip to the Greek isles" in Midtown, this "classy bit of Santorini"
proves its "flair for fish" with "fresh", "simply grilled" catch right "from
the ice" served in an "airy", "high-energy" room; it's "deservedly popular", despite "loud acoustics" and "per-pound" pricing that "approaches the national debt."

Awash *Ethiopian*
21 | 13 | 17 | $24

E Village | 338 E. Sixth St. (bet. 1st & 2nd Aves.) | 212-982-9589
W 100s | 947 Amsterdam Ave. (bet. 106th & 107th Sts.) |
212-961-1416
www.awashnyc.com

The "hands-on" (i.e. "no utensils") approach can get "a little messy", but
these "modest" Ethiopians still satisfy with their "flavorful", "finger-
licking-good" stews scooped up with spongy injera bread; "uninspiring" decor and "lackadaisical" service detract, but not the tabs.

Azul Bistro ❶ *Argentinean/Steak*
20 | 18 | 19 | $43

LES | 152 Stanton St. (Suffolk St.) | 646-602-2004 |
www.azulnyc.com

Hipsters in the "mood for meat" head for this "small" LES Argentinean
specializing in "dynamite" steaks and "good" gaucho grub paired with
imported reds; the "cool, offbeat" digs are as "inviting" as the prices,
yet it's best known to locals and expats.

	FOOD	DECOR	SERVICE	COST

Azuri Cafe ⊄ *Israeli* 25 | 4 | 10 | $15

W 50s | 465 W. 51st St. (bet. 9th & 10th Aves.) | 212-262-2920 |
www.azuricafe.com

"Masterfully prepared" falafel and other "incredible", "cheap-as-hell"
Israeli kosher eats warrant the "schlep" west to this "tiny" Hell's
Kitchen "dive"; since you'll have to abide a "gritty" setting and "un-
friendly" owner ("Danny Meyer he isn't"), "don't bring a date."

Z Babbo ● *Italian* 27 | 23 | 25 | $79

G Village | 110 Waverly Pl. (bet. MacDougal St. & 6th Ave.) | 212-777-0303 |
www.babbonyc.com

"Still a wow", the Batali-Bastianich boys' "boffo" Village "linchpin" is
"always on" with "transcendent" Italian cooking, "primo" wines and
"well-informed service"; the handsome restored carriage house quarters are always "jammed" with "cacophonic" crowds, who say that the
"hassle to get a table" and the check afterwards are "beyond worth it."

Bacchus *French* 21 | 19 | 20 | $39

Boerum Hill | 409 Atlantic Ave. (bet. Bond & Nevins Sts.) | Brooklyn |
718-852-1572 | www.bacchushistro.com

A "sweet" spot near BAM, this Boerum Hill bistro "aims to please"
with "très terrific" French food and "interesting" wines ferried by a
"welcoming" team; with its "shabby-chic charm", "divine" garden and
$25 "prix fixe steal", locals label it a "winner."

Back Forty *American* 22 | 18 | 21 | $38

E Village | 190 Ave. B (bet. 11th & 12th Sts.) | 212-388-1990 |
www.backfortynyc.com

"Farm-to-table" fanatics tout Peter Hoffman's East Village "locavore
haunt" for its "flavorful", "conscientiously sourced" New American
menu built around an "out-of-this-world" burger; "comforting",
"country-style" vibes and a "great backyard" complete the picture.

Bagatelle ● *French* 18 | 20 | 16 | $66

Meatpacking | 409 W. 13th St. (bet. 9th Ave. & Washington St.) |
212-675-2400 | www.bistrotbagatelle.com

"Euros go wild" at this "fist-pumping" Meatpacking bistro where the
French food plays second fiddle to the "bottles of champagne" and DJs
spinning "techno" music (the "table-dancing" Saturday brunch is "an
event in itself"); it's way "overpriced", but then again, "you don't come
here to eat, you come to party."

NEW Balaboosta *Mediterranean* – | – | – | E

NoLita | 214 Mulberry St. (bet. Prince & Spring Sts.) | 212-966-7366
From the husband-and-wife team behind the falafel phenom Taïm, this
"wonderful addition to NoLita" serves sophisticated, somewhat pricey
iterations of traditional dishes both Mediterranean (bouillabaisse)
and Middle Eastern (lamb with Persian lime sauce); the rustic, window-
lined space features an open kitchen visible from the sidewalk.

Z Balthazar ● *French* 23 | 23 | 20 | $56

SoHo | 80 Spring St. (bet. B'way & Crosby St.) | 212-965-1414 |
www.balthazarny.com

"Unabashedly fabulous", Keith McNally's "grand pillar of SoHo" is a
"like-Paris-used-to-be" brasserie whose "infectious allure" attracts

everyone from "celebs" to "out-of-towners" for "scrumptious" Gallic eats served in a "big, bright, bustling" space; it's "always buzzing", even in the AM when regulars relish its "breakfast of champions."

Baluchi's *Indian*
18 | 14 | 16 | $28

E 50s | 224 E. 53rd St. (bet. 2nd & 3rd Aves.) | 212-750-5515
E 80s | 1724 Second Ave. (bet. 89th & 90th Sts.) | 212-996-2600
Murray Hill | 329 Third Ave. (bet. 24th & 25th Sts.) | 212-679-3434
SoHo | 193 Spring St. (bet. Sullivan & Thompson Sts.) | 212-226-2828
TriBeCa | 275 Greenwich St. (Warren St.) | 212-571-5343
W 50s | 240 W. 56th St. (bet. B'way & 8th Ave.) | 212-397-0707
Park Slope | 310 Fifth Ave. (bet. 2nd & 3rd Sts.) | Brooklyn | 718-832-5555
Forest Hills | 113-30 Queens Blvd. (bet. 76th Ave. & 76th Rd.) | Queens | 718-520-8600
www.baluchis.com

Notwithstanding the "Italian-sounding name", this "omnipresent" local chain is a "competent" supplier of "basic" Indian grub at a "fair" cost; the "half-price lunch specials" are a "great value" if you can tolerate "perfunctory" service and "blah" settings – though "they also deliver."

Bamonte's *Italian*
23 | 16 | 21 | $45

Williamsburg | 32 Withers St. (bet. Lorimer St. & Union Ave.) | Brooklyn | 718-384-8831

"Family-run" since 1900, this "old-line" Williamsburg Italian stays "on the money" with "genuine" "red-gravy" standards served by a "tuxedo-clad" crew who have "worked here longer than you've been alive"; sure, it's well worn, but "satisfied customers" find it a "comforting throwback to another time."

Banjara ● *Indian*
22 | 15 | 18 | $33

E Village | 97 First Ave. (6th St.) | 212-477-5956 | www.banjaranyc.com

Bringing some "class" to the Sixth Street scene around the corner, this East Village "standout" satisfies with "delicious", "perfectly spiced" Northern Indian dishes that "you don't find everywhere else"; true, the service and setting may be "unmemorable", but "affordable" prices compensate.

Bann *Korean*
22 | 22 | 20 | $48

W 50s | Worldwide Plaza | 350 W. 50th St. (bet. 8th & 9th Aves.) | 212-582-4446 | www.bannrestaurant.com

Do-it-yourselfers dig the tabletop hibachis at this "higher-end" Korean in Midtown's Worldwide Plaza, a "quiet" sibling of Woo Lae Oak offering "excellent" chow and "solicitous" service; alright, "you can find cheaper" elsewhere, but for a "classy change of pace", this one's "on the front burner."

Bann Thai *Thai*
19 | 17 | 19 | $31

Forest Hills | 69-12 Austin St. (bet. 69th Rd. & Yellowstone Blvd.) | Queens | 718-544-9999 | www.bannthairestaurant.com

One of Forest Hills' "better bets" for Thai, this "easygoing" "neighborhood" spot is a "good deal" for "tasty" eats, "solicitous" service and a "lovely" setting decorated with "puppets and masks"; it's a bit out of the way but "still going strong" thanks to "steady regulars."

	FOOD	DECOR	SERVICE	COST

Baoguette ⊄ *Vietnamese* — 21 | 8 | 14 | $12

NEW **Financial District** | 9 Maiden Ln. (B'way) | 212-233-3400 Ⓢ
Murray Hill | 61 Lexington Ave. (bet. 25th & 26th Sts.) | 212-532-1133 Ⓢ
W Village | 120 Christopher St. (Bedford St.) | 212-929-0877

Baoguette Cafe ❶⊄ *Vietnamese*

E Village | 37 St. Marks Pl. (bet. 2nd & 3rd Aves.) | 212-380-1487
www.baoguette.com

While not yet "on every corner", Michael 'Bao' Huynh's Vietnamese chainlet is spreading thanks to "terrific" banh mi sandwiches served up "fast" and "cheap"; however, given the "disorganized" service and "cramped", "dumpy" settings, regulars bao out and guette it "to go."

NEW **BaoHaus** ⊄ *Chinese* — - | - | - | I

LES | 137 Rivington St. (bet. Norfolk & Suffolk Sts.) | 646-684-3835 |
www.baohausnyc.com

Courtesy of enfant terrible Eddie Huang, this tiny, stool-lined LES snackery offers Taiwanese *bao* (steamed buns) stuffed with beef, fried chicken, pork belly or tofu; the menu also includes misleadingly named 'fries' (*bao* pieces drizzled with sweet syrup) and soup.

Bao Noodles *Vietnamese* — 19 | 12 | 15 | $27

Gramercy | 391 Second Ave. (bet. 22nd & 23rd Sts.) | 212-725-7770 |
www.baonoodles.com

"Much needed" in Gramercy, this "casual" venue plies "fresh" pho and other Vietnamese comfort items for a "pittance"; service is "lacking" and it's "not much to look at", yet it still draws lots of "noisy" "young" things.

Bar Americain *American* — 23 | 23 | 23 | $62

W 50s | 152 W. 52nd St. (bet. 6th & 7th Aves.) | 212-265-9700 |
www.baramericain.com

Bobby Flay "gets it right" at this Midtowner where "flay-nomenal" American brasserie favorites are served in a "glamorous" setting by "engaging" staffers; despite "big prices", a cross-section of "corporate" and "pre-theater" sorts keeps it "loud" and "happening."

Baraonda ❶ *Italian* — 19 | 17 | 16 | $48

E 70s | 1439 Second Ave. (75th St.) | 212-288-8555 | www.baraondany.com

"Things get going late" at this "hedonistic" UES "hot spot" where "Euros" and "yuppies" pile in for a "hopping scene" that's "a floor show in itself"; despite "so-so" Italian food and "spotty service", it's a destination for "fun" lovers for whom "price is no object."

Barbès ❶ *French/Moroccan* — 19 | 18 | 20 | $42

Murray Hill | 21 E. 36th St. (bet. 5th & Madison Aves.) | 212-684-0215 |
www.barbesrestaurantnyc.com

In the "shadow of the Morgan Library" lies this "unexpected", "under-the-radar" Murray Hill "charmer", a bès bet for "tempting" French-Moroccan chow delivered by "amicable" folks; the "intimate", "sultry" space reminds some of a "genie's bottle", albeit a "crowded" one.

Ⓩ **Barbetta** ❶ⓈⓂ *Italian* — 20 | 23 | 21 | $63

W 40s | 321 W. 46th St. (bet. 8th & 9th Aves.) | 212-246-9171 |
www.barbettarestaurant.com

A "perennial" Theater District destination since 1906, this "well-oiled" Italian is favored for its "high-style" cooking and "refined service", enhanced by an "elegant", "villalike" setting and "glorious garden"; "discerning" diners with traditional tastes figure it's a must-try.

Barbone *Italian*
24 | 18 | 22 | $45

E Village | 186 Ave. B (bet. 11th & 12th Sts.) | 212-254-6047 | www.barbonenyc.com

Somewhat of a "best-kept secret", this "little" Alphabet City "gem" offers "lip-smacking" Italiana via a "genial" team overseen by a "host-with-the-most" owner; "decent prices" and a "charming garden" seal the deal.

Bar Boulud *French*
23 | 20 | 21 | $61

W 60s | 1900 Broadway (bet. 63rd & 64th Sts.) | 212-595-0303 | www.danielnyc.com

"*Bravissima*" is the word on Daniel Boulud's "sleek" wine bar "just steps from Lincoln Center", where the "well-crafted" French bistro fare including "second-to-none" charcuterie makes for "chic" eating pre- or post-curtain; it's "not cheap" and the "spartan", "tunnellike interior" can get "loud", but ultimately it's a "huge boost" for the neighborhood.

Barbounia *Mediterranean*
21 | 23 | 20 | $49

Flatiron | 250 Park Ave. S. (20th St.) | 212-995-0242 | www.barbounia.com

The "impressive", vaulted-ceilinged setting and "good-looking" clientele are a "feast for the eyes" at this "sceney" Flatiron Med where "buzzing" crowds convene for "delish" food and drink from an "accommodating" team; sure, it's "pricey" and "not for conversation", but that doesn't hurt its "popularity."

Bar Breton *French*
19 | 15 | 18 | $43

Chelsea | 254 Fifth Ave. (bet. 28th & 29th Sts.) | 212-213-4999 | www.barbreton.com

Breton chef Cyril Renaud (of bygone yet still "beloved Fleur de Sel") brings his native cuisine to this "casual" North Chelsea yearling, serving French "comfort food" in "humble" digs; though he "nails it" with "fabulous" galettes and crêpes, nonfans still shrug "nothing special."

Barbuto *Italian*
23 | 19 | 21 | $53

W Village | 775 Washington St. (bet. Jane & W. 12th Sts.) | 212-924-9700 | www.barbutonyc.com

Top toque Jonathan Waxman works some "serious magic" with Italian "market cuisine" at this West Village "winner", a "sceney hangout" set in a "cool" converted garage; it's agreeably "lively" if "a little loud", and when it gets warm enough, they roll up the walls.

BareBurger *Burgers*
23 | 17 | 19 | $20

Astoria | 33-21 31st Ave. (34th St.) | Queens | 718-777-7011 | www.bareburger.com

"All-organic" and "oh-so-tasty", this "earthy" Astoria venue vends "eco-friendly" burgers – from grass-fed beef to "rarities like elk, bison and ostrich" – accompanied by "freshly cut" fries; "helpful" staffers make "paying a premium" easier to bear.

NEW Bar Henry 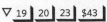 *American*
∇ 19 | 20 | 23 | $43

G Village | 90 W. Houston St., downstairs (bet. La Guardia Pl. & Thompson St.) | 646-448-4559 | www.barhenry.com

A "subterranean surprise", this new Village bistro–cum–wine bar appeals to "worldly" oenophiles with an "awesome" vino lineup served with "genuine warmth" in "intimate", ultrarustic digs; "worthy" American bites also figure into the equation, though some say the "food's an afterthought."

Bark Hot Dogs ● *Hot Dogs*   21 | 16 | 17 | $15

Park Slope | 474 Bergen St. (bet. 5th & 6th Aves.) | Brooklyn | 718-789-1939 | www.barkhotdogs.com

"Environmentally sensitive" enthusiasts woof down "artisanal" tubesteaks and "homemade" organic condiments at this Park Slope "haute dog" nook set in a space made out of "recycled" materials; it's collaring the "stroller set", though some growl it's a little "pricey" for a wiener.

Barmarché ● *American*   21 | 21 | 19 | $40

NoLita | 14 Spring St. (Elizabeth St.) | 212-219-2399 | www.barmarche.com

Something of a "neighborhood secret", this NoLita bistro is a "low-key refuge" where habitués slip in for "well-done" New Americana and cocktails at a "good price"; the "cute" "vintage" setting is a perfect match for the "pretty" crowd.

☑ Barney Greengrass Ⓜ⊄ *Deli*   24 | 8 | 15 | $29

W 80s | 541 Amsterdam Ave. (bet. 86th & 87th Sts.) | 212-724-4707 | www.barneygreengrass.com

"Unchanged for generations", this circa-1908 UWS "landmark" is "still the genuine item" for "ambrosial" smoked fish and other premium Jewish deli fare that make for a "not-to-be-missed NYC experience"; despite "dumpy" digs, a "cash-only" policy and "long waits", this is "one of the great constants in life."

Barolo *Italian*   19 | 21 | 19 | $55

SoHo | 398 W. Broadway (bet. Broome & Spring Sts.) | 212-226-1102 | www.nybarolo.com

Life is good under the "tree blossoms" of this SoHo stalwart's "gorgeous" garden, a "lovely retreat" for "middle-of-the-road" Italian food backed up by an "impressive", extensive wine list; though it's "a bit pricey" and "Euro-pretentious", the open-air "respite" makes it a winning option.

Barosa *Italian*   22 | 17 | 20 | $38

Rego Park | 62-29 Woodhaven Blvd. (62nd Rd.) | Queens | 718-424-1455
www.barosas.com

Italian "old-school" dining is in session at this "solid" supplier of "generously portioned" "red-sauce" standards in Rego Park; since "weekend crowds" are as probable as a "pinky-ring" sighting, "be prepared to wait."

NEW Bar Paya ● *Peruvian*   - | - | - | M

E Village | 65 Second Ave. (bet. 3rd & 4th Sts.) | 212-777-6965 | www.barpaya.com

Raw-food enthusiast Matthew Kenney switches gears by firing up the stoves at this upscale East Village Peruvian offering a mostly small-plates menu of ceviche, causa (dumplings), paya (flatbreads) and plancha items; the rustic setting includes communal seats, a central bar and plenty of sidewalk tables.

	FOOD	DECOR	SERVICE	COST

Bar Pitti ●🖘 Italian
22 | 14 | 17 | $41

G Village | 268 Sixth Ave. (bet. Bleecker & Houston Sts.) | 212-982-3300
"See and be seen" at this Village Italian, a "perennial favorite" for "star sightings", "bustling" alfresco action and "dynamite" pastas at "relatively modest prices"; even with "rushed" service, "sparse" decor, no reservations and no plastic, "trendy" types keep it "going strong."

Barrio Mexican
17 | 15 | 16 | $31

Park Slope | 210 Seventh Ave. (3rd St.) | Brooklyn | 718-965-4000 | www.barriofoods.com
Park Slopers are sweet on the "fun bar" and "nice patio" at this "neighborhood" Mexican, but aren't as jazzed by the "ordinary" eats and service; sympathizers suggest it "could be a treasure" with some tinkering, provided the "kid-friendly" attitude stays on.

Bar Stuzzichini Italian
20 | 18 | 18 | $44

Flatiron | 928 Broadway (bet. 21st & 22nd Sts.) | 212-780-5100 | www.barstuzzichini.com

Stuzzicheria Italian
NEW **TriBeCa** | 305 Church St. (bet. Lispenard & Walker Sts.) | 212-219-4037
Sampling lots of "inventive" small plates is the way to go at this "cavernous" Flatiron Italian (and its new TriBeCa spin-off), especially when they're paired with its "great wine selection"; "gentle prices" help its "youthful professional" following forgive the "iffy" service.

Bar Tano ● Italian
▽ 21 | 23 | 21 | $31

Park Slope | 457 Third Ave. (9th St.) | Brooklyn | 718-499-3400 | www.bartano.com
Although "on the edge of nowhere", this "quaint" Bar Toto sibling is a "marvelous" Park Slope discovery where "tasty" Italian nibbles are served "with panache" in "atmospheric" digs heavy on the pressed tin; all in all, it's an "easy" option with "good prices" to boot.

Bar Toto ● Italian
21 | 20 | 19 | $29

Park Slope | 411 11th St. (6th Ave.) | Brooklyn | 718-768-4698 | www.bartoto.com
There are "no pretenses" at this "popular", "sweet" Park Sloper that covers the "basics" with "well-priced" Italian fare; its "neighborhood vibe" works, but note that it's as "kid-friendly" as *Romper Room*."

Bar Vetro 🖾 Italian
▽ 22 | 17 | 22 | $40

E 50s | 222 E. 58th St. (bet. 2nd & 3rd Aves.) | 212-308-0112 | www.vivolonyc.com
One of the East Side's few "secrets", this "civilized" Italian "couldn't be more hospitable" with its good, "dependable" food and wine, "pro" staffers and "affordable" tabs; the "modern decor" appeals to "younger" types mixing it up at the glass-topped bar "after work."

Basilica ● Italian
20 | 13 | 20 | $34

W 40s | 676 Ninth Ave. (bet. 46th & 47th Sts.) | 212-489-0051
Despite ungodly "tight" dimensions, this Theater District Italian is a "satisfying" option for non-claustrophobes headed to a show; the $28 "prix fixe with a complimentary bottle of wine" is a "terrific buy", though some wonder "how they do it for the price."

	FOOD	DECOR	SERVICE	COST

Basso56 *Italian* — 23 | 18 | 23 | $49

W 50s | 234 W. 56th St. (bet. B'way & 8th Ave.) | 212-265-2610 |
www.basso56.com

"Calm", "consistent" and "convenient" to Carnegie Hall, this "high-performance" Theater District Italian is "popular" with showgoers who applaud its "simple, albeit creative" dishes and "personable" staffers; the "long, narrow room" and midlevel pricing are less exciting.

Basta Pasta *Italian* — 23 | 16 | 20 | $44

Flatiron | 37 W. 17th St. (bet. 5th & 6th Aves.) | 212-366-0888 |
www.bastapastanyc.com

"Japanese-style Italian food" might sound "bizarre", but somehow "they manage to pull it off" for a "reasonable" sum at this longtime Flatiron favorite; those seeking "spectacle" ignore the "minimalist" digs, focussing instead on its legendary "pasta tossed in a huge wheel of cheese."

Battery Gardens *American/Continental* — 17 | 24 | 18 | $48

Financial District | SW corner of Battery Park (State St.) | 212-809-5508 |
www.batterygardens.com

It's all about the "outdoor tables" with a "spectacular NY harbor view" at this "remote" Battery Park hideaway; the American-Continental cooking is "enjoyable" enough, and if it's "slow" to arrive, "watching the ships go by" distracts.

Bay Leaf *Indian* — 21 | 18 | 19 | $40

W 50s | 49 W. 56th St. (bet. 5th & 6th Aves.) | 212-957-1818 |
www.bayleafnyc.com

"Flavorful dishes that don't cost too many rupees" clinch the deal for curry fans at this Midtown Indian near Carnegie Hall; the setting may feel "a bit tired", but at least the "unrushed" ambiance allows you to linger over that "bargain" $16 lunch buffet.

Bayou *Cajun* — 23 | 19 | 21 | $34

Staten Island | 1072 Bay St. (bet. Chestnut & St. Mary's Aves.) |
718-273-4383 | www.bayoustatenisland.com

Folks gung-ho for gumbo in Staten Island tout this "funky" Rosebank nod to N'Awlins as the "authentic" article, citing its "tried-and-true" Cajun favorites and "friendly" atmosphere; indeed, this "great little place" is now "better than ever" thanks to a "recent renovation."

B. Café *Belgian* — 21 | 17 | 19 | $38

E 70s | 240 E. 75th St. (bet. 2nd & 3rd Aves.) | 212-249-3300 |
W 80s | 566 Amsterdam Ave. (bet. 87th & 88th Sts.) | 212-873-1800 |
www.bcafe.com

Those in the mood for mussels tout these crosstown Belgian bistros for their "awesome" variety of moules, "irresistible" frites and "world-class beers" served in "lively", "pubby" environs; the narrow settings are often "cheek-by-jowl", but they're "popular for a reason."

Beacon *American* — 22 | 21 | 22 | $61

W 50s | 25 W. 56th St. (bet. 5th & 6th Aves.) | 212-332-0500 |
www.beaconnyc.com

Waldy Malouf's trademark "wood-fired" flame still burns bright at this Midtown "mainstay", grilling "exceptional" New Americana served in a "gracious" setting by an "attentive" crew; though "business" types don't mind the "costly" tabs, "deal"-hunters love its "value"-packed prix fixes.

Beast *Mediterranean* | 21 | 16 | 18 | $33 |

Prospect Heights | 638 Bergen St. (Vanderbilt Ave.) | Brooklyn | 718-399-6855 | www.brooklynbeast.com

"Really good" Mediterranean tapas tame wild appetites at this "casual" Prospect Heights hangout that hosts a "popular weekend brunch"; though the small plates are "moderately priced", overall it's "not cheap" since the tabs "can add up" quickly.

Becco ● *Italian* | 23 | 19 | 22 | $46 |

W 40s | 355 W. 46th St. (bet. 8th & 9th Aves.) | 212-397-7597 | www.becco-nyc.com

"Good value" is the main attraction at Joe and Lidia Bastianich's *molto* "busy" Restaurant Row Italian with a "home-run" hook: "amazing", "all-you-can-eat" pasta for $23, washed down with a "fab" $25-a-bottle wine list; even better, the "accommodating" staffers "get you to the show on time without compromising quality."

Beccofino *Italian* | 20 | 15 | 20 | $37 |

Bronx | 5704 Mosholu Ave. (bet. Fieldston Rd. & Spencer Ave.) | 718-432-2604

"Plentiful" portions of "reasonably priced" red-sauce standards served by "helpful" staffers have Riverdale residents raving about this "neighborhood" Italian; no surprise, the "tiny" dimensions and no-reservations policy translate into "long" weekend waits.

Belcourt *European* | 19 | 16 | 16 | $38 |

E Village | 84 E. Fourth St. (2nd Ave.) | 212-979-2034 | www.belcourtnyc.com

"Completely down to earth", this East Villager offers "hearty" Pan-European eats and "well-made cocktails" at a "fair price"; ambiance-wise, it's "got the French bistro thing going on", i.e. "antique", Parisian-cafe furnishings, "detached service" and "noisy" acoustics.

Bella Blu ● *Italian* | 21 | 18 | 19 | $52 |

E 70s | 967 Lexington Ave. (bet. 70th & 71st Sts.) | 212-988-4624 | www.baraondany.com

"Pasta, pearls and plastic surgery" collide at this "lively" UES Italian where the *"delizioso"* dishes, "fab" brick-oven pizzas and "busy bar" are designed to suit its "stylish" patrons; though both the decibels and the tabs can be "too high", at least the "great people-watching" is gratis.

Bella Via *Italian* | 23 | 17 | 20 | $34 |

LIC | 47-46 Vernon Blvd. (48th Ave.) | Queens | 718-361-7510 | www.bellaviarestaurant.com

LIC "locals" wonder "why schlep into Manhattan?" when this "home-style Italian" supplies "solid" pastas and "out-of-this-world" brick-oven pizzas in their own backyard; the big-windowed storefront's "airy" feel and overall "friendly" vibe ratchet up the "value" factor.

Belleville *French* | 18 | 19 | 18 | $38 |

Park Slope | 330-332 Fifth St. (5th Ave.) | Brooklyn | 718-832-9777 | www.bellevillebistro.com

The "look and feel of Paris" is spot-on at this "pleasant" Park Slope French bistro, from its "charming" Left-Bank-by-way-of-Balthazar atmosphere to the leisurely service; critics say the "so-so" chow needs a dash of "American ambition", but at least "the price is right."

Bello *Italian*

 21 | 17 | 22 | $48

W 50s | 863 Ninth Ave. (56th St.) | 212-246-6773 | www.bellorestaurant.com

An "old standout" in Hell's Kitchen, this Italian proves that a "sedate" scene doesn't preclude "enjoyable" dining given "consistently good" food and "pro" service; the "throwback" mood even extends to the next-door garage, where you can enjoy "free parking."

Bello Sguardo ● *Mediterranean*

20 | 16 | 19 | $39

W 70s | 410 Amsterdam Ave. (bet. 79th & 80th Sts.) | 212-873-6252

On an UWS strip that's "back-to-back with restaurants", this "trusty" joint holds its own with a "modestly priced" Mediterranean menu that's "great for grazing"; service is "friendly", and if the interior's "not flashy" enough, sidewalk seating is a "pleasant" alternative.

Ben & Jack's Steak House *Steak*

23 | 18 | 23 | $70

E 40s | 219 E. 44th St. (bet. 2nd & 3rd Aves.) | 212-682-5678
Murray Hill | 255 Fifth Ave. (bet. 28th & 29th Sts.) | 212-532-7600
www.benandjackssteakhouse.com

These East Side contenders in the "Peter Luger clone wars" serve up "seriously fine" steaks with all the "familiar" trimmings – "bring on the bacon!" – in "spacious" venues overseen by "pro" teams; ultimately, "there are no surprises here", but "at these prices" there shouldn't be.

Ben Benson's *Steak*

24 | 18 | 22 | $70

W 50s | 123 W. 52nd St. (bet. 6th & 7th Aves.) | 212-581-8888 |
www.benbensons.com

"Gargantuan" slabs of "buttery steaks", "awesome sides" and "birdbath-size" martinis delivered by "seasoned" waiters make "manly men" maxi-merry at this "oldie but goodie" Midtowner; natch, it's "expensive as hell", but considering the "class operation", "you get what you pay for."

NEW Benchmark Ⓜ *American/Steak*

– | – | – | E

Park Slope | 339A Second St. (bet. 4th & 5th Aves.) | Brooklyn |
718-965-7040 | www.benchmarkrestaurant.com

Park Slope finally gets a bona fide steakhouse with the arrival of this diminutive eatery that also offers a roster of New American starters and salads; tabs are predictably steep, but its hidden location behind Loki Lounge supplies some hip mystique.

Benjamin Steak House *Steak*

25 | 22 | 24 | $72

E 40s | Dylan Hotel | 52 E. 41st St. (bet. Madison & Park Aves.) |
212-297-9177 | www.benjaminsteakhouse.com

In an "unusual location" south of Grand Central, this hotel steakhouse serves *"Flintstones"*-size cuts of "quality" beef in a "civilized", chandeliered setting under the watch of an "attentive" crew; the "pleasant" departures from the genre formula don't extend to the tabs, however, which require "corporate card"–caliber purchasing power.

Benoit ⓢ *French*

20 | 21 | 20 | $61

W 50s | 60 W. 55th St. (bet. 5th & 6th Aves.) | 646-943-7373 |
www.benoitny.com

After a "rocky start" and subsequent refinements, Alain Ducasse's Midtown bistro "seems to have found its stride" thanks to chef Pierre

Schaedelin's "expert" French cooking and the venue's "attractive new look"; still, some report an "uneven" performance that ultimately "disappoints" given the "names attached" – and "what you pay."

Ben's Best *Deli*

23 | 10 | 17 | $24

Rego Park | 96-40 Queens Blvd. (bet. 63rd Rd. & 64th Ave.) | Queens | 718-897-1700 | www.bensbest.com

Among the "last of a dying breed", this circa-1945 Jewish deli in Rego Park is a fresser's best friend for "top-notch" meats and other "cholesterol-be-damned" kosher delicacies; insiders don't mind the "zero" ambiance and "Borscht Belt service" since the "indigestion is just like my bubbe gave me."

Ben's Kosher Deli *Deli*

19 | 12 | 16 | $26

Garment District | 209 W. 38th St. (bet. 7th & 8th Aves.) | 212-398-2367
Bayside | Bay Terrace | 211-37 26th Ave. (211th St.) | Queens | 718-229-2367
www.bensdeli.net

Paging "Dr. Brown's" – these "decent" kosher delis in the Garment District and Bayside will "cure your cravings" for a "Jewish soul food" fix; "low-budget" ambiance and service as salty as the food stay true to the "old-fashioned", "nothing-fancy" genre.

Bereket   *Turkish*

19 | 5 | 14 | $14

LES | 187 E. Houston St. (Orchard St.) | 212-475-7700

Nothing soothes a "stomach full of booze" at 2 AM like the "delicious" doner kebabs and other "cheap" Turkish chow at this serve-yourself cafeteria parked on a "busy" LES corner; its 24/7 open-door policy trumps the "cruddy" decor and "punk"-heavy crowd.

NEW B.E.S. *Mediterranean*

‑ | ‑ | ‑ | M

Chelsea | 559 W. 22nd St. (11th Ave.) | 212-414-8700 | www.boutiqueeatshop.com

West Chelsea's art gallery district is the appropriate site for this new arrival where much of the artwork is for sale – or at least available for underwriting (the proceeds are split between the artist and a nonprofit, but you can't take the item home); expect a Med-American menu served in a sunny, window-lined setting.

NEW Betel *Asian*

▽ 25 | 24 | 20 | $50

W Village | 51 Grove St. (bet. Bleecker St. & 7th Ave. S.) | 212-352-0460 | www.betelnyc.com

There's "a little bit of a scene" in progress at this "trendy" new West Villager serving "standout" SE Asian street food to a "too-cool-for-school" crowd; the rough-hewn room (dominated by a large communal table) is a "slick" mix of brick walls, dark wood and silk lanterns.

Bettola  *Italian*

20 | 15 | 17 | $38

W 70s | 412 Amsterdam Ave. (bet. 79th & 80th Sts.) | 212-787-1660 | www.bettolanyc.com

"Good bet" UWS Italian purveying "wonderful" thin-crust pizzas and "reliable" pastas at a fair price; sidewalk seating with dandy "people-watching" possibilities makes the "small", "crowded" interior and "inconsistent service" much easier to swallow.

	FOOD	DECOR	SERVICE	COST

Beyoglu *Turkish* — 22 | 17 | 18 | $36

E 80s | 1431 Third Ave. (81st St.) | 212-650-0850

"Always packed and for a good reason", this "shoulder-to-shoulder" UES Turk serves "marvelous meze" and other "tasty" bites in a "lively" split-level space; service veers between "friendly" and "rude", but "excellent value" keeps them coming.

Bianca ⊭ *Italian* — 24 | 18 | 20 | $33

NoHo | 5 Bleecker St. (bet. Bowery & Elizabeth St.) | 212-260-4666 | www.biancanyc.com

"Knockout" cooking inspired by Italy's Emilia-Romagna region and a "tiny" yet "charming" backdrop explain why it's "packed evening after evening" at this NoHo "gem"; throw in "great prices" and no wonder the no-res, no-plastic policies pose no problem.

Bice *Italian* — 21 | 20 | 20 | $63

E 50s | 7 E. 54th St. (bet. 5th & Madison Aves.) | 212-688-1999 | www.bicenewyork.com

"Euro-trendy" types who fancy a "power scene with pasta" keep this Midtown Italian standby "hopping", thanks to food as "stylish" as the "Botox-city" crowd; it "never disappoints but never excites", save for the "outrageous prices."

Big Nick's Burger Joint *Burgers* — 18 | 6 | 15 | $18

W 70s | 2175 Broadway (77th St.) | 212-362-9238 | www.bignicksnyc.com ☽

W 70s | 70 W. 71st St. (bet. Columbus Ave. & CPW) | 212-799-4444 | www.bignicksny.com

"They serve everything under the sun" at these separately owned West Side "mega-dumps" whose "gigantic burgers" and "classic pizzas" "hit the spot" for "rock-bottom" dough; they're a "quintessential NY" solution to "any food emergency", and the Broadway original is open 24/7.

Big Wong ⊭ *Chinese* — 22 | 5 | 12 | $14

Chinatown | 67 Mott St. (bet. Bayard & Canal Sts.) | 212-964-0540

No search for the "essence of old Chinatown" is complete until you visit this Cantonese "legend" favored for its congee, roasted meats and "real cheap" tabs; sure, "Laundromat" decor and "service without a smile" earn few style points, but hey, "what a name!"

NEW Bill's Bar & Burger ☽ *Burgers* — 20 | 13 | 17 | $21

Meatpacking | 22 Ninth Ave. (13th St.) | 212-414-3003 | www.billsbarandburger.com

Steve Hanson takes on the "burger craze" at this "gentle-on-the-wallet" Meatpacking joint where the "pretty darn good" patties are made from a custom blend of "Pat LaFrieda" beef; set in the former Hog Pit pen, it has a "dive bar" feel, though the mood should be more refined at its planned Rock Center sib, currently in the works.

NEW Bino *Italian* — - | - | - | M

Carroll Gardens | 276 Smith St. (bet. Degraw & Sackett Sts.) | Brooklyn | 718-875-1980 | www.binobrooklyn.com

It started life as an offshoot of the Village Italian institution Pó, but following an ownership split this cute-as-a-button facsimile on Carroll

Gardens' Smith Street strip has gone indie and taken on a new name; otherwise the scene remains much the same, with midpriced rustic fare served up in convivial environs to a faithful local following.

Bistro Cassis *French*

20 | 17 | 17 | $45

W 70s | 225 Columbus Ave. (bet. 70th & 71st Sts.) | 212-579-3966 | www.bistrocassisnyc.com

When UWS types want to feel like "Americans in Paris", they head for this Gallic "charmer"; while it's "too bad" about the "no-reservations" policy and overly "authentic" service (*vive la* "indifference"), "consistent" cooking and "reasonable" rates compensate.

Bistro Chat Noir *French*

19 | 17 | 20 | $54

E 60s | 22 E. 66th St. (bet. 5th & Madison Aves.) | 212-794-2428 | www.bistrochatnoir.com

"Well-heeled" "white-shoe" types feel *très bien* at this "pleasant" "copycat Parisian" off Madison Avenue that plies "pricey" French bistro "classics" in an "intimate" townhouse setting; it's a default choice for those who "miss La Goulue" and its "late neighbor, Frederick's."

Bistro Citron *French*

19 | 18 | 19 | $44

W 80s | 473 Columbus Ave. (bet. 82nd & 83rd Sts.) | 212-400-9401 | www.bistrocitronnyc.com

"Decent" Gallic dishes for "digestible" tabs earn this Bistro Cassis sibling a "reliable" rep in the Upper West *arrondissement*; as for the secret behind its "easygoing" mien: the crew's "Parisian attitude" actually tilts toward "friendly."

Bistro Les Amis ● *French*

21 | 17 | 21 | $44

SoHo | 180 Spring St. (Thompson St.) | 212-226-8645 | www.bistrolesamis.com

Friends of this "cozy" SoHo bistro show up for its "well-executed" French food, "reasonable" pricing and "eager-to-please" service; "lack of pretense" and prime "people-watching opportunities" from sidewalk seats burnish its "*très charmant*" vibe.

Bistro 61 *French*

19 | 16 | 20 | $42

E 60s | 1113 First Ave. (61st St.) | 212-223-6220 | www.bistro61.com

Set in the "nowhereland" around the Queensboro Bridge, this "pleasant" French bistro offers a "fairly priced" "slice of the Left Bank" with "satisfying food" and "courteous" service; granted, it's more "handy" than trendy, but those "album covers as menu jackets" do "set a fun tone."

Bistro Ten 18 *American*

19 | 18 | 20 | $42

W 100s | 1018 Amsterdam Ave. (110th St.) | 212-662-7600 | www.bistroten18.com

The Columbia U. crowd "doesn't have to travel downtown" for "comfortable" dining thanks to this "solid" New American bistro in Morningside Heights; "hardworking" staffers, a "cozy fireplace" and a "great view" of St. John the Divine across the street help "make it a destination."

Bistro 33 *French/Japanese*

∇ 20 | 16 | 19 | $34

Astoria | 19-33 Ditmars Blvd. (21st St.) | Queens | 718-721-1933 | www.bistro33nyc.com

At this "eclectic" Astoria bistro, a "creative fusion" of Japanese and French flavors yields "tasty" results that rev up a "local" dining scene starved for variety; its lofty ambitions aren't diminished by the "small" setting, and fair prices and "welcoming" service ice the cake.

NEW Bistro Vendôme French

21 | 19 | 21 | $56

E 50s | 405 E. 58th St. (bet. 1st Ave. & Sutton Pl.) | 212-935-9100 | www.bistrovendomenyc.com

The "early signs are good" at this "civilized" newcomer in the former March space offering a midpriced, traditional French bistro menu (think escargots and sole meunière); aside from "noise-level" issues, fans say this "welcoming" duplex is just what Sutton Place needed.

Black Duck American/Seafood

21 | 19 | 21 | $51

Murray Hill | Park South Hotel | 122 E. 28th St. (bet. Lexington Ave. & Park Ave. S.) | 212-448-0888 | www.blackduckny.com

Decidedly "under the radar", this Murray Hill "sleeper" serves "delicious" New Americana with a seafood focus in a "dark", "London" publike setting; "attentive" service, a "romantic fireplace" and weekend "live jazz" earn it "definite repeat" status.

Black Iron Burger Shop ●∌ Burgers

20 | 15 | 17 | $18

E Village | 540 E. Fifth St. (bet. Aves. A & D) | 212-677-6067 | www.blackironburger.com

A contender in the "current burger craze", this "unassuming" East Villager pairs "juicy" patties with "crispy" fixin's, washed down with a beer; the "small", "saloon"-like setting has the "rustic/grungy" thing down pat, while "late"-night hours keep barhoppers happy.

Black Whale American

20 | 18 | 19 | $30

Bronx | 279 City Island Ave. (Hawkins St.) | 718-885-3657 | www.dineatblackwhale.com

This "nautical"-themed City Island "institution" is a "local favorite" that also reels in mainlanders with its "friendly" ambiance and "affordable" New American grub (including an $11 "all-you-can-eat" weekend brunch); in good weather, "sit in the garden for the full effect."

Blaue Gans ● Austrian/German

22 | 18 | 20 | $47

TriBeCa | 139 Duane St. (bet. Church St. & W. B'way) | 212-571-8880 | www.kg-ny.com

The "spaetzle's so light it almost floats" at Kurt Gutenbrunner's "unique" TriBeCan serving "delightful" Austro-German specialties along with a "fine beer selection"; the "simple but atmospheric" setting reminds some of "Berlin", while the "pleasant" service and relatively "gentle prices" also induce feelings of *freude*.

Bliss Bistro French

21 | 20 | 21 | $38

Sunnyside | 45-20 Skillman Ave. (46th St.) | Queens | 718-729-0778 | www.blissbistro.com

It may be "off the beaten path", but this Sunnyside "gem" is right on the money with its "well-prepared" French bistro items, "attentive" service and prices that are a "fraction" of what you'd pay in Manhattan; P.S. insiders say "dining in the garden is an unforgettable experience."

Blockheads Burritos Mexican

16 | 10 | 15 | $19

E 50s | 954 Second Ave. (bet. 50th & 51st Sts.) | 212-750-2020
E 80s | 1563 Second Ave. (bet. 81st & 82nd Sts.) | 212-879-1999

(continued)

(continued)

Blockheads Burritos

Financial District | Courtyard at 4 World Financial Ctr. (North & Vesey Sts.) | 212-619-8226
Murray Hill | 499 Third Ave. (bet. 33rd & 34th Sts.) | 212-213-3332
W 50s | Worldwide Plaza | 322 W. 50th St. (bet. 8th & 9th Aves.) | 212-307-7029
W 100s | 951 Amsterdam Ave. (bet. 106th & 107th Sts.) | 212-662-8226
www.blockheads.com

These "cheap", "Americanized" Mexican filling stations "keep the crowds coming" with "burritos the size of Buicks" and $3 margaritas that catapult their "young" fans into "spring-break" mode; for a more sedate experience, delivery and takeout are "fast, easy" alternatives.

Blossom *Vegan/Vegetarian*

22 | 17 | 20 | $36

Chelsea | 187 Ninth Ave. (bet. 21st & 22nd Sts.) | 212-627-1144
W 80s | 466 Columbus Ave. (bet. 82nd & 83rd Sts.) | 212-875-2600
www.blossomnyc.com

They do "great things with vegetables" at this "healthier-than-thou" vegan duo where the "savory", "feel-good" fare can convince carnivores to "take a break from steak"; partisans praise the "knowledgeable" staff, but pricewise, some are surprised by the "meat on the bill."

NEW BLT Bar & Grill *American*

- | - | - | M

Financial District | W Hotel Downtown | 123 Washington St. (bet. Albany & Carlisle Sts.) | 646-826-8666 | www.bltrestaurants.com

The latest in the BLT empire – now sans chef Laurent Tourondel – this casual W Downtown hotel outpost serves classic Americana in a distressed-industrial setting that mirrors the construction upheavals in the Financial District; laid out over two high-ceilinged floors, it's a hit with both young turks and out-of-towners.

BLT Burger *Burgers*

21 | 15 | 17 | $27

G Village | 470 Sixth Ave. (bet. 11th & 12th Sts.) | 212-243-8226 | www.bltburger.com

The most "casual" member of the "BLT restaurant family", this Villager draws "throngs" with its "high-quality" burgers and "delicious spiked shakes"; pricewise, it's "not exactly a value" and neither decor nor service impress, but diehards still find it "too good to resist."

Z BLT Fish *Ⓢ Seafood*

24 | 21 | 22 | $62

Flatiron | 21 W. 17th St. (bet. 5th & 6th Aves.) | 212-691-8888 | www.bltfish.com

Seafood "as fresh as if you caught it yourself" is "impeccably pre-pared" and presented by "solicitous" staffers at this "top-flight" Flatiron piscatorium set in a "lovely, skylit" room; those feeling clammy over the tabs stick to the simpler "New England–style fish shack" downstairs.

BLT Market *American*

22 | 21 | 22 | $68

W 50s | Ritz-Carlton Central Park | 1430 Sixth Ave. (CPS) | 212-521-6125 | www.bltmarket.com

Although no longer involved with the rest of the BLT empire, chef Laurent Tourondel still has a hand in this "inviting" New American in Midtown's Ritz-Carlton, where "market-fresh" food and "superb" wines arrive in an "airy" setting that's a cross between a "farmhouse" and a "hotel lobby"; "alfresco" seating makes the "expensive" checks easier to overlook.

BLT Prime *Steak* | 25 | 22 | 23 | $73 |

Gramercy | 111 E. 22nd St. (bet. Lexington Ave. & Park Ave. S.) | 212-995-8500 | www.bltprime.com

"Lick-your-plate"-worthy cuts of beef and "excellent wines" are steered your way by "top-notch" servers at this "artfully contemporary" Gramercy steakhouse; admirers say "it's worth going just for the popovers", and speaking of which, don't forget to "bring lots of dough."

☑ BLT Steak ⓈSteak | 25 | 22 | 23 | $77 |

E 50s | 106 E. 57th St. (bet. Lexington & Park Aves.) | 212-752-7470 | www.bltsteak.com

"Everything's first-class" at this "spiffy" Midtown chop shop – the original outpost of the BLT empire – that supplies "cooked-to-perfection" steaks, "memorable" sides and "air-kissy" vibes; granted, "they ain't giving it away", so it's best savored "on the company dime."

Blue Fin ◑ *Seafood* | 22 | 22 | 21 | $56 |

W 40s | W Hotel Times Sq. | 1567 Broadway (47th St.) | 212-918-1400 | www.brguestrestaurants.com

An "oasis amid the Times Square madness", Steve Hanson's "enjoyable" seafooder "opposite TKTS" reels in tourists and showgoers with fish "cooked just right" and dispatched by an amiable (if at times "distracted") crew; veterans "eat upstairs" since it's more "serene" than the "frenetic" ground floor, but either way, an "expense account" comes in handy.

Blue Ginger *Asian* | 22 | 18 | 20 | $40 |

Chelsea | 106 Eighth Ave. (bet. 15th & 16th Sts.) | 212-352-0911

"Consistently good" sushi and "inventive rolls" are the stars of the show at this Chelsea Pan-Asian, a "useful neighborhood" nexus that's also "ideal pre-Joyce Theater"; "fair prices" and "savvy service" overcome the "unexciting" atmosphere.

☑ Blue Hill *American* | 27 | 23 | 27 | $82 |

G Village | 75 Washington Pl. (bet. MacDougal St. & 6th Ave.) | 212-539-1776 | www.bluehillfarm.com

The "farm-to-table" philosophy is in full bloom at Dan Barber's "civilized" Villager – the *real* Fresh Direct – where uncommon "respect for ingredients" translates into "simply sublime" American cooking; its "earthy" ethos is echoed in the "warm" environs and "knowledgeable" service, and though undeniably "expensive", the biggest hurdle is scoring a reservation – especially since "Barack and Michelle" had dinner.

☑ Blue Ribbon ◑ *American* | 25 | 19 | 22 | $53 |

SoHo | 97 Sullivan St. (bet. Prince & Spring Sts.) | 212-274-0404
Park Slope | 280 Fifth Ave. (bet. 1st St. & Garfield Pl.) | Brooklyn | 718-840-0404
www.blueribbonrestaurants.com

Team Bromberg makes fans "feel like kids in a candy store" at these "sure-bet" SoHo-Park Slope New Americans where the "extensive", "burgers-to-bone-marrow" menus can be had "late into the night"; despite "packed" quarters and "upscale" prices, it's "worth the bucks, and the wait."

Blue Ribbon Bakery ● *American* | 24 | 19 | 21 | $43 |

W Village | 35 Downing St. (Bedford St.) | 212-337-0404 |
www.blueribbonrestaurants.com

"You'll want to fill up on bread" (and the "delicious" New American
comfort chow) at the Bromberg brothers' "quintessential Village"
bistro-bakery; an aromatic "joy" any time of day, it's particularly "terrific for brunch" and the sort of place "every neighborhood should be
so lucky to have."

☑ Blue Ribbon Sushi ● *Japanese* | 26 | 19 | 21 | $58 |

SoHo | 119 Sullivan St. (bet. Prince & Spring Sts.) | 212-343-0404
Park Slope | 278 Fifth Ave. (bet. 1st St. & Garfield Pl.) | Brooklyn |
718-840-0408
www.blueribbonrestaurants.com

"Pristine sushi" with "caught-within-the-hour" freshness is yours at
these "casual" Japanese "revelations" from the Brombergs, in SoHo
and Park Slope; despite "steep" tabs and prime-time "long waits", it's
an experience that's "worth every cent."

Blue Ribbon Sushi Bar & Grill ● *Japanese* | 24 | 20 | 21 | $64 |

W 50s | 6 Columbus Hotel | 308 W. 58th St. (bet. 8th & 9th Aves.) |
212-397-0404 | www.blueribbonrestaurants.com

Bringing their "popular downtown" dining formula to Columbus Circle,
the Bromberg brothers have rolled out a "varied" menu of "blissful"
sushi and grilled items at this hotel Japanese; their trademark "quality
service", "late-night" hours and "not-for-the-faint-of-budget" bills
also made the journey north.

Blue Smoke *BBQ* | 21 | 17 | 19 | $41 |

Murray Hill | 116 E. 27th St. (bet. Lexington Ave. & Park Ave. S.) |
212-447-7733
Flushing | Citi Field | 126th St. & Roosevelt Ave. (behind the scoreboard) |
Queens
www.bluesmoke.com

"Prepare to get messy" at Danny Meyer's "upscale" Murray Hill rib joint,
a "spirited, family-friendly" furnisher of "finger-lickin'" BBQ
accompanied by a "wide selection" of beer and bourbon; there's some
debate about whether the 'cue is "done right" or dang "New Yawk-ified",
but the "downstairs jazz club" is indisputably *smokin'*; P.S. there's a
satellite at Citi Field.

☑ Blue Water Grill *Seafood* | 23 | 22 | 21 | $56 |

Union Sq | 31 Union Sq. W. (16th St.) | 212-675-9500 |
www.brguestrestaurants.com

Steve Hanson's 15-year-old Union Square juggernaut is ever the "seafood staple", with "first-rate" fin fare ferried by "cordial" crewmem-
bers in a "classy", "remodeled bank"; the "energetic" scene spills over
into a "downstairs jazz room" as well as a "heavenly" outdoor veranda,
with a predictably "pricey" undercurrent.

Boathouse *American* | 18 | 26 | 18 | $54 |

E 70s | Central Park | Central Park Lake, enter on E. 72nd St. (Park Dr. N.) |
212-517-2233 | www.thecentralparkboathouse.com

A veritable "oasis" in Central Park, this perennial American is famed
for its "Impressionistic" lakeside view that's "unmatched" for "roman-

tic" encounters, "celebrations" and the like; both food and service are "dicey" and the asking price "steep", but most "grin and bear it" given the "picturesque" setting.

Bobby Van's Steakhouse Steak   22 | 20 | 22 | $68

E 40s | 230 Park Ave. (46th St.) | 212-867-5490 🖄
E 50s | 131 E. 54th St. (bet. Lexington & Park Aves.) | 212-207-8050
Financial District | 25 Broad St. (Exchange Pl.) | 212-344-8463 🖄
Jamaica | JFK Airport | American Airlines Terminal 8 | Queens | 718-553-2100

Bobby Van's Grill Steak

W 50s | 135 W. 50th St. (bet. 6th & 7th Aves.) | 212-957-5050
www.bobbyvans.com

"Pro" staffers at this "solid" steakhouse mini-chain serve up "dependable" slabs and "fine" wines in fittingly "masculine" milieus ("sit in the bank vault" at the Financial District branch); some rank it "just below top-shelf", though its "masters-of-the-universe" price tags are on par for the genre.

Bobo American   21 | 24 | 20 | $59

W Village | 181 W. 10th St. (7th Ave. S.) | 212-488-2626 | www.bobonyc.com
The "scene" is the thing at this "clandestine" Village brownstone filled with "Euros" and "beautiful yuppies" who gravitate to its antiques-laden dining room and "transporting" outdoor deck; the New American eats are "creative" if "costly", so some stick with liquids in the "thumping" downstairs bar.

Boca Chica Pan-Latin   21 | 16 | 17 | $32

E Village | 13 First Ave. (1st St.) | 212-473-0108
"Huge portions" of "inexpensive", "no-frills" Pan-Latin grub are washed down with "killer drinks" at this "colorful" East Village vet that's a hit with younger folk; the "small" quarters get "noisy" fast, and at peak times there's usually a "wait" to get in.

Bocca Italian   23 | 20 | 22 | $49

Flatiron | 39 E. 19th St. (bet. B'way & Park Ave. S.) | 212-387-1200 | www.boccanyc.com
"There's much to like" about this Flatiron cousin of Cacio e Pepe, from its "really tasty" Roman menu (led by a "crowd-pleasing" pasta served in a pecorino wheel) to its "warm" hospitality and "hip vibe"; supporters sum it up in two words: "good value."

Bocca di Bacco ❶ Italian   22 | 21 | 18 | $43

W 50s | 828 Ninth Ave. (bet. 54th & 55th Sts.) | 212-265-8828 | www.boccadibacconyc.com
"Dramatic wood doors" open onto this "rustic" Italian, a "bare-brick-walled" Hell's Kitchen operation offering "creative takes on old favorites" and an "extensive wine list" to boot; surveyors salute the "decent" pricing but split on the service: "helpful" vs. "should be better."

Bocca Lupo ❶ Italian   24 | 21 | 20 | $33

Cobble Hill | 391 Henry St. (Warren St.) | Brooklyn | 718-243-2522
"Big-windowed" and "laid-back", this Cobble Hill enoteca is prized by locals for its "affordable" lineup of "delicious" small plates and "well-chosen" wines; a "heavenly brunch" and "family-friendly" service earn it extra "neighborhood appreciation."

Bocelli *Italian*

25 | 22 | 25 | $52

Staten Island | 1250 Hylan Blvd. (bet. Old Town Rd. & Parkinson Ave.) |
718-420-6150 | www.bocellirest.com

Staten Islanders salute this "old-school" Grasmere Italian as a supplier of generously portioned seafood specialties and devout practitioner of "keep-the-customers-happy" hospitality; additionally, valet
parking and live weekend music help justify the "pricey" tabs.

Bodrum *Mediterranean/Turkish*

20 | 16 | 19 | $38

W 80s | 584 Amsterdam Ave. (bet. 88th & 89th Sts.) | 212-799-2806 |
www.bodrumnyc.com

Definitely "not humdrum", this moderately priced UWS Med mixes up
its "diverse" menu with everything from "tasty" Turkish meze to "quality"
brick-oven pizza, all presented by a "courteous" crew; since "space
can be tight", it's best experienced at an "outdoor table."

Bogota Latin Bistro *Pan-Latin*

23 | 18 | 18 | $31

Park Slope | 141 Fifth Ave. (bet. Lincoln & St. Johns Pls.) | Brooklyn |
718-230-3805 | www.bogotabistro.com

"Colorful lights" and "loud music" greet you at this "cheerful" Park
Slope Pan-Latin serving first-rate "authentic" grub and "killer mojitos"
for "reasonable" sums; the all-seasons backyard patio absorbs the
overflow when the main room gets too "tight."

Bôi *Vietnamese*

20 | 12 | 18 | $25

E 40s | 246 E. 44th St. (bet. 2nd & 3rd Aves.) | 212-681-6541
Bôi Noodles ⊠ *Vietnamese*
🆕 **W 40s** | 240 W. 40th St. (bet. 7th & 8th Aves.) | 212-575-0088
Bôi Sandwich ⊠ *Vietnamese*
E 40s | 708 Third Ave. (bet. 44th & 45th Sts.) | 212-682-1117
www.boi-restaurant.com

For "real Vietnamese food" near Grand Central, try this "efficient"
boutique chainlet's "fresh", affordable Saigon specialties, available in
both sit-down and takeaway formats; P.S. the new, noodle-focused
number near the NYT Building opened post-Survey.

Bo-Ky ⌿ *Noodle Shop*

22 | 5 | 11 | $15

Chinatown | 80 Bayard St. (bet. Mott & Mulberry Sts.) | 212-406-2292
🆕 **Little Italy** | 216 Grand St. (Elizabeth St.) | 212-219-9228
These "juror havens" are renowned for their "tasty" Chinese and
Vietnamese noodle soups; "bargain-basement" tabs make the "glaringly
fluorescent" settings and "rush-you-in-and-out" service more bearable.

Bombay Palace ◑ *Indian*

19 | 17 | 18 | $40

W 50s | 30 W. 52nd St. (bet. 5th & 6th Aves.) | 212-541-7777 |
www.bombay-palace.com

"Expensive" for the genre but still "reliable", this longtime Midtown
Indian serves "classic" fare in a once "opulent" setting that's become a
bit "frayed"; the jewel in its crown is the "outstanding" $16 lunch buffet.

Bombay Talkie *Indian*

20 | 18 | 17 | $42

Chelsea | 189 Ninth Ave. (bet. 21st & 22nd Sts.) | 212-242-1900 |
www.bombaytalkie.com

"Unique" interpretations of "Indian street food" are paired with
"tasty" cocktails at this "modern" Chelsea retreat that pays "hip"

homage to Bollywood on a split-level stage; though there's praise for its "novel" concept, critics nix the portion-to-price ratio and "iffy" supporting cast.

Bon Chon Chicken *Chicken* | 20 | 10 | 12 | $18 |

E Village | 9 St. Marks Pl. (bet. 2nd & 3rd Aves.) | 212-228-2887 ◑
NEW **Financial District** | 104 John St. (Cliff St.) | 646-682-7747
NEW **Garment District** | 207 W. 38th St. (bet. 7th & 8th Aves.) | 212-221-3339 ◑
NEW **Murray Hill** | 325 Fifth Ave. (bet. 32nd & 33rd Sts.) | 212-686-8282 ◑
TriBeCa | 98 Chambers St. (Church St.) | 212-227-2375
Bayside | 45-37B Bell Blvd. (bet. 45th Dr. & 45th Rd.) | Queens | 718-225-1010
www.bonchon.com

"Sorry, Colonel, there's a new KFC in town" – Korean fried chicken, that is – and converts "can't stop craving" this import chain's "crispy" lacquered Seoul specialty; given "utilitarian" digs and "long waits" required for cooked-to-order preparation, "calling ahead for takeout" is preferable.

Bond 45 ◑ *Italian* | 19 | 18 | 19 | $52 |

W 40s | 154 W. 45th St. (bet. 6th & 7th Aves.) | 212-869-4545 | www.bond45.com

"Everything's big" at Shelly Fireman's "fast-paced" Times Square Italian housed in the former Bond clothing store, from its "extensive" menu (featuring some "can't-be-beat antipasto") to the "humongous" "old-NY" setting; "carnival"-worthy noise levels aside, it's a secure "asset."

Bondi Road ◑ *Australian* | 17 | 15 | 20 | $26 |

LES | 153 Rivington St. (bet. Clinton & Suffolk Sts.) | 212-253-5311 | www.bondiroad.com

Even the "authentic fish 'n' chips" are "supplemental" to the "boozy" action at the bar of this "cheap" LES Aussie; "cute" staffers, a "sweet" all-you-can-drink brunch and "surf"-themed decor (notably a huge "mural of Bondi Beach") keep its "young" patrons loyal.

Z Bond Street ◑ *Japanese* | 25 | 23 | 21 | $63 |

NoHo | 6 Bond St. (bet. B'way & Lafayette St.) | 212-777-2500 | www.bondstrestaurant.com

The "people-watching is almost as good as the food" at this seasoned Japanese "swank"-atorium in NoHo, where "skinny" folks toy with "amazing" sushi in "chichi" digs patrolled by "pretty servers"; whether upstairs or in the "fantastic" lower-level lounge, "you can't go wrong" – if you've got the bucks.

Boqueria ◑ *Spanish* | 22 | 19 | 19 | $46 |

Flatiron | 53 W. 19th St. (bet. 5th & 6th Aves.) | 212-255-4160
SoHo | 171 Spring St. (bet. Thompson St. & W. B'way) | 212-343-4255
www.boquerianyc.com

"One delicious thing after another" comes your way at these "unique", "Barcelona"-esque tapas dispensers that are always "buzzing" in spite of "cramped quarters", bills that "add up quickly" and a "no-rez policy" producing "long waits"; still, many say "you're in for a treat."

	FOOD	DECOR	SERVICE	COST

Bottega del Vino *Italian*   22 | 19 | 21 | $61

E 50s | 7 E. 59th St. (bet. 5th & Madison Aves.) | 212-223-2724 |
www.bottegadelvinonyc.com

"Wealthy Euros" wistful for the Verona original (or looking to drop sur-
plus dollars "post-Bergdorf's") settle into this Midtown Italian "hideaway" for "expensive" but "enjoyable" meals, enhanced by an "incredible
wine list"; fittingly, the "dolce vita" vibe includes "obliging" service.

Bottino *Italian*   20 | 18 | 18 | $45

Chelsea | 246 10th Ave. (bet. 24th & 25th Sts.) | 212-206-6766 |
www.bottinonyc.com

"You could be rubbing elbows with the next Banksy" at this West Chelsea
canteen, an "art-scene staple" with "consistent" Tuscan chow that
sates "gallery-hoppers"; the "simple modern" setting is "pleasant, not
pretentious", but "most relaxing" of all is that "wonderful garden."

Bouchon Bakery *American/French*   24 | 15 | 18 | $29

W 60s | Time Warner Ctr. | 10 Columbus Circle, 3rd fl. (60th St. at B'way) |
212-823-9366 | www.bouchonbakery.com

"On-the-go" types in the Time Warner Center turn to Thomas Keller's
"middle-of-the-mall" cafe/patisserie for a "light" New American "re-
prieve" via "delicious sandwiches" and "even better pastries"; if the
venue's basically bland, at least the Central Park view is pretty "spectacular"; P.S. a new Rock Center outpost is in the works.

☑ Bouley ● *French*   27 | 27 | 26 | $102

TriBeCa | 163 Duane St. (Hudson St.) | 212-964-2525 |
www.davidbouley.com

On the rise again, David Bouley's "dazzling" TriBeCa flagship is "elegance personified", from its "impeccable" French country cooking to
the "opulent", "no-expense-spared" setting and "seamless service";
those who "can't afford it in this economy" opt for the $36 prix fixe
lunch, a "remarkable value" and perhaps the "best show in town";
P.S. the private parties here are "as good as it gets."

Bourbon Street Café *Cajun/Southern*   17 | 16 | 18 | $34

Bayside | 40-12 Bell Blvd. (bet. 40th & 41st Aves.) | Queens | 718-224-2200 |
www.bourbonstreetny.com

"As close to New Orleans" as you'll find in Queens, this Bayside "fave"
honors the Big Easy with "affordable" spins on Cajun cuisine and other
Americana; "festive" folk make like it's Mardi Gras at the "great bar."

Braai *South African*   21 | 21 | 21 | $45

W 50s | 329 W. 51st St. (bet. 8th & 9th Aves.) | 212-315-3315 |
www.braainyc.com

The "novelty of South African cuisine" plays well with open-minded
palates at this "intriguing" Hell's Kitchen braai (or BBQ) specialist;
decked out like an "upscale" hut and staffed with an "attentive" team,
it's a "welcome" refuge, especially for the "pre-theater" tribe.

Braeburn *American*   21 | 19 | 22 | $54

W Village | 117 Perry St. (Greenwich St.) | 212-255-0696 |
www.braeburnrestaurant.com

"Innovative yet unfussy" New Americana with a "seasonal" slant is the
"well-conceived" idea behind this "under-the-radar" Village "neighbor-

	FOOD	DECOR	SERVICE	COST

hood spot" from chef Brian Bistrong; the "comfortable" "country lodge" setting and "friendly staff" earn kudos, but not the "noisy" acoustics.

Brasserie *French* | 20 | 21 | 20 | $53 |

E 50s | Seagram Bldg. | 100 E. 53rd St. (bet. Lexington & Park Aves.) | 212-751-4840 | www.patinagroup.com

"Business" and leisure diners alike "take a turn on the catwalk" to enter this "ultramodern" Midtowner where "fine" French food delivered by "gracious" servers stokes the "cool" scene; drawbacks include "pricey" tabs and a "loud" din, yet some insist it's an "essential NYC" experience.

Brasserie Cognac ● *French* | 19 | 18 | 18 | $49 |

W 50s | 1740 Broadway (55th St.) | 212-757-3600 | www.cognacrestaurant.com

For a "Gallic interlude" in Midtown, this "homage" to the French brasserie supplies "tried-and-true" standards, "courteous" service and an "attractive" setting; "convenient" to Carnegie Hall and City Center, it also draws the overflow from Serafina across the street.

Brasserie 8½ *French* | 22 | 23 | 22 | $59 |

W 50s | 9 W. 57th St. (bet. 5th & 6th Aves.) | 212-829-0812 | www.patinagroup.com

The spiral staircase makes for "dramatic" entrances at this "mod" Midtowner, a "spacious" subterranean lair offering both "intimate" dining and "lively bar" action; opinions vary on the "updated" French menu, but there's agreement that the $29 Sunday brunch is one "great value."

Brasserie Julien *French* | 18 | 18 | 18 | $46 |

E 80s | 1422 Third Ave. (bet. 80th & 81st Sts.) | 212-744-6327 | www.brasseriejulien.com

Upper Eastsiders with a soft spot for this "neighborhood resource" cite "reasonable" tabs, "consistent" French brasserie dishes and "homey" atmospherics as reasons for its "staying power"; live weekend jazz ratchets up its "cool" quotient, and noise level.

Brasserie Ruhlmann *French* | 19 | 21 | 19 | $56 |

W 50s | 45 Rockefeller Plaza (enter on 50th St., bet. 5th & 6th Aves.) | 212-974-2020 | www.brasserieruhlmann.com

Smack in the middle of Rock Center, this "classy" brasserie showcases Laurent Tourondel's "attractively prepared" French cooking in a swanky, salute-to-art-deco setting; it's predictably "pricey", comes with a "fantastic" patio and for some reason is usually "sans tourists."

Bravo Gianni *Italian* | 22 | 16 | 21 | $69 |

E 60s | 230 E. 63rd St. (bet. 2nd & 3rd Aves.) | 212-752-7272 | www.bravogiannirestaurant.com

Eponymous chef Gianni Garavelli "rules the roost" with a "welcoming" touch at this "timeless" UES "standby" that's been turning out "top-drawer" Northern Italiana since 1983; the interior may be "dated" and the prices "high", but this doesn't faze its "well-heeled" following.

🆕 Bread and Butter *American* | ▽ 18 | 19 | 21 | $39 |

Brooklyn Heights | 46 Henry St. (bet. Cranberry & Middagh Sts.) | Brooklyn | 718-858-9605 | www.breadandbutterbk.com

"Good but not distinguished" Americana with a Southern accent fills out the menu of this midpriced new Brooklyn Heights arrival set in a

"manicured", Colonial-style room; although both the kitchen and service are still "finding their stride", at least they "get the basics right."

Bread Tribeca *Italian*　　20 | 17 | 16 | $32

TriBeCa | 301 Church St. (Walker St.) | 212-334-8282 | www.breadtribeca.com

Bread ● *Sandwiches*

NoLita | 20 Spring St. (bet. Elizabeth & Mott Sts.) | 212-334-1015 | www.orderbreadsoho.com

"Hip atmospheres" lure locals to these "casual", separately owned spots in NoLita and TriBeCa known for "great panini" and other "simple" Italian dishes; "surprisingly affordable" tabs help leaven criticism of "nonexistent" service and unremarkable decor.

Breeze *French/Thai*　　22 | 14 | 18 | $29

W 40s | 661 Ninth Ave. (bet. 45th & 46th Sts.) | 212-262-7777 | www.breezenyc.com

A "nice change of pace", this slick Hell's Kitchen "find" plates "tasty" Thai-French fusion dishes in a "funky", "neon orange" setting; "inexpensive" tabs and "quick" turnaround draw "pre-theater" eaters.

Brennan & Carr ●⊄ *Sandwiches*　　21 | 9 | 16 | $17

Sheepshead Bay | 3432 Nostrand Ave. (Ave. U) | Brooklyn | 718-646-9559

At this circa-1938 Sheepshead Bay "landmark", roast beef sandwiches "double-dipped" ("bread and all") in au jus are the beloved "soppy" specialty; "healthy eating it ain't", but for such "cheap" sums, no one cares about nutrition, or the "old, dark" decor.

Z NEW Breslin, The ● *British*　　21 | 21 | 17 | $53

Chelsea | Ace Hotel | 16 W. 29th St. (bet. B'way & 5th Ave.) | 212-679-1939 | www.thebreslin.com

The latest from Ken Friedman and April Bloomfield (Spotted Pig), this "sceney" Chelsea newcomer in the Ace Hotel vends a "decadent", meat-centric British menu to "teeming masses of hipsters" in a "dark", "hunting lodge"–esque setting; great "people-watching" distracts from the "junior-varsity" service, "crazy" decibel levels and "looong waits" caused by its "no-reservations" policy.

Brgr *Burgers*　　19 | 13 | 14 | $17

Chelsea | 287 Seventh Ave. (bet. 26th & 27th Sts.) | 212-488-7500
NEW E 60s | 1026 Third Ave. (bet. 60th & 61st Sts.) | 212-588-0080
www.brgr.us

Part of the "haute beef-patty circuit", these "casual" counter-service joints vend "prty gd" burgers made from beef, turkey or veggies backed up by "incredible" shakes; still, some find it "a little pricey" for "fast food–style" dining.

Bricco *Italian*　　19 | 17 | 20 | $47

W 50s | 304 W. 56th St. (bet. 8th & 9th Aves.) | 212-245-7160

Bricco Blu *Italian*

NEW W 40s | 650 W. 42nd St. (bet. 11th & 12th Aves.) | 212-967-2250
www.bricconyc.com

"Within shouting distance of Carnegie Hall", this "steady" Hell's Kitchen Italian draws theatergoers with "flavorful" wood-oven pizzas and pastas served by a "congenial" team; lipsticked kisses on the ceiling supply the kitsch factor, while a new 42nd Street satellite provides variety.

Brick Cafe *French/Italian* 22 | 20 | 20 | $32

Astoria | 30-95 33rd St. (31st Ave.) | Queens | 718-267-2735 | www.brickcafe.com

"Hip and cool" comes to Astoria via this "busy" bistro that draws "mostly young" ones with its "delicious" Franco-Italian fare; the "intimate", "exposed-brick" setting opens onto sidewalk tables in the summer, where locals "nurse a coffee" and "watch the world go by."

Brick Lane Curry House *Indian* 21 | 14 | 18 | $30

E 50s | 235 E. 53rd St. (bet. 2nd & 3rd Aves.) | 212-339-8353 | www.bricklanetoo.com

E Village | 306-308 E. Sixth St. (bet. 1st & 2nd Aves.) | 212-979-2900 | www.bricklanecurryhouse.com

Fire-eaters who "fancy curry" hurry to this East Side duo for "superspicy", "British-style" Indian dishes; the East Village original is "a notch above the Sixth Street fray", while the "tiny" Midtown spin-off sports "one long communal table" – too bad the decor's not so hot in either.

Bridge Cafe *American* 22 | 19 | 22 | $48

Financial District | 279 Water St. (Dover St.) | 212-227-3344 | www.bridgecafenyc.com

A bona fide "bit of olde NY", this "quaint" New American occupying a circa-1794 tavern "under the Brooklyn Bridge" endures thanks to "thoughtfully prepared" entrees, "accommodating" service and a "spectacular" view of the underbelly of the span; relatively "reasonable" rates don't hurt either.

Brio *Italian* 20 | 16 | 19 | $43

E 60s | 137 E. 61st St. (Lexington Ave.) | 212-980-2300 | www.brionyc.com

"Thin pizza" and "hearty" Italiana turn up at this "upscale" spot near Bloomie's that's "been around forever" and works particularly well for lunch or "*après* shopping"; critics call it a "Serafina wannabe", but fans commend its "friendly service" and "outside seating."

Brioso *Italian* 25 | 20 | 23 | $49

Staten Island | 174 New Dorp Ln. (9th St.) | 718-667-1700 | www.briosoristorante.com

"Renowned pastas" and "creative" specials make this "comfortable" New Dorp Italian a "Staten Island standby"; paisans praise the "attentive" personnel but advise "going early" to sidestep "high noise levels" that "make conversation impossible."

NEW Broken English *Italian*   - | - | - | M

Cobble Hill | 68 Bergen St. (bet. Court & Smith Sts.) | Brooklyn | 718-488-3906

Simple Roman dishes like fresh egg pasta with pecorino cheese are the focus at this new Cobble Hill Italian, whose industrial-edged open space and midrange pricing should translate well for Brooklynites; the ample bar stays open past kitchen hours while the weekend brunch provides a welcome option for the Smith Street crowd.

Brooklyn Diner USA ☽ *Diner* 17 | 14 | 16 | $34

W 40s | 155 W. 43rd St. (bet. B'way & 6th Ave.) | 212-265-5400

(continued)

(continued)

Brooklyn Diner USA

W 50s | 212 W. 57th St. (bet. B'way & 7th Ave.) | 212-977-2280
www.brooklyndiner.com

"Convenient" to theaterland, Shelly Fireman's Midtown twosome pulls in "tourists" and "families" with "oversized plates" of "basic" Americana served in "nostalgic" takes on a diner; though a few find "more kitsch than kitchen" here, most say it's "good for what it is", especially for breakfast.

Brooklyn Fish Camp ☒ *Seafood* | 23 | 15 | 19 | $42 |

Park Slope | 162 Fifth Ave. (bet. Degraw & Douglass Sts.) | Brooklyn | 718-783-3264 | www.brooklynfishcamp.com

For ultra-"fresh" seafood "without the drive to the beach", check out this "informal" Park Slope spin-off of Mary's Fish Camp famed for "first-rate" lobster rolls; "unpretentious service" and a "lovely garden" compensate for tabs that may make you feel you got hooked.

Brother Jimmy's BBQ *BBQ* | 16 | 12 | 15 | $27 |

E 40s | Grand Central | lower level (42nd St. & Vanderbilt Ave.) | 212-661-4022

E 70s | 1485 Second Ave. (bet. 77th & 78th Sts.) | 212-288-0999 ◑

E 90s | 1644 Third Ave. (92nd St.) | 212-426-2020 ◑

Garment District | 416 Eighth Ave. (31st St.) | 212-967-7603 ◑

NEW Gramercy | 116 E. 16th St. (bet. Irving Pl. & Union Sq. E.) | 212-673-6465 ◑

Murray Hill | 181 Lexington Ave. (31st St.) | 212-779-7427 ◑

W 80s | 428 Amsterdam Ave. (bet. 80th & 81st Sts.) | 212-501-7515 ◑

www.brotherjimmys.com

"Noisy, greasy and fun", these "raucous" 'cue shacks dispense "cheap", "generic" Southern grub that's overshadowed by the "fishbowls of booze" that accompany it; "sticky floors", "scatterbrained service" and the raging "fratmosphere" make a good case for "delivery."

Brown Café *American* | ▽ 22 | 15 | 18 | $36 |

LES | 61 Hester St. (bet. Essex & Ludlow Sts.) | 212-477-2427 | www.greenbrownorange.com

Given its "postage-stamp" dimensions, small wonder that this LES 20-seater remains "relatively unknown"; but locals love its "sumptuous", yet affordable, New American menu, while the rustic-verging-on-"rough" decor embellishes the joint's "super-casual" vibe.

Bruckner Bar & Grill ◑ *American* | ▽ 19 | 16 | 22 | $24 |

Bronx | 1 Bruckner Blvd. (3rd Ave.) | 718-665-2001 | www.brucknerbar.com

A "true oasis" in a "gritty" stretch of the South Bronx, this "hip" New American "hidden under the Third Avenue Bridge" serves "solid", "inexpensive" meals to a "diverse" boho crowd; the "no-frills" setting is enlivened by "interesting art on the walls" and a "fun weekend brunch."

Bryant Park Grill/Cafe *American* | 18 | 22 | 18 | $49 |

W 40s | behind NY Public Library | 25 W. 40th St. (bet. 5th & 6th Aves.) | 212-840-6500 | www.arkrestaurants.com

"Location, location, location" makes this Bryant Park "indoor/outdoor" American duo a "tourist magnet"; the "handsome" Grill works best for "special events", while the "charming" alfresco Cafe is more suitable for "casual" nibbling, but at either the food is "unexciting" – so "stick to basics and enjoy the view."

B. Smith's Restaurant Row *Southern* | 19 | 19 | 20 | $48 |

W 40s | 320 W. 46th St. (bet. 8th & 9th Aves.) | 212-315-1100 | www.bsmith.com

Theatergoers go for the "Southern comfort" dispensed at this "busy" Restaurant Row "standby" owned by TV personality Barbara Smith; besides "down-home vittles with a contemporary twist", you can B sure of "fast-paced" service before the show.

Bubba Gump Shrimp Co. ◐ *American/Seafood* | 14 | 15 | 17 | $33 |

W 40s | 1501 Broadway (bet. 43rd & 44th Sts.) | 212-391-7100 | www.bubbagump.com

A "typical chain" offering amid the "bright lights of Times Square", this "tribute to *Forrest Gump*" serves "mostly fried" American seafood to "tourists in a hurry on a budget"; it works best for those "16 or younger" who don't mind "pedestrian" grub, "overly cheery" service and an "amusement-park" vibe.

Bubby's *American* | 18 | 15 | 16 | $32 |

TriBeCa | 120 Hudson St. (N. Moore St.) | 212-219-0666 ◐
Dumbo | 1 Main St. (bet. Plymouth & Water Sts.) | Brooklyn | 718-222-0666 ⊟
www.bubbys.com

The "trillion-calorie" Sunday brunch is an "institution" at these "crowd-pleasing" Americans in TriBeCa and Dumbo purveying "tasty", "homestyle" eats in "unpretentious", diner-ish settings; on weekends, brace yourself for "glacial" service, "nightmarish" acoustics and "mobs of kids" and hipsters.

⚡ Buddakan ◐ *Asian* | 24 | 27 | 22 | $65 |

Chelsea | 75 Ninth Ave. (bet. 15th & 16th Sts.) | 212-989-6699 | www.buddakannyc.com

The decor's a "total knockout" at Stephen Starr's "dazzling" Chelsea showplace, a "huge", "over-the-top" double-decker where "fashionable" "young" things toy with "expensive", "glammed-up" Asian dishes, "deftly" served by a "super" crew; but those not in the mood for a "never-ending party" find the "cacophonous" "bacchanal" "more theater than restaurant."

Buenos Aires ◐ *Argentinean/Steak* | 23 | 14 | 20 | $45 |

E Village | 513 E. Sixth St. (bet. Aves. A & B) | 212-228-2775 | www.buenosairesnyc.com

Steaks the "size of your forearm" crowd the plates at this "lively" East Village Argentinean chophouse where the grass-fed beef is so "tender" that "no knives are needed"; "marvelous Malbecs", "attentive" service and "great value" make up for the "bare, spare" brick-walled setting.

Bukhara Grill *Indian* | 23 | 15 | 19 | $39 |

E 40s | 217 E. 49th St. (bet. 2nd & 3rd Aves.) | 212-888-2839 | www.bukharany.com

Regulars rave about the "flavorful" $17 lunch buffet at this U.N.-area Indian offering "authentic" subcontinental specialties "cooked with care" and served by an "aim-to-please" team; dinner is quieter, but sari decor leads aesthetes to murmur "delivery is better."

Bull & Bear ● *Steak* 21 | 22 | 22 | $66

E 40s | Waldorf-Astoria | 301 Park Ave. (enter on Lexington Ave. & 49th St.) | 212-872-1275 | www.bullandbearsteakhouse.com

A "total throwback" to dining *"Mad Men"*-style, this "clubby" Waldorf-Astoria steakhouse offers "Type A personality" chops and "generous" pops ferried by a "well-tuned" team; expect an "old-boy" crowd "right out of the '50s" and decidedly more contemporary pricing.

Burger Heaven *Burgers* 16 | 10 | 15 | $20

E 40s | 20 E. 49th St. (bet. 5th & Madison Aves.) | 212-755-2166
E 40s | 291 Madison Ave. (bet. 40th & 41st Sts.) | 212-685-6250
E 50s | 536 Madison Ave. (bet. 54th & 55th Sts.) | 212-753-4214
E 50s | 9 E. 53rd St. (bet. 5th & Madison Aves.) | 212-752-0340
E 60s | 804 Lexington Ave. (62nd St.) | 212-838-3580
E 80s | 1534 Third Ave. (bet. 86th & 87th Sts.) | 212-722-8292
www.burgerheaven.com

Though "hardly heaven", these East Side patty palaces provide "reliable", "straightforward" chow at an "inexpensive" price point; despite "poor" service and "dreary" "diner environments", there's just "something comforting about them."

Burger Joint at Le Parker Meridien ●●⊄ *Burgers* 24 | 11 | 12 | $17

W 50s | Le Parker Meridien | 119 W. 56th St. (bet. 6th & 7th Aves.) | 212-708-7414 | www.parkermeridien.com

The "best thing hidden behind a curtain since the Wizard of Oz", this "no-frills" "burger speakeasy" incongruously set in the "fancy-schmancy" Parker Meridien lobby is again voted tops in the genre for its "super-juicy" patties "grilled to perfection"; even though the lines are "ridiculous", the room "ain't much" and the staff is "curt", wags tag it the *real* "burger heaven."

Burger Shoppe Ⓩ *Burgers* 21 | 12 | 14 | $18
(aka Wall Street Burger Shoppe)

Financial District | 30 Water St. (bet. Broad St. & Coenties Slip) | 212-425-1000 | www.burgershoppenyc.com

"Throwback to the '50s" decor sets the "retro" mood at this FiDi burger joint that vends "White Castle–size" patties with "interesting" toppings plus "awesome" malteds; fans prefer the "cozy" upstairs tavern to the "tiny" diner below, but either way you may have to shoppe for service.

Butter Ⓩ *American* 22 | 23 | 20 | $63

E Village | 415 Lafayette St. (bet. Astor Pl. & 4th St.) | 212-253-2828 | www.butterrestaurant.com

Although better known as a "hip nightlife destination", this "sleek", "chic" New American duplex near the Public Theater boasts "serious" cooking via chef Alex Guarnaschelli; diners prefer the "cathedral"-like ground-floor dining room, while scenesters head downstairs for drinking and "celebrity hoopla", but it's "expensive" wherever you sit.

Buttermilk Channel *American* 24 | 21 | 22 | $42

Carroll Gardens | 524 Court St. (Huntington St.) | Brooklyn | 718-852-8490 | www.buttermilkchannelnyc.com

"Familiar, comforting" cooking is the hallmark of this "eco-conscious" Carroll Gardens New American churning out "sophisticated" takes on old favorites in "airy", "communal-tabled" digs; it "lives up to the hype" for both "families" and "hipsters", though everyone wishes they'd "take reservations."

BXL Café ❶ *Belgian*   19 | 14 | 17 | $33
W 40s | 125 W. 43rd St. (bet. B'way & 6th Ave.) | 212-768-0200
BXL East ❶ *Belgian*
E 50s | 210 E. 51st St. (bet. 2nd & 3rd Aves.) | 212-888-7782
www.bxlcafe.com
Mussels are the "star of the show" at these "boisterous" Midtown Belgians where the "serviceable" grub is paired with "excellent" regional brews in "sports-bar" settings; for the "best bargain in town", check out the "all-you-can-eat-moules" deal on Sundays and Mondays.

Cabana ❶ *Nuevo Latino*   21 | 18 | 18 | $37
E 60s | 1022 Third Ave. (bet. 60th & 61st Sts.) | 212-980-5678
Seaport | Pier 17 | 89 South St. (Fulton St.) | 212-406-1155
Forest Hills | 107-10 70th Rd. (bet. Austin St. & Queens Blvd.) |
Queens | 718-263-3600
www.cabanarestaurant.com
"Right on the money", this "splashy" trio dishes out "huge portions" of Nuevo Latino food in "loud", "busy" rooms; "courteous" but "slow" service reinforces the "vacation" vibe, further enhanced by the "fab water view" from the deck of the Seaport branch.

Cabrito ❶ *Mexican*   17 | 13 | 16 | $35
W Village | 50 Carmine St. (bet. Bedford & Bleecker Sts.) | 212-929-5050 |
www.cabritonyc.com
"Younger" types tout the "flavorful" namesake roasted goat at this "hip" West Village Mexican that also does the job for a "taco and margarita fix"; too bad the "good prices" don't overcome the "cooler-than-thou" service, "loud" sound levels and only "decent" cooking.

Cacio e Pepe *Italian*   21 | 16 | 20 | $42
E Village | 182 Second Ave. (bet. 11th & 12th Sts.) | 212-505-5931
The thing to order at this "reliable" East Village Italian is its "eponymous" pasta "theatrically presented" inside a "massive wheel" of Parmesan, though all of its Roman offerings are "tasty" and "reasonably priced"; "pleasant service" and a "peaceful" back garden are also part of the package.

Cacio e Vino ❶ *Italian*   22 | 17 | 20 | $39
E Village | 80 Second Ave. (bet. 4th & 5th Sts.) | 212-228-3269 |
www.cacioevino.com
Akin to a "ticket to Palermo", this "off-the-radar" East Villager serves a "simple but wonderful" Sicilian menu that includes "excellent" wood-oven pizzas; "value" pricing and "welcoming" service make up for the "cramped" digs.

Cafe Asean ⊄ *Asian*   21 | 14 | 19 | $28
W Village | 117 W. 10th St. (bet. Greenwich & 6th Aves.) | 212-633-0348 |
www.cafeasean.com
"Fragrant, spicy" SE Asian fare turns up across the street from the Jefferson Market Library at this "tiny" West Village "find"; it's "not much to look at" and there's a "cash-only" rule, but payoffs include "bargain" tabs and a "swell", "neighborhood-secret" back garden.

	FOOD	DECOR	SERVICE	COST

Cafe Bar ◐ *Greek/Mediterranean* ▽ 20 | 18 | 18 | $23

Astoria | 32-90 36th St. (34th Ave.) | Queens | 718-204-5273 | www.cafebarastoria.com

Appreciated by Astorians for its cheap, "hearty" Greek-Med eats and "funky" "retro" mien, this "come-as-you-are-stay-as-long-as-you-like" joint is as "informal" as they come – but so is the service, so be sure to bring some "patience" along with you.

☑ Café Boulud *French* 27 | 24 | 26 | $82

E 70s | Surrey Hotel | 20 E. 76th St. (bet. 5th & Madison Aves.) | 212-772-2600 | www.danielnyc.com

It's "first class all the way" at Daniel Boulud's "*extraordinaire*" Uptown annex where Gavin Kaysen's "heavenly" French cuisine, "spectacular" wines, a "sophisticated" setting and "cosseting" service draw a "well-heeled" UES crowd; sure, the "prices are not 'cafe'", but the $35 prix fixe lunch is accessible to "mere mortals"; P.S. it now adjoins a smart new cocktail lounge, Bar Pleiades.

Cafe Centro ☒ *Mediterranean* 20 | 18 | 20 | $49

E 40s | MetLife Bldg. | 200 Park Ave. (45th St.) | 212-818-1222 | www.patinagroup.com

This "upscale" mega-brasserie near Grand Central is a "client lunch" magnet thanks to "reliable" Med cooking and efficient service; while it can be "hectic" midday, after dark it's noticeably more "sedate", and it's "always Restaurant Week" here given the nightly $35 prix fixe.

Cafecito *Cuban* 22 | 14 | 16 | $26

E Village | 185 Ave. C (bet. 11th & 12th Sts.) | 212-253-9966

Dishing out "Cuban soul food" that's about as "authentic" as it gets "this side of Miami", this Avenue C double storefront is a "great find" for those wanting to be transported "back to Havana"; "low prices" help obscure its decor and service issues.

Cafe Cluny ◐ *American/French* 21 | 20 | 20 | $47

W Village | 284 W. 12th St. (W. 4th St.) | 212-255-6900 | www.cafecluny.com

"Classic" French-American cookery, a "chic rep" and a "*très charmant*" setting are the lures at this "cozy", "quintessential West Village" boîte; it's a "popular date-night" venue weeknights, but the "hordes pile in" for its "awesome" weekend brunch.

NEW Café Colette *American* - | - | - | M

Williamsburg | 79 Berry St. (N. 9th St.) | Brooklyn | no phone | www.cafe-colette.com

Replacing Williamsburg's Silent H, this new bistro goes in a more mainstream direction with affordable American fare running the gamut from BBQ pork ribs to a steak-and-cheese sandwich; a checkered floor and vintage wooden fridge lend a retro note to the proceedings.

Cafe Con Leche *Cuban/Dominican* 18 | 12 | 16 | $26

W 80s | 424 Amsterdam Ave. (bet. 80th & 81st Sts.) | 212-595-7000
W 90s | 726 Amsterdam Ave. (bet. 95th & 96th Sts.) | 212-678-7000

"Stick-to-your-ribs" Cuban-Dominican comfort chow and the great "namesake drink" are on offer at these "authentic" little UWS "stand-bys"; Latin lovers don't mind the "slow" service, "loud" acoustics and "keep-your-eyes-shut" decor when the prices are this "low."

Café d'Alsace ❶ *French* | 21 | 18 | 19 | $45 |

E 80s | 1695 Second Ave. (88th St.) | 212-722-5133 | www.cafedalsace.com
Upper Eastsiders "got lucky" with the arrival of this Yorkville "god-send" serving "hearty" Alsatian favorites along with an "extensive beer list" (curated by its very own suds sommelier); the only drawback is "it's noisy when crowded, and it's always crowded."

Café du Soleil *French/Mediterranean* | 19 | 17 | 16 | $41 |

W 100s | 2723 Broadway (104th St.) | 212-316-5000 | www.cafedusoleilny.com
Bringing a "taste of France to the UWS", this "bustling" bistro near Columbia is a local "go-to" for "reliable", moderately priced French-Med cooking; the downsides are "erratic" service and "loud" acoustics ("sit outdoors" if you "plan to have a conversation").

Cafe Español ❶ *Spanish* | 20 | 15 | 20 | $37 |

G Village | 172 Bleecker St. (bet. MacDougal & Sullivan Sts.) | 212-505-0657
W Village | 78 Carmine St. (bet. Bedford St. & 7th Ave. S.) | 212-675-3312 www.cafeespanol.com
A "garlic-lover's dream", these "value-priced", separately owned Village vets vend "throwback" Spanish food and "wonderful" sangria; though the interiors could use some "sprucing up" and some find the overall experience "predictable", you "can't beat their prices."

Café Evergreen *Chinese* | 19 | 12 | 18 | $33 |

E 60s | 1288 First Ave. (bet. 69th & 70th Sts.) | 212-744-3266 | www.cafeevergreenchinese.com
For "downtown"-style dim sum, Upper Eastsiders point to this "consistent" Cantonese where the "tasty" morsels come via a "want-to-please" crew; "dull" decor may detract, but the prices are fine and "Sino oenophiles" say that the wines are surprisingly good.

Cafe Fiorello ❶ *Italian* | 20 | 17 | 19 | $52 |

W 60s | 1900 Broadway (bet. 63rd & 64th Sts.) | 212-595-5330 | www.cafefiorello.com
An "unbeatable" location facing Lincoln Center and "marvelous" pizzas and pastas have made this "convivial" Italian a pre-theater scene for 40 years; insiders tout its "scrumptious" antipasto bar, best enjoyed at sidewalk seats offering equally scrumptious "people-watching."

Café Frida *Mexican* | 20 | 16 | 18 | $40 |

W 70s | 368 Columbus Ave. (bet. 77th & 78th Sts.) | 212-712-2929
NEW **W 90s** | 768 Amsterdam Ave. (bet. 97th & 98th Sts.) | 212-749-2929 www.cafefrida.com
Champions cheer "olé for the mole" at this "congenial" UWS cantina where the Mexican fare is "flavorful" and the margaritas "strong"; dumpy digs and "have-it-our-way" service may mar the otherwise "fun" experience; P.S. the Amsterdam Avenue outpost opened post-Survey.

Cafe Gitane ❶ *French/Moroccan* | 20 | 20 | 16 | $31 |

NoLita | 242 Mott St. (Prince St.) | 212-334-9552 ⌐
NEW **W Village** | Jane Hotel | 113 Jane St. (bet. Washington & West Sts.) | 212-255-4113
It "feels like Rick's Cafe from *Casablanca*" at this "sceney" NoLita French-Moroccan where a "groovy crowd" tucks into "delicious", well-

priced grub while tolerating the "snooty" service and prime-time "waits"; its new Jane Hotel sibling differentiates itself by accepting plastic and reservations, as well as having "more room to stretch out."

Café Habana ● *Cuban/Mexican* `22` `15` `15` `$24`
NoLita | 17 Prince St. (Elizabeth St.) | 212-625-2001 | www.cafehabana.com

Habana Outpost ●⊄ *Cuban/Mexican*
Fort Greene | 755-757 Fulton St. (S. Portland Ave.) | Brooklyn | 718-858-9500 | www.ecoeatery.com

"Scrumptious" Mexican-Cuban "haute street food" and "diabolically good" grilled corn have "hip-and-happenin'" hordes enduring "insane waits" at this "crazy busy" NoLita joint and its more "ecologically sensitive" Fort Greene sibling; "dirt-cheap" prices are another reason for the "overcrowding."

Café Henri ● *French* `20` `16` `18` `$24`
W Village | 27 Bedford St. (Downing St.) | 212-243-2846
LIC | 10-10 50th Ave. (bet. Jackson Ave. & Vernon Blvd.) | Queens | 718-383-9315

The only thing missing is "the Seine" at this "casual", low-budget French duo in LIC and the Village specializing in "fabulous crêpes" and "real-deal" café au lait; "just like Paris", the service is "extremely leisurely", but no one cares.

Cafe Joul *French* `18` `14` `19` `$44`
E 50s | 1070 First Ave. (bet. 58th & 59th Sts.) | 212-759-3131

Though not exactly the "crown joul of Sutton Place", this "convenient", affordable local bistro does provide its "older" audience with "consistent", "authentically French" cooking "served with good cheer"; too bad the "tight", "ordinary" setting has diners sitting cheek by jowl.

Café Katja *Austrian* ▽ `24` `17` `23` `$35`
LES | 79 Orchard St. (bet. Broome & Grand Sts.) | 212-219-9545 | www.cafe-katja.com

Sure it's "small" – "or in NYC speak, 'cozy'" – but this "off-the-beaten-path" Lower East Side "hideaway" purveys big flavors in its "real-thing" Austrian menu, accompanied by an array of "must-try" international brews; "charming" service and modest tabs make regulars feel spaetzle.

Cafe Loup ● *French* `19` `18` `20` `$45`
W Village | 105 W. 13th St. (bet. 6th Ave. & 7th Ave. S.) | 212-255-4746 | www.cafeloupnyc.com

"Nothing much has changed" at this "old reliable" West Villager, on the scene since 1977 and renowned for "satisfying" French bistro fare, "attentive" service and prices that "won't throw you for a loop"; the "bohemian" yet "civilized" room also hosts "popular" Sunday jazz sessions.

Cafe Luluc ⊄ *French* `20` `15` `18` `$31`
Cobble Hill | 214 Smith St. (Baltic St.) | Brooklyn | 718-625-3815

"*Très* French", this "comfortable", "friendly" Cobble Hill bistro rolls out "quality" Gallic grub, including "Brooklyn's fluffiest pancakes"; "low" prices offset the "cash-only" rule, and since "brunch is the big draw", insiders show up off-peak for quick, "in-and-out" dining.

	FOOD	DECOR	SERVICE	COST

☑ Cafe Luxembourg *French* | **20** | **18** | **20** | **$53**

W 70s | 200 W. 70th St. (bet. Amsterdam & West End Aves.) |
212-873-7411 | www.cafeluxembourg.com

Primo "performing-arts" people-watching ("was that Jude and
Sienna?") comes with "fine" French food at this UWS bastion of "sophistication personified"; boasting "stylish" digs, "super-flattering
lighting" and a "sexy bar scene", it's usually "packed tighter than
a dance belt."

Cafe Mogador ● *Moroccan* | **22** | **16** | **18** | **$30**

E Village | 101 St. Marks Pl. (bet. Ave. A & 1st Ave.) | 212-677-2226 |
www.cafemogador.com

"Terrific", "tangy" cooking "makes you forget how close you are to the
next table" at this longtime East Village Moroccan decorated in a
"delightfully funky" style; "affordable" tabs and late-night hours
balance out the "long waits" and dinnertime "din."

Cafe Ronda *Mediterranean/S American* | **20** | **16** | **18** | **$36**

W 70s | 249-251 Columbus Ave. (bet. 71st & 72nd Sts.) | 212-579-9929 |
www.caferonda.com

Regulars ronda-vous at this UWS Med–South American for "tasty"
tapas (plus larger plates) offered at "fair prices"; if the "intimate"
room sometimes feels "too small for the traffic", the sidewalk tables
are a sensible option.

Café Sabarsky/Café Fledermaus *Austrian* | **23** | **24** | **20** | **$44**

E 80s | Neue Galerie | 1048 Fifth Ave. (86th St.) | 212-288-0665 |
www.wallse.com

"Old-world charm" and "new-world prices" collide at Kurt
Gutenbrunner's "*wunderbar*" Viennese *kaffehaus* in the Neue Galerie
offering "stupendous" pastries and light bites in an atmospheric "fin
de siècle" chamber; downstairs sibling Fledermaus serves the "same
menu" with less waiting.

Café Select ● *Swiss* | ▽ **19** | **17** | **17** | **$35**

SoHo | 212 Lafayette St. (bet. Broome & Spring Sts.) | 212-925-9322 |
www.cafeselectnyc.com

This "cool" SoHo spot draws "attractive young" types with "modern
takes" on "rustic" Swiss cooking served in a smart setting recalling a
European railway cafe; service may be "relaxed", but so are the prices;
P.S. insiders tout the "private room behind the kitchen."

Cafe S.F.A. *American* | **18** | **17** | **18** | **$35**

E 40s | Saks Fifth Ave. | 611 Fifth Ave., 8th fl. (bet. 49th & 50th Sts.) |
212-940-4080

"When your feet get tired", this "convenient" New American in Saks
supplies "high-quality" nibbles accessorized with "glorious" views of
St. Patrick's and Rock Center; still, a few find the enterprise "uninspired" and "pricey for what it is."

Cafe Steinhof *Austrian* | **20** | **16** | **18** | **$28**

Park Slope | 422 Seventh Ave. (14th St.) | Brooklyn | 718-369-7776 |
www.cafesteinhof.com

Park Slopers praise this "unpretentious" Austrian as a great "bang for
the buck", citing "hearty, heavy" eats paired with "out-of-this-world"

brews; "movie nights" and Monday's $6 "goulash special" embellish its "best-deal" status.

Cafeteria ● American

FOOD	DECOR	SERVICE	COST
19	16	15	$33

Chelsea | 119 Seventh Ave. (17th St.) | 212-414-1717 |
www.cafeteriagroup.com

"Comfort food for hipsters" is yours at this affordable 24/7 Chelsea American where most go to "see and be seen", "not hear and be heard"; though trendoids yawn it's "over the hill" scenewise, the "ridiculous" lines, "flippant" service and "glaring pretension" remain in place.

Cafe Un Deux Trois ● French

17	15	18	$43

W 40s | 123 W. 44th St. (bet. B'way & 6th Ave.) | 212-354-4148 |
www.cafeundeuxtrois.biz

The "Energizer bunny of bistros", this Times Square perennial (since '77) can be a "madhouse pre-theater", when it morphs into a "noisy" mix of "tourists", "crayons and paper tablecloths"; though most report a "solid meal for a fair price", there are "no surprises" here, save for how "stale" the decor has become.

Caffe Cielo ● Italian

20	17	21	$46

W 50s | 881 Eighth Ave. (bet. 52nd & 53rd Sts.) | 212-246-9555 |
www.caffecielonyc.com

Now celebrating its 25th anniversary, this "edge-of-the-Theater-District" Italian produces "well-prepared" meals served by "true professionals"; even though the "decor leaves something to be desired", it does offer "reasonable pricing" and "no tourists."

Caffe Grazie Italian

20	17	20	$47

E 80s | 26 E. 84th St. (bet. 5th & Madison Aves.) | 212-717-4407 |
www.caffegrazie.com

"Convenient" to Museum Mile, this "charming" Italian attracts "devoted regulars" (including the "ladies-who-lunch" set) with "consistent" cooking and a "cheerful welcome"; most overlook the "too-tight" quarters – especially when its $15 prix fixe lunch is served.

Calexico Ⓜ☞ Mexican

25	10	16	$14

Carroll Gardens | 122 Union St. (bet. Columbia & Hicks Sts.) | Brooklyn |
718-488-8226 | www.calexicocart.com

Devotees of this come-as-you-are, cash-only Carroll Gardens "taco temple" are in "pork heaven" thanks to the "cheap", "addictive" Mexican eats; given the bargain tabs, fans willingly ignore the decor and service.

Calle Ocho Nuevo Latino

21	21	19	$46

W 80s | 446 Columbus Ave. (bet. 81st & 82nd Sts.) | 212-873-5025 |
www.calleochonyc.com

"High-energy" scenemakers flock to this UWS Nuevo Latino for "delicious" dishes and "marvelous" mojitos served in a "glitzy Havana" setting that could "win a Tony for theatrics"; alright, it's "very loud", but no one cares when the "unlimited sangria brunch" is in full swing.

CamaJe ● American/French

∇ 22	16	22	$40

G Village | 85 MacDougal St. (bet. Bleecker & Houston Sts.) | 212-673-8184 |
www.camaje.com

"Surprisingly sophisticated" Franco-American fare with a "wallet-friendly" price tag is the hallmark of this "tiny", "eccentric" Villager helmed by chef Abigail Hitchcock; there are also "cooking classes" and "dark dining" nights when you eat blindfolded.

Campagnola ● *Italian* | 24 | 18 | 21 | $72 |

E 70s | 1382 First Ave. (bet. 73rd & 74th Sts.) | 212-861-1102
Like a "private club" for "celebs", "wiseguys" and the "painted ladies" who love them, this "buzzing" "old-school" Italian merges the "charm of Portofino" with the "class of the UES"; it's "best if you're a regular", and though the prices are "insane", the "food is insanely good."

NEW Campo de' Fiori *Pizza* | - | - | - | M |

Park Slope | 187 Fifth Ave. (Berkeley Pl.) | Brooklyn | 347-763-0933
Park Slope's busy Fifth Avenue strip is home to this new pizzeria specializing in Roman-style square pies, along with salumi and antipasti; its basic, sunny quarters with an open kitchen put the focus on its simple, well-priced fare.

Canaletto *Italian* | 21 | 17 | 22 | $56 |

E 60s | 208 E. 60th St. (bet. 2nd & 3rd Aves.) | 212-317-9192
An "island of mellow civility", this "upscale" Italian "close to Bloomie's" offers "quiet", "reliable" dining as a relief in a "frenzied shopping" zone; it's "traditional", verging on "stuffy" – and that suits its "adult", "kissy-face" fan base just fine.

Candle Cafe *Vegan/Vegetarian* | 23 | 14 | 19 | $32 |

E 70s | 1307 Third Ave. (bet. 74th & 75th Sts.) | 212-472-0970 | www.candlecafe.com
Look for "tofu to die for" at Candle 79's "less expensive", "more fun" sibling, an UES vegetarian with heavenly vegan vittles and an "earthy vibe"; "great value and quality", if not decor, explain why there's "almost always a line."

Candle 79 *Vegan/Vegetarian* | 24 | 21 | 23 | $47 |

E 70s | 154 E. 79th St. (bet. Lexington & 3rd Aves.) | 212-537-7179 | www.candlecafe.com
There's "nary a Birkenstock or untweezed hippie in sight" at this "sophisticated" UES vegan/vegetarian vending "exquisitely prepared" fare that proves the genre "need not be boring or tasteless"; the "passionate staffers" are "great cheerleaders", making the semi-"pricey" tabs easy to digest.

Canyon Road *Southwestern* | 20 | 17 | 18 | $38 |

E 70s | 1470 First Ave. (bet. 76th & 77th Sts.) | 212-734-1600 | www.arkrestaurants.com
The "spicy" Southwestern eats, "high-test" margaritas and prices that "aren't crazy expensive" keep this "unassuming" UES cantina buzzing with "workaholic bankers" and their "blond" companions; it's typically "loud" and "crowded", so conversationalists "request a table away from the bar."

Capital Grille *Steak* | 24 | 23 | 24 | $69 |

E 40s | Chrysler Ctr. | 155 E. 42nd St. (bet. Lexington & 3rd Aves.) | 212-953-2000
NEW **Financial District** | 120 Broadway (Nassau & Pine Sts.) | 212-374-1811 ⊠

(continued)

(continued)

Capital Grille

W 50s | Time-Life Building | 120 W. 51st St. (bet. 6th & 7th Aves.) |
212-246-0154
www.thecapitalgrille.com

This "top-tier" steakhouse trio offers "quality dry-aged beef", "charm-school" service and "humming" bar scenes – "you'd never know it was a chain" – though you'll "need a lot of capital" when the check arrives; P.S. the Chrysler Building satellite has the splashiest setting.

Capsouto Frères *French*   24 | 23 | 24 | $59

TriBeCa | 451 Washington St. (Watts St.) | 212-966-4900 |
www.capsoutofreres.com

Although "in the middle of nowhere", this "charming" TriBeCa "pioneer" is worth seeking out for its "home-run" French bistro cooking, "wonderful" wines and "warm", "family" feel; plentiful parking, "impeccable service" and a "lovely", brick-walled setting enhance the "civilized" experience; P.S. save room at the end – the "soufflé is a must."

Caracas Arepa Bar *Venezuelan*   24 | 14 | 18 | $21

E Village | 93½ E. Seventh St. (bet. Ave. A & 1st Ave.) | 212-529-2314

Caracas Brooklyn *Venezuelan*

Williamsburg | 291 Grand St. (bet. Havemeyer & Roebling Sts.) |
Brooklyn | 718-218-6050

Caracas to Go *Venezuelan*

E Village | 91 E. Seventh St. (1st Ave.) | 212-228-5062
www.caracasarepabar.com

"Always packed", this "cheap" and "casual" East Villager specializes in "authentic" arepas (Venezuelan corn-flour rounds with an array of fillings) served in a "tiny" space; as an "alternative to waiting", check out the neighboring "to-go" outpost or the newer, larger Williamsburg entry.

Cara Mia *Italian*   21 | 16 | 20 | $39

W 40s | 654 Ninth Ave. (bet. 45th & 46th Sts.) | 212-262-6767 |
www.caramiany.com

A "good choice before or after a show", this "not fancy" Hell's Kitchen Italian turns out "solid", "reasonably priced" homemade pastas and the like with "efficient" speed; just be prepared for a "tight" fit: a "subway at rush hour has more space."

Caravaggio *Italian*   23 | 23 | 24 | $96

E 70s | 23 E. 74th St. (bet. 5th & Madison Aves.) | 212-288-1004

You'll "rub elbows with power players" at this "posh" UES Italian in the "old Coco Pazzo" digs; catering to the "over-50 crowd" with "excellent", "old-style" cooking and "extraordinarily accommodating" service (the "captain bowed so often he almost broke in two"), it's – no surprise – "exorbitantly expensive."

Caravan of Dreams ⊽ *Vegan/Vegetarian*   22 | 16 | 18 | $27

E Village | 405 E. Sixth St. (1st Ave.) | 212-254-1613 |
www.caravanofdreams.net

"Every type of veg head" is accommodated at this 20-year-old East Villager known for its "dream-come-true" kosher vegan dishes that make folks "feel good about what they're eating"; though "cash only" is a buzzkill, nightly "live music" bolsters the "bohemian" vibe.

Carl's Steaks *Cheesesteaks* `20` `5` `13` `$12`
Murray Hill | 507 Third Ave. (34th St.) | 212-696-5336 ◐
TriBeCa | 79 Chambers St. (bet. B'way & Church St.) |
212-566-2828
www.carlssteaks.com
For a "little piece of Philadelphia in NY" – "griminess included" – check out these "budget-conscious" cheesesteak houses popular with the "post-bar crowd" for their "sloppy, gooey" sandwiches; they both "get the job done" and "keep cardiologists in business."

⚡ Carlyle Restaurant *French* `23` `27` `25` `$85`
E 70s | Carlyle Hotel | 35 E. 76th St. (Madison Ave.) | 212-570-7192 |
www.thecarlyle.com
The "epitome of old-world UES civility", this "upper-crust" hotel dining room is a "NY must" for its "grand" New French cooking, "flawless courtesy" and "elegant" design; just be aware it's so pricey that "you may have to disinherit your children"; P.S. jackets (remember them?) are required at dinner.

Carmine's *Italian* `20` `16` `18` `$42`
W 40s | 200 W. 44th St. (bet. B'way & 8th Ave.) | 212-221-3800 ◐
W 90s | 2450 Broadway (bet. 90th & 91st Sts.) | 212-362-2200
www.carminesnyc.com
"Heroic" family-style portions of "super-garlicky" red-sauce Italiana ensure that "you'll always take home a doggy bag" from these hugely popular Westsiders; "loud" and "bustling" with "groups", "tourists" and "theatergoers", they can be "difficult to get into" without a "wait."

⚡ Carnegie Deli ◐⊄ *Deli* `22` `10` `14` `$29`
W 50s | 854 Seventh Ave. (55th St.) | 212-757-2245 |
www.carnegiedeli.com
"They pile the meat on mile-high" at this "cash-only", "one-and-only" Midtown deli that "Woody Allen" put on everybody's "must-go-at-least-once list"; the sandwiches – and prices – may leave you with "lockjaw" (and the seating may involve locked elbows), but most say the "shtick" is worth the sticker shock.

Carol's Cafe ⓈⓂ *Eclectic* `26` `18` `21` `$55`
Staten Island | 1571 Richmond Rd. (bet. Four Corners Rd. & Seaview Ave.) |
718-979-5600 | www.carolscafe.com
A "labor of love" in Staten Island, Carol Frazzetta's "homey" Dongan Hills "staple" serves "imaginative" Eclectic eats in a simple setting recalling dining "with family"; sure, it's "expensive" for these parts, but where else will a "hands-on" chef actually "teach you how to make the dish you like"?

NEW Casa Lever Ⓢ *Italian* `23` `25` `22` `$75`
E 50s | 390 Park Ave. (enter on 53rd St., bet. Madison & Park Aves.) |
212-888-2700 | www.casalever.com
"Chic and modern", this "buzzy" new power canteen in Midtown's Lever House delivers a "high-energy" scene, "sophisticated" Milanese cuisine and "ultracool" design with "Warhols" lining the walls; brought to you by the Sant Ambroeus team, it's a "movers-and-

shakers" magnet at lunch, but whenever you show up, bring your "expense account."

Casa Mono ● *Spanish*   26 | 18 | 20 | $57

Gramercy | 52 Irving Pl. (17th St.) | 212-253-2773 | www.casamononyc.com

For "gourmet grazing" on "exotic" tapas and "sublime" wines, check out Mario Batali's "tiny" Gramercy Spaniard; it's "like being in Barcelona", though "steep tabs", "zero elbow room" and "pretentious" service come with the territory; if you can't get in, around-the-corner sibling Bar Jamon is a "good alternative."

Z NEW Cascabel ● *Mexican*   25 | 15 | 18 | $24

E 80s | 1542 Second Ave. (bet. 80th & 81st Sts.) | 212-717-7800 | www.nyctacos.com

"Huge crowds" assemble at this "amazing" new UES taqueria with "good reason": "delicious", "off-the-charts" tacos made with "top-notch" ingredients for "cheap" tabs; indeed, it's such a hit that it's already relocating from its original "beyond-tiny setting" to bigger digs two doors down the street at 1538 Second Avenue.

NEW Ça Va *French*   − | − | − | E

W 40s | InterContinental NY Times Sq. | 310 W. 44th St. (8th Ave.) | 212-803-4545 | www.cavatoddenglish.com

Busy chef Todd English touches down in Times Square via this new French brasserie in the InterContinental Hotel (also home to the latest Shake Shack); though the overall design and neutral palette has a faint suburban vibe, the roomy setting offers three squares a day and covers all the bases by including a lounge, take-out market and private dining room.

Caviar Russe ● *American*   25 | 24 | 24 | $82

E 50s | 538 Madison Ave., 2nd fl. (bet. 54th & 55th Sts.) | 212-980-5908 | www.caviarrusse.com

"Like dining at Catherine the Great's", this "opulent", second-floor New American tucked away on Madison Avenue supplies "sterling" service and a "sumptuous" menu of caviar and sushi; if you don't feel like "emptying the trust fund", there's always the $20 weekday prix fixe lunch.

Cávo ● M *Greek*   20 | 26 | 20 | $42

Astoria | 42-18 31st Ave. (bet. 42nd & 43rd Sts.) | Queens | 718-721-1001 | www.cavoastoria.com

"Athens" alights in Astoria at this "trendy" taverna serving "tasty" Greek dishes in its big, "bustling" dining room and "amazing", waterfall-enhanced garden; be prepared to "pay for the scenery", though, and "bring earplugs" late-night when it morphs into a "Euro-clubby" party.

Cebu ● *Continental*   22 | 19 | 18 | $38

Bay Ridge | 8801 Third Ave. (88th St.) | Brooklyn | 718-492-5095 | www.cebubrooklyn.com

"One of the better Bay Ridge hangouts", this "cool" Continental bistro transitions from "tranquil" and "charming" during the dinner hour to a bona fide "pickup scene" later on (it's open nightly till 3 AM); "recently expanded", it's "still as good" – and "busy" – as ever.

	FOOD	DECOR	SERVICE	COST

Celeste ⏸ *Italian*
24 **11** **16** **$34**

W 80s | 502 Amsterdam Ave. (bet. 84th & 85th Sts.) | 212-874-4559
Devotees of this "wonderful little" UWS trattoria tout its "unbelievably fresh" Neapolitan cooking, "to-die-for" cheese plates and "bargain-basement" tabs; despite no reservations, "cramped quarters" and an "unfortunate cash-only" policy, "long lines" are the norm here.

Cellini *Italian*
22 **18** **22** **$59**

E 50s | 65 E. 54th St. (bet. Madison & Park Aves.) | 212-751-1555 | www.cellinirestaurant.com
"Classic old-style" Italian dishes fill out the menu of this "corporate" Midtown "business club" that's "best for lunch", though "more enjoyable" (and quieter) at dinner; "service that makes you feel like you own the restaurant" keeps regulars regular.

Centolire *Italian*
21 **20** **20** **$60**

E 80s | 1167 Madison Ave. (bet. 85th & 86th Sts.) | 212-734-7711 | www.pinoluongo.com
Pino Luongo's "attractive" Carnegie Hill duplex draws an "older neighborhood crowd" with "sumptuous" Tuscan cooking and "quality" service; its "pleasant" downstairs cafe – a panini specialist – is less expensive than the "more formal" upstairs dining room.

Centrico *Mexican*
20 **19** **18** **$47**

TriBeCa | 211 W. Broadway (Franklin St.) | 212-431-0700 | www.myriadrestaurantgroup.com
"Fancy" takes on Mexican food are yours at this "upscale yet unpretentious" TriBeCan helmed by TV celeb chef Aarón Sanchez; though "service leaves a bad taste" in some mouths, the "lively" mood, "lofty" setting and "moderate pricing" are fine as is.

Centro Vinoteca ● *Italian*
21 **19** **19** **$51**

W Village | 74 Seventh Ave. S. (Barrow St.) | 212-367-7470 | www.centrovinoteca.com
It's "all about the wine" and small-plate *piccolini* at this West Village Italian that's generally "delicious", though some say it "lost some luster" after "too much turnover" in the kitchen; the bi-level setting boasts a "fun downstairs bar", but insiders "eat upstairs" in order to "hear what people are saying."

Cercle Rouge ● *French*
19 **19** **19** **$47**

TriBeCa | 241 W. Broadway (N. Moore St.) | 212-226-6252 | www.cerclerougeresto.com
For the "feel of Paris" in TriBeCa, check out this "lovely" French brasserie where the "country cooking", pro service and warm, banquette-lined setting transport fans to the "Rive Gauche"; "reasonable" tabs and sidewalk seats score bonus points.

'Cesca *Italian*
23 **21** **21** **$60**

W 70s | 164 W. 75th St. (Amsterdam Ave.) | 212-787-6300 | www.cescanyc.com
At this "sociable" UWS Southern Italian, there's usually a "lively crowd" thanks to its "sublime" dishes, "warm atmosphere" and "first-rate" service; although it skews a bit "pricey", Monday night's "half-price wine deal" is a hit with the budget-minded.

Chadwick's *American*
23 | **18** | **23** | **$47**

Bay Ridge | 8822 Third Ave. (89th St.) | Brooklyn | 718-833-9855 | www.chadwicksny.com

A "dependable" Bay Ridge local, this circa-1987 "oldie but goodie" is known for serving first-rate Traditional Americana in an "old-style, white-tablecloth" setting; "welcoming" service, "valet parking" and good deal prix fixes ($17 lunch, $25 dinner) add bang for the buck.

Char No. 4 ❂ *Southern*
22 | **20** | **20** | **$40**

Cobble Hill | 196 Smith St. (bet. Baltic & Warren Sts.) | Brooklyn | 718-643-2106 | www.charno4.com

"Go for the bourbon" and "stay for the bourbon" at this "slice-of-heaven" Cobble Hill Southerner with a "pork-inflected" menu and a decided "bacon fetish"; while the grub's midpriced, the drinks can run up, but the "hipsters" lost in its "amber-hued" glow don't seem to mind.

Chef Ho's Peking Duck Grill *Chinese*
21 | **14** | **19** | **$33**

E 80s | 1720 Second Ave. (bet. 89th & 90th Sts.) | 212-348-9444

There's "no need to go downtown" for Peking duck thanks to this 20-year-old Yorkville Chinese "standby" where the "mouthwatering" signature dish is the "must"-order item; "Chinatown prices" and "pro service" make up for the "small", spare setting.

Chennai Garden *Indian/Vegetarian*
21 | **12** | **15** | **$22**

Murray Hill | 129 E. 27th St. (Park Ave. S.) | 212-689-1999

"Sure, there are fancier joints in Curry Hill", but the "delish" dosas and "just-out-of-the-oven" breads at this vegetarian Indian are "priced to please" – and kosher to boot; its bountiful $7 lunch buffet makes fans forget the "lackluster" service and "sterile" decor.

Chestnut Ⓜ *American*
23 | **20** | **22** | **$45**

Carroll Gardens | 271 Smith St. (bet. Degraw & Sackett Sts.) | Brooklyn | 718-243-0049 | www.chestnutonsmith.com

One of "Smith Street's best", this "platonic ideal of a neighborhood restaurant" is a "textbook Brooklyn" kind of place with "inventive" New American cooking, "reasonable prices", "hipster waiters" and a "glorious" backyard; though its "compact" setting has been "expanded", it still feels "cozy."

Chez Jacqueline ❂ *French*
20 | **19** | **20** | **$48**

G Village | 72 MacDougal St. (bet. Bleecker & Houston Sts.) | 212-505-0727 | www.chezjacquelinerestaurant.com

"Quaint" and "quiet", this "throwback" Village standby continues to delight fans with its "simple" French bistro fare, "moderate" pricing and "charming" atmosphere; though some say this "old standard" "isn't the same" sans Jacqueline, at least it "always makes you feel welcome."

Chez Josephine ❂Ⓜ *French*
20 | **21** | **21** | **$53**

W 40s | 414 W. 42nd St. (bet. 9th & 10th Aves.) | 212-594-1925 | www.chezjosephine.com

Whether the curtains rise or fall on Broadway, the show goes on at this Theater District "shrine" to Josephine Baker, helmed by her "flamboyant", "worth-the-price-of-admission" son, Jean-Claude; "reliable" French cooking, an "ivory-tickling" pianist and an "over-the-top", "gay Paree" setting have kept this one going strong for 25 years.

Chez Lucienne *French*

FOOD	DECOR	SERVICE	COST
22	18	20	$40

Harlem | 308 Lenox Ave. (bet. 125th & 126th Sts.) | 212-289-5555 |
www.chezlucienne.com

For the "South of France in the middle of Harlem", check out this "welcome" spot serving the "most ambitious" French food you'll find "down the block from Bill Clinton's office"; "*tout de suite*" service and fair tabs make it a natural "pre–Apollo Theater."

Chez Napoléon ⊠ *French*

FOOD	DECOR	SERVICE	COST
21	15	21	$48

W 50s | 365 W. 50th St. (bet. 8th & 9th Aves.) | 212-265-6980 |
www.cheznapoleon.com

One of the Theater District's "last old-fashioned, family-run" French restaurants, this circa-1960 "constant companion" draws "mature" types with its "Julia-Child-lives" cooking and "sweet" service; "time only burnishes its charm", even if it "looks like it hasn't been painted since Piaf died."

Chez Oskar ● *French*

FOOD	DECOR	SERVICE	COST
19	17	19	$33

Fort Greene | 211 DeKalb Ave. (Adelphi St.) | Brooklyn | 718-852-6250 |
www.chezoskar.com

Dishing out "funky French" fare on DeKalb Avenue, this Fort Greene bistro lures "youthful" locals who dig the "European" feel and "bustling" vibe; though the cooking's a bit "inconsistent" and service skews "slow", Brooklyn prices and "great" live jazz are sufficient offsets.

Chiam Chinese Cuisine *Chinese*

FOOD	DECOR	SERVICE	COST
22	19	21	$47

E 40s | 160 E. 48th St. (bet. Lexington & 3rd Aves.) | 212-371-2323 |
www.chiamnyc.com

Midtowners migrate to this "upscale" Chinese for "upgraded" cuisine and service that's "much better than the standard in Chinatown"; of course, the "fancy food" comes at a "fancy price", though the $21 prix fixe lunch is a "reasonable" alternative.

Chickpea *Mideastern*

FOOD	DECOR	SERVICE	COST
19	10	15	$12

E Village | 210 E. 14th St. (bet. 2nd & 3rd Aves.) | 212-228-3445
Flatiron | 688 Sixth Ave. (bet. 21st & 22nd Sts.) | 212-243-6275 ●
www.getchickpea.com

"Flavorful" and "quick", this Mideast duo is known for serving "falafel that never saw a deep fryer"; since the digs are "cramped" and the food can be "hit-or-miss", "price is the best feature" here.

ChikaLicious *Dessert*

FOOD	DECOR	SERVICE	COST
25	15	20	$18

E Village | 203 E. 10th St. (bet. 1st & 2nd Aves.) | 212-995-9511 |
www.chikalicious.com
E Village | 204 E. 10th St. (bet. 1st & 2nd Aves.) | 212-475-0929 |
www.dessertclubnyc.com ●

A "one-of-a-kind experience", this "tiny" East Village dessert specialist seduces sweet tooths with "dazzling", three-course prix fixes and "ingenious wine pairings"; the counter-service adjunct across the street "handles the overflow."

Chimichurri Grill ● *Argentinean/Steak*

FOOD	DECOR	SERVICE	COST
23	16	20	$50

W 40s | 609 Ninth Ave. (bet. 43rd & 44th Sts.) | 212-586-8655 |
www.chimichurrigrill.com

Theatergoers get a "red-meat fix" at this Hell's Kitchen "carnivore's delight" that's priced "below the bigger steakhouses" yet still offers

| | FOOD | DECOR | SERVICE | COST |

"incredibly flavorful" Argentine specialties; some say that the across-the-street location has "lost the charm" of its original site.

Chimu *Peruvian*   ▽ 25 | 15 | 20 | $30

Williamsburg | 482 Union Ave. (bet. Meeker & Metropolitan Aves.) | Brooklyn | 718-349-1208

Out of the way in Williamsburg and "out of this world" in the kitchen, this "quaint little" seafood-heavy Peruvian serves an "explosion of authentic flavors" without scorching your wallet; since the ambiance "leaves a little to be desired", insiders gravitate outside to the patio.

China Chalet *Chinese*   18 | 14 | 19 | $30

Financial District | 47 Broadway (bet. Exchange Pl. & Morris St.) | 212-943-4380
Staten Island | Eltingville Shopping Ctr. | 4326 Amboy Rd. (bet. Armstrong & Richmond Aves.) | 718-984-8044
www.chinachalet.com

There are "no surprises" to be found at these purveyors of "typical, Americanized" Chinese chow in the FiDi and Staten Island that put out "plentiful" portions for "reasonable" prices and even boast "pleasant" service; but "old-looking" decor leads critics to say "don't bring anyone you want to impress."

☒ China Grill *Asian*   22 | 21 | 20 | $56

W 50s | 60 W. 53rd St. (bet. 5th & 6th Aves.) | 212-333-7788 | www.chinagrillmgt.com

Ever the "fun Midtown melting pot", this "timeless" "powerhouse" caters to "business" folk with a "flashy", "consistently delicious" Asian menu that's a match for its great big "glam" setting; sure, it's "spendy" and the bar is a "pickup palace", but it's not true that "they pipe the noise in."

Chinatown Brasserie *Chinese*   22 | 22 | 19 | $48

NoHo | 380 Lafayette St. (Great Jones St.) | 212-533-7000 | www.chinatownbrasserie.com

Channeling a Shanghai "movie set", this "over-the-top" NoHo Chinese wows patrons with its "lush" looks, "exquisite" dim sum and "delicious" Peking duck; it's every bit "as good as Chinatown", but since it comes at "twice the price", some are sure to gripe.

☒ Chin Chin ◐ *Chinese*   23 | 18 | 22 | $53

E 40s | 216 E. 49th St. (bet. 2nd & 3rd Aves.) | 212-888-4555 | www.chinchinny.com

A "tried-and-true" nexus for Midtown "business lunching", this circa-1987 "favorite" offers "reliable" Chinese cuisine for a "high-end" tab, but the "creative" dishes – like the "superb", "off-the-menu" Grand Marnier shrimp – are "worth every penny"; though the servers "aim to please", it "helps to be a regular."

Chinese Mirch *Asian*   20 | 12 | 16 | $28

Murray Hill | 120 Lexington Ave. (28th St.) | 212-532-3663 | www.chinesemirch.com

Fans say the "stranger the dish sounds, the better it will be" at this "spicy" Chinese-Indian hybrid in Murray Hill where the merch is "affordable" fusion "at its best"; given that there's "zero ambiance", "takeout may be the best route."

	FOOD	DECOR	SERVICE	COST

ChipShop *British*
| | 19 | 14 | 18 | $23 |

Brooklyn Heights | 129 Atlantic Ave. (Henry St.) | Brooklyn | 718-855-7775 ●
Park Slope | 383 Fifth Ave. (bet. 6th & 7th Sts.) | Brooklyn | 718-832-7701 ⊅
www.chipshopnyc.com

These Brooklyn temples of "gluttony" salute "jolly old England" with "greasy" British menus highlighted by classic fish 'n' chips and "God's gift to mankind", the "deep-fried candy bar"; it's a "guilty pleasure" for many, even though you'll "feel your veins throb" when you exit.

Chocolate Room *Dessert*
| | 24 | 18 | 20 | $18 |

Cobble Hill | 269 Court St. (bet. Butler & Douglass Sts.) | Brooklyn | 718-246-2600
Park Slope | 86 Fifth Ave. (bet. Prospect Pl. & St. Marks Ave.) | Brooklyn | 718-783-2900
www.thechocolateroombrooklyn.com

For an "unparalleled chocolate experience", try these "luscious" Brooklyn sweets specialists where the "decadent" desserts can be paired with wines to "help cut the sugar shock"; both share "old-school" decor, but the Cobble Hill outpost is the "roomier" of the two.

Cho Dang Gol *Korean*
| | 23 | 15 | 17 | $31 |

Garment District | 55 W. 35th St. (bet. 5th & 6th Aves.) | 212-695-8222 | www.chodanggolny.com

"Sublime homemade tofu" is the specialty at this "traditional" Garment District Korean, a "vegan's dream" near Macy's; "large" portions and fair prices offset the "indifferent" service and decor.

Chola *Indian*
| | 24 | 16 | 20 | $39 |

E 50s | 232 E. 58th St. (bet. 2nd & 3rd Aves.) | 212-688-4619 | www.fineindiandining.com

An "encyclopedic menu" – "if they don't make it, it doesn't exist" – is the hook at this "splendid" East Side Indian parked on 58th Street's "mini–Curry Row"; though the $14 lunch buffet is an "incredible bargain", the à la carte pricing is quite "reasonable" too.

NEW Chom Chom *Korean*
| | - | - | - | M |

W 50s | 40 W. 56th St. (bet. 5th & 6th Aves.) | 212-213-2299 | www.chomchomny.com

Korean tapas (dubbed 'kapas') are the standouts at this new Midtowner where the relaxed pricing belies the semi-swank, pink neon-lit setting; it also serves standards like bibimbop paired with creative cocktails.

NEW Choptank ● *American/Seafood*
| | 17 | 18 | 15 | $49 |

W Village | 308 Bleecker St. (bet. Grove St. & 7th Ave. S.) | 212-675-2009 | www.choptanknyc.com

This new West Village seafooder serves a "Maryland-inspired" menu that's "more than ho-hum but not quite oh-boy" in a "contemporary" setting with a "cool deck"; sinkers see "service kinks" and "overpricing", but at least it's always "easy to get in."

Christos Steak House ●Ⓜ *Steak*
| | 23 | 19 | 22 | $64 |

Astoria | 41-08 23rd Ave. (41st St.) | Queens | 718-777-8400 | www.christossteakhouse.com

"Phenomenal" cuts of beef arrive "cooked to order" at this "classy" Astoria steakhouse, a "great local" joint that throws some Greek apps into the mix; be prepared for "Manhattan prices", but a "comfortable atmosphere" and free "valet parking" cushion the blow.

Churrascaria Plataforma ◐ *Brazilian/Steak*   23 | 19 | 22 | $74

W 40s | 316 W. 49th St. (bet. 8th & 9th Aves.) | 212-245-0505 | www.churrascariaplataforma.com

Churrascaria TriBeCa ◐ *Brazilian/Steak*

TriBeCa | 221 W. Broadway (bet. Franklin & White Sts.) | 212-925-6969 | www.churrascariatribeca.com

At these "festive", "eat-till-you-drop" Brazilian rodizios, skewer-bearing servers rush "succulent" cuts "from spit to tabletop" until carnivores "cry uncle"; there's also a "huge" salad bar, but given the "not-cheap" tabs, it's best to "keep the greens to a minimum."

Ciaobella ◐ *Italian*   20 | 19 | 18 | $45

E 80s | 1640 Second Ave. (85th St.) | 212-794-9494 | www.ciaobellanyc.com

This "chic" UES duplex (and Baraonda sibling) makes it hard to focus on the "delicious" Italian food with so many "beautiful, noisy people" milling about; dining on the "upstairs balcony" makes some feel "very continental", but "if you want decent service, be good-looking."

Cibo *American/Italian*   21 | 19 | 21 | $47

E 40s | 767 Second Ave. (41st St.) | 212-681-1616 | www.cibonyc.com

Diners in the "gastronomic desert" around the U.N. and Tudor City praise this Tuscan–New American for its "excellent" meals assembled from "fresh seasonal ingredients"; "warm service", "reasonable" tabs and "white-tablecloth" looks make for "great value" here.

Cilantro *Southwestern*   17 | 15 | 16 | $32

E 70s | 1321 First Ave. (71st St.) | 212-537-4040 ◐
E 80s | 1712 Second Ave. (bet. 88th & 89th Sts.) | 212-722-4242 ◐
W 80s | 485 Columbus Ave. (bet. 83rd & 84th Sts.) | 212-712-9090
www.cilantronyc.com

"Not for the faint of hearing", this "always buzzing" Southwestern trio is a magnet for uptown cowpokes hankering for "cheap 'n' cheerful" dining; "deadly margaritas" make up for the "bland" chow, "*mañana*" service and decor that's as "cheesy" as the quesadillas.

Cipriani Dolci ◐ *Italian*   20 | 20 | 18 | $55

E 40s | Grand Central | West Balcony (42nd St. & Vanderbilt Ave.) | 212-973-0999 | www.cipriani.com

An "exciting environment" – Grand Central's cavernous Concourse – is home to this mezzanine Venetian, a "people-watcher's delight" that makes "waiting for a train" actually enjoyable; though the food's "delicious" (especially with a "signature Bellini"), it's even tastier if "someone else is paying."

Cipriani Downtown ◐ *Italian*   22 | 21 | 20 | $75

SoHo | 376 W. Broadway (bet. Broome & Spring Sts.) | 212-343-0999 | www.cipriani.com

"Right out of a Fellini movie", this too-"chic" SoHo Italian is the kind of place where "models and their rich uncles" show up to sip Bellinis and nibble on some of the "most expensive pasta in the world"; sure, it's "show-offy", but let's face it honey, the real show here is "not on the plate."

Circus *Brazilian/Steak* | 21 | 19 | 21 | $53 |

E 60s | 132 E. 61st St. (bet. Lexington & Park Aves.) | 212-223-2965 | www.circusrestaurante.com

Still "something of a secret", this East Side "sleeper" offers good, "dependable" Brazilian food in "pleasant" digs tended by "congenial" servers; though it "may not be a high-flying act", at least the "whimsical" clown decor gets more amusing with every "knockout" caipirinha.

Citrus Bar & Grill *Asian/Nuevo Latino* | 19 | 18 | 18 | $42 |

W 70s | 320 Amsterdam Ave. (75th St.) | 212-595-0500 | www.citrusnyc.com

Sushi and salsa share table space at this "hopping" UWS Latin-Asian hybrid where the "good but not extraordinary" food plays second fiddle to the swinging "young singles" scene; all that high "energy" gets "noisy", but no one seems to care – "if you're over 40, you're old here."

City Bakery *Bakery* | 22 | 13 | 15 | $19 |

Flatiron | 3 W. 18th St. (bet. 5th & 6th Aves.) | 212-366-1414 | www.thecitybakery.com

"Scrumptious" baked goods and a "greenmarket" salad bar/buffet are the lures at this Flatiron bakery, but don't forget its "velvety" hot chocolate and "resistance-is-futile" pretzel croissant; despite "self-service", "uncomfortable" seating and "pricey", by-the-pound tabs, most "can't wait to return."

City Crab & Seafood Co. *Seafood* | 19 | 16 | 18 | $45 |

Flatiron | 235 Park Ave. S. (19th St.) | 212-529-3800 | www.citycrabnyc.com

Flatiron finatics favor this "dependable" bi-level seafooder to "shuck and slurp" to their hearts' content in a "massive" setting (with a menu to match); "modest" pricing and an "energetic bar scene" trump the "suburban" vibe and "erratic" service.

City Hall ☒ *Seafood/Steak* | 21 | 21 | 21 | $57 |

TriBeCa | 131 Duane St. (bet. Church St. & W. B'way) | 212-227-7777 | www.cityhallnyc.com

"Power brokers" and assorted "muckety-mucks" patronize Henry Meer's "polished" TriBeCa surf 'n' turfer for its "excellent" cooking and "entertaining" people-watching; "personable" staffers and a "manly", "old-NY" setting make for "enjoyable" repasts – so long as "cost is not an issue"; P.S. good private party rooms are available.

City Island Lobster House ❶ *Seafood* | 19 | 16 | 18 | $47 |

Bronx | 691 Bridge St. (City Island Ave.) | 718-885-1459 | www.cilobsterhouse.com

A "seafood stalwart" that's "worth the drive" to City Island, this "family"-friendly shellfish "standby" turns out "consistent" crustaceans for "reasonable" dough; inside, the decor's getting "tired", but the "water views" from the deck make everything taste better.

City Lobster & Steak *Seafood* | 19 | 17 | 18 | $51 |

W 40s | 121 W. 49th St. (6th Ave.) | 212-354-1717 | www.citylobster.com

"Tourists" and theatergoers take the bait at this "convenient dock" near Rock Center where "delicious" surf 'n' turf arrives in a "comfortable", "steakhouse"-style setting; crabs carp about "nothing-special" vittles and "erratic service", but admit the prix fixes are a "value" catch.

	FOOD	DECOR	SERVICE	COST

City Winery ◑ *Mediterranean* — 16 | 21 | 16 | $42

SoHo | 155 Varick St. (Vandam St.) | 212-608-0555 | www.citywinery.com

Combining a "working winery" with a restaurant, wine bar and concert venue, this "cavernous", "multipurpose" West SoHo spot serves "up-scale" Med small plates that are "not bad" but "nothing fancy"; "all-over-the-place service" suggests that it's still "looking for its legs."

Clinton St. Baking Co. *American* — 24 | 14 | 17 | $26

LES | 4 Clinton St. (bet. Houston & Stanton Sts.) | 646-602-6263 | www.clintonstreetbaking.com

Gird yourself for "huge lines" for the "fluffy, buttery" brunch at this "tiny" LES American bakery/cafe best known for its "incredible" pancakes (that aren't "laced with crack" as rumored); it's "easier" to access at the dinner hour, provided you don't mind "glorified coffee-shop" decor.

Co. *Pizza* — 22 | 16 | 18 | $32

Chelsea | 230 Ninth Ave. (24th St.) | 212-243-1105 | www.co-pane.com

"Crust is king" at Jim Lahey's "couture pizza joint", a "perpetually crowded" Chelsea spot vending pies made from "billowy dough" and laden with "strong toppings"; the "industrial" space seems to be "carbo-load" central, even if the "communal tables" and "new-wave" creations are "not for everyone."

Coals ⊠ *Pizza* — ▽ 23 | 14 | 18 | $21

Bronx | 1888 Eastchester Rd. (Morris Park Ave.) | 718-823-7002 | www.coalspizza.com

Ok, it's "out of the way" in Morris Park and only open on weekdays, but this "friendly" Bronx pizzeria is "worth the travel" given its "different" thin-crust pies, which are *grilled* to "smoky" perfection; "awesome" panini and "good salads" fill out the menu.

Coco Roco *Peruvian* — 19 | 13 | 16 | $28

Cobble Hill | 139 Smith St. (bet. Bergen & Dean Sts.) | Brooklyn | 718-254-9933
Park Slope | 392 Fifth Ave. (bet. 6th & 7th Sts.) | Brooklyn | 718-965-3376
www.cocorocorestaurant.com

"Stick-to-your-ribs" Peruvian comfort grub led by a "juicy" rotisserie chicken draws "locals" to this Brooklyn pair that encourages repeat business by being an "excellent value"; given the "unbearable" din and "nothing-to-look-at" decor, it's probably "better for carryout."

Coffee Shop ◑ *American/Brazilian* — 15 | 13 | 12 | $31

Union Sq | 29 Union Sq. W. (16th St.) | 212-243-7969 | www.thecoffeeshopnyc.com

The "clientele is hotter than the food" at this Union Square Brazilian-American that's still "buzzing" 20 years into its run, though the "after-thought" chow and "run-down" digs could stand a "shot of caffeine"; the "bored", "beautiful" staffers "couldn't care less", but hey, the "slow service" allows more time for "people-watching."

Cole's Dock Side *Continental/Seafood* — ▽ 18 | 13 | 19 | $40

Staten Island | 369 Cleveland Ave. (Hylan Blvd.) | 718-948-5588 | www.colesdockside.com

"Nice views" of Great Kills Harbor are the hook at this "simple" Staten Island seafooder that offers "fresh" fish and "neighborly" vibes for

	FOOD	DECOR	SERVICE	COST

"budget" tabs; the patio's perfect for summer boat-watching, while the "salty-dog bar scene" is just what it sounds like.

NEW Colicchio & Sons *American* | 23 | 25 | 24 | $80 |

Chelsea | 85 10th Ave. (bet. 15th & 16th Sts.) | 212-400-6699 | www.colicchioandsons.com

Top Chef's Tom Colicchio gives his former Craftsteak a "reboot" via this new West Chelsea "work in progress" where "inventive", "expertly prepared" Americana arrives in an "airy", "theatrical" setting; though it's priced for "boom times", the "cheaper", more "informal" Tap Room is a hit with light lunchers and weekend brunchers.

NEW Collective, The ● *Eclectic* | ▽ 21 | 24 | 23 | $57 |

Meatpacking | 1 Little W. 12th St. (9th Ave.) | 212-255-9717 | www.collectivecafe.com

Kooky, costly new Meatpacking Eclectic flaunting "recycled" decor (think "pill-bottle lamps", coat-hanger chandeliers) and a menu that salutes various NYC neighborhoods (e.g. Harlem chicken and waffles); but "off-the-wall" acoustics suggest this one's more scene than cuisine.

Commerce *American* | 23 | 20 | 20 | $59 |

W Village | 50 Commerce St. (Barrow St.) | 212-524-2301 | www.commercerestaurant.com

Starting with an "exceptional" signature bread basket, this West Village "hidden jewel" is home to a "tasty" array of "market-oriented" New Americana served in a "stylish" room; oh boy, it's "lively" – verging on "ear-splitting" – and there's an odd "no-cash policy", but seers say this one "will be around for a long time."

NEW Commodore, The ● *Southern* | - | - | - | I |

Williamsburg | 366 Metropolitan Ave. (Havemeyer St.) | Brooklyn | 718-218-7632

This Williamsburg dive bar stands out from the fray thanks to ambitious, Southern-inflected bar fare from a former Pies-n-Thighs chef; as there's no table service, all the grub is ordered at the bar, then consumed in a kitschy space done up with flea-market art and vintage Hawaiian prints.

Community Food & Juice *American* | 22 | 17 | 18 | $33 |

W 100s | 2893 Broadway (bet. 112th & 113th Sts.) | 212-665-2800 | www.communityrestaurant.com

"Always packed" with the "Columbia crowd", this "deservedly popular", easily affordable New American "fills a gap" in Morningside Heights with "organic", "guilt-free" options" presented in "functional" environs; just be prepared for "long" weekend brunch waits.

Z Compass *American* | 22 | 23 | 22 | $59 |

W 70s | 208 W. 70th St. (bet. Amsterdam & West End Aves.) | 212-875-8600 | www.compassrestaurant.com

"Not far from Lincoln Center", this "grown-up" UWS New American offers a "first-rate" menu that runs "pricey", though there's "value" in its "spectacular", three-pound lobster special; overall, the watchword is "relaxing", from its "well-spaced tables" and seamless service to the "blissfully quiet" acoustics.

	FOOD	DECOR	SERVICE	COST

Congee Bowery ● *Chinese* | 21 | 12 | 14 | $25

LES | 207 Bowery (bet. Rivington & Spring Sts.) | 212-766-2828

Congee Village ● *Chinese*

LES | 100 Allen St. (bet. Broome & Delancey Sts.) | 212-941-1818 |
www.congeevillagerestaurants.com

The "awesome" namesake rice porridge soothes Lower Eastsiders at these separately owned Cantonese that are "authentic", "price-is-right" options so long as you can abide the "nonservice"; the "tacky" decor is a match for the "festive", near-"chaotic" ambiance.

Ⓩ Convivio *Italian* | 26 | 23 | 24 | $76

E 40s | 45 Tudor City Pl. (42nd St., bet. 1st & 2nd Aves.) | 212-599-5045 |
www.convivionyc.com

"Dressy foodies" and "U.N. dignitaries" alike patronize this "aptly named" Southern Italian in "secluded" Tudor City, where chef Michael White's "originality and finesse" is most evident in the "blow-you-away" pastas; "spot-on" service, "modern" looks and a "fabulous" outdoor patio are part of the package, along with a $62 prix fixe that may supply the "best quality-to-price ratio in town."

Ⓩ Convivium Osteria *Mediterranean* | 26 | 23 | 23 | $53

Park Slope | 68 Fifth Ave. (bet. Bergen St. & St. Marks Ave.) | Brooklyn |
718-857-1833 | www.convivium-osteria.com

"Romance" is in the air at this "charming" Park Slope taverna that "transports" diners with "hearty", "seriously good" Med dishes dispensed in a space recalling a "rustic" "Tuscan farmhouse"; the wine cellar is equally "cozy", ditto the "bonus" back garden.

Cookshop ● *American* | 22 | 19 | 20 | $53

Chelsea | 156 10th Ave. (20th St.) | 212-924-4440 |
www.cookshopny.com

A "locavore's dream", this "farm-to-table" Chelsea American from the "Five Points family" puts out a "perfectly executed" menu in "airy" digs conveniently located "near an entrance to the High Line"; it's a "brunch must", provided you can stand the "din" kicked up by its "trendy" following.

Coppola's *Italian* | 20 | 17 | 19 | $41

Murray Hill | 378 Third Ave. (bet. 27th & 28th Sts.) | 212-679-0070

W 70s | 206 W. 79th St. (bet. Amsterdam Ave. & B'way) |
212-877-3840

www.coppolas-nyc.com

Think "red sauce" and "anything smothered in cheese" to get the gist of these "neighborhood" Southern Italians that not only get the job done, but do it for "reasonable" dough; sure, they may be rather "nondescript", but at least "you know what to expect."

Cornelia Street Cafe ● *American/French* | 19 | 16 | 18 | $37

W Village | 29 Cornelia St. (bet. Bleecker & W. 4th Sts.) | 212-989-9319 |
www.corneliastreetcafe.com

Maybe this "venerable" West Villager won't "knock your socks off", but regulars have been "going for years" for its "hearty", "affordable" French-Americana and "awesome brunch"; what's more, a "warm and fuzzy" downstairs performance space features jazz and poetry readings.

	FOOD	DECOR	SERVICE	COST

Corner Bistro ●⊅ Burgers | 22 | 10 | 13 | $18

W Village | 331 W. Fourth St. (Jane St.) | 212-242-9502 |
www.cornerbistrony.com

"Juicy", "mind-blowing" burgers that soak right through the "paper plates" produce "endless" lines at this "grungy" West Village burger-and-brew dispenser; downsides include "frat-boy" crowds and the fact that you'll leave smelling like "cheap beer."

NEW Corsino ● Italian | 20 | 18 | 19 | $43

W Village | 637 Hudson St. (Horatio St.) | 212-242-3093 |
www.corsinocantina.com

Restaurateur Jason Denton ('Ino, 'Inoteca) is the mind behind this "promising" new West Villager serving modestly priced Italian small plates (with an emphasis on "delicious" crostini); the warm, "welcoming" setting features lots of slate, dark wood and "noise."

☑ Corton ☒ French | 26 | 23 | 25 | $118

TriBeCa | 239 W. Broadway (bet. Walker & White Sts.) | 212-219-2777 |
www.cortonnyc.com

"Genius abounds" at this TriBeCa "stunner" via Drew Nieporent and chef Paul Liebrandt, where the "experimental" New French cuisine is "gorgeous to look at and even better to taste"; though the all-white setting divides surveyors ("serene" vs. "stark"), there's agreement on the "impeccable" service and "Goldman-Sachs-bonus-money" tabs.

Così Sandwiches | 16 | 10 | 13 | $15

E 40s | 38 E. 45th St. (bet. Madison & Vanderbilt Aves.) | 212-370-0705
E 50s | 60 E. 56th St. (bet. Madison & Park Aves.) | 212-588-1225
Financial District | World Financial Ctr. | 200 Vesey St. (West St.) |
212-571-2001
Flatiron | 700 Sixth Ave. (bet. 22nd & 23rd Sts.) | 212-645-0223
G Village | 53 E. Eighth St. (bet. B'way & Mercer St.) | 212-260-1507
G Village | 841 Broadway (bet. 13th & 14th Sts.) | 212-614-8544 ●
Murray Hill | 461 Park Ave. S. (31st St.) | 212-634-3467
W 40s | 11 W. 42nd St. (bet. 5th & 6th Aves.) | 212-398-6662
W 50s | Paramount Plaza | 1633 Broadway (50th St.) | 212-397-9838
W 70s | 2186 Broadway (bet. 77th & 78th Sts.) | 212-595-5616
www.getcosi.com
Additional locations throughout the NY area

Churning out "quick, tasty" lunches for "on-the-run" types, this "serviceable", all-over-town sandwich chain is touted for its "addictive", "fresh-baked" flatbreads and "free WiFi"; but "convenience" comes at a cost, namely "hectic" crowds, "formulaic" looks and "slo-mo" service.

Counter ● Vegan/Vegetarian | 21 | 18 | 20 | $38

E Village | 105 First Ave. (bet. 6th & 7th Sts.) | 212-982-5870 |
www.counternyc.com

Proving that vegetarian food can be "delicious", this "upbeat" East Villager seduces "even omnivores" with its "earthy" bounty and "organic wines and spirits"; a "courteous" crew provides "warmth without hippie-dippy attitude" in a setting that's "more elegant" than the genre's norm.

Covo ● Italian | 22 | 21 | 19 | $34

Harlem | 701 W. 135th St. (12th Ave.) | 212-234-9573 | www.covony.com
Harlem's "12th Avenue Restaurant Row" is home to this "relaxed" Italian proffering "flavorful", inexpensive fare (and "excellent pizza")

in "rustic", brick-walled digs; the "laid-back" upstairs lounge hosts art exhibits and late-night jazz.

Cowgirl *Southwestern* | 16 | 17 | 17 | $31 |

W Village | 519 Hudson St. (W. 10th St.) | 212-633-1133 | www.cowgirlnyc.com

Cowgirl Sea-Horse *Southwestern*

Seaport | 259 Front St. (Dover St.) | 212-608-7873 | www.cowgirlseahorse.com

There's enough "deep-fried", "down-home" Southwestern grub to "feed a hungry ranch hand" at this "funky" Villager done up in "kitschy", "trailer-trash" style; "family"-friendly by day, it caters to the "margaritas-and-corndogs" set after dark; the Seaport spin-off offers all the above plus seafood.

Craft *American* | 25 | 23 | 24 | $78 |

Flatiron | 43 E. 19th St. (bet. B'way & Park Ave. S.) | 212-780-0880 | www.craftrestaurant.com

Top Chef's Tom Colicchio has his "craft down to a science" at this 10-year-old Flatiron "original" where the "modern" New Americana "unlocks amazing flavors" within farm-fresh ingredients; sure, as you "design your meal" the à la carte pricing adds up, but "superlative" service and a "sophisticated" setting help make the splurge "memorable."

Craftbar *American* | 23 | 20 | 20 | $52 |

Flatiron | 900 Broadway (bet. 19th & 20th Sts.) | 212-461-4300 | www.craftrestaurant.com

Aka "Craft Lite", this more "casual" spin-off of Tom Colicchio's Flatiron flagship offers "just as delicious" New Americana at a somewhat "cheaper" price point; the "nonchalant chic" setting is populated by a "noisy" "young" crowd that keeps its phone number on "speed dial."

Crema *Mexican* | 23 | 18 | 20 | $47 |

Chelsea | 111 W. 17th St. (bet. 6th & 7th Aves.) | 212-691-4477 | www.cremarestaurante.com

Chef Julieta Ballesteros dresses up south-of-the-border fare with French flair at this "fancified" Chelsea Nuevo Mexicano where the "sophisticated" preparation is truly the "Crema the crop"; an "unassuming", "low-key" atmosphere and "affordable" tabs round out the picture.

Crispo ◑ *Italian* | 23 | 19 | 20 | $48 |

W Village | 240 W. 14th St. (bet. 7th & 8th Aves.) | 212-229-1818 | www.crisporestaurant.com

"Rightly famous" for its spaghetti carbonara, this "enjoyable" West Villager follows through with an "exceptional" Northern Italian menu that's priced "reasonably"; since the "high-energy" interior tends toward "tight" and "loud", insiders retreat to its "charming", all-seasons back patio.

NEW Crosby Bar *Eclectic* | ▽ 19 | 24 | 19 | $53 |

SoHo | Crosby Street Hotel | 79 Crosby St. (bet. Prince & Spring Sts.) | 212-226-6400 | www.firmdale.com

Both "locals and travelers" alike frequent this "trendy" newcomer in SoHo's Crosby Street Hotel, where "fancy" Eclectic food (and afternoon tea) is served in "stunning" digs festooned with avant-garde art; still, the "upbeat" mood can turn "rocky" due to "over-the-top" drink prices.

	FOOD	DECOR	SERVICE	COST

✴ Cru ⊠ *American/French*
25 | 22 | 25 | $95

G Village | 24 Fifth Ave. (bet. 9th & 10th Sts.) | 212-529-1700 | www.cru-nyc.com

"Big-night-out" dining for a "big-bucks price" is the "pre-recession concept" at this Village "oenophile paradise" renowned for its "phone book–size wine lists"; "contemporary" Franco-American cooking, "highly trained" staffers and "soothing" atmospherics are further reasons to "punish your credit card" here.

Cuba *Cuban*
22 | 18 | 20 | $40

G Village | 222 Thompson St. (bet. Bleecker & W. 3rd Sts.) | 212-420-7878 | www.cubanyc.com

Everything's "authentic" at this "atmospheric" Villager, from the "outstanding", "affordable" Cuban cooking to the complimentary "cigars hand-rolled" while you dine; everyone's "havana great time" too, thanks to its "killer" mojitos and "loud" live Latin music.

Cubana Café ⊭ *Cuban*
20 | 14 | 18 | $26

G Village | 110 Thompson St. (bet. Prince & Spring Sts.) | 212-966-5366

Carroll Gardens | 272 Smith St. (bet. Degraw & Sackett Sts.) | Brooklyn | 718-858-3980

NEW Park Slope | 80 Sixth Ave. (St. Marks Pl.) | Brooklyn | 718-398-9818

This "casual", "cash-only" Cuban trio may share "small" dimensions but they're worth the "tight squeeze" when "hearty", "inexpensive" chow is the payoff; "nothing-fancy" decor and "island-time" service from "shamelessly flirty waiters" come with the territory.

Cucina di Pesce *Italian*
19 | 14 | 17 | $31

E Village | 87 E. Fourth St. (bet. Bowery & 2nd Ave.) | 212-260-6800 | www.cucinadipesce.com

Now 25 years old, this East Village Italian seafooder serves a "reliable" menu in a "no-frills" setting; it's beloved for its "secret backyard" and a "bargain-of-the-century" $14 early-bird, though some caution "you get what you pay for . . ."

Cupping Room Café ● *American*
18 | 15 | 17 | $31

SoHo | 359 W. Broadway (bet. Broome & Grand Sts.) | 212-925-2898 | www.cuppingroomcafe.com

A "funky holdover from olde SoHo", this circa-1977 American slings comfort food in a "homey" setting complete with a potbellied stove; "affordable" tabs gloss over the "hit-or-miss" cooking and "patchy" service.

Curry Leaf *Indian*
18 | 11 | 16 | $28

Murray Hill | 99 Lexington Ave. (27th St.) | 212-725-5558 | www.curryleafnyc.com

"Flavorful", "well-spiced" Indian food comes at a bargain price at this "dependable" Curry Hiller from the "good folks who run Kalustyan's"; those who "expected more" are bummed by the "eyesore" decor and rushed, "no-lingering-allowed" service.

Da Andrea *Italian*
22 | 16 | 20 | $38

G Village | 35 W. 13th St. (bet. 5th & 6th Aves.) | 212-367-1979 | www.daandreanyc.com

Since relocating to bigger, "brighter" digs, this Villager is "going gang-busters" thanks to "hearty" Emilia-Romagna dishes at "recession-proof" tabs; what's "vibrant" to some is "ridiculously noisy" to others, but overall it's the kind of place where "real NYers eat."

Da Ciro *Italian/Pizza*

22	18	20	$47

Murray Hill | 229 Lexington Ave. (bet. 33rd & 34th Sts.) | 212-532-1636 | www.daciro.com

Best known for its "have-to-have" item – the signature focaccia Robiola – this "neighborhood" Murray Hill Italian follows through with "reliable" classics and pizza from a "wood-burning oven"; upstairs is best for "quiet conversation", but wherever you sit, service is "polished."

Dafni Greek Taverna *Greek*

20	15	20	$35

W 40s | 325 W. 42nd St. (bet. 8th & 9th Aves.) | 212-315-1010 | www.dafnitaverna.com

Staking claim to the "barren Port Authority area", this "unexpectedly" good Greek taverna purveys "simple", "affordable" Hellenica in a modest, "low-key" setting; it's a no-brainer pre- or post-theater.

Daisy May's BBQ USA *BBQ*

22	7	13	$25

W 40s | 623 11th Ave. (46th St.) | 212-977-1500 | www.daisymaysbbq.com
The "down 'n' dirty" BBQ evokes "squeals of delight" at Adam Perry Lang's "cafeteria-style" Hell's Kitchen joint where "off-the-hook" ribs and "finger-lickin'-good" sides are slung for "bargain-basement" rates; "truck-stop" looks and occasional "raucous" crowds come with the territory.

Dallas BBQ ● *BBQ*

15	10	14	$24

Chelsea | 261 Eighth Ave. (23rd St.) | 212-462-0001
E 70s | 1265 Third Ave. (bet. 72nd & 73rd Sts.) | 212-772-9393
E Village | 132 Second Ave. (St. Marks Pl.) | 212-777-5574
Washington Heights | 3956 Broadway (bet. 165th & 166th Sts.) | 212-568-3700
W 40s | 241 W. 42nd St. (bet. 7th & 8th Aves.) | 212-221-9000
W 70s | 27 W. 72nd St. (bet. Columbus Ave. & CPW) | 212-873-2004
Bronx | 281 W. Fordham Rd. (Major Deegan Expwy.) | 718-220-2822
Downtown Bklyn | 180 Livingston St. (bet. Hoyt & Smith Sts.) | Brooklyn | 718-643-5700
www.dallasbbq.com

"Quasi-authentic" BBQ and "bathtub-size" drinks for "dirt-cheap" dough draw "Texas-size" crowds to these all-over-town destinations; given the "chainlike" feel, "chaotic" atmosphere and "ordinary" grub, they're best approached with modest expectations.

Danal *French/Mediterranean*

20	20	20	$40

G Village | 59 Fifth Ave. (bet. 12th & 13th Sts.) | 212-982-6930 | www.danalnyc.com

"Just like home – only the food is better" – this Greenwich Village duplex rolls out "delicious" French-Med food in a "comfy-cozy" "living room" setting; "polite" service led by a "gracious host" and "fair" pricing make it a "popular" destination.

Da Nico *Italian*

22	18	21	$40

Little Italy | 164 Mulberry St. (bet. Broome & Grand Sts.) | 212-343-1212 | www.danicoristorante.com

For some of "da best" traditional Italian cooking on Mulberry Street, try this "tried-and-true" Little Italy "staple" where the "generous" helpings come at a "great value"; it's even more "charming" in the summer when the "beautiful" backyard garden becomes a "secret oasis."

☑ Daniel 🅢 French
28 | 28 | 28 | $137

E 60s | 60 E. 65th St. (bet. Madison & Park Aves.) | 212-288-0033 | www.danielnyc.com

When it comes to "jacket-required", "special-occasion" dining, star chef Daniel Boulud's eponymous East Side flagship is the "gold standard" thanks to "perfection-on-a-plate" New French cooking, a "superb" wine list and "service with the precision of a symphony orchestra"; in short, such "seamless decadence" "should be on everyone's bucket list" as "you will leave your table richer – despite the bill"; P.S. the main room is prix fixe only, the more casual lounge à la carte.

Danny Brown Wine
26 | 21 | 24 | $48
Bar & Kitchen Ⓜ European

Forest Hills | 104-02 Metropolitan Ave. (71st Dr.) | Queens | 718-261-2144 | www.dannybrownwinekitchen.com

"Manhattan quality at Queens prices" turns up at this "sophisticated" Forest Hills European that's a "standout" in a neighborhood with "limited fine-dining choices"; "delicious" food, "eager" service and "pleasant" environs make this one a "smart" choice anytime, and it's recently added a "top-notch" Sunday brunch to its repertoire.

Da Noi Italian
23 | 19 | 22 | $48

Staten Island | 138 Fingerboard Rd. (Tompkins Ave.) | 718-720-1650
Staten Island | 4358 Victory Blvd. (Service Rd.) | 718-982-5040
www.danoirestaurant.com

"Always jumping", these "inviting" Staten Island Italians feature "perfectly al dente" pastas and "amazing" specials that translate into "serious crowds"; "knowledgeable" servers and "hospitable owners" seal the deal, so long as you can stand "da noise."

Darbar Indian
21 | 15 | 18 | $35

E 40s | 152 E. 46th St. (bet. Lexington & 3rd Aves.) | 212-681-4500 | www.darbarny.com

Darbar Grill Indian

E 50s | 157 E. 55th St. (bet. Lexington & 3rd Aves.) | 212-751-4600 | www.darbargrill.com

"Fresh", "flavorful" Indian dishes and a "remarkable" $12 lunch buffet keep customers coming back to this toothsome twosome in Midtown; "dependable" service and "decent"-enough settings lift them "a cut above" the competition.

Da Silvano ➊ Italian
21 | 17 | 18 | $65

G Village | 260 Sixth Ave. (Bleecker St.) | 212-982-2343 | www.dasilvano.com
The "tasty" eats play second fiddle to the "famous faces" at this "sceney" Tuscan celeb magnet that brings "la dolce vita" to the Village (right down to the "paparazzi" lurking out front); both the attitude and tabs can be "a bit much", but who cares when "Beyoncé" is two tables away?

Da Tommaso ➊ Italian
21 | 16 | 20 | $49

W 50s | 903 Eighth Ave. (bet. 53rd & 54th Sts.) | 212-265-1890 | www.datommasony.com

"Convenience" is key to this Hell's Kitchen Italian that works for biz dining as well as pre-theater; everything about it is "throwback" –

from the "old-school" service to the "well-worn" decor – but the "wonderful" cooking is timeless and the prices are right.

Da Umberto ☒ *Italian* | 25 | 20 | 23 | $65 |

Chelsea | 107 W. 17th St. (bet. 6th & 7th Aves.) | 212-989-0303 |
www.daumbertonyc.com

Bringing "old-world flair" to "ultramodern Chelsea", this "gracious" Northern Italian is like "time suspended" with its "sublime" cooking, "subdued" atmosphere and "superb" service; sure, it's "expensive", but what else would you expect for such a "memorable" experience?

David Burke Townhouse *American* | 24 | 24 | 24 | $71 |

E 60s | 133 E. 61st St. (bet. Lexington & Park Aves.) | 212-813-2121 |
www.davidburketownhouse.com

"Ladies who lunch" and other "ritzy" UES types applaud David Burke's "creative genius" at this recently "revamped" "tony townhouse" known for "exciting", "whimsically presented" New Americana (i.e. "cheesecake lollipops") and "lap-of-luxury" service; wow, it's "expensive" and boy, it's "cramped", but admirers insist "close encounters were never so worthwhile."

Dawat *Indian* | 23 | 19 | 21 | $48 |

E 50s | 210 E. 58th St. (bet. 2nd & 3rd Aves.) | 212-355-7555 |
www.dawatrestaurant.com

"Authentic", "deftly spiced" Indian fare is yours at this "sure-thing" Midtowner via chef/cookbook author Madhur Jaffrey; despite grumbles that this 25-year-old "gem" has "lost some of its luster", "engaging" service and good food make it "worth every rupee."

☑ DB Bistro Moderne *French* | 25 | 22 | 23 | $67 |

W 40s | City Club Hotel | 55 W. 44th St. (bet. 5th & 6th Aves.) |
212-391-2400 | www.danielnyc.com

Daniel Boulud's "bustling" Theater District French bistro lures "chic" crowds with an appropriately "*moderne*" setting, "first-class service" and a "deliciously decadent" menu led by its "signature" $32 burger; *bien sûr,* it's "pricey", though the $45 pre-theater prix fixe is easier on d-wallet.

☑ DBGB ◑ *French* | 22 | 23 | 21 | $50 |

E Village | 299 Bowery (bet. 1st & Houston Sts.) | 212-933-5300 |
www.danielnyc.com

Chef Daniel Boulud gets "hip" at this "trendy" Bowery yearling where the "meat-centric" French menu is built around burgers and sausages washed down with an "expansive" beer list; the "open kitchen" and "industrial decor" (think "copper pots" and "concrete floors") make for "can't-hear-yourself-chew" acoustics, but everyone's having too much "fun" to care.

Dean's *Pizza* | 18 | 15 | 15 | $28 |

E 40s | 801 Second Ave. (bet. 42nd & 43rd Sts.) | 212-878-9600 |
TriBeCa | 349 Greenwich St. (bet. Harrison & Jay Sts.) | 212-966-3200 |
W 80s | 215 W. 85th St. (bet. Amsterdam Ave. & B'way) | 212-875-1100 |
www.deansnyc.com

For best results, you "must love kids" to enjoy this "family-oriented" pizzeria trio known for its "awesome square pies" and "decent" Italian standards; service can be "harried" and the settings "noisy", but "wallet-friendly" prices keep them "very popular."

	FOOD	DECOR	SERVICE	COST

Dee's Ⓜ *Mediterranean/Pizza* — 21 | 17 | 19 | $30

Forest Hills | 107-23 Metropolitan Ave. (74th Ave.) | Queens |
718-793-7553 | www.deesnyc.com

"Crowd-pleasing" Forest Hills pizzeria offering "dependable"
brick-oven pies plus a "wide range" of "basic" Mediterranean eats; the
"family-friendly", "no-rush" vibe and "reasonable" pricing earn it
"local-favorite" status.

Defonte's Sandwich Shop *Sandwiches* — 22 | 8 | 18 | $14

Gramercy | 261 Third Ave. (21st St.) | 212-614-1500
Red Hook | 379 Columbia St. (Luquer St.) | Brooklyn |
718-625-8052 🅿🕿
www.defontesofbrooklyn.com

It's "sandwich heaven" at this "old-school" duo dispensing "honking"
heros that are a "two-hand experience" and "delicious" to boot; you'll
"rub shoulders with longshoremen" at the circa-1922 Red Hook
original, while the Gramercy yearling imports an "authentic Brooklyn"
vibe to Manhattan.

DeGrezia Ⓢ *Italian* — 24 | 22 | 25 | $66

E 50s | 231 E. 50th St. (bet. 2nd & 3rd Aves.) | 212-750-5353 |
www.degreziaristorante.com

They "make you feel pampered" at this "below-street-level" East Side
Italian sleeper where the "romantic" atmosphere and "old-world for-
mality" feel like something "out of a black-and-white movie"; though
it's "not cheap", the "top-notch food" and "charming" environs make
this a must-try.

🆉 Degustation *French/Spanish* — 27 | 21 | 25 | $74

E Village | 239 E. Fifth St. (bet. 2nd & 3rd Aves.) | 212-979-1012 |
www.degustationnyc.com

"Counter seating" gets a "foodie" spin at Jack and Grace Lamb's
"stunning" East Village tasting bar where the "lucky few" experience
"theater *and* a meal" as they watch the chef compose "sublime"
Franco-Spanish small plates; "attention-to-detail" service rounds out
the "one-of-a-kind" dining experience that leaves patrons "happy",
despite the "expensive" denouement.

🆉 Del Frisco's ◐ *Steak* — 25 | 23 | 23 | $77

W 40s | 1221 Sixth Ave. (bet. 48th & 49th Sts.) | 212-575-5129 |
www.delfriscos.com

"Perfectly cooked" steaks and "treat-you-like-a-king" service draw a
"sea of ties" to this "first-class" Midtown chop shop set in a high-
ceilinged, mahogany-lined space that's a "meat market" in every way;
it "doesn't come cheap" so it's best to go for the $32 prix fixe lunch
"steal"; P.S. there are a variety of private party rooms available.

Delhi Palace *Indian* — ▽ 21 | 14 | 16 | $26

Jackson Heights | 37-33 74th St. (bet. 37th Ave. & 37th Rd.) |
Queens | 718-507-0666

A longtime Jackson Heights "standby", this circa-1975 Indian offers
"well-prepared" classics to "loyal" followers who especially tout its
"lavish" $10 lunch buffet; though decor and service are "typical" for
the genre, at least it's "quieter" than its archrival, Jackson Diner,
two doors down.

	FOOD	DECOR	SERVICE	COST

Delicatessen ● *American*
19 | 19 | 16 | $38

NoLita | 54 Prince St. (Lafayette St.) | 212-226-0211 |
www.delicatessennyc.com

"Don't be fooled by the name" – this "hip" NoLita duplex offers "clever spins" on "affordable" American comfort food in a "sleek" room equipped with retractable walls; many of its "trendy" followers "go to be seen, not to eat", particularly at the "secret downstairs bar."

Dell'anima ● *Italian*
25 | 19 | 20 | $53

W Village | 38 Eighth Ave. (Jane St.) | 212-366-6633 | www.dellanima.com

"Young, beautiful" types are dell'ighted by this "tiny", "lively" West Villager where the "tantalizing" Italian cooking is best enjoyed "at the counter by the open kitchen"; despite "tight" seating, "pricey" tabs and "hard-to-get reservations", it's always "crowded"; equally "popular" is Anfora, its new next-door wine bar/holding pen.

Delmonico's ☒ *Steak*
23 | 23 | 23 | $69

Financial District | 56 Beaver St. (S. William St.) | 212-509-1144 | www.delmonicosny.com

Ever a "FiDi favorite", this storied chophouse on the scene since the 1830s now specializes in steaks "cooked just right"; its "gentlemen's club" setting and "above-and-beyond" service similarly hark back to its Diamond Jim Brady days, though the tabs are strictly contemporary.

☑ Del Posto *Italian*
26 | 26 | 25 | $94

Chelsea | 85 10th Ave. (bet. 15th & 16th Sts.) | 212-497-8090 | www.delposto.com

The "Batali-Bastianich dynasty" provides an experience that's "as much opera as restaurant" at this Way West Chelsea "luxe Italian" where the "divine", "complex" cooking meets its match in the "spectacular wine list"; "perfect" service and a "drop-dead", "marble-and-mahogany" setting (like the Excelsior in Rome) make fans "feel warm all over", even if it might be cheaper to fly there.

Delta Grill ● *Cajun/Creole*
19 | 15 | 18 | $33

W 40s | 700 Ninth Ave. (48th St.) | 212-956-0934 | www.thedeltagrill.com

For the "Big Easy" in the "Big Apple", check out this "down-home" Hell's Kitchen joint dishing out "massive portions" of Cajun-Creole chow at "N'Awlins prices"; the "partylike atmosphere" builds on weekends, when "great live music" ratchets up the "boisterous" mood.

Demarchelier *French*
18 | 16 | 16 | $48

E 80s | 50 E. 86th St. (bet. Madison & Park Aves.) | 212-249-6300 | www.demarchelierrestaurant.com

"True to the French bistro experience", this longtime UES "hangout" offers "simple" fare, a "hopping" bar scene and "attractive" tabs (led by a "bargain" $26 prix fixe); "indifferent" service and "tired" looks are also part of the very "Gallic" package.

Denino's Pizzeria ∌ *Pizza*
26 | 10 | 19 | $21

Staten Island | 524 Port Richmond Ave. (bet. Hooker Pl. & Walker St.) | 718-442-9401

"In crust we trust" could be the motto of this "old-time" Staten Island pizzeria that's been a "rite of passage" in Port Richmond since 1937;

"tasty" pies, "affordable" tabs and "family-friendly" atmospherics trump the "no-frills" service and "finished-basement" decor.

Dervish ● *Mediterranean*   19 | 15 | 19 | $38

W 40s | 146 W. 47th St. (bet. 6th & 7th Aves.) | 212-997-0070 | www.dervishrestaurant.com

"More exotic" than the norm in the Theater District, this "reliable" Med plies an "authentic", "easy-on-the-budget" menu in a location that couldn't be more "convenient"; the "faded decor" is easily overlooked given the "prompt" service and "good-value" $28 early-bird prix fixe.

Deux Amis *French*   19 | 17 | 21 | $48

E 50s | 356 E. 51st St. (bet. 1st & 2nd Aves.) | 212-230-1117

A "great owner" who's like a "one-man welcoming committee" sets the "convivial" tone at this East Midtown French bistro, a "casual" stop for "steady" traditional cooking; the "small" dimensions aren't as bothersome in warm weather when there's "pleasant" outdoor seating.

☒ Dévi *Indian*   23 | 21 | 22 | $58

Flatiron | 8 E. 18th St. (bet. D'way & 5th Ave.) | 212-691-1300 | www.devinyc.com

"Not your typical Indian", this "upscale" Flatiron venue helmed by chef Suvir Saran takes subcontinental cooking to "another level" with its "unusual", "deftly spiced" delicacies; a "romantic", "colorful" setting and "gracious" service help justify the tabs.

Dhaba ● *Indian*   23 | 17 | 18 | $29

Murray Hill | 108 Lexington Ave. (bet. 27th & 28th Sts.) | 212-679-1284 | www.highwaydhaba.com

"Even the mild dishes pack a punch" at this "high-energy" Curry Hill Indian where "spicy means spicy" and the "fantastic" menu provides "super value"; the name translates as 'truck stop', though its "bright", "Bollywood-chic" decor and "cool", "noisy" crowd are anything but.

☒ Di Fara Ⓜ⟊ *Pizza*   27 | 3 | 8 | $17

Midwood | 1424 Ave. J (15th St.) | Brooklyn | 718-258-1367 | www.difara.com

Again voted NYC's No. 1 pizzeria, this Midwood "mecca" has pilgrims raving about "rock-star" Dom DeMarco's "work-of-art" pies and tolerating the circa-1964 "fluorescent"-and-"Formica" decor; what with the "eternal waits" it may be "quicker to fly to Italy", but fans say it's worth it to sample "di-best."

Dim Sum Go Go *Chinese*   20 | 10 | 15 | $24

Chinatown | 5 E. Broadway (Chatham Sq.) | 212-732-0797

"Tasty" dim sum served "à la carte rather than from a cart" (and available "any time of day") is the gimmick at this C-towner, though purists protest "it loses something" without the trolleys; still, fans of this "user-friendly" spot overlook the "factorylike" decor and suggest you "go go."

Diner ● *American*   22 | 16 | 18 | $39

Williamsburg | 85 Broadway (Berry St.) | Brooklyn | 718-486-3077 | www.dinernyc.com

"Hipster-than-thou" servers ferry "hearty" seasonal New Americana at this "casual" South Williamsburg joint housed in a circa-1927 din-

| | FOOD | DECOR | SERVICE | COST |

ing car; while the "bland retro" decor and "overcrowded" conditions are a drag, the "excellent brunch" is "right on the money."

Dinosaur Bar-B-Que *BBQ*
22 | 16 | 17 | $32

Harlem | 646 W. 131st St. (12th Ave.) | 212-694-1777 | www.dinosaurbarbque.com

"Mouthwatering" 'cue and "swoon-worthy" sides chased with "buckets of beer" are yours at this "rockin'" West Harlem BBQ joint done up like a "biker bar", complete with "picnic tables" and "sticky floors"; "Middle America" pricing and "lightning-speed" service make the "long waits" easier to swallow; P.S. it's due to move across the street to 2276 12th Avenue.

Dirt Candy ☒Ⓜ *Vegetarian*
27 | 18 | 23 | $47

E Village | 430 E. Ninth St. (bet. Ave. A & 1st Ave.) | 212-228-7732 | www.dirtcandynyc.com

"Extraordinary presentation" is one of the secrets of this "avant-garde" East Village vegetarian where chef-owner Amanda Cohen's "passionate" cooking "takes vegetables to otherworldly places"; despite a "tiny", "hole-in-the-wall" setting, this one's an "original" that's "definitely worth trying."

Dishes *Sandwiches*
21 | 12 | 12 | $17

E 40s | 6 E. 45th St. (bet. 5th & Madison Aves.) | 212-687-5511 ☒
E 40s | Grand Central | lower level (42nd St. & Vanderbilt Ave.) | 212-808-5511
E 50s | Citigroup Ctr. | 399 Park Ave. (54th St.) | 212-421-5511 ☒
www.dishestogo.com

Midtown desk jockeys swear by the "outrageously good" soups, salads and sandwiches vended by this "packed-to-the-rafters" trio; true, it takes "stamina" to navigate the "chaotic" lunchtime mobs and it's "not inexpensive", but even so the lines make it "look like they're giving away the food."

Ditch Plains ◑ *Seafood*
18 | 17 | 18 | $38

W Village | 29 Bedford St. (Downing St.) | 212-633-0202 | www.ditch-plains.com

Named after the Montauk surfing beach, Marc Murphy's "casual", low-budget West Villager reels in "cell-phone" users with "unfussy seafood" served in spare but "lively" digs; though some think they should "up their game", others praise its "fun, laid-back" mood; P.S. an UWS spin-off is in the works.

Docks Oyster Bar *Seafood*
19 | 17 | 19 | $51

E 40s | 633 Third Ave. (40th St.) | 212-986-8080 | www.docksoysterbar.com

"Simple but delicious" seafood is the raison d'être of this "high-energy" "oldie but goodie" near Grand Central that's been "running like clockwork" since '87; despite "industrial" service and a "loud racket", it's ever "popular" thanks to fair tabs and a "lively" after-work "bar scene."

Do Hwa *Korean*
21 | 18 | 19 | $40

W Village | 55 Carmine St. (Bedford St.) | 212-414-1224 | www.dohwanyc.com

For "expertly prepared" Korean dishes "without the crush of K-town" but with the "same quality", bibimboppers bop by this West Villager for its "cool" looks and "hip" crowd; it's "not a factory"

| | FOOD | DECOR | SERVICE | COST |

like many of its competitors, and interactive types find "cooking at the table" a "super" option.

Dominick's ⊄ *Italian*
| 23 | 10 | 18 | $39 |

Bronx | 2335 Arthur Ave. (bet. Crescent Ave. & E. 187th St.) | 718-733-2807

1966-vintage "prototypical Arthur Avenue" Italian, famed for "enormous" portions of "delicious" grub served at "communal tables"; the "no-frills" experience here includes "no reservations", "no credit cards", "no menus" ("just ask the waiter") and "no bill" (you get a "verbal total"), yet just about everyone "walks out happy."

Donguri Ⓜ *Japanese*
| 27 | 15 | 24 | $68 |

E 80s | 309 E. 83rd St. (bet. 1st & 2nd Aves.) | 212-737-5656 | www.dongurinyc.com

"Real-deal" Japanese fare – sans sushi – is yours at this UES "gem" featuring "beautifully presented" dishes from Japan's Kansai region (with particularly "superb" soba and udon); though the digs are beyond "tiny" and the tabs "steep", "aim-to-please" service and a "calming" ambiance make for a "special" night out.

Don Pedro's *Caribbean/European*
| 22 | 17 | 21 | $44 |

E 90s | 1865 Second Ave. (96th St.) | 212-996-3274 | www.donpedros.net

A "true UES sleeper", this "upscale" Euro-Caribbean dishes out "large portions" of "spicy" grub that's even tastier with some "killer mojitos" or sangria; supporters sidestep the "Second Avenue subway" construction outside, touting the "modern" mien and "extremely attentive" staff.

Don Peppe Ⓜ⊄ *Italian*
| 26 | 12 | 19 | $47 |

Ozone Park | 135-58 Lefferts Blvd. (bet. 135th & 149th Aves.) | Queens | 718-845-7587

"Serious" eaters "never leave hungry" from this "old-school" Ozone Park "garlic heaven" where the "red-sauce" Italiana is served family-style and everyone seems to be named "Dominic"; sure, it's "cash only" and "not much to look at", but all those "Lincolns parked on the sidewalk" are there for a reason.

Dos Caminos *Mexican*
| 20 | 19 | 18 | $43 |

E 50s | 825 Third Ave. (bet. 50th & 51st Sts.) | 212-336-5400
NEW **Meatpacking** | 675 Hudson St. (14th St.) | 212-699-2400
Murray Hill | 373 Park Ave. S. (bet. 26th & 27th Sts.) | 212-294-1000
SoHo | 475 W. Broadway (bet. Houston & Prince Sts.) | 212-277-4300
www.brguestrestaurants.com

"Major margaritas" and super guacamole made tableside get "dos thumbs up" at Steve Hanson's "contemporary" quartet, supplying midpriced Mexican chow to a "young", "loud" crowd; service can be "inconsistent", but no one cares given the "hopping social scene."

NEW Dos Toros *Mexican*
| 24 | 11 | 18 | $12 |

E Village | 137 Fourth Ave. (13th St.) | 212-677-7300 | www.dostorosnyc.com

East Villagers are bullish on this new, "Bay Area–inspired" Mexican taqueria, doling out "sublime tacos" and "excellent burritos" in an "eco-friendly" storefront; "cheap" tabs and "minimal" seating keep the "tiny" digs "jam-packed", so "takeout" may be the best way out.

	FOOD	DECOR	SERVICE	COST

Double Crown *Eclectic*   20 | 23 | 20 | $52

NoHo | 316 Bowery (Bleecker St.) | 212-254-0350 |
www.doublecrown-nyc.com

Transporting diners from "the Bowery to colonial SE Asia", this "chic"-but-"chill" NoHo Eclectic serves an "inventive" Indo-Asian menu in a "Raj"-like, AvroKO-designed room that's as "gorgeous" as the crowd; tipplers tout its Madam Geneva "gin lounge" for post-dinner sipping.

Z Dovetail *American*   26 | 22 | 25 | $72

W 70s | 103 W. 77th St. (Columbus Ave.) | 212-362-3800 |
www.dovetailnyc.com

The UWS takes a giant "culinary leap forward" via John Fraser's "world-class" New American duplex offering "incredibly tasty" food, "seamless" service and an "understated" setting; altogether, it's a "top-notch experience" that more than justifies the "East Side prices"; P.S. Sunday 'suppa' is a "fantastic bargain."

Dressler *American*   25 | 23 | 23 | $58

Williamsburg | 149 Broadway (bet. Bedford & Driggs Aves.) | Brooklyn | 718-384-6343 | www.dresslernyc.com

For "grown-up" dining in "hipster Williamsburg", this "stylish" New American gets it right with a "mind-blowing" seasonal menu, "charming" staffers and a "striking", "retro-techno" setting; some dub it Brooklyn's answer to "Gramercy Tavern", an idea reinforced by the "Manhattan prices."

Duane Park *American*   21 | 21 | 22 | $55

TriBeCa | 157 Duane St. (bet. Hudson St. & W. B'way) | 212-732-5555 |
www.duaneparknyc.com

"Off the radar" in TriBeCa, this New American unrolls an on-point menu injected with "Southern flair" in a "fanciful", neo-classical setting; given the "charming" service, "live jazz" and "throwback burlesque" acts, many wonder why it's "still undiscovered."

Due ◑ *Italian*   21 | 16 | 21 | $48

E 70s | 1396 Third Ave. (bet. 79th & 80th Sts.) | 212-772-3331 |
www.duenyc.com

"Mature" folk "feel at home" at this "respectable" Upper East Side Northern Italian well regarded for its "consistent" cooking and "cozy" atmosphere; "helpful" staffers and "affordable" tariffs help explain its longevity (since 1988), though modernists suggest "a little revamping" is due.

DuMont *American*   23 | 16 | 18 | $30

Williamsburg | 432 Union Ave. (bet. Devoe St. & Metropolitan Ave.) | Brooklyn | 718-486-7717

DuMont Burger ◑ *American*

Williamsburg | 314 Bedford Ave. (bet. S. 1st & 2nd Sts.) | Brooklyn | 718-384-6127

www.dumontnyc.com

Williamsburg hipsters in "skinny jeans" hype this New American for its "hearty" comfort chow, "everyday prices" and "stay-all-night" back garden; the Bedford Avenue spin-off is a more "casual" option for "marvel-of-grillery" burgers in a room so "close" that you will "get to know your neighbors very well."

	FOOD	DECOR	SERVICE	COST

Dumpling Man ◑ *Chinese*   `20` `9` `16` `$12`
E Village | 100 St. Marks Pl. (bet. Ave. A & 1st Ave.) | 212-505-2121 | www.dumplingman.com

"Addictive", "fluffy" dumplings "handmade from scratch" are the bait at this East Village Chinese where the goods are as "delicious" as the prices; but a "hole-in-the-wall" setting "smaller than a mini-storage unit" makes "takeout" a best bet.

Dylan Prime *Steak*   `24` `23` `23` `$71`
TriBeCa | 62 Laight St. (Greenwich St.) | 212-334-4783 | www.dylanprime.com

"Not for guys only", this "stylish" TriBeCa steakhouse is a "great place to bring a lady" given its "tasty" chops, "giant martinis" and "dark, sexy" digs; granted, the "more happening" adjoining barroom draws plenty of "frat-boy bankers" oblivious to the "expensive" tabs.

Earthen Oven *Indian*   `20` `13` `19` `$36`
W 70s | 53 W. 72nd St. (bet. Columbus Ave. & CPW) | 212-579-8888

"Above-average" Indian eats (including unusual regional specialties) are purveyed at this "casual" Upper Westsider that's both "authentic" and "dependable"; "cheerful" service and "affordable" deals like the $14 all-you-can-eat lunch buffet distract from the "blah decor."

East Manor *Chinese*   `19` `14` `12` `$27`
Flushing | 46-45 Kissena Blvd. (bet. Kalmia & Laburnum Aves.) | Queens | 718-888-8998

Known for its "can't-go-wrong" dim sum, this "huge" Flushing Chinese also rolls out an "over-the-top buffet" with "plentiful variety" for low dough; despite "couldn't-care-less" service and "showing-its-age" decor, it still draws the "masses", especially on "chaotic" weekends.

NEW East Side Social Club ◑ *American/Italian*   `17` `18` `17` `$54`
E 50s | The Pod Hotel | 230 E. 51st St. (bet. 2nd & 3rd Aves.) | 212-355-9442

"Downtown" lands in Midtown via this "sceney" newcomer serving "pricey" Italian-Americana in an old-school, checkered-tablecloth setting modeled after a Little Italy social club; too bad the chow "doesn't live up to the hype", but the "cool bar" and "hot crowd" do.

E.A.T. *American*   `20` `12` `15` `$39`
E 80s | 1064 Madison Ave. (bet. 80th & 81st Sts.) | 212-772-0022 | www.elizabar.com

Thirty years on, Eli Zabar's "casual" UES New American remains a destination for "museum"-goers and "shoppers" seeking "superior" sandwiches and deli items; but the "chutzpah" factor includes "condescending" service and pricing so high that you may want to "get an estimate first."

NEW Eataly *Italian*   `-` `-` `-` `E`
Flatiron | 200 Fifth Ave. (bet. 23rd & 24th Sts.) | 212-927-3565 | www.eataly.com

Cloned from the Turin original, this colossal Italian food hall opposite Madison Square Park has illustrious backers (Mario Batali, Joe and Lidia Bastianich) and features over 20 departments, including produce, seafood, cheese, pasta and pizza stations, as well as a coffee bar, wine store and a small steakhouse called Manzo; while the sprawling space is primarily a retail operation, the casual mood (and luscious offerings) encourages spontaneous dining, with counters, barstools and tables scattered throughout.

Eatery ● *American* | 20 | 16 | 17 | $33 |

W 50s | 798 Ninth Ave. (53rd St.) | 212-765-7080 | www.eaterynyc.com
"Energetic" Hell's Kitchen New American known for "affordable" comfort food "with a twist" (i.e. the "killer" mac 'n' jack) served in "stylishly spare" digs; brace yourself for a "gay-friendly", "see-and-be-seen" crowd that's "way too loud."

Ecco ⊠ *Italian* | 22 | 18 | 21 | $58 |

TriBeCa | 124 Chambers St. (bet. Church St. & W. B'way) | 212-227-7074 | www.eccorestaurantny.com
"Old-world" is the word on this "been-there-forever" TriBeCa "favorite" that serves "consistent" Italian "classics" to the tune of a live weekend pianist; regulars allow it's a tad "expensive" and advise you "wait for the chalkboard to come around" before choosing what to eat.

Edison Cafe ⊄ *Coffee Shop* | 15 | 8 | 14 | $22 |

W 40s | Edison Hotel | 228 W. 47th St. (bet. B'way & 8th Ave.) | 212-840-5000
Everyone from "producers" to "pit musicians" turns up at this "old-time" Theater District coffee shop (aka the "Polish Tea Room") where "sassy staffers" dish out "cheap", "basic" Jewish soul food; despite "luncheonette" looks and "bad lighting", most "hope it never changes."

NEW Ed's Chowder House ● *Seafood* | 19 | 21 | 19 | $58 |

W 60s | Empire Hotel | 44 W. 63rd St., mezzanine (bet. B'way & Columbus Ave.) | 212-956-1288 | www.chinagrillmgt.com
This "satisfying" seafooder "just a hop across the street to Lincoln Center" serves "good but not amazing" grub in a "spacious" setting that's "fancier than the name suggests"; though some "kinks need to be worked out", overall it's an "appealing" addition to the area.

Ed's Lobster Bar *Seafood* | 23 | 17 | 19 | $43 |

NoLita | 222 Lafayette St. (bet. Kenmare & Spring Sts.) | 212-343-3236 | www.lobsterbarnyc.com
For an "authentic New England experience", try this "straightforward" NoLita seafooder famed for its "fresh-off-the-boat" lobster roll; the "narrow", "Nantucket-esque" space may be "cool", but insiders say the food tastes best at the "long bar" rather than the "cramped" tables.

Egg ⊄ *Southern* | 23 | 12 | 17 | $23 |

Williamsburg | 135A N. Fifth St. (bet. Bedford Ave. & Berry St.) | Brooklyn | 718-302-5151 | www.pigandegg.com
"Eggspectations" are eggceeded at this "calorie-packed", "cash-only" Williamsburg joint where the "ambrosial" Southern eats are largely "locally grown"; you won't have to shell out much dough, but you'll probably wait in "really long lines."

EJ's Luncheonette ⊄ *Diner* | 16 | 10 | 14 | $23 |

E 70s | 1271 Third Ave. (73rd St.) | 212-472-0600
W 80s | 447 Amsterdam Ave. (bet. 81st & 82nd Sts.) | 212-873-3444
Brace yourself for "Maclaren-stroller" gridlock at these "family-friendly" "upscale greasy spoons" slinging a "something-for-everyone" menu of

"good old American food"; "rushed" service and "inexplicably long" weekend waits are trumped by the "recession-buster" tabs.

Elaine's ● *American/Italian*   14 | 14 | 15 | $59

E 80s | 1703 Second Ave. (bet. 88th & 89th Sts.) | 212-534-8103

Once *the* "see-and-be-seen" nexus for "literati" and "show" folk, Elaine Kaufman's UES Italian-American is now "past its heyday" with "snobby service" and "overpriced, undergood" food; still, regulars are extremely loyal and compare it to a comfortable old shoe.

El Almacén ⊽ *Argentinean*   ∇ 24 | 23 | 20 | $41

Williamsburg | 557 Driggs Ave. (bet. N. 6th & 7th Sts.) | Brooklyn | 718-218-7284

"Meat eaters" unite behind this "solid" Argentinean, an "exceptional", "well-priced" option for a "taste of Buenos Aires" in the "heart of Billyburg"; while its rustic, "all-wooden interior" may be "cozy" enough for some, others describe it as "packed tight."

NEW El Ay Si Ⓜ *American*   - | - | - | I

LIC | 47-38 Vernon Blvd. (bet. 47th Rd. & 48th Ave.) | Queens | 718-389-8781 | www.elaysi.com

The hipster aesthetic lands in LIC via this dark, narrow newcomer equipped with distressed brick walls, Edison lightbulbs and an ironic moniker; the pared-down American menu is similarly of the moment, featuring standard comfort-food items (i.e. fried chicken, mac 'n' cheese) at Queens prices.

El Charro Español *Spanish*   22 | 17 | 23 | $44

W Village | 4 Charles St. (bet. Greenwich & 7th Aves.) | 212-242-9547 | www.el-charro-espanol.com

The sangria's "strong", the cooking "satisfying" and the prices "reasonable" at this "bygone-world" Spaniard that's occupied the same West Village basement since 1925; though the decor may need some "serious freshening up", admirers feel it "gets better with age."

Elephant, The ●Ⓜ *French/Thai*   ∇ 21 | 17 | 17 | $35

E Village | 58 E. First St. (bet. 1st & 2nd Aves.) | 212-505-7739 | www.theelephantrestaurant.com

Ironically monikered, this "tiny" East Villager crams diners in "like sardines" thanks to "delish" Thai-French cooking washed down with "fun" cocktails; it's "pretty cheap" too, hence its popularity with the younger set.

Elephant & Castle ● *Pub Food*   18 | 15 | 18 | $28

W Village | 68 Greenwich Ave. (bet. Perry St. & 7th Ave. S.) | 212-243-1400 | www.elephantandcastle.com

A "Village staple" since 1974, this "dependable" joint decked out in "coffee-shop" style draws locals with its "solid" pub grub and "affordable brunch"; though the setting is getting "a bit worn", it's usually "crowded" and especially "jammed on weekends."

Ⓩ Eleven Madison Park Ⓢ *French*   28 | 27 | 27 | $163

Flatiron | 11 Madison Ave. (24th St.) | 212-889-0905 | www.elevenmadisonpark.com

Everything an "upscale NYC restaurant should be", Danny Meyer's "knockout" New French off Madison Square Park is set in a "splendid" deco bank space that "makes a grand stage" for chef Daniel Humm's "world-class" work, shuttled by hospitable servers; though the prix fixe-only meals come with "soaring" price tags, there's agreement that such "pure elegance" is "worth every penny."

El Faro ● M _Spanish_
22 | 11 | 18 | $42

W Village | 823 Greenwich St. (bet. Horatio & Jane Sts.) | 212-929-8210 | www.elfaronyc.com

"Paella is the staple" at this "heavy-on-the-garlic" Village Spaniard, a "veritable antique" that's "never changed" since it opened in 1927; though some say the "tatty" decor "needs an update", there's nothing wrong with its "tasty" vittles and "moderate" pricing.

Eliá M _Greek_
26 | 20 | 24 | $49

Bay Ridge | 8611 Third Ave. (bet. 86th & 87th Sts.) | Brooklyn | 718-748-9891 | www.eliarestaurant.com

Like visiting "Greece without a passport", this "exceptional" Bay Ridge Hellenic offers an "excellent" menu that "takes Greek to a whole new level"; "hospitable" service, "fair prices" and a "comfortable" setting (including a "charming" back garden deck) make it a neighborhood "favorite."

Elias Corner ●⌿ _Greek/Seafood_
23 | 9 | 16 | $39

Astoria | 24-02 31st St. (24th Ave.) | Queens | 718-932-1510

There are "no bells and whistles" at this "straightforward", "cash-only" Astoria Greek, just "right-off-the-boat" seafood "simply grilled" and ferried by waiters as "fresh" as the fish; despite "no menus" and a somewhat plain setting, it's been around 25 years for a reason.

Z Elio's ● _Italian_
24 | 17 | 20 | $66

E 80s | 1621 Second Ave. (bet. 84th & 85th Sts.) | 212-772-2242

"Air kisses" abound at this "clubby", "high-style" Italian where "Upper East Side royalty" and "boldface names" schmooze over "expensive", "wonderfully prepared" Italian fare; unless you're a regular or "look the part", "be prepared to be ignored" in all the "fabulous" "hustle and bustle."

Elizabeth ● _Eclectic_
18 | 21 | 19 | $45

NoLita | 265 Elizabeth St. (bet. Houston & Prince Sts.) | 212-334-2426 | www.elizabethny.com

This NoLita "escape" exudes "indoor-outdoor" appeal with its "pretty" interior and "fantastic" all-seasons back garden; the "reliable" Eclectic menu is equally "delicious", particularly when it's washed down with a "creative cocktail" shaken by one of its "engaging mixologists."

El Malecon ● _Dominican_
22 | 10 | 16 | $20

Washington Heights | 4141 Broadway (175th St.) | 212-927-3812
W 90s | 764 Amsterdam Ave. (bet. 97th & 98th Sts.) | 212-864-5648
Bronx | 5592 Broadway (231st St.) | 718-432-5155

In the "competitive field" of rotisserie chicken, this Uptown/Bronx trio features a "garlicky", "fall-off-the-bone" version that's particularly "flavorful", as well as "heaping platters" of "honest" Dominican chow; it's "cheap" and "quick", even though the decor is "cheesy."

	FOOD	DECOR	SERVICE	COST

El Parador Café *Mexican*
22 | 17 | 21 | $46

Murray Hill | 325 E. 34th St. (bet. 1st & 2nd Aves.) | 212-679-6812 | www.elparadorcafe.com

Though around since 1959, this venerable Murray Hill Mexican remains "largely undiscovered" despite "terrific" cooking, "fair" prices and "knock-your-socks-off margaritas"; sure, it could stand an "upgrading", but fans say it demonstrates that "new isn't always improved."

El Paso Taqueria *Mexican*
23 | 16 | 19 | $27

E 100s | 1643 Lexington Ave. (104th St.) | 212-831-9831 ●
E 90s | 64 E. 97th St. (bet. Madison & Park Aves.) | 212-996-1739
Harlem | 237 E. 116th St. (3rd Ave.) | 212-860-4875 ●
www.elpasotaqueria.com

"Real-deal" Mexican food that's "several notches above the standard" is yours at this Uptown trio that also boasts "friendly" service and "great prices"; given the "small", "tight" settings, many opt for "quick" delivery, though the Lexington Avenue outpost has an "attractive" back patio.

El Pote Ⓩ *Spanish*
22 | 14 | 21 | $42

Murray Hill | 718 Second Ave. (bet. 38th & 39th Sts.) | 212-889-6680 |
www.elpote.com

"Big servings" of "delicious" paella and other Spanish "staples" keep the trade brisk at this "old-style" Murray Hill "sleeper" on the scene since '77; though the "tight" quarters "aren't exciting", the combo of good food and service guarantees its further longevity.

El Quijote ● *Spanish*
21 | 14 | 18 | $43

Chelsea | 226 W. 23rd St. (bet. 7th & 8th Aves.) | 212-929-1855
Like "stepping into a time warp", this vintage-1930 Spaniard near the Chelsea Hotel is renowned for its "cheap lobster", "fantastic sangria" and "Spanglish"-speaking staff; no question, the decor is "wondrously tacky", but that's part of its charm.

El Quinto Pino ● *Spanish*
21 | 16 | 20 | $34

Chelsea | 401 W. 24th St. (bet. 9th & 10th Aves.) | 212-206-6900 | www.elquintopinonyc.com

"Adventurous" types tout this "tiny" Chelsea tapas bar (now owned by the Txikito team) for its "new rotating menu" exploring "different regions of Spain"; despite a table-free setting with "bar seating only" and checks that can "add up quickly", fans summarize it as "adorable."

Embers *Steak*
21 | 15 | 19 | $49

Bay Ridge | 9519 Third Ave. (bet. 95th & 96th Sts.) | Brooklyn | 718-745-3700
Locals give glowing reviews to this Bay Ridge chop shop where "top-quality" beef is served at "hard-to-beat" prices; while the crowd's right out of *Steakhouse, a film by Martin Scorsese*, the "too-close" tables and "tired" decor need a rewrite.

Empanada Mama ● *South American*
22 | 12 | 15 | $18

W 50s | 763 Ninth Ave. (bet. 51st & 52nd Sts.) | 212-698-9008 | www.empmamanyc.com

Now open 24/7, this Hell's Kitchen South American slings "little pieces of heaven" in a space that's as "small" as its namesake specialty; it's "always crowded" and so loud that "conversation is an exercise in futility", but insiders order the "Viagra" version and "go home happy."

	FOOD	DECOR	SERVICE	COST

Empire Szechuan ● *Chinese*

16 | 10 | 15 | $25

Washington Heights | 4041 Broadway (bet. 170th & 171st Sts.) |
212-568-1600
W 60s | 193 Columbus Ave. (bet. 68th & 69th Sts.) | 212-496-8778
W 100s | 2642 Broadway (bet. 100th & 101st Sts.) | 212-662-9404
W Village | 173 Seventh Ave. S. (bet. Perry & W. 11th Sts.) | 212-243-6046
www.empiretogo.com
Always a "safe bet", these Manhattan mini-chain "survivors" purvey
an "extensive" selection of "standard" Chinese dishes (plus sushi)
priced for the "budget-minded"; "bleak" digs and "stingy-with-the-
fortune-cookies" service lead many to opt for "lightning-fast delivery."

Employees Only ● *European*

20 | 21 | 19 | $47

W Village | 510 Hudson St. (bet. Christopher & W. 10th Sts.) |
212-242-3021 | www.employeesonlynyc.com
It's "all about the cocktails" at this "speakeasy"-ish West Villager
that's a "night-owl" nexus into the wee hours; the European chow is
"tasty" enough and brunch in the garden "lovely", but ultimately "it's
a lounge first, restaurant second."

Emporio *Italian*

21 | 20 | 18 | $42

NoLita | 231 Mott St. (bet. Prince & Spring Sts.) | 212-966-1234 |
www.auroraristorante.com
"Earthy, imaginative" Italian food comes to NoLita via this Aurora
spin-off parked in a high-ceilinged industrial space crowned by a
dramatic skylight; the "cool vibe" and "reasonable prices" make up for
"having to pretend you can hear what your date is saying."

Energy Kitchen *Health Food*

17 | 9 | 15 | $14

Chelsea | 307 W. 17th St. (bet. 8th & 9th Aves.) | 212-645-5200
E 40s | 300 E. 41st St. (2nd Ave.) | 212-687-1200
E 50s | 1089 Second Ave. (bet. 57th & 58th Sts.) | 212-888-9300
E 80s | 1628 Second Ave. (bet. 84th & 85th Sts.) | 212-288-8484
Financial District | 71 Nassau St. (bet. Fulton & John Sts.) | 212-577-8989
Flatiron | 18 W. 23rd St. (bet. 5th & 6th Aves.) | 212-989-2323
W 40s | 417 W. 47th St. (bet. 9th & 10th Aves.) | 212-333-3500
W Village | 82 Christopher St. (bet. Bleecker St. & 7th Ave. S.) | 212-414-8880
www.energykitchen.com
"Health nuts" hail this "guilt-free" fast-food chain as a "diet savior",
citing its "calorie-conscious" burgers, wraps and salads at "good-for-
you" prices; so-so service and "hospitallike" decor result in "a lot
of take-out customers."

EN Japanese Brasserie *Japanese*

24 | 25 | 23 | $65

W Village | 435 Hudson St. (Leroy St.) | 212-647-9196 | www.enjb.com
En-thusiasts en-joy this "exquisite" West Village Japanese where the
"wow factor" centers around the "silky housemade" tofu and "airy",
"stunningly beautiful" room; add "exotic" small plates, an "extensive
sake list" and "outstanding" service, and the "high prices" don't
sting as much.

Enoteca Maria Ⓜ⌷ *Italian*

23 | 18 | 21 | $46

Staten Island | 27 Hyatt St. (Central Ave.) | 718-447-2777 |
www.enotecamaria.com
The "unique concept" at this Staten Island wine bar in St. George is
having different "Italian nonnas" take turns "cooking from their re-

gions of Italy"; the resultant "ever-changing menu" makes for an "experience like no other", even if the small-plate prices can run up.

Enzo's *Italian*   23 | 17 | 21 | $41

Bronx | 1998 Williamsbridge Rd. (Neill Ave.) | 718-409-3828
Bronx | 2339 Arthur Ave. (bet. Crescent Ave. & E. 186th St.) | 718-733-4455
www.enzosofthebronx.com

These "big-plate, big-flavor" Bronx Italians dish out "red-sauce" classics in portions so "large" that "plenty of leftovers" are virtually guaranteed; "budget-minded" tabs and "service with gusto" make the "so-so decor" and "no-rez" rule easy to swallow.

Epices du Traiteur *Mediterranean/ Tunisian*   21 | 16 | 20 | $43

W 70s | 103 W. 70th St. (Columbus Ave.) | 212-579-5904

"Unique" for "pre–Lincoln Center" types, this UWS Med-Tunisian offers an "exotic" menu that's both "fortifying" and "affordable"; when the "narrow", "shoebox"-size space gets "cramped", regulars escape to its "delightful garden" – or show up after 8 when it's "more relaxed."

Erawan *Thai*   23 | 20 | 20 | $37

Bayside | 213 11 09th Ave. (Bell Blvd.) | Queens | 718-229-1620
Bayside | 42-31 Bell Blvd. (bet. 42nd & 43rd Aves.) | Queens | 718-428-2112

"Excellent" Thai food featuring more "contemporary" recipes is yours at this Bayside duo where "wonderful" service and "soothing" vibes make it "hard to get a seat" at prime times; the "cavernous" 39th Avenue branch features "fantastic" surf 'n' turf à la Siam.

Erminia ⊠ *Italian*   25 | 24 | 24 | $69

E 80s | 250 E. 83rd St. (bet. 2nd & 3rd Aves.) | 212-879-4284 |
www.erminiaristorante.com

"Special-occasion" venues don't get much more "charming" than this "transporting" UES "rendezvous" where many "renew their vows" over a "delicious" Roman menu; the "rustic", "candlelit" space is so "romantic" that the "tiny" dimensions and "expensive" tabs barely register.

⊠ Esca ❶ *Italian/Seafood*   25 | 21 | 22 | $72

W 40s | 402 W. 43rd St. (9th Ave.) | 212-564-7272 | www.esca-nyc.com

"Sublime" Italian seafood (and "mouthwatering" pastas and crudo) "graciously served" are the hooks at this "chic" Hell's Kitchen port of call from the Batali-Bastianich-Pasternack team; despite "high price tags", it works well both "pre-theater or sans theater" thanks to "brilliant execution on every level."

Ess-a-Bagel *Deli*   23 | 7 | 13 | $12

E 50s | 831 Third Ave. (bet. 50th & 51st Sts.) | 212-980-1010
Gramercy | 359 First Ave. (21st St.) | 212-260-2252
www.ess-a-bagel.com

"Doughy", "mutant"-size bagels schmeared with "any topping you can imagine" are the specialty of this East Side deli duo; noshers nix the "grungy" digs, service "out of *Seinfeld*" and "weekend lines out the door", but it's all part of the "authentic NY experience."

Essex ❶ *American*   18 | 16 | 15 | $32

LES | 120 Essex St. (Rivington St.) | 212-533-9616 | www.essexnyc.com

An "infamous", ultra-"cheap" boozy brunch draws hordes of "hipsters" to this Lower Eastsider done up in "warehouse-chic" style; the rest of the week, the New American menu with Jewish-Latin accents is "decent" enough, though "poor service" and "crushing noise" are downers.

NEW Estiatorio Rafina *Greek*

| − | − | − | E |

Murray Hill | 630 First Ave. (37th St.) | 212-532-2234 | www.rafinanyc.com

Crispy whole-roasted fish is the specialty of this new Hellenic seafooder in Murray Hill just off the East River, where stucco walls, a blue-lit bar and sidewalk seating supply the vaguely Mediterranean atmosphere.

Etcetera Etcetera Ⓜ *Italian*

| 21 | 19 | 22 | $50 |

W 40s | 352 W. 44th St. (bet. 8th & 9th Aves.) | 212-399-4141 | www.etcrestaurant.com

A "hipper", "gayer" version of sibling ViceVersa, this Hell's Kitchen Italian offers "quality" dining in a "contemporary", "MoMA"-esque setting; it's "totally geared up to get you to the curtain on time", either on the "loud" ground floor or the more "conversation"-friendly upstairs.

Ethos *Greek*

| 21 | 16 | 19 | $43 |

E 50s | 905 First Ave. (51st St.) | 212-888-4060
Murray Hill | 495 Third Ave. (bet. 33rd & 34th Sts.) | 212-252-1972
www.ethosrestaurants.com

"Really fresh fish" is the focus of these "upscale" Hellenic tavernas where the "authentic" cooking makes for "delectable" dining; the Sutton Place spin-off is "fancier" than the Murray Hill original, though both boast "inviting" service and "unchallenging" prices.

Euzkadi *Spanish*

| 20 | 17 | 19 | $39 |

E Village | 108 E. Fourth St. (bet. 1st & 2nd Aves.) | 212-982-9788 | www.euzkadirestaurant.com

"Delectable" Basque tapas, "wonderful sangria" and live Tuesday night flamenco lend a "festive" feel to this "authentic, affordable" East Villager; "friendly" vibes and a "cool, dark" setting keep its hip young patrons happy.

Excellent Dumpling House ⊘ *Chinese*

| 20 | 6 | 12 | $15 |

Chinatown | 111 Lafayette St. (bet. Canal & Walker Sts.) | 212-219-0212

Whether the name "says it all" or is just "wishful thinking", most agree this Chinatowner is a natural for "jury duty lunch breaks" thanks to good Shanghainese chow at "below-market prices"; given the "bare-bones" looks and "rude service", it's "not a place to linger."

Extra Virgin *Mediterranean*

| 21 | 18 | 16 | $43 |

W Village | 259 W. Fourth St. (Perry St.) | 212-691-9359 | www.extravirginrestaurant.com

"Pretty people" pop by this West Village Med for its "tasty" cooking, "upbeat" mood and outdoor tables rated "second to none"; the "cranky" service is another story, but regardless, this "ever popular" place is "always jammed."

Fabio Piccolo Fiore *Italian*

| 22 | 19 | 23 | $51 |

E 40s | 230 E. 44th St. (bet. 2nd & 3rd Aves.) | 212-922-0581 | www.fabiopiccolofiore.com

A "secret hideaway" near bustling Grand Central, this "charming" Italian is known for "first-class food" prepared by a chef with a "total willingness to modify things if you ask"; "warm, warm, warm" service and "well-spaced tables" distinguish it from its peers.

| | FOOD | DECOR | SERVICE | COST |

Fairway Cafe *American* `18` `10` `12` `$26`
W 70s | 2127 Broadway, 2nd fl. (74th St.) | 212-595-1888
Red Hook | 480-500 Van Brunt St. (Reed St.) | Brooklyn | 718-694-6868
www.fairwaymarket.com
Shoppers "rest their dogs" at these grocery store cafes offering "decent", "inexpensive" American grub (and steaks at the UWS outlet); there's "not much ambiance" or service, but there are views of the "mighty NY harbor" and Lady Liberty in Red Hook.

Falai *Italian* `25` `19` `22` `$61`
LES | 68 Clinton St. (bet. Rivington & Stanton Sts.) | 212-253-1960
Falai Panetteria *Italian*
LES | 79 Clinton St. (Rivington St.) | 212-777-8956
Caffe Falai *Italian*
SoHo | 265 Lafayette St. (Prince St.) | 212-274-8615
www.falainyc.com
Chef Iacopo Falai's "deftly prepared" Italian food thrills fans at this "innovative" Lower Eastsider, an "all-white", "Ferragamo shoe box"–size place where regulars "get the gnudi", then "lick the plate clean"; the nearby Panetteria and SoHo's Caffe, besides being more casual and affordable than the parent, also serve breakfast and lunch.

F & J Pine Restaurant *Italian* `22` `19` `19` `$37`
Bronx | 1913 Bronxdale Ave. (bet. Matthews & Muliner Aves.) | 718-792-5956 | www.fjpine.com
"Everyone leaves with a doggy bag" from this "old-faithful" Bronx Italian where "giant portions" of "red-sauce" standards and "Yankee" sightings will "keep you sated"; low prices and "terrific sports memorabilia" make the weekend "waits" more tolerable.

Farm on Adderley *American* `24` `20` `21` `$37`
Ditmas Park | 1108 Cortelyou Rd. (bet. Stratford & Westminster Rds.) | Brooklyn | 718-287-3101 | www.thefarmonadderley.com
"Up-and-coming" yet still "underserved", Ditmas Park is "eating better" thanks to this "imaginative" American bistro that uses "fresh", "locally sourced" ingredients in its "crave-worthy" menu; "genuine" service, a "nice" garden and "Brooklyn prices" ice the cake.

Fatty Crab ● *Malaysian* `20` `13` `16` `$44`
W 70s | 2170 Broadway (77th St.) | 212-496-2722
W Village | 643 Hudson St. (bet. Gansevoort & Horatio Sts.) | 212-352-3590
www.fattycrab.com
"Zingy" Malaysian street eats are purveyed at this "dark", "noisy" duo via the "clever" Zak Pelaccio; both locations share a "too-cool-for-school" vibe with "tattooed hipsters" supplying "my-way-or-the-highway" service; P.S. the UWS spin-off has "more elbow room" than the "rinky-dink" Village original.

NEW Fatty 'Cue ● *Asian/BBQ* ▽ `23` `16` `18` `$43`
Williamsburg | 91 S. Sixth St. (Berry St.) | Brooklyn | 718-599-3090 | www.fattycue.com
Zak Pelaccio "strikes again" with this new Williamsburg "carnivore's delight" that merges "amazing" American barbecue with "Southeast Asian flavors", covering "territory from Memphis to Malaysia"; the "casual", "hipster"-friendly digs are arranged on several floors.

	FOOD	DECOR	SERVICE	COST

NEW Fatty Fish *Asian* — ▽ 22 | 17 | 22 | $33

E 60s | 406 E. 64th St. (bet. 1st & York Aves.) | 212-813-9338 |
www.fattyfishnyc.com

New, "delightfully delicious" addition to the UES serving "excellent"
Asian fusion items for "reasonable" dough in a "minimalist" room; the
"lovely" back patio, "anxious-to-please" service and no-corkage-fee
BYO policy are all "nice surprises."

NEW Faustina *Italian* — 23 | 21 | 22 | $67

E Village | Cooper Square Hotel | 25 Cooper Sq. (bet. 5th & 6th Sts.) |
212-475-3400 | www.faustinanyc.com

Ensconced on the "now-hip" Bowery, Scott Conant's new Italian in the
Cooper Square Hotel offers a "simply marvelous" menu with "awesome pastas" and a "wonderful" raw bar as standouts; the "modern"
setting and pricing get mixed marks, however, and the loos are so "far
away" you'll "need a miner's hat to find them."

Felice ● *Italian* — 21 | 21 | 20 | $47

E 60s | 1166 First Ave. (64th St.) | 212-593-2223 | www.felicewinebar.com
The "atmosphere is great" at this "sexy" UES wine bar that's a magnet
for gals seeking a *"Sex and the City"* experience; the "simple" Italian
menu is "not terribly diverse", but the "reasonable" tabs and "from-
the-heart" service are felicitous.

Felidia *Italian* — 26 | 22 | 24 | $78

E 50s | 243 E. 58th St. (bet. 2nd & 3rd Aves.) | 212-758-1479 |
www.lidiasitaly.com

Thirty years later, Lidia Bastianich's "memorable" East Side Italian
"hasn't lost its luster", offering "stunning" meals, "perfect" service
and a "dignified" townhouse setting; maybe the tables are "too close
together" and the room "needs revamping", but overall it's worth "every one of the many pennies it will cost."

Félix ● *French* — 17 | 17 | 15 | $43

SoHo | 340 W. Broadway (Grand St.) | 212-431-0021 | www.felixnyc.com
"People-watching" at the sidewalk tables is the "best thing on the
menu" at this SoHo French bistro that seduces "Euro-chic" types and
"model wannabes" despite "not-special" food and "lackadaisical"
service; supporters say there's "always something crazy going on", especially during Sunday's "loco brunch."

Ferrara ● *Bakery* — 23 | 17 | 17 | $20

Little Italy | 195 Grand St. (bet. Mott & Mulberry Sts.) | 212-226-6150 |
www.ferraracafe.com

"Leave the money, take the cannoli" and "never mind the tourists" at
this circa-1892 Little Italy bakery vending "tasty" Italian desserts and
espresso; "you can put on weight simply by looking at the pastry
cases", but many can't resist and "order everything."

Z Fette Sau *BBQ* — 25 | 15 | 15 | $27

Williamsburg | 354 Metropolitan Ave. (bet. Havemeyer & Roebling Sts.) |
Brooklyn | 718-963-3404 | www.fettesaubbq.com

Again voted Top BBQ in town, this "funky" Williamsburger set in a
converted garage sends "hipsters" into "meat comas" with its "self-
serve", pay-by-the-pound 'cue washed down with "terrific bourbons"

and "growlers of beer"; on the downside, the "mason jars", "paper towels" and "picnic tables" recall "Boy Scout camping" to some.

15 East ⓩ *Japanese*

`25` `22` `23` `$83`

Union Sq | 15 E. 15th St. (bet. 5th Ave. & Union Sq. W.) | 212-647-0015 | www.15eastrestaurant.com

"Fish bliss" awaits at the sushi bar of this "refined" Union Square Japanese from the Tocqueville team; the "exquisite omakases" are "on par with the best" in town, while the "calming", "quiet" milieu and "pro service" are "perfect accompaniments" to a meal as "unforgettable" as the "mind-blowing" tabs.

Fig & Olive *Mediterranean*

`20` `20` `18` `$47`

E 50s | 10 E. 52nd St. (bet. 5th & Madison Aves.) | 212-319-2002
E 60s | 808 Lexington Ave. (bet. 62nd & 63rd Sts.) | 212-207-4555
Meatpacking | 420 W. 13th St. (bet. 9th Ave. & Washington St.) | 212-924-1200
www.figandolive.com

"Creative use" of olive oils enriches the menus of these "Mediterranean marvels" offering a "satisfying", "affordable" array of "tasty" small plates and mains; the Eastsiders are best for "taking a break" from shopping, while the Meatpacking location is "more spacious" and "high-ceilinged", and draws a more "bouncy" crowd.

Filippo's Ⓜ *Italian*

`▽ 25` `19` `23` `$57`

Staten Island | 1727 Richmond Rd. (bet. Buel & Seaver Aves.) | 718-668-9091 | www.filipposrestaurant.com

A "step above most Staten Island places", this Dongan Hills Italian presents an "excellent" menu abetted by a "long list of specials" recited by "informative" waiters; though the "bill can be breathtaking" – especially given the "strip-mall" setting – locals insist it's "well worth it."

F.illi Ponte ⓩⓂ *Italian*

`22` `21` `22` `$69`

TriBeCa | 39 Desbrosses St. (bet. Washington & West Sts.) | 212-226-4621 | www.filliponte.com

"Tucked away" in Far West TriBeCa, this long-"established", 1967-vintage Italian keeps locals and "South Jersey" types "happy" with "good traditional" cooking, including its "outstanding" signature 'angry lobster'; Hudson River views and "warm" service make the "pricey" tabs more palatable.

Fiorentino's *Italian*

`21` `13` `19` `$37`

Gravesend | 311 Ave. U (bet. McDonald Ave. & West St.) | Brooklyn | 718-372-1445

The "prices are low but the food quality's high" at this Gravesend "neighborhood favorite" specializing in "gigantic portions" of "hearty" Neapolitan food served in a "vintage Brooklyn" atmosphere; "older folks love it", despite the "noise" and "no-reservations" rule.

Fiorini ⓩ *Italian*

`22` `18` `22` `$59`

E 50s | 209 E. 56th St. (bet. 2nd & 3rd Aves.) | 212-308-0830 | www.fiorinirestaurant.com

One of the few "well-kept secrets" in Midtown, Lello Arpaia's "old-school" Italian serves a "solid" Neapolitan menu to "well-dressed grown-ups"; ok, it's "pricey", but in return you get "friendly" service and a "refined" setting "quiet" enough to "have a conversation in peace."

	FOOD	DECOR	SERVICE	COST

❷ FireBird Ⓜ Russian
20 | 26 | 21 | $66

W 40s | 365 W. 46th St. (bet. 8th & 9th Aves.) | 212-586-0244 |
www.firebirdrestaurant.com

Like dining "with the czar and czarina", this "ornate" Restaurant Row
Russian townhouse is a "feast for the eyes" thanks to a collection of
"gorgeous artifacts"; some say the "decor outclasses" the "costly" chow,
but the "last-century" service and "dizzying" vodka list are fine as is.

Firenze ❶ Italian
20 | 20 | 22 | $49

E 80s | 1594 Second Ave. (bet. 82nd & 83rd Sts.) | 212-861-9368 |
www.firenzeny.com

Doing its "namesake" proud, this "old-fashioned" UES hideaway
serves "classic" Tuscan dishes "made with TLC" in a "warm", brick-
lined room that exudes "romance"; the "very attentive" service makes
fans feel like they're "dining in a private home."

Fish Seafood
21 | 14 | 19 | $37

W Village | 280 Bleecker St. (Jones St.) | 212-727-2879

There's "nothing fancy" going on at this Village "fish shack" that channels "Ocean City, MD", with its "extremely fresh" seafood and refresh-
ingly "reasonable" tabs; despite "tight seating" and "noisy" decibels,
"you get what you pay for here – and then some."

Fishtail Seafood
23 | 23 | 22 | $64

E 60s | 135 E. 62nd St. (bet. Lexington & Park Aves.) | 212-754-1300 |
www.fishtaildb.com

Those angling for "refined" UES dining are hooked on this David Burke
"winner" where "perfectly prepared" seafood and "eager-to-please"
service provide the "wow factor"; there's also a "classy" townhouse
setting, leaving the "big-bucks" price tags as the only sticking point.

Five Guys Burgers
20 | 8 | 14 | $13

NEW **E 40s** | 690 Third Ave. (bet. 43rd & 44th Sts.) | 646-783-5060
G Village | 496 La Guardia Pl. (bet. Bleecker & Houston Sts.) | 212-228-6008
NEW **W 40s** | 36 W. 48th St. (bet. 5th & 6th Aves.) | 212-997-1270
W 50s | 43 W. 55th St. (bet. 5th & 6th Aves.) | 212-459-9600
W Village | 296 Bleecker St. (7th Ave. S.) | 212-367-9200 ❶
Bay Ridge | 8510 Fifth Ave. (bet. 85th & 86th Sts.) | Brooklyn | 718-921-9380
Brooklyn Heights | 138 Montague St. (bet. Clinton & Henry Sts.) |
Brooklyn | 718-797-9380
Park Slope | 284 Seventh Ave. (bet. 6th & 7th Sts.) | Brooklyn | 718-499-9380
College Point | 132-01 14th Ave. (132nd St.) | Queens | 718-767-6500
Glendale | 73-25 Woodhaven Blvd. (bet. 74th & Rutledge Aves.) |
Queens | 718-943-3483
www.fiveguys.com
Additional locations throughout the NY area

Setting a "new standard for fast-food" chains, these all-over-town
"burger temples" flip "handmade" patties that are "good enough for
Obama" and could be the "East Coast answer to In-N-Out"; "nice
prices" and "free peanuts" offset the "grease-city" decor.

Five Leaves ❶ American
∇ 25 | 24 | 20 | $32

Greenpoint | 18 Bedford Ave. (bet. Lorimer St. & Manhattan Ave.) |
Brooklyn | 718-383-5345 | www.fiveleavesny.com

"Hordes of hipsters" squeezed into the "skinniest jeans" assemble at this
Greenpoint New American for its "simple" takes on "down-home" clas-

sics with Australian touches; "motivated" service and "tight" dimensions mean it's "always packed" and has "super-long" weekend lines.

5 Napkin Burger ● *Burgers* | 21 | 17 | 18 | $30

W 40s | 630 Ninth Ave. (bet. 44th & 45th Sts.) | 212-757-2277
NEW **W 80s** | 2315 Broadway (84th St.) | 212-333-4488
NEW **Astoria** | 35-01 36th St. (35th Ave.) | Queens | 718-433-2727
www.5napkinburger.com

It takes "at least five napkins" to handle the "hefty", "succulent" burgers at this "'fast-paced" Hell's Kitchen patty palace (and its new UWS/Astoria offspring); even though it can be "louder than a train station at rush hour", fans "like the atmosphere" and "credit crunch-friendly" pricing.

5 Ninth *American* | 19 | 22 | 19 | $49

Meatpacking | 5 Ninth Ave. (bet. Gansevoort & Little W. 12th Sts.) | 212-929-9460 | www.5ninth.com

A "perfect hideaway" for Meatpacking "date nights", this "quaint" tri-level townhouse offers a "clever" New American menu served in "warm", "rustic" rooms or outside in the "lovely garden"; it's "a touch pricey" with "middling" service, but the "building is the star of the show" here.

Five Points *American/Mediterranean* | 22 | 21 | 21 | $48

NoHo | 31 Great Jones St. (bet. Bowery & Lafayette St.) | 212-253-5700 | www.fivepointsrestaurant.com

Even though it's "named after one of old NY's worst slums", this "lovely" NoHo Med–New American inhabits a "sun-dappled", "Zen-like" room complete with a "babbling brook" and serves "amazing", "reasonably priced" food; service is equally "terrific", even during its "killer brunch."

Flatbush Farm *American* | 21 | 19 | 18 | $38

Park Slope | 76 St. Marks Ave. (Flatbush Ave.) | Brooklyn | 718-622-3276 | www.flatbushfarm.com

"Homey" is the word on this "excellent" Park Sloper, a "locavore's delight" offering "farm-to-table" New Americana in a setting that's a cross between a "barn and a tavern"; though service can skew "ditzy", it's easier to overlook in the "super-fab garden."

Flea Market Cafe ● *French* | 19 | 17 | 17 | $31

E Village | 131 Ave. A (bet. 9th St. & St. Marks Pl.) | 212-358-9282 | www.fleamarketcafe.com

The "name says it all" about this "microcosm of the East Village" vending "basic" French bites in a "quirky" room where some of the "mish-mash" decor is "also for sale"; "value" tabs make up for the "slow" service and "dime-a-dozen" brunch.

Flex Mussels *Seafood* | 23 | 17 | 19 | $45

E 80s | 174 E. 82nd St. (bet. Lexington & 3rd Aves.) | 212-717-7772 | www.flexmusselsny.com

"Fresh, fleshy" mussels are prepared "every which way to Sunday" at this "cheery" UES spin-off of a Prince Edward Island seafooder; "deafening" decibels and "boring" decor don't seem to faze its "youthful" habitués one bit – in fact, it's so popular that a West Village outpost at 154 West 13th Street is in the works.

Flor de Mayo ◑ *Chinese/Peruvian* · 20 · 10 · 17 · $24

W 80s | 484 Amsterdam Ave. (bet. 83rd & 84th Sts.) | 212-787-3388

W 100s | 2651 Broadway (bet. 100th & 101st Sts.) | 212-663-5520

"Fantastic" rotisserie chicken has Upper Westsiders clucking about these Chinese-Peruvians that are usually "mob scenes" thanks to the can't-miss combination of "huge portions" and "low prices"; given "humble" decor and "disappearing" staffers, many opt for "takeout."

Flor de Sol *Spanish* · 20 · 19 · 19 · $46

TriBeCa | 361 Greenwich St. (bet. Franklin & Harrison Sts.) | 212-366-1640 | www.flordesolnyc.com

Even though it's "too dark to read the menu", no one cares at this "sexy" TriBeCa tapas dispenser since the Spanish tidbits are "really good" and the sangria's "even better"; "flamenco dancing" and "live music" ratchet up the ambiance.

Fonda Ⓜ *Mexican* · 24 · 20 · 22 · $39

Park Slope | 434 Seventh Ave. (bet. 14th & 15th Sts.) | Brooklyn | 718-369-3144 | www.fondarestaurant.com

An "instant favorite" in the South Slope, this "hits-all-the-right-notes" yearling offers an "upscale", "honestly Mexican" menu in "small", "cozy" digs; even though the "seating's "tight" and the music "loud", fans are kinda fonda its "sublime margaritas" and "active little bar."

Forlini's ◑ *Italian* · 20 · 15 · 21 · $41

Chinatown | 93 Baxter St. (Walker St.) | 212-349-6779

Whether you're "on a break from jury duty" or "just getting out of jail", this 1956-vintage Italian near the courthouses is a "reliable" respite; still, uncivil servants think it's "time to modernize" the "middling" chow.

Fornino *Pizza* · 23 · 15 · 19 · $26

NEW **Park Slope** | 256 Fifth Ave. (bet. Carroll St. & Garfield Pl.) | Brooklyn | 718-399-8600

Williamsburg | 187 Bedford Ave. (bet. 6th & 7th Sts.) | Brooklyn | 718-384-6004

www.forninopizza.com

"Crafted with love" and "fresh ingredients", the "innovative" wood-fired pies at this Williamsburg pizzeria are "among the city's best"; maybe the setting "leaves something to be desired", but overall it's "solid" enough to have spawned a Park Slope sibling post-Survey.

44 & X ◑ *American* · 21 · 19 · 20 · $46

W 40s | 622 10th Ave. (44th St.) | 212-977-1170

44½ ◑ *American*

W 40s | 626 10th Ave. (bet. 44th & 45th Sts.) | 212-399-4450

www.heaveninhellskitchen.com

"Pretty-boy" waiters with "Broadway aspirations" serve comfort food with "zing" to a "*très* gay" audience at these "winning" Hell's Kitchen New Americans; the "smart" settings stay on the "right side of trendy."

Z Four Seasons ⊠ *American* · 26 · 28 · 27 · $96

E 50s | 99 E. 52nd St. (bet. Lexington & Park Aves.) | 212-754-9494 | www.fourseasonsrestaurant.com

"Deserving all its accolades", this "iconic" Midtown "institution" designed by Philip Johnson and helmed by Alex von Bidder and Julian

Niccolini draws "famous" folk, "blue bloods" and corporate moguls with its "outstanding" New American food ferried by a "serve-with-verve" staff; whether for "power-lunching" in the Grill Room or "romantic" wining and dining in the Pool Room, fans wonder "can it get any chicer?"; P.S. jackets required, ditto "gold cards."

Fragole *Italian*   24 | 17 | 21 | $36

Carroll Gardens | 394 Court St. (bet. Carroll St. & 1st Pl.) | Brooklyn | 718-522-7133 | www.fragoleny.com

"Small in size but huge on flavor", this "charming" Carroll Gardens Italian is known for its *"delizioso"* pastas and "decent" tabs; the "epitome of a cozy neighborhood joint", it "lavishes its attention on the food rather than the decor."

Francisco's Centro Vasco *Spanish*   22 | 13 | 18 | $48

Chelsea | 159 W. 23rd St. (bet. 6th & 7th Aves.) | 212-645-6224 | www.centrovasco.ypguides.net

"Crustacean cravers" are crazy about this "old-fashioned" Chelsea Spaniard famed for "giga-size" lobsters that "weigh more than you do" served at "relative hargain" prices; it's a "delicious but messy" dining, complete with "working-class" decor and "rush-you-out" service.

Frank ●⊟ *Italian*   24 | 15 | 17 | $34

E Village | 88 Second Ave. (bet. 5th & 6th Sts.) | 212-420-0202 | www.frankrestaurant.com

"Teeny-weeny", cash-only East Villager plying "cheap", "labor-of-love" Italiana in "close" quarters with "disregard-the-decor" decor; "jostled" service and an "annoying" no-reservations policy are turn-offs, but the payoff is "straight-up fantastic" eating.

Frankie & Johnnie's Steakhouse ⊠ *Steak*   23 | 15 | 20 | $64

Garment District | 32 W. 37th St. (bet. 5th & 6th Aves.) | 212-947-8940
W 40s | 269 W. 45th St., 2nd fl. (bet. B'way & 8th Ave.) | 212-997-9494 ●
www.frankieandjohnnies.com

The 85-year-old Times Square outpost of this steakhouse duo is right out of "Damon Runyon", with "rickety stairs", "bow-tied" waiters and a "speakeasy"-ish vibe, while its "more refined" Garment District cousin is set in "John Barrymore's former townhouse"; both offer "frankly fine", "not-cheap" chops with "no pretense."

Frankies Spuntino *Italian*   24 | 18 | 20 | $38

LES | 17 Clinton St. (bet. Houston & Stanton Sts.) | 212-253-2303 ●
Carroll Gardens | 457 Court St. (bet. 4th Pl. & Luquer St.) | Brooklyn | 718-403-0033 ⊟
www.frankiesspuntino.com

"Every detail" is "spot on" at this "casual" Italian duo proffering a "spunky" menu of "excellent small plates" in "rustic", "Tuscany"-like settings; though both feature "no-reservation" policies, the Carroll Gardens original has an "enchanting" garden and its LES offspring takes credit cards.

Franny's *Pizza*   24 | 16 | 19 | $37

Prospect Heights | 295 Flatbush Ave. (bet. Prospect Pl. & St. Marks Ave.) | Brooklyn | 718-230-0221 | www.frannysbrooklyn.com

For "knock-your-socks-off" pizza crafted from "fresh local ingredients", look no further than this Prospect Heights "destination" that also supplies "memorably delicious" starters and cocktails; "ridiculous waits" and rather "steep" tabs (by pizza standards) are offset by "pleasant" service and overall "attention to detail."

Fratelli Italian 21 | 18 | 21 | $38

Bronx | 2507 Eastchester Rd. (Mace Ave.) | 718-547-2489
They "treat you like family" at this "neighborhood" Bronx Italian where "all the locals" go for "delicious" red-sauce cooking, and "plenty of it"; "reasonable" costs and "accommodating" service complete the "quality" picture.

Fred's at Barneys NY American/Italian 21 | 19 | 19 | $48

E 60s | Barneys NY | 660 Madison Ave., 9th fl. (60th St.) | 212-833-2200
"Ladies who lunch for hours" take a break from the "rigors of shopping" at this Midtown department-store canteen where the "surprisingly good" Italian-American food is as "chic" as the setting; it's more "calming" at dinnertime, though wags say the prices explain why everyone here is "so thin."

Freemans ◑ American 21 | 22 | 18 | $48

LES | Freeman Alley (off Rivington St., bet. Bowery & Chrystie St.) | 212-420-0012 | www.freemansrestaurant.com
Well "hidden on a LES back alley", this "quirky" New American draws "tragically hip" types with "hearty", "decently priced" chow and "eye-catching", "Addams Family"–esque decor; even though the servers don't "know how to smile", it's so achingly "trendy" that "interminable waits" are a given.

French Roast ◑ French 17 | 16 | 16 | $30

G Village | 78 W. 11th St. (bet. 5th & 6th Aves.) | 212-533-2233
W 80s | 2340 Broadway (85th St.) | 212-799-1533
www.frenchroastny.com
"Always busy", this "laid-back" Village/UWS duo dishes out "basic", if "uninspiring", French chow for "moderate" dough; a 24/7 open-door policy is the secret to their success, not the "snotty" service and "glorified coffee-shop" decor.

Fresco by Scotto ⌧ Italian 22 | 18 | 20 | $55

E 50s | 34 E. 52nd St. (bet. Madison & Park Aves.) | 212-935-3434

Fresco on the Go ⌧ Italian

E 50s | 40 E. 52nd St. (bet. Madison & Park Aves.) | 212-754-2700
Financial District | 114 Pearl St. (Hanover Sq.) | 212-635-5000
www.frescobyscotto.com
Known for its "warm welcome" and *"Today Show"*–cast regulars, this "family-run" Midtowner supplies "sophisticated" Tuscan food delivered by a "prompt" team; sure, it's "pricey" and "mobbed" for lunch, but the casual 'on-the-go' outlets do takeout with "panache."

Friend of a Farmer American 19 | 18 | 17 | $32

Gramercy | 77 Irving Pl. (bet. 18th & 19th Sts.) | 212-477-2188 | www.friendofafarmernyc.com
"Upstate New York" lands in Gramercy Park via this "folksy" 25-year-old vending "farmer's portions" of "bring-a-smile-to-your-face" Early Americana; though it's "affordable" and feels "homey", foes cluck about the "hippie" mood, "spotty" service and "intimidating brunch lines."

| | FOOD | DECOR | SERVICE | COST |

Fuleen Seafood ◕ *Chinese/Seafood*　　22 | 7 | 15 | $27
Chinatown | 11 Division St. (Bowery) | 212-941-6888
"Cheap", "squirming fresh" fish prepared Hong Kong-style hooks fi-natics at this "terrific" Chinatown seafooder that's less revered for its "nonexistent decor" and "uncivil service"; it's a natural for "jury duty" or even after a night on the town, thanks to its 2:30 AM closing time.

Fulton *Seafood*　　21 | 18 | 20 | $57
E 70s | 205 E. 75th St. (bet. 2nd & 3rd Aves.) | 212-288-6600 | www.fultonnyc.com
"Obviously, seafood is the strong suit" of this UES yearling via the "Citarella folks" around the corner, where "delish fish" is purveyed in a "lovely", brick-walled room; alright, it's a bit "expensive", but at least service is "attentive" and it's "easy to have a conversation" here.

Fushimi *Japanese*　　23 | 21 | 20 | $48
Bay Ridge | 9316 Fourth Ave. (bet. 93rd & 94th Sts.) | Brooklyn | 718-833-7788
Staten Island | 2110 Richmond Rd. (Lincoln Ave.) | 718-980-5300
www.fushimi.usacom
There's "no need to visit Manhattan" given the "creative" sushi on of-fer at this outer-borough Japanese duo that also "pays attention to aesthetics" with "stylish", "nightclub"-like looks; "upscale" tabs, "loud" decibels and "raucous" late-night crowds right out of *Jersey Shore* come with the territory.

Gabriela's *Mexican*　　18 | 18 | 17 | $38
W 90s | 688 Columbus Ave. (bet. 93rd & 94th Sts.) | 212-961-9600 | www.gabrielas.com
"Bring the kids" – "everyone else does" – to this "solid" UWS Mexican revered for its "fantastic" roast chicken and margaritas; despite "crowded, noisy" conditions and "absent" service, "good value" and a "fabulous patio" keep locals loyal.

Gabriel's ☒ *Italian*　　22 | 19 | 23 | $62
W 60s | 11 W. 60th St. (bet. B'way & Columbus Ave.) | 212-956-4600 | www.gabrielsbarandrest.com
"Spacious" and "gracious", Gabriel Aiello's "adult" Columbus Circle Italian serves "wonderfully prepared" classics in a "convenient" location that's "perfect pre–Lincoln Center"; "solicitous" service and "enter-tainment industry" celeb-watching make the "splurge" dinner pricing more palatable – and lunch is a bargain.

Gahm Mi Oak ◕ *Korean*　　20 | 13 | 15 | $26
Garment District | 43 W. 32nd St. (bet. B'way & 5th Ave.) | 212-695-4113
"Customers come at all hours" to this 24/7 Garment District Korean for "belly-warming" *sollongtang* beef soup (a "secret hangover rem-edy") as well as other "affordable" specialties; despite little decor or service, regulars say it "gets the job done."

Gallagher's Steak House ◕ *Steak*　　21 | 18 | 19 | $68
W 50s | 228 W. 52nd St. (bet. B'way & 8th Ave.) | 212-245-5336 | www.gallaghersnysteakhouse.com
"Brontosaurus-size" steaks "house-aged" in a glass-lined "meat locker" are the draw at this "real-deal", 1927-vintage Theater District chop

shop; its "good ol' boys" fan base relishes its "old-school" service, red-checkered tablecloths and sports pictures, but not the "expensive" tabs.

Gargiulo's *Italian* | 22 | 19 | 22 | $47 |

Coney Island | 2911 W. 15th St. (bet. Mermaid & Surf Aves.) | Brooklyn | 718-266-4891 | www.gargiulos.com

This "huge", circa-1907 Coney Islander features an equally "monumental menu" of "red-sauce" Southern Italian standards delivered by a "tuxedoed" pro crew; it's a "taste of Brooklyn the way it used to be" with a bonus "possibility of winning a free meal" in the nightly raffle.

☑ Gari *Japanese* | 27 | 15 | 21 | $83 |

W 70s | 370 Columbus Ave. (bet. 77th & 78th Sts.) | 212-362-4816

☑ Sushi of Gari ☾ *Japanese*

E 70s | 402 E. 78th St. (bet. 1st & York Aves.) | 212-517-5340

☑ Sushi of Gari 46 ☾ *Japanese*

W 40s | 347 W. 46th St. (bet. 8th & 9th Aves.) | 212-957-0046
www.sushiofgari.com

The "gold-standard omakase" is the "way to go" at this "outstanding" Japanese trio where "master" chef Gari Sugio "continues to astound" sushi aficionados with "inventive", "pristine" morsels; despite "austere" quarters, the "revolutionary tastes" here are well "worth paying the arm and the leg."

Gascogne *French* | 21 | 20 | 20 | $51 |

Chelsea | 158 Eighth Ave. (bet. 17th & 18th Sts.) | 212-675-6564 | www.gascognenyc.com

"Gascony" comes to Chelsea's Eighth Avenue runway via this "quint-essential" French bistro offering "accessible" traditional dishes ferried by a "knows-its-stuff" staff; pricing is fairly "reasonable", while a "moonlit garden" eases the "tight" crush indoors.

Gazala Place *Mideastern* | 23 | 8 | 19 | $27 |

W 40s | 709 Ninth Ave. (bet. 48th & 49th Sts.) | 212-245-0709
NEW **W 70s** | 380 Columbus Ave., upstairs (78th St.) | 212-873-8880
www.gazalaplace.com

"Terrific" Druse cooking is the specialty of this Hell's Kitchen Mideasterner where the "superbly made", low-priced chow and equally "delectable" BYO policy compensate for the "comically cramped" digs; P.S. a roomier UWS spin-off opened post-Survey.

Geido ⓜ *Japanese* | 24 | 15 | 21 | $31 |

Prospect Heights | 331 Flatbush Ave. (7th Ave.) | Brooklyn | 718-638-8866

There are "no frills and no gimmicks" at this longtime, "perpetually packed" Prospect Heights Japanese, just a "dependable" assortment of "superb" sushi that doesn't "strain the pocketbook"; "neighborly" service and "quirky" "Basquiat-esque" wall art enhance its "real-deal" appeal.

Geisha ⓩ *Japanese* | 23 | 21 | 21 | $65 |

E 60s | 33 E. 61st St. (bet. Madison & Park Aves.) | 212-813-1113 | www.geisharestaurant.com

"Sexy and sophisticated", this UES Japanese duplex seduces an "interesting" crowd with a "not-traditional", French-accented menu accessorized with an "excellent" cocktail list; although "expensive for what it is", it's more reasonable "when you factor in the scene."

| | FOOD | DECOR | SERVICE | COST |

Gemma ● *Italian*
20 **22** **19** **$49**

E Village | Bowery Hotel | 335 Bowery (bet. 2nd & 3rd Sts.) | 212-505-9100 | www.theboweryhotel.com

Gawking at "models and musicians" is a favorite pastime at this "sceney" Italian trattoria in the Bowery Hotel; regulars report "authentic", well-priced fare and a "rustic farmhouse" setting that really "shines" – thanks to about "a million candles."

General Greene *American*
20 **16** **18** **$33**

Fort Greene | 229 DeKalb Ave. (Clermont Ave.) | Brooklyn | 718-222-1510 | www.thegeneralgreene.com

Perfect "before the Brooklyn Flea", this "low-key" Fort Greene New American lures "locavores" with affordably priced "seasonal" small plates; those who "wish they could cook this at home" are pleased that a back-room grocery now sells the same ingredients served up front.

Gennaro ⊟ *Italian*
24 **15** **19** **$40**

W 90s | 665 Amsterdam Ave. (bet. 92nd & 93rd Sts.) | 212-665-5348

"Dostoevsky-loaded Kindles" help diners "endure the wait" at this no-rezzie, no-plastic Italian, the "worst-kept secret" on the UWS thanks to "scrumptious" eats at "terrifically low" prices; a recent "expansion" eases the "squeeze", but the "deafening" acoustics remain.

Ghenet *Ethiopian*
▽ **23** **17** **19** **$28**

Park Slope | 348 Douglass St. (bet. 4th & 5th Aves.) | Brooklyn | 718-230-4476 | www.ghenet.com

"Authentic", "well-spiced" Ethiopian food draws adventurous eaters to this "friendly", "off-the-beaten-path" Park Slope spot; low tabs and share-worthy platters make it especially "great for groups."

Gigino Trattoria *Italian*
21 **20** **19** **$47**

TriBeCa | 323 Greenwich St. (bet. Duane & Reade Sts.) | 212-431-1112 | www.gigino-trattoria.com

Gigino at Wagner Park *Italian*

Financial District | 20 Battery Pl. (West St.) | 212-528-2228 | www.gigino-wagnerpark.com

TriBeCans swear there's "fresh Tuscan air" wafting through the casual "farmhouse" setting of this "easygoing" trattoria known for its pleasing pizzas and pastas; the "hard-to-find" Wagner Park offshoot boasts "whew!" views of "Miss Liberty" from its waterfront terrace.

☒ Gilt ⧉Ⓜ *American*
24 **27** **26** **$116**

E 50s | NY Palace Hotel | 455 Madison Ave. (bet. 50th & 51st Sts.) | 212-891-8100 | www.giltnewyork.com

A "24-karat experience" awaits at this "luxurious" New American in the Palace Hotel, where the "inventive" prix fixe–only menu is served by a "polished" team in a "beautiful old-NY setting" once owned by the Archdiocese of New York; needless to say, all this "over-the-top" "elegance" comes at a comparable cost.

Giorgione *Italian*
24 **20** **21** **$57**

SoHo | 307 Spring St. (bet. Greenwich & Hudson Sts.) | 212-352-2269 | www.giorgionenyc.com

"As-good-as-it-gets" pizza and pasta draw "hip" locals to this "energetic" West SoHo Italiano equipped with a fireplace and wood-burning oven; owner Giorgio DeLuca (Dean & DeLuca) is often a "welcoming" presence in the "contemporary" room.

Giorgio's of Gramercy *American*　　21 | 18 | 21 | $47

Flatiron | 27 E. 21st St. (bet. B'way & Park Ave. S.) | 212-477-0007 | www.giorgiosofgramercy.com

"Still going strong", this longtime Flatiron New American offers "dependable" eats that "won't break the bank" in a "narrow", "softly lit" setting; fans say it's an "underappreciated" "neighborhood secret" that deserves greater recognition.

Giovanni Venticinque *Italian*　　▽ 23 | 19 | 24 | $69

E 80s | 25 E. 83rd St. (bet. 5th & Madison Aves.) | 212-988-7300 | www.giovanniventicinque.com

"Steps from the Met", this "intime" UES Tuscan "cossets" its "blue-hair" fan base with "terrific" food, "wonderful" service and an overall "old-world" mien; though it's "pricey", the $25 prix fixe lunch is a steal.

Girasole *Italian*　　23 | 18 | 22 | $61

E 80s | 151 E. 82nd St. (bet. Lexington & 3rd Aves.) | 212-772-6690

"Pleasantly adult" and "somewhat clubby", this longtime UES Italian attracts a "well-deserved local following" with "top-notch", "expensive" food and "old-school" service; though the decor "needs updating", the "warm welcome" is fine as is.

Glass House Tavern ● *American*　　21 | 21 | 22 | $46

W 40s | 252 W. 47th St. (bet. B'way & 8th Ave.) | 212-730-4800 | www.glasshousetavern.com

There's "something for everyone" on the New American menu of this "cheery", "upscale" player in the Theater District; "top-notch" service, a "spiffy" bi-level setting, "good value" and the chance for some "Broadway stargazing" make it worthy of an "encore."

Gnocco ● *Italian*　　24 | 17 | 20 | $39

E Village | 337 E. 10th St. (bet. Aves. A & B) | 212-677-1913 | www.gnocco.com

"Delicious" Emilian eats, "tasty pizzas" and the "not-to-be-missed" golden-fried namesake dish are dispatched by an "efficient" crew at this "snug" East Village Italian featuring "fantastic wines" from The Boot to boot; a "romantic", "gorgeous garden" seals the deal.

Gobo *Vegan/Vegetarian*　　22 | 18 | 19 | $35

E 80s | 1426 Third Ave. (81st St.) | 212-288-5099
W Village | 401 Sixth Ave. (bet. 8th St. & Waverly Pl.) | 212-255-3242
www.goborestaurant.com

Uptown and down, these "crowd-pleasers" turn out "tantalizing" Asian-accented vegan/vegetarian fare so "alive with flavor" that even "flesh-eating skeptics" consider going "herbivorous"; "moderate costs", pleasantly "Zen" surroundings and "swift service" supplement the "surprisingly satisfying" experience.

Golden Unicorn *Chinese*　　21 | 12 | 14 | $27

Chinatown | 18 E. Broadway, 2nd fl. (Catherine St.) | 212-941-0911 | www.goldenunicornrestaurant.com

Brace yourself for a "loud, frenetic blur" at this "very big, very fast", very crowded C-town dim sum palace where "parading carts" roll out an

| | FOOD | DECOR | SERVICE | COST |

"endless variety" of tidbits; prices are "low", the "garish" digs "tumultuous" and the service "brusque" – in short, "there's nothing else like it."

Good *American* | 19 | 16 | 18 | $37 |

W Village | 89 Greenwich Ave. (bet. Bank & W. 12th Sts.) | 212-691-8080 | www.goodrestaurantnyc.com

"Surprisingly good" – given the "modest name" – this "simple" West Villager dispenses "reliable" New American mains plus "heavenly seasonal desserts" for a "reasonable" tariff; just plan on "long waits" and "absentminded" service at its "amazing brunch."

Goodburger *Burgers* | 17 | 9 | 13 | $15 |

E 40s | 800 Second Ave. (42nd St.) | 212-922-1700
E 50s | 636 Lexington Ave. (54th St.) | 212-838-6000
NEW **Financial District** | 101 Maiden Ln. (Pearl St.) | 212-797-1700
Flatiron | 870 Broadway (bet. 17th & 18th Sts.) | 212-529-9100
W 40s | 23 W. 45th St. (bet. 5th & 6th Aves.) | 212-354-0900
NEW **W 50s** | 977 Eighth Ave. (bet. 57th & 58th Sts.) | 212-245-2200
www.goodburgerny.com

"Aptly named", this burger chain churns out "made-to-order" chargrilled "hangover cures" along with "great skinny fries" and "waist-enhancing shakes"; despite "spendy" tabs, "muddled service" and "ghastly loud music", they're "always crowded."

Good Enough to Eat *American* | 20 | 15 | 17 | $27 |

W 80s | 483 Amsterdam Ave. (bet. 83rd & 84th Sts.) | 212-496-0163 | www.goodenoughtoeat.com

An UWS "standby" for 30 years, this "popular" American suits with "top-flight comfort food" served in a "cute farmhouse setting", right down to the white picket fence out front; service is just "ok", but its "ultimate" brunch is "good enough to wait in a long line for."

Good Fork ⓜ *Eclectic* | 25 | 19 | 22 | $43 |

Red Hook | 391 Van Brunt St. (bet. Coffey & Van Dyke Sts.) | Brooklyn | 718-643-6636 | www.goodfork.com

"Getting there is an adventure" but the payoff is "seriously good eats" at this "laid-back" Red Hook Eclectic turning out "sophisticated", Asian-accented chow at "reasonable" tabs; a "friendly" crew mans the "diminutive", "rustic" space while the "delightful backyard" eases the crush.

Gordon Ramsay ⓈⓂ *French* | 23 | 22 | 22 | $143 |

W 50s | London NYC Hotel | 151 W. 54th St. (bet. 6th & 7th Aves.) | 212-468-8888 | www.gordonramsay.com

Although the "firebrand" himself is now just a consultant, Gordon Ramsay's "recipes live on" at this "stylish" prix fixe–only Midtown French where an "on-top-of-it" team totes top-flight fare in "sleek" "modern" digs exuding "luxury"; still, cynics nix the "astronomical prices" and say it's just "not as good without the master" – sort of like *Hell's Kitchen* without Gordon.

🅩 Gotham Bar & Grill *American* | 27 | 25 | 26 | $79 |

G Village | 12 E. 12th St. (bet. 5th Ave. & University Pl.) | 212-620-4020 | www.gothambarandgrill.com

"Still wowing" Gotham "after all these years", this "simply marvelous" Villager strikes all the "right chords", from "master chef" Alfred Portale's "glorious", "towering" New American dishes to the "soaring" setting and "exemplary" service; it's worth the "zillion-dollar tabs" for such a "thoroughly enjoyable", "first-class experience", though bargain-hunters tout its "amazing" $31 lunch.

Gottino ● *Italian* | 22 | 20 | 20 | $39

W Village | 52 Greenwich Ave. (bet. Charles & Perry Sts.) | 212-633-2590 | www.ilmiogottino.com

"Imaginative", "well-executed" Italian nibbles and a "wonderful" vino selection make this "atmospheric" Village enoteca a "convivial" desti-nation; despite "tight quarters", the vibe's "comfortable", especially in the "tiny back garden."

Grace's Trattoria *Italian* | 18 | 16 | 19 | $44

E 70s | 201 E. 71st St. (bet. 2nd & 3rd Aves.) | 212-452-2323 | www.gracestrattoria.net

A "low-key local", this UES Italian is a "dependable favorite" for "sim-ple", "competently prepared" food that matches the standards of owner Grace's Marketplace next door; "retirees" and "ladies doing lunch" applaud the "unrushed service" but not the "boring" decor.

Gradisca *Italian* | 23 | 17 | 20 | $52

W Village | 126 W. 13th St. (bet. 6th Ave. & 7th Ave. S.) | 212-691-4886 | www.gradiscanyc.com

"Superb" homemade pasta makes the grade at this "cozy" Village trat-toria whose "traditional" Italian dishes feature an "original touch"; "charming", sometimes "flirty", service keeps things "romantic" even as the "noise level" rises, muting the suspicion that "prices have gone up."

Graffiti Ⓜ *Eclectic* | 25 | 15 | 22 | $48

E Village | 224 E. 10th St. (bet. 1st & 2nd Aves.) | 212-677-0695 | www.graffitinyc.com

"Foodies looking for nirvana" find something close to it at chef Jehangir Mehta's "tiny" East Village Eclectic dispensing "heavenly" small plates with "spirited" Indian spins at "fair prices"; you get "more legroom fly-ing economy" than at the communal table, but it's "worth the squish."

Ⓩ Gramercy Tavern *American* | 28 | 26 | 27 | $112

Flatiron | 42 E. 20th St. (bet. B'way & Park Ave. S.) | 212-477-0777 | www.gramercytavern.com

"Firmly established as one of the city's finest" (and again voted Most Popular), Danny Meyer's "perfecto" Flatiron "powerhouse" dazzles thanks to chef Michael Anthony's "dash-of-panache" New American cuisine, "tone-perfect" service and a "flower-festooned", "country-chic" setting that "oozes charm"; it's certainly worth the "steep prices" in the "stately", prix fixe–only main room, though the front bar is a "wonderful" alternative that "will save you some bucks."

Grand Sichuan *Chinese* | 22 | 9 | 14 | $27

Chelsea | 229 Ninth Ave. (24th St.) | 212-620-5200 ●
Chinatown | 125 Canal St. (Chrystie St.) | 212-625-9212 ⊄
E 50s | 1049 Second Ave. (bet. 55th & 56th Sts.) | 212-355-5855
E Village | 19-23 St. Marks Pl. (bet. 2nd & 3rd Aves.) | 212-529-4800
Murray Hill | 227 Lexington Ave. (bet. 33rd & 34th Sts.) | 212-679-9770
NEW W 40s | 368 W. 46th St. (bet. 8th & 9th Aves.) | 212-969-9001
W Village | 15 Seventh Ave. S. (bet. Carmine & Leroy Sts.) | 212-645-0222

(continued)

Grand Sichuan

Rego Park | 98-108 Queens Blvd. (bet. 66th Rd. & 67th Ave.) | Queens | 718-268-8833
www.thegrandsichuan.com

"Spice is king" at this "incendiary" Chinese chain churning out an "amazing array" of "superior" Sichuan dishes for "chump change"; it's "no-frills" all the way, however, with "zero decor" and "perfunctory service", so it may be best to "order in" or "take out."

Grand Tier ⊠ *Italian*   20 | 26 | 24 | $83

W 60s | Metropolitan Opera House, 2nd fl. | Lincoln Center Plaza (bet. 63rd & 65th Sts.) | 212-799-3400 | www.patinagroup.com

"Grand is the word" for the "glitter-and-glitz" balcony setting of this Lincoln Center Italian "overlooking the Met foyer", where the "polite" staff is more than "adept at timing"; "prices are as high as a soprano", but "nothing's more chic than eating at the opera" – and the "food's not bad", either.

Gray's Papaya ●♥ *Hot Dogs*   20 | 4 | 14 | $7

Garment District | 539 Eighth Ave. (37th St.) | 212-904-1588
G Village | 402 Sixth Ave. (8th St.) | 212-260-3532
W 70s | 2090 Broadway (72nd St.) | 212-799-0243

These "no-fuss-no-muss" counter-service "institutions" dole out "hot-diggity dogs" with a "juicy snap" washed down with frothy fruit drinks to a very "mixed" crowd; despite the "glorious heartburn", they're "Big Apple rituals" that are open 24/7 and "dirt-cheap" to boot.

Great Jones Cafe ● *Cajun*   20 | 14 | 16 | $28

NoHo | 54 Great Jones St. (bet. Bowery & Lafayette St.) | 212-674-9304 | www.greatjones.com

"Unpretentious", cheap Cajun cooking draws fans to this "tiny", "down-home" NoHo "dive" best known for its "soul-satisfying" brunch; there's always a wait at "peak hours", despite the "noise" and "slow service."

Great NY Noodle Town ●♥ *Noodle Shop*   22 | 5 | 11 | $18

Chinatown | 28½ Bowery (Bayard St.) | 212-349-0923

Usually "mobbed", this "elbow-to-elbow" C-towner dishes out "abundant" amounts of "delectable noodles" and "salt-baked seafood"; "cheaper-than-cheap" tabs for terrific food trump the "greasy-spoon" decor and "language-problem" service.

Greek Kitchen *Greek*   19 | 13 | 19 | $31

W 50s | 889 10th Ave. (58th St.) | 212-581-4300 | www.greekkitchennyc.com

A "short stroll" from Lincoln Center and thus "convenient for concert-goers", this "low-key" Hell's Kitchen taverna pairs "tasty" "traditional" Greek cooking with "prompt service"; true, the setting's "not fancy", but it's hard to beat "for the price."

Greenhouse Café *American*   19 | 19 | 20 | $35

Bay Ridge | 7717 Third Ave. (bet. 77th & 78th Sts.) | Brooklyn | 718-833-8200 | www.greenhousecafe.com

Whether for a "casual date" or a "romantic dinner", this longtime Bay Ridge "favorite" fits the bill with "quality" New Americana delivered by a "genuinely friendly" staff; the glassed-in greenhouse room is "lovely" and, capping it off, "the price is right."

	FOOD	DECOR	SERVICE	COST

Greenwich Grill/
Sushi Azabu *Japanese/Mediterranean*

▽ 25 | 21 | 23 | $60

TriBeCa | 428 Greenwich St. (bet. Laight & Vestry Sts.) | 212-274-0428 | www.greenwichgrill.com

Behind the "nondescript door" of this "cool" TriBeCa "sleeper" lies some "delicious", "truly unusual" Japanese-Mediterranean fusion fare on the ground floor, and sushi that "ranks with the best" downstairs; the staff is "attentive", and the fair "value" means you'll likely leave "glowing."

Grifone ⓩ *Italian*

23 | 18 | 24 | $66

E 40s | 244 E. 46th St. (bet. 2nd & 3rd Aves.) | 212-490-7275 | www.grifonenyc.com

"Service reminiscent of a bygone era" is the calling card of this "superior" Northern Italian near the U.N. serving a "solid" selection of classic dishes; ok, it's "hard on the wallet" but it's easy to have a "quiet conversation" in the "old-fashioned", "1960s"-style digs.

Grimaldi's ⊄ *Pizza*

24 | 11 | 15 | $22

Dumbo | 19 Old Fulton St. (bet. Front & Water Sts.) | Brooklyn | 718-858-4300
Douglaston | Douglaston Plaza | 242-02 61st Ave. (bet. Douglaston Pkwy. & 244th St.) | Queens | 718-819-2133
www.grimaldis.com

Pie-eyed pilgrims profusely praise the "perfect pizzas" at this "iconic", cash-only Dumbo "destination" where "painful waits" and "rushed-in-and-out" service are part of the package; there are "no lines" at the Queens outlet, and a scaled-down version in the Flatiron's Limelight Marketplace is in the works.

ⓩ Grocery, The ⓢⓜ *American*

26 | 17 | 25 | $61

Carroll Gardens | 288 Smith St. (bet. Sackett & Union Sts.) | Brooklyn | 718-596-3335 | www.thegroceryrestaurant.com

"Consistently brilliant", "locavore"-leaning New American cuisine makes this Carroll Gardens destination a top "contender" in the "lively Smith Street scene"; a "beautiful garden" eases the squeeze in the minimalist, "matchbox"-esque dining room, while "personal attention" from a "gracious" staff renders the "splurge"-worthy tabs more palatable.

Grotta Azzurra ☽ *Italian*

17 | 15 | 17 | $44

Little Italy | 177 Mulberry St. (Broome St.) | 212-925-8775 | www.grottaazzurrany.com

"Homestyle" Southern Italian comfort food and "gruff service" lend a "classic Little Italy" feel to this re-creation of the 1908 antecedent; sure, it's "touristy" and a "far cry from the original", but there's a "catacombs"-like feel in the wine cellar and "good value" in the specials.

Gruppo *Pizza*

24 | 11 | 18 | $24

E Village | 186 Ave. B (bet. 11th & 12th Sts.) | 212-995-2100 | www.gruppothincrust.com

"Hipsters" report that the "delicious", "paper-thin"-crust pizza at this "small" East Villager "refuses to droop", even after the "marvelous" "high-end" toppings are piled on; it's often "hard to get a seat" but they do "deliver to your door."

	FOOD	DECOR	SERVICE	COST

Gusto *Italian*
23 | 20 | 20 | $49

W Village | 60 Greenwich Ave. (Perry St.) | 212-924-8000 |
www.gustonyc.com

Despite "revolving-door chefs", the "innovative" cooking at this
Village Italian remains "delicious", with "standout specials" and prix
fixe "bargains"; an "accommodating" team mans the "modern" space,
but "forget having a conversation" when the "scene" gains gusto.

Gyu-Kaku *Japanese*
21 | 20 | 19 | $46

E 40s | 805 Third Ave., 2nd fl. (bet. 49th & 50th Sts.) | 212-702-8816
E Village | 34 Cooper Sq. (bet. Astor Pl. & 4th St.) | 212-475-2989
www.gyu-kaku.com

Folks fond of "playing with fire" plug these "stylish" Japanese fran-
chises, the "ultimate in interactive dining" where you can "cook your
own" meals on charcoal braziers; it's a "blast", even if all those "small
portions" can mount up to a "big tab."

Hale & Hearty Soups *Sandwiches/Soup*
19 | 8 | 13 | $12

Chelsea | Chelsea Mkt. | 75 Ninth Ave. (bet. 15th & 16th Sts.) |
212-255-2400
E 40s | 685 Third Ave. (bet. 43rd & 44th Sts.) | 212-681-6460 ⊠
E 40s | Grand Central | lower level (42nd St. & Vanderbilt Ave.) |
212-983-2845
E 60s | 849 Lexington Ave. (bet. 64th & 65th Sts.) | 212-517-7600
Financial District | 55 Broad St. (bet. Beaver St. & Exchange Pl.) |
212-509-4100 ⊠
Garment District | 462 Seventh Ave. (35th St.) | 212-971-0605 ⊠
W 40s | 30 Rockefeller Plaza (49th St.) | 212-265-2117 ⊠
W 40s | 49 W. 42nd St. (bet. 5th & 6th Aves.) | 212-575-9090 ⊠
W 50s | 55 W. 56th St. (bet. 5th & 6th Aves.) | 212-245-9200 ⊠
Brooklyn Heights | 32 Court St. (Remsen St.) | Brooklyn |
718-596-5600 ⊠
www.haleandhearty.com
Additional locations throughout the NY area

"Flavorful" soups plus "freshly made" sandwiches and salads soothe
the "harried" working-class masses at this all-over-town counter-
service chain; "utilitarian" digs, "not-so-swift" service and "madhouse" atmospheres at lunchtime come with the territory.

Hallo Berlin *German*
18 | 8 | 13 | $22

W 40s | 626 10th Ave. (bet. 44th & 45th Sts.) | 212-977-1944 |
www.halloberlinrestaurant.com

"Solid Teutonic feasts" featuring the "best wursts" and "good draft"
brews are the lure at this "basic" Hell's Kitchen Deutschlander;
das tabs are "cheap", but the "dumpy" decor drives diners to the
"mini-beer garden."

Hampton Chutney Co. *Indian*
20 | 10 | 14 | $17

SoHo | 68 Prince St. (bet. Crosby & Lafayette Sts.) | 212-226-9996
W 80s | 464 Amsterdam Ave. (bet. 82nd & 83rd Sts.) |
212-362-5050
www.hamptonchutney.com

Putting a "fusion spin" on its "damn good dosas", this toothsome
Indian twosome is a "healthy", "cheap" alternative to the typical fast-
food options; they're "reliable fueling stations" for the SoHo set and
"popular with the baby-carriage crowd" on the UWS.

	FOOD	DECOR	SERVICE	COST

Hanci Turkish Cuisine *Turkish* — 22 | 13 | 20 | $34

W 50s | 854 10th Ave. (bet. 56th & 57th Sts.) | 212-707-8144 |
www.hanciturkishnyc.com

Enlivening a far-out stretch of 10th Avenue, this "endearing", family-
run Hell's Kitchen Turk turns out "bright, zesty" grub in "shareable
portions"; "congenial" service and "inexpensive" pricing trumps
the "bare-bones" setting.

Hanco's *Vietnamese* — 21 | 7 | 14 | $11

Boerum Hill | 85 Bergen St. (bet. Hoyt & Smith Sts.) | Brooklyn |
718-858-6818 ⌷

Park Slope | 350 Seventh Ave. (10th St.) | Brooklyn | 718-499-8081
www.hancosny.com

"Filled to brimming", the sandwiches at this Vietnamese duo deliver
"banh-mi bliss" with a "spicy kick", washed down with "tasty bubble
teas"; the newer Park Slope outpost is roomier than the Boerum Hill
original, but both are "priced right" and "ever busy."

☑ HanGawi *Korean* — 24 | 24 | 23 | $47

Murray Hill | 12 E. 32nd St. (bet. 5th & Madison Aves.) | 212-213-0077 |
www.hangawirestaurant.com

"Transportive" is the word on this Murray Hill vegetarian where "dazzling" Korean dishes, "marvelous" service and "peaceful" environs
leave acolytes feeling "soothed"; though a bit "pricey", most feel it's
"good value", but be sure to "wear your best socks" – "shoes come off
at the door."

Harrison, The *American* — 24 | 21 | 23 | $61

TriBeCa | 355 Greenwich St. (Harrison St.) | 212-274-9310 |
www.theharrison.com

A "class act all-around", this "sophisticated" TriBeCan offers "sublime", Med-inspired New Americana, "unobtrusive" service and a setting exuding "low-key elegance"; it's "not cheap", but its "dressed-
up", "energetic crowd" digs the "adult dining" experience; P.S. Jimmy
Bradley is taking over from Amanda Freitag in the kitchen.

Harry Cipriani ❶ *Italian* — 21 | 21 | 21 | $93

E 50s | Sherry-Netherland Hotel | 781 Fifth Ave. (bet. 59th & 60th Sts.) |
212-753-5566 | www.cipriani.com

Home to the "priciest air kisses in Manhattan", this Sherry-Netherland
"institution" is mostly about "rubbing elbows with the elite" but the
Venetian victuals are also appealing; "unbeatable Bellinis" and prime
people-watching distract from the "off-the-wall" tabs, yet still some
shrug "leave it to the glitterati."

Harry's Cafe ❶☒ *Steak* — 23 | 21 | 22 | $54

Financial District | 1 Hanover Sq. (bet. Pearl & Stone Sts.) |
212-785-9200

Harry's Steak ☒ *Steak*

Financial District | 97 Pearl St. (bet. Broad St. & Hanover Sq.) |
212-785-9200
www.harrysnyc.com

Practically "synonymous with Wall Street", this Financial District duo
in the landmark India House provides "power" types with "top-notch
steaks" in the "old-school" downstairs chop shop and "straightfor-

ward" Eclectic eats in the cafe above; the wow-worthy wine cellar is one of the city's best.

Harry's Italian   *Italian*
| 21 | 18 | 20 | $33 |

Financial District | 2 Gold St. (bet. Maiden Ln. & Platt St.) | 212-747-0797 | www.harrysitalian.com

A "new favorite in the FiDi", this recent addition to the Harry's empire features "amazing pizzas" and "tasty" Italian standards, served by a "helpful" team; rates are "wallet-friendly", while the "outdoor seating is a bonus", given the "rumpus-room" racket within.

Haru   *Japanese*
| 20 | 17 | 18 | $42 |

E 40s | 280 Park Ave. (enter on 48th St., bet. Madison & Park Aves.) | 212-490-9680
E 70s | 1327 Third Ave. (76th St.) | 212-452-1028 ●
E 70s | 1329 Third Ave. (76th St.) | 212-452-2230 ●
Financial District | 1 Wall Street Ct. (bet. Beaver & Pearl Sts.) | 212-785-6850
Flatiron | 220 Park Ave. S. (18th St.) | 646-428-0989 ●
W 40s | 205 W. 43rd St. (bet. B'way & 8th Ave.) | 212-398-9810 ●
W 80s | 433 Amsterdam Ave. (bet. 80th & 81st Sts.) | 212-579-5655 ●
www.haruaousni.com

Those craving a "sushi fix" tout this "safe-bet" Japanese chain for its "whale-size" pieces of "glistening fish" dispensed at "won't-break-the-bank" prices; the settings are "spare", the pacing "frenzied" and the mood beyond "lively" thanks to the "loud, loud, loud" acoustics.

Hasaki ● *Japanese*
| 24 | 14 | 18 | $46 |

E Village | 210 E. Ninth St. (bet. 2nd & 3rd Aves.) | 212-473-3327 | www.hasakinyc.com

On the East Village scene since '84, this "tiny" Japanese offers "beautiful presentations" of "fresh, delectable" sushi plus "outstanding hot dishes" for an "ok price"; despite "tight quarters" and no reservations, it's a "local favorite", so regulars "bear the lines or eat early."

Hatsuhana   ☒ *Japanese*
| 25 | 17 | 22 | $57 |

E 40s | 17 E. 48th St. (bet. 5th & Madison Aves.) | 212-355-3345
E 40s | 237 Park Ave. (46th St.) | 212-661-3400
www.hatsuhana.com

The 48th Street flagship was one of the first to introduce sushi to Midtown in 1976, and today these "exceptional" Japanese still supply "first-quality" delicacies perfect for business-lunching; the only caveat: the "modest" settings seem rather "stale" when compared to the fish.

Havana Alma de Cuba   *Cuban*
| 21 | 16 | 18 | $39 |

W Village | 94 Christopher St. (bet. Bedford & Bleecker Sts.) | 212-242-3800 | www.havananyc.com

"Familiar" Cuban "favorites" washed down with "awesome" sangria keep "cool crowds" coming to this "funky" Villager; "attentive" service, a "hidden" garden and "reasonable" rates make for a "festive" mood.

Havana Central   *Cuban*
| 18 | 16 | 16 | $33 |

Union Sq | 22 E. 17th St. (bet. B'way & 5th Ave.) | 212-414-4999
W 40s | 151 W. 46th St. (bet. 6th & 7th Aves.) | 212-398-7440
W 100s | 2911 Broadway (bet. 113th & 114th Sts.) | 212-662-8830
www.havanacentral.com

A "party atmosphere" prevails at these "noisy" Cuban "theme parks" known for "simple", "serviceable" grub, "potent" "love potion–type" drinks, "live Latin music" and prices that "aren't bad"; service is "sketchy", but the "young" crowd is having too "mucho fun" to notice.

Haveli ● Indian
21 | 15 | 20 | $32

E Village | 100 Second Ave. (bet. 5th & 6th Sts.) | 212-982-0533 | www.havelinyc.com

Rated "a notch above" its Sixth Street kin, this East Village Indian offers "delicately prepared" food and "solicitous" service in "humble" digs; since it's "not run of the mill", the slightly higher tariffs are "reasonable."

Hearth American/Italian
24 | 19 | 23 | $64

E Village | 403 E. 12th St. (1st Ave.) | 646-602-1300 | www.restauranthearth.com

Bringing "true dining" to the funky East Village, this "memorable" Tuscan-American foodie favorite leaves fans "blown away" by Marco Canora's "soulful" cooking, backed up by "congenial" service; sure, it's "pricey", but ultimately this place "never disappoints"; for best results, "snag a spot at the counter overlooking the kitchen."

Heartland Brewery Pub Food
14 | 14 | 15 | $30

Garment District | Empire State Bldg. | 350 Fifth Ave. (34th St.) | 212-563-3433
Seaport | 93 South St. (Fulton St.) | 646-572-2337
Union Sq | 35 Union Sq. W. (bet. 16th & 17th Sts.) | 212-645-3400
W 40s | 127 W. 43rd St. (bet. B'way & 6th Ave.) | 646-366-0235
NEW W 40s | Port Authority | 625 Eighth Ave. (41st St.) | 646-214-1000
W 50s | 1285 Sixth Ave. (51st St.) | 212-582-8244
www.heartlandbrewery.com

"Beer is the star" of the show at this "generic" microbrewery chain that some dub an "upscale T.G.I. Friday's"; despite "pedestrian" pub grub and "lackluster" service, these "boisterous" joints come alive at "happy hour" when they're flooded with young NYers and "tourists."

NEW Hecho en Dumbo ● Mexican
▽ 25 | 20 | 18 | $35

NoHo | 354 Bowery (bet. 4th & Great Jones Sts.) | 212-937-4245 | www.hechoendumbo.com

"Mexico City street food" fills out the small-plates menu of this "buzzy" newcomer, a Dumbo cult favorite now relocated to the Bowery; the food's "fantastic", the tabs "cheap", the decor "sparse" and the "prime" seats are at the "counter facing the kitchen."

Heidelberg German
20 | 17 | 18 | $38

E 80s | 1648 Second Ave. (bet. 85th & 86th Sts.) | 212-628-2332 | www.heidelbergrestaurant.com

A "last vestige" of "old Yorkville", this circa-1938 "bastion of German cuisine" specializes in "*der beste* wursts" and "das boots" of beer in a "wonderfully schmaltzy" setting; maybe it's "hokey", but "lively music" and staffers in "traditional garb" keep the mood "*gemütlich.*"

NEW Hello Pasta Italian
- | - | - | I

E 40s | 708 Third Ave. (bet. 44th & 45th Sts.) | 212-557-2782
E 50s | 649 Lexington Ave. (bet. 54th & 55th Sts.) | 212-557-2782
www.hellopasta.com

This new, fast-casual Italian chainlet offers an affordable lineup of pasta and sauces that can be mixed and matched; though there's limited seating available, it's geared to takeout or delivery.

	FOOD	DECOR	SERVICE	COST

Hell's Kitchen *Mexican* | 23 | 16 | 19 | $44

W 40s | 679 Ninth Ave. (bet. 46th & 47th Sts.) | 212-977-1588 |
www.hellskitchen-nyc.com

"High energy" meets "high-end" Nuevo Mexicana at this "crowded"
Clinton cantina where the food is even more "tasty" when paired with a
"head-spinning" margarita; "fair prices" and "considerate" service
make it a natural "pre-theater", even though it can get "hellishly noisy."

NEW **Henry Public** ●⇆ *Pub Food* | ▽ 17 | 21 | 18 | $31

Cobble Hill | 329 Henry St. (bet. Atlantic & Pacific Sts.) | Brooklyn |
718-852-8630 | www.henrypublic.com

Exuding an "old NY tavern feel" that's the "new Brooklyn formula",
this "nifty" Cobble Hill American offers a "limited menu" focused
around a "killer burger" and an "amazing turkey sandwich"; some say
it's more bar than restaurant, but agree it's a "wonderful addition."

Henry's End *American* | 24 | 15 | 23 | $47

Brooklyn Heights | 44 Henry St. (bet. Cranberry & Middagh Sts.) |
Brooklyn | 718-834-1776 | www.henrysend.com

Famed for its "wonderful wild game", this longtime Brooklyn Heights
"institution" also assembles "amazing" New American dishes in its "tiny
open kitchen"; a "loyal clientele" appreciates the "gracious" service and
"well-priced" tabs, but wishes it weren't so "claustrophobically small."

Hibino *Japanese* | 25 | 18 | 21 | $34

Cobble Hill | 333 Henry St. (Pacific St.) | Brooklyn | 718-260-8052 |
www.hibino-brooklyn.com

"They know tofu" at this "unusual", "destination-worthy" Cobble Hill
Japanese that also vends "unusual sushi" and "craveable" Kyoto-style
obanzai (small plates) that change daily; "courteous" service and "excellent value" add to the pleasantly "chill" vibe.

NEW **Hide-Chan** ●⑤ *Noodle Shop* | – | – | – | I

E 50s | 248 E. 52nd St., 2nd fl. (bet. 2nd & 3rd Aves.) | 212-813-1800

Warm, rich woods and slate floors add a touch of class to this otherwise basic East Midtowner, a ramen-slinging member of the Totto
family set in the former Yakitori Torys space; its affordable offerings
include a creamy, porky *tonkotsu* broth, its signature dish.

NEW **Highpoint Bistro** *American* | – | – | – | M

Chelsea | 216 Seventh Ave. (bet. 22nd & 23rd Sts.) | 646-410-0120 |
www.highpointnyc.com

Set in the former Porters digs in Chelsea, this New American
arrival offers a midpriced menu served in a long, narrow space
simply appointed with exposed brick and blond wood; light boxes
feature scenes from the Hudson Valley, where the kitchen sources
many of its ingredients.

Hill Country *BBQ* | 22 | 16 | 15 | $34

Flatiron | 30 W. 26th St. (bet. B'way & 6th Ave.) | 212-255-4544 |
www.hillcountryny.com

"Urban cowboys" tout the "true Texas BBQ" at this "hectic" Flatiron "ar-
tery clogger" where the "finger-lickin'" eats are sold "by the pound" in
a great "big" double-decker space; despite "awkward" "do-it-yourself
service", it's "a hoot", and the "sides are as good as the meat.'"

| | FOOD | DECOR | SERVICE | COST |

Hillstone *American* — 21 | 19 | 20 | $41
(fka Houston's)
E 50s | Citicorp Building | 153 E. 53rd St. (enter on 3rd Ave. & 54th St.) |
212-888-3828
Murray Hill | NY Life Bldg. | 378 Park Ave. S. (27th St.) | 212-689-1090
www.hillstone.com
If "hopping" bar scenes, "can't-go-wrong" American eats and
"addictive spinach dip" aren't enough, this "popular" chain (fka
Houston's) ices the cake with "stylish" settings and seamless service; ultimately, you "get what you pay for" here, which explains why
it's "perpetually jammed."

HK ◑ *American* — 18 | 18 | 17 | $35
Garment District | 523 Ninth Ave. (39th St.) | 212-947-4208 |
www.hkhellskitchen.com
A "refuge" in an "area with few choices", this "hip" American parked
behind Port Authority attracts a "stylish", "gay-friendly" crowd with its
"trendy vibes", "good food" and "even better people-watching"; it's
"hectic" at brunch, "more sedate" for dinner and well priced all the time.

Holy Basil ◑ *Thai* — 21 | 18 | 18 | $32
E Village | 149 Second Ave., 2nd fl. (bet. 9th & 10th Sts.) | 212-460-5557 |
www.holybasilrestaurant.com
"Dark and sexy", this East Village Thai "standby" has all the ingredients for a "modest first date": "spicy" chow, "attentive" service and
"ridiculously reasonable" rates; regulars report it's "best on the balcony" to avoid the "noisy" main floor.

Home *American* — 22 | 17 | 20 | $44
W Village | 20 Cornelia St. (bet. Bleecker & W. 4th Sts.) | 212-243-9579 |
www.homerestaurantnyc.com
"Homey and then some", this West Villager "lives up to its name" with
"comfortingly delicious" American grub, "friendly" service and a
"cozy" atmosphere; though the "hallway"-size space can be too
"close" for some, the back patio is a "delightful" escape.

Hope & Anchor *Diner* — 19 | 15 | 19 | $24
Red Hook | 347 Van Brunt St. (Wolcott St.) | Brooklyn | 718-237-0276
Popular for "brunch, beers and banter", this "funky" diner in Red
Hook's "no-subway zone" matches a "massive menu" of "hearty"
Americana with "down-home service" and bargain-basement tabs;
it's "full of characters", especially for its "drag karaoke" on weekends.

Hotel Griffou ◑ *American* — 19 | 25 | 21 | $61
G Village | 21 W. Ninth St., downstairs (bet. 5th & 6th Aves.) | 212-358-0228
The "stellar bar scene" nearly outshines the "expensive" New American
cooking at this "cool" Village townhouse, though there's word the "food
is improving"; the subterranean "speakeasy" setting with five themed
dining chambers is just as "eye-popping" as the "eye-candy" crowd.

House, The ◑ *American* — 22 | 25 | 23 | $55
Gramercy | 121 E. 17th St. (bet. Irving Pl. & Park Ave. S.) | 212-353-2121 |
www.thehousenyc.com
Just plain "lovely" for a "romantic tête-à-tête" or drinks beside a "cozy"
fireplace", this Gramercy triplex follows through with a delightful ar-

ray of New American small plates delivered by an "attentive" staff; "everything here says special", from the "charming" 1854 carriage house setting to the serious tabs.

NEW Hudson Eatery *American*

FOOD	DECOR	SERVICE	COST
-	-	-	M

W 50s | 601 W. 57th St. (bet. 11th & 12th Aves.) | 212-265-2300

At this new, all-day Hell's Kitchen option, well-priced Americana is served in a cafeteria-meets-nightclub setting, done up in copper, leather and concrete; the airy, wide-open space echoes its airy, wide-open neighborhood, the car-dealership stretch of Way West 57th Street.

NEW Hudson Hall *American*

FOOD	DECOR	SERVICE	COST
-	-	-	M

W 50s | Hudson Hotel | 356 W. 58th St. (bet. 8th & 9th Aves.) | 212-554-6000 | www.morganshotelgroup.com

The former Hudson Cafeteria in the Hudson Hotel may have changed its name, but has morphed into an actual cafeteria where patrons help themselves to a variety of New American small plates; it's retained the same Gothic vibe and communal tables as before, now jazzed up with a wraparound video installation on the walls.

Hudson River Café *American/Seafood*

FOOD	DECOR	SERVICE	COST
21	22	20	$51

Harlem | 697 W. 133rd St. (12th Ave.) | 212-491-9111 | www.hudsonrivercafe.com

Helping "change the neighborhood", this "upscale" West Harlem American offers a satisfying, seafood-centric menu along with "lots to look at" (i.e. the "amazing" river views from its "beautiful" outdoor patios); "great service" and "live jazz" sweeten the pot.

Hummus Place *Israeli/Vegetarian*

FOOD	DECOR	SERVICE	COST
22	11	16	$17

E Village | 109 St. Marks Pl. (bet. Ave. A & 1st Ave.) | 212-529-9198 ●
G Village | 99 MacDougal St. (bet. Bleecker & W. 3rd Sts.) | 212-533-3089 ⊟
W 70s | 305 Amsterdam Ave. (bet. 74th & 75th Sts.) | 212-799-3335 ●
W 90s | 2608 Broadway (bet. 98th & 99th Sts.) | 212-222-1554 ●
W Village | 71 Seventh Ave. S. (bet. Barrow & Bleecker Sts.) | 212-924-2022 ●
www.hummusplace.com

These "low-tech", "bare-bones" Israeli joints "deliver on a simple promise": "super-creamy" hummus scooped up with "hot", "pillowy" pita bread; perfect for a "late-night snack", it's a "budget" stop that belongs on "every vegetarian's short list."

Hundred Acres *American*

FOOD	DECOR	SERVICE	COST
19	21	20	$45

SoHo | 38 MacDougal St. (Prince St.) | 212-475-7500 | www.hundredacresnyc.com

"Barnyard-chic" decor provides a fitting backdrop for the "fresh" "farm-to-table" grub served at this "breezy" SoHo New American (from the same stable as Cookshop and Five Points); "efficient service", "fair pricing" and a "fantastic brunch" all harvest praise.

NEW Hurricane Club ● *Polynesian*

FOOD	DECOR	SERVICE	COST
-	-	-	E

Flatiron | 360 Park Ave. S. (26th St.) | 212-951-7111 | www.thehurricaneclub.com

Restaurateur Michael Stillman and design team AvroKO (Quality Meats) blow into the Flatiron via this new Polynesian supper club that will serve a self-described 'decisively inauthentic' menu (with a pronounced Pan-Asian accent), washed down with a slew of deadly rum cocktails;

the wide-open setting features cozy, sectioned-off dining areas, in an atmosphere that's more Angkor Wat than tacky tiki.

Ici Ⓜ *American/French*   ∇ 22 | 19 | 21 | $39

Fort Greene | 246 DeKalb Ave. (bet. Clermont & Vanderbilt Aves.) | Brooklyn | 718-789-2778 | www.icirestaurant.com
"Lovingly prepared" with "super-fresh" organic ingredients, the "terrific" Franco-American food at this "earnest" Fort Greene boîte is also modestly priced; "friendly servers", an "understated" room and "lovely back garden" complete the picture.

I Coppi *Italian*   22 | 20 | 21 | $48

E Village | 432 E. Ninth St. (bet. Ave. A & 1st Ave.) | 212-254-2263 | www.icoppinyc.com
A "lush" year-round garden is the star of the show at this East Village "charmer" where the "true Tuscan experience" extends from the "farmhouse"-like interior to the "wonderful" Northern Italian cooking; "fine service" and midrange tabs round out the "inviting" picture.

Il Bagatto ◑Ⓜ *Italian*   24 | 17 | 19 | $42

E Village | 192 E. Second St. (bet. Aves. A & B) | 212-228-0977 | www.ilbagattonyc.com
It's "easy to be happy" at this "unpretentious" East Villager known for "down-home" Italian cooking, particularly its "handmade pastas"; "personal service" and "affordable" tabs make up for the "noise", "long waits" and "difficult prime-time reservations."

Il Bambino *Italian*   ∇ 24 | 17 | 22 | $20

Astoria | 34-08 31st Ave. (bet. 34th & 35th Sts.) | Queens | 718-626-0087 | www.ilbambinonyc.com
"Good vibes" emanate from this "neat little" Astoria pressed-sandwich specialist offering "damn good" panini along with other "delicious" Italian nibbles, all "priced right"; "helpful" staffers and a "great garden" lend it "neighborhood-favorite" status.

Il Bastardo ◑ *Italian/Steak*   18 | 16 | 17 | $40

Chelsea | 191 Seventh Ave. (bet. 21st & 22nd Sts.) | 212-675-5980 | www.ilbastardonyc.com
"Consistently good" cooking for "decent" dough – not to mention a cameo on *The Hills* – draws "young" diners to this Chelsea Tuscan steakhouse beloved for its "boozy brunch"; the next-door enoteca, Bar Baresco, offers "essentially the same menu" in more casual digs.

Ⓩ Il Buco ◑ *Italian/Mediterranean*   26 | 24 | 22 | $65

NoHo | 47 Bond St. (bet. Bowery & Lafayette St.) | 212-533-1932 | www.ilbuco.com
"Off-the-charts" Med-Italian cuisine made from "artisanal ingredients" is served by a "congenial" crew at this NoHo "celeb" magnet set in a transporting, "antiques"-laden "Tuscan-rustic" room; sure, it's "expensive", but fans call it "last meal"–worthy – especially in its "romantic wine cellar."

Il Cantinori *Italian*   23 | 22 | 22 | $65

G Village | 32 E. 10th St. (bet. B'way & University Pl.) | 212-673-6044
"Impressive in every way", this "luxe", circa-1983 Villager attracts "stylish" folk with its "casually perfect" Northern Italiana and "affable"

service; the "beautiful", "flower-bedecked" setting is just the ticket for a "hot date", although the prices lead wags to tag it "Il Cantaffordi."

Il Corallo Trattoria *Italian* | 22 | 12 | 17 | $28 |

SoHo | 176 Prince St. (bet. Sullivan & Thompson Sts.) | 212-941-7119

The "largest pasta menu you've ever seen" comes "priced for today's economy" at this SoHo Italian; it's "not much to look at" and "cramped as all get-out", but no one minds since it's "one of the best deals going."

Il Cortile *Italian* | 23 | 20 | 21 | $54 |

Little Italy | 125 Mulberry St. (bet. Canal & Hester Sts.) | 212-226-6060 | www.ilcortile.com

So good that "non-tourists seek it out", this "upscale" Italian has been a "Mulberry Street mainstay" since 1975 thanks to *delizioso* cucina ferried by an "experienced" crew; though "a tad pricey", it's worth it just to sit in the "beautiful" garden atrium.

Il Gattopardo ● *Italian* | 25 | 20 | 25 | $64 |

W 50s | 33 W. 54th St. (bet. 5th & 6th Aves.) | 212-246-0412 | www.ilgattopardonyc.com

"Convenient to MoMA" – and a "work of art itself" – this "first-class" Neapolitan is a hit with the "wealthy and the powerful" given its "outstanding" food and "gracious, hard-working" staff; though "expensive", it's "not unreasonable" thanks to the "beautiful" townhouse setting and "sophisticated" milieu.

Il Giglio ⊠ *Italian* | 25 | 18 | 23 | $74 |

TriBeCa | 81 Warren St. (bet. Greenwich St. & W. B'way) | 212-571-5555 | www.ilgigliorestaurant.com

Starting with the "free antipasto", this "first-rate" TriBeCa Tuscan is known for its "sumptuous" repasts served by a "bow-tied" staff that "makes you feel like family"; sure, it's "expensive" and the facilities may "need a face-lift", but it's still "terrific for special occasions."

Ilili *Lebanese* | 24 | 23 | 22 | $51 |

Chelsea | 236 Fifth Ave. (bet. 27th & 28th Sts.) | 212-683-2929 | www.ililinyc.com

"High-style" Chelsea Lebanese "change of pace" where the "innovative" small-plates menu ("try the Brussels sprouts") works well with the "stunning", "Frank Lloyd Wright"–esque setting; despite its "trendy" feel, fans report that service is "timely" and the prices "non-exorbitant."

NEW Il Matto ⊠ *Italian* | – | – | – | E |

TriBeCa | 281 Church St. (White St.) | 212-226-1607 | www.ilmattonyc.com

Its name means 'the madman', and this upscale new TriBeCan revels in the offbeat with both its creative Italian cooking and its whimsical design; the dishes comprise traditional ingredients in unexpected combinations, while the cocktails are even more surprising given components like ricotta cheese and lettuce leaves.

Il Mattone ⊠ *Italian/Pizza* | ∇ 21 | 13 | 18 | $36 |

TriBeCa | 413 Greenwich St. (Hubert St.) | 212-343-0030 | www.ilmattonenyc.com

Brick-oven pizzas are the thing at this low-budget TriBeCa Italian, a "very casual" staple in a neighborhood that needs it; still, it flies under the radar, probably due to its "biker bar" look and "rushed" service.

| | FOOD | DECOR | SERVICE | COST |

⒵ Il Mulino ⑤ *Italian* | 27 | 19 | 24 | $87 |

G Village | 86 W. Third St. (bet. Sullivan & Thompson Sts.) | 212-673-3783 | www.ilmulino.com

"Voluminous", "voluptuous" dining is the calling card of this "one-of-a-kind" Village Italian where the "stunning" meals begin with a "bounty of freebies" served by a "marvelous staff" in black tie; despite soaring prices, it's always "jam-packed" and "ridiculously hard" to get into, so "ask Bill Clinton to call for a reservation" or go at lunchtime when both access and prices are "easier."

Il Postino ● *Italian* | 23 | 20 | 21 | $68 |

E 40s | 337 E. 49th St. (bet. 1st & 2nd Aves.) | 212-688-0033

After extending a "warm welcome", the waiters inhale and recite a "list of specials as long as your arm" at this "outstanding" Midtown Italian; granted, it skews "expensive", but its "U.N. crowd" doesn't seem to care given the "enjoyable" fare and "great atmosphere."

Il Punto *Italian* | ▽ 21 | 17 | 21 | $48 |

Garment District | 507 Ninth Ave. (38th St.) | 212-244-0088 | www.ilpuntoristorante.com

Bringing "well-prepared" Puglian food to an "unlikely location" behind Port Authority, this Garment District Italian (once Osteria Gelsi) also features "eager-to-please" service and fair tabs; fans tout it pre-theater, since it's "not as noisy and crowded" as its peers.

Il Riccio ● *Italian* | 22 | 16 | 20 | $52 |

E 70s | 152 E. 79th St. (bet. Lexington & 3rd Aves.) | 212-639-9111

"Like a club" for certain Upper Eastsiders (including "the mayor"), this "agreeable" Southern Italian serves "quality" traditional cuisine in a "small" but "cheerful" setting; the staffers exude "sincere warmth", while a "charming" courtyard garden helps relieve the "cramped" dimensions in warm weather.

⒵ Il Tinello ⑤ *Italian* | 25 | 20 | 25 | $73 |

W 50s | 16 W. 56th St. (bet. 5th & 6th Aves.) | 212-245-4388

"Well-dressed" patrons convene at this 25-year-old Midtown Italian where the "serious", "world-class" menu is delivered by a "responsive", "tuxedo"-clad staff; it's "quiet" and "refined" enough to pitch some "woo", but you'll need to be a "big spender" to do it.

Inakaya *Japanese* | ▽ 19 | 20 | 20 | $64 |

W 40s | NY Times Bldg. | 231 W. 40th St. (bet. 7th & 8th Aves.) | 212-354-2195 | www.inakayany.com

An "authentic" robatayaki experience awaits at this "cool" Japanese in the NYT building, where the staff's shout-and-response "show" accompanies "solid" grilled fare; the "entertaining spectacle" distracts from the rather "expensive" tabs.

Indochine ● *French/Vietnamese* | 21 | 21 | 18 | $54 |

E Village | 430 Lafayette St. (bet. Astor Pl. & 4th St.) | 212-505-5111 | www.indochinenyc.com

This "time machine back to the '80s" near the Public Theater is "still going strong", offering "enjoyable" French-Vietnamese dishes served by a "reed-thin" staff in "exotic" digs right out of a "1930s movie"; some sniff it's "losing its edge", but most maintain it "never ages."

	FOOD	DECOR	SERVICE	COST

Indus Valley *Indian*
23 | 16 | 20 | $33

W 100s | 2636 Broadway (100th St.) | 212-222-9222 |
www.indusvalleyus.com

"Inviting" and "peaceful" ambiancewise, this UWS Indian jazzes up its
menu with "spicy", "flavorful" items that include some "fiery" dishes
fit for "heat freaks"; though the tabs run "slightly upscale" compared
to the Sixth Street scene, the $14 lunch buffet is a "true bargain."

'Ino ● *Italian*
24 | 15 | 18 | $30

W Village | 21 Bedford St. (bet. Downing St. & 6th Ave.) | 212-989-5769 |
www.cafeino.com

"Amazing panini" and "sublime truffled egg toast" paired with "interesting" Italian wines are the draws at this low-budget, "studio apart-
ment"–size Village wine bar; since it's usually "crowded" with tables
"closer than hillbilly cousins", insiders reserve it for a "rainy night."

'Inoteca ● *Italian*
22 | 18 | 19 | $42

LES | 98 Rivington St. (Ludlow St.) | 212-614-0473
Murray Hill | 323 Third Ave. (24th St.) | 212-683-3035
www.inotecanyc.com

"Hip", "under-30" types populate these "busy" wine bars known for their
"sensational" small plates and "fair prices"; "knowledgeable" staffers
help "decode" the Italian-language menu, but given the "LaGuardia
runway" noise levels, it's best to brush up on your "sign language."

Inside Park at St. Bart's *American*
17 | 21 | 18 | $43

E 50s | 325 Park Ave. (50th St.) | 212-593-3333 | www.insideparknyc.com
A "refuge" in St. Bart's "beautiful" community hall, this Park Avenue
American works best for a "relaxing" lunch or "after-work drinks" on
its "wonderful terrace" (aka "Outside Park"); since the eats may be a
bit "ordinary", supplicants "pray for improvement."

Insieme *Italian*
23 | 20 | 22 | $70

W 50s | Michelangelo Hotel | 777 Seventh Ave. (bet. 50th & 51st Sts.) |
212-582-1310 | www.restaurantinsieme.com

"Interesting" cuisine, "minimalist" decor and "thoughtful" service make
this "modern" Italian a "classy" option in "honky-tonk" Times Square;
true, the price tags are "a bit high" given chef Marco Canora's departure, but ultimately it works for "understated sophisticated" dining.

Ippudo ● *Noodle Shop*
25 | 20 | 19 | $28

E Village | 65 Fourth Ave. (bet. 9th & 10th Sts.) | 212-388-0088 |
www.ippudo.com/ny

"Energetic" staffers "shout out greetings" at this "destination" East
Village noodle shop, but slurpers say the "real reason to cheer" is its
"gold-standard" ramen in a "rich, flavorful" broth; since it's voted Tops
in its genre, the "insane waits" to get in should come as no surprise.

Isabella's *American/Mediterranean*
20 | 19 | 20 | $44

W 70s | 359 Columbus Ave. (77th St.) | 212-724-2100 |
www.brguestrestaurants.com

"Quite the scene", Steve Hanson's "upbeat" UWS Med-American offers
"crowd-pleasing" fare at "moderate" rates, along with the "best darn
brunch" (with the "waits to prove it"); there's also primo "people-
watching", whether in the "airy" interior or the coveted sidewalk seats.

	FOOD	DECOR	SERVICE	COST

Ise *Japanese* | 21 | 12 | 17 | $39 |

E 40s | 151 E. 49th St. (bet. Lexington & 3rd Aves.) | 212-319-6876
Financial District | 56 Pine St. (bet. Pearl & William Sts.) | 212-785-1600 |
www.iserestaurant.com
W 50s | 58 W. 56th St. (bet. 5th & 6th Aves.) | 212-707-8702
"First-rate" sushi and "affordable" Japanese home cooking keep these
"rudimentary" izakayas popular with expats and "businesspeople",
especially for their "excellent lunch specials"; despite "hurried" service,
"no decor" and "language barriers", fans insist they're the "real deal."

Island Burgers & Shakes *Burgers* | 21 | 9 | 16 | $18 |

W 50s | 766 Ninth Ave. (bet. 51st & 52nd Sts.) | 212-307-7934 |
www.islandburgersny.com
"Massive, perfectly cooked" burgers with a "multitude" of toppings
are yours at this bare-bones, low-budget Hell's Kitchen "dive"; "sinful,
straw-clogging shakes" supply the "calorie surge" and compensate for
the inexplicable "lack of fries."

I Sodi ❶ *Italian* | 25 | 19 | 22 | $56 |

W Village | 105 Christopher St. (bet. Bleecker & Hudson Sts.) |
212-414-5774 | www.isodinyc.com
"Simple but sophisticated" Italian cuisine backed up by an "interesting
wine list" (and house specialty Negronis) seduces "true foodies" at
this "sleek" West Villager; when the "tiny" sliver of a setting gets
"elbow-to-elbow", regulars opt for a seat at the "beautiful bar."

Italianissimo *Italian* | 24 | 19 | 23 | $50 |

E 80s | 307 E. 84th St. (bet. 1st & 2nd Aves.) | 212-628-8603 |
www.italianissimonyc.net
"From-the-heart" cooking and "treat-you-like-family" service are the
draws at this "tiny" UES Italian where the "cozy" ambiance makes up
for the "unfortunate name"; the pricing is "decent", and the $22 early-
bird is impossible to resist.

Ithaka *Greek/Seafood* | 22 | 18 | 21 | $48 |

E 80s | 308 E. 86th St. (bet. 1st & 2nd Aves.) | 212-628-9100 |
www.ithakarestaurant.com
The feeling is pure "Santorini" at this Yorkville Greek taverna where
"whitewashed walls", "laid-back" vibes and "whole fish grilled to perfection" lead to "transporting" experiences; "genial service" and moderate tabs complete the pleasing picture.

I Tre Merli *Italian* | 19 | 19 | 19 | $45 |

SoHo | 463 W. Broadway (bet. Houston & Prince Sts.) | 212-254-8699
W Village | 183 W. 10th St. (W. 4th St.) | 212-929-2221 ❶
www.itremerli.com
While the Italian food's good, the people-watching's "great" at this "big-
windowed" SoHo "oldie but goodie" where "Claudia Schiffer and Naomi
Campbell" once held court but which now hosts a "NJ" crowd; its smaller
Village sibling shares the same moderate prices and "aloof" service.

I Trulli *Italian* | 23 | 21 | 21 | $60 |

Murray Hill | 122 E. 27th St. (bet. Lexington Ave. & Park Ave. S.) |
212-481-7372 | www.itrulli.com
Boasting i "truly *fantastico*" track record, this longtime Murray Hill
Italian features "marvelous" Pugliese dishes "served with aplomb",

plus "superb" wines from the adjoining enoteca; an all-weather destination thanks to a "delightful fireplace" and "lush garden", it has "getaway" written all over it.

Itzocan ⊄ Mexican

22 | 10 | 18 | $35

E 100s | 1575 Lexington Ave. (101st St.) | 212-423-0255 |
www.itzocanbistro.com
E Village | 438 E. Ninth St. (bet. Ave. A & 1st Ave.) | 212-677-5856 |
www.itzocanrestaurant.com ●

"Upscale" Mexican chow arrives in "downscale" digs at this "inventive" duo offering "mouthwatering" fare at the East Village original and a more "interesting" Mex-French mix Uptown; both are "tiny" and "cash only", with servers doing their best to "handle the masses."

Ivo & Lulu ☑⊄ Caribbean/French

19 | 12 | 14 | $33

SoHo | 558 Broome St. (bet. 6th Ave. & Varick St.) | 212-226-4399
"Low-key celebration" central, this "out-of-the-way" SoHo French-Caribbean features dishes accented with "bold spices" and "island flair"; "cramped" dimensions and "inattentive" service are offset by the "BYO factor" and great overall "bang for the buck."

Jack's Luxury Oyster Bar ☒ Continental/French

▽ 27 | 17 | 24 | $65

E Village | 101 Second Ave. (bet. 5th & 6th Sts.) | 212-979-1012
"Great things come in small packages" at Jack Lamb's East Village French-Continental where the "inventive", seafood-centric menu features "fresh ingredients in novel combinations"; the "matchbox"-size setting may be "awkward" but "welcoming" service and luxe on the plate are adequate offsets.

Jackson Diner Indian

22 | 10 | 15 | $24

Jackson Heights | 37-47 74th St. (bet. Roosevelt & 37th Aves.) |
Queens | 718-672-1232 | www.jacksondiner.com
"Subtly flavored" Indian "comfort food" – and "lots of it" – keeps fans "riding the subway" to this longtime Jackson Heights joint; "low" costs trump the "uneven" service and "mess-hall" decor, while the $10 lunch buffet is a not-to-be-missed "excellent value."

Jackson Hole Burgers

17 | 10 | 15 | $22

E 60s | 232 E. 64th St. (bet. 2nd & 3rd Aves.) | 212-371-7187 ●
E 80s | 1611 Second Ave. (bet. 83rd & 84th Sts.) | 212-737-8788 ●
E 90s | 1270 Madison Ave. (91st St.) | 212-427-2820
Murray Hill | 521 Third Ave. (35th St.) | 212-679-3264 ●
W 80s | 517 Columbus Ave. (85th St.) | 212-362-5177
Bayside | 35-01 Bell Blvd. (35th Ave.) | Queens | 718-281-0330 ●
Jackson Heights | 69-35 Astoria Blvd. (70th St.) | Queens | 718-204-7070 ●
www.jacksonholeburgers.com

"Students" and "locals of all ages" tout the "big sloppy burgers" and "massive sides" dispensed by this longtime mini-chain; the "vintage '50s", "Frankie Avalon"–ready settings may be "nothing to write home about" (ditto the service), but hey, the tabs are real "cheap."

Jack the Horse Tavern American

22 | 20 | 20 | $45

Brooklyn Heights | 66 Hicks St. (Cranberry St.) | Brooklyn | 718-852-5084 |
www.jackthehorse.com
Earning "high marks" for its "excellent" American food and grog, this "distinctive" tavern is one of the "few adult restaurants in Brooklyn

Heights"; a "pretty" setting, "efficient" service and "modest prices" cement its "neighborhood-standby" appeal.

Jacques *French* `19` `17` `18` `$44`
E 80s | 206 E. 85th St. (bet. 2nd & 3rd Aves.) | 212-327-2272
NoLita | 20 Prince St. (bet. Elizabeth & Mott Sts.) | 212-966-8886
www.jacquesnyc.com

The "marvelous" moules frites are "always special" at these "steady" French brasseries, serving all the "classics" Uptown with some North African spins in NoLita; the "pleasant" Gallic ambiance extends to the staff's "authentic hauteur", but "fair" prices make them "safe bets."

Jaiya Thai *Thai* `22` `13` `16` `$29`
Murray Hill | 396 Third Ave. (28th St.) | 212-889-1330 | www.jaiya.com

"Even mild is spicy" at this "high-quality" Murray Hill Siamese where the "hotness ratings" are "scaled to Thai tastes" (and fiery enough to "burn off your extra pounds"), while the tabs are "inexpensive"; a recent "spruce-up" is not yet reflected in the Decor score.

Jake's Steakhouse *Steak* `24` `20` `21` `$55`
Bronx | 6031 Broadway (242nd St.) | 718-581-0182 | www.jakessteakhouse.com

"Downtown-caliber" cuts of beef for "less than Manhattan prices" can be had at this "quality" Riverdale steakhouse run by "serious" meat wholesalers; "go-out-of-their-way" service and a "great view of Van Cortlandt Park" from the upstairs dining room are bonuses.

James *American* `24` `22` `23` `$48`
Prospect Heights | 605 Carlton Ave. (St. Marks Ave.) | Brooklyn | 718-942-4255 | www.jamesrestaurantny.com

Tucked away on a "tree-lined residential block", this "seductive" Prospect Heights American radiates "Brooklyn chic", with "delicious" "seasonal" fare served in a "sophisticated" setting; "amiable service" and relative "bargain" pricing help keep the "hipster" hordes happy here.

Jane *American* `21` `17` `18` `$40`
G Village | 100 W. Houston St. (bet. La Guardia Pl. & Thompson St.) | 212-254-7000 | www.janerestaurant.com

Putting out "upscale" New American eats for "won't-break-the-bank" tabs, this "informal" Villager hits the "comfort spot" for many, reaching "mob-scene" proportions during weekend brunch; despite "noise" issues and a "modest" setting, the bottom line is "satisfying."

Japonais ⧄ *Japanese* `20` `23` `19` `$57`
Gramercy | 111 E. 18th St. (bet. Irving Pl. & Park Ave. S.) | 212-260-2020 | www.japonaisnewyork.com

Japanese fusion fare with a French twist plays second fiddle to the "dark", "sleek" setting at this "cool" Gramercy Japanese that draws "pretty" folks with its "fantastic cocktails" and "prime location"; "so-so service" and "pricey" tabs come with the territory.

Japonica *Japanese* `24` `16` `21` `$48`
G Village | 100 University Pl. (12th St.) | 212-243-7752 | www.japonicanyc.com

A longtime "Village tradition", this "gold-standard" Japanese is renowned for "sparklingly fresh" "super-size" sushi served by a "thoughtful" team; despite "tired" decor and prices that suggest "you can't afford to walk out full", you "get what you pay for" here.

Jean Claude ⊄ *French* | 22 | 16 | 21 | $46 |

SoHo | 137 Sullivan St. (bet. Houston & Prince Sts.) | 212-475-9232 | www.jeanclauderestaurant.com

For a short so-French sojourn "without the attitude", try this circa-1992 SoHo bistro where the "delicious" cooking and "warm" service are equally "down to earth"; it's the "ultimate neighborhood joint", with one "small negative": the "cash-only" rule.

☑ Jean Georges ☒ *French* | 28 | 27 | 28 | $127 |

W 60s | Trump Int'l Hotel | 1 Central Park W. (bet. 60th & 61st Sts.) | 212-299-3900 | www.jean-georges.com

"Everything it's cracked up to be", Jean-Georges Vongerichten's "magical" Columbus Circle New French is a "pleasure all the way" from the "inventive", "wow-inducing" cuisine to the understatedly elegant "modernist" decor and service that "silently anticipates your wants"; all that "luxe" makes the "splurge"-worthy tabs easier to digest, while the $29 prix fixe lunch may be NYC's best dining value.

☑ Jean Georges' Nougatine *French* | 27 | 23 | 25 | $64 |

W 60s | Trump Int'l Hotel | 1 Central Park W. (bet. 60th & 61st Sts.) | 212-299-3900 | www.jean-georges.com

For the "thrill of Jean Georges'" formal dining room at a more palatable price, try this "relaxed" front room serving "sublime" Nouveau French cuisine in a "tasteful" setting manned by "cosseting" staffers; the $26 prix fixe three-course lunch is a fantastic "bargain", and it also hosts a "power breakfast" for those who "don't need to be seen."

☑ Jewel Bako ☒ *Japanese* | 26 | 21 | 22 | $81 |

E Village | 239 E. Fifth St. (bet. 2nd & 3rd Aves.) | 212-979-1012

Owners Grace and Jack Lamb preside over this "almost-Tokyo" East Village Japanese where connoisseurs convene for "incredible, jet-set sushi" served in "ever-so-chic" bamboo-lined digs; though the dimensions are "tiny" and the costs large, overall it's a "superb" experience.

Jewel of India *Indian* | 20 | 19 | 18 | $42 |

W 40s | 15 W. 44th St. (bet. 5th & 6th Aves.) | 212-869-5544 | www.jewelofindiarestaurant.com

The tables are "well spaced" and the food well spiced at this "inviting" Midtown Indian providing "reliable" eats for "reasonable" dough; "business folks" favor the $17 lunch buffet served upstairs.

J.G. Melon ●⊄ *Pub Food* | 21 | 12 | 16 | $27 |

E 70s | 1291 Third Ave. (74th St.) | 212-744-0585

Seemingly "frozen in time", this "perennially crowded" UES pub enjoys a "cultlike following" among "preppy" types thanks to its "phenomenal" burgers and cottage fries; despite "snippy" service and a "no-plastic" rule, its "ribbon-belted" fan base touts its "hometown feeling."

Jimmy's No. 43 ● *American* | ▽ 22 | 18 | 18 | $34 |

E Village | 43 E. Seventh St., downstairs (bet. 2nd & 3rd Aves.) | 212-982-3006 | www.jimmysno43.com

"Surprisingly sophisticated" for its off-the-radar "cellar" location, this "too-cool" East Villager doles out "inspired" American small plates from a reasonably tabbed, "rotating" menu; the rathskeller-esque digs can be "claustrophobic", but an expansive beer list helps to distract.

Jing Fong *Chinese* | 19 | 11 | 11 | $22 |

Chinatown | 20 Elizabeth St. (bet. Bayard & Canal Sts.) | 212-964-5256

The "Disneyland of dim sum", this "massive" C-towner may "blow your mind" with its sea of "racing carts" stocked with "reliable but unimaginative" Hong Kong–style morsels; insiders say the "early bird gets the dumpling" here, and advise showing up before the "good stuff is gone."

JJ's Asian Fusion Ⓜ *Asian* | ▽ 24 | 14 | 19 | $27 |

Astoria | 37-05 31st Ave. (bet. 37th & 38th Sts.) | Queens | 718-626-8888 | www.jjsfusion.com

Renowned for its "famous" edamame potstickers, this "seriously good" Astoria Asian fusion practitioner also slices up "wonderfully fresh sushi"; though the "small", "plain" digs are "not much to speak of", the "bargain" tabs and "friendly" vibes merit a mention.

Joe Allen ◑ *American* | 17 | 16 | 18 | $44 |

W 40s | 326 W. 46th St. (bet. 8th & 9th Aves.) | 212-581-6464 | www.joeallenrestaurant.com

"Dependably comforting" American chow comes with a side of "Broadway buzz" at this Restaurant Row "institution", a "showbiz hangout" since '63; manned by "waiters waiting for a break", it runs "full-throttle" pre-theater, though the "stargazing" is best after the shows.

Joe & Pat's *Italian/Pizza* | 23 | 12 | 17 | $25 |

Staten Island | 1758 Victory Blvd. (Manor Rd.) | 718-981-0887

A "pillar of Staten Island pizza" since 1960, this "family favorite" purveys classic thin-crust pies crowned with "tangy" accoutrements; "chintzy" decor and "distracted" service are part of the package, along with "waits in line" at prime times.

JoeDoe *American* | ▽ 23 | 15 | 21 | $45 |

E Village | 45 E. First St. (bet. 1st & 2nd Aves.) | 212-780-0262 | www.chefjoedoe.com

"Gutsy" New Americana with some "Jewish soul food" influences is served with "unique beer cocktails" at this "offbeat" little East Villager; the "unassuming", "laid-back" enterprise exudes such "heartfelt" vibes that fans think it "should be more popular than it is."

Joe's Ginger ⊘ *Chinese* | 20 | 9 | 13 | $23 |

Chinatown | 25 Pell St. (Doyers St.) | 212-285-0333 | www.joeginger.com

"Immensely satisfying soup dumplings" are the specialty of this C-town Shanghainese that's a "less crowded" alternative to its popular sibling, Joe's Shanghai; though service runs "cold" and the decor skews "bland", at least the eats come "cheap" and satisfying.

Joe's Pizza *Pizza* | 23 | 6 | 14 | $10 |

W Village | 7 Carmine St. (bet. Bleecker St. & 6th Ave.) | 212-255-3946 ◑
Midwood | 1621 Kings Hwy. (E. 16th St.) | Brooklyn | 718-339-4525 ⊘
Park Slope | 137 Seventh Ave. (bet. Carroll St. & Garfield Pl.) | Brooklyn | 718-398-9198
www.joespizza.com

Piezanos hit these separately owned pie purveyors for "textbook NY street pizza" that's appropriately "hot, greasy, gooey" and available "by the slice"; given the "gruff service" and "dumpy" digs, they're best reserved for a quick "pit stop."

Joe's Shanghai   *Chinese* | 22 | 9 | 14 | $26 |

Chinatown | 9 Pell St. (bet. Bowery & Mott St.) | 212-233-8888 ⌐
W 50s | 24 W. 56th St. (bet. 5th & 6th Aves.) | 212-333-3868
Flushing | 136-21 37th Ave. (bet. Main & Union Sts.) | Queens | 718-539-3838 ⌐
www.joeshanghairestaurants.com

"Piping hot" soup dumplings are the "star attraction" at this Shanghainese trio that's usually "jam-packed" at all hours; "tired" looks, "insane" lines and "slapdash" service are trumped by the "addictive" food – and everyone "loves the bill."

John's of 12th Street ⌐ *Italian* | 21 | 14 | 19 | $33 |

E Village | 302 E. 12th St. (2nd Ave.) | 212-475-9531 |
www.johnsof12thstreet.com

"Tried-and-true" since 1908, this East Village Italian is "wonderfully retro", from its "home-cooked" "red-sauce" dishes and "old-time prices" to "decor from many moons ago"; "low lights" and "appreciative" service enhance its "simpler-times" vibe.

☒ John's Pizzeria   *Pizza* | 22 | 13 | 16 | $24 |

E 60s | 408 E. 64th St. (bet. 1st & York Aves.) | 212-935-2895
W 40s | 260 W. 44th St. (bet. B'way & 8th Ave.) | 212-391-7560 ◑
W Village | 278 Bleecker St. (bet. 6th Ave. & 7th Ave. S.) | 212-243-1680 ◑⌐
www.johnspizzerianyc.com

"Meccas for pizza lovers", this low-budget trio dispenses "divine" brick-oven pies with "thin, crispy" crusts, but unfortunately "no slices"; the vintage-1929 Bleecker Street original is a "shrine" for purists, though the Times Square spin-off in a "converted church" is "perfect" pre-theater.

JoJo   *French* | 25 | 23 | 24 | $67 |

E 60s | 160 E. 64th St. (bet. Lexington & 3rd Aves.) | 212-223-5656 |
www.jean-georges.com

Still "on target", Jean-Georges Vongerichten's 20-year-old Upper Eastsider emits an unmistakable "glow" thanks to its "classy" French bistro fare, "genteel" service and "lovely" duplex setting; it's a "civilized" option for the "fabulously dressed" – and a "primo lunch choice" via the $26 prix fixe.

Jolie   *French* | 21 | 20 | 20 | $41 |

Boerum Hill | 320 Atlantic Ave. (bet. Hoyt & Smith Sts.) | Brooklyn | 718-488-0777 | www.jolierestaurant.com

Everything's "Gallic and good" at this "restful" Boerum Hill boîte where an "upbeat staff" ferries "well-prepared" French favorites in a "pretty" dining room or a "lovely garden"; factor in "prix fixe bargains" and *tout* is *jolie* indeed.

Josephina ◑ *American* | 18 | 16 | 18 | $48 |

W 60s | 1900 Broadway (bet. 63rd & 64th Sts.) | 212-799-1000 |
www.josephinanyc.com

Just "steps from Lincoln Center", this "solid" New American has been "catering to the pre-theater crowd" with "satisfying" chow served at "warp speed" for 20 years now; its audience tolerates the "close tables", "ordinary decor" and "fierce noise level" given its "good value."

Joseph Leonard ◗ American

22	20	22	$47

W Village | 170 Waverly Pl. (Grove St.) | 646-429-8383 |
www.josephleonard.com

An instant "hot spot", Gabe Stulman's "hip", open-all-day Village yearling purveys "ridiculously good" New American food served in a "tiny rustic" space equipped with a "fabulous zinc bar"; throw in moderate tabs, "eager-to-please" service and a "chill atmosphere" and, no surprise, "there's always a wait."

Josie's Eclectic

19	15	17	$34

Murray Hill | 565 Third Ave. (37th St.) | 212-490-1558
W 70s | 300 Amsterdam Ave. (74th St.) | 212-769-1212
www.josiesnyc.com

Everyone from carnivores to vegans "feels virtuous" at this "wholesome" Eclectic duo specializing in "guilt-free" organic grub; although the decor is "drab" and the service "awkward", they're "light on the pocketbook" and catnip for "groups of girlfriends."

Joya ⊅ Thai

23	17	18	$23

Cobble Hill | 215 Court St. (bet. Warren & Wyckoff Sts.) | Brooklyn | 718-222-3484

"Skinny jeans"–wearers and those who love them swear by this "terminally hip" Cobble Hill Thai that pulls in the "young and noisy" with "fabulous" food, "Manhattan-cool" design and "astonishingly low prices"; for a respite from the "unbearable decibels" within, check out the "lovely garden."

Jubilee French

23	16	20	$50

E 50s | 347 E. 54th St. (bet. 1st & 2nd Aves.) | 212-888-3569 |
www.jubileeny.net

"Nothing compares to the mussels" at this "*très charmant*" Sutton Place French bistro where the "traditional" offerings are "delicious" but the mollusks "divine"; its "mature" following is willing to overlook the "tired" decor, but the "tight tables" are another story.

Jules ◗ French

20	18	18	$41

E Village | 65 St. Marks Pl. (bet. 1st & 2nd Aves.) | 212-477-5560 |
www.julesbistro.com

This "laid-back" East Village bistro conjures up images of the "Left Bank" with its "solid" traditional French cooking and nightly "live jazz"; "intimate" in size and "funky" by nature, it seals the deal with "reasonable" tabs.

Junior's Diner

17	12	16	$27

E 40s | Grand Central | lower level (42nd St. & Vanderbilt Ave.) |
212-983-5257
W 40s | Shubert Alley | 1515 Broadway (enter on 45th St., bet. B'way & 8th Ave.) | 212-302-2000 ◗
Downtown Bklyn | 386 Flatbush Ave. Ext. (DeKalb Ave.) | Brooklyn | 718-852-5257 ◗
www.juniorscheesecake.com

Its "world-class cheesecake" is the "raison d'être" of this diner trio serving "filling" "soda-fountain" grub and "reliable" deli for "decent" dough; the Downtown Brooklyn branch (where the "legend" began) is the "real one", but you can "meet fun tourists" at all three.

Kabab Café M⊘ *Egyptian* ▽ 25 | 14 | 19 | $34
Astoria | 25-12 Steinway St. (25th Ave.) | Queens | 718-728-9858
Regulars at this "eccentric" Astoria cafe bypass the "outstanding", affordable Egyptian offerings and let "friendly chef" Ali El Sayed prepare something "off the menu"; though "tiny" and "cramped", it compensates with a BYO policy, "good shawarma and good karma."

Kafana ⊘ *Serbian* ▽ 24 | 18 | 22 | $34
E Village | 116 Ave. C (bet. 7th & 8th Sts.) | 212-353-8000 |
www.kafananyc.com
"Off the beaten path" in more ways than one, this East Village Serbian serves "mouthwatering grilled meats", signature *cevapi* (beef-pork-lamb sausages) and other "unusual" eats that are hard to find "this side of Zagreb"; the low tabs and "simple" setting match its laid-back mood.

Kajitsu M *Japanese/Vegetarian* ▽ 27 | 24 | 27 | $90
E Village | 414 E. Ninth St. (bet. Ave. A & 1st Ave.) | 212-228-4873 |
www.kajitsunyc.com
"Soothing is the word for this East Village Japanese kaiseki "vegetarian temple" serving "simply amazing" *shojin* cuisine that originated in Buddhist monasteries; "seamless service" and a "restrained aesthetic" burnish the "Zen" mood, which is only broken by the profane tabs.

Kang Suh ● *Korean* 22 | 12 | 16 | $35
Garment District | 1250 Broadway (32nd St.) | 212-564-6845
"Delicious", "do-it-yourself" Korean BBQ is the "main attraction" at this Garment District longtimer where "bubbling soup pots" and sushi also "hit the spot"; "service could improve", ditto the decor, but the 24/7 open-door policy is fine as is.

Kanoyama ● *Japanese* 26 | 17 | 19 | $55
E Village | 175 Second Ave. (11th St.) | 212-777-5266 | www.kanoyama.com
"Beautifully presented", "hard-to-find" cuts of "ocean-fresh" sushi keep this "phenomenal" East Village Japanese "swarming" with finatics; prices are "reasonable" given the "extraordinary quality", and a recent expansion has added a "cool sake bar" to the mix.

Kati Roll Co. *Indian* 21 | 6 | 13 | $11
Garment District | 49 W. 39th St. (bet. 5th & 6th Aves.) |
212-730-4280
G Village | 99 MacDougal St. (bet. Bleecker & W. 3rd Sts.) | 212-420-6517 ●
www.thekatirollcompany.com
"Street-food heaven", this Indian duo doles out "fantastic" burrito-style rolls with "lots of flavor" at "dirt-cheap" prices; they're great for a "late-night" nosh or "on the go", but be prepared for "hole-in-the-wall" decor and "disgruntled" service.

Katsu-Hama *Japanese* 21 | 13 | 16 | $28
E 40s | 11 E. 47th St. (bet. 5th & Madison Aves.) | 212-758-5909
W 50s | 45 W. 55th St., 2nd fl. (bet. 5th & 6th Aves.) | 212-541-7145 ●
www.katsuhama.com
"Beloved by expats" for their "terrific" Japanese comfort food, these Midtown tonkatsu parlors specialize in "succulent" pork cutlets breaded

| | FOOD | DECOR | SERVICE | COST |

and "fried to perfection"; though there's "no decor" and not much service, they're "quick and cheap" enough to draw "midday lines."

☑ Katz's Delicatessen *Deli*
`24` `9` `13` `$24`

LES | 205 E. Houston St. (Ludlow St.) | 212-254-2246 | www.katzdeli.com

One of the last "real-deal" LES delis, this circa-1888 "quintessential Noo Yawk" fixture is famed for its "mouthwatering" sandwiches, latkes and kosher dogs; despite "zero decor" (apart from the "Formica tables") and "army-bootcamp" service, fans of this "lovable dump" say there's "nothing else like it in the world"; P.S. maybe Meg Ryan "wasn't faking it."

NEW Kaz An Nou Ⓜ⊄ *French/Caribbean*
`-` `-` `-` `I`

Prospect Heights | 53 Sixth Ave. (bet. Bergen & Dean Sts.) | Brooklyn | 718-938-3235 | www.kazannou.com

"Deservedly popular" new French-Caribbean in Prospect Heights from the originators of the SoHo cult hit Ivo & Lulu; the "tiny", "homey" room fills up fast thanks to "excellent" cooking, "can't-be-beat" pricing and a "no-corkage-fee BYO" policy, making the "no-reservations" and cash-only rules easier to swallow.

☑ Keens Steakhouse *Steak*
`25` `23` `23` `$70`

Garment District | 72 W. 36th St. (bet. 5th & 6th Aves.) | 212-947-3636 | www.keens.com

You'll "leave the 21st century behind" at this 1885 Garment District steakhouse-cum-"museum", renowned for its "superlative mutton chop", "mind-bending" single-malt list and "impressive" displays of historical "memorabilia" (including 88,000 clay pipes on the ceiling); everything here is "old world", except for the "modern" prices.

Kefi *Greek*
`22` `16` `18` `$39`

W 80s | 505 Columbus Ave. (bet. 84th & 85th Sts.) | 212-873-0200 | www.kefirestaurant.com

There's a "real NY buzz" in the air at Michael Psilakis' "top-flight" Upper West Side Greek, now ensconced in a "bigger" double-decker setting but still supplying the same "zesty" Hellenica; though some say it's a "victim of its own fame" with "roaring" crowds and "rush-you-in-and-out" service, at least the "fair prices" let you "feast and not worry about the bill."

Kellari Taverna ● *Greek*
`22` `21` `21` `$51`

W 40s | 19 W. 44th St. (bet. 5th & 6th Aves.) | 212-221-0144 | www.kellari.us

Kellari's Parea ● *Greek*

Flatiron | 36 E. 20th St. (bet. B'way & Park Ave. S.) | 212-777-8448 | www.kellari-parea.com

It's "almost like Greece" at this "easygoing" Hellenic duo dispensing "grilled-to-perfection" fish for "not ridiculously expensive prices"; the Theater District outpost is "perfect for a business lunch" or before a show, while the "more casual" Flatiron sibling is "great for a date."

NEW Kenmare ● *American/Mediterranean*
▽ `21` `20` `21` `$60`

Little Italy | 98 Kenmare St. (bet. Lafayette & Mulberry Sts.) | 212-274-9898 | www.kenmarenyc.com

Little Owl chef Joey Campanaro is behind the burners at this "sceney" new Med-American in Little Italy launched amid "lots of hype" but "still working out the kinks"; look for a "good-looking" crowd sampling "simple" but "creative" fare in a dark space with a nightclubbish vibe and "deafening" acoustics.

Keste Pizza e Vino *Pizza*

25	14	19	$28

W Village | 271 Bleecker St. (bet. Cornelia & Jones Sts.) | 212-243-1500 | www.kestepizzeria.com

The "first-rate" Napoli-style pies are the "genuine article" at this West Village pizzeria, "prepared by a master chef" who's president of the Italian Association of Neapolitan Pizza; "cramped" tables and "hallway" dimensions are part of the package, along with a wait in "queue purgatory."

Killmeyer's Old Bavaria Inn *German*

20	20	20	$33

Staten Island | 4254 Arthur Kill Rd. (Sharrotts Rd.) | 718-984-1202 | www.killmeyers.com

"Ample portions" of "basic" German grub washed down with an "amazing" suds selection have locals saying *"ja wohl"* to this "homey" Staten Islander in Charleston; "classic beer hall" decor and "waitresses in dirndl skirts" add to its "Teutonic" appeal.

Kings' Carriage House *American*

23	26	24	$65

E 80s | 251 E. 82nd St. (bet. 2nd & 3rd Aves.) | 212-734-5490 | www.kingscarriagehouse.com

"Excellent everything" is on hand at this "sweetly elegant" UES New American with a "fancy" "English country house" setting, "perfect service" and a "delightful host" to buttress the "superb" cooking; granted, the prix fixe–only repasts are on the "expensive" side, but "you feel special just by walking in."

Kingswood ● *American*

19	21	17	$48

W Village | 121 W. 10th St. (bet. Greenwich & 6th Aves.) | 212-645-0018 | www.kingswoodnyc.com

"Fashionable" "under-30" types who show up for the "bar scene" at this "buzzworthy" Villager say that the Australian-accented American gastropub fare is equally appealing; though tabs run "a little steep" and service can be "uppity", this "cool" joint is still a "hot spot."

Ki Sushi *Japanese*

∇ 26	21	21	$34

Boerum Hill | 122 Smith St. (bet. Dean & Pacific Sts.) | Brooklyn | 718-935-0575 | www.ki-sushi.com

"Delicate", "impeccably fresh" fish is sliced into "top-rate sushi" at this "lovely" Boerum Hill Japanese where "unobtrusive service" and a "soothing", "minimalist" setting add to the "Zen-like" mood; "affordable" rates are another reason why it's a "must-try."

Kitchenette *Southern*

19	14	16	$25

Harlem | 1272 Amsterdam Ave. (bet. 122nd & 123rd Sts.) | 212-531-7600
TriBeCa | 156 Chambers St. (bet. Greenwich St. & W. B'way) | 212-267-6740
www.kitchenetterestaurant.com

It's useless to "skimp on the calories" at these "shabby-chic" Southerners where the "homestyle comfort food" is so "tempting" you'll want to have "biscuits with everything"; service is "pokey", but brunch is "terrific" and so "affordable" you won't mind the "wait."

	FOOD	DECOR	SERVICE	COST

Kittichai *Thai*
23 | **26** | **21** | **$56**

SoHo | 60 Thompson Hotel | 60 Thompson St. (bet. Broome & Spring Sts.) | 212-219-2000 | www.kittichairestaurant.com

"Orchids and candles" float in a reflecting pool at this "glossy magazine-worthy" SoHo Thai where the "glamour" extends to the "sophisticated" Siamese cuisine and "overconfident" staffers; sure, it's "a bit expensive", but priced right for a "celebratory night out."

Klee Brasserie *American/European*
19 | **17** | **20** | **$53**

Chelsea | 200 Ninth Ave. (bet. 22nd & 23rd Sts.) | 212-633-8033 | www.kleebrasserie.com

One "smooth operation", this "upscale" Chelsea Euro-American manages to meld "offbeat" but "spot-on" eats, "warm" service and "modernist decor" into one "relaxed" "neighborhood" package; some fault the "smallish", "overpriced" portions, but admit it's a "change of pace."

Klong ● *Thai*
20 | **16** | **17** | **$25**

E Village | 7 St. Marks Pl. (bet. 2nd & 3rd Aves.) | 212-505-9955 | www.klongnyc.com

This "solid" East Village Thai emits a "cool vibe" and offers "better-than-average" Bangkok street eats at "lower-than-average" tabs; the "dim" space suggests "date spot", save for the "klong"-like sound levels.

Knickerbocker
Bar & Grill ● *American*
20 | **18** | **20** | **$49**

G Village | 33 University Pl. (9th St.) | 212-228-8490 | www.knickerbockerbarandgrill.com

"Casual, comfortable" and "reliable", this 1977-vintage Village American multitasks as a "tasty T-bone" steakhouse, "solid" burger joint and "lively" locals' bar; though the digs may be "dated", "exceptional" weekend jazz has the joint jumping like a "honky-tonk."

Koi *Japanese*
23 | **24** | **21** | **$65**

W 40s | Bryant Park Hotel | 40 W. 40th St. (bet. 5th & 6th Aves.) | 212-921-3330 | www.koirestaurant.com

The Bryant Park Hotel provides the "glam setting" for "top-notch sushi" and "outrageously good" Asian fusion fare at this "lush" Japanese where "fashionistas" who "don't mind overpaying" gather for "trendy" grazing; just note, the "hot scene" can generate "lots of noise."

NEW Kouzina by Trata *Greek*
- | **-** | **-** | **E**

E 70s | 1331 Second Ave. (bet. 70th & 71st Sts.) | 212-535-3800

With a name that translates as 'kitchen', this pricey UES newcomer replaces the longtime Trata (and its fresh fish focus) with a basic Greek menu emphasizing traditional meat dishes and *mezedakia* (small plates); the revamped setting features plenty of room, plus outdoor seating perfect for Second Avenue people-watching.

Kuma Inn *Filipino/Thai*
25 | **13** | **21** | **$38**

LES | 113 Ludlow St., 2nd fl. (bet. Delancey & Rivington Sts.) | 212-353-8866 | www.kumainn.com

This "original" LES "hideaway" is known for its "zesty" Filipino-Thai small plates; "friendly service" compensates for a "quirky" setting that's "thin on ambiance", while a BYO policy buttresses the "bargain" costs.

	FOOD	DECOR	SERVICE	COST

Kum Gang San ● *Korean*
21 | 15 | 17 | $35

Garment District | 49 W. 32nd St. (bet. B'way & 5th Ave.) | 212-967-0909
Flushing | 138-28 Northern Blvd. (bet. Bowne & Union Sts.) | Queens |
718-461-0909
www.kumgangsan.net

"Smoke and sizzle" perfume the air at these "cavernous" 24/7 Korean BBQ palaces where "delicious" marinated meats can be "cooked at the table"; although the decor's "cheesy", the prices are "cheap" and it's a given "you won't leave hungry."

Kuruma Zushi ⊠ *Japanese*
▽ 26 | 15 | 21 | $133

E 40s | 7 E. 47th St., 2nd fl. (bet. 5th & Madison Aves.) | 212-317-2802 |
www.kurumazushi.com

Purists tout the "hard-to-find" sushi at this "hard-core" Midtown mezzanine and suggest you "put yourself in the hands" of "brilliant master" chef Toshihiro Uezu for "sublime omakase"; granted, you need "wheelbarrows of money" to pay, but then again this one is "in a class by itself."

Kyochon Chicken *Chicken*
20 | 15 | 16 | $18

NEW Murray Hill | 319 Fifth Ave. (bet. 32nd & 33rd Sts.) |
212-725-9292 ●
Bayside | 61-02 Springfield Blvd. (Horace Harding Expwy.) | Queens |
718-224-9292
Flushing | 156-50 Northern Blvd. (bet. 156th & 157th Sts.) | Queens |
718-939-9292 ●
www.kyochon.com

Think "upscale Asian KFC" to get the gist of this Korean fried chicken chainlet churning out "crispy", "super-spicy" wings, drumsticks and strips accompanied by "dynamite dipping sauces"; portions are "small" but so are prices, making them perfect for a "quick bite."

Kyotofu ●Ⓜ *Dessert/Japanese*
23 | 19 | 19 | $30

W 40s | 705 Ninth Ave. (bet. 48th & 49th Sts.) | 212-974-6012 |
www.kyotofu-nyc.com

Proving that the "lowly soybean" can be "truly delicious", this "unusual" Hell's Kitchen Japanese dispenses "wonderful desserts" and "fantastic soft-serve", all made from tofu; the "candlelit" setting and "seductive sakes" conjure up "romance" with a "touch of Zen."

Kyo Ya ●Ⓜ *Japanese*
26 | 22 | 24 | $91

E Village | 94 E. Seventh St., downstairs (1st Ave.) | 212-982-4140

Offering "otherworldly kaiseki", this "hidden" East Village Japanese presents "exquisitely prepared" multicourse meals that look like "edible" art; "slow" pacing, "lovely" service and an elegantly "spare" setting add up to an experience that's "flawless", except for the cost.

La Baraka *French*
21 | 16 | 24 | $44

Little Neck | 255-09 Northern Blvd. (2 blocks east of Little Neck Pkwy.) |
Queens | 718-428-1461

You "really feel welcome" at this "reliable" Little Neck veteran, where the "old-fashioned" Moroccan-accented French fare is deemed a "steal for the quality"; regulars "never tire" of "truly caring" service led by "charming hostess" Lucette, so never mind if the decor needs "refreshing."

	FOOD	DECOR	SERVICE	COST

La Bergamote *Bakery/French*
| 24 | 14 | 16 | $18 |

Chelsea | 169 Ninth Ave. (20th St.) | 212-627-9010
W 50s | 515 W. 52nd St. (bet. 10th & 11th Aves.) | 212-586-2429
www.labergamotenyc.com

"Am I in Paris?" wonder patrons of these French patisserie-cafes, where it's "easy to overdo it" on "exquisite" baked goods and savory "light eats"; whether at the "teeny" Chelsea original or its full-menu Hell's Kitchen counterpart, they don't come more "authentic" – or "aloof" – unless you "hop a plane."

La Boîte en Bois *French*
| 22 | 17 | 21 | $53 |

W 60s | 75 W. 68th St. (bet. Columbus Ave. & CPW) | 212-874-2705 | www.laboitenyc.com

"Convenient" to Lincoln Center, this long-running French bistro's "enticing" classics are served with "curtain times studiously considered"; just bring a "shoehorn", as the "value"-intensive pre-theater prix fixe keeps the "minuscule" space "tightly packed."

La Bonne Soupe *French*
| 18 | 14 | 16 | $30 |

W 50s | 48 W. 55th St. (bet. 5th & 6th Aves.) | 212-586-7650 | www.labonnesoupe.com

"After decades", this "no-nonsense" Midtown bistro still "does the trick" with its "beloved onion soup" and other French "usual suspects" at "bargain" rates; the "casual" quarters can get "mobbed" at prime times, so just plan on some "togetherness."

L'Absinthe *French*
| 22 | 22 | 21 | $68 |

E 60s | 227 E. 67th St. (bet. 2nd & 3rd Aves.) | 212-794-4950 | www.labsinthe.com

"Well-to-do" regulars declare this "very UES" "Parisian-style brasserie" "has it all", from "delightful belle epoque surroundings" to "fine" French cuisine served by a "welcoming" staff; *naturellement* "you pay for it", but it's justifiably a "local favorite."

La Carbonara *Italian*
| 19 | 16 | 18 | $37 |

W Village | 202 W. 14th St. (bet. 7th & 8th Aves.) | 212-255-2060 | www.lacarbonaranyc.com

"Bargain"-hunters rate this West Villager a "real find" for "tasty" Italian "basics" at modest prices (all entrees are under $15); it's "not much to look at" and "tends to be noisy", but when the check comes "all is forgiven."

Lady Mendl's *Tearoom*
| 21 | 26 | 22 | $43 |

Gramercy | Inn at Irving Pl. | 56 Irving Pl. (bet. 17th & 18th Sts.) | 212-533-4466 | www.ladymendls.com

"As classic English as you can get", this "gracious" Gramercy tearoom channels "high" "Victorian style" with its finger sandwiches and scones served in an "enchanting" "antique setting"; the price is "a bit steep", but for "bridal showers" or a "ladies' afternoon out" it's "truly a treat."

La Esquina   *Mexican*
| 22 | 20 | 16 | $42 |

Little Italy | 114 Kenmare St. (bet. Cleveland Pl. & Lafayette St.) | 646-613-7100 | www.esquinanyc.com

The "*delicioso*" eats will "cure your sorrows" at this Little Italy Mexican's "late-night taco shack" and upstairs cafe, but the "chic crowd" slips "past the doorman" into a "Maxwell Smart" "passageway through the kitchen" to access the "awesomely" "cool, happening" cellar – it's "quite a scene", and reservations are a "hassle."

La Fonda del Sol *Spanish*

22 | 21 | 21 | $57

E 40s | MetLife Bldg. | 200 Park Ave. (enter on 44th St. & Vanderbilt Ave.) | 212-867-6767 | www.patinagroup.com

Inspired by the namesake '60s "favorite", this "cheerful" Grand Central–area Spaniard has chef Josh DeChellis lending "creative" "zing" to an "enticing" lineup of tapas in the "lively bar" and full-size dishes in the "civilized" rear dining room; maybe it's "a far cry from the original", but it's got "a lot of *sol.*"

NEW La Gazzetta ● *Italian*

- | - | - | M

Meatpacking | 55 Gansevoort St. (bet. Greenwich & Washington Sts.) | 212-924-5559 | www.villapacri.com

From the Bagatelle folks comes this Meatpacking cafe – part of a tri-level complex including a posh upstairs dining room and basement lounge – where hip young things collect for casual, well-priced Italian sandwiches and such; it features tiled floors, cafe tables and French doors that open out to the street in fair weather.

☑ La Grenouille ☒ *French*

28 | 28 | 28 | $109

E 50s | 3 E. 52nd St. (bet. 5th & Madison Aves.) | 212-752-1495 | www.la-grenouille.com

NYC's "surviving grande dame" of "traditional haute French" cuisine, Charles Masson's Midtown "treasure" remains the "essence" of "luxe" with its "flawless" cooking, "splendid" setting bedecked with "flowers galore" and black-tie service fit for "Louis XIV"; it's "worth the big bucks" to be "swept away", though you can have the "bargain" $29 prix fixe lunch in the charming upstairs "artist's studio."

Lake Club *Continental/Eclectic*

∇ 23 | 27 | 22 | $47

Staten Island | 1150 Clove Rd. (Victory Blvd.) | 718-442-3600 | www.lake-club.com

"Nestled on the shore" of a private island "in the middle of Clove Lake park", this Staten Islander sets a "lovely" scene for "well-prepared" Continental-Eclectic fare and "eager-to-please" service; the "romantic" location's the main attraction, so "bring your loved one" and "rekindle the spark."

La Lunchonette *French*

21 | 15 | 20 | $45

Chelsea | 130 10th Ave. (enter on 18th St., bet. 10th & 11th Aves.) | 212-675-0342

"Way before the High Line", this stalwart West Chelsea bistro was a "quirky" "haven" for "consistently tasty French standards" in "unassuming" environs overseen by a "cheery" staff; as ever, "the check won't drain your wallet", and on Sundays there's even an "accordion player."

La Mangeoire *French*

20 | 20 | 21 | $50

E 50s | 1008 Second Ave. (bet. 53rd & 54th Sts.) | 212-759-7086 | www.lamangeoire.com

It's "been there forever" (well, since 1975), and this Midtown French bistro continues to "hold its own" with "solid" Provençal "country cooking" in a *"très jolie"* "farmhouse" setting; "moderate pricing" and "unpretentious" service ensure it stays "popular" with "locals."

	FOOD	DECOR	SERVICE	COST

La Masseria *Italian* — 22 | 19 | 22 | $56

W 40s | 235 W. 48th St. (bet. B'way & 8th Ave.) | 212-582-2111 | www.lamasserianyc.com

Showgoers "depend on" this "convenient" Theater District resource for "hearty" Southern Italian cooking that's "well above average" and service that's "mindful" of "curtain time"; "word seems to have spread", though, so the "faux country-house" digs can get "packed and loud."

NEW Lambs Club *American* — - | - | - | E

W 40s | Chatwal Hotel | 132 W. 44th St. (bet. 6th & 7th Aves.) | 212-997-5262 | www.thelambsclub.com

Chef Geoffrey Zakarian (Town, Country) returns to the scene via this splashy new entry in the Theater District's Chatwal Hotel, offering a high-end New American menu of self-described 'luxury bar and grill' items; the swish setting – recalling a 1940s deco nightclub – features red leather banquettes and dark-wood paneling, but the focal point of the room is an enormous, circa-1920 limestone fireplace.

La Mirabelle *French* — 23 | 19 | 24 | $53

W 80s | 102 W. 86th St. (bet. Amsterdam & Columbus Aves.) | 212-496-0458 | www.lamirabelleny.com

An UWS "old standby", this "family-operated" bistro provides "traditional French" fare with "no bells and whistles" via a staff that gives the "warmest of welcomes" and even "occasionally breaks into song"; though its prices aren't bad, overall it may seem "a bit long in the tooth."

Land *Thai* — 22 | 16 | 19 | $29

E 80s | 1565 Second Ave. (bet. 81st & 82nd Sts.) | 212-439-1847
W 80s | 450 Amsterdam Ave. (bet. 81st & 82nd Sts.) | 212-501-8121
www.landthaikitchen.com

It's easy to imagine you've "landed in Bangkok" at this "simple" crosstown duo, where the "scintillating" Thai staples satisfy "spice cravings" for "next to nothing"; the "shoebox-size" digs are "frequently full" ("like eating on a bus"), but delivery "comes in minutes."

L & B Spumoni Gardens *Dessert/Pizza* — 24 | 11 | 16 | $22

Bensonhurst | 2725 86th St. (bet. W. 10th & 11th Sts.) | Brooklyn | 718-449-6921 | www.spumonigardens.com

At this seriously "retro" (circa 1939) Bensonhurst "landmark", it's "all about" the "mouthwatering" "thick Sicilian squares" and "must-have" spumoni – "simple pleasures" that "leave you smiling ear to ear"; sure, the outside seating is "no-frills", but there's lotsa "local color."

Landmarc *French* — 20 | 19 | 19 | $49

TriBeCa | 179 W. Broadway (bet. Leonard & Worth Sts.) | 212-343-3883
W 60s | Time Warner Ctr. | 10 Columbus Circle, 3rd fl. (60th St. at B'way) | 212-823-6123
www.landmarc-restaurant.com

With their "quality" "midpriced" bites and "minimally marked-up" wines, this "informal" French duo from Marc Murphy is a "crowd-pleaser", especially with "the stroller mafia"; the TriBeCa original's more "neighborly" than its "cavernous" TWC spin-off, but both get "rollicking" and "noisy" during peak hours.

		FOOD	DECOR	SERVICE	COST

Landmark Tavern *American/Irish* | 18 | 19 | 19 | $39 |

W 40s | 626 11th Ave. (46th St.) | 212-247-2562 |
www.thelandmarktavern.org

Around since 1868, this way West Side "haunt" is "still serviceable" for "meat-and-potatoes" American-Irish pub fare in a setting that's "steeped" in "yesteryear"; those who claim the food's "just fair" can always "unwind" and "savor the vintage atmosphere" and brews instead.

Lantern Thai Kitchen *Thai* | 19 | 18 | 18 | $27 |

Gramercy | 311 Second Ave. (18th St.) | 212-777-2770
Brooklyn Heights | 101 Montague St. (bet. Henry & Hicks Sts.) |
Brooklyn | 718-237-2594
www.lanternthai.com

Neighborhood "bright spots", these Gramercy and Brooklyn Heights Thais are an "easy option" for "enjoyable" "basics" served up "fast" in casually "modern" quarters; maybe they're "nothing exceptional", but light tabs ensure they remain "popular with the locals."

Lanza *Italian* | 18 | 14 | 18 | $34 |

E Village | 168 First Ave. (bet. 10th & 11th Sts.) | 212-674-7014

It's been "around forever" (well, since 1904), and this East Village Southern Italian still dispenses "solid, affordable red-sauce" standards in "appropriately old-timey" digs; maybe it's "past its prime", but it's "reliable for its type" – and "people are happy in that room."

La Paella *Spanish* | 20 | 16 | 18 | $37 |

E Village | 214 E. Ninth St. (bet. 2nd & 3rd Aves.) | 212-598-4321 |
www.lapaellanyc.com

For "dates and groups" disposed to "sharing", this "cozy" East Village Spaniard "hits the spot" with tapas and the namesake dish washed down with pitchers of "the best sangria"; prices are "reasonable", and "warm" "Barcelona" vibes give the "quaint" space a lift.

La Palapa ◐ *Mexican* | 20 | 16 | 18 | $35 |

E Village | 77 St. Marks Pl. (bet. 1st & 2nd Aves.) | 212-777-2537
W Village | 359 Sixth Ave. (bet. Washington Pl. & W. 4th St.) | 212-243-6870
www.lapalapa.com

"Dependable" and "down to earth", this cross-Village Mexican twosome turns out "well-prepared" grub with "little fanfare" at an "affordable" cost; the settings are on the "simple" side, but the "potent margaritas" and general "conviviality" get you "feeling pretty good."

La Petite Auberge *French* | 21 | 17 | 23 | $49 |

Murray Hill | 116 Lexington Ave. (bet. 27th & 28th Sts.) | 212-689-5003 |
www.lapetiteaubergeny.com

"Old-fashioned" "to the teeth", this "very French" bistro in Murray Hill "keeps humming along" "year after year" with "classic" dishes "done right" and "ultracourteous" service; the decor "could use updating", but "the price is right" – traditionalists only "wish there were more like it."

La Pizza Fresca Ristorante *Italian* | 23 | 18 | 18 | $40 |

Flatiron | 31 E. 20th St. (bet. B'way & Park Ave. S.) | 212-598-0141 |
www.lapizzafrescaristorante.com

Known for its "delish", "authentic" Neapolitan pizza, this Flatiron Italian is also a "neighborhood find" for "tasty pastas" and a "surprisingly" "decent" wine list; the "cozy", brick-lined space is "adult" enough, but have *pazienza* as "service can be iffy."

La Ripaille *French*

20	17	21	$51

W Village | 605 Hudson St. (bet. Bethune & W. 12th Sts.) | 212-255-4406 | www.laripailleny.com

"True to its heritage", this longtime West Village French bistro is a "*très charmant*" "hideaway" for "quiet conversation" over "delightful" "traditional" dishes; it's something of a "chestnut", but "caring" servers led by a "winning" chef-owner ensure most "leave happy."

L'Artusi *Italian*

24	21	22	$59

W Village | 228 W. 10th St. (bet. Bleecker & Hudson Sts.) | 212-255-5757 | www.lartusi.com

"Pretty people" flock to this West Village Italian from "the folks behind Dell'anima", a "stylish" duplex staffed by a "l'artful" team where the "terrific" small plates (and "extensive wine list") are "best shared"; it's a "scene for sure", so be ready for a "high" "buzz level."

La Sirène ⊅ *French*

▽ 22	13	21	$48

SoHo | 558½ Broome St. (Varick St.) | 212-925-3061 | www.lasirenenyc.com

"Everyone's a VIP" at this West SoHo BYO "joint" that treats you well with "inventive", seafood-centric French fare from a chef-owner who's "your new best friend after just one visit"; though unassuming and "off the beaten path", it's "tiny" and "gets booked up" fast, so "don't tell."

Las Ramblas ● *Spanish*

24	16	22	$39

W Village | 170 W. Fourth St. (bet. Cornelia & Jones Sts.) | 646-415-7924 | www.lasramblasnyc.com

Although "miniature", this "inviting" Village Spaniard packs a "powerful punch" thanks to its "exceptional" tapas that evoke "memories of Madrid"; "cozy in the extreme", with "super-sweet" service led by owner/"perfect hostess" Natalie Sanz, it's "definitely worth" a try.

La Superior ●⊅ *Mexican*

▽ 24	11	16	$22

Williamsburg | 295 Berry St. (bet. S. 2nd & 3rd Sts.) | Brooklyn | 718-388-5988 | www.lasuperiornyc.com

Those seeking "proper" "Mexican street food" at "bargain" rates "can't miss" at this Williamsburg "hole-in-the-wall", which boasts a "superior" lineup of "wonderful" mini-tacos and the like; it's a "quirky" setup, but "purists" keep it "packed", especially now that it has a liquor license.

La Taqueria *Mexican*

20	13	16	$20

Park Slope | 72 Seventh Ave. (bet. Berkeley & Lincoln Pls.) | Brooklyn | 718-398-4300

Rachel's Taqueria *Mexican*

Park Slope | 408 Fifth Ave. (bet. 7th & 8th Sts.) | Brooklyn | 718-788-1137

"Loosen your belt a notch" before digging into the "voluptuous burritos" and other "tasty" Mexican eats "on the cheap" at these "friendly", "hippie-California" Park Slope twins; those who don't savor the laid-back "'70s" "rock 'n' roll" vibe can always opt for "takeout."

La Taza de Oro ⊠⊅ *Puerto Rican*

▽ 21	9	19	$14

Chelsea | 96 Eighth Ave. (bet. 14th & 15th Sts.) | 212-243-9946

"NYC needs more places" like this "cheap and quick" circa-1957 Chelsea coffee shop doling out "fresh", "tasty" Puerto Rican comfort fare plus

| | FOOD | DECOR | SERVICE | COST |

"cafe con leche the way *abuelita* makes it"; it's on the "greasy" side, but the portions are "large" and the mood "charming."

☑ L'Atelier de Joël Robuchon   French   27 | 25 | 27 | $128
E 50s | Four Seasons Hotel | 57 E. 57th St. (bet. Madison & Park Aves.) | 212-829-3844 | www.fourseasons.com
Most maintain a "front-row seat" at the counter "is the way to go" at "über-chef" Joël Robuchon's "opulent" Midtown "gastronomic experi ence", which "inspires and entertains" with its "ingenious", Japanese-accented French small plates and air of "true luxury"; it's designed to "knock your socks off", but given the "exorbitant price tag" ("bring your first-born"), a few say they "expected more."

Lattanzi ● Italian   22 | 18 | 21 | $56
W 40s | 361 W. 46th St. (bet. 8th & 9th Aves.) | 212-315-0980 | www.lattanzinyc.com
It's a "good bet" pre-theater, but "after 8 PM" this "soothing" Restaurant Row Italian gets "dialed up a notch" with "delicious Roman-Jewish dishes" (fried artichokes are a "must-try") that make for a "treat"; "skilled" service and a "lovely" terrace help soften any "sticker shock."

Laut ⊠ Malaysian/Thai   23 | 14 | 20 | $28
Union Sq | 15 E. 17th St. (bet. B'way & 5th Ave.) | 212-206-8989
"Assertive spices" inspire "serious cravings" at this "friendly" Asian off Union Square, where the "expansive menu" presents a "zingy" Thai-Malaysian-Singaporean merger; it's casual and "pleasant", with "low tabs" ensuring that lauts of "twentysomethings" fill the tables.

Lavagna   Italian   23 | 19 | 21 | $48
E Village | 545 E. Fifth St. (bet. Aves. A & B) | 212-979-1005 | www.lavagnanyc.com
Outwardly it's "unassuming", but "locals" know this midpriced East Village trattoria as a "delight" for "wonderful" "homestyle" Italian paired with a "serious" but "accessible" wine list; the ultra-"cozy" quarters are often "mobbed", but it's worth the effort to "shoulder your way in."

La Villa Pizzeria   Pizza   21 | 16 | 18 | $28
Mill Basin | Key Food Shopping Ctr. | 6610 Ave. U (bet. 66th & 67th Sts.) | Brooklyn | 718-251-8030
Park Slope | 261 Fifth Ave. (bet. 1st St. & Garfield Pl.) | Brooklyn | 718-499-9888 | www.lavillaparkslope.com
Howard Bch | Lindenwood Shopping Ctr. | 82-07 153rd Ave. (82nd St.) | Queens | 718-641-8259
"Predictable in a good way", this "unpretentious" interborough three-some plies "awesome" "wood-fired pizzas" plus "reliable" Italian "ba-sics" in "portion sizes like mom's"; "decent prices" cement their "popularity" with a "family crowd."

Lazzara's   Pizza   21 | 10 | 15 | $22
Garment District | 221 W. 38th St., 2nd fl. (bet. 7th & 8th Aves.) | 212-944-7792 ⊠
W 40s | 617 Ninth Ave. (bet. 43rd & 44th Sts.) | 212-245-4440 ●
www.lazzaraspizza.com
They often "escape notice", but these "homey" joints have "pizza lovers" "impressed" by their "high-quality", "crispy-crusted" square pies; the

Garment District original occupies a "hidden", "only-in-NY" upstairs space, but the Hell's Kitchen "storefront" is the only one to serve slices.

Le Barricou ●🖘 *French* ▽ 21 | 21 | 19 | $33

Williamsburg | 533 Grand St. (bet. Lorimer St. & Union Ave.) | Brooklyn | 718-782-7372 | www.lebarricouny.com

"Hipster Francophiles" make this "comfy" East Williamsburg bistro their "neighborhood spot" for French favorites in authentically "laid-back" environs that get "busy" at brunch; some speak of "snarky" service, but "good value" helps it "hold its own."

☒ Le Bernardin ☒ *French/Seafood* 29 | 27 | 28 | $146

W 50s | 155 W. 51st St. (bet. 6th & 7th Aves.) | 212-554-1515 | www.le-bernardin.com

"You've reached the top of the line" at this Midtown "champ", once again voted NYC's No. 1 for Food, a "reserved", art-filled "temple" co-owned by the lovely Maguy LeCoze and "perfectionist" chef Eric Ripert, where diners "rejoice" over "unmatched" French seafood and "discreetly" "synchronized" service; prices are "heady" (prix fixe–only dinner starts at $112), but you can "save a few bucks" by going at lunch; P.S. the "small" upstairs rooms are "nice for a private party."

Le Bilboquet *French* 23 | 18 | 16 | $59

E 60s | 25 E. 63rd St. (bet. Madison & Park Aves.) | 212-751-3036

See the "beautiful" "air-kissing" folk "in action" at this East Side French bistro that's something of an "exclusive party" for the "chic Euros" and "socialites" "packed" into its "loud, tight space"; the "expensive" food's surprisingly "good", but service can be "haughty" – it "depends on who you are."

🆕 Le Caprice ● *European* 17 | 24 | 20 | $79

E 60s | Pierre Hotel | 2 E. 61st St. (5th Ave.) | 212-940-8195 | www.lecapriceny.com

A branch of the sceney "London original", this Pierre Hotel newcomer appeals to UES "adults" with an "elegant" black-and-white backdrop and updated "Noël Coward atmosphere"; its "glam setting" trumps the "passable" modern European cuisine, but the Park Avenue plutocrats don't seem to mind.

Le Charlot *French* ▽ 21 | 17 | 19 | $55

E 60s | 19 E. 69th St. (bet. Madison & Park Aves.) | 212-794-1628

It's a "buzzy" "air-kiss" scene at this "upbeat" UES bistro, which "caters to regulars in a big way" with "fine", "authentic French" fare and "excellent outdoor seating"; it's a "local" "go-to" despite "laissez-faire" service, "frenetic" crowds and tables that are a "tight fit."

☒ Le Cirque ☒ *French* 24 | 26 | 24 | $95

E 50s | One Beacon Court | 151 E. 58th St. (bet. Lexington & 3rd Aves.) | 212-644-0202 | www.lecirque.com

After 37 years and three venues, Sirio Maccioni still "outdoes himself" at this "famed" Midtown "class act", which "shines" with "exquisite" French cuisine, "pro" service and a "glamorous" setting for "the rich and famous"; a few fret over "lapses", but it's "still special" if "your bankbook holds out" – and there's always the $28 lunch prix fixe in the informal cafe to spare you the "splurge."

	FOOD	DECOR	SERVICE	COST

L'Ecole *French* | 24 | 20 | 23 | $54 |

SoHo | Intl. Culinary Ctr. | 462 Broadway (Grand St.) | 212-219-3300 | www.frenchculinary.com

Education "has never been so good" as at this "understated" SoHo culinary school "practice arm", where "budding chefs" produce "gourmet" French prix fixes at an "amazing value for the quality"; but while the students often "ace it", the less impressed note they're "still learning."

Le Colonial *French/Vietnamese* | 21 | 22 | 20 | $57 |

E 50s | 149 E. 57th St. (bet. Lexington & 3rd Aves.) | 212-752-0808 | www.lecolonialnyc.com

Like you've "time-traveled" to "colonial Hanoi", this "stylish" Midtown French-Vietnamese serves "piquant" fusion dishes in "atmospheric", "frond-filled" surroundings "straight out of Graham Greene"; the "cool upstairs" lounge shares "the mood" too, though a few feel it's all "a bit dated" – except for the prices.

Le Gigot *French* | 24 | 18 | 22 | $57 |

W Village | 18 Cornelia St. (bet. Bleecker & W 4th Sts.) | 212-627-0714 | www.legigotrestaurant.com

West Villagers have long "relied" on this "quaint little" French bistro for "first-rate" Provençal "comfort food" "cheerfully served" in "cozy, convivial" quarters; it "ain't cheap" and "claustrophobes might have a problem", but the "homey" meals are "always a pleasure."

Le Jardin Bistro *French* | 20 | 19 | 19 | $43 |

NoLita | 25 Cleveland Pl. (bet. Kenmare & Spring Sts.) | 212-343-9599 | www.lejardinbistro.com

Screened by a "cover of real vines", the "lovely back garden" is a "definite" plus at this NoLita bistro supplier of "hearty" French favorites "without attitude"; "decent prices" have "neighborhood" types "returning again and again."

Le Magnifique ● *French* | 20 | 18 | 17 | $48 |

E 70s | 1022A Lexington Ave. (73rd St.) | 212-879-6190

"Not bad for a neighborhood bistro", this UES French is a "welcome" "retreat" for "moderately priced" bites in "intimate" digs; there's a choice of a downstairs bar, second-floor dining room and outdoor seating, but sticklers cite "spotty" service and "tight" tables.

Le Marais *French/Steak* | 22 | 16 | 17 | $55 |

W 40s | 150 W. 46th St. (bet. 6th & 7th Aves.) | 212-869-0900 | www.lemarais.net

The "quality" meat "just happens to be kosher" at this Theater District French steakhouse, a convenient provider of "delicious" beef at fair prices; service is "erratic" and the "packed" room's "not much on ambiance", but it gets points for having its own "built-in butcher shop."

Le Monde *French* | 17 | 18 | 16 | $36 |

W 100s | 2885 Broadway (bet. 112th & 113th Sts.) | 212-531-3939 | www.lemondenyc.com

A "known quantity" in the "Columbia area", this "lively" Morningside Heights bistro is "popular with profs" and students gobbling "reliable" French "basics" in an "informal" setting including a "sidewalk cafe"; moderate prices offset "uneven" service.

	FOOD	DECOR	SERVICE	COST

Lemongrass Grill *Thai*   17 | 11 | 15 | $25

Financial District | 84 William St. (Maiden Ln.) | 212-809-8038 |
www.lemongrassgrillnyc.com
Murray Hill | 138 E. 34th St. (bet. Lexington & 3rd Aves.) |
212-213-3317 | www.lemongrassgrill34thst.com
Cobble Hill | 156 Court St. (bet. Dean & Pacific Sts.) | Brooklyn |
718-522-9728
Park Slope | 61A Seventh Ave. (bet. Berkeley & Lincoln Pls.) |
Brooklyn | 718-399-7100

"Serviceable", "if not mind-blowing", this "generic" chainlet's Thai
standards "fill you up" at "very affordable" rates; some are sour on the
"disappointing" service and decor, but there's always carryout or
"super-speedy delivery."

Lenny's *Sandwiches*   17 | 8 | 15 | $15

E 50s | 1024 Second Ave. (54th St.) | 212-355-5700
E 60s | 1269 First Ave. (68th St.) | 212-288-0852
E 70s | 1481 Second Ave. (77th St.) | 212-288-5288
Financial District | 108 John St. (bet. Cliff & Pearl Sts.) | 212-385-2828
Flatiron | 16 W. 23rd St. (bet. 5th & 6th Aves.) | 212-462-4433
G Village | 418 Sixth Ave. (9th St.) | 212-353-0300
W 40s | 60 W. 48th St. (bet. 5th & 6th Aves.) | 212-997-1969
W 40s | 613 Ninth Ave. (43rd St.) | 212-957-7800
W 70s | 302 Columbus Ave. (74th St.) | 212-580-8300
W 80s | 489 Columbus Ave. (bet. 84th & 85th Sts.) | 212-787-9368
www.lennysnyc.com
Additional locations throughout the NY area

A "model of efficiency", this "convenient" chain is a "no-brainer" for
"satisfying sandwiches" swiftly "made to order" from any fixing "under the sun" ("decisions, decisions"); it's "nothing fancy", but "fair
prices" explain why it's "spreading all over."

Leo's Latticini 🈂Ⓜ *Deli/Italian*   ▽ 26 | 10 | 21 | $14

(aka Mama's of Corona)

Corona | 46-02 104th St. (46th Ave.) | Queens | 718-898-6069

Run by a "sweet family", this '20s-era Corona deli keeps "tradition
alive" vending what cognoscenti call "definitive Italian heros" and "the
freshest" imaginable housemade mozzarella in "unchanging" "old-
school" digs; it "isn't elegant dining", but it packs good "value."

Le Pain Quotidien *Bakery/Belgian*   18 | 15 | 14 | $23

E 60s | 833 Lexington Ave. (bet. 63rd & 64th Sts.) | 212-755-5810
E 70s | 252 E. 77th St. (bet. 2nd & 3rd Aves.) | 212-249-8600
E 80s | 1131 Madison Ave. (bet. 84th & 85th Sts.) | 212-327-4900
Flatiron | ABC Carpet & Home | 38 E. 19th St. (bet. B'way & Park Ave. S.) |
212-673-7900
G Village | 10 Fifth Ave. (8th St.) | 212-253-2324
G Village | 801 Broadway (11th St.) | 212-677-5277
SoHo | 100 Grand St. (bet. Greene & Mercer Sts.) | 212-625-9009
W 50s | 922 Seventh Ave. (58th St.) | 212-757-0775
W 60s | 60 W. 65th St. (bet. B'way & CPW) | 212-721-4001
W 70s | 50 W. 72nd St. (bet. Columbus Ave. & CPW) | 212-712-9700
www.painquotidien.com
Additional locations throughout the NY area

"So handy", this "omnipresent" Belgian bakery/cafe chain is a
"safe bet" for "super" baked goods and "wholesome" "organic"

noshes in "faux-folk" settings equipped with "trademark" "communal farm tables"; service is "scattered", but the "easy" "refueling" "serves its purpose."

NEW Le Parisien *French*   — | — | — | I

Murray Hill | 163 E. 33rd St. (bet. Lexington & 3rd Aves.) | 212-889-5489 | www.leparisiennyc.com

Art nouveau posters, arched windows and a record player pile on the retro charm at this snug Murray Hill French bistro evoking a Parisian trip back in time; a petite bar, budget-friendly tabs and pleasantly served French staples are already earning it warm welcomes from the locals.

Le Perigord *French*   25 | 22 | 25 | $76

E 50s | 405 E. 52nd St. (bet. FDR Dr. & 1st Ave.) | 212-755-6244 | www.leperigord.com

One of NYC's "last bastions" of "old-guard" "fine dining", owner Georges Briguet's Sutton Place "charmer" (since 1964) seems "suspended in time" with its *magnifique* "traditional" French fare and "lovely" "dress-up" setting matched with "gracious" service: "you pay the piper", but its "well-heeled" clientele doesn't seem to mind.

Le Pescadeux ●Ⓜ *French/Seafood*   ▽ 23 | 19 | 24 | $52

SoHo | 90 Thompson St. (bet. Prince & Spring Sts.) | 212-966-0021 | www.lepescadeux.com

SoHo pescatarians have "welcomed" this "cozy" "neighborhood" berth for its "outstanding", Quebec-style French seafood best sampled via dishes featuring "two half-portions" of different fish; the "congenial" staff sets a "down-to-earth" tone "rarely seen" hereabouts.

Le Relais de Venise L'Entrecôte *Steak*   20 | 17 | 19 | $42

E 50s | 590 Lexington Ave. (52nd St.) | 212-758-3989 | www.relaisdevenise.com

Feeling "indecisive"? – then this Paris-based French meatery in East Midtown is your ticket: it offers only a "set menu" of steak frites and salad, "priced right" at $24 and served "quick" in "faux-bistro" digs; *oui*, it's "formulaic", but for "consistency" and "value", it's hard to beat.

Le Rivage *French*   20 | 17 | 21 | $47

W 40s | 340 W. 46th St. (bet. 8th & 9th Aves.) | 212-765-7374 | www.lerivagenyc.com

Operating since 1958, this Restaurant Row "staple" still "delivers" pre-theater with "solid old-style French" fare "hustled out to you" by a "totally reliable" staff; it's "satisfying", if due for "a sprucing up", and after 8 PM the $25 prix fixe is an "excellent deal."

Les Halles ● *French*   20 | 17 | 17 | $46

Financial District | 15 John St. (bet. B'way & Nassau St.) | 212-285-8585
Murray Hill | 411 Park Ave. S. (bet. 28th & 29th Sts.) | 212-679-4111
www.leshalles.net

These "straightforward" French bistros "efficiently" turn out "fab" steak frites and other "honest" classics for fair fares; you can expect plenty of "hustle and bustle" and a serious "din", but don't look for onetime chef Anthony Bourdain in the kitchen – he's "long gone."

	FOOD	DECOR	SERVICE	COST

Le Singe Vert ● *French*
| | 18 | 15 | 17 | $42 |

Chelsea | 160 Seventh Ave. (bet. 19th & 20th Sts.) | 212-366-4100 | www.lesingevert.com

Like "stepping into the Left Bank", this Chelsea "neighborhood boîte" "earns its chevrons" with French bistro fare "done properly" in "unpretentious" quarters; "moderate prices" keep it "full of locals", and there's "outdoor seating" for singular "people-watching."

L'Express ● *French*
| | 18 | 15 | 16 | $35 |

Flatiron | 249 Park Ave. S. (20th St.) | 212-254-5858 | www.lexpressnyc.com

A 24/7 "go-to", this Flatiron French bistro "reliably" provides the "standards" *sans* fanfare" at prices that "won't make you gasp"; "hopping" crowds lead to high "decibels" and "hit-or-miss" service, but "when you're hungry" at 4 AM it's a no-brainer.

Le Zie 2000 ● *Italian*
| | 22 | 15 | 20 | $42 |

Chelsea | 172 Seventh Ave. (bet. 20th & 21st Sts.) | 212-206-8686 | www.lezie.com

"Still going strong", this "casual" Chelsea Italian is "beloved" by "local regulars" for "wonderful" "Venetian-style" food served "without attitude" at the "right price"; just "bring your earplugs" for the "loud" front "echo chamber" – or "opt for the back room" "if you want to talk."

Libertador ●◐⊟ *Argentinean*
| | ▽ 21 | 18 | 17 | $39 |

E 80s | 1725 Second Ave. (89th St.) | 212-348-6222 | www.libertador-nyc.com

"Buzzing" and "moderately priced", this Yorkville yearling specializes in "quality" Argentinean "grilled meat" prepared "pampas"-style and slathered with "yummy chimichurri"; add a "friendly" feel, and though service is "spotty", it's a "winner" when the pesos run low.

Liebman's *Deli*
| | 22 | 9 | 17 | $22 |

Bronx | 552 W. 235th St. (Johnson Ave.) | 718-548-4534 | www.liebmansdeli.com

"After all these years", this "genuine" Bronx kosher deli is still a "contender" where you can "stuff your face" with "piled-high" sandwiches and other "luscious" "traditional" noshes at "can't-go-wrong" prices; decor is "nonexistent", but hey, it's "one of the few remaining."

Lil' Frankie's Pizza ●⊟ *Pizza*
| | 23 | 16 | 17 | $32 |

E Village | 19 First Ave. (bet. 1st & 2nd Sts.) | 212-420-4900 | www.lilfrankies.com

With a wood-burning oven producing "awesome" "thin-crust" Neapolitan pizzas and other "casual" Italian eats, this "easygoing" East Village offshoot of Frank is just "the coolest"; however, its "funky" space is a "tight fit" for the "young" fans drawn by a serious "bang for your buck."

Lime Jungle *Mexican*
| | – | – | – | I |

NEW W 50s | 741 Ninth Ave. (50th St.) | 212-582-5599 ●
W 50s | 803 Ninth Ave. (bet. 53rd & 54th Sts.) | 212-586-6032 | www.limejunglenyc.com

This Hell's Kitchen twosome packs in Midtown lunchers for low-cost tacos, burritos and other nothing-fancy Mexican standards; come dinnertime, the margaritas start to flow in the small but convivial spaces done up with colorful tropical artwork.

Limon *Turkish* ▽ 24 | 10 | 19 | $31

Murray Hill | 238 E. 24th St. (bet. 2nd & 3rd Aves.) | 212-213-3343
"Tiny, tiny", this Murray Hill "sleeper" is a "real find" for "sensational" kebabs and other Turkish staples, especially given the wallet-friendly BYO policy; the staff is "friendly", but the space "lacks" both size and "personality" – "thank goodness for delivery."

NEW Lina Frey ● *French* - | - | - | M

LES | 201 E. Houston St. (bet. Ludlow & Orchard Sts.) | 212-995-5546
A tranquil Lower East Side respite, this airy bistro boasts an outdoor garden with flower-filled watering cans, slatted benches and a retractable roof; French proteins come in two categories (*de la terre* and *de la mer*) for under $12, and sweet and savory crêpes can be ordered at a walk-up window.

NEW Lincoln *Italian* - | - | - | VE

W 60s | Lincoln Ctr. | 142 W. 65th St. (bet. Amsterdam Ave. & B'way) | 212-359-6500 | www.patinagroup.com
Debuting at Lincoln Center with one of the city's more striking restaurant spaces, this Modern Italian showstopper from the Patina Group inhabits a freestanding, Diller Scofidio & Renfro–designed glass wedge beside the Henry Moore reflecting pool, with a sloping, grass-planted roof that doubles as a picnic perch; the room – under a curved wood ceiling with windows on all sides – is centered around a glass-walled kitchen, whose daily changing, market-based menu from chef Jonathan Benno (ex Per Se) is served in the main area, lounge, bar or out on the plaza.

NEW Lion, The ● *American* - | - | - | E

G Village | 62 W. Ninth St. (bet. 5th & 6th Aves.) | 212-353-8400 | www.thelionnyc.com
The "gorgeous" old-NY setting – replete with skylight, soaring ceilings and walls lined salon-de-Paris style with crime-blotter photos and Basquiat paintings – makes a fitting backdrop for the Traditional Americana at this "buzzing" new Villager that's been a "glitterati" magnet from day one; no surprise, prime-time rezzies (and the choice mezzanine-level table) are near-impossible to snag.

Lisca *Italian* 20 | 14 | 21 | $38

W 90s | 660 Amsterdam Ave. (bet. 92nd & 93rd Sts.) | 212-799-3987 | www.liscanyc.com
UWS "neighborhood folks" count on this "genial", "family-owned" trattoria for "tasty" Tuscan fare delivered by an "attentive" staff at "recession-friendly" rates; given its "consistency" and "homey" atmospherics, it's "the kind of place you'd want on your block."

Little Giant *American* 23 | 16 | 20 | $43

LES | 85 Orchard St. (Broome St.) | 212-226-5047 | www.littlegiantnyc.com
"Tiny" but "impressive", this "inviting" LES New American turns out "terrific" "homestyle" cooking for "adventurous" "locavores"; the "cramped" space can get "tricky" at "rush hour" since its giant "hipster" following keeps "coming back", notably for "excellent brunch."

	FOOD	DECOR	SERVICE	COST

Little Owl   *American/Mediterranean* | 25 | 19 | 22 | $55

W Village | 90 Bedford St. (Grove St.) | 212-741-4695 |
www.thelittleowlnyc.com

"Inch for inch one of the best", chef-owner Joey Campanaro's West
Village "micro"-eatery is "always a treat" with "inspired" Med–New
American dishes "warmly" served in the "coziest" "nest-size" space; it
"retains its cachet" with "foodie" types, so "wise" diners reserve
"way in advance."

Lobster Box ● *Seafood* | 18 | 15 | 16 | $45

Bronx | 34 City Island Ave. (bet. Belden & Rochelle Sts.) | 718-885-1952 |
www.lobsterboxrestaurant.com

A "classic City Island joint" dating from 1946, this "nothing-fancy"
seafooder is still a source for "reasonably priced lobsters" and such,
though the views of Long Island Sound are really what you "come for";
critics call it a "glorified diner" with "tourist trap" tendencies.

Locale   *Italian*   ▽ | 21 | 21 | 20 | $34

Astoria | 33-02 34th Ave. (33rd St.) | Queens | 718-729-9080 |
www.localeastoria.com

"Not your father's Italian", this "appealing" Astorian takes a "modern
approach" with its "fresh, delicious" cuisine and stylishly "airy" digs
where you'll "feel like lingering"; popular for brunch, it's a "neighborhood favorite" that would cost far "more in Manhattan."

Locanda Verde   *Italian* | 24 | 23 | 20 | $61

TriBeCa | Greenwich Hotel | 377 Greenwich St. (N. Moore St.) |
212-925-3797 | www.locandaverdenyc.com

Chef Andrew Carmellini has "done it again" at this justified "hit",
where a "very TriBeCa" crowd collects for "nuanced" versions of
"zesty" Italian dishes; pricing is naturally "upscale", but its "pleasingly
funky" premises are "usually packed", and a "boisterous" "din" under-
scores the fact: it's the "place to be."

Locanda Vini & Olii Ⓜ *Italian*   ▽ | 27 | 24 | 24 | $51

Clinton Hill | 129 Gates Ave. (bet. Cambridge Pl. & Grand Ave.) |
Brooklyn | 718-622-9202 | www.locandany.com

At this "tucked-away" "restored old pharmacy" in Clinton Hill, they're
serving "delicious", "out-of-the ordinary" Tuscan cuisine made from
"carefully sourced" ingredients; "knowledgeable" service and relatively "affordable" rates are two more reasons it's rated a "must-visit."

Lombardi's ⊕ *Pizza* | 23 | 13 | 16 | $25

NoLita | 32 Spring St. (bet. Mott & Mulberry Sts.) | 212-941-7994 |
www.firstpizza.com

This "old-fashioned", "cash-only" NoLita stalwart remains in favor for
"perfectly blistered" "coal-oven" pizzas fired as "God intended"; the
hordes of "tourists" and pie-sanos can produce "long waits" at prime
times, but for most it's "well worth it."

Londel's Supper Club Ⓜ *Southern*   ▽ | 20 | 19 | 20 | $37

Harlem | 2620 Frederick Douglass Blvd. (bet. 139th & 140th Sts.) |
212-234-6114 | www.londelsrestaurant.com

"Classy", "comfortable" and cost-conscious, this Southerner on Strivers'
Row in Harlem is a "friendly" fixture offering "tasty" eats and a "jazz

| | FOOD | DECOR | SERVICE | COST |

combo on weekends"; Sundays it's an after-church "gathering place" with a "great" buffet brunch – "what more could a neighborhood want?"

London Lennie's *Seafood*
| | 22 | 18 | 20 | $44 |

Rego Park | 63-88 Woodhaven Blvd. (bet. Fleet Ct. & Penelope Ave.) | Queens | 718-894-8084 | www.londonlennies.com

Ever a "local" "fave", this "longtime" (since 1959) Rego Park fish house lures a "big following" with "the freshest" seafood "done right" in "busy", "family-friendly" digs; it's "not too stylish", but "the formula still works" – and you won't have to sink your "next mortgage payment."

Long Tan ◑ *Thai*
| | ▽ 20 | 17 | 18 | $27 |

Park Slope | 196 Fifth Ave. (bet. Berkeley Pl. & Union St.) | Brooklyn | 718-622-8444 | www.long-tan.com

"Reliable", inexpensive Thai chow and a "pleasantly hip" space tantalize the twentysomethings at this "eager-to-please" Park Sloper; it's also favored for "terrific drinks" that fuel a "late-night scene" at the bar.

Lorenzo's *Italian*
| | ▽ 23 | 26 | 25 | $50 |

Staten Island | Hilton Garden Inn | 1100 South Ave. (Lois Ln.) | 718-477-2400 | www.lorenzosdining.com

"Forget about Atlantic City" – this "upscale" Staten Islander in Bloomfield's Hilton Garden Inn hosts cabaret shows on select Fridays to supplement its well-rated Italian menu; "hands-on" owners oversee the "super" staff, and if it's generally a little "pricey", the Sunday jazz brunch is a "value."

Los Dos Molinos Ⓜ *Southwestern*
| | ▽ 21 | 20 | 17 | $34 |

Gramercy | 119 E. 18th St. (bet. Irving Pl. & Park Ave. S.) | 212-505-1574 | www.losdosmolinosnyc.com

"Bring a fire extinguisher" to handle the "delish" "*caliente*" SW cooking at this "colorful" Gramercy chain "favorite"; the youngish clientele kicks up a "deafening" din, but after a "big margarita" or two "you won't even notice."

NEW Los Feliz ◑ *Mexican*
| | ▽ 20 | 21 | 16 | $38 |

LES | 109 Ludlow St. (bet. Delancey & Rivington Sts.) | 212-228-8383 | www.losfeliznyc.com

This new LES Mexican from the Spitzer's Corner folks dispenses "awesome tacos" and other midpriced fare from chef Julieta Ballesteros (Crema), washed down with "excellent" libations; its "La Esquina lite" tri-level setting with a cantina, catacomb-like dining room and banquette-lined lounge is already a "raucous" "scene."

Lucali ⊘ *Pizza*
| | 26 | 18 | 17 | $25 |

Carroll Gardens | 575 Henry St. (bet. Carroll St. & 1st Pl.) | Brooklyn | 718-858-4086

"Masterfully crafted", "life-affirming" pizza and calzones put this cash-only Carroll Gardens BYO in the "top tier" of NYC's pie parlors, making a trip to its "small", "no-nonsense" site way "worth it"; however, the "secret" is long out, so be prepared for an "insane wait."

Lucien ◑ *French*
| | 22 | 18 | 19 | $45 |

E Village | 14 First Ave. (1st St.) | 212-260-6481 | www.luciennyc.com

As if "you've left the East Village" on a quick trip to "Paris", this "informal" French bistro provides "flavorsome" fare at "fair prices" amid "ambiance galore"; it's a "squeeze" and service can be "frazzled", but the "hoot" of an owner, Lucien Bahaj, "creates authentic bonhomie."

Lucky Strike ◑ *French*

17 | 17 | 17 | $36

SoHo | 59 Grand St. (bet. W. B'way & Wooster St.) | 212-941-0772 | www.luckystrikeny.com

An "old SoHo standby" that keeps "rolling along", Keith McNally's "neighborhood" bistro "fills the bill" for late-night burgers and "casual French" meals at "reasonable prices"; the "bohemian vibe" is "still cool", though critics of the "tired" menu quip it's "more like a spare."

NEW Luke's Lobster *Seafood*

25 | 11 | 18 | $20

E 80s | 242 E. 81st St. (bet. 2nd & 3rd Aves.) | 212-249-4241
E Village | 93 E. Seventh St. (bet. Ave. A & 1st Ave.) | 212-387-8487
www.lukeslobster.com

"Simple is best" at these East Village–UES newcomers supplying "succulent" lobster rolls made from "incredibly fresh" crustaceans "brought in daily from Maine", with minimal mayo and no "superfluous filler"; "tiny" storefronts with "sparse seating" keep the cost "affordable" but encourage "takeout."

Lunetta Ⓜ *Italian*

▽ 22 | 17 | 19 | $40

Boerum Hill | 116 Smith St. (bet. Dean & Pacific Sts.) | Brooklyn | 718-488-6269 | www.lunetta-ny.com

"Not your usual" "local Italian" joint, this "cozy" Smith Streeter keeps things "interesting" with "amazing seasonal" small-plates fare made with "locally sourced ingredients"; the "cheerful" setting includes a five-seat bar fronting the open kitchen and a "bamboo garden" out back.

Ⓩ Lupa ◑ *Italian*

25 | 18 | 22 | $56

G Village | 170 Thompson St. (bet. Bleecker & Houston Sts.) | 212-982-5089 | www.luparestaurant.com

Batali groupies on a "budget" gush *molto grazie* as they "revel" in the "honest", "earthy" Roman cooking and a "smart" wine list "without the high price tag" at this "relaxed" Village trattoria, aka "Babbo's little brother"; its "cozy, rustic" digs are typically "packed" and a bit "chaotic", so it may be a "hassle" getting in at prime times.

Lure Fishbar *Seafood*

23 | 22 | 20 | $55

SoHo | 142 Mercer St., downstairs (Prince St.) | 212-431-7676 | www.lurefishbar.com

Evoking the "wood-paneled" "interior of a yacht", this "below-ground" SoHo seafooder remains a "happening" harbor for "fantastic fish" and "superb" sushi; just be aware that the "buzzing" bar can be "noisy", and pricing "expensive."

Lusardi's *Italian*

24 | 19 | 24 | $63

E 70s | 1494 Second Ave. (bet. 77th & 78th Sts.) | 212-249-2020 | www.lusardis.com

"Adoring" regulars affirm that this circa-1982 Upper East Side standby "hasn't lost its touch" for "civilized" dining, with a "highly professional" staff (led by "gracious" owner Mauro Lusardi) and "superb" Northern Italian fare; it's a "subdued" retreat for "mature patrons" who don't mind shelling out "upper-end" sums to "feel special and well fed."

Luz *Nuevo Latino* ▽ 24 | 18 | 21 | $35

Fort Greene | 177 Vanderbilt Ave. (bet. Myrtle Ave. & Willoughby St.) | Brooklyn | 718-246-4000 | www.luzrestaurant.com

"One of the best" in the zip code, this "creative" Fort Greene "gem" offers "off-the-hook" Nuevo Latino cuisine and "killer drinks"; "helpful" servers oversee the modern, "low-key" quarters, and at these prices you can't go wrong.

Luzzo's *Pizza* 22 | 14 | 17 | $29

E Village | 211 First Ave. (bet. 12th & 13th Sts.) | 212-473-7447

Ovest Pizzoteca ● *Pizza*

NEW Chelsea | 513 W. 27th St. (bet. 10th & 11th Aves.) | 212-967-4392

Pie-sanos praise this "rustic" East Villager for its coal-oven pizzas whose "crusts as thin as paper" are topped with "the freshest ingredients"; the new Chelsea spin-off turns out its "ethereal" specimens in a "lively", "industrial"-looking space, and a TriBeCa branch is in the works at 275 Church Street.

NEW **L'Ybane** ● *Mediterranean* - | - | - | I

W 40s | 709 Eighth Ave. (bet. 44th & 45th Sts.) | 212-582-2012 | www.lybane.com

The sole outpost of a lounge in Nice, this new West 40s wine bar/Med eatery features a wall of bottles, crimson-hued velvets and oil lamps, with golden armchairs and exotic plants adding a dollop of swank; the menu's low-priced small plates pair well with the vintages.

NEW **Lychee House** *Chinese* ▽ 25 | 18 | 22 | $29

E 50s | 141 E. 55th St. (Lexington Ave.) | 212-753-3900 | www.lycheehouse.com

Considered a "big step above your typical Chinese", this Midtowner adds "adventurous" "Shanghai specialties", Malaysian curries and dim sum to its "outstanding" roster; the setting's been "slightly upgraded" since its Our Place days, as has the service.

Macao Trading Co. ● *Chinese/Portuguese* 18 | 24 | 18 | $54

TriBeCa | 311 Church St. (bet. Lispenard & Walker Sts.) | 212-431-8750 | www.macaonyc.com

Boasting a "fabulous", "exotic" setting (think "1940s" "Macao port"), this "intriguing" TriBeCan is out to "tease the palate" with small plates "mixing Chinese and Portuguese" flavors; too bad some say the "sexy" digs and "stellar" drinks upstage the "lackluster cuisine."

NEW **Macbar** *American* ▽ 19 | 16 | 13 | $15

SoHo | 54 Prince St. (Lafayette St.) | 212-226-8877 | www.macbar.net

An adjunct to Delicatessen, this "tiny SoHo comfort station" peddles a dozen "sinful" varieties of mac 'n' cheese, from classic to "outrageous" (e.g. the fontina-and-duck Mac Quack); its "cute" cheddar-hued space is sized like a "walk-in closet", so do "takeout" or "expect to wait."

Macelleria *Italian/Steak* 22 | 20 | 20 | $57

Meatpacking | 48 Gansevoort St. (bet. Greenwich & Washington Sts.) | 212-741-2555 | www.macelleriarestaurant.com

A "carnivore's delight" in the Meatpacking District, this Italian steakhouse serves "buonissimo" beef with "no surprises" in a "boisterous" space appointed with a "butcher shop theme"; a few find it "kind of uninspiring" for the "high price", but at least they act like they're glad to have you.

Macondo ◐ *Pan-Latin*   ▽ 23 | 19 | 20 | $41
LES | 157 E. Houston St. (bet. Allen & Eldridge Sts.) | 212-473-9900 | www.macondonyc.com
"Bold" Spanish and South American flavors mark the "delicious" Pan-Latin street food at this "cute" LES adjunct of Rayuela, whose "innovative" small plates are chased with "yummy drinks"; with an "accommodating" staff and a "happening" bar, it's a "late-night-bite" "favorite."

Madangsui *Korean*   ▽ 23 | 13 | 21 | $38
Garment District | 35 W. 35th St. (6th Ave.) | 212-564-9333 | www.madangsui.com
"Formerly a best-kept secret", this Garment District Korean specializes in "awesome" BBQ grilled at your table by "efficient" servers, preceded by "tasty" *banchan* – little nibbles that amount to "free appetizers"; as for the digs, "what it lacks in decor it makes up for in taste" and value.

Madiba ◐ *African*   22 | 22 | 21 | $33
Fort Greene | 195 DeKalb Ave. (Carlton Ave.) | Brooklyn | 718-855-9190 | www.madibarestaurant.com
"Eat, drink and socialize" at this "chill" Fort Greene "original", a "favorite" for "playful" South African fare, "warm" service and "upbeat" atmospherics boosted by "funky" "live music"; the menu, including pricing, is a "winner", but the "cool" vibe's what people "really come for."

Madison's *Italian*   22 | 18 | 20 | $40
Bronx | 5686 Riverdale Ave. (259th St.) | 718-543-3850
Aiming for "Manhattan-style ambiance" where "you'd least expect it", this Riverdale Italian comes through with "fine" cuisine, "attentive" service and "comfortable" (even "romantic") surroundings; it strikes a few as "slightly overpriced", but the locals know it's "satisfying" "in a pinch."

NEW Maialino *Italian*   25 | 23 | 24 | $67
Gramercy | Gramercy Park Hotel | 2 Lexington Ave. (21st St.) | 212-777-2410 | www.maialinonyc.com
Danny Meyer goes Italian and "nails it again" at this "hot" newcomer in the Gramercy Park Hotel, a "marvelous" Roman trattoria mock-up with "mouthwatering" "rustic" fare (the "delectable" eponymous roast pig "is the thing") and "impressive" wines served with "no pretense" by a "sensational" staff; it's "not cheap", but "energetic" "throngs" make it "tough to get a reservation" – though the "wonderful" front wine bar accepts walk-ins.

Maison ◐ *French*   19 | 17 | 18 | $37
W 50s | 1700 Broadway (53rd St.) | 212-757-2233 | www.maisonnyc.com
"Conveniently located" near Carnegie Hall and City Center, this "casual" "24/7" brasserie is "popular" with "theater and tourist" types seeking "acceptable" French "favorites" at "decent" prices; in fair weather, the roomy "alfresco" terrace adds to the experience.

Malagueta ⓜ *Brazilian*   ▽ 25 | 16 | 21 | $35

Astoria | 25-35 36th Ave. (28th St.) | Queens | 718-937-4821 |
www.malaguetany.com

"If you can find it", this "small, family-run" Brazilian on a "quiet" Astoria
stretch is a "major bargain" for "first-rate", "authentic" cuisine; the
"relaxed" space "may be modest", but the "fabulous" flavors and
"warm" service keep customers coming.

Malatesta Trattoria ⬤⊘ *Italian*   24 | 17 | 18 | $36

W Village | 649 Washington St. (Christopher St.) | 212-741-1207 |
www.malatestatrattoria.com

West Villagers vouch for the "deeply flavorful" Northern Italian fare at
this "relaxed" "local tratt", where well-priced "straightforward dishes"
served by "handsome waiters" leave fans "totally satisfied"; maybe the
"cash-only" policy's a "headache", but that doesn't dent its "popularity."

Maloney & Porcelli *Steak*   23 | 20 | 22 | $69

E 50s | 37 E. 50th St. (bet. Madison & Park Aves.) | 212-750-2233 |
www.maloneyandporcelli.com

A "trusted standby" for the "meat-and-martini" set, Alan Stillman's
"bustling", "high-testosterone" Midtown steakhouse delivers "excellent", "brontosaurus"-size slabs (check out the signature pork shank);
it's advisable to "go on an expense account", though insiders "salud"
the weekend wine dinners as the "best deal around."

Mamajuana Cafe ⬤ *Dominican/Nuevo Latino*   20 | 21 | 18 | $40

Inwood | 247 Dyckman St. (bet. Payson & Seaman Aves.) | 212-304-0140 |
www.mamajuana-cafe.com

"Definitely a super-cool" scene, this Inwood standout serves "wonderful" Dominican–Nuevo Latino specialties in a "gorgeous" Spanish colonial space that's "hopping" with mojito-fueled "energy"; while "not
the place for a quiet rendezvous", it's a "people-watching heaven."

Mamá Mexico ⬤ *Mexican*   19 | 17 | 18 | $36

E 40s | 214 E. 49th St. (bet. 2nd & 3rd Aves.) | 212-935-1316
W 100s | 2672 Broadway (102nd St.) | 212-864-2323
www.mamamexico.com

You can live the "*vida loca*" at these East 40s–UWS Mexicans, where
"reliably good" food comes in settings as "gaudy" as "the inside of a
piñata"; "jam-packed" "fiestas" with "strolling mariachis" and "lethal"
margs, at times they get so "raucous" you "can't hear yourself eat."

Mama's Food Shop ⊘ *American*   ▽ 20 | 11 | 17 | $16

E Village | 200 E. Third St. (bet. Aves. A & B) | 212-777-4425 |
www.mamasfoodshop.com

As "reliable as mom", this cash-only East Village American lets you
"load up" on "more-than-generous" portions of "honest", "homestyle"
grub at "amazing-value" rates; the "no-frills" setup is "perfect for
takeout", since "comfort" applies to "the food, not the ambiance."

Mancora ⬤ *Peruvian*   ▽ 21 | 15 | 19 | $31

E Village | 99 First Ave. (6th St.) | 212-253-1011 |
www.mancorarestaurantandbar.com

"Thank the Peruvian gods" for this East Village "find", where the "traditional" lineup includes "terrific" rotisserie chicken and "must-have"

ceviche; the "hospitality", "fair prices" and pisco sours help offset "humble" quarters with "inadequate" illumination ("bring a flashlight").

Mandarin Court *Chinese*

FOOD	DECOR	SERVICE	COST
20	8	14	$23

Chinatown | 61 Mott St. (bet. Bayard & Canal Sts.) | 212-608-3838
Dim sum carts "wheeling past" bear an "endless succession" of "flavorful" "wonders" at this "dependable", "budget-friendly" Chinatown "joint"; the service is "not so cheerful" and the "big room has virtually "no decor", but "there's a reason" that the lines "extend out the door" on weekends.

Mandoo Bar *Korean*

FOOD	DECOR	SERVICE	COST
20	11	16	$22

Garment District | 2 W. 32nd St. (bet. B'way & 5th Ave.) | 212-279-3075
With "delicious, fresh mandoo" (dumplings) handmade "right in the window", this "simple" Garment District "hole-in-the-wall" makes a "top-notch" choice for a "Korean quickie"; if the space is "rather limited", the eating's bound to be "cheap" and "satisfying."

Manducatis *Italian*

FOOD	DECOR	SERVICE	COST
23	14	21	$48

LIC | 13-27 Jackson Ave. (47th Ave.) | Queens | 718-729-4602 | www.manducatis.com
"Red-sauce" lovers report it's "worth schlepping" to this "ancient" LIC Italian for "real-deal" "homestyle" cooking and a "fab" wine list, even if it resembles "your grandparents' living room, circa '78"; insiders advise "don't bother with the menu" – trust the server's "discretion."

Mangia 🖹 *Mediterranean*

FOOD	DECOR	SERVICE	COST
20	12	13	$24

E 40s | 16 E. 48th St. (bet. 5th & Madison Aves.) | 212-754-7600
Flatiron | 22 W. 23rd St. (bet. 5th & 6th Aves.) | 212-647-0200
W 50s | 50 W. 57th St. (bet. 5th & 6th Aves.) | 212-582-5882
www.mangiatogo.com
"Popular" with the "office crowd", this "easy in, easy out" Mediterranean threesome provides a "super" sandwich, salad bar and prepared foods "array" that'll "satisfy the tummy" way "better than fast food"; the "quality" comes at "higher prices", but "when you're in a hurry" it "fits the bill."

Maoz Vegetarian *Mideastern/Vegetarian*

FOOD	DECOR	SERVICE	COST
21	8	15	$11

G Village | 59 E. Eighth St. (bet. B'way & University Pl.) | 212-420-5999
Union Sq | 38 Union Sq. E. (bet. 16th & 17th Sts.) | 212-260-1988
NEW W 40s | 200 W. 40th St. (7th Ave.) | 212-777-0820 ◖
W 70s | 2047A Broadway (enter on Amsterdam Ave., bet. 70th & 71st Sts.) | 212-362-2622 ◖
NEW W 100s | 2857 Broadway (bet. 110th & 111th Sts.) | 212-222-6464
www.maozusa.com
You "feel almost virtuous" at this Netherlands-based Middle Eastern vegetarian chain, where the "fab" "fresh falafel" sandwiches come with "limitless toppings" from the "fixin's bar"; the "cool concept" and "bargain" prices are "addictive", though given the "sterile" setups, many "stick to takeout."

NEW Má Pêche *French/Vietnamese*

FOOD	DECOR	SERVICE	COST
22	18	21	$48

W 50s | Chambers Hotel | 15 W. 56th St. (bet. 5th & 6th Aves.) | 212-757-5878 | www.momofuku.com
"Momo moves near MoMA" with the arrival of David Chang's upscale yet "informal" French-Vietnamese eatery inside Midtown's Chambers

Hotel, with former Ssäm Bar chef Tien Ho overseeing the kitchen; early reports favor the "spicy", "flavorful" fare over the "noisy" "bi-level" digs done up with trademark-Chang "minimalism" (complete with communal "X table"), but all agree the front take-out branch of Momofuku Milk Bar is "divine."

NEW Mappamondo ● *Italian* | - | - | - | M |

W Village | 11 Abingdon Sq. (8th Ave., bet. Bleecker & W. 12th Sts.) | 212-206-9330 | www.mappamondonyc.com

"Back with a vengeance" in the "cozy" West Village digs it inhabited in the '90s (preceding Shag), this "quirky" wayfarer is adorned with maps and "globes galore"; the menu stays in Italy, however, with anti-pasti, pastas and mains priced as affordably as the wine list.

Mara's Homemade *Cajun* | 22 | 10 | 20 | $36 |

E Village | 342 E. Sixth St. (bet. 1st & 2nd Aves.) | 212-598-1110 | www.marashomemade.com

To ease that "hankering for N'Awlins", hit this East Villager whose "killer" Cajun cooking is the "next best" thing to being "on the hayou"; its "cramped" space is strictly "no-frills", but the "engaging" owner makes everyone "feel at home" and there's "no chance you'll leave hungry."

Marc Forgione *American* | 24 | 23 | 23 | $61 |

TriBeCa | 134 Reade St. (bet. Greenwich & Hudson Sts.) | 212-941-9401 | www.marcforgione.com

A "hidden" TriBeCa "jewel" from chef-owner Marc Forgione (son of chef Larry), this "inviting" New American gets top marks for its "refined" "farm-to-table" cuisine, "warm" service and "earthy", "candlelit" space; all in all it's an "unpretentious" "winner", but for its prices.

NEW Marcony ⑧ *Italian* | ▽ 22 | 21 | 24 | $71 |

Murray Hill | 184 Lexington Ave. (bet. 31st & 32nd Sts.) | 646-837-6020 | www.marconyusa.com

Capri sails to Murray Hill via this breezy Italian whose nautical colors, translucent balcony and Murano chandelier – not to mention "polite" crew – evoke a yacht cruising in the Mediterranean; its "pricey" classics include pastas made fresh or imported from Naples.

☑ Marea *Italian/Seafood* | 27 | 26 | 25 | $96 |

W 50s | 240 Central Park S. (bet. B'way & 7th Ave.) | 212-582-5100 | www.marea-nyc.com

Co-owners Chris Cannon and chef Michael White (of Alto and Convivio renown) turn "the wow factor" way up for "sophisticated diners" at this "sumptuous" Central Park South slice of "la dolce vita" that's voted NYC's No. 1 Italian thanks to its "transcendent" seafood-focused cuisine; "impeccable" service and "opulent" "modern" surroundings complete the "breathtaking" experience.

Maria Pia *Italian* | 20 | 17 | 20 | $38 |

W 50s | 319 W. 51st St. (bet. 8th & 9th Aves.) | 212-765-6463 | www.mariapianyc.com

Expect "no gimmicks" at this Theater District Italian, a "reliable" pre-show "go-to" for "sturdy" "standard" dishes that "don't break the bank"; the "plain-Jane" setting gets "crowded" and "deafening" during the rush, but the "back garden is nice" and "quiet."

Marina Cafe *Seafood*
| 20 | 22 | 19 | $43 |

Staten Island | 154 Mansion Ave. (Hillside Terr.) | 718-967-3077 | www.marinacafegrand.com

"Stupendous" waterfront views over Great Kills Harbor make this Staten Island "stalwart" a "solid choice", though the "pretty setting" is a bigger draw than the "well-prepared" seafood; given its tiki bar and live music in warm weather, customers consider it a "staycation."

Marinella *Italian*
| 23 | 18 | 24 | $41 |

W Village | 49 Carmine St. (Bedford St.) | 212-807-7472

"Tried-and-true", this "quaint" West Village trattoria is a "longtime" "delight" for Italian classics (look for the "specials board on wheels") and "sweet service"; prices are "reasonable" and you can "always get a seat" – no wonder the "locals love it."

Mario's Ⓜ *Italian*
| 21 | 15 | 21 | $42 |

Bronx | 2342 Arthur Ave. (bet. 184th & 186th Sts.) | 718-584-1188 | www.mariosrestarthurave.com

You can step "back in time" at this Arthur Avenue Southern Italian, which dates to 1919 as a "mainstay" for "quintessential red-sauce" standards (and "terrific" pizzas) served with "no pretenses"; it's "old-school and looks it", but "when you've got it right, why change?"

Mari Vanna ❶ *Russian*
| ▽ 20 | 24 | 22 | $65 |

Flatiron | 41 E. 20th St. (bet. B'way & Park Ave. S.) | 212-777-1955 | www.ginzaproject.ru

"Trendy" "expats" frequent this "charming" Flatiron yearling for "tasty" Russian bites (think caviar, borscht and blini) like "babushka" used to make; it's "expensive", but between the "pretty" "antique" decor, "model-esque" staff and "impressive" house-infused vodkas, it's bound to "win you over."

NEW Mark, The ❶ *American*
| 24 | 24 | 22 | $73 |

E 70s | Mark Hotel | 25 E. 77th St. (bet. 5th & Madison Aves.) | 212-606-3030 | www.themarkrestaurantnyc.com

"The Upper East Side has met its match" in Jean-Georges Vongerichten's "upscale" newcomer in the Mark Hotel, which regales "chic" Park to Fifth sorts with a "plush" layout and a "top-notch" menu mixing gourmet pizza and burgers with a raw bar and "high-end" New American fare; it's "already a favorite" with a "buzzy" "bar scene" – just "be prepared for the bill."

Market Table *American*
| 23 | 20 | 21 | $53 |

W Village | 54 Carmine St. (Bedford St.) | 212-255-2100 | www.markettablenyc.com

"Greenmarket-fresh" ingredients yield "genuinely exciting" seasonal New American cuisine at this "impressive" West Villager, an "always-busy" neighborhood "gem"; the "attractive room" is overseen by a "wonderful" staff, but "popular" demand makes it a "tough reservation."

MarkJoseph Steakhouse Ⓩ *Steak*
| 24 | 18 | 22 | $79 |

Financial District | 261 Water St. (Peck Slip) | 212-277-0020 | www.markjosephsteakhouse.com

"Mammoth" cuts of "prime meat" and a "fantastic" bacon appetizer may "take a year off of your life" at this Financial District steakhouse,

	FOOD	DECOR	SERVICE	COST

which caters to "Wall Street types" undaunted by the "high prices"; unlike its peers, it's "a bit out of the way" and can be "almost serene."

Markt *Belgian*

	19	17	17	$41

Flatiron | 676 Sixth Ave. (21st St.) | 212-727-3314 | www.marktrestaurant.com

This "heavily trafficked" Flatiron Belgian is marked by "slammin'" moules frites and a "massive" imported beer list that "makes everything taste better"; the "claustrophobic" quarters may get "noisy", but it's a "safe bet" for an "unpretentious" bite.

Marlow & Sons ● *American*

	24	17	18	$45

Williamsburg | 81 Broadway (bet. Berry St. & Wythe Ave.) | Brooklyn | 718-384-1441 | www.marlowandsons.com

"Quirky" but "cool", this Williamsburg American salutes "local cuisine" with "toothsome" small plates served in "casual", rough-hewn digs that feature a tiny market up front; "get there early", as the "cozy" space gets "crowded" at prime times with "neighborhoodies" sporting "plastic eyeglasses and lopsided haircuts."

Marseille *French/Mediterranean*

	20	19	19	$49

W 40s | 630 Ninth Ave. (bet. 44th & 45th Sts.) | 212-333-3410 | www.marseillenyc.com

While "nothing flashy", this "well-situated" pre-theater "fave" in Hell's Kitchen "keeps humming along" with "satisfying" and "moderately priced" French-Med fare in an "airy" brasserie stage set; as for being "out in time for the curtain", the "efficient" servers have it "down to a science."

Maruzzella ● *Italian*

	23	17	22	$47

E 70s | 1483 First Ave. (bet. 77th & 78th Sts.) | 212-988-8877 | www.maruzzellanyc.com

A "warm greeting" awaits at this "homey" UES standby, where "winning" owners lead a "caring" crew that serves up "consistently" "wonderful" Northern Italian standards "without the East Side prices"; devoted "local" followers feel it "would be a favorite anywhere" ("they should clone it").

Mary Ann's *Tex-Mex*

	15	11	14	$27

Chelsea | 116 Eighth Ave. (16th St.) | 212-633-0877 ⊘
E Village | 80 Second Ave. (bet. 4th & 5th Sts.) | 212-475-5939 ⊘
TriBeCa | 353 Greenwich St. (Harrison St.) | 212-766-0911
www.maryannsmexican.com

"Young crowds" on a "low budget" populate these "standard-issue" Tex-Mex fixtures, washing down "so-so" "cheap eats" with "powerful margaritas"; just try to "drink enough" to cancel out the "drab" digs and "mindless" service.

Mary's Fish Camp ⊠ *Seafood*

	25	14	19	$43

W Village | 64 Charles St. (W. 4th St.) | 646-486-2185 | www.marysfishcamp.com

A "lobster roll for the ages" is the signature of this "all-star" West Village "fish joint", an "offbeat" "treasure" that's "deservedly popular" for its "delectable" dockside "delights" delivered by a "warm" crew; the "tight" space shore can get "crazy busy", though – "go early" or camp out in line.

	FOOD	DECOR	SERVICE	COST

Z Mas ● *American* | 27 | 24 | 26 | $87 |

W Village | 39 Downing St. (bet. Bedford & Varick Sts.) | 212-255-1790 |
www.masfarmhouse.com

"One to remember", this "intimate", "understated" New American
"represents the best of the Village" with "innovative" chef Galen
Zamarra's "masterful" market-driven cuisine and "effortlessly" "courteous" service; though it's still something of a "secret gem", for those
willing to "run up a notable tab" it's an "incredible experience."

Z Masa 🗷 *Japanese* | 27 | 24 | 26 | $520 |

W 60s | Time Warner Ctr. | 10 Columbus Circle, 4th fl. (60th St. at B'way) |
212-823-9800

Z Bar Masa 🗷 *Japanese*

W 60s | Time Warner Ctr. | 10 Columbus Circle, 4th fl. (60th St. at B'way) |
212-823-9800
www.masanyc.com

Yes, it's "masa-vely expensive", but "save up" because the Time
Warner Center's "reigning king" of "high-end Japanese" is an "inimi-
table" "church of sushi" where renowned chef Masayoshi Takayama
presents his "exquisite" prix fixes (starting at $400) in "luxurious",
"Zen-like" surroundings; while "still not cheap", the "sedate" next-
door bar's à la carte menu offers "a glimpse" of the same "exceptional" fare at a lower price.

NEW Masala Times ● *Indian* | – | – | – | I |

G Village | 194 Bleecker St. (bet. MacDougal St. & 6th Ave.) | 212-477-3333 |
www.masalatimesnyc.com

Bollywood comes to the Village via this vibrant Indian storefront specializing in Bombay BBQ items like chicken seekh and fish tikka;
tricked out with pink mirrored walls, it's targeted toward NYU types
with counter service, late-night hours and cheap tabs.

Matilda ⊘ *Italian/Mexican* | ∇ 23 | 19 | 22 | $39 |

E Village | 647 E. 11th St. (bet. Aves. B & C) | 212-777-3355 |
www.matildarestaurant.com

The "odd combination" of Tuscan and Mexican cuisines "actually
works" at this "welcoming" East Villager finding "innovative" ways to
"please the palate" with "flavorful" fusion fare; in a "low-key" contemporary space run by "lovely owners", it has fans waltzing back despite
kinda "tight" conditions.

Matsugen *Japanese* | 23 | 22 | 21 | $64 |

TriBeCa | 241 Church St. (Leonard St.) | 212-925-0202 |
www.jean-georges.com

Jean-Georges Vongerichten does Japanese "exceptionally well" at this
"serene" TriBeCan, a "stylish", "minimalist" venue for "savoring" "silken"
housemade soba along with "excellent" sushi and shabu-shabu; "you
pay" for the "quality", but the $38 prix fixe dinner is a "real deal."

Z Matsuri ● *Japanese* | 22 | 25 | 21 | $62 |

Chelsea | Maritime Hotel | 369 W. 16th St., downstairs (9th Ave.) |
212-243-6400 | www.matsurinyc.com

"Hidden" in "very cool" "underground" digs, this "cavernous" West
Chelsea Japanese houses chef Tadashi Ono's "sumptuous" sushi and
a "vast" sake selection in a "fantastic" space filled with "mobs" of

"models, hipsters and clubgoers"; while still steeply priced, some say scenewise it's "slipping."

Max *Italian*   21 | 15 | 17 | $32

E Village | 51 Ave. B (bet. 3rd & 4th Sts.) | 212-539-0111
TriBeCa | 181 Duane St. (bet. Greenwich & Hudson Sts.) | 212-966-5939
www.max-ny.com

Devotees declare "they should be charging more" for the "hearty portions" of "killer" pastas and other classics at this "rustic Italian" East Village-TriBeCa twosome; then again, "hit-or-miss" service and "small", "funky" setups may account for the "amazing value."

Max Brenner ❶ *Dessert*   20 | 19 | 15 | $28

G Village | 841 Broadway (bet. 13th & 14th Sts.) | 212-388-0030 |
www.maxbrenner.com

"Sweet tooths" make a beeline for this "high-traffic" Village dessert place, where chocolate is a "basic food group" and the sugary "novelties" are "irresistible to kids" and "tourists"; however, tarter types find the "hectic" setting "too cute" and "frazzled" service "enervating."

Max SoHa ❶⊅ *Italian*   20 | 14 | 16 | $30

W 100s | 1274 Amsterdam Ave. (123rd St.) | 212-531-2221
Max Caffe ❶ *Italian*
W 100s | 1262 Amsterdam Ave. (122nd St.) | 212-531-1210
www.maxsoha.com

"Students" assemble "elbow-to-elbow" at these "casual" Upper West Side Italian "favorites" "on the outskirts of Columbia" for their "tasty" "homestyle" fare and "extremely affordable" tabs; "glacial" service, "squished" seating and "flea-market" decor are all part of "slummin' it."

Maya *Mexican*   24 | 20 | 20 | $52

E 60s | 1191 First Ave. (bet. 64th & 65th Sts.) | 212-585-1818 |
www.modernmexican.com

"Definitely a step up" from the "typical" Mexican, this "sophisticated" Upper Eastsider "stands out" with "delicious", "serious" cuisine ("no combo plates here") and "magical margaritas" served by a "cheerful" staff; "lively" compadres consider it "a hit" despite the "deafening noise" and "high bill."

Maze *French*   22 | 21 | 20 | $71

W 50s | London NYC Hotel | 151 W. 54th St. (bet. 6th & 7th Aves.) |
212-468-8889 | www.gordonramsay.com

The London Hotel's "sleek" sidekick to the more "formal" Gordon Ramsay, this "stylish" Midtowner specializes in "imaginative" New French small plates at prices "cheaper" than its neighbor's (though it's still "easy to rack up big bills"); a four-point Food score drop since the last Survey suggests something's up in the kitchen.

Maz Mezcal *Mexican*   20 | 17 | 20 | $40

E 80s | 316 E. 86th St. (bet. 1st & 2nd Aves.) | 212-472-1599 |
www.mazmezcal.com

For a "non-trendy" "Mexican fix", this "long-standing" UES "family-run" "favorite" plies "mighty fine" food and margaritas that'll "knock your socks off"; "cheery" vibes and prices that "won't break the bank" ensure it's generally "packed."

| | FOOD | DECOR | SERVICE | COST |

McCormick & Schmick's *Seafood* — 20 | 18 | 20 | $53

W 50s | 1285 Sixth Ave. (enter on 52nd St., bet. 6th & 7th Aves.) | 212-459-1222 | www.mccormickandschmicks.com

"Not bad for a chain", this "convenient" Rock Center–area "fish house" "fills the bill" for "well-prepared" seafood "standards" in a "cookie-cutter" space; "corporate" types call it "completely serviceable", but mutineers shrug "you could be in Denver."

NEW Meatball Shop ● *Sandwiches* — 22 | 17 | 20 | $22

LES | 84 Stanton St. (bet. Allen & Orchard Sts.) | 212-982-8895 | www.themeatballshop.com

You "build your own" subs and sliders from a "superior" lineup of "homemade" meatballs and sauces at this new LES sandwich shop, whose "genius" concept is perfect for "late-night" "cheap eats"; alas, "tight" quarters and "long lines" lead to "huge waits."

Mediterraneo ● *Italian* — 20 | 16 | 18 | $42

E 60s | 1260 Second Ave. (66th St.) | 212-734-7407 | www.mediterraneonyc.com

"Enough accents to make your head spin" fill this "sceney" Upper East Side Italian, a "perennial favorite" among "pretty things" where "air kisses are the norm" and "outdoor tables are fought over"; otherwise, it's "reliable" for pizza and pasta if you don't mind "disinterested" service.

Mee Noodle Shop *Noodle Shop* — 17 | 4 | 12 | $17

E 40s | 922 Second Ave. (49th St.) | 212-888-0027
Murray Hill | 547 Second Ave. (bet. 30th & 31st Sts.) | 212-779-1596
W 50s | 795 Ninth Ave. (53rd St.) | 212-765-2929 | www.meenoodleshopnyc.com

"When you're feeling poor", this separately owned Chinese three-some slings "slurpy", "filling" noodle soups at "lightning speed" for an "incredibly low" cost; the "trade-off" is "downright shabby" decor and service that's "not the friendliest."

☑ Megu *Japanese* — 24 | 26 | 23 | $83

TriBeCa | 62 Thomas St. (bet. Church St. & W. B'way) | 212-964-7777 | www.megunyc.com

☑ Megu Midtown *Japanese*

E 40s | Trump World Tower | 845 United Nations Plaza (1st Ave. & 47th St.) | 212-964-7777 | www.megurestaurants.com

"You're in another world" at this "classy" TriBeCa–East Midtown Japanese duo, where the "stunning" surroundings (including signature "giant Buddha" ice sculptures), "fabulous" food and "exemplary" service are "fit for an emperor"; it's "really special" when you're out to "celebrate" or "impress" – if "you can afford" megu-bucks.

Melba's *American* — ▽ 25 | 20 | 20 | $29

Harlem | 300 W. 114th St. (Frederick Douglass Blvd.) | 212-864-7777 | www.melbasrestaurant.com

"Comfort food" takes on some "soulful flair" at this "warm" Harlem American, which delivers "big-time flavors" in a "classy setting" overseen by a "charming" staff; fair prices and a "serious" weekend brunch are good reasons to "keep going back."

	FOOD	DECOR	SERVICE	COST

Meltemi *Greek*
– | – | – | M

E 70s | 1481 York Ave. (bet. 78th & 79th Sts.) | 212-327-0950

Saving Upper Eastsiders a trip to Greece – or at least Astoria – this unassuming Midtown transplant looks as if it's always inhabited this off-the-radar stretch of York Avenue; the midpriced menu reprises the usual taverna favorites, while a full bar, patio seating and moderate prices further sweeten the baklava.

Menchanko-tei *Noodle Shop*
20 | 11 | 16 | $22

E 40s | 131 E. 45th St. (bet. Lexington & 3rd Aves.) | 212-986-6805
W 50s | 43-45 W. 55th St. (bet. 5th & 6th Aves.) | 212-247-1585
www.menchankotei.com

Business folks sit "elbow-to-elbow" at these "real-deal" Midtown Japanese noodleramas, downing "hearty", "slurpalicious" bowls of udon and ramen "for not much cash"; the "dreary" digs are the "downside", but "there's a reason" for the "absolute mob scene" at lunch.

Mercadito *Mexican*
23 | 16 | 18 | $37

E Village | 179 Ave. B (bet. 11th & 12th Sts.) | 212-529-6490
Mercadito Cantina ◕ *Mexican*
E Village | 172 Ave. B (bet. 10th & 11th Sts.) | 212-388-1750
Mercadito Grove *Mexican*
W Village | 100 Seventh Ave. S. (bet. Bleecker & Grove Sts.) | 212-647-0830
www.mercaditorestaurants.com

"Big" flavors "come in small packages" at these cross-Village Mexican "cubbyholes", where "scrumptious" tacos and a "must-get" guac sampler arrive in "mini" portions; "potent" margaritas seal the deal – not to mention "prime outdoor seating" at the Seventh Avenue spot.

Mercat *Spanish*
20 | 19 | 19 | $47

NoHo | 45 Bond St. (bet. Bowery & Lafayette St.) | 212-529-8600 |
www.mercatnyc.com

"True to its mission", this NoHo Spaniard "gets the taste buds going" with "authentic Catalan cuisine" in the form of "high-end tapas"; the "urban-chic" setting is made for "date night", though things get "expensive" for plates that "err on the small side."

Mercer Kitchen ◕ *American/French*
22 | 22 | 19 | $56

SoHo | Mercer Hotel | 99 Prince St. (Mercer St.) | 212-966-5454 |
www.jean-georges.com

By now a "classic", Jean-Georges Vongerichten's "fashionable" underground "lair" attracts "the 'in' crowd" with "artfully prepared" French-New American fare in "dimly lit, sexy" digs with a "hip SoHo vibe"; "doing-you-a-favor" service adds sting to the "steep" prices.

Mermaid Inn *Seafood*
21 | 18 | 19 | $43

E Village | 96 Second Ave. (bet. 5th & 6th Sts.) | 212-674-5870
W 80s | 568 Amsterdam Ave. (bet. 87th & 88th Sts.) | 212-799-7400
Mermaid Oyster Bar *Seafood*
NEW **G Village** | 79 MacDougal St. (bet. Bleecker & Houston Sts.) |
212-260-0100
www.themermaidnyc.com

Like a "Nantucket getaway", these "quaint", "casual" seafarers – including a new raw bar–focused Village outpost – serve "fantabulous" fish and "luscious" "lobstah rolls" "without pretense" to a "lively" clientele; they "don't sink your budget", and the "complimentary chocolate pudding" is a "sweet finish."

Mesa Coyoacan ● *Mexican* ▽ 24 | 21 | 24 | $33

Williamsburg | 372 Graham Ave. (bet. Conselyea St. & Skillman Ave.) | Brooklyn | 718-782-8171 | www.mesacoyoacan.com

Short of "flying to Mexico City", this Williamsburg *cucina* is as "authentic as it gets" for "superb" regional Mexican cooking and "phenomenal margaritas"; other reasons those who know it say it's "top rank" include low-peso prices, a "nice" rustic space with communal seating and "super" service.

☒ Mesa Grill *Southwestern* 23 | 20 | 21 | $58

Flatiron | 102 Fifth Ave. (bet. 15th & 16th Sts.) | 212-807-7400 | www.mesagrill.com

"His food tastes even better than it looks on TV" fawn fans of "Food Network" lothario Bobby Flay's "high-energy" Flatiron Southwestern, whose "bright flavors" are "still a crowd-pleaser"; some give the "dated" setting a chili reception, but "affable" service keeps things copacetic.

Meskerem *Ethiopian* 22 | 11 | 17 | $25

G Village | 124 MacDougal St. (bet. Bleecker & W. 3rd Sts.) | 212-777-8111
W 40s | 468 W. 47th St. (bet. 9th & 10th Aves.) | 212-664-0520

Eating with "no utensils" is a mess of "exotic" "fun" at these "dependable" Ethiopians proffering "delicious" stews and such that you "pick up with your hands" using injera bread; "affordable" tabs make "lackadaisical" service and "short-on-atmosphere" digs easy to abide.

Metrazur ☒ *American* 21 | 22 | 19 | $52

E 40s | Grand Central | East Balcony (42nd St. & Vanderbilt Ave.) | 212-687-4600 | www.charliepalmer.com

The "people-watching is half the fun" at this mezzanine New American perched over the Grand Central Concourse and affording "fantastic views" of the "commuter scramble"; the balance of the action comes via Charlie Palmer's "appealing" cuisine and "generous" prix fixe "deals."

Mexicana Mama ☒ *Mexican* 23 | 12 | 18 | $35

G Village | 47 E. 12th St. (bet. B'way & University Pl.) | 212-253-7594
W Village | 525 Hudson St. (bet. Charles & W. 10th Sts.) | 212-924-4119 ⊄

It's "worth every minute of waiting" to score a seat at this ever-mobbed West Village "hole-in-the-wall" whose "high-quality" Mexican eats are "some of the best" going; the Greenwich Village outpost duplicates the "delicious" fun with one notable benefit: "it takes credit cards."

Mexican Radio ● *Mexican* 20 | 14 | 16 | $32

NoLita | 19 Cleveland Pl. (bet. Kenmare & Spring Sts.) | 212-343-0140 | www.mexrad.com

"Flavorful", affordable *comida* and "amazing margaritas" are the chart-toppers at this "unpretentious" NoLita Mexican; the "adequate" service and "divey" decor get a weak reception, and, depending on your wavelength, the dialed-up "party vibe" is either "tons of fun" or "too noisy."

	FOOD	DECOR	SERVICE	COST

Mezzaluna ● *Italian*   20 | 14 | 17 | $45

E 70s | 1295 Third Ave. (bet. 74th & 75th Sts.) | 212-535-9600 |
www.mezzalunany.com

Pizza Mezzaluna ⊘ *Pizza*

G Village | 146 W. Houston St. (MacDougal St.) | 212-533 1242 |
www.pizzamezzalunanyc.com

Yes, it's "cramped" and "noisy" at this "real Italian" UES "closet", but
to most its "ridiculously good" pastas and wood-fired pizzas are worth
the "squeeze"; the mostly take-out Village offshoot is even tinier.

Mezzogiorno *Italian*   21 | 18 | 20 | $45

SoHo | 195 Spring St. (Sullivan St.) | 212-334-2112 | www.mezzogiorno.com

"From pizza to pasta and beyond", you could "throw a dart at the
menu" and have a "*buonissimo*" meal at this "consistent"-as-they-
come Italian, a SoHo "fixture" since 1987; given its "prime location",
in warm weather "sit outside" to "enjoy the scenery."

Mia Dona *Italian*   20 | 17 | 18 | $53

E 50s | 206 E. 58th St. (bet. 2nd & 3rd Aves.) | 212 750 0170 |
www.miadona.com

Donatella Arpaia has relaunched her Italian Eastsider with a "satisfying"
new menu of Pugliese specialties served in remodeled but still "unpretentious" digs; fans of its former chef Michael Psilakis may sigh "the
thrill is gone", but "Bloomie's shoppers" tout the "scaled-down prices."

Michael Jordan's
The Steak House NYC *Steak*   21 | 21 | 19 | $65

E 40s | Grand Central | Northwest Balcony (43rd St. & Vanderbilt Ave.) |
212-655-2300 | www.michaeljordansnyc.com

Its "unbeatable" "view from above" is worthy of His Airness at this
steakhouse overlooking the Grand Central Concourse and offering "well-
executed", "high-priced" standards and a "fun" bar scene; service runs
"hot and cold", but commuters say it works before "the train home."

Z Michael's 🅂 *Californian*   21 | 22 | 23 | $70

W 50s | 24 W. 55th St. (bet. 5th & 6th Aves.) | 212-767-0555 |
www.michaelsnewyork.com

Members of the "media power elite" eat "expensive", "very good"
Californian fare in between "air kisses" at this "artwork"-adorned
Midtown "classic"; the "celeb-gazing" is best during "breakfast and
lunch", so come early if you want to "say hi to Barry Diller."

Mike's Bistro *Kosher*   ▽ 26 | 20 | 23 | $62

W 70s | 228 W. 72nd St. (bet. B'way & West End Ave.) | 212-799-3911 |
www.mikesbistro.com

"If you think glatt kosher" joints "can't do the gourmet thing", a sampling of this Upper Westsider's "creative", "vegetarian"-friendly cuisine may "change your mind"; sure, it's "expensive", but who's to
question cooking that "answers to a higher authority"?

NEW Mile End *Deli*   25 | 14 | 17 | $18

Boerum Hill | 97A Hoyt St. (bet. Atlantic & Pacific Sts.) | Brooklyn |
718-852-7510 | www.mileendbrooklyn.com

"It's all about the meats" smoked and cured in-house at this new Boerum
Hill "Montreal-style" Jewish deli that takes NYC's top ranking for the

genre with its "amazing sandwiches" deemed a "Canadian revelation"; its "tiny" digs "fill up" fast and supplies of the "tasty" goods do "run out", so "get there early."

Mill Basin Kosher Deli *Deli* | 22 | 15 | 19 | $25 |

Mill Basin | 5823 Ave. T (59th St.) | Brooklyn | 718-241-4910 | www.millbasindeli.com

This circa-1972 Mill Basin deli's "overstuffed sandwiches" and other Jewish "delights" still get a hearty "thumbs-up"; it's also an art gallery with "museum-quality" works, so you get "a side of" Erté, Lichtenstein and Chagall "with your corned beef on rye" – "now that's livin'!"

☒ Milos, Estiatorio ◑ *Greek/Seafood* | 27 | 24 | 23 | $81 |

W 50s | 125 W. 55th St. (bet. 6th & 7th Aves.) | 212-245-7400 | www.milos.ca

"If it swims, they have it" displayed on ice, ready to be "perfectly grilled" at this "energetic" Midtown Greek "seafood-lover's dream"; add the "airy" "resortlike" space manned by a "knowledgeable" crew and one might conclude "the gods of Olympus don't have it this good"; P.S. to control "way-high" by-the-pound pricing, consider making a meal of the "fabulous appetizers."

Mimi's Hummus *Mideastern*   ▽ | 25 | 18 | 23 | $24 |

Ditmas Park | 1209 Cortelyou Rd. (Westminster Rd.) | Brooklyn | 718-284-4444 | www.mimishummus.com

Ditmas Park is humming about the "extraordinary hummus" ("never had it so smooth!") and "fluffiest pita" at this "cute little" BYO specializing in "simple", "deliciously fresh" Middle Eastern fare; staffers "like family", reasonable rates and a "next-door market" are other reasons it's already a local "favorite."

Minca ◑⇗ *Noodle Shop*   ▽ | 21 | 9 | 17 | $19 |

E Village | 536 E. Fifth St. (bet. Aves. A & B) | 212-505-8001

Though "not as well known" as its "trendy" competitors on the East Village's ramen circuit, this "sleeper" is a respected supplier of "cheap" bowls of "hot, slurpy goodness"; per the genre, just expect your stint in "noodle heaven" to be a "fast", "no-frills" affair.

☒ Minetta Tavern ◑ *French* | 24 | 21 | 21 | $64 |

G Village | 113 MacDougal St. (bet. Bleecker & W. 3rd Sts.) | 212-475-3850 | www.minettatavernny.com

Keith McNally's "got it goin' on" at this "sensational", "sceney" "remake" of an "old Village favorite", from its "über-cool", "classic NY" ambiance to the "first-rate" French bistro fare (its Food score is up four points since the last Survey), including a "decadent" $26 burger and "don't-miss" côte de boeuf (don't ask the price) that actually "live up to the hype"; in sum, "you'll eat like a star" and probably see a few – but "good luck getting a reservation."

Mingala Burmese *Burmese*   ▽ | 21 | 11 | 18 | $29 |

E 70s | 1393B Second Ave. (bet. 72nd & 73rd Sts.) | 212-744-8008

For a "different kind of Asian food experience" that's "delicious" and a "fantastic bargain" to boot, Upper Eastsiders suggest this "welcoming" Burmese "standout"; given the chance to try "a cuisine rarely found around town", most overlook the "uninspired" decor.

	FOOD	DECOR	SERVICE	COST

Mint *Indian* ▽ 22 | 19 | 20 | $44
E 50s | San Carlos Hotel | 150 E. 50th St. (bet. Lexington & 3rd Aves.) | 212-644-8888 | www.mintny.com
Curry connoisseurs find "nothing heavy-handed" about this Midtown Indian boasting a "refreshing", "hipper"-than-usual setting and "flavorful" upscale cuisine "capably served"; though tabs tilt a tad toward "expensive", admirers assure "it's worth it for what you get."

Miranda *Italian/Pan-Latin* ▽ 23 | 20 | 25 | $37
Williamsburg | 80 Berry St. (N. 9th St.) | Brooklyn | 718-387-0711 | www.mirandarestaurant.com
"Why hasn't it been tried more often?" wonder Williamsburg foodies about the "odd" yet "delicious" fusion of Italian and Pan-Latin cuisines featured at this local "must"; another mystery is how such a "cozy", affordable joint run by "super-friendly" folks "hasn't caught on" more.

Miriam *Israeli/Mediterranean* 22 | 18 | 19 | $32
Park Slope | 79 Fifth Ave. (Prospect Pl.) | Brooklyn | 718-622-2250 | www.miriamrestaurant.com
A local "favorite" for "distinct", "delicious", "reasonably priced" Israeli-Med cuisine, this Park Slope "charmer" does it all with "warm" hospitality; its narrow space "gets crowded" during the "wonderful" weekend brunch, so "go early" or expect a "long wait."

Mishima *Japanese* 24 | 12 | 21 | $37
Murray Hill | 164 Lexington Ave. (bet. 30th & 31st Sts.) | 212-532-9596 | www.mishimany.com
It's definitely "not the fanciest" Japanese joint in town, but this "unsung" Murray Hiller reels 'em in nonetheless with "fresh", "satisfying" sushi that's "well priced" "for the quality"; "attentive" service seals its status as a solid "neighborhood option."

Miss Mamie's *Soul Food/Southern* ▽ 20 | 11 | 16 | $24
Harlem | 366 W. 110th St. (bet. Columbus & Manhattan Aves.) | 212-865-6744
Miss Maude's *Soul Food/Southern*
Harlem | 547 Lenox Ave. (bet. 137th & 138th Sts.) | 212-690-3100 | www.spoonbreadinc.com
When a Southern "comfort" craving strikes, these Harlem "homes away from home" bring "some good cookin'" your way, and at "bargain" rates; maybe service and decor "could use improvement", but most "just enjoy" the transporting "genuine soul food" experience on its own terms.

Mizu Sushi ⊠ *Japanese* 24 | 15 | 18 | $39
Flatiron | 29 E. 20th St. (bet. B'way & Park Ave. S.) | 212-505-6688
"Young, hip" types gravitate to this Flatironer for "fabulous" sushi and sake "fixes" in a "party atmosphere"; the "absolutely fresh", "priced-right" fish comes with a "loud techno" soundtrack, so sensitive ears eat in the quieter bar area or go at "less-noisy" lunchtime.

Mo-Bay *Caribbean/Soul Food* ▽ 21 | 18 | 16 | $33
Harlem | 17 W. 125th St. (bet. 5th & Lenox Aves.) | 212-876-9300 | www.mobayuptownnyc.com
"Fine food" and a "festive" air is the MO of this "cozy" Harlem hangout featuring a budget-priced Caribbean–soul food menu plus the "added

bonus" of "live music" on weekends; "iffy service" is the only blot on its otherwise "reliable" rep.

Z Modern, The Ⓩ *American/French*   26 | 27 | 25 | $114
W 50s | Museum of Modern Art | 9 W. 53rd St. (bet. 5th & 6th Aves.) | 212-333-1220 | www.themodernnyc.com
"Art on a plate" with art as a backdrop makes for a "*très* sophisticated" meal at Danny Meyer's MoMA "triumph", where "splendid" staffers ferry Gabriel Kreuther's "refined", "luxury"-priced French–New American cuisine to a "chic" crowd; the venue boasts two "gorgeous" options: the "formal", prix fixe–only, jacket-required dining room overlooking the museum's sculpture garden or the "lively", comparatively "less-expensive" front bar/cafe.

Moim Ⓜ *Korean*   23 | 23 | 19 | $40
Park Slope | 206 Garfield Pl. (bet. 7th & 8th Aves.) | Brooklyn | 718-499-8092 | www.moimrestaurant.com
"Rethinking tradition", this Park Slope "gem" puts subtle "modern twists" on Korean cuisine that satisfy Seoul food fans and the "uninitiated" alike; its "sleek" setup, complete with a "beautiful outdoor garden", provides a "serene" outer-borough alternative to "the bustle of K-town."

Mojo *American*   ▽ 21 | 21 | 21 | $41
Harlem | 185 St. Nicholas Ave. (enter on 119th St.) | 212-280-1924 | www.mojo-harlem.com
"Harlem's upswing" is in evidence at this "small", "funky" newcomer, a "cozy" corner joint done up in deep-purple hues and plying an offbeat, "reasonably priced" New American menu; the "chill" vibe is regularly enhanced by live jazz, DJs and the like.

Molé *Mexican*   25 | 17 | 20 | $34
LES | 205 Allen St. (Houston St.) | 212-777-3200 ⑂
NEW **W Village** | 57 Jane St. (Hudson St.) | 212-206-7559
www.molenyc.com
"Wonderful", "you're-in-Mexico" flavors plus "the best" happy-hour specials keep things "crowded" at these LES–West Village "holes-in-the-wall"; "friendly" service and "down-to-earth" pricing offset "any discomfort from sitting in your neighbor's lap"; P.S. a Williamsburg outpost is in the works.

Molly's ◐ *Pub Food*   20 | 17 | 21 | $25
Gramercy | 287 Third Ave. (bet. 22nd & 23rd Sts.) | 212-889-3361 | www.mollysshebeen.com
This Gramercy "classic" is a "real-deal" Irish pub complete with "sawdust on the floor", "cracklin' fireplace" and "friendly" staff "from the Auld Sod"; grub options include "big, tasty burgers" and other "filling" fare designed to pair perfectly with a "proper pint."

Molyvos ◐ *Greek*   23 | 19 | 20 | $56
W 50s | 871 Seventh Ave. (bet. 55th & 56th Sts.) | 212-582-7500 | www.molyvos.com
"No need to travel to Mykonos" – this "upscale" taverna provides "wonderfully prepared", "authentic" Greek cuisine within a stone's throw of Carnegie Hall; "attentive" service is part of the package, as are kinda "pricey" tabs, though the $37 prix fixe is a "bargain."

	FOOD	DECOR	SERVICE	COST

Momofuku Bakery & Milk Bar *Bakery* | 22 | 11 | 15 | $16 |

E Village | 207 Second Ave. (enter on 13th St., bet. 2nd & 3rd Aves.) | 212-475-7899 ◐

NEW **W 50s** | Chambers Hotel | 15 W. 56th St. (bet. 5th & 6th Aves.) | 212-757-5878

www.momofuku.com

From "rich" soft-serve ice cream in "clever", "intense" flavors to "funky", "addictive" cakes and pies, your "sweet tooth" will celebrate at David Chang's "playful" East Village dessert specialist; those famously "tasty pork buns" are "reason enough to come", "long lines", "slacker" service and "dumpy", standing-room-only digs notwithstanding; P.S. there's now an offshoot in Chang's Midtown eatery, Má Pêche.

Momofuku Ko *American* | 27 | 18 | 23 | $163 |

E Village | 163 First Ave. (bet. 10th & 11th Sts.) | 212-475-7899 | www.momofuku.com

It's "heaven on a barstool" say the "fortunate" few who've snagged a near-"impossible" online rez at David Chang's "austere" East Village "crown jewel", where a "sublime", "superinventive" multicourse parade of Asian-accented New Americana is "masterfully prepared" in full view of the 12-capacity crowd; you "pay a price" for the privilege ($125, prix fixe-only), and the seating's "most uncomfortable", but any "die-hard foodie" "must eat here."

Momofuku Noodle Bar *American* | 24 | 16 | 18 | $36 |

E Village | 171 First Ave. (bet. 10th & 11th Sts.) | 212-777-7773 | www.momofuku.com

David Chang shows what "keeping it simple" can do at his empire's "ragingly popular" ("expect to fight the crowds") East Village original, a "small", "hectic" hub whose "creative" American "homage" to Japanese cuisine includes "slurp-a-licious" ramen and "to-die-for" pork buns; in short, it "lives up to the hype" and is "affordable" too.

Momofuku Ssäm Bar ◐ *American* | 25 | 16 | 19 | $48 |

E Village | 207 Second Ave. (13th St.) | 212-254-3500 | www.momofuku.com

From "succulent pork buns" to a "bucket list"-worthy *bo ssäm* hog "feast" (reserved in advance online), it's a "delight" to "pig out on pig" at David Chang's "stellar" Asian-inflected New American in the East Village; despite its "barely controlled chaos" and "less-than-cozy" digs, converts are eager as ever to queue up and "play it again, *ssäm*."

Momoya *Japanese* | 22 | 19 | 19 | $42 |

Chelsea | 185 Seventh Ave. (21st St.) | 212-989-4466

W 80s | 427 Amsterdam Ave. (bet. 80th & 81st Sts.) | 212-580-0007

www.themomoya.com

"Tasty", "creative" rolls that rank "above the usual" sushi yet come "without the prices of a high-end" purveyor set this Chelsea-UWS Japanese duo apart from the pack; the "sleek" settings are "utilitarian, but not unpleasant", with fittingly "efficient" service to match.

Z **Monkey Bar** ◐▢ *American* | 17 | 23 | 20 | $68 |

E 50s | Elysée Hotel | 60 E. 54th St. (bet. Madison & Park Aves.) | 212-308-2950 | www.monkeybarnewyork.com

Vanity Fair editor Graydon Carter is the top banana behind this "insiders' hot spot", a "handsome" mural-bedecked Midtown "club" "buzzing" with "celebs", "bankers" and other "exclusivity"-seekers; scoring a rez may be easier now, either by phone or e-mail (reservations@monkeybarnewyork.com), but as the "expensive" New American eats really "don't impress", the key may be to "just go for drinks" with the gorgeous crowd in the "happening bar."

Monster Sushi *Japanese*
18 | 11 | 16 | $33

Chelsea | 158 W. 23rd St. (bet. 6th & 7th Aves.) | 212-620-9131 ◑
W 40s | 22 W. 46th St. (bet. 5th & 6th Aves.) | 212-398-7707
www.monstersushi.com
Even "Godzilla would get his fill" at this "name-says-it-all" Chelsea–West 40s Japanese duo doling out "huge", low-cost sushi rolls via a "polite" staff in "no-atmosphere" environs; some sniff "quantity doesn't mean quality", but to "value"-seekers it's a "gimmick" that delivers.

Mont Blanc ◑ *Austrian/Swiss*
▽ 21 | 16 | 21 | $45

W 40s | 315 W. 48th St. (bet. 8th & 9th Aves.) | 212-582-9648 |
www.montblancrestaurant.com
"Wonderful fondue" and other "hearty" Swiss-Austrian staples are the forte of this Theater District standby outfitted with a "delightful garden room in back"; "attentive" servers and "reasonable prices" help make it a peak pre-theater performer.

Montebello 🗷 *Italian*
24 | 20 | 25 | $54

E 50s | 120 E. 56th St. (bet. Lexington & Park Aves.) | 212-753-1447 |
www.montebellonyc.com
"Try any item on the menu" urge admirers of this "quiet, cozy" Midtown "gem" whose "excellent" Tuscan classics and "pro" service make it a favored area option for both "business" and "romance"; enthusiasts only wonder "why it's not better known."

Montenapo 🗷 *Italian*
▽ 21 | 24 | 18 | $66

W 40s | NY Times Bldg. | 250 W. 41st St. (bet. 7th & 8th Aves.) |
212-764-7663 | www.montenaporestaurant.com
Now run by the Salute! folks following an ownership shuffle, this Italian yearling's high point remains its "soaring" space overlooking the garden atrium of the NY Times building; early reports on the "pricey" new Italian menu are mostly positive, especially the "bargain" prix fixe options.

Morandi ◑ *Italian*
22 | 20 | 20 | $52

W Village | 211 Waverly Pl. (Charles St.) | 212-627-7575 |
www.morandiny.com
"Rustic" trattoria and "trendy hot spot" rolled into one, Keith McNally's "buzzing" (i.e. "noisy") Village hive for "the young and pretty" does "simple", "authentic" Italiana "very well" – and the "people-watching" thing "even better"; a "smart" crew and "perfect outdoor seating" batten down a "tight ship."

Morgan, The 🅼 *American*
20 | 21 | 20 | $44

Murray Hill | The Morgan Library & Museum | 225 Madison Ave.
(bet. 36th & 37th Sts.) | 212-683-2130 | www.themorgan.org
"Wonderfully located" within the "jewel" that is the Morgan Library, this "civilized" lunch-only Murray Hiller offers its New American repasts in either the atrium or the "elegant" dining room once used by J. Pierpont himself; not surprisingly, the "old-NY" experience comes at an up-to-date price.

	FOOD	DECOR	SERVICE	COST

☒ Morimoto *Japanese* — 25 | 26 | 24 | $81

Chelsea | 88 10th Ave. (bet. 15th & 16th Sts.) | 212-989-8883 | www.morimotonyc.com

"Not an Iron Chef for nothing", Masaharu Morimoto "reigns supreme" with his "divine" Japanese cuisine delivered by a "diligent" crew at this "ultrahip", "spaceship"-like Chelsea destination; just bring a "pot of cash" to pay for it – or two to go for the "fabulous omakase"; P.S. check out the "funky" high-tech bathrooms.

Morrell Wine Bar & Cafe *American* — 19 | 17 | 18 | $48

W 40s | 1 Rockefeller Plaza (49th St., bet. 5th & 6th Aves.) | 212-262-7700 | www.morrellwinebar.com

Whether you're "new to wine or a seasoned connoisseur", this Rock Center standby supplies a "no-snobbery" setting for sampling a "vast" inventory at "reasonable-for-Midtown" prices; if the New American edibles "aren't the draw", you're bound to enjoy the "great people-watching" from the patio.

Morton's The Steakhouse *Steak* — 24 | 21 | 23 | $75

E 40s | 551 Fifth Ave. (45th St.) | 212-972-3315
Downtown Bklyn | NY Marriott Brooklyn | 339 Adams St. (bet. Tillary & Willoughby Sts.) | Brooklyn | 718-596-2700
www.mortons.com

"Consistency rules" at these "clubby", "wood-paneled" links of the Chicago chophouse chain, from their "always excellent" slabs and "delish sides" to the "attentive" staffers who deliver them; a few "could do without" the pre-meal "plastic-wrapped steak" spiel, but along with major league prices, it's a "traditional steakhouse" experience.

Motorino ● *Pizza* — 24 | 14 | 18 | $28

E Village | 349 E. 12th St. (bet. 1st & 2nd Aves.) | 212-777-2644
Williamsburg | 319 Graham Ave. (Devoe St.) | Brooklyn | 718-599-8899
www.motorinopizza.com

"Fantastic" "thin-crusted" Neapolitan pies topped with "interesting" goodies propel this Williamsburg–East Village duo into NYC's "pizza pantheon"; "friendly" vibes offset "long lines" and "cramped" quarters, with the masses claiming it's "worth it" to be "blown away."

Moustache *Mideastern* — 21 | 12 | 16 | $26

E 100s | 1621 Lexington Ave. (102nd St.) | 212-828-0030 ●
E Village | 265 E. 10th St. (bet. Ave. A & 1st Ave.) | 212-228-2022 ⊟
W Village | 90 Bedford St. (Grove St.) | 212-229-2220 ●⊟
www.moustachepitza.com

They're "dumpy" and service can be "slow", but this Mideastern threesome is "usually crowded" all the same thanks to "tasty" staples (oh that "heavenly pitza") priced "cheap"; the East Village branch boasts a roomy garden, while the UES outpost takes plastic.

Mr. Chow ● *Chinese* — 22 | 21 | 20 | $75

E 50s | 324 E. 57th St. (bet. 1st & 2nd Aves.) | 212-751-9030
Mr. Chow Tribeca ● *Chinese*
TriBeCa | 121 Hudson St. (N. Moore St.) | 212-965-9500
www.mrchow.com

"The '80s" live at Michael Chow's "glamorous" Chinese duo, where "prominent" sorts dine on "delicious" eats (including chicken satay that's "a form of legal crack") in swank "ultramodern" digs; the "no-menu format" isn't to everyone's liking, ditto the "part-time job needed to pay the tab", and most "prefer the flagship on 57th" over the TriBeCa spin-off.

Mr. K's *Chinese*　　　　　23 | 23 | 23 | $61
E 50s | 570 Lexington Ave. (51st St.) | 212-583-1668 | www.mrksny.com
The "arrival of an emperor" wouldn't raise eyebrows at this royally "upscale" Chinese Eastsider, an art deco "oasis of plush pinkness" staffed with "white-glove" servers ferrying "darn good" chow; tabs match the "over-the-top" milieu, but commoners can still have a go via the $28 prix fixe lunch.

M Shanghai Bistro & Den ◑ *Chinese*　▽ 21 | 16 | 19 | $21
Williamsburg | 292 Grand St. (bet. Havemeyer & Roebling Sts.) | Brooklyn | 718-384-9300 | www.newmshanghai.com
M Noodle Shop ◑ *Chinese*
NEW **Williamsburg** | 549 Metropolitan Ave. (bet. Lorimer & Union Sts.) | Brooklyn | 718-384-8008 | www.mnoodleshop.com
"Chinatown meets hipsterville" at this "terrific" Williamsburg duo whose "tasty" Chinese fare with a "modern flair" comes at "modest" rates; the "nicely designed" Bistro & Den, with its red bar and back garden, excels at dim sum, while the newer Noodle Shop slings "delish" slurps.

Mughlai *Indian*　　　　　20 | 15 | 19 | $36
W 70s | 320 Columbus Ave. (75th St.) | 212-724-6363
Upper Westsiders seeking an Indian fix turn "time and again" to this "unchanged-in-years" "neighborhood staple" for "consistently good" cooking carried by a "courteous" crew; its slightly high-for-the-genre prices and "small, unassuming" digs are naan-issues.

Mundo *Argentinean/Mideastern*　▽ 22 | 18 | 23 | $30
Astoria | 31-18 Broadway (enter on 32nd St.) | Queens | 718-777-2829 | www.mundoastoria.com
A "delicious" "departure from the everyday", this "cute" Astorian's "exotic" menu marries Argentine and Turkish flavors and is "vegan"-friendly to boot; the "cozy" quarters are "ridiculously tiny", but "solicitous" staffers and low prices make it a "pleasure to frequent" nonetheless.

NEW **M. Wells** Ⓜ *Diner*　　　　- | - | - | I
LIC | 21-17 49th Ave. (21st St.) | Queens | 718-425-6917 | www.mwellsdiner.com
This old-school Long Island City diner teetering on the edge of a wind-swept rail yard is far from a greasy spoon, offering contemporary Latin and Québécois spins on traditional coffee-shop fare; it's currently open weekdays for breakfast and lunch, with dinner and weekend hours in the works.

NEW **Mxco** *Mexican*　　　　18 | 17 | 17 | $34
E 70s | 1491 Second Ave. (78th St.) | 212-249-6080
"Creative takes on the taco" and other "fresh" Mexican dishes go down well with "huge margaritas" at this "lively" arrival to the UES's former Vynl space, a "welcome addition" to an area that "needed" it; prices are "reasonable", though a few grumble about "skimpy" portions.

	FOOD	DECOR	SERVICE	COST

Nam *Vietnamese* | 22 | 18 | 19 | $40 |

TriBeCa | 110 Reade St. (W. B'way) | 212-267-1777 | www.namnyc.com
A toothsome tour of Vietnam is the net effect of sampling the "fresh",
"flavorful" Saigon specialties prepared at this "pleasing" TriBeCan;
"good prices", "efficient" service and digs more "refined" than many in
the genre keep the traffic coming to its "off-the-beaten-track" location.

Nanni ⊠ *Italian* | 25 | 15 | 23 | $59 |

E 40s | 146 E. 46th St. (bet. Lexington & 3rd Aves.) | 212-697-4161
Silver hair and angel hair unite in "old-school" harmony at this circa-
1968 Italian "standby" near Grand Central, where "excellent" classics
are ferried by "been-there-forever" waiters; "pricey" tabs and "tired"
decor come with the territory, but regulars insist "you'll leave happy."

Nanoosh *Mediterranean* | 19 | 13 | 15 | $19 |

E 60s | 1273 First Ave. (bet. 68th & 69th Sts.) | 917-677-7575
NEW **G Village** | 111 University Pl. (bet. 12th & 13th Sts.) | 212-387-0744
NEW **Murray Hill** | 173 Madison Ave. (bet. 33rd & 34th Sts.) |
212-447-4348 ⊠
W 60s | 2012 Broadway (bet. 68th & 69th Sts.) | 212-362-7922
www.nanoosh.com
"Delicious hummus" is the thing at this "reliable", "inexpensive" Med
chainlet that's a lunchtime standby thanks to its "wholesome" wraps and
"fresh" salads made from "quality" ingredients; "no-nonsense" service
and "minimal" ambiance favor "takeout" or "quick meals" on the go.

Naples 45 ⊠ *Italian* | 17 | 15 | 16 | $36 |

E 40s | MetLife Bldg. | 200 Park Ave. (45th St.) | 212-972-7001 |
www.patinagroup.com
"Convenience" is the clincher at this "big, loud" pizza-palooza near
Grand Central, where "decent" Neapolitan pies, pastas and other
Southern Italian standards arrive "quick" for "biz lunchers" and "commuters"; "Naples it's not", but those who "work nearby" are "happy"
to have it.

Natsumi ❶ *Italian/Japanese* | 24 | 19 | 22 | $45 |

W 50s | Amsterdam Court Hotel | 226 W. 50th St. (bet. B'way & 8th Ave.) |
212-258-2988 | www.natsuminyc.com
"Fresh, inventive sushi" and a variety of Japanese cooked entrees –
some with "hints of Italian" influence – are the "well-priced" stars at
this "classy" Theater Districter; "efficient" service bolsters its pre-
curtain cred, and tipplers dig the "energetic scene" in its lounge.

Naya *Lebanese* | 23 | 21 | 20 | $41 |

E 50s | 1057 Second Ave. (bet. 55th & 56th Sts.) | 212-319-7777 |
www.nayarestaurants.com
The "mod", "otherworldly" design scheme is an "offbeat" counter-
point to the "classic" Lebanese cuisine dished up at this "narrow" East
Midtown "gem"; its "generous meze portions" and fair prices are
points of praise, as is the "pleasant" service.

Neary's ❶ *Pub Food* | 18 | 15 | 21 | $44 |

E 50s | 358 E. 57th St. (1st Ave.) | 212-751-1434 | www.nearys.com
"No one pours a more generous drink" than "leprechaun"-like "perfect
host" Jimmy Neary, whose "welcoming" East Midtown pub has been a

beloved hangout and Irish "comfort-food" station since 1967; its "loyal" regulars ("some well-known") are largely "pre–baby boomer" and "feel at home" in the "old-fashioned" setting.

Negril ● *Caribbean/Jamaican*　21　17　17　$41

G Village | 70 W. Third St. (bet. La Guardia Pl. & Thompson St.) | 212-477-2804 | www.negrilvillage.com

The next best thing to an "island getaway" is this "colorful" Village Jamaican where you get "delicious" Caribbean flavors and "sweet tropical drinks" minus the flight; any service miscues are easy to abide when you're doing some "good ol' partying" to "live music" downstairs.

Nello ● *Italian*　18　17　16　$96

E 60s | 696 Madison Ave. (bet. 62nd & 63rd Sts.) | 212-980-9099

The East Side's unofficial "who's who" HQ, this Italian vet serves its upscale fare to a mix of "celebs", "Euros" and other "upper-crust" types who provide a prime people-watching "show"; just know that the "scene" includes "snobbish" service and "underwhelming" fare at prices that lead some to call it "the Madoff of restaurants."

New Hawaii Sea ● *Chinese*　▽ 22　22　22　$32

Bronx | 1475 Williamsbridge Rd. (bet. St. Raymond's Ave. & Silver St.) | 718-863-7900

Around since 1980, this "spacious", incongruously named Bronx Chinese bastion continues to serve "consistently good", "old-fashioned" favorites, plus sushi; "reasonable prices", "fancy" Polynesian-inspired drinks and a staff that "doesn't rush you" are other keys to its longevity.

New Leaf Ⓜ *American*　21　24　21　$47

Washington Heights | Fort Tryon Park | 1 Margaret Corbin Dr. (190th St.) | 212-568-5323 | www.nyrp.org

The "bucolic" scenery's more "upstate" than uptown at this "charming" Fort Tryon Park "hideaway" run by "Bette Midler's nonprofit" NY Restoration Project; the New American food's "tasty", staff "welcoming" and clientele – from Cloisters-goers to families – at complete "peace."

Nha Trang *Vietnamese*　22　7　15　$19

Chinatown | 148 Centre St. (bet. Walker & White Sts.) | 212-941-9292

Chinatown | 87 Baxter St. (bet. Bayard & Canal Sts.) | 212-233-5948

This Chinatown duo trafficking in "wonderful pho" and other Vietnamese "standouts" is a favored "jury-duty stop" thanks to "lightning-fast" turnaround ("food arrives almost before you finish ordering") and "ridiculously cheap" tabs; as for decor, "no-frills" is putting it mildly.

Nice Green Bo ⇪ *Chinese*　23　4　13　$18

Chinatown | 66 Bayard St. (bet. Elizabeth & Mott Sts.) | 212-625-2359

"Dingy" digs, "communal tables" and "surly" service are mere "cosmetic flaws" at this C-towner, since sympathists swear the "superb" soup dumplings and other Shanghainese specialties are worth "running across hot coals" for; "can't-be-beat" prices are another reason the "line's out the door."

	FOOD	DECOR	SERVICE	COST

Nice Matin *French/Mediterranean*

| 20 | 18 | 18 | $46 |

W 70s | 201 W. 79th St. (Amsterdam Ave.) | 212-873-6423 |
www.nicematinnyc.com

At this "convivial", "deservedly popular" Upper Westsider, "reliably
good" French-Med fare and a "strong" wine list "transport you to the
Côte d'Azur"; its "civilized brunch" and "lovely sidewalk seating" offset "noisy" acoustics and sometimes "slow" service.

Nick & Stef's Steakhouse 🖪 *Steak*

| 21 | 17 | 21 | $63 |

Garment District | 9 Penn Plaza (enter on 33rd St., bet. 7th & 8th Aves.) |
212-563-4444 | www.patinagroup.com

A clutch performer "pre-Garden", this Midtown chophouse with a
"direct entrance" into MSG serves up "delicious hunks of beef" while
getting ticket-holders "in and out" quick; it's "expensive" but arguably
"your best option" in an area with "few reliable" players; P.S. it's temporarily closed for renovations but expected to reopen in late 2010.

Nick & Toni's Cafe *Mediterranean*

| 19 | 16 | 18 | $49 |

W 60s | 100 W. 67th St. (bet. B'way & Columbus Ave.) | 212-496-4000 |
www.nickandtoniscafe.com

Though not as hot as its "East Hampton parent", this pre-concert "performer" near Lincoln Center keeps its "spartan" setting "warm" with
the wood-burning oven that produces its pizzas and other
"dependable", "uncomplicated" Med fare; "ABC media types" in
regular attendance add interest.

Nick's *Pizza*

| 23 | 14 | 18 | $24 |

E 90s | 1814 Second Ave. (94th St.) | 212-987-5700 |
www.nicksnyc.com
Forest Hills | 108-26 Ascan Ave. (bet. Austin & Burns Sts.) | Queens |
718-263-1126 ⊉

"Perfectly charred" brick-oven pizza is the thing at this Forest Hills pie
parlor and its UES offshoot, which serves pastas and other Italian basics as well; they won't impress with either service or ambiance, but
the Manhattan outlet gets some slack for "surviving the Second
Avenue subway dig."

Nicky's
Vietnamese Sandwiches ⊉ *Sandwiches*

| 21 | 7 | 16 | $11 |

E Village | 150 E. Second St. (Ave. A) | 212-388-1088
Boerum Hill | 311 Atlantic Ave. (bet. Hoyt & Smith Sts.) | Brooklyn |
718-855-8838
www.nickyssandwiches.com

"Freakin' awesome" banh mi with "perfectly toasted baguettes and
luscious fillings" come "quick" and "cheap" at this Vietnamese duo; the
Boerum Hill offshoot also offers "very good pho" and has a few more
seats than its East Village parent, but "no decor" describes them both.

🆉 Nicola's ● *Italian*

| 22 | 17 | 21 | $61 |

E 80s | 146 E. 84th St. (bet. Lexington & 3rd Aves.) | 212-249-9850

Membership has its privileges at this "clubby" UES "staple" frequented by "upscale neighborhood" types partial to "very good
Italian" classics prepared "however they like it"; outsiders who report
"standoffish" service are advised to "return a few times" for improved
treatment – just secure a line of credit first.

Nina's Argentinian Pizzeria *Italian* | ▽ 23 | 15 | 21 | $26 |

E 90s | 1750 Second Ave. (91st St.) | 212-426-4627

"Zesty pizzas" and "excellent empanadas" coexist in "delicious" multi-cultural harmony at this UES Argentine-Italian; "cordial" service and "easy-on-the-wallet" tabs are appreciated by a "local" following that doesn't mind if the "hole-in-the-wall" setting isn't much.

99 Miles to Philly ◐⇻ *Cheesesteaks* | 19 | 8 | 15 | $13 |

E Village | 94 Third Ave. (bet. 12th & 13th Sts.) | 212-253-2700 | www.99milestophilly.net

Bringing the "gooey pleasures" of a Philly cheesesteak to NYC, this East Village "hole-in-the-wall" mimics the "real deal" with just the "right amount of grease" and Cheez Whiz; though it's certainly "quicker than taking the bus", purists insist "something got lost on the turnpike."

Ninja *Japanese* | 17 | 25 | 23 | $64 |

TriBeCa | 25 Hudson St. (bet. Duane & Reade Sts.) | 212-274-8500 | www.ninjanewyork.com

"Restaurant and amusement park" converge at this TriBeCan where the "fun gimmick" has you dining in a faux "Japanese village" under the watch of costumed "ninja"-waiters who also perform "magic"; the food's less than *sensei*-tional and "pricey" too, so try to "be in a playful mood."

Nino's ◐ *Italian* | 20 | 18 | 21 | $55 |

E 70s | 1354 First Ave. (bet. 72nd & 73rd Sts.) | 212-988-0002

Nino's Bellissima Pizza *Pizza*

E 40s | 890 Second Ave. (bet. 47th & 48th Sts.) | 212-355-5540

Nino's Positano *Italian*

E 40s | 890 Second Ave. (bet. 47th & 48th Sts.) | 212-355-5540

Nino's Tuscany *Italian*

W 50s | 117 W. 58th St. (bet. 6th & 7th Aves.) | 212-757-8630

Nino's 208 *Italian*

E 50s | 208 E. 58th St. (bet. 2nd & 3rd Aves.) | 212-750-7766 | www.ninony.com

"Quintessential host" Nino Selimaj's mini-fiefdom of "old-school" Italian eateries "gets the job done" with "dependable" (albeit "high-priced") cuisine served by a staff that "treats you well"; the "nostalgia"-rich settings tilt toward "fine dining", except for the casual Positano link and its adjunct pizzeria.

Nippon ⓩ *Japanese* | ▽ 21 | 17 | 20 | $61 |

E 50s | 155 E. 52nd St. (bet. Lexington & 3rd Aves.) | 212-758-0226 | www.restaurantnippon.com

Where NYers "first tried sushi" back in the '60s, this Midtown institution remains a "standby" for "excellent" Japanese standards, including "super soba"; though a bit "expensive" and "run-down", fans declare it's "still as wonderful" as ever.

Nirvana *Indian* | ▽ 23 | 21 | 22 | $47 |

Murray Hill | 346 Lexington Ave. (bet. 39th & 40th Sts.) | 212-983-0000 | www.nirvanany.com

A bit more upscale than many in Murray Hill, this under-the-radar Indian features "traditional favorites" as well as some "interesting variations" (e.g. rabbit stew) ferried by "attentive" staffers; the upstairs room is deemed "Zen-like", while the "exotic" street-level lounge is livelier.

	FOOD	DECOR	SERVICE	COST

Nizza 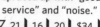 *French/Italian* — 20 | 16 | 18 | $37

W 40s | 630 Ninth Ave. (bet. 44th & 45th Sts.) | 212-956-1800 | www.nizzanyc.com

"Tasty" French-Italian small plates straight out of Nice ("the socca is so good") make for "memorable" "Riviera-style" meals at this "bustling" Hell's Kitchen "favorite"; with "quick" turnaround, "inexpensive" tabs and late-night hours, it's a "good bet" both "before and after the theater."

☑ Nobu *Japanese* — 26 | 23 | 23 | $81

TriBeCa | 105 Hudson St. (Franklin St.) | 212-219-0500

☑ Nobu 57 ● *Japanese*

W 50s | 40 W. 57th St. (bet. 5th & 6th Aves.) | 212-757-3000

☑ Nobu, Next Door *Japanese*

TriBeCa | 105 Hudson St. (bet. Franklin & N. Moore Sts.) | 212-334-4445 www.noburestaurants.com

Nobu Matsuhisa offers NYers three "upbeat", "celeb-peppered" venues in which to sample his Japanese-Peruvian culinary "ingenuity": the "still-fabulous", "tough-to-reserve" TriBeCa flagship, its "more relaxed", "cheaper" next door adjunct and the "classy", newer Midtown outpost; "pro" service and "dazzling" decor ensure it's "worth every Benjamin."

Nocello *Italian* — 21 | 18 | 21 | $52

W 50s | 257 W. 55th St. (bet. B'way & 8th Ave.) | 212-713-0224 | www.nocello.net

For an Italian "charmer" that's "close to Carnegie Hall and City Center", you "can't go wrong" with this "refined enclave" where "well-prepared" Tuscan classics are served by a "caring" ensemble; factor in "fair prices" and it's plain to see why so many "keep coming back."

Noche Mexicana *Mexican* — 22 | 10 | 18 | $20

W 100s | 852 Amsterdam Ave. (bet. 101st & 102nd Sts.) | 212-662-6900 | www.noche-mexicana.com

"No atmosphere" is *no problema* at this recently "expanded" but still no-frills UWS "sleeper" serving "outstanding" Mexican fare at "rock-bottom" rates; since "language can be an issue" with the "sweetheart" servers, it helps "if you speak a little Spanish."

NoHo Star ● *American* — 17 | 14 | 17 | $35

NoHo | 330 Lafayette St. (Bleecker St.) | 212-925-0070 | www.nohostar.com

A NoHo "staple" since forever, this "glorified coffee shop" plies a "varied" (if "uninspired") New American menu that's spruced up with "good Chinese" options at dinner; downsides are "iffy service" and "noise."

Nomad *African/Spanish* — ▽ 21 | 16 | 20 | $34

E Village | 78 Second Ave. (4th St.) | 212-253-5410 | www.nomadny.com

A post-Survey menu revamp has added Spanish-Med tapas to the lineup at this "welcoming" East Village North African that still serves the likes of pastilla and tagines; check out the "attractive back garden."

Noodle Bar *Asian* — 20 | 13 | 18 | $21

LES | 172 Orchard St. (Stanton St.) | 212-228-9833
W Village | 26 Carmine St. (bet. Bedford & Bleecker Sts.) | 212-524-6800 www.noodlebarnyc.com

Oodles flock to this Village-LES Pan-Asian pair, where "lots of choices" from "hearty soups" to "tasty" wok-works supply a "filling", "inexpensive" fix; cash-only policies and "small" spaces are part of the "simple" package, though "watching your food be prepared" in the open kitchen adds interest.

Noodle Pudding ⓂⒼ *Italian*

24 | **17** | **22** | **$39**

Brooklyn Heights | 38 Henry St. (bet. Cranberry & Middagh Sts.) | Brooklyn | 718-625-3737
An "odd name" doesn't hold back this Brooklyn Heights Italian "standout" – it's "always packed" due to its "terrific" "traditional" Italian cooking at retro prices; however, the "quality" offerings come with a few "annoyances": "cash only", "no reservations", "long waits" and "noise."

Nook Ⓖ *Eclectic*

22 | **12** | **18** | **$33**

W 50s | 746 Ninth Ave. (bet. 50th & 51st Sts.) | 212-247-5500
The "name says it all" about this "teeny", "convivial" Hell's Kitchen "hole-in-the-wall", where "quality" Eclectic cooking is delivered by a "competent" (if sometimes "curt") crew; it's cash-only and takes no reservations, but the BYO policy "saves you a bundle."

Norma's *American*

25 | **18** | **19** | **$42**

W 50s | Le Parker Meridien | 119 W. 56th St. (bet. 6th & 7th Aves.) | 212-708-7460 | www.normasnyc.com
Midtown's "high temple of breakfast" and brunch, this New American hoteler "pushes the envelope" of "decadence" with its "delicious", "incredibly rich" morning fare priced for "power" and "trust-fund" types; it gets "hectic", so "make a reservation" or "prepare to wait."

🆕 Northern Spy Food Company *American*

23 | **18** | **18** | **$32**

E Village | 511 E. 12th St. (bet. Aves. A & B) | 212-228-5100 | www.northernspyfoodco.com
Preliminary intel is positive on this new East Villager's "locally" focused, "fair-priced" American cuisine, served by an "engaging" staff in "small, quirky" quarters; it takes its name from an upstate apple variety, and fittingly there's a "market in back selling regional foods."

North Square *American*

23 | **19** | **21** | **$47**

G Village | Washington Square Hotel | 103 Waverly Pl. (MacDougal St.) | 212-254-1200 | www.northsquareny.com
"Worth" unearthing, this "hidden gem" near NYU offers "wonderful" New American fare delivered by "attentive" servers in "peaceful" digs; factor in moderate prices, and no wonder regulars are "reluctant to tell others how good it is."

No. 7 ●Ⓜ *American*

23 | **17** | **19** | **$35**

Fort Greene | 7 Greene Ave. (bet. Cumberland & Fulton Sts.) | Brooklyn | 718-522-6370 | www.no7restaurant.com

No. 7 Sub *Sandwiches*

🆕 **Chelsea** | Ace Hotel | 1188 Broadway (bet. 28th & 29th Sts.) | 212-532-1680 | www.no7sub.com
"Delicate" New American cooking energized by a "healthy dose of imagination" is the hot number at this "relaxed", "stylish" and "cordial" Fort Greene standout; the same "inventive" spirit infuses its new counter-service spin-off in Chelsea's Ace Hotel, whose "amazing" subs make "all other sandwiches seem boring."

	FOOD	DECOR	SERVICE	COST

No. 28 ⊄ *Pizza* | 23 | 13 | 17 | $27 |

NEW E Village | 176 Second Ave. (11th St.) | 212-777-1555 ◗
NEW SoHo | 196 Spring St. (bet. Sullivan & Thompson Sts.) |
212-219-9020
W Village | 28 Carmine St. (bet. Bedford & Bleecker Sts.) |
212-463 9653
www.numero28.com

Pizzaphiles are enthused about the "charred-to-perfection" Neapolitan pies supplied by these "reasonably priced" East and West Villagers and their takeout-oriented SoHo satellite, which vends "delicious" Roman-style slices; a cash-only policy, "uneven" service and nothing-fancy digs come with 'za territory.

Nove ⬚ *Italian* | ▽ 25 | 24 | 23 | $50 |

Staten Island | 3900 Richmond Ave. (Amboy Rd.) | 718-227-3286 |
www.noveitalianbistro.com

Staten Islanders are stoked about this "warm", upscale South Shore Italian bistro whose "impressive" midpriced fare is delivered by staffers who "can't do enough for you"; "fancy", "trendy" decor and "live music" also hit the right notes with hot spot–starved locals.

Novecento ◗ *Argentinean/Steak* | ▽ 23 | 18 | 20 | $47 |

SoHo | 343 W. Broadway (bet. Broome & Grand Sts.) | 212-925-4706 |
www.novecento.com

"Perfect if you're hankering" for Argentine specialties like "wonderful grilled meats" and "authentic empanadas", this "stylish" SoHo standby draws an "eat-and-be-merry" expat crowd; P.S. once for "music and partying", the upstairs lounge now hosts private events only.

Novitá *Italian* | 24 | 18 | 21 | $58 |

Gramercy | 102 E. 22nd St. (bet. Lexington Ave. & Park Ave. S.) |
212-677-2222 | www.novitanyc.com

Touted as a "Gramercy find", this "understated" Italian wins fans with its "consistently fine" "contemporary" Northern Italian cooking and "congenial" service; yes, it can get "cramped and noisy", but that's "forgivable" given the overall "pleasant" experience and "fair" (if "not cheap") prices.

NEW Nuela *Latin* | - | - | - | E |

Flatiron | 43 W. 24th St. (bet. B'way & 6th Ave.) | 212-929-1200 |
www.nuelany.com

Once poised for chef Douglas Rodriguez's return to NYC, this cavernous new Flatironer instead has his protégé, Adam Schop, at the burners, sending out "flavorful", pricey Pan-Latin dishes from small plates to roast suckling pig; the "gorgeous" space has been done up in vivid guava and passionfruit tones and has a ceviche bar at its center.

Num Pang ⊄ *Cambodian* | 26 | 7 | 15 | $13 |

G Village | 21 E. 12th St. (bet. 5th Ave. & University Pl.) | 212-255-3271 |
www.numpangnyc.com

Its name means 'bread' in Khmer, and this Cambodian-inspired sandwich shop in the Village assembles "ridiculously good" baguette-based "marvels" that give the banh mi a run for its money; it's value-priced but cash-only, with "tiny" dimensions that have many declaring it "best for takeout."

	FOOD	DECOR	SERVICE	COST

Nurnberger Bierhaus *German* ▽ 21 | 16 | 19 | $34

Staten Island | 817 Castleton Ave. (bet. Davis & Pelton Aves.) |
718-816-7461 | www.nurnbergerbierhaus.com

Staten Island *volk* vouch for this North Shore beer hall's "traditional"
Bavarian eats, which come in "huge portions" tailor-made for soaking
up the many German suds on tap; other "authentic" nods to Teutonia
include a "lively outdoor garden" and the waitresses' traditional garb.

Nyonya ⏀ *Malaysian* 21 | 13 | 14 | $24

Little Italy | 199 Grand St. (bet. Mott & Mulberry Sts.) | 212-334-3669 ☽
Bensonhurst | 2322 86th St. (bet. 23rd & 24th Aves.) | Brooklyn |
718-265-0888
Sunset Park | 5323 Eighth Ave. (54th St.) | Brooklyn | 718-633-0808 ☽
www.penangusa.com

When craving Asian fare that's "a little different", check out these
Malaysians dishing up a "flavorful" array of "just-like-in-Penang"
dishes for "cheap"; despite "uneven" service, "lacking" decor and a
cash-only policy, they're "usually crowded."

NYY Steak *Steak* 21 | 21 | 20 | $70

Bronx | Yankee Stadium | 1 E. 161st St., Gate 6 (River Ave.) | 646-977-8325 |
www.nyysteak.com

Look for "current or former Yankees" downing "steaks branded with pin-
stripes" at this meatery "in the house that George built"; it "scores" with
"quality" beef and a "fun" setting, but prepare for "ballpark prices."

Oak Room *American* 20 | 26 | 22 | $71

W 50s | Plaza Hotel | 10 Central Park S. (bet. 5th & 6th Aves.) |
212-758-7777 | www.oakroomny.com

Its "fantastic", oak-lined, century-old room was refreshed in 2008, and
this "clubby" Plaza Hotel "landmark" now has a new chef delivering "very
good" American fare via a "polished" crew; diehards "liked the original
better", but to most it's a "definite-visit" despite the "outrageous" tab.

Oceana *American/Seafood* 23 | 23 | 22 | $79

W 40s | McGraw Hill Bldg. | 120 W. 49th St. (bet. 6th & 7th Aves.) |
212-759-5941 | www.oceanarestaurant.com

Now docked in a "spacious" Rockefeller Center berth, this seafooder
provides "splendid" "culinary voyages" featuring an "incredible raw
bar" and "dignified" service, all at "expense account"–worthy prices;
supporters declare this ship "revitalized", but a mutinous few maintain its "corporate" new incarnation "misses the boat."

Ocean Grill *Seafood* 24 | 21 | 22 | $56

W 70s | 384 Columbus Ave. (bet. 78th & 79th Sts.) | 212-579-2300 |
www.brguestrestaurants.com

Pescatarians "dive in" to Steve Hanson's Upper Westsider for "mouthwatering" seafood, including sushi, delivered by an "accommodating"
crew; the "big-city" vibe includes being "packed like herring" along with
"problematic" acoustics – unless you hook "prime outside seating."

Odeon, The ☽ *American/French* 20 | 18 | 19 | $47

TriBeCa | 145 W. Broadway (bet. Duane & Thomas Sts.) | 212-233-0507 |
www.theodeonrestaurant.com

Still "going strong" after 30 years, this TriBeCa "pioneer" relies on a
"perfect formula" of "solid" French-American bistro classics, an "eclec-

tic" clientele ("young hipsters" to "professionals" to "families") and "energetic" ambiance; it's especially "welcoming" in the wee hours.

NEW Ofrenda *Mexican* ▽ 25 | 18 | 24 | $39

W Village | 113 Seventh Ave. S. (bet. Christopher & W. 10th Sts.) | 212-924-2305 | www.ofrendanyc.com

Not your average cantina, this "friendly" West Village arrival in "simple" but spacious digs is serious about its "upscale", modern Mexican cuisine, and offers its "outstanding" dishes in the under-$20 range; "fierce cocktails" and an outdoor seating area are other appeals.

Old Homestead *Steak* 24 | 18 | 21 | $73

Meatpacking | 56 Ninth Ave. (bet. 14th & 15th Sts.) | 212-242-9040 | www.theoldhomesteadsteakhouse.com

As "excellently aged" as its "two-doggy-bag" slabs, this Meatpacking chophouse is a "whir of activity" presided over by waiters who've seemingly "been there since the place opened" in 1868; it's "not cheap", and some find it "inconsistent", but to most it's "one of the city's best no-frills steak experiences."

Olea *Mediterranean* ▽ 23 | 19 | 21 | $36

Fort Greene | 171 Lafayette Ave. (Adelphi St.) | Brooklyn | 718-643-7003 | www.oleabrooklyn.com

At this "casual", "whitewashed" Fort Greene taverna, the "wonderful", well-priced Med menu consists largely of "outstanding tapas" offering "something for everybody"; it's a "fave" of BAM-goers and "mobbed" at brunch – "earnest service and modest tabs" are part of the reason.

NEW Olio ● *Pizza* - | - | - | M

W Village | 3 Greenwich Ave. (bet. Christopher St. & 6th Ave.) | 212-243-6546 | www.olionyc.com

Authentic Neapolitan pies are the specialty of this casual new West Village pizzeria from a master pizzaiolo whose numerous awards are listed on the menu; an airy setting, sidewalk seating and a cocktail list via an Employees Only alum add to its allure.

Olives *Mediterranean* 23 | 20 | 20 | $57

Union Sq | W Hotel Union Sq. | 201 Park Ave. S. (17th St.) | 212-353-8345 | www.toddenglish.com

"Celeb chef" Todd English's "Manhattan flagship" in the W Union Square is still "bustling" thanks to its "bold" Mediterranean cooking; servers tending the "commodious" room "know their stuff" too, but "pricey" tabs and "noise" from the adjacent bar can be the pits.

Olive's *Sandwiches* ▽ 22 | 14 | 16 | $29

SoHo | 120 Prince St. (bet. Greene & Wooster Sts.) | 212-941-0111 | www.olivesnyc.com

For a "quick bite" in SoHo, this "hip", "tiny take-out place" fills the bill with its "wide selection" of "excellent" sandwiches, soups and treats served up "quick"; yes, there are "crazy lines at lunch", but "superb people-watching" helps the time pass.

Ollie's *Chinese* 16 | 10 | 13 | $24

W 40s | 411 W. 42nd St. (bet. 9th & 10th Aves.) | 212-868-6588
W 60s | 1991 Broadway (bet. 67th & 68th Sts.) | 212-595-8181

(continued)

(continued)

Ollie's

NEW | **W 80s** | 2425 Broadway (bet. 89th & 90th Sts.) | 212-877-2298
W 100s | 2957 Broadway (116th St.) | 212-932-3300 ●

When "hungry and hurried", Westsiders hasten to this "utilitarian" Cantonese chainlet for "decent", "hot, cheap" noodles and other "filling" chow, "tossed at you" in "about 3½ minutes"; homebodies hail "magical" delivery guys who seem to "work at the speed of sound."

☑ Omai *Vietnamese*

23 | 16 | 20 | $44

Chelsea | 158 Ninth Ave. (bet. 19th & 20th Sts.) | 212-633-0550 |
www.omainyc.com

"Oh my" swoon surveyors sampling the "savory", "addictive" Vietnamese fare at this "friendly", "reasonably priced" Chelsea "hideaway", whose "pleasant" space is so "minimalist" it's signless; "cheerful" regulars who kick up a "crowded, noisy" scene plead "expand already."

Omen ● *Japanese*

∇ 24 | 18 | 22 | $59

SoHo | 113 Thompson St. (bet. Prince & Spring Sts.) | 212-925-8923

"Still incredible after all these years", this "bit of Kyoto in SoHo" serves "stunning" sashimi and noodles to an "arty", "celeb"-heavy clientele; "preternaturally kind" staffers man a "serene" setting that's "so peaceful you can float through" without noticing the "kick to your wallet."

Omonia Cafe ● *Greek*

20 | 16 | 16 | $21

Bay Ridge | 7612-14 Third Ave. (bet. 76th & 77th Sts.) | Brooklyn | 718-491-1435
Astoria | 32-20 Broadway (33rd St.) | Queens | 718-274-6650
www.omoniacafe.com

Expect "instant sugar shock" upon entering these "long-standing" Astoria–Bay Ridge coffeehouses known for "big fat Greek desserts" ("best baklava outside Athens") plus a "solid" slate of "tasty" savories; "cordial" service "can be slow at times", but "the price is right."

Once Upon a Tart . . . *Coffeehouse*

21 | 14 | 16 | $16

SoHo | 135 Sullivan St. (bet. Houston & Prince Sts.) | 212-387-8869 |
www.onceuponatart.com

Known for "wonderful" baked goods and "wacky window displays", this counter-service SoHo stalwart inspires tales of "fragrant" pastries plus "special" sandwiches and soups; the space is "teensy" so consider "takeout" – unless you're "lucky enough to snag" a sidewalk table.

One 83 *Italian*

19 | 20 | 21 | $52

E 80s | 1608 First Ave. (bet. 83rd & 84th Sts.) | 212-327-4700 |
www.one83restaurant.com

"You can actually converse" "without shouting" at this "modern", "roomy" Yorkville Italian, where Tuscan "standards" share the menu with more "innovative" options; "courteous" service and a "pretty patio" ideal for "warm summer evenings" help make it a "neighborhood favorite."

☑ One if by Land, Two if by Sea *American*

24 | 27 | 25 | $101

W Village | 17 Barrow St. (bet. 7th Ave. S. & W. 4th St.) | 212-228-0822 |
www.oneifbyland.com

"Love is busting out all over" at this "sumptuous" Village "classic" that was once Aaron Burr's carriage house and is now a favored place to "get engaged" over "oysters and beef Wellington" or other prix fixe-only New Americana served with "attention to detail"; maybe the ambiance "exceeds the menu", but to most it's "well worth" a "splurge."

101 *American/Italian*   20 | 18 | 19 | $44

Bay Ridge | 10018 Fourth Ave. (101st St.) | Brooklyn | 718-833-1313
"Locals" tout this fairly priced Bay Ridge fixture as "better than most" for "solid" Italian-American fare served in "casual" digs with a "nice view" of the Verrazano Bridge; however, unless "you're young and like it loud", the "weekend bar scene" can be "overbearing."

Orchard, The ☒ Ⓜ *American*   23 | 21 | 20 | $58

LES | 162 Orchard St. (bet. Rivington & Stanton Sts.) | 212-353-3570 | www.theorchardny.com
"Irresistible flatbreads" lead the "excellent" New American offerings at this "upscale" LES "retreat", whose "amber lighting" is as kind to diners as the "warm, unobtrusive" staff; just know that in this zip code, you "need a passport if you're over 50."

☒ Oriental Garden *Chinese/Seafood*   24 | 11 | 15 | $34

Chinatown | 14 Elizabeth St. (bet. Bayard & Canal Sts.) | 212-619-0085
"Fine, fresh" fin fare elicits fanfare at this veteran Chinatown Cantonese, where marine "critters" from on-site tanks practically "swim to your table"; "typical C-town" Formica decor and "hurried" service are part of the package, as are "long lines on weekends" for its "first-rate" dim sum.

Orsay *French*   18 | 20 | 18 | $59

E 70s | 1057 Lexington Ave. (75th St.) | 212-517-6400 | www.orsayrestaurant.com
"Truly Parisian" from the "art nouveau" styling to the "tasty" French standards, this UES brasserie makes "chic Euro" types feel at home; the less-enamored cite "mediocre-for-the-price" offerings, "deafening" acoustics and staffers who serve up "attitude on a plate."

Orso ◑ *Italian*   22 | 18 | 22 | $56

W 40s | 322 W. 46th St. (bet. 8th & 9th Aves.) | 212-489-7212 | www.orsorestaurant.com
It's a longtime "theater celebrity" haunt, but even "non–Page Six types" get "genial" service and "terrific" Tuscan fare – if they "can get a reservation" – at this "comfortable, unpretentious" Restaurant Row "haven"; "quick in-and-out" pacing is another reason it's a "superior" choice pre- or post-curtain – orso they say.

Osaka *Japanese*   ▽ 22 | 15 | 18 | $33

Cobble Hill | 272 Court St. (bet. Butler & Douglass Sts.) | Brooklyn | 718-643-0044 | www.osakany.com
This "friendly" Cobble Hill Japanese proffers "generous", well-priced servings of "artfully wrought" sushi in "unpretentious" environs; it's especially "popular" in the "warmer months" when tables in the "huge garden" augment its "Lilliputian" dining room.

Osso Buco *Italian*   19 | 15 | 19 | $38

E 90s | 1662 Third Ave. (93rd St.) | 212-426-5422 | www.ossobuco2010.com
"Though not gourmet", this amiable Upper East Side Italian eatery is "popular" with neighbors for "abundant" family-style platters of "tasty

red-sauce" standards at "reasonable prices"; it's ideal for "groups and kids", and also boasts a location "convenient to the 92nd Street Y."

Osteria al Doge Italian   20 | 17 | 19 | $49

W 40s | 142 W. 44th St. (bet. B'way & 6th Ave.) | 212-944-3643 | www.osteria-doge.com

"Hearty", "straightforward" Northern Italian classics are executed "very well" at this "lively", "midpriced" Venetian that's located just a "gondola's row" from Times Square and has a crew that "understands theater time constraints"; insiders suggest "for less noise, sit upstairs."

Osteria del Circo ● Italian   22 | 23 | 21 | $64

W 50s | 120 W. 55th St. (bet. 6th & 7th Aves.) | 212-265-3636 | www.osteriadelcirco.com

A "carousel of Maccionis" is "always on hand" to welcome *amici* to this Tuscan "Le Cirque offshoot", a "whimsical", circus-themed culinary "celebration" near City Center; "excellent" pastas and pizzas plus plenty of prix fixe "steals" make the "expensive" rates easy to tolerate.

Osteria Laguna ● Italian   19 | 17 | 19 | $46

E 40s | 209 E. 42nd St. (bet. 2nd & 3rd Aves.) | 212-557-0001 | www.osteria-laguna.com

Filling a niche near Grand Central and the U.N., this "useful" East Midtown Venetian proffers "decent", "fair-priced" traditional dishes in a zone "lacking many good choices"; "by no means haute", it's "pleasant" enough, especially when the French doors are open "on nice days."

Otto ● Pizza   22 | 19 | 18 | $39

G Village | 1 Fifth Ave. (enter on 8th St., bet. 5th Ave. & University Pl.) | 212-995-9559 | www.ottopizzeria.com

"All aboard" – "NYU students", "tourists" and "families" travel to this train-themed Batali-Bastianich enoteca/pizzeria in the Village for "inventive" pies, an "insanely long" Italian wine list and "must-have" gelato; despite "waits", "din" and *mezzo-mezzo* service, most say you "really otto go" for the "Mario experience" at a "decent price."

ⓩ Ouest American   24 | 21 | 22 | $63

W 80s | 2315 Broadway (bet. 83rd & 84th Sts.) | 212-580-8700 | www.ouestny.com

"Year after year" Tom Valenti's UWS "charmer" turns out "sophisticated" American "comfort" fare "accommodatingly served" in a setting whose "spacious" circular booths and "swanky" vibe suggest a "1940s supper club"; it's "not cheap", but the prix fixe menus are a "bargain."

Outback Steakhouse Steak   15 | 13 | 17 | $34

E 50s | 919 Third Ave. (enter on 56th St., bet. 2nd & 3rd Aves.) | 212-935-6400
Flatiron | 60 W. 23rd St. (bet. 5th & 6th Aves.) | 212-989-3122
Dyker Heights | 1475 86th St. (15th Ave.) | Brooklyn | 718-837-7200
Bayside | Bay Terrace | 23-48 Bell Blvd. (26th Ave.) | Queens | 718-819-0908
Elmhurst | Queens Pl. | 88-01 Queens Blvd. (56th Ave.) | Queens | 718-760-7200
Staten Island | 280 Marsh Ave. (Platinum Ave.) | 718-761-3907
www.outback.com

"Luger's it isn't", but penny-wise patrons pick this "reliable" steakhouse chain for "decent" meat at a "modest price", "competently" served;

"snobs" give eye-rolls to the "Australian kitsch" and "over-salted" offerings, but that "OMG bloomin' onion" still "brings 'em back."

☒ Oyster Bar ⑤ *Seafood* 22 | 18 | 18 | $49

E 40s | Grand Central | lower level (42nd St. & Vanderbilt Ave.) |
212-490-6650 | www.oysterbarny.com

This "landmark cavern" below Grand Central has been "packing 'em in" since 1913 for "bewilderingly delicious" bivalves, pan roasts, "chowder and chatter"; just "muscle" up to the bar, "ask a counterman" which fish to order and "be blown away" – but be aware, "cheap it ain't."

Pacificana *Chinese* 25 | 17 | 20 | $25

Sunset Park | 813 55th St., 2nd fl. (8th Ave.) | Brooklyn |
718-871-2880

At this "sprawling" Sunset Park "dim sum palace", a Sinophile can "feast like an emperor" for a "peasant's wages"; beyond the "plentiful" carts' "succession of succulence", a "wide array" of Cantonese cookery is on offer, with an "excellent" staff to "help you figure out what to order."

Padre Figlio ⑤ *Italian* ▽ 22 | 21 | 23 | $58

E 40s | 310 E. 44th St. (bet. 1st & 2nd Aves.) | 212-286-4310 |
www.padrefiglio.com

The "omnipresent" father and son who run this "lively", "expensive" East Midtown Italian steakhouse "want every detail to be perfect", and its "outstanding" eats (including "attractive" prix fixe options) "don't disappoint"; on weekends it all comes with a side of "terrific" live jazz.

☒ Palm, The *Steak* 24 | 18 | 22 | $71

E 40s | 837 Second Ave. (bet. 44th & 45th Sts.) | 212-687-2953 ⑤
E 40s | 840 Second Ave. (bet. 44th & 45th Sts.) | 212-697-5198
TriBeCa | 206 West St. (bet. Chambers & Warren Sts.) |
646-395-6391
W 50s | 250 W. 50th St. (bet. B'way & 8th Ave.) | 212-333-7256
www.thepalm.com

"Clubby" with "caricatures" and "cartoons" for decor, these chain chophouses (including the circa-1926 "template" at 837 Second Avenue) turn out "superior" steaks and lobsters the size of "small cars"; the "seasoned waiters" can be "surly" and a "fat wallet" is required, but even so, contented carnivores come away "feeling sorry for vegetarians."

Palma ❶ *Italian/Mediterranean* 22 | 20 | 21 | $53

W Village | 28 Cornelia St. (bet. Bleecker & W. 4th Sts.) | 212-691-2223 |
www.palmanyc.com

A "rustic" former speakeasy now adorned with "gorgeous fresh flowers on the bar" and a "cozy" garden, this "pocket-size" Villager delivers "excellent" Italian-Med eats via an "aim-to-please" crew; the carriage house in back is "wonderful" for private parties.

Palm Court *American* – | – | – | VE

W 50s | Plaza Hotel | 768 Fifth Ave. (59th St.) | 212-546-5302 |
www.theplaza.com

Newly restored and back in business following a hiatus, the Plaza Hotel's "quiet", "beautiful" palm-lined courtyard is just the ticket for "elegant" American breakfasts, lunches and afternoon tea complete with "white-glove" service; true, a "scary bill" is part of the experience, but it's considered a particular treat for "out-of-town" guests.

	FOOD	DECOR	SERVICE	COST

Palo Santo *Pan-Latin*
| | 25 | 22 | 23 | $43 |

Park Slope | 652 Union St. (bet. 4th & 5th Aves.) | Brooklyn |
718-636-6311 | www.palosanto.us

A "serene" "oasis" nestled in a Park Slope brownstone, this "friendly"
Pan-Latin "sleeper" presents a "high-quality" "flavor extravaganza"
based on "local" ingredients paired with South American wines; its
"funky" interior makes a "homey but chic" backdrop.

Pampano *Mexican/Seafood*
| | 24 | 22 | 22 | $57 |

E 40s | 209 E. 49th St. (bet. 2nd & 3rd Aves.) | 212-751-4545 |
www.modernmexican.com

A duet by co-owner Plácido Domingo and chef Richard Sandoval, this
East Midtown Mexican orchestrates "elegant" Veracruz-style seafood
served by a "savvy" staff; the "airy" "hacienda" interior is augmented
with a "can't-be-beat" terrace, so never mind if the bill hits the
"C notes"; P.S. an around-the-corner taqueria does delivery and takeout.

Pam Real Thai Food ⊄ *Thai*
| | 23 | 9 | 17 | $24 |

W 40s | 402 W. 47th St. (bet. 9th & 10th Aves.) | 212-315-4441 Ⓜ
W 40s | 404 W. 49th St. (bet. 9th & 10th Aves.) | 212-333-7500
www.pamrealthaifood.com

Theatergoers happily "trek a few extra blocks West" to these "bargain-
priced", cash-only Hell's Kitchen twins whose "delicious" Thai cuisine in
"large portions" ranges from "flavorful" to "fiery"; "courteous", "reed-
thin" staffers "maneuver valiantly" through the "tight", "no-decor" digs.

Paola's *Italian*
| | 22 | 18 | 20 | $58 |

E 90s | Hotel Wales | 1295 Madison Ave. (92nd St.) | 212-794-1890 |
www.paolasrestaurant.com

Still under the "watchful" eye of "matriarch Paola", this "upscale" trattoria, relocated in 2009, now draws a "decidedly Carnegie Hill crowd"
for its "delicious" Italiana, including some "unusual regional dishes";
the "glossier" setting causes a few grumbles about "noisy" acoustics.

Pappardella ● *Italian*
| | 20 | 17 | 18 | $37 |

W 70s | 316 Columbus Ave. (75th St.) | 212-595-7996 |
www.pappardella.com

Hosting Upper Westsiders practically "since the time of the Romans",
this "attractive" Italian remains a "staple" for its "glorious antipasto" and
"toothsome" pastas at "reasonable" rates; the "homey" room is on the
"tight" side, so go for the "people-watching"-perfect sidewalk tables.

Paradou ● *French*
| | 21 | 18 | 18 | $46 |

Meatpacking | 8 Little W. 12th St. (bet. Greenwich & Washington Sts.) |
212-463-8345 | www.paradounyc.com

"Given its trendy locale", some are "surprised" that such a "small, rustic"
Meatpacking vet proffers such "sophisticated" French bistro fare; another "secret" is the tented garden that's especially "lovely" at brunch,
when "charming" staffers keep "refilling" the champagne glasses.

Park, The ● *Mediterranean*
| | 17 | 23 | 16 | $41 |

Chelsea | 118 10th Ave. (bet. 17th & 18th Sts.) | 212-352-3313 |
www.theparknyc.com

A "beautiful" setting for cocktails "near the High Line", this "huge"
multilevel Chelsea nightspot is aptly named given its "gorgeous"

glassed-in garden that feels "alfresco" "even in winter"; if only the "ok" Med eats and "underwhelming" service "matched the atmosphere."

☑ Park Avenue . . . *American* | 25 | 26 | 23 | $73 |

E 60s | 100 E. 63rd St. (bet. Lexington & Park Aves.) | 212-644-1900 | www.parkavenyc.com

"Celebrate the changing seasons" at this East Side showplace that keeps things "interesting" for its "posh" clientele by rotating its name, menu and decor quarterly; "fantastic" New American fare, "spectacular" AvroKO-designed settings and "gracious" treatment mean it's "worth" the serious "splurge."

Park Side ● *Italian* | 24 | 19 | 21 | $48 |

Corona | 107-01 Corona Ave. (51st Ave.) | Queens | 718-271-9321 | www.parksiderestaurant.com

A "plate of pasta and a glass of the house wine" and you're in "red-sauce heaven" at this "bustling" Corona Italian where even first-timers "eat like part of the family"; an "upscale" feel and "un-Manhattan prices" help keep this "old-world" bastion "going strong" ("reserve way ahead").

Parlor Steakhouse *Steak* | 22 | 21 | 21 | $59 |

E 90s | 1600 Third Ave. (90th St.) | 212-423-5888 | www.parlorsteakhouse.com

Carnegie Hillers rate this "smart" steakhouse "female-friendly" given that its "solid" beef is joined by "gourmet appetizers" and "excellent fish", and the service is "attentive"; "UES prices" and what some call "inconsistent" output don't dampen the "hopping bar scene."

Parma ● *Italian* | 22 | 14 | 22 | $59 |

E 70s | 1404 Third Ave. (bet. 79th & 80th Sts.) | 212-535-3520

This UES trattoria is a "home away from home" for "Park Avenue" types who like that the "plain" (and "pricey") Italian fare comes in "generous" portions and the fact that "the maitre d' knows them"; its decor was recently redone, but surveyors say the "time-warp" feel remains.

Pascalou *French* | 21 | 14 | 19 | $44 |

E 90s | 1308 Madison Ave. (bet. 92nd & 93rd Sts.) | 212-534-7522

With a "zillion choices" on its menu of "savory", "well-priced" New French dishes, this UES "shoebox" attracts "ladies who not only lunch, but want a satisfying meal"; "friendly" staffers show they "want you here", but given the "petite" dimensions, expect to "sit cheek to cheek."

Pasha *Turkish* | 20 | 19 | 20 | $42 |

W 70s | 70 W. 71st St. (bet. Columbus Ave. & CPW) | 212-579-8751 | www.pashanewyork.com

Given its scarlet walls, skylights and bar resembling a "pumpkin coach lined with carpets", this "quiet" UWS Turk is something a bit "out of the ordinary" fairly "close to Lincoln Center"; staffers happy to "explain" about the "delicious" dishes and a "bargain" prix fixe are other draws.

Pasquale's Rigoletto *Italian* | 21 | 16 | 19 | $44 |

Bronx | 2311 Arthur Ave. (Crescent Ave.) | 718-365-6644

"Pleasingly gaudy", this Arthur Avenue "old standby" "outdoes the neighbors" with "solid Italian standards" in "huge portions" – happily it's "roomy" and "comfortable" inside; "old-school" crooners on Saturday nights and free parking are other reasons loyalists "love this place."

Pastis *French*

21 | 21 | 18 | $50

Meatpacking | 9 Ninth Ave. (Little W. 12th St.) | 212-929-4844 | www.pastisny.com

"Still trendy" after a decade in the Meatpacking District, Keith McNally's "theatrical Paris facsimile" dispenses "delectable" bistro classics to "celeb-spotting" customers while "too-cool" servers "try their best" to maneuver; dinner can be "deafening" and "huge lines" make brunch a "contact sport", but breakfast is almost "subdued."

Pastrami Queen *Deli*

20 | 5 | 13 | $25

E 70s | 1125 Lexington Ave. (bet. 78th & 79th Sts.) | 212-734-1500 | www.pastramiqueen.com

Basically a "take-out counter with a few tables", this "inelegant" Upper Eastsider is heralded for its "deli-icious" meats (especially signature "boffo" pastrami) stuffed into "skyscraper-high" sandwiches; "fairly rude" service is one more reason to go for "prompt delivery" or takeout.

Patricia's *Italian*

22 | 13 | 20 | $31

Bronx | 1082 Morris Park Ave. (bet. Haight & Lurting Aves.) | 718-409-9069

Patricia's of Tremont *Italian*

Bronx | 3883 E. Tremont Ave. (Cross Bronx Expwy.) | 718-918-1800 | www.patriciasoftremont.com

The "specialty is pizza" at these "hospitable" Bronx Italians, separately owned but equally touted for "authentic" eats and "generous" wine pours; their "busy" rooms are "designed for crowds, not style", leading some to say "delivery is best."

Patroon ⊠ *American*

22 | 22 | 23 | $66

E 40s | 160 E. 46th St. (bet. Lexington & 3rd Aves.) | 212-883-7373 | www.patroonrestaurant.com

"Perfect for power lunches" and "client dinners", Ken Aretsky's "clubby-in-a-good-way" Eastsider remains "reliable" for "marvelous" steaks and New American standards ferried by an "attentive" team; its "soothing" rooms are full of "amazing" vintage photos, but upwardly mobile types make for the "new roof deck."

Patsy's *Italian*

22 | 17 | 20 | $56

W 50s | 236 W. 56th St. (bet. B'way & 8th Ave.) | 212-247-3491 | www.patsys.com

Once a "Sinatra hangout", this Midtown "temple to red sauce" "brings you back to the 1950s" with "robust" Neapolitan "comfort" fare served by "old-world" waiters in a "throwback" setting; maybe it's "the world's most expensive spaghetti", but it's cheap for the "nostalgia."

Patsy's Pizzeria *Pizza*

20 | 12 | 15 | $26

Chelsea | 318 W. 23rd St. (bet. 8th & 9th Aves.) | 646-486-7400
E 60s | 1312 Second Ave. (69th St.) | 212-639-1000
E 60s | 206 E. 60th St. (bet. 2nd & 3rd Aves.) | 212-688-9707
G Village | 67 University Pl. (bet. 10th & 11th Sts.) | 212-533-3500
Harlem | 2287-91 First Ave. (bet. 117th & 118th Sts.) | 212-534-9783
Murray Hill | 509 Third Ave. (bet. 34th & 35th Sts.) | 212-689-7500
W 70s | 61 W. 74th St. (bet. Columbus Ave. & CPW) | 212-579-3000
www.patsyspizzeriany.com

"Don't be discouraged by the chain factor" because these pizzerias provide "perfectly charred" "primo" pies with "quality" toppings, plus

| | | FOOD | DECOR | SERVICE | COST |

"generous" salads, which are especially outstanding at the sprawling First Avenue branch; "ambiance is nonexistent" and "squealing off-spring" abound, so consider "takeout."

NEW Patty & Bun ● *Burgers*

▽ 20 | 17 | 19 | $26

G Village | 61 W. Eighth St. (bet. MacDougal St. & 6th Ave.) | 212-477-1850 | www.pattyandbun.com

Surveyors who've discovered this "casual" new Village burger specialist say its "excellent" patties on "substantial buns" are "worth the impending heart attack"; "attractive" dark-wood decor, a full bar and "knowledgeable" service add up to a "burger version of a steakhouse."

Peacefood Café *Vegan*

21 | 17 | 18 | $21

W 80s | 460 Amsterdam Ave. (82nd St.) | 212-362-2266 | www.peacefoodcafe.com

"Yummm" sigh "health"-minded types who turn to this "inexpensive" UWS cafe for "delicious vegan food" ("usually an oxymoron"), including desserts so "decadent" "you'll forget" they're dairy-free; the "sincere" service can be "slow", but it's "worth" it if you can "spare the time."

Peaches *Southern*

▽ 22 | 20 | 20 | $23

Bed-Stuy | 393 Lewis Ave. (bet. Decatur & MacDonough Sts.) | Brooklyn | 718-942-4162 | www.peachesbrooklyn.com

Peaches HotHouse Ⓜ *Southern*

NEW Bed-Stuy | 415 Tompkins Ave. (Hancock St.) | Brooklyn | 718-483-9111 | www.peacheshothouse.com

The few surveyors who've "found their way" to this Bed-Stuy duo tout its "creatively" updated Southern "favorites" made with "wonderfully fresh" local ingredients; "friendly" staffers foster a "make-yourself-at-home" vibe that extends to the original's "relaxing" patio.

Peanut Butter & Co. *Sandwiches*

19 | 12 | 17 | $14

G Village | 240 Sullivan St. (bet. Bleecker & W. 3rd Sts.) | 212-677-3995 | www.ilovepeanutbutter.com

"How can you not love this place?" muse PB&J-fiends smitten with the "original" peanut butter sandwich combos at this Village "novelty spot"; it can be "tough to find a seat" in the "tiny", "diner"-like digs, but jars of its "gourmet" spreads-to-go mean you can "do the same at home" for even cheaper.

❷ Pearl Oyster Bar ☒ *Seafood*

26 | 15 | 20 | $46

W Village | 18 Cornelia St. (bet. Bleecker & W. 4th Sts.) | 212-691-8211 | www.pearloysterbar.com

You feel "miles from Manhattan" at Rebecca Charles' "tiny" West Village "fish shack" whose "freaking delicious" seafood includes "NYC's best lobster roll"; you'll spend "a few pearls", and the no-rez policy spells "waaay long lines", but short of New England, you "won't find better."

Pearl Room *Seafood*

22 | 21 | 22 | $51

Bay Ridge | 8201 Third Ave. (82nd St.) | Brooklyn | 718-833-6666

A Bay Ridge locals' "favorite", this "pricey" seafooder makes a splash with "Manhattan-quality" cuisine, "excellent" service and a "fun, noisy" bar scene; a few shrug it's "nothing to write home about", but they're outvoted by those who say there's nowhere in the area with "fresher fish."

	FOOD	DECOR	SERVICE	COST

Peasant Ⓜ *Italian*　　24 | 22 | 20 | $57
NoLita | 194 Elizabeth St. (bet. Prince & Spring Sts.) | 212-965-9511 |
www.peasantnyc.com
The height of "rustic chic", this "charming" NoLita Italian offers "simple yet elegant" dishes from a "massive" wood-burning oven in "dark", "romantic" quarters complete with a "candlelit" downstairs wine bar; just bear in mind that it's "priced for royalty, not peasants."

NEW Peels *Eclectic*　　- | - | - | M
E Village | 325 Bowery (2nd St.) | 646-602-7015
The latest from William Tigertt and Taavo Somer, the hippest restaurateurs in town, this new Bowery comer serves the same quirky Americana as their freshman effort, Freemans, this time with a slight Southern drawl; the whitewashed, bi-level space features a ground-floor cafe with a take-out counter and a long communal table, while upstairs there are booths, banquettes and a bar for more traditional dining.

Peep *Thai*　　20 | 21 | 18 | $27
SoHo | 177 Prince St. (bet. Sullivan & Thompson Sts.) | 212-254-7337 |
www.peepsoho.net
With its "pink neon lighting", "tasty", low-cost Thai fare and "nice-size bar" – not to mention "cool" "one-way-mirrored bathrooms" – this "clublike" SoHo "trendster" is "definitely worth a peep"; "quick" service and "killer lunch deals" make it a "terrific" midday stop too.

Peking Duck House *Chinese*　　23 | 14 | 18 | $41
Chinatown | 28 Mott St. (bet. Mosco & Pell Sts.) | 212-227-1810
E 50s | 236 E. 53rd St. (bet. 2nd & 3rd Aves.) | 212-759-8260
www.pekingduckhousenyc.com
The eponymous fowl "carved tableside" with "crispy skin and just the right amount of fat" "is the star" at this "otherwise ordinary" Chinese duo; it's "perfect for groups" and "birthday parties on a budget" – especially the more "downscale" BYO C-town branch.

Pellegrino's *Italian*　　23 | 17 | 23 | $46
Little Italy | 138 Mulberry St. (bet. Grand & Hester Sts.) | 212-226-3177
When "your out-of-town guests want to go to Little Italy", this "old-school" Italian "is *the* place", given its "fairly priced" red-sauce classics served up by "tuxedoed" waiters; sit outside in summer to savor the "wonderful block party feel" – "watching the tourists is part of the fun."

Penelope *American*　　22 | 18 | 18 | $25
Murray Hill | 159 Lexington Ave. (30th St.) | 212-481-3800 |
www.penelopenyc.com
Think of an "inn in Vermont" and you've got this "adorable", "shabby-chic" Murray Hill New American that's a "sweet place" for a "reasonably priced" repast; still, the "hippie vibe" ("Alice B. Toklas would love it") and "long lines" require "patience" – especially at the "mobbed" brunch.

NEW Penny Farthing *American*　　- | - | - | M
E Village | 103 Third Ave. (13th St.) | 212-387-7300 |
www.thepennyfarthingnyc.com
On the East Village's college-bar stretch, this bustling tavern has an Industrial Era throwback feel complete with exposed brick and beams, Edison bulbs and antique wheels of the namesake bicycle; well-priced

gastropub grub goes down well with beers and cocktails at the dining area next to the bar.

Pepe Giallo To Go *Italian* | 21 | 13 | 16 | $23 |
Chelsea | 253 10th Ave. (bet. 24th & 25th Sts.) | 212-242-6055
Pepe Rosso Caffe *Italian*
E 40s | Grand Central | lower level (42nd St. & Vanderbilt Ave.) | 212-867-6054
Pepe Rosso To Go *Italian*
SoHo | 149 Sullivan St. (bet. Houston & Prince Sts.) | 212-677-4555
Pepe Verde To Go *Italian*
W Village | 559 Hudson St. (bet. Perry & W. 11th Sts.) | 212-255-2221
www.peperossotogo.com

"Fresh", "fast" and "cheap", this Italian mini-chain's pastas and panini are just the ticket if you're "in a hurry" or "on a budget"; "DIY service" and "tiny", "no-frills" setups mean it's "best to take away" – unless you hit Chelsea's "hidden garden."

Pepolino *Italian* | 25 | 18 | 23 | $56 |
TriBeCa | 281 W. Broadway (bet. Canal & Lispenard Sts.) | 212-966-9983 | www.pepolino.com

A "serious sleeper", this "out-of-the-way" TriBeCa trattoria offers "ridiculously good" Tuscan fare served by "hot waiters" with "no attitude" in "convivial" bi-level digs; some say "pasta shouldn't be so expensive", but those in-the-know "can't stay away."

Pera *Mediterranean* | 21 | 21 | 20 | $50 |
E 40s | 303 Madison Ave. (bet. 41st & 42nd Sts.) | 212-878-6301 | www.peranyc.com

"Convenient to Grand Central" and boasting a big "open-flame grill" and "popular bar", this "lovely", "cosmopolitan" Med "exemplifies what Turkish cuisine can and should be"; grumbles about "pricey tabs" aside, most agree it's "a jewel waiting to be found."

Perbacco ◑ *Italian* | 23 | 16 | 19 | $50 |
E Village | 234 E. Fourth St. (bet. Aves. A & B) | 212-253-2038 | www.perbacconyc.com

A "true gastronomic" experience, this "often-brilliant" Italian offers "Alphabet City hole-in-the-wall dining at its best"; by East Village standards it's "pricey", but the bill's a "pittance" given such "innovative" fare and "friendly" (if occasionally "flighty") service.

Peri Ela *Turkish* | 19 | 16 | 19 | $41 |
E 90s | 1361 Lexington Ave. (bet. 90th & 91st Sts.) | 212-410-4300 | www.periela.com

"Shoebox"-size it may be, but this Carnegie Hill Turkish "neighborhood joint" "convenient to the 92nd Street Y" "packs a punch" with "delicious" meze and such; it's "cramped and loud", but "couldn't-be-friendlier" service makes you feel "like you're at a family dinner."

Perilla *American* | 26 | 21 | 24 | $59 |
W Village | 9 Jones St. (bet. Bleecker & W. 4th Sts.) | 212-929-6868 | www.perillanyc.com

"Dollar for dollar one of the best dining experiences" in the Village, this "civilized" New American from "*Top Chef* winner" Harold Dieterle delivers with "wonderful", "inventive" cuisine and "warm", "unobtru-

| | FOOD | DECOR | SERVICE | COST |

sive" service; if the "simple" setting doesn't quite live up to the "re-fined" food, most are too "content" to care.

Periyali   Greek   24 | 20 | 22 | $56
Flatiron | 35 W. 20th St. (bet. 5th & 6th Aves.) | 212-463-7890 |
www.periyali.com
"You'll think you're on the island of Mykonos" at this "longtime"
Flatiron "Aegean jewel" that "continues to please" with "fabulous"
grilled seafood and other "first-rate" classics delivered with "wonder-ful hospitality"; such "upscale" experiences don't come cheap, but
then neither does "a trip to Greece."

Per Lei ◑ Italian   21 | 19 | 19 | $53
E 70s | 1347 Second Ave. (71st St.) | 212-439-9200 | www.perleinyc.com
"Hyper-Euro" and a "scene at night", this "pricey", "chic" UES Italian
offers "surprisingly good food" for the kind of "beautiful-people" mag-net where "girls dance on tables" in the later hours; in summer, "sit
outside" if you're averse to "noise and crowds."

Perry St.   American   25 | 24 | 24 | $67
W Village | 176 Perry St. (West St.) | 212-352-1900 | www.jean-georges.com
"Cool, sophisticated and casual", this way West Village "star in the
Vongerichten firmament "wows" with "fabulous" New American
dishes, "pro" service and a "calm", "austere" Richard Meier–designed
setting; it's a bit "out of the way" but well "worth the trip", especially
for its "bargain" prix fixe options.

☑ Per Se   American/French   28 | 28 | 29 | $303
W 60s | Time Warner Ctr. | 10 Columbus Circle, 4th fl. (60th St. at B'way) |
212-823-9335 | www.perseny.com
"Words aren't adequate" to describe Thomas Keller's "food-lover's
paradise" in the TWC, a "once-in-a-lifetime experience" hailed for its
"utterly professional" service (rated NYC's No. 1) and $275 prix fixe–only "four-hour cavalcade" of "perfectly prepared", "divine" French–New
American dishes presented in a "beautiful", "minimalist" room with
views over Central Park; yes, the bill is "shocking" but "worth every
penny" – especially "if you can't make it to Napa" to its sister, the French
Laundry; P.S. à la carte small-plates dining is available in the salon.

Persephone ☑ Greek   21 | 19 | 21 | $57
E 60s | 115 E. 60th St. (bet. Lexington & Park Aves.) | 212-339-8363 |
www.persephoneny.com
This "lovely little" "upscale" Greek by Bloomie's enchants with clas-sics like grilled whole fish ferried by a "graceful" staff; most find it all
perfectly "pleasant", with a $24 lunch prix fixe to sweeten the pot, but
upstarts declare the "dated" decor a bit of a "yawn."

Persepolis   Persian   21 | 17 | 20 | $42
E 70s | 1407 Second Ave. (bet. 73rd & 74th Sts.) | 212-535-1100 |
www.persepolisnyc.com
Among NYC's "best" in an "under-represented category", this Upper
East Side Persian offers no "pretense", just "wonderful", "true Iranian"
cooking, including "not-to-be-missed" sour cherry rice; downsides are
decor that "could use refreshing" and subway construction that
"hides" its facade.

	FOOD	DECOR	SERVICE	COST

Pershing Square *American*

15 | 15 | 15 | $37

E 40s | 90 E. 42nd St. (Park Ave.) | 212-286-9600 | www.pershingsquare.com
"Corporate" types collect for "power breakfasts" at this "crowded" American brasserie opposite Grand Central, where those in-the-know "get a booth" – or bring "earplugs"; though its simple grub and "warm weather" alfresco dining are bright spots, critics say it tilts "tourist trap."

Petaluma *Italian*

17 | 16 | 19 | $47

E 70s | 1356 First Ave. (73rd St.) | 212-772-8800 |
www.petalumarestaurant.com
"Home away from home" for its UES neighbors, this "staid" circa-1986 Italian offers "no-surprises" pastas and pizzas in "relaxed" environs; it's a fallback for everyone from "families" with "young children" to "first dates" and the Sotheby's crowd, even if it's "slightly overpriced."

ⓩ Peter Luger Steak House ⊄ *Steak*

27 | 15 | 20 | $78

Williamsburg | 178 Broadway (Driggs Ave.) | Brooklyn | 718-387-7400 | www.peterluger.com
"The Godfather of steakhouses", ranked NYC's No. 1 for the 27th year in a row, this "essential" "Williamsburg institution" is as "aged to perfection" as its slabs of "sizzling porterhouse" sliced by "sarcastic" waiters who contribute to its "old-school" brauhaus "charm"; "nightmare"-to-nab reservations and a "cash-only" policy vex, but "if you're a beef lover", it's a "must-go from anywhere on earth."

Pete's Tavern ❶ *Pub Food*

16 | 18 | 18 | $34

Gramercy | 129 E. 18th St. (Irving Pl.) | 212-473-7676 | www.petestavern.com
The "ghost" of "O. Henry" haunts this "atmospheric" circa-1864 Gramercy Park tavern, as do plenty of "local characters" who hail the trinity of "burger, fries and beer"; the pub food's "nondescript", but never mind – it's affordable and at "Christmas" it's a "jolly" good time.

Petite Abeille *Belgian*

18 | 14 | 16 | $31

Flatiron | 44 W. 17th St. (bet. 5th & 6th Aves.) | 212-727-2989
Gramercy | 401 E. 20th St. (1st Ave.) | 212-727-1505
TriBeCa | 134 W. Broadway (Duane St.) | 212-791-1360
W Village | 466 Hudson St. (Barrow St.) | 212-741-6479 ⊄
www.petiteabeille.com
Stick with the "excellent" moules frites and you can't go wrong at this "cute, cozy" and "cheap" Belgian mini-chain that "would stand up well even in Bruges"; however, you may have to indulge in the "solid beer selection" to stomach the "noisy crowds" and "nonchalant" service.

Petite Crevette ⊄ *Seafood*

▽ 24 | 15 | 19 | $36

Carroll Gardens | 144 Union St. (enter on Hicks St., bet. President & Union Sts.) | Brooklyn | 718-855-2632
"Shoehorn" yourself into this "cramped", "quirky" Carroll Gardens seafooder for "exceptionally fresh" fish that's a real "value", especially given the "BYO" policy; just remember to bring "cash" and an open mind, as "you will make friends with the neighbors here."

Petrossian *Continental/French*

23 | 24 | 23 | $79

W 50s | 182 W. 58th St. (7th Ave.) | 212-245-2214 | www.petrossian.com
You expect to run into "Nick and Nora" at this "sumptuous" "grande dame" near Carnegie Hall featuring "thrilling" art deco decor, "gracious"

"pro" service and "superbly decadent" French-Continental fare starring "caviar, vodka and champagne"; for those short on "petro-dollars", check out the "prix fixe deals" – $24 at lunch, $35 pre-theater.

Philip Marie Ⓜ American   20 | 18 | 20 | $44

W Village | 569 Hudson St. (W. 11th St.) | 212-242-6200 |
www.philipmarie.com
"Perfect for a date" and "popular for brunch", this "genuinely friendly" West Village "charmer" dishes up "well-priced" New American fare with a "personal touch"; Wednesday jazz nights and a "romantic" wine room for two further endear it to the neighborhood.

Philippe ◗ Chinese   23 | 21 | 21 | $69

E 60s | 33 E. 60th St. (bet. Madison & Park Aves.) | 212-644-8885 |
www.philippechow.com
"'Excellent' doesn't do it justice" gush groupies of the "mind-blowing" fare (not to mention the "costly" tab) at this "dark, sceney" East Side "chic Chinese"; at prime times the "noise" approaches "dance-club" levels, but that's no surprise since the "celeb-spotting" is "as good as the eats."

Philoxenia Ⓜ Greek   21 | 20 | 19 | $38

Astoria | 32-07 34th Ave. (bet. 32nd & 33rd Sts.) | Queens |
718-626-2000 | www.philoxeniarestaurant.com
A far cry from Astoria's "faded-out Greek" standbys, this "rustic, romantic" find "away from the hustle of Ditmars" impresses with its "refined" Hellenic dishes and "charming" vibe; service here lives up to the name ("hospitality"), though it can be "slooow."

Pho Bang ⊄ Vietnamese   20 | 5 | 12 | $16

Little Italy | 157 Mott St. (bet. Broome & Grand Sts.) |
212-966-3797
Elmhurst | 82-90 Broadway (Elmhurst Ave.) | Queens |
718-205-1500
Flushing | 41-07 Kissena Blvd. (Main St.) | Queens | 718-939-5520
When you "gotta have" your "pho phix", this Vietnamese trio does a bang-up job, serving "excellent" versions of the "namesake" soup and other noodle "classics"; "don't expect culinary surprises", just a "cheap" meal "fit for a well-traveled palate", served "fast" by a "smileless" staff.

Phoenix Garden ⊄ Chinese   24 | 9 | 15 | $31

E 40s | 242 E. 40th St. (bet. 2nd & 3rd Aves.) | 212-983-6666 |
www.thephoenixgarden.com
"True Cantonese spirit" infuses this BYO East Midtown vet whose "flavorful", "low-priced" Chinese fare is "fit for a last supper"; cares about the "shoddy", "low-ceilinged" decor and cash-only policy "melt away" once that "worship"-worthy salt and pepper shrimp hits the table.

Pho Viet Huong Vietnamese   22 | 10 | 16 | $22

Chinatown | 73 Mulberry St. (bet. Bayard & Canal Sts.) | 212-233-8988 |
www.phoviethuongnyc.com
A "must for jurors" and "judges" alike, this "ridiculously cheap" Vietnamese eatery near the courts wins favor for its "uniformly excellent" pho and noodle dishes; "grungy" digs are a given and the "monstrous menu can be challenging" but it's all well "worth the effort."

	FOOD	DECOR	SERVICE	COST

☑ Piano Due ⑤ *Italian* — 24 | 25 | 25 | $71

W 50s | Equitable Center Arcade | 151 W. 51st St., 2nd fl. (bet. 6th & 7th Aves.) | 212-399-9400 | www.pianoduenyc.net

A "blissfully quiet" "refuge for adults" hidden "halfway down" a Midtown breezeway, this "luxurious" second-floor Italian "defines elegant dining" with "smooth" service and "terrific" cooking from chef Michael Cetrulo; yes, it's "pricey" – but this is the "stuff memories are made of"; P.S. the Sandro Chia mural in the Palio bar downstairs is "worth a visit in itself."

Piccola Venezia *Italian* — 25 | 17 | 24 | $59

Astoria | 42-01 28th Ave. (42nd St.) | Queens | 718-721-8470 | www.piccola-venezia.com

"Forget the menu – just say 'feed me'" at this "pricey" pasta-palace "throwback" that's "worth the schlep" to Astoria; it's "not the pinky rings" that make this "gem" "sparkle" – it's the "outstanding" "old-school" Italian cooking and "warm welcomes" from the "tuxedo-clad" staff.

Piccolo Angolo Ⓜ *Italian* — 25 | 13 | 22 | $45

W Village | 621 Hudson St. (Jane St.) | 212-229-9177 | www.piccoloangolo.com

Locals "love" this "spirited" "little" West Villager for its "staying power", "old-world" sensibility and "humongous" "family-style" portions "like your Italian mama would dish out"; owner Renato Migliorini "treats you like an old friend" – and your neighbors may too given the "cramped" elbow-to-elbow setup; P.S. "reservations are a must."

☑ Picholine ⑤ *French/Mediterranean* — 27 | 26 | 26 | $120

W 60s | 35 W. 64th St. (bet. B'way & CPW) | 212-724-8585 | www.picholinenyc.com

"Off-the-charts" French-Med cuisine, including the city's "best cheese course", is served in "exquisite" formal surroundings at Terrance Brennan's prix fixe–only "crown jewel" near Lincoln Center; sure, it can strain your budget, but it's bound to be a "memorable" experience – and now there's a $28 lunch deal too; P.S. "try its marvelous wines" and fromages at the "pleasant" non-reserving front bar, or go for a party-perfect private room.

Picnic Market & Café *French* — 20 | 15 | 21 | $40

W 100s | 2665 Broadway (bet. 101st & 102nd Sts.) | 212-222-8222 | www.picnicmarket.com

"No pretensions, no disappointments" is the general consensus on this UWS "welcome touch of Alsace-Lorraine" delivering "simple", "fresh" French bistro fare plus picnic provisions to go; factor in "friendly" service, and "what more could you ask for when you don't want to cook?"

Pies-n-Thighs ●⑦ *Soul Food* — ∇ 23 | 13 | 19 | $20

Williamsburg | 166 S. Fourth St. (Driggs Ave.) | Brooklyn | 347-529-6090 | www.piesnthighs.com

Following a hiatus, this Williamsburg soul food "haven" is back in new digs near its original site, delivering fried chicken to "make you cluck for joy" plus "old-school pies" evoking "visits to grandma"; roomier outdoor area aside, "you don't go" for the "bare-bones" decor or service.

Pietrasanta *Italian*

18 | 15 | 18 | $39

W 40s | 683 Ninth Ave. (47th St.) | 212-265-9471

"A-ok" for "pre-theater", this "crowded" yet "welcoming" Hell's Kitchen Italian delivers its "solid" (if "not extraordinary") pastas and such pronto, ensuring you "make your curtain"; on warm nights when you have time to "linger", snag a table by the open windows for the "alfresco" effect.

Pietro's ⌧ *Italian/Steak*

24 | 14 | 22 | $66

E 40s | 232 E. 43rd St. (bet. 2nd & 3rd Aves.) | 212-682-9760 | www.pietros.com

"Mature, well-dressed" types (think "AARP") convene at this "comfortable", "expensive" circa-1932 Eastside "clubhouse" for "classic Italian" specialties and "superb" steaks "professionally served"; that there's "no buzz here" suits regulars fine – it's a "satisfying" "no-rush" experience that "never leaves you hungry."

Pigalle ◐ *French*

17 | 17 | 17 | $39

W 40s | Hilton Garden Inn | 790 Eighth Ave. (48th St.) | 212-489-2233 | www.pigallenyc.com

The "old-time Parisian" feel of this Theater District brasserie is so "authentic", you half expect to see "Toulouse-Lautrec" at the next table; instead, it's "packed" with "tourists" as well as showgoers who say its "sensibly priced" French "comfort food" is a "godsend" pre-"curtain."

Pig Heaven ◐ *Chinese*

20 | 13 | 19 | $36

E 80s | 1540 Second Ave. (bet. 80th & 81st Sts.) | 212-744-4333 | www.pigheaven.biz

A "porcine theme" pervades this UES Chinese "favorite" where "gracious hostess" Nancy Lee "remembers all of her guests" and "all things" pork rule the pen; oinkers who report the digs are "getting a bit tired in the trotter" suggest "take your piggy home."

Ping's Seafood *Chinese/Seafood*

22 | 11 | 14 | $27

Chinatown | 22 Mott St. (bet. Chatham Sq. & Pell St.) | 212-602-9988 ◐
Elmhurst | 83-02 Queens Blvd. (Goldsmith St.) | Queens | 718-396-1238

"Your wallet stays as full as your belly" at these Hong Kong–style seafooders, "delights" for "introducing uninitiated friends to the art of dim sum and fish served whole"; never mind the "brusque" service and "sketchy" decor – you can "eat and eat" and "never lack for anything."

Pink Tea Cup ◐ *Soul Food/Southern*

– | – | – | M

W Village | 88 Seventh Ave. S. (bet. Barrow & Grove Sts.) | 212-255-2124 | www.thepinkteacup.com

With new owners and roomier digs, this reincarnated Village soul food institution is less campy and more upscale than the old place, and boasts a full bar, performance space and sidewalk patio; the prices on its Southern menu are more up-to-date too.

Pinocchio Ⓜ *Italian*

22 | 16 | 24 | $45

E 90s | 1748 First Ave. (bet. 90th & 91st Sts.) | 212-828-5810

It's "tiny" ("like a relative's cramped dining room"), but this "romantic" UES Italian has a "big heart" thanks to a "gracious" owner who really "cares"; the "wonderful" fare is "reasonable" too – "every neighborhood" should have a "jewel" like this.

	FOOD	DECOR	SERVICE	COST

Pintaile's Pizza *Pizza*   21 | 7 | 16 | $17

E 80s | 1573 York Ave. (bet. 83rd & 84th Sts.) | 212-396-3479
E 90s | 26 E. 91st St. (bet. 5th & Madison Aves.) | 212-722-1967
"Gourmet" pies with "really thin" whole-wheat crusts and "creative" toppings add up to "healthy" "masterpieces" at this UES pizza pair; "hole-in-the-wall" digs with limited seating means for most it's "to-go."

Pio Pio *Peruvian*   22 | 13 | 17 | $25

E 90s | 1746 First Ave. (bet. 90th & 91st Sts.) | 212-426-5800
Murray Hill | 210 E. 34th St. (bet. 2nd & 3rd Aves.) | 212-481-0034
W 40s | 604 10th Ave. (bet. 43rd & 44th Sts.) | 212-459-2929
W 90s | 702 Amsterdam Ave. (94th St.) | 212-665-3000
Bronx | 264 Cypress Ave. (bet. 138th & 139th Sts.) | 718-401-3300
Jackson Heights | 84-02 Northern Blvd. (bet. 84th & 85th Sts.) | Queens | 718-426-1010
Rego Park | 62-30 Woodhaven Blvd. (62nd Rd.) | Queens | 718-458-0606 ⊅
www.piopionyc.com
Cognoscenti "never tire" of this Peruvian chain's "juicy", "dirt-cheap" rotisserie chicken and "addictive" "spicy green sauce", offered in hefty portions; besides the "roomy", "modern" Theater District branch, set-ups are "tiny, cramped and noisy" – no wonder many do "takeout."

Pipa *Spanish*   22 | 24 | 19 | $45

Flatiron | ABC Carpet & Home | 38 E. 19th St. (bet. B'way & Park Ave. S.) | 212-677-2233
"Chandeliers everywhere" boost the "romance" factor ("if you ignore" the dangling price tags) at this "very social" Flatiron Spaniard, a "first date" and "small group" "favorite" for "chic" tapas and *muy delicioso* sangria; now if only the "so-so" service "matched up."

Pisticci *Italian*   23 | 19 | 21 | $38

W 100s | 125 La Salle St. (B'way) | 212-932-3500 | www.pisticcinyc.com
Consider "bringing a Tolstoy tome to fit in" with the "Columbia prof" clientele at this "charming", "affordable" Morningside Heights "favorite"; its "highly satisfying" Italian "comfort food", "attentive" service and "live Sunday jazz" ensure it's the local pasta place "of choice."

Pizza 33 ⦿ *Pizza*   19 | 7 | 12 | $12

Chelsea | 268 W. 23rd St. (8th Ave.) | 212-206-0999
G Village | 527 Sixth Ave. (14th St.) | 212-255-6333
Murray Hill | 489 Third Ave. (33rd St.) | 212-545-9191
www.pizza33nyc.com
This "open-late" trio's "better-than-average" pizza "hits the spot" after a "night of trolling the bars"; "you're guaranteed to see some happy drunks at the counter" – chances are they don't mind the "brusque" service and "no-ambiance-at-all" digs with "barely any seating."

P.J. Clarke's ⦿ *Pub Food*   17 | 16 | 17 | $37

E 50s | 915 Third Ave. (55th St.) | 212-317-1616
P.J. Clarke's at Lincoln Square ⦿ *Pub Food*
W 60s | 44 W. 63rd St. (bet. B'way & Columbus Ave.) | 212-957-9700
P.J. Clarke's on the Hudson *Pub Food*
Financial District | 4 World Financial Ctr. (Vesey St.) | 212-285-1500
www.pjclarkes.com
"Packed to the brick walls", this "nostalgic" vintage saloon is an East Midtown "institution" for "out-of-this-world" burgers and other pub

staples; its offshoots have designer-"history" but are "so handy" for Lincoln Center–goers and "Wall Streeters" who spend happy hour "overlooking the Hudson."

Place, The *American/Mediterranean* | 21 | 23 | 21 | $46 |

W Village | 310 W. Fourth St. (bet. Bank & 12th Sts.) | 212-924-2711 | www.theplaceny.com

Especially "cozy" by the fireplace in "winter", this "quaint" subterranean West Villager seduces with "sexy" midpriced Med–New American fare and a "sooo romantic" vibe; it's "small", but the "quiet" mood and "attentive-without-being-in-your-face" service "create a sense of privacy" perfect for "intimate" evenings.

NEW Plaza Food Hall *Eclectic*   ∇ | 22 | 25 | 20 | $41 |

W 50s | Plaza Hotel | 1 W. 59th St., lower level (5th Ave.) | 212-986-9260 | www.theplazafoodhall.com

The trick is finding it ("a GPS is indispensable"), but once inside Todd English's "informal" new all-day dining operation on the lower level of the Plaza Hotel, you'll uncover a "lovely" "European-style food hall"; the "well-prepared", "pricey" Eclectic offerings at a raw bar, grill, sushi bar, pizza station, noodle/dumpling bar and wine bar are consumed at "limited" counter seating throughout, or gotten to go.

NEW Plein Sud *French*   ∇ | 18 | 21 | 15 | $53 |

TriBeCa | Smyth Hotel | 85 W. Broadway (bet. Chambers & Warren Sts.) | 212-204-5555 | www.pleinsudnyc.com

A busy TriBeCa intersection is home to this "big, airy" new brasserie from restaurateur Frederick Lesort, with a "pretty", "clean-lined" design via AvroKO that's meant to suggest the south of France; the pricey menu features "French classics with a twist", and as it's the in-house eatery of the Smyth Hotel, it serves three meals a day.

Pó *Italian* | 24 | 16 | 22 | $52 |

W Village | 31 Cornelia St. (bet. Bleecker & W. 4th Sts.) | 212-645-2189 | www.porestaurant.com

"Compact" and "convivial", this West Village po-werhouse "unfailingly" delivers "sublime" Italian "feasts" that will have you thinking "there's an old *nonna* in the kitchen"; it's "hugely popular", ergo "crowded and noisy", but the only real complaint is that reservations are "so hard to come by."

Poke ⊠⊄ *Japanese* | 25 | 13 | 18 | $41 |

E 80s | 343 E. 85th St. (bet. 1st & 2nd Aves.) | 212-249-0569

One of the "great recession steals" on the UES, this "cash-only" Japanese BYO delivers "outstanding" sushi ("rolls from heaven") at "affordable prices"; the setup is "no-frills" and the lines "long", but any drawbacks "melt" away with that "first bite."

Pomaire *Chilean* | 20 | 16 | 20 | $46 |

W 40s | 371 W. 46th St. (bet. 8th & 9th Aves.) | 212-956-3056 | www.pomairenyc.com

A rare taste of "Chile in the Big Apple", this Restaurant Row "sleeper" run by a "sociable owner" "transports" diners with "colorful", "hearty" dishes and "authentic" pisco sours; it "makes a nice change of pace", and the $25 dinner prix fixe is a "bargain-hunter's" dream.

FOOD | DECOR | SERVICE | COST

Pomodoro Rosso *Italian* 21 | 16 | 21 | $44

W 70s | 229 Columbus Ave. (bet. 70th & 71st Sts.) | 212-721-3009 |
www.pomodororossonyc.com

"Warm and welcoming", this "popular" "red-sauce" Italian "convenient
to Lincoln Center" dishes up well-priced portions so "humongous", a
doggy bag provides "lunch for the next day"; arrive well before "curtain" time or "prepare to wait" since it's a "no-reservations" act.

Pongal *Indian/Vegetarian* 22 | 15 | 17 | $27

Murray Hill | 110 Lexington Ave. (bet. 27th & 28th Sts.) | 212-696-9458 |
www.pongalnyc.com

They may be "too spicy for gentle souls", but bolder palates declare
every "well-seasoned" kosher-vegetarian dish (including "wonderful
dosas") a "winner" at this Curry Hill South Indian; "penny-pincher"
prices make "down-at-the-heel" decor and "spotty" service easy to take.

Pongsri Thai *Thai* 20 | 12 | 17 | $27

Chelsea | 165 W. 23rd St. (bet. 6th & 7th Aves.) | 212-645-8808
Chinatown | 106 Bayard St. (Baxter St.) | 212-349-3132
W 40s | 244 W. 48th St. (bet. B'way & 8th Ave.) | 212-582-3392
www.pongsri.com

This long-standing "cheap and cheerful" Thai trio is "still strutting its
stuff" with "oh-so-good" traditional dishes; the "blah" settings are
"nothing to write home about", ditto the "rushed" service, but there's
always "takeout" or "lightning-fast" delivery.

Ponticello *Italian* ▽ 24 | 19 | 23 | $51

Astoria | 46-11 Broadway (bet. 46th & 47th Sts.) | Queens | 718-278-4514 |
www.ponticelloristorante.com

"Contented regulars" tout this "old-world" Astoria Italian for "delicious
and plentiful" dishes delivered by a "caring" crew that "caters to re-
quests"; there's also a "fantastic private" wine-cellar room if you "need
to impress clients", but it all comes with a "pricey-for-Queens" tab.

Ponty Bistro ❷ *African/French* ▽ 23 | 17 | 22 | $39

Gramercy | 218 Third Ave. (bet. 18th & 19th Sts.) | 212-777-1616 |
www.pontybistro.com

For a "happy surprise", try this Gramercy French–Senegalese whose
dishes conjured by a "delightful" chef-owner exhibit "flair and imagination"; it's "small" and "easy to miss", but devotees declare it a "value"-
oriented "gem" worth unearthing for its "warmth and authenticity."

NEW Pop Art Bar *Mediterranean* - | - | - | M

E 60s | 345 E. 62nd St. (bet. 1st & 2nd Aves.) | 212-308-0900

Bringing some pizzazz to a sleepy UES side street, this ritzy newcomer
offers a midpriced Med menu in a glossy space adorned with modern art
(including some from the erstwhile Chanterelle); a Hamptons-esque
back patio and basement bar complete the showy picture.

Pop Burger ❷ *Burgers* 18 | 14 | 13 | $18

E 50s | 14 E. 58th St. (bet. 5th & Madison Aves.) | 212-991-6644
Meatpacking | 58-60 Ninth Ave. (bet. 14th & 15th Sts.) |
212-414-8686
www.popburger.com

For a "tasty break after the Apple Store", hit these "mod" Meatpacking-
Midtown "slider spots", which also fill the bill "late-night" when the

| | FOOD | DECOR | SERVICE | COST |

"loud" soundtrack's "popping"; still, "can it really take that long to make a tiny burger?"; P.S. a Village branch at 57 E. 11th Street is in the works.

Popover Cafe *American* | 19 | 15 | 17 | $27 |

W 80s | 551 Amsterdam Ave. (bet. 86th & 87th Sts.) | 212-595-8555 | www.popovercafe.com

"Brunch is king" at this "homey" (some say "chintzy") Upper West Side "treasure" that lures "hungry" hordes for "heavenly" popovers "as big as your head"; but psst, those "pillows of deliciousness" grace nearly every "hearty" American meal here, so "go midweek" – "you'll be glad you did."

Porchetta *Italian* | 23 | 9 | 15 | $17 |

E Village | 110 E. Seventh St. (bet. Ave. A & 1st Ave.) | 212-777-2151 | www.porchettanyc.com

At "food genius" Sara Jenkins' "super" East Village Italian "nook", "pork-lovers" oink out on "divine" "succulently roasted" pig, offered either in a sandwich or on a platter alongside beans and veggies; the "postage stamp"–size space has but six stools, so you may have to "take it to go."

Porter House New York *Steak* | 24 | 25 | 24 | $77 |

W 60s | Time Warner Ctr. | 10 Columbus Circle, 4th fl. (60th St. at B'way) | 212-823-9500 | www.porterhousenewyork.com

"Regal" and "clubby" with "plenty of table room and comfy chairs", chef Michael Lomonaco's "high-end" wood-paneled Time Warner Center steakhouse is the "perfect" "pricey" perch "pre–Lincoln Center" – or any time; from the "outstanding" beef and "professional" service to the "amazing panoramic" Columbus Circle and Central Park views, all aspects "impress."

Portofino *Italian/Seafood* | 21 | 21 | 22 | $43 |

Bronx | 555 City Island Ave. (Cross St.) | 718-885-1220 | www.portofinocityisland.com

"Summer nights on the deck overlooking Eastchester Bay" are part of the "charm" of this City Island "landmark" dishing up traditional "tastes of old Italy" with a seafood focus; "friendly" service adds to the "pleasurable" experience, while "reasonable" lunch rates provide an alternative to kinda "pricey" dinner.

Positano ◑ *Italian* | ▽ 23 | 20 | 22 | $39 |

Little Italy | 122 Mulberry St. (bet. Canal & Hester Sts.) | 212-334-9808 | www.positanoatlittleitaly.com

"Quaint yet appropriate" for "treating that special someone" to an "old-world" Italian "red-sauce" meal and "cannoli too", this longtimer is rated a Little Italy standout; a few dismiss its milieu as positively "touristy", but even they admit "your taste buds leave well satisfied."

Post House *Steak* | 24 | 20 | 23 | $76 |

E 60s | Lowell Hotel | 28 E. 63rd St. (bet. Madison & Park Aves.) | 212-935-2888 | www.theposthouse.com

Embodying "old-school-NY" "charm" thanks to its collection of Americana, this "classy" UES steakhouse proffers "monster cuts" of "top-quality" meat, "excellent sides" and "perfectly dry martinis" via an "impeccable" staff; you'll leave feeling like you've "been somewhere special" – and you have.

		FOOD	DECOR	SERVICE	COST

Posto *Pizza* | **24** | **14** | **18** | **$28** |

Gramercy | 310 Second Ave. (18th St.) | 212-716-1200 |
www.postothincrust.com

"Perfect" "crispy crust" coupled with the "right toppings" induces pizza "cravings" aplenty at this "funky", "no-frills" joint "tucked away in Gramercy"; "long waits" in its "small digs" can be a "downer", so addicts who "need a fix" often do delivery, or "dine outside" in summer.

Pranna *Asian* | **20** | **24** | **18** | **$50** |

Murray Hill | 79 Madison Ave. (bet. 28th & 29th Sts.) | 212-696-5700 |
www.prannarestaurant.com

An "exotic", "swanky" space "heightens" the experience at this "modern", multilevel Murray Hiller proffering "pricey", "above-average" Southeast Asian cuisine; its "bar scene" is just as "stimulating" given its "killer drinks" and "cool" vibe – now if only the staff would "lose the 'tude."

Press 195 *Sandwiches* | **21** | **14** | **17** | **$20** |

Park Slope | 195 Fifth Ave. (bet. Berkeley Pl. & Union St.) | Brooklyn | 718-857-1950

Bayside | 40-11 Bell Blvd. (bet. 40th & 41st Aves.) | Queens | 718-281-1950
www.press195.com

The "impressive" panini lineup and "awesome" fries "disappear off your plate" – and are worth the "waits and elbows" – at this Bayside-Park Slope sandwich duo; to bide your time, have something from the "strong beer selection" in the "lovely" garden.

Pret A Manger *Sandwiches* | **18** | **11** | **15** | **$14** |

E 40s | 205 E. 42nd St. (bet. 2nd & 3rd Aves.) | 212-867-1905
E 40s | 287 Madison Ave. (bet. 40th & 41st Sts.) | 212-867-0400 🅢
E 50s | 400 Park Ave. (bet. 54th & 55th Sts.) | 212-207-4101 🅢
E 50s | 630 Lexington Ave. (bet. 54th & 55th Sts.) | 646-497-0510 🅢
Financial District | 60 Broad St. (Beaver St.) | 212-825-8825 🅢
Garment District | 530 Seventh Ave. (bet. 38th & 39th Sts.) |
646-728-0750 🅢
W 40s | 11 W. 42nd St. (bet. 5th & 6th Aves.) | 212-997-5520
W 40s | 30 Rockefeller Plaza, concourse level (bet. 49th & 50th Sts.) |
212-246-6944 🅢
W 50s | 135 W. 50th St. (bet. 6th & 7th Aves.) | 212-489-6458 🅢
W 50s | 1350 Sixth Ave. (enter on 55th St., bet. 5th & 6th Aves.) |
212-307-6100 🅢
www.pret.com
Additional locations throughout the NY area

Considered the "perfect grab-and-go" chain, this "enlightened" "fast-food" concept "born in London" offers a plethora of "delicious" "pre-boxed" sandwiches and salads made with "quality ingredients" and served "quick"; "every detail is done right" – including the policy of giving daily leftovers to charity.

Prime Grill *Steak* | **22** | **20** | **19** | **$79** |

E 40s | 60 E. 49th St. (bet. Madison & Park Aves.) | 212-692-9292 |
www.theprimegrill.com

"Melt-in-your-mouth" steaks and "wonderful" sushi that "happens to be kosher"? – "call the rabbi" because this "classic" East Side steakhouse "can hold its own" with the city's "quality" meat palaces; it'll "wow your guests", "observant or not", and the "pricey" tab may too.

	FOOD	DECOR	SERVICE	COST

Primehouse New York *Steak* — 24 | 23 | 23 | $68

Murray Hill | 381 Park Ave. S. (27th St.) | 212-824-2600 |
www.brguestrestaurants.com

Beef "dry-aged" so long it "could collect Social Security" is the "fantas-tic" specialty of Steve Hanson's "buzzy" Murray Hill steakhouse, whose "eclectic" wine list is "as thick as a bible"; "terrific" service and an "expensive-but-worth-it" tab complete the "big-city" picture.

Prime Meats ● *American* — 24 | 22 | 22 | $54

Carroll Gardens | 465 Court St. (Luquer St.) | Brooklyn | 718-254-0327 |
www.frankspm.com

A "solid hit" from the Frankies folks, this "happening" Carroll Gardens arrival delights with its "quirky", "Prohibition era" look and "amazing", meat-centric, German-accented New American fare; admirers only wish the waits weren't so "long", though "fantastic" retro cocktails "lovingly prepared by mustachioed hipsters" help the time pass.

Primola ● *Italian* — 23 | 16 | 20 | $64

E 60s | 1226 Second Ave. (bet. 64th & 65th Sts.) | 212-758-1775

"Strictly for the 'in' crowd", this East Side Italian is "filled with regulars" and a "smattering of celebs" schmoozing over "pasta cooked to perfec-tion" and other "delicious" "classics" "graciously" delivered, "at a price"; if you're "unknown", expect "rush-act" service with a seat in "Siberia."

NEW Print *American* — ▽ 25 | 25 | 23 | $56

W 40s | Ink48 Hotel | 653 11th Ave. (bet. 47th & 48th Sts.) | 212-757-2224 |
www.printrestaurant.com

The few surveyors who've "hiked" to far west Hell's Kitchen report that this new hoteler is serving "marvelous" farm-to-table American fare in a modern, Rockwell-designed room that brings a new level of "gorgeous" to 11th Avenue; "maybe when it gets busier there will be buzz in the air."

Provence en Boite *Bakery/French* — 20 | 19 | 17 | $33

Carroll Gardens | 263 Smith St. (Degraw St.) | Brooklyn | 718-797-0707 |
www.provenceenboite.com

"Ideal for decadent" pastries, this "charming" husband and wife-run Carroll Gardens French bakery/bistro also woos locals with "amazing crêpes" and other savories; "pleasant" "Parisian" ambiance and af-fordable prices outweigh any instances of "amateurish" service.

Provini ● *Italian* — ▽ 22 | 23 | 20 | $42

Park Slope | 1302 Eighth Ave. (13th St.) | Brooklyn | 718-369-2154

To a "restaurant-starved section of Park Slope" comes this Italian cafe from the Bar Toto/Bar Tano folks, whose "beautiful" "go-to-Italy" space and "delicious" pastas and other classics make for a "perfectly pitched" experience; it's "teeni" and often "packed", but "super-nice" staffers keeps things "relaxed."

Prune *American* — 24 | 15 | 20 | $48

E Village | 54 E. First St. (bet. 1st & 2nd Aves.) | 212-677-6221 |
www.prunerestaurant.com

Chef-owner Gabrielle Hamilton's "magic touch" is evident in the "stel-lar", "deceptively simple" New American cuisine (e.g. "interesting of-fal") that changes with the season at this "tiny", "unassuming" East

Village "foodie's paradise"; downsides are "sardine" seating and a "crazy wait" for the "superb" brunch.

❷ Public ◐ *Eclectic*　　　24 | 25 | 22 | $58

NoLita | 210 Elizabeth St. (bet. Prince & Spring Sts.) | 212-343-7011 | www.public-nyc.com

"Sexy" "old public school library" is not an oxymoron at this NoLita "sophisticate" that "indulges" the senses with "gorgeous retrofitted" furnishings and "stellar" Eclectic cooking with an "Australia-NZ" accent; it's more "swanky" than the name implies, with "first-rate" service and prices to match.

Pukk *Thai/Vegetarian*　　　▽ 21 | 17 | 19 | $21

E Village | 71 First Ave. (bet. 4th & 5th Sts.) | 212-253-2742 | www.pukknyc.com

This "dirt-cheap" Thai is an East Village "fail-safe" for "creative", competently served vegetarian dishes that live up to "omnivore standards"; though the "white-tiled", "futuristic hole-in-the-wall" look isn't for everyone, all agree that the "super-modern" loo is worth a visit.

NEW Pulino's ◐ *Pizza*　　　19 | 20 | 20 | $41

NoLita | 282 Bowery (E. Houston St.) | 212-226-1966 | www.pulinosny.com

"Pretty people eating pizza" sums up Keith McNally's latest, a "buzzy" Bowery "boîte" where "helpful" servers deliver "haute" pies in a "Schiller's-like" space featuring lots of brick and subway tile; it's "quite the scene", despite the "deafening noise" and "incommodious tables."

Pure Food & Wine *Vegan/Vegetarian*　　　23 | 22 | 22 | $53

Gramercy | 54 Irving Pl. (bet. 17th & 18th Sts.) | 212-477-1010 | www.purefoodandwine.com

"How'd they do that?" is the refrain at this "bold, creative" vegan performing "raw-food miracles" in "peaceful" Gramercy Park digs; the "tantalizing" tastes and "lovely garden" make even "omnivores smile", but the "clean-food high" comes with tabs that are less than "guilt-free."

NEW Purple Yam *Asian*　　　23 | 19 | 21 | $35

Ditmas Park | 1314 Cortelyou Rd. (bet. Argyle & Rugby Rds.) | Brooklyn | 718-940-8188 | www.purpleyamnyc.com

"Diverse", "original" Pan-Asian dishes packing "deep" flavors are the deal at this "brilliant arrival" to Ditmas Park's burgeoning "Cortelyou Restaurant Row"; its "sleek, small" room gets "crowded" quickly, but "friendly" service and "reasonable" tabs compensate.

Puttanesca *Italian*　　　19 | 16 | 18 | $40

W 50s | 859 Ninth Ave. (56th St.) | 212-581-4177 | www.puttanesca.com

"Well placed" near Lincoln Center, this "large, comfy" Hell's Kitchen haunt is known for "generous portions" of "straightforward" Italian fare, "prompt" service and "budget" prices; it's a "reliable oldie" whose "contagious party atmosphere" lends a "frisky" air, especially during "all-you-can-drink" brunch.

Pylos ◐ *Greek*　　　25 | 22 | 22 | $48

E Village | 128 E. Seventh St. (bet. Ave. A & 1st Ave.) | 212-473-0220 | www.pylosrestaurant.com

"From the amphora-clad ceiling" to the "vibrant" Hellenic fare, this "earthy" East Villager "spirits you to Greece" for "deftly" crafted

	FOOD	DECOR	SERVICE	COST

dishes that are made "to share"; factor in "thoughtful" service, a "laid-back" vibe and "reasonable" tabs, and it "hits the spot" every time.

NEW Qi *Asian* ▽ 22 | 22 | 22 | $26

Union Sq | 31 W. 14th St. (bet. 5th & 6th Aves.) | 212-929-9917 | www.qirestaurant.com

The multiculti (Indian, Thai, Vietnamese) fare is not only "wonderful", it's meant to promote healthy energy flow at this affordable Union Square arrival with macrobiotic and ayurvedic leanings; eco-friendly and "startlingly modern", its digs, done up with abacuses and suspended boats, are deemed a "knockout."

Q Thai Bistro *Thai* 20 | 17 | 18 | $39

Forest Hills | 108-25 Ascan Ave. (bet. Austin & Burns Sts.) | Queens | 718-261-6599 | www.qthaibistrony.com

"Tucked away" in Forest Hills, this "tiny" Thai "wins over" locals with its "flavorful" dishes and "nice bar scene"; it's "not the cheapest", but the "dark" and "whimsical" decor makes it a "divine" date destination.

Quaint *American* ▽ 25 | 21 | 25 | $34

Sunnyside | 46-10 Skillman Ave. (bet. 46th & 47th Sts.) | Queens | 917-779-9220 | www.quaintnyc.com

At this "friendly" "neighborhood" Sunnysider, the New American cooking "packs a delicious punch" with "local, organic" ingredients and "revelatory specials"; "warm, attentive" service, "cozy" digs that "live up to the name" and a "lovely" garden make for a "relaxing" experience.

Quality Meats *American/Steak* 24 | 22 | 22 | $71

W 50s | 57 W. 58th St. (bet. 5th & 6th Aves.) | 212-371-7777 | www.qualitymeatsnyc.com

"Overindulgence is required" at this "cavernous" Midtown chop shop whose "sumptuous" steaks and "to-die-for housemade ice cream" come in "funky", "1920s butcher shop"–inspired quarters; the tab may tip the scales, but it's "worth it" when "quality" everything is factored in.

Quantum Leap *Health Food/Vegetarian* 20 | 11 | 18 | $22

E Village | 203 First Ave. (bet. 12th & 13th Sts.) | 212-673-9848 | www.quantumleapeastvillage.com
G Village | 226 Thompson St. (bet. Bleecker & W. 3rd Sts.) | 212-677-8050 | www.quantumleapwestvillage.com

"Hearty" veggie vittles at "inexpensive" rates are the draw at this "unpretentious" cross-Village duo; the "health food" lineup (including fish) is "surprisingly satisfying", but the "college-y" atmosphere and sometimes "sleepy" service mean that many take the leap of "takeout."

Quatorze Bis *French* 21 | 19 | 20 | $59

E 70s | 323 E. 79th St. (bet. 1st & 2nd Aves.) | 212-535-1414

A "home away from home" for "mature" Eastsiders, this French bistro gets it "right" from the Parisian feel to the "efficient" staff; "worn" digs contrast with "splurge"-worthy tabs, but fans hope it "never changes."

NEW Quattro Gastronomia Italiana *Italian* ▽ 21 | 25 | 24 | $76

SoHo | Trump SoHo Hotel | 246 Spring St. (bet. 6th Ave. & Varick St.) | 212-842-4500 | www.quattronewyork.com

Inside the long-awaited new Trump SoHo Hotel is this offshoot of a chic Northern Italian eatery in Miami's South Beach; the "upmarket" seasonal cuisine is served three meals a day in "beautiful", "buzzy" bi-level digs whose emerald-green hue is fitting given the monied clientele and seriously "pricey" tab.

Quattro Gatti *Italian*
21 | 18 | 21 | $48

E 80s | 205 E. 81st St. (bet. 2nd & 3rd Aves.) | 212-570-1073
Every visit to this "old-fashioned" UES trattoria is like a "step back in time", what with the "veteran servers" proffering "rich and authentic" Italian fare at "easy-to-swallow" (for the zip code) prices; with a "casual", "charming and quiet" feel, it keeps the "regulars" regular.

Queen *Italian*
24 | 14 | 21 | $46

Brooklyn Heights | 84 Court St. (bet. Livingston & Schermerhorn Sts.) | Brooklyn | 718-596-5955 | www.queenrestaurant.com
"Delightful" red-sauce Italian dishes are the crowning specialty of this circa-1958 Brooklyn Heights "institution" overseen by a "welcoming" staff; the "lawyer and politico" crowd "disregards the generic" white-tablecloth setting and "counts on" "going home sated and happy."

Queen of Sheba ❶ *Ethiopian*
23 | 13 | 17 | $27

W 40s | 650 10th Ave. (bet. 45th & 46th Sts.) | 212-397-0610 | www.shebanyc.com
You "eat with your fingers" – or rather injera bread – at this "crowded, energetic" Hell's Kitchen Ethiopian, whose "budget"-friendly fare in-cludes "irresistible" veggie options and "fiery" flavors too; "preoccupied" service and no-decor digs don't detract much from the "royal" feast.

Quercy *French*
21 | 15 | 19 | $40

Cobble Hill | 242 Court St. (bet. Baltic & Kane Sts.) | Brooklyn | 718-243-2151
This "charming" Cobble Hill country French offshoot of La Lunchonette "deserves more attention" for its "well-prepared" fare and "unpreten-tious" vibe; add in "sweet" service and "affordable tabs", and locals are "mystified" that it's not more difficult to get in.

🆕 Rabbit in the Moon ❶ *British*
- | - | - | E

G Village | 47 W. Eighth St. (bet. 5th & 6th Aves.) | 212-473-2800
With its ivy-covered-townhouse space on the Village's collegiate-happy Eighth Street, this upscale gastropub feels like the library of an English cottage, complete with fireplace, portraits and taxidermy; its pricey cocktails and Modern British bites can be enjoyed in the up-stairs dining parlor or the loungier first floor.

Rachel's American Bistro ❶ *American*
17 | 13 | 16 | $38

W 40s | 608 Ninth Ave. (bet. 43rd & 44th Sts.) | 212-957-9050
A "reliable" fallback in the Theater District, this "cozy" New American "packs 'em in" for "tasty basics" at "reasonable" rates; the "narrow" space can be a "tight squeeze", but the "down-to-earth" staff navigat-ing it will "get you out fast" for the show.

Rack & Soul *BBQ/Southern*
21 | 12 | 17 | $28

W 100s | 258 W. 109th St. (B'way) | 212-222-4800 | www.rackandsoul.com
"Sublime" soul food "fixin's" and "flavorful" BBQ in "bountiful" serv-ings await at this Columbia-area Southerner, where the staff is "friendly" and "the price is right"; even so, supporters suggest "stick-ing to delivery" to skirt the "plain", "sticky" surrounds.

	FOOD	DECOR	SERVICE	COST

Radegast Hall ◑ *European* — 18 | 21 | 14 | $24

Williamsburg | 113 N. Third St. (Berry St.) | Brooklyn | 718-963-3973 | www.radegasthall.com

At this low-cost Williamsburg beer hall, the "stunning suds selection" and "soaring" "Bavarian biergarten" space complete with picnic tables and a retractable roof overshadow the "no-frills", "sausage-tastic" Euro grub; even with so-so service from the staff of dirndl-clad "maidens", it's always "packed" and "rowdy."

Rai Rai Ken ◑⇗ *Noodle Shop* — 22 | 11 | 16 | $16

E Village | 214 E. 10th St. (bet. 1st & 2nd Aves.) | 212-477-7030

For a "Tokyo-like experience", enthusiasts "sit at the counter and slurp" "toothsome" ramen at this "affordable", "authentically divey" East Village noodle shop; waiting for a seat is "worth it", even if "squeezing into" the "compressed" space is akin to "eating in coach."

NEW Ramen Kuidouraku *Noodle Shop* — - | - | - | I

E Village | 141 First Ave. (bet. 9th St. & St. Marks Pl.) | 212-529-2740 ◑

LES | 121 Ludlow St. (bet. Delancey & Rivington Sts.) | 212-979-0105

These East Village–LES arrivals on the ramen scene offer hot and cold versions of the noodles flavored with soy or salt and pork aplenty; minimalist digs and minimal prices keep things simple, while a BYO policy makes the new Ludlow Street locale especially wallet-friendly.

Ramen Setagaya *Noodle Shop* — 18 | 10 | 15 | $17

E Village | 34A St. Marks Pl. (bet. 2nd & 3rd Aves.) | 212-387-7959

Flushing | 37-02 Prince St. (37th Ave.) | Queens | 718-321-0290

"Comforting bowls" of "springy, flavorful ramen" served "quick" consistently "hit the spot" at these "well-priced" noodle shops in the East Village and Flushing; the "random Japanese" shows on TV lend an "authentic" air to the "tiny", no-decor settings.

Rao's ⊠⇗ *Italian* — 22 | 15 | 22 | $75

Harlem | 455 E. 114th St. (Pleasant Ave.) | 212-722-6709 | www.raos.com

"Snagging a reservation" at Frank Pellegrino's "primo" – and perpetually "sold-out" – "old-school" East Harlem Italian is near-"impossible", but the "chosen ones" affirm that the "scene is straight out of a [Bogart or Cagney] movie", "peppered with celebs" and "exclusive" types – oh, and the "red sauce" is as good as "grandma's"; those less "fortunate" will have to make do with the "Vegas offshoot."

Raoul's ◑ *French* — 23 | 19 | 21 | $61

SoHo | 180 Prince St. (bet. Sullivan & Thompson Sts.) | 212-966-3518 | www.raouls.com

A "hot spot" since before SoHo was SoHo, this perpetually "cool" French bistro attracts a "cacophonous" mix of "hipsters and neighborhood types" for costly, "outstanding" classics ferried by staffers "you want to be friends with"; its "dark, bohemian" and "mysterious" interior and "sexy" back garden complete the overall "seductive" scene.

Rare Bar & Grill *Burgers* — 21 | 15 | 16 | $33

NEW Chelsea | Fashion 26 Hotel | 152 W. 26th St. (bet. 6th & 7th Aves.) | 212-807-7273

(continued)

Rare Bar & Grill

Murray Hill | Shelburne Murray Hill Hotel | 303 Lexington Ave. (37th St.) |
212-481-1999
www.rarebarandgrill.com

"Upscale burgers" with "fun toppings" and "must-have fries" are the
hallmarks of this Chelsea-Murray Hill patty pair with a "young, boisterous" following; downsides include "slow" service and setups that
are "nothing spectacular" – except for the view from the rooftop bars.

Ravagh *Persian*

21 | 13 | 18 | $31

E 60s | 1237 First Ave. (bet. 66th & 67th Sts.) | 212-861-7900
Murray Hill | 11 E. 30th St. (bet. 5th & Madison Aves.) | 212-696-0300
This "exotic" East Side twosome "satisfies" with inexpensive classic
Persian cooking "like someone's mama made", including "heavenly"
rice and grill dishes; the service is "pleasant and courteous", but locals
put off by "crowds" and iffy decor often opt for "takeout."

Rayuela *Pan-Latin*

23 | 24 | 20 | $59

LES | 165 Allen St. (bet. Rivington & Stanton Sts.) | 212-253-8840 |
www.rayuelanyc.com

"Fantastic" Pan-Latin small plates pair with "tantalizing cocktails" at
this "jovial" Lower Eastsider, where a live olive tree "right in the middle" of its "sleek" space lends an "ethereal" air; just know it's "easy to
run up the bill" while soaking up the "electric" atmosphere here.

Real Madrid *Spanish*

∇ 22 | 14 | 19 | $40

Staten Island | 2075 Forest Ave. (Union Ave.) | 718-447-7885 |
www.realmadrid-restaurant.com

Named after Spain's famous soccer club, this Staten Island "standby"
maintains a faithful fan base for its "delicious" Spanish classics,
including "pretty darn good" lobster dishes and paella; factor in fair
prices and "attentive" service, and no one minds if the *fútbol*-themed
decor "needs updating."

NEW Recette ❶ *American*

24 | 19 | 21 | $62

W Village | 328 W. 12th St. (Greenwich St.) | 212-414-3000 |
www.recettenyc.com

"Little plates" bring "spectacular tastes" at this "great addition" to the
West Village serving "exceptional" (and "pricey") New American fare;
though some want to reset the menu's "confusing" snacks-vs.-plates
setup, all appreciate the "personable" service and "buzzing" vibe.

Recipe *American*

22 | 16 | 21 | $43

W 80s | 452 Amsterdam Ave. (bet. 81st & 82nd Sts.) | 212-501-7755 |
www.recipenyc.com

"Market-fresh ingredients" in "unfussy" New American preparations
are the thing at this "homespun" UWS yearling presided over by a
"cheerful" crew; prices are "reasonable" too, but as its 26-seat "nook"
is a "tight squeeze", regulars wish to "keep this recipe in the family."

Red Cat *American/Mediterranean*

24 | 19 | 22 | $56

Chelsea | 227 10th Ave. (bet. 23rd & 24th Sts.) | 212-242-1122 |
www.theredcat.com

After "gallery-hopping" or High Line strolling, an "eclectic" crowd collects at this "hip" West Chelsea vet for "delicious", "ever-changing",

slightly "pricey" Mediterranean–New American dishes; "gracious" service and a "convivial", "unpretentious" vibe keep this "chatty cat" bustling "year after year."

Red Egg *Chinese*

21 | 16 | 18 | $32

Little Italy | 202 Centre St. (Howard St.) | 212-966-1123 | www.redeggnyc.com

On the Little Italy–Chinatown border, this specialist in "upscale", yet low-cost, "made-to-order" dim sum delivers its "fab" tidbits via a staff so "friendly" you "won't miss the carts"; its "mod" space was redone post-Survey to enlarge the bar, which is known for its "amazing happy hour."

Redeye Grill ● *American/Seafood*

20 | 20 | 20 | $56

W 50s | 890 Seventh Ave. (56th St.) | 212-541-9000 | www.redeyegrill.com

"Kitschy", "touristy" and "lots of fun", Shelly Fireman's "lively" New American seafooder offers "fresh" catch at "reasonable"-for-Midtown rates in handsome, "noisy", "cavernous" digs; best of all, the "competent" staff gets the Carnegie Hall–bound "in and out in a hurry."

Redhead, The ● *American*

22 | 14 | 18 | $39

E Village | 349 E. 13th St. (bet. 1st & 2nd Aves.) | 212-533-6212 | www.theredheadnyc.com

"Never judge a book by its cover" advise admirers of this East Village "charmer" in "dive bar" clothing, which dishes up "insanely tasty" New American vittles with a Southern slant; a "friendly" staff, moderate tabs and "stellar" drinks are other reasons local wish to "keep it a secret."

☑ Regency *American*

▽ 19 | 23 | 23 | $75

E 60s | Loews Regency Hotel | 540 Park Ave. (61st St.) | 212-339-4050 | www.loewshotels.com

Long a "power-breakfast mecca" for those in business and politics, this Tisch family East Midtown New American is the place to "see and be seen" in the morning; "after hours", it transforms into the cabaret den Feinstein's, offering "substantial meals" and "the most potent drinks around."

Remi *Italian*

23 | 23 | 22 | $63

W 50s | 145 W. 53rd St. (bet. 6th & 7th Aves.) | 212-581-4242 | www.remi-ny.com

"Business-lunchers" and "pre-theater people" find "respite from the Midtown hustle" at this long-standing Venetian whose "terrific" Italian fare comes in a "striking" space sporting a 90-ft. mural of the Grand Canal; "pricey" tabs are offset by "pleasant service", "conversation"-friendly acoustics and lighting that "makes you look 10 years younger."

Republic *Asian*

18 | 14 | 15 | $24

Union Sq | 37 Union Sq. W. (bet. 16th & 17th Sts.) | 212-627-7172 | www.thinknoodles.com

The "young" and budget-minded "pack into communal tables" for "big, steaming noodle bowls" and other Pan-Asian eats "on the cheap" at this "frenetic" Union Square "standby"; "thunderous" decibels and "hard benches" are balanced by "short waits" and "speedy" service.

		FOOD	DECOR	SERVICE	COST

Re Sette ◐ *Italian* — 19 | 17 | 19 | $54

W 40s | 7 W. 45th St. (bet. 5th & 6th Aves.) | 212-221-7530 | www.resette.com

"Well located" near Times Square, this "charming", "pricey" Italian proffers "pleasant" (if "not extraordinary") Barese regional dishes made for "business lunches" and pre-theater repasts; "prompt" service is a plus, as is the upstairs King's Table for private parties.

Resto ◐ *Belgian* — 21 | 16 | 19 | $43

Murray Hill | 111 E. 29th St. (bet. Lexington Ave. & Park Ave. S.) | 212-685-5585 | www.restonyc.com

Burgers, moules frites and other "blissful" Belgian bistro fare that's well priced and backed by a "phenomenal beer selection" keeps this "hip" Murray Hill gastropub humming; a few peace-seekers lament "crowds" and "noise", but the resto relish the "happy, social" vibe.

Ricardo Steak House *Steak* — ▽ 22 | 20 | 20 | $42

Harlem | 2145 Second Ave. (bet. 110th & 111th Sts.) | 212-289-5895 | www.ricardosteakhouse.com

Up in East Harlem, this "lively" chophouse has gained a rep for "consistently good" steaks in a "small" candlelit space decked out with local artwork; add patio seating, a "pleasant" staff and "bargain" tabs, and you've got "a winner."

Rice ⊄ *Eclectic* — 19 | 15 | 16 | $22

NoHo | 292 Elizabeth St. (bet. Bleecker & Houston Sts.) | 212-226-5775 ◐
Dumbo | 81 Washington St. (bet. Front & York Sts.) | Brooklyn | 718-222-9880
Fort Greene | 166 DeKalb Ave. (Cumberland St.) | Brooklyn | 718-858-2700
www.riceny.com

"Creative" preparations of "the stuff it's named for" with lots of "veggie" options is what's on offer at this "basic", "cash-only" Eclectic trio that manages to provide a bit of "style and eco-consciousness" at "bargain" rates; "courteous" service ices the cake.

Riingo *American* — 21 | 20 | 19 | $54

E 40s | Alex Hotel | 205 E. 45th St. (bet. 2nd & 3rd Aves.) | 212-867-4200 | www.riingo.com

Marcus Samuelsson is no longer involved, and the "pricey" menu of "flavorful" New American fare received some post-Survey tweaks that removed the Japanese influences at this Midtown vet; still, a crowd heavy on "business-lunchers" collects in its "quiet", "ultramodern" digs.

Risotteria *Italian* — 22 | 10 | 18 | $27

W Village | 270 Bleecker St. (Morton St.) | 212-924-6664 | www.risotteria.com

"Gluten-free goodness" abounds at this "popular" West Village Italian that's a sensitive eater's "delight" given its "abundance" of affordable, "addictive" risottos and "wheat-free pizzas"; its "luncheonette-like" space is "tiny" and "always crowded", but "takeout" is always an option.

⊠ River Café *American* — 26 | 28 | 26 | $127

Dumbo | 1 Water St. (bet. Furman & Old Fulton Sts.) | Brooklyn | 718-522-5200 | www.rivercafe.com

"Nestled beneath the Brooklyn Bridge", Buzzy O'Keeffe's "impeccable", jackets-required Dumbo doyenne is an all-around "divine" experience, from the "inventive" New American cuisine proffered by "attentive" servers to the "mesmerizing" views of Lower Manhattan and the Harbor; the "over-the-top" milieu is matched with "splurge-worthy" tabs (prix fixe–only dinner is $98), but to most it's "worth every penny" for such a "magical event."

Riverview *American*

20 | 23* | 20 | $50

LIC | 2-01 50th Ave. (East River & 49th Ave.) | Queens | 718-392-5000 | www.riverviewny.com

"Good" New American fare, "unrushed" service and an "attractive" setting embellish the "romantic" mood at this Long Island City waterfronter; after dinner, insiders stroll along the river and admire the "stunning skyline view."

Rizzo's Pizza *Pizza*

▽ 23 | 9 | 19 | $12

Astoria | 30-13 Steinway St. (bet. 30th & 31st Aves.) | Queens | 718-721-9862 | www.rizzosfinepizza.com

This veteran Astoria pie peddler is known for its "delicious" square pizzas with "thin crusts" and "flavorful, fresh" toppings, proffered by a "friendly" crew; some say it's a mite "pricey" for a no-frills "slice" joint, but to the majority there's "no reason to go anywhere else."

NEW Robataya Ⓜ *Japanese*

▽ 23 | 24 | 23 | $48

E Village | 231 E. Ninth St. (bet. 2nd & 3rd Aves.) | 212-979-9674 | www.robataya-ny.com

"Food becomes theater" at this "lively" new East Village Japanese, where you can "sit at the robata counter" and "watch the chefs" grill up meats, fish and veggies, "yelling" all the while; there are also "delicious" small plates, but either way, it's not cheap.

NEW Robert ❶ *American*

19 | 24 | 19 | $58

W 50s | Museum of Arts and Design | 2 Columbus Circle, 9th fl. (bet. B'way & 8th Ave.) | 212-299-7730 | www.robertnyc.com

"High above" Columbus Circle, this new museum eatery is noted mostly for its "wow!"-worthy views (plead for a "table by the window") and "brilliant" mod decor; hopefully the "hit-or-miss" New American fare will soon "catch up", but for now you may want to "go for drinks" in the lounge.

Roberta's ❶⊅ *Pizza*

▽ 23 | 16 | 16 | $30

Bushwick | 261 Moore St. (Bogart St.) | Brooklyn | 718-417-1118 | www.robertaspizza.com

"Quietly emerging" as a destination for "insanely good" "wood-fired" pizzas, this far-flung Bushwick "hipster" magnet is also home to an "Internet radio station" and a "rooftop garden" that supplies the kitchen; both the "industrial" interior and "outdoor tiki bar" are "always full", so "expect to wait."

Ⓩ Roberto Ⓢ *Italian*

27 | 18 | 22 | $54

Bronx | 603 Crescent Ave. (Hughes Ave.) | 718-733-9503 | www.roberto089.com

"Sensational" Salerno specialties prepared "under the watchful eye" of chef Roberto Paciullo will make you "swear you're in Italy" rather than the Bronx at this Arthur Avenue–area perennial "star"; the prices are "reasonable" given the "enormous portions" and the "pro" service is "pleasant" – now "if only they'd take reservations."

	FOOD	DECOR	SERVICE	COST

Rocco ⓜ *Italian*
21 17 23 $40

G Village | 181 Thompson St. (bet. Bleecker & Houston Sts.) |
212-677-0590 | www.roccorestaurant.com

The "menu never changes" at this "quaint" Villager, an "old-timer"
(circa 1922) whose "dependable" Northern Italian classics and
"bargain" tabs keep it "popular with the NYU crowd"; thanks to the
"wonderful" staff, "eating here is like dropping in on old friends" – "ya
gotta love it."

Rock Center Café *American*
18 22 18 $52

W 50s | Rockefeller Ctr. | 20 W. 50th St. (bet. 5th & 6th Aves.) |
212-332-7620 | www.patinarestaurantgroup.com

It's "all about" the "view of the skating rink" in winter and "peaceful
outdoor seating" in summer at this Rock Center American "tourist haven", a NYers' "must" with the kids "when the Christmas tree is up";
the "decent" but "high-priced" food is almost beside the point.

Rocking Horse Cafe *Mexican*
20 15 17 $38

Chelsea | 182 Eighth Ave. (bet. 19th & 20th Sts.) | 212-463-9511 |
www.rockinghorsecafe.com

"Fresh", "modern" Mexican fare and "fantastic" cocktails are what
keep this "vibrant" Chelsea vet "bustling"; "reasonable" tabs and
"quick" (some say "rushed") service offset "cramped" digs and "rock-
ing" noise levels; P.S. the $15 brunch prix fixe is an "amazing bargain."

Roebling Tea Room ⓞ *Tearoom*
▽ 19 21 15 $33

Williamsburg | 143 Roebling St. (Metropolitan Ave.) | Brooklyn |
718-963-0760 | www.roeblingtearoom.com

"British tearoom" meets "hipster haven" at this "cool" Williamsburg
eatery serving "honest" American fare and "great teas" in a "lovely"
remodeled "old warehouse"; wear your "skinny black jeans and flannel
shirt" – and be prepared for service that's "sweet but neglectful."

Rolf's *German*
14 20 15 $38

Gramercy | 281 Third Ave. (22nd St.) | 212-477-4750

"You come for the Christmas spectacle" at this "blast-from-the-past"
Gramercy German, whose "over-the-top" yuletide decorations out-
dazzle the just-"ok" fare; bah-humbugers cite "tight" seating and "un-
interested" service, but still appreciate that this is one of "NYC's few"
remaining Teutonic bastions.

Roll-n-Roaster ⓞ *Sandwiches*
21 10 14 $14

Sheepshead Bay | 2901 Emmons Ave. (bet. Nostrand Ave. & 29th St.) |
Brooklyn | 718-769-5831 | www.rollnroaster.com

On a roll since 1970, this Sheepshead Bay "institution" is famed for
its "greasy, delicious", "double-dipped" roast beef sandwiches and
the option to "put cheez on anything"; "time-warp" decor, "late-
night" hours and low rates ensure it's a hit with "teenagers" and
old-timers alike.

Room Service ⓞ *Thai*
21 22 18 $30

Chelsea | 166 Eighth Ave. (bet. 18th & 19th Sts.) | 212-691-0299
W 40s | 690 Ninth Ave. (bet. 47th & 48th Sts.) | 212-582-0999

"Done up like hotels" complete with "sparkling chandeliers", these
"snazzy" twins draw a "fun" crowd with their "tasty Thai" fare and "sexy"

"disco" vibe; the "thumping" soundtrack "makes conversation impossible", but "affordable" tabs have most squealing "get a room, baby."

Rosa Mexicano *Mexican*

| 22 | 21 | 20 | $50 |

E 50s | 1063 First Ave. (58th St.) | 212-753-7407 ◐
Flatiron | 9 E. 18th St. (bet. B'way & 5th Ave.) | 212-533-3350
W 60s | 61 Columbus Ave. (62nd St.) | 212-977-7700 ◐
www.rosamexicano.com

"Glorious guacamole" "made at your table" plus "lethal" pomegranate margaritas equals lots of "happy campers" at these "stylish" outlets for "high-end Mexican" that "pack 'em in" and leave patrons "craving *mas*"; "welcoming" service only adds to the "fiesta-time" spirit.

Rosanjin ◪ *Japanese*

| ▽ 27 | 24 | 27 | $115 |

TriBeCa | 141 Duane St. (bet. Church St. & W. B'way) | 212-346-0664 | www.rosanjintribeca.com

"Top-notch but under the radar", this "serene" TriBeCa "haute Japanese" offers "outstanding" kaiseki dinners prepared with the "utmost attention to presentation and detail"; the "geishalike" service is "impeccable" and the "tiny" space "beautiful", but you'll practically "leave your wallet" when the bill comes – unless you go for the $40 mini-kaiseki menu.

Rose Water *American*

| 25 | 19 | 24 | $45 |

Park Slope | 787 Union St. (6th Ave.) | Brooklyn | 718-783-3800 | www.rosewaterrestaurant.com

Among "the first in the Slope" to make "fresh, local ingredients" a focus, this "tiny", decade-old New American remains a "foodie" favorite for "sustainable fine dining"; service is "warm" and the prices "aren't ruinous", so "the only negative" is the "cramped" space – and "DMV-length" lines for the "amazing brunch."

Rossini's *Italian*

| 24 | 21 | 25 | $61 |

Murray Hill | 108 E. 38th St. (bet. Lexington & Park Aves.) | 212-683-0135 | www.rossinisrestaurant.com

"They don't make 'em like this anymore" sigh mature fans of this "romantic" Murray Hill Northern Italian that's a "mainstay" for "old-world gracious" service and "superior" classic cuisine; factor in live music ("piano weekdays, opera on Saturday") and most diners happily stomach the pricey tab.

Rothmann's *Steak*

| 23 | 20 | 22 | $72 |

E 50s | 3 E. 54th St. (bet. 5th & Madison Aves.) | 212-319-5500 | www.rothmannssteakhouse.com

"Carnivores with corporate cards" fuel the "busy businessperson scene" at this Midtown moo house whose "solid", "pricey" steaks come via a "friendlier-than-average" staff; insiders note "the real action is at the bar and outside" where the "macho men smoke cigars."

🆕 Rothschild's ⊅ *American*

| – | – | – | M |

Boerum Hill | 411 Atlantic Ave. (bet. Bond & Nevins Sts.) | Brooklyn | 718-596-3110 | www.rothschilds-restaurant.com

The owners of the erstwhile Boerum Hiller Stan's Place have opened this new arrival in its former digs, with a menu that features New Orleans classics familiar from the old place plus some New American additions; the nifty vintage neon sign out front is in tune with the old-timey look of the space, which includes a second-floor lounge.

	FOOD	DECOR	SERVICE	COST

Rouge Tomate ⓔ *American*   23 | 25 | 23 | $65

E 60s | 10 E. 60th St. (bet. 5th & Madison Aves.) | 646-237-8977 | www.rougetomatenyc.com

"Foodies", "locavores" and "nutritionists" alike go giddy for the "creative", "healthy" New American plates at this "gorgeous", "understated" East Side duplex manned by a "refined" crew; "ladies who lunch organically" don't mind the "pricey" "little" portions – and anyway, there's always the "bargain prix fixe."

Royal Siam Ⓜ *Thai*   20 | 15 | 21 | $30

Chelsea | 240 Eighth Ave. (bet. 22nd & 23rd Sts.) | 212-741-1732

"Better-than-usual" Thai fare, "prompt" service and "reasonable prices" set this Chelsea vet apart from the crowd; regulars give the "recent remodeling" a "thumbs-up" and hope the restaurant preserves its "low profile" ("please don't tell").

RUB BBQ *BBQ*   21 | 10 | 16 | $29

Chelsea | 208 W. 23rd St. (bet. 7th & 8th Aves.) | 212-524-4300 | www.rubbbq.net

A "Kansas City–style" BBQ joint declared "the real thing", this "noisy" and "gritty" Chelsea pit stop is "authentic" down to the "paper plates", "fluorescent lights", "sassy" service and "reasonable" rates; just "get there early" because those coveted "burnt ends" from the brisket "go fast."

Ruby Foo's *Asian*   19 | 20 | 18 | $46

W 40s | 1626 Broadway (49th St.) | 212-489-5600 | www.brguestrestaurants.com

"Boisterous", "loud" and smack dab "in the heart of tourist central", this "cavernous", ever-"packed" Times Square Pan-Asian "theme" palace is tailor-made for "out-of-towners and kids"; the "over-the-top" "Charlie Chan"–worthy decor "pleases" most, and the eats are "surprisingly decent" too.

Rue 57 ❶ *French*   18 | 19 | 17 | $47

W 50s | 60 W. 57th St. (6th Ave.) | 212-307-5656 | www.rue57.com

"Tourists" and "shoppers" hit this "lively" Midtown "Parisian" brasserie facsimile at "any time of day" for "above-average" eats that are an "odd blend" of "French and sushi"; don't mind the "take-you-for-granted" service or "thumping techno music" – it's all about the "convenient" location and "fair" prices.

Rughetta *Italian*   22 | 16 | 22 | $50

E 80s | 347 E. 85th St. (bet. 1st & 2nd Aves.) | 212-517-3118 | www.rughetta.com

This Yorkville Italian "neighborhood charmer" "remains solid" a decade on according to "loyal locals" who laud its "well-crafted" Roman cuisine and "warm" staff; ever since the space was "expanded", it's no longer so "tight", although the prices may have grown a bit too.

Russian Samovar ❶ *Continental*   20 | 18 | 17 | $52

W 50s | 256 W. 52nd St. (bet. B'way & 8th Ave.) | 212-757-0168 | www.russiansamovar.com

There's "never a dull moment" at this "convivial" Midtown Russian-Continental, which is "frequented by émigrés" who come for the free-flowing "infused vodkas", "decadent" grub and "nightly music from a white baby grand"; just "bring your passport – and your wallet."

Russian Tea Room   *Continental*   19 | 25 | 20 | $72

W 50s | 150 W. 57th St. (bet. 6th & 7th Aves.) | 212-581-7100 | www.russiantearoomnyc.com

It's not the "legend" "your mother knew", but this Russian-accented Continental "institution" in Midtown still "delights" with its "dazzling" "over-the-top" setting and requisite "blini and caviar"; cynics citing "hit-or-miss" fare and "hefty prices" say it's strictly "for out-of-towners."

Ruth's Chris Steak House   *Steak*   24 | 21 | 23 | $71

W 50s | 148 W. 51st St. (bet. 6th & 7th Aves.) | 212-245-9600 | www.ruthschris.com

"Steak connoisseurs" "drool" over "aged-to-perfection" meats "in sizzling butter" at this "first-class" Midtown franchise where the "especially nice service" and "pleasant" dark wood–paneled setting are a "sure bet" for "impressing clients"; just "watch your cholesterol – and your wallet."

Rye   *American*   ▽ 23 | 22 | 22 | $47

Williamsburg | 247 S. First St. (bet. Havemeyer & Roebling Sts.) | Brooklyn | 718-218-8047 | www.ryerestaurant.com

A "true hidden gem", this "darkly sexy", "speakeasy-style" Williamsburg New American has "hip" folks grooving on "fresh" seasonal fare and "top-notch" cocktails from a "grandiose antique bar"; "friendly" service takes the sting out of tabs deemed "a bit expensive" for the area.

Sac's Place   *Pizza*   23 | 14 | 19 | $30

Astoria | 25-41 Broadway (29th St.) | Queens | 718-204-5002 | www.sacsplace.com

"When it comes to coal-fired, brick-oven pizza", this Astoria "corner Italian" may be the real "king of Queens" thanks to its "amazing", "crispy-crust" pies; as for the "regular menu", it's "standard" "red-sauce" all the way, and the service and decor "could use some help."

Sahara ◐ *Turkish*   22 | 14 | 16 | $30

Gravesend | 2337 Coney Island Ave. (bet. Aves. T & U) | Brooklyn | 718-376-8594 | www.saharapalace.com

"Big portions, big taste" is the "low-priced" deal at this "busy" Gravesend Turk whose "tasty" grill dishes and other classics draw a mixed crowd, from "families with kids to dates"; those put off by the "cavernous", "noisy" digs do "takeout", or hit the "lovely garden."

Sahara's Turkish Cuisine   *Turkish*   22 | 16 | 21 | $35

Gramercy | 513 Second Ave. (bet. 28th & 29th Sts.) | 212-532-7589 | www.saharaturkishrestaurant.com

"Order many plates, they're meant for sharing" advise regulars of this no-frills Gramercy Turk offering "delicious" meze and other classics at a "price-to-quality ratio" that leaves "belly and wallet very happy"; another virtue is service so "helpful" you almost "feel you're not in NYC."

Saigon Grill ◐ *Vietnamese*   21 | 12 | 16 | $27

G Village | 91-93 University Pl. (bet. 11th & 12th Sts.) | 212-982-3691
W 90s | 620 Amsterdam Ave. (90th St.) | 212-875-9072

"Crazy-delicious" Vietnamese fare at "easy-on-your-wallet" rates means this "loud and lively" Village-UWS duo is always "mobbed", despite "assembly-line" service and "zero decor"; P.S. the publicized "labor dispute" is "finally over", so delivery from the Amsterdam Avenue branch is back.

Sakagura ● *Japanese* | 24 | 21 | 22 | $56

E 40s | 211 E. 43rd St., downstairs (bet. 2nd & 3rd Aves.) | 212-953-7253 | www.sakagura.com

"Top-notch" small plates and a "sake-lovers'" wish list are the lures at this "hard-to-find, worth-the-search" Japanese izakaya in the "basement of a Midtown office building"; the overall effect is "authentic" Tokyo, complete with yenlike tabs that "add up fast."

Sala *Spanish* | 22 | 19 | 20 | $41

Flatiron | 35 W. 19th St. (bet. 5th & 6th Aves.) | 212-229-2300
NoHo | 344 Bowery (Great Jones St.) | 212-979-6606
www.salanyc.com

"Pitchers of sangria fly by" and "wonderful" tapas kick up a "party in your mouth" at these "fun, friendly", relatively "affordable" NoHo-Flatiron Spaniards; "dimly lit" and "loungelike", they host an "incredibly loud" "young" "trendster" scene in the later hours "amus."

Salaam Bombay *Indian* | 22 | 17 | 19 | $33

TriBeCa | 319 Greenwich St. (bet. Duane & Reade Sts.) | 212-226-9400 | www.salaambombay.com

Regulars say it's "always a wonderful meal" at this "friendly" TriBeCa Indian, but the "best" is its "diverse", "way-above-average" weekday lunch buffet, a mega-"bargain" at $14; maybe the decor "needs a redo", but "don't be fooled" – everything else is just fine.

Sala Thai *Thai* | 21 | 14 | 19 | $31

E 80s | 1718 Second Ave. (bet. 89th & 90th Sts.) | 212-410-5557

A "long-standing" UES "neighborhood favorite", this Thai traffics in tongue-tingling "fixes" in "nothing-fancy" (though recently "updated") surroundings; modest prices and an "accommodating" crew are other secrets to its longevity.

Salt *American* | 23 | 19 | 20 | $45

SoHo | 58 MacDougal St. (bet. Houston & Prince Sts.) | 212-674-4968

Salt Bar ● Ⓜ⇗ *American*

LES | 29A Clinton St. (bet. Houston & Stanton Sts.) | 212-979-8471 | www.saltnyc.com

"Varied and exciting" "seasonal" cookery keeps 'em "squishing" into the "communal" tables "meal after meal" at this "friendly" and "vibrant" SoHo New American; the Lower East Side outpost is more about "wonderful drinks" and "bar snacks", but both are declared "thoroughly enjoyable."

NEW Saltie Ⓜ⇗ *Sandwiches* | ▽ 25 | 12 | 17 | $14

Williamsburg | 378 Metropolitan Ave. (bet. Havemeyer St. & Marcy Ave.) | Brooklyn | 718-387-4777 | www.saltieny.com

"Heavenly sandwiches" with seafarin' names (the Captain's Daughter, Scuttlebutt), "innovative combos" and "unerringly fresh ingredients" are the bait at this Williamsburg arrival from vets of Marlow & Sons and Diner; a dinghy-size space and service on the "salty" side makes takeout a good tack.

	FOOD	DECOR	SERVICE	COST

NEW Salumè Sandwiches
| - | - | - | I |

SoHo | 330 W. Broadway (Grand St.) | 212-226-8111 |
www.salumenewyork.com

With 20-odd sandwiches made with cured Italian meats and cheeses on crusty bread – and left unpressed – this new SoHo panini shop is off to a good start; there are also Euro desserts, served in minimalist-chic digs that are just big enough for table service.

Salumeria Rosi Parmacotto Italian
| 24 | 17 | 19 | $45 |

W 70s | 283 Amsterdam Ave. (bet. 73rd & 74th Sts.) | 212-877-4800 |
www.salumeriarosi.com

It's "salami and prosciutto heaven" at Cesare Casella's UWS enoteca/salumeria where "top-notch" cured meats from its retail counter and "Tuscan tapas" allow you to "try a sliver of this and a slice of that" with "lovely wines"; it's always "crowded and noisy", but that's part of its *vero Italiano* charm.

Salute! Italian
| 19 | 19 | 18 | $52 |

Murray Hill | 270 Madison Ave. (39th St.) | 212-213-3440 |
www.salutenyc.com

Those looking to "talk business" collect at this "clubby" Murray Hill Italian during "bustling lunch" and tuck into "solid", "expensive" fare; after work, it's all about the "hot bar crowd" (expect "lots of little black dresses"), peppered with "attitude" from the staff.

Sambuca Italian
| 20 | 17 | 20 | $41 |

W 70s | 20 W. 72nd St. (bet. Columbus Ave. & CPW) | 212-787-5656 |
www.sambucanyc.com

"Gargantuan" "family-style platters" of red-gravy dishes delivered by a "helpful" staff is the deal at this "cavernous", "noisy", "low-cost" UWS "local"; it fills the bill when you're feeding "large families and groups" – or "can't get into Carmine's"; P.S. the "gluten-free menu" is a plus.

Sammy's Fishbox ● Seafood
| ▽ 20 | 13 | 17 | $42 |

Bronx | 41 City Island Ave. (Rochelle St.) | 718-885-0920 |
www.sammysfishbox.com

"You gotta love" the combo of "good basic seafood" and "fun" "honky-tonk" atmosphere at this "nothing-fancy" Bronx fish house that supplies "large portions" of "very fresh" catch and a "real City Island experience"; no surprise, it gets "extremely crowded" in summertime.

Sammy's Roumanian Jewish
| 20 | 10 | 18 | $56 |

LES | 157 Chrystie St. (Delancey St.) | 212-673-0330

"Ear-splitting 'Hava Nagila' music" sets the tone at this "cheesy", "helluva-lotta-fun" LES "Jewish soul food" "institution" famed for "schmaltz on the table", "ice-encased vodka" bottles and steaks that drape "over the sides of your plate"; its "borscht-belt humor" leaves most cheering *"l'chaim!"*, "kitschy basement" decor and "heartburn be damned."

Sandro's ● Italian
| 24 | 15 | 20 | $64 |

E 80s | 306 E. 81st St. (bet. 1st & 2nd Aves.) | 212-288-7374 |
www.sandrosnyc.com

"Colorful", "caring" chef-owner Sandro Fioriti and his "fabulous Roman specialties" inspire "repeat visits" to this "treat" of an UES trat-

| | FOOD | DECOR | SERVICE | COST |

toria; regulars say "don't miss the lemon pasta", and "don't mind" Sandro's "crazy pants" – or the so-so decor and "pricey" tabs.

Sandwich Planet *Sandwiches*   ▽ 22 | 10 | 16 | $14
Garment District | 522 Ninth Ave. (39th St.) | 212-273-9768 | www.sandwichplanet.com

Those who know this mighty mite "near Port Authority" nominate its "fantastic" sandwiches and burgers for "best on planet"; everything's ordered from a "huge" menu that includes nearly any "seriously creative, fresh" combo "you can dream of", served up in "tiny, crowded" digs that have most doing delivery.

🆕 San Pietro 🏛 *Italian*   25 | 21 | 25 | $88
E 50s | 18 E. 54th St. (bet. 5th & Madison Aves.) | 212-753-9015 | www.sanpietro.net

"Top-firm CEOs" and other "power players" lunch on "fantastic" Southern Italian classics at this Midtown "business-dining" "paragon"; "extremely cordial" waiters help you "remember what service is about", but you may suffer "sticker-shock" when the bill comes.

Sant Ambroeus *Italian*   21 | 19 | 20 | $59
E 70s | 1000 Madison Ave. (bet. 77th & 78th Sts.) | 212-570-2211
W Village | 259 W. Fourth St. (Perry St.) | 212-604-9254
www.santambroeus.com

"Memorable as a Fellini movie", these "chic" cafes are "escapes" to Milan for "monied" types seeking to be "coddled" over "real-deal" Italian nibbles and even "better desserts"; the UES original is a "ladies-who-lunch" magnet, while the West Villager is a "prime people-watching" perch, "daah-ling", so be "pretty and well dressed"; P.S. "your 401(k) will be a 201(k) after you eat here."

Sapori D'Ischia Ⓜ *Italian*   23 | 16 | 20 | $48
Woodside | 55-15 37th Ave. (56th St.) | Queens | 718-446-1500

"Hidden" in a Woodside "warehouse district", this "Italian food market" by day morphs into a "fantastic" Neapolitan eatery come dinnertime; the signature dish, "pasta tossed in a huge Parmesan wheel", is deemed "worth the trip" alone, ditto the "meandering opera singers" on Thursday nights.

Sapphire Indian *Indian*   21 | 19 | 18 | $44
W 60s | 1845 Broadway (bet. 60th & 61st Sts.) | 212-245-4444 | www.sapphireny.com

The "reigning rajah" of Lincoln Center–area Indian dining, this Columbus Circle stalwart offers "fresh, richly flavored" food, "pretty" decor and service that ensures you "make your seats on time"; it's a bit "pricey" for the genre, but the "boffo" $15 lunch buffet is a "terrific bargain."

Sarabeth's *American*   20 | 17 | 18 | $36
Chelsea | Chelsea Mkt. | 75 Ninth Ave. (bet. 15th & 16th Sts.) | 212-989-2424 | www.sarabeth.com
E 90s | 1295 Madison Ave. (92nd St.) | 212-410-7335 | www.sarabeth.com
Garment District | Lord & Taylor | 424 Fifth Ave., 5th fl. (bet. 38th & 39th Sts.) | 212-827-5068 | www.sarabeth.com
W 50s | 40 Central Park S. (bet. 5th & 6th Aves.) | 212-826-5959 | www.sarabethscps.com

(continued)

(continued)

Sarabeth's

W 80s | 423 Amsterdam Ave. (bet. 80th & 81st Sts.) | 212-496-6280 | www.sarabeth.com

This mini-"empire of American comfort cuisine" remains the "brunch gold standard", whose "loyal", "carb-starved" following queues up for "to-die-for" scones and jams in "Laura Ashley"–inspired digs; it's a "packed", "noisy" scene, but dinner is "quieter."

Saravanaas *Indian*

25 | 10 | 14 | $22

Murray Hill | 81 Lexington Ave. (26th St.) | 212-679-0204

"Heavenly" dosas and other "cheap", "wonderful vegetarian" dishes elevate this "unassuming" Murray Hill South Indian miles above "your usual curry joint"; "regimented" service and "cafeteria"-like decor don't deter the "crowds", so "be prepared to stand in line."

Sardi's Ⓜ *Continental*

17 | 22 | 19 | $55

W 40s | 234 W. 44th St. (bet. B'way & 8th Ave.) | 212-221-8440 | www.sardis.com

You "dine surrounded by a who's who" of theatrical "caricatures" – not to mention "Broadway players" and "tourists" – at this circa-1921 Theater District "icon" where the "better-than-you-think" Continental fare is served by "crusty" waiters; though it's "not what it once was", it's "still a favorite" for its "showbiz history."

Sarge's Deli ❶ *Deli*

20 | 9 | 15 | $26

Murray Hill | 548 Third Ave. (bet. 36th & 37th Sts.) | 212-679-0442 | www.sargesdeli.com

This "old-school" Murray Hill deli's "humongous" corned beef and pastrami sandwiches and other "Jewish comfort" classics come at "bang-for-the-buck" prices; the staff is "not cordial" and the decor's "shabby", but it's "open 24/7" – hopefully your cardiologist's is too.

☒ Sasabune ⓈⓂ *Japanese*

29 | 11 | 21 | $102

E 70s | 401 E. 73rd St. (bet. 1st & York Aves.) | 212-249-8583

"You have no choice" but to "trust the master" at Kenji Takahashi's omakase-only UES Japanese, a "close-to-Tokyo" "must" where the chef doles out "NYC's finest sushi" and acolytes "beg for more"; the only drawbacks are the "not-fancy" venue and "extremely expensive" bill.

☒ Saul *American*

26 | 21 | 25 | $63

Boerum Hill | 140 Smith St. (bet. Bergen & Dean Sts.) | Brooklyn | 718-935-9844 | www.saulrestaurant.com

"Everything's divine" at this Boerum Hill "class act", a "relaxed" refuge where chef-owner Saul Bolton makes "superb" New American cuisine "look easy" working with "market-fresh" ingredients; near-"perfect" service and "pretty" storefront digs further justify the "high prices."

Savoia *Pizza*

20 | 16 | 19 | $34

Carroll Gardens | 277 Smith St. (bet. Degraw & Sackett Sts.) | Brooklyn | 718-797-2727

"Delicious" "thin-crust" pizzas from the "wood-burning oven" are the highlight at this "casual" Italian that's a Carroll Gardens "fixture"; "attentive" service, "reasonable prices" and "ample sidewalk seating" are other endearments.

| | FOOD | DECOR | SERVICE | COST |

Savoy *American/Mediterranean* | 24 | 20 | 22 | $60 |

SoHo | 70 Prince St. (Crosby St.) | 212-219-8570 | www.savoynyc.com

A "locavore" eatery "before the word was invented", Peter Hoffman's SoHo standby is "still an exemplar" for "fab" "farm-to-table" Med-New American cooking; its "rustic, two-story charmer" space ("especially upstairs" by the "fireplace") and "friendly pro" service add to the "special" experience.

Sazon *Puerto Rican* | ∇ 23 | 21 | 21 | $41 |

TriBeCa | 105 Reade St. (bet. Church St. & W. B'way) | 212-406-1900 | www.sazonnyc.com

This "hip" TriBeCa "sister to Sofrito" is a "high-end Puerto Rican" "*caliente* spot" serving "delicious interpretations" of the classics plus sangria "that'll make you salsa like nobody's business" when the DJ spins; in sum, "the food is off the hook and the scene is happening."

Scaletta *Italian* | 21 | 20 | 23 | $52 |

W 70s | 50 W. 77th St. (bet. Columbus Ave. & CPW) | 212-769-9191 | www.scalettaristorante.com

"Civilized" and "attractive", this UWS Italian boasts a "gracious" staff that delivers "solid" standards to "staid" "regulars" who find the kinda "pricey" rates "easy to digest"; its "spacious" setting allows for "quiet dining" – meaning you can "actually enjoy the conversation."

Z Scalinatella ● *Italian* | 24 | 17 | 21 | $86 |

E 60s | 201 E. 61st St., downstairs (3rd Ave.) | 212-207-8280

"Down a flight" of steps you'll find this "expensive" Italian "grotto" that's "tightly packed" with "well-heeled UES" types who appreciate its "superb" "Capri-style" fare and "entertaining" waiters; as for its infamous "unpriced" specials list, regulars warn "hold on to your wallet."

Z Scalini Fedeli 图 *Italian* | 27 | 24 | 25 | $86 |

TriBeCa | 165 Duane St. (bet. Greenwich & Hudson Sts.) | 212-528-0400 | www.scalinifedeli.com

"Exquisite" Northern Italian cooking in a "romantic", "high"-vaulted-ceilinged setting that recalls "Tuscany", matched with an "impressive wine list" and "first-class" service, make Michael Cetrulo's "wonderful" TriBeCan a favored "special-occasion" destination; it's far from cheap (prix fixe–only dinner is $65), but "such a memorable evening" is "worth every penny."

Scalino *Italian* | ∇ 24 | 12 | 24 | $35 |

Park Slope | 347 Seventh Ave. (10th St.) | Brooklyn | 718-840-5738

"Every neighborhood should have" a "treasure" like this "homey", reasonably priced Park Slope Italian owned by "two brothers who treat you like an old friend" while sending out "simply delicious" traditional dishes; as for the "small", "no-frills" setup, "manage your expectations."

Scarlatto ● *Italian* | 20 | 17 | 19 | $46 |

W 40s | 250 W. 47th St. (bet. B'way & 8th Ave.) | 212-730-4535 | www.scarlattonyc.com

Reviewers rate this Theater Districter a "keeper" thanks to its "upscale" "Italiano" offerings at "affordable" prices and "quick", "amiable" staff; the space is "pleasant" enough too, with *Roman Holiday* film stills to "transport" diners abroad; P.S. at $29, the prix fixe dinner is a "bargain."

	FOOD	DECOR	SERVICE	COST

☑ Scarpetta   *Italian*   26 | 22 | 23 | $71

Chelsea | 355 W. 14th St. (bet. 8th & 9th Aves.) | 212-691-0555 |
www.scarpettanyc.com

Scott Conant's "delectably extravagant" "high-concept Italian" on
14th Street "lives up to its hype", eliciting "oohs and aahs" with its "exceptional" cuisine (including the "best spaghetti ever"), "ultrapro"
service and "elegant" yet "hip" setting; it's "worth breaking the bank"
for – assuming you "can get a reservation."

Schiller's ● *Eclectic*   19 | 19 | 17 | $39

LES | 131 Rivington St. (Norfolk St.) | 212-260-4555 | www.schillersny.com

"Balthazar for the under-35 set", Keith McNally's "sceney" LES Eclectic
features patented "Paris bistro" decor, "solid", "well-priced" standards
and "handcrafted cocktails" served into the wee hours; to talk, plan on
"screaming" – how do the "models and hipsters hear each other"?

Schnipper's Quality Kitchen   *American*   19 | 13 | 14 | $16

W 40s | NY Times Bldg. | 620 Eighth Ave. (41st St.) | 212-921-2400 |
www.schnippers.com

A "welcome option" for "satisfying comfort food" in Times Square, this
"cafeteria-style" contender dispenses "delicious burgers" and other
"affordable" basics "made to order"; with "huge windows" and Port
Authority across the street, it's also a "people-watching" perch.

Scottadito Osteria Toscana Ⓜ *Italian*   ▽ 21 | 18 | 20 | $36

Park Slope | 788A Union St. (bet. 6th & 7th Aves.) | Brooklyn |
718-636-4800 | www.scottadito.com

"Tasty", "affordable" Tuscan fare comes in "rustic farmhouse" digs at
this Park Slope Northern Italian; if a "fireplace" weren't enough, it
boasts a few sidewalk seats and a "terrific" $18 brunch.

NEW SD26   *Italian*   22 | 23 | 22 | $69

Murray Hill | 19 E. 26th St. (bet. 5th & Madison Aves.) | 212-265-5959 |
www.sd26ny.com

In a *"molto chic"* "soaring", "contemporary" space opposite Madison
Park, this "sexier" San Domenico "reincarnation" puts forth "innovative"
Italian cuisine in your choice of a "terrific" front wine bar or "loft"-like
dining room, both "presided over with grace" by "father-daughter"
team Tony and Marisa May; a few mind the "relentlessly modern" decor and "pricey" tabs, but to most it's simply a "winner."

Sea ● *Thai*   21 | 22 | 17 | $30

Meatpacking | 835 Washington St. (Little W. 12th St.) | 212-243-3339
Williamsburg | 114 N. Sixth St. (Berry St.) | Brooklyn | 718-384-8850
www.seathainyc.com

At this Williamsburg-Meatpacking Thai duo, "awesome", "ridiculously
inexpensive" Thai fare comes in downright "chic" quarters ("sit near the
pool" or "stare at the Buddha"); at night it's "loud and clubby" with
servers "eager to turn your table", but by day it's "all peace and serenity."

Sea Grill ☒ *Seafood*   24 | 25 | 23 | $70

W 40s | Rockefeller Ctr. | 19 W. 49th St. (bet. 5th & 6th Aves.) |
212-332-7610 | www.theseagrillnyc.com

Nab a "table by the window" overlooking the rink and "you can't go
wrong" at this "Rock Center standout" whose "amazing" skater views

| | FOOD | DECOR | SERVICE | COST |

are matched with "superior" seafood, "plush" decor and "beyond-charming" service; sure, it's a "tourist mecca" and tabs are high, but it's a "must-go" when the "Christmas tree" is up.

⧲ Seasonal Austrian

25 | 19 | 24 | $69

W 50s | 132 W. 58th St. (bet. 6th & 7th Aves.) | 212-957-5550 | www.seasonalnyc.com

"Leave your lederhosen at home", because this "sleek", "refined", "wonderful" Midtown Austrian is all about "contemporary" takes on "traditional" dishes using "top" "seasonal" ingredients; "friendly, professional" service and a location "near Carnegie Hall" are added reasons to go, expense notwithstanding.

2nd Ave Deli ✪ Deli

22 | 12 | 17 | $28

Murray Hill | 162 E. 33rd St. (bet. Lexington & 3rd Aves.) | 212-689-9000 | www.2ndavedeli.com

Ok, the "original Second Avenue location" is just a "memory", but this off-Third-Avenue Murray Hill "revival" still "holds up" with "gargantuan", "artery-blocking" sandwiches and other "traditional" Jewish deli favorites ("you won't leave hungry"), despite "cramped quarters", "rough-and-tumble" service and "chutzpah prices", it still "draws crowds."

NEW Seersucker Ⓜ Southern

- | - | - | M

Carroll Gardens | 329 Smith St. (bet. Carroll & President Sts.) | Brooklyn | 718-422-0444 | www.seersuckerbrooklyn.com

Lovers of Southern classics like chicken 'n' dumplings and pimento cheese have a new go-to in this midpriced Smith Street arrival bringing contemporary polish to the genre and emphasizing local ingredients; the narrow dining room is separated from the kitchen by a wall of jarred housemade pickles, a homey touch in an otherwise clean-lined space.

Sel de Mer ✪ Mediterranean/Seafood

▽ 24 | 18 | 20 | $34

Williamsburg | 374 Graham Ave. (bet. Conselyea St. & Skillman Ave.) | Brooklyn | 718-387-4181

A "clever" approach to seafood – think mussels Roquefort and fish-cake sliders – informs the "fantastic" Mediterranean offerings at this young salt in Williamsburg, which appeases landlubbers with steaks and burgers; pricing is as modest as the room's pressed-tin wainscoting and brown-paper tablecloths.

Sentosa ✪⇕ Malaysian

▽ 23 | 14 | 17 | $24

Flushing | 3907 Prince St. (39th Ave.) | Queens | 718-886-6331

"Excellent", "spicy" curries and other "value"-priced Malaysian "home-cooking" classics are the draw at this casual Flushing find; pleasant wood-lined quarters and "warm" service complete the picture; P.S. in summer, "go for the shaved ice desserts."

Seo Japanese

▽ 21 | 17 | 20 | $51

E 40s | 249 E. 49th St. (bet. 2nd & 3rd Aves.) | 212-355-7722

"Udon and soba at its best" are the highlights at this "reliable" noodle-and-sushi joint near the U.N. that "transports" eaters to "Japan"; maybe its "so-fresh" fare "isn't cheap" and its digs tilt "claustrophobic", but to devotees it's "well worth" the outlay and the squeeze.

	FOOD	DECOR	SERVICE	COST

Serafina ● *Italian* | 19 | 16 | 17 | $42

E 50s | 38 E. 58th St. (bet. Madison & Park Aves.) | 212-832-8888 Ⓢ
E 60s | 29 E. 61st St. (bet. Madison & Park Aves.) | 212-702-9898
E 70s | 1022 Madison Ave., 2nd fl. (79th St.) | 212-734-2676
W 40s | Time Hotel | 224 W. 49th St. (bet. B'way & 8th Ave.) | 212-247-1000
W 50s | Dream Hotel | 210 W. 55th St. (B'way) | 212-315-1700
www.serafinarestaurant.com

These "casual Italians" are "crowd-pleasers" – hence "there's always a crowd" for their pizzas and other "decent" "basics" in "lively", "loud" environs; "could-be-better" service is part of the "Euro-chic" package.

Serendipity 3 ● *Dessert* | 19 | 20 | 15 | $30

E 60s | 225 E. 60th St. (bet. 2nd & 3rd Aves.) | 212-838-3531 |
www.serendipity3.com

"Throngs of children" and "tourists" "pack" this "legendary" East Side dessert parlor/gift shop for "sinful", "high-priced" sundaes and famous "frozen hot chocolate"; "patience is a must" to handle "out-the-door lines" and – once you "wedge yourself in" – "spotty" service.

Serge *French* | ▽ 20 | 17 | 21 | $45

Murray Hill | 165 Madison Ave. (bet. 32nd & 33rd Sts.) | 212-679-8077 |
www.brasseriecafecreme.com

Those who know this "tiny", "homey" Murray Hill French brasserie call it an "inviting" "hideaway" whose "simple menu" of "solid" classics sports equitable prices; a chef-owner who "sings along" with the "French standards playing" heightens the all-around "good vibe."

Sette *Italian* | 20 | 18 | 19 | $35

Park Slope | 207 Seventh Ave. (3rd St.) | Brooklyn | 718-499-7767 |
www.setteparkslope.com

"Dependable" thin-crust pizzas and pastas served in "pleasant", "low-key" environs ensure that this Park Slope Southern Italian remains a "local standby"; the "can't-be-beat" $12 weekend brunch and "terrific outdoor space" are added attractions.

Sette Mezzo ⊘ *Italian* | 22 | 16 | 21 | $74

E 70s | 969 Lexington Ave. (bet. 70th & 71st Sts.) | 212-472-0400

"Jockeying for table position" is the pastime at this "solid" UES Italian, where dining among the "neo-rich" feels like being "admitted" into an "expensive" club (it's "cash-only" for non-regulars); the space recently underwent a "deft face-lift" – not unlike many of its "clients' faces" – while service remains "as sweet as ever."

718 *French* | 22 | 19 | 19 | $39

Astoria | 35-01 Ditmars Blvd. (35th St.) | Queens | 718-204-5553 |
www.718restaurant.com

It's "worth leaving 212" to check out this "unexpectedly hip" Astoria "gem" for "well-executed", Spanish-accented French food ferried by a "helpful" crew that "never rushes you"; while "kind of pricey" for Queens, it's "great for brunch" and a bona fide "neighborhood favorite."

Sevilla ● *Spanish* | 22 | 14 | 20 | $42

W Village | 62 Charles St. (W. 4th St.) | 212-929-3189 |
www.sevillarestaurantandbar.com

A "garlic heaven" since way back, this West Village Spaniard has "changed little" in 70 years, and "that's a good thing"; from the "well-priced" sangria, paella and other Iberian "favorites" to the "throwback" decor and "seasoned" staffers, it's a "beloved" "institution" – "go early" or "wait."

Sezz Medi' *Mediterranean/Pizza*　　20 | 15 | 15 | $36

W 100s | 1260 Amsterdam Ave. (122nd St.) | 212-932-2901 | www.sezzmedi.com

Wood-fired brick-oven pizza is the "best bet" at this simple and "unpretentious" Morningside Heights Mediterranean, a "neighborhood" highlight that's often "jammed" with Columbia "students and faculty"; "indifferent service" aside, it's a "good buy."

Sfoglia *Italian*　　23 | 19 | 21 | $62

E 90s | 1402 Lexington Ave. (92nd St.) | 212-831-1402 | www.sfogliarestaurant.com

"Excellent homestyle" Northern Italian cuisine has made this Carnegie Hill "favorite" near the 92nd Street Y "insanely difficult to get into"; if you do score a rez, expect "dedicated" service and a check that seems "pricey" this far Uptown.

Shabu-Shabu 70 *Japanese*　　22 | 15 | 21 | $35

E 70s | 314 E. 70th St. (bet. 1st & 2nd Aves.) | 212-861-5635

This "little slice of Tokyo" on the UES has earned a "loyal following" for its well-priced shabu-shabu ("cook-your-own" meat-and-vegetable "hot pots") and sushi; "polite" staffers who greet you "like long lost friends" add warmth to decor that's getting a bit "tired and bleak."

Shabu-Tatsu *Japanese*　　∇ 20 | 12 | 18 | $35

E Village | 216 E. 10th St. (bet. 1st & 2nd Aves.) | 212-477-2972 | www.tic-nyc.com

For "fun DIY" Japanese, hit this East Village shabu-shabu/sukiyaki specialist where "NYU students" and others simmer "delectably thin slices" of meat and veggies in tableside "hot pots"; "amiable" service and affordable tabs are other reasons "there's always a wait."

Shake Shack *Burgers*　　23 | 11 | 14 | $16

NEW **E 80s** | 154 E. 86th St. (bet. Lexington & 3rd Aves.) | 646-237-5035
Flatiron | Madison Square Park | 23rd St. (Madison Ave.) | 212-889-6600
NEW **W 40s** | InterContinental NY Times Sq. | 300 W. 44th St. (8th Ave.) | 646-435-1035 ●
W 70s | 366 Columbus Ave. (77th St.) | 646-747-8770
Flushing | Citi Field | 126th St. & Roosevelt Ave. (behind the scoreboard) | Queens
www.shakeshack.com

"Unforgettable burger perfection" and "close-to-heaven" frozen custards draw "amusement park lines" to these proliferating "high-end fast-food" joints and are "worth every extra minute on the treadmill"; though they're "part of the Danny Meyer empire", prices are "far from shakedown", so go ahead and "queue up" – and "have fun finding a seat."

Shalezeh ● *Persian*　　∇ 21 | 18 | 21 | $42
(fka Shalizar)

E 80s | 1420 Third Ave. (bet. 80th & 81st Sts.) | 212-288-0012 | www.shalezeh.com

This "sister to Persepolis" is rated a "sophisticated" UES "find" for Persian cuisine "done right", including especially "marvelous" rice dishes; locals call it a "pleasant change of pace", with "calm", "modern" digs, "friendly" service and "fair prices" ensuring their endorsement.

Shang ☒Ⓜ *Chinese*

	FOOD	DECOR	SERVICE	COST
	21	23	20	$59

LES | Thompson LES Hotel | 187 Orchard St. (bet. Houston & Stanton Sts.) | 212-260-7900 | www.shangrestaurant.com

"Dang" – the "high-end" Chinese cuisine "sings" at Susur Lee's LES "standout", as does its "striking", "sexy" space; but those who find the vibe "surprisingly sedate" wonder "why isn't this place more popular?"; P.S. to avoid climbing the "steep stairs", "enter through the hotel on Allen Street."

Shanghai Café ⊘ *Chinese*

	FOOD	DECOR	SERVICE	COST
	21	8	11	$18

Little Italy | 100 Mott St. (bet. Canal & Hester Sts.) | 212-966-3988

"Exceptional" – and "exceptionally cheap" – soup dumplings are the lure at this "frenzied", "quick-fix", cash-only Little Italy Chinese; the "lightning-fast" servers "can't wait to get you out", and given the "ambiance-free" setting, that may well be what you want.

Shanghai Cuisine ⊘ *Chinese*

	FOOD	DECOR	SERVICE	COST
	▽ 22	10	14	$25

Chinatown | 89 Bayard St. (Mulberry St.) | 212-732-8988

"Delicious, delicate" Shanghai-style soup dumplings and other "authentic" goodies make this Chinatown joint "very popular", especially with the "jury duty" crowd; prices are "great", but the same can't be said of the cash-only policy, vintage-movie-poster-plastered decor and functional service.

Shanghai Pavilion *Chinese*

	FOOD	DECOR	SERVICE	COST
	21	16	18	$38

E 70s | 1378 Third Ave. (bet. 78th & 79th Sts.) | 212-585-3388 | www.shanghaipavilionnyc.com

A solid "neighborhood favorite", this "upscale" UES Shanghainese offers "well-prepared" fare that leaves locals marveling "who would've thought that Chinese outside of C-town could be so good?"; a "pleasant" vibe and "reasonable" rates seal the deal.

Sheep Station ⊘ *Pub Food*

	FOOD	DECOR	SERVICE	COST
	▽ 18	17	21	$26

Park Slope | 149 Fourth Ave. (Douglass St.) | Brooklyn | 718-857-4337 | www.sheepstation.net

One of Park Slope's "friendliest places" is this "relaxed" Aussie dispensing solid, fair-priced "pub food" and "excellent" Down Under suds in tastefully rough-hewn digs with a "fireplace in back"; no wonder it's a locals' favorite "for a beer and a soccer match."

Shelly's Trattoria ◐ *Italian*

	FOOD	DECOR	SERVICE	COST
	20	18	21	$55

W 50s | 41 W. 57th St. (bet. 5th & 6th Aves.) | 212-245-2422 | www.shellysnewyork.com

Shelly Fireman's Midtown Italian near Carnegie Hall gets good notices for its seafood-centric menu, staffers who "treat you like you're in their home" and Milan-inspired triplex digs; in sum, it's the perfect "overture to your concert" – if you can afford to buy a ticket afterwards.

Shorty's ◐ *Cheesesteaks*

	FOOD	DECOR	SERVICE	COST
	▽ 24	11	19	$17

W 40s | 576 Ninth Ave. (bet. 41st & 42nd Sts.) | 212-967-3055 | www.shortysnyc.com

The City of Brotherly Love "comes to NYC" via this "upbeat" – as in "loud" – Midtown "sports bar" notable for its "authentic" "Philly-style" cheesesteaks ("without the two-hour drive!") and "huge selection" of "specialty beers"; "don't even try to get a table during Eagles games."

Shorty's.32 _American_
21 | 17 | 21 | $51

SoHo | 199 Prince St. (bet. MacDougal & Sullivan Sts.) | 212-375-8275 | www.shortys32.com

Fans find "nothing short about the food quality" at Josh Eden's "upscale" American comfort fooder, a "quirky" 32-seat "shoebox" in the "heart of SoHo"; "fun, interactive" staffers, an "interesting crowd" and a "come-back-soon" vibe have most declaring it "delightful."

☑ SHO Shaun Hergatt ☒ _French_
26 | 27 | 26 | $91

Financial District | 40 Broad St., 2nd fl. (Exchange Pl.) | 212-809-3993 | www.shoshaunhergatt.com

"There aren't enough oohs and aahs" to describe the "top-shelf-all-the-way" experience at Shaun Hergatt's "glamorously modern" Financial District stunner, where the "seriously inventive and skilled" Asian-inflected French cuisine takes "taste buds to nirvana" and the kitchen provides a "show" via its glass wall; naturally it's "expensive" (prix fixe-only dinner starts at $69), but non "overpaid bankers" can eat à la carte at lunch, or dine in the Pearl Room bar.

Shula's
Steak House _Steak_
20 | 18 | 19 | $67

W 40s | Westin Times Sq. Hotel | 270 W. 43rd St. (bet. B'way & 8th Ave.) | 212-201-2776 | www.westinny.com

Perhaps best appreciated by "football buffs", this Times Square link of coach Don Shula's namesake steakhouse chain gets points for its "decent" beef and "memorabilia"-packed setting; however, some on the sidelines cite "high prices" and "nothing-special" output, concluding "they've dropped the pass here."

Shun Lee Cafe ◑ _Chinese_
21 | 17 | 19 | $43

W 60s | 43 W. 65th St. (bet. Columbus Ave. & CPW) | 212-769-3888 | www.shunleewest.com

Carts "loaded" with dim sum "meander from table to table" at this "hectic" Lincoln Center–area Chinese that's "more fun" and "less pricey" than its "big sister next door"; hazards are "checkerboard" decor and "calories and cost" that can "sneak up on you."

☑ Shun Lee Palace ◑ _Chinese_
24 | 21 | 23 | $57

E 50s | 155 E. 55th St. (bet. Lexington & 3rd Aves.) | 212-371-8844 | www.shunleepalace.com

New York's "original gourmet Chinese", Michael Tong's East Midtown "benchmark" (now in its fourth decade) can still be "counted on" for "excellent" repasts ferried by "uniformed" staffers in "elegant", old-fashioned environs; yes, it "comes at a price", but it's a "quantum leap" above the norm.

Shun Lee West ◑ _Chinese_
22 | 20 | 21 | $55

W 60s | 43 W. 65th St. (bet. Columbus Ave. & CPW) | 212-595-8895 | www.shunleewest.com

The "haute" Chinese fare at this Lincoln Center–area "warhorse" is in "another league" from "the usual", distinguished by "palate-pleasing" dishes, "quick", "elegant" service and "wonderful" (if slightly "faded") "dragon"-centric decor, all of which help "justify the cost."

	FOOD	DECOR	SERVICE	COST

Siam Inn ● *Asian* | 21 | 15 | 18 | $37 |

W 50s | 251 W. 51st St. (bet. B'way & 8th Ave.) | 212-246-3330 | www.bluechilinewyork.com

"Hopping" and "noisy", this handy Theater District Thai (fka bluechili) gets applause for "flavorful dishes" at "low"-for-the-area prices and "phenomenal" cocktails; depending on your perspective, the "ever-changing" "neon background lighting" is either "cool" or something "to put up with."

Siam Square Ⓜ *Thai* | ▽ 23 | 17 | 21 | $31 |

Bronx | 564 Kappock St. (Henry Hudson Pkwy.) | 718-432-8200 | www.siamsq.com

"One of the hidden gems" in Riverdale, this Thai "sleeper" can be counted on for "creative" fare at low prices supplied by agreeable staffers; the setting may be "unexciting", but the kitchen provides ample zing – "when they say spicy, they're not kidding."

Sinigual *Mexican* | 21 | 21 | 20 | $40 |

E 40s | 640 Third Ave. (41st St.) | 212-286-0250 | www.sinigualrestaurants.com

This "friendly", "fancified" Mexican near Grand Central "hits all the right mariachi notes" with "upscale" eats and killer cocktails at modest cost; it's not the place for "quiet conversation", but to those in search of a "fun", "bustling" scene, it "rocks."

Sip Sak *Turkish* | 20 | 14 | 16 | $36 |

E 40s | 928 Second Ave. (bet. 49th & 50th Sts.) | 212-583-1900 | www.sip-sak.com

The "winning combo" of "fresh" Turkish fare and "inexpensive" tabs makes this U.N.-area eatery a "favorite" "go-to"; a "recent refurbishing" has given the space a "needed lift", but insiders say you still have to "get past" the sometimes "abrasive" owner.

Ⓩ Sistina *Italian* | 26 | 19 | 23 | $77 |

E 80s | 1555 Second Ave. (bet. 80th & 81st Sts.) | 212-861-7660

"Sublime" Northern Italian cuisine, an "outstanding" wine cellar and a host who pays "special attention to regulars" has "insiders" wishing to keep this "intimate" UES gem a "secret" (too late!); its crowd of "celebs" and Park Avenue types doesn't blink at the "eye-popping" prices.

67 Burger *Burgers* | 21 | 13 | 16 | $18 |

Fort Greene | 67 Lafayette Ave. (Fulton St.) | Brooklyn | 718-797-7150 | www.67burger.com

"Drippy burgers" customized with "inventive toppings" for a "reasonable price" explain why this Fort Greene venue is such a "popular" draw despite the "stark decor" and cafeteria-style ordering; it's a "viable" option for a "quick pre-BAM" bite and a beer.

S'MAC *American* | 21 | 11 | 15 | $16 |

E Village | 345 E. 12th St. (bet. 1st & 2nd Aves.) | 212-358-7912 | www.smacnyc.com

"Very cheesy", this East Village "niche" restaurant is "devoted" to "gooey and delicious" mac 'n' cheese, offered in "create-your-own" renditions and served in "hot skillets" for little dough; it's a "guilty pleasure" despite "apathetic service" and "no-decor" digs.

Smith, The ⏺ *Pub Food* — 19 | 16 | 17 | $33

E Village | 55 Third Ave. (bet. 10th & 11th Sts.) | 212-420-9800 |
www.thesmithnyc.com

"Trendy" pub food "in its best form" steers "scenesters" to this "popular", "affordable" East Village New American that's "massive" and "always fun"; "loud doesn't begin to describe" the decibel levels, but its "young" "late-night" crowd couldn't care less.

☒ Smith & Wollensky *Steak* — 24 | 19 | 21 | $73

E 40s | 797 Third Ave. (49th St.) | 212-753-1530 |
www.smithandwollensky.com

One part "steak lovers' landmark", one part "man cave", this "classic" Midtown beef "emporium" delivers "top-notch" "slabs" and "big-fisted cocktails" to a "parade of suits"; "seasoned" waiters "love to be part of the act", which includes packing a "megaphone" to speak over the din and accepting the "corporate cards" at the end.

Smoke Joint *BBQ* — 22 | 11 | 16 | $24

Fort Greene | 87 S. Elliott Pl. (Lafayette Ave.) | Brooklyn | 718-797-1011 |
www.thesmokejoint.com

"Addictive", low-budget BBQ beckons "locals" and the "BAM crowd" to this "hip", "no-frills" shack in Fort Greene, where you can smell the "smokin'" vittles a "block away"; get there "early" to "pig out on pig" and beat the "thundering hordes."

Smorgas Chef *Scandinavian* — 19 | 16 | 18 | $36

Financial District | 53 Stone St. (William St.) | 212-422-3500
Murray Hill | Scandinavia Hse. | 58 Park Ave. (bet. 37th & 38th Sts.) |
212-847-9745
W Village | 283 W. 12th St. (4th St.) | 212-243-7073 ⏺
www.smorgas.com

"Love-'em meatballs" and other "satisfying Scandinavian specialties" highlight this trio offering "much more" than the "Ikea" menu, delivered by a staff that's "friendly but slow"; it's a "good fallback" when you crave an affordable "trip" to "Stockholm."

Snack *Greek* — 22 | 13 | 18 | $30

SoHo | 105 Thompson St. (bet. Prince & Spring Sts.) | 212-925-1040

As "small in size" as it is "big in flavor", this SoHo Greek makes up for its "matchbox" dimensions with "fresh", "low-priced" food; just "bring a snack" to tide you over as you "wait outside to get in."

Snack Taverna *Greek* — 22 | 17 | 20 | $43

W Village | 63 Bedford St. (Morton St.) | 212-929-3499

Snack's "more upscale", roomier (but still "crowded") West Village offshoot offers "delectable", "full-flavored" Greek cuisine prepared with a "contemporary twist"; a "cozy" corner setting, "hospitable" service and "fair prices" have neighbors calling it "lovely" all around.

sNice *Sandwiches* — 20 | 13 | 18 | $16

NEW **SoHo** | 150 Sullivan St. (bet. Houston & Prince Sts.) | 212-253-5405
W Village | 45 Eighth Ave. (bet. Horatio & Jane Sts.) | 212-645-0310
Park Slope | 315 Fifth Ave. (bet. 2nd & 3rd Sts.) | Brooklyn | 718-788-2121 ⊘

Sure, a "tempeh Reuben" "may sound funny", but these "friendly" "hangouts" proffer vegetarian sandwiches and salads so "tasty" even a "carnivore can love" 'em; a crowd heavy on "crunchy types working on their novels" collects in the "sunny", "laid-back" spaces.

SobaKoh *Noodle Shop*
▽ 24 | 16 | 20 | $37

E Village | 309 E. Fifth St. (bet. 1st & 2nd Aves.) | 212-254-2244

A "mesmerizing" "noodle-making station in the front" of this "serene", still largely "undiscovered" East Village Japanese hints at the house specialty: "exceptionally delicious" buckwheat soba, made fresh daily; "attentive" service and "jazz" in the background seal the deal.

Soba Nippon *Noodle Shop*
23 | 16 | 21 | $43

W 50s | 19 W. 52nd St. (bet. 5th & 6th Aves.) | 212-489-2525 | www.sobanippon.com

"You can taste the quality" at this "peaceful" Midtown Japanese that specializes in "incredibly fresh" soba noodles "made from buckwheat from their own farm"; "professional and pleasant" waiters are another reason it's "worth a premium" price.

Soba Totto ✪ *Noodle Shop*
21 | 18 | 19 | $48

E 40s | 211 E. 43rd St. (bet. 2nd & 3rd Aves.) | 212-557-8200 | www.sobatotto.com

"Yummy" yakitori and "delicious soba" are the twin attractions at this "courteous" Grand Central–area Japanese that's "not quite Tokyo, but close"; just be sure you've got enough yen to cover the "elevated" check.

Soba-ya *Noodle Shop*
24 | 17 | 20 | $31

E Village | 229 E. Ninth St. (bet. 2nd & 3rd Aves.) | 212-533-6966 | www.sobaya-nyc.com

"Slurping noodle soup is an unforgettable experience" at this "civilized" East Village Japanese that's well loved for its "fresh, amazing" soba and udon, as well as prices that'll have your "wallet thanking you"; the catch is "insane" lines at "peak times."

Socarrat Paella Bar *Spanish*
24 | 16 | 20 | $46

Chelsea | 259 W. 19th St. (bet. 7th & 8th Aves.) | 212-462-1000 | www.socarratpaellabar.com

This "hip", "convivial" "sliver of Spain in Chelsea" specializes in "mind-blowing" paella and tapas, proffered by an "attentive" team; the "skinny" "communal" space gets "crowded", but it's an overall "pleasant experience" with the "adjoining wine bar" offsetting long "waits."

Sofrito ✪ *Puerto Rican*
22 | 20 | 19 | $43

E 50s | 400 E. 57th St. (bet. 1st Ave. & Sutton Pl.) | 212-754-5999 | www.sofritony.com

The "humongous portions" of midpriced Puerto Rican eats are nearly upstaged by the "booming scene" at this Sutton Place "celebration spot"; expect plenty of *cumpleaños feliz* parties and "Page Six" types – and plan to "pass notes to carry on a conversation."

Sojourn ✪ *Eclectic*
22 | 21 | 21 | $45

E 70s | 244 E. 79th St. (bet. 2nd & 3rd Aves.) | 212-537-7745 | www.sojournrestaurant.com

A "surprising delight", this "lively" Upper East Side Eclectic has built a following for its "inspired" small plates, "solid" wine list and "cheerful" service; its "young crowd" may make you think you've gone "downtown", but the "checks are very much UES."

Solera *Spanish*   21 | 18 | 22 | $57

E 50s | 216 E. 53rd St. (bet. 2nd & 3rd Aves.) | 212-644-1166 |
www.soleranyc.com

"Wonderful tapas" stand out at this "pleasant" East Midtowner offering a "traditional Spanish experience" including a "fine" Iberian wine
selection and "truly pleasing", "detail"-oriented service; amigos only
wish the tabs were a little less.

Solo *Mediterranean*   ▽ 26 | 24 | 24 | $79

E 50s | 550 Madison Ave. (bet. 55th & 56th Sts.) | 212-833-7800 |
www.solonyc.com

It's the "be-all, end-all" of "gourmet" glatt kosher restaurants according to devotees of this "trendy" Midtown Mediterranean that's "tops
in every way", from the "upscale" offerings to the "very pricey" check;
"friendly" staffers keep the "bustling" "scene" copacetic.

Son Cubano *Cuban*   21 | 21 | 19 | $49

Meatpacking | 405 W. 14th St. (bet. 9th Ave. & Washington St.) |
212-366-1640 | www.soncubanonyc.com

"Hot, hot, hot! - and that's "just the clientele" at this "hopping"
"Havana-style" Meatpacking Cuban featuring "rich, satisfying" island
classics; "live music" "makes talking impossible" but the mojito-
fueled "fun never stops."

Song ✍ *Thai*   23 | 15 | 17 | $22

Park Slope | 295 Fifth Ave. (bet. 1st & 2nd Sts.) | Brooklyn |
718-965-1108

"One of the best deals in Park Slope", this Fifth Avenue Thai ("Joya's
next of kin") offers "huge, delicious portions" at "wildly inexpensive"
rates; part of the bargain is "loud" DJ-spun tunes and a "fun, raucous"
vibe – for a "quieter experience", "go early" or try the back garden.

Sookk *Thai*   21 | 18 | 19 | $27

W 100s | 2686 Broadway (bet. 102nd & 103rd Sts.) | 212-870-0253 |
www.sookkrestaurant.com

It's "high time" the UWS got a contemporary Thai, and this "favorite"
offers "novel dishes" inspired by Bangkok "street food", made with
"fresh ingredients"; "friendly" service, "small"-but-"attractive" digs
and modest rates are more reasons it's a "wonderful find."

Sorella ●Ⓜ *Italian*   ▽ 24 | 20 | 19 | $49

LES | 95 Allen St. (bet. Broome & Delancey Sts.) | 212-274-9595 |
www.sorellanyc.com

"Delightful", "varied" small plates come with "quite good" Italian
wines at this "elegant" LES Italian; the "educated" staff and spare,
"well-designed" space create a "welcoming vibe", so the only question
is whether this "little gem" will stay "pleasantly uncrowded."

Sosa Borella ● *Argentinean/Italian*   19 | 15 | 19 | $44

W 50s | 832 Eighth Ave. (50th St.) | 212-262-7774 |
www.sosaborella.com

An "Italian-Argentinean mix" that cooks "just right" and is offered at
"fair prices" keeps this "dependable" Hell's Kitchen duplex packed
with a "fun, local crowd"; it's a "favorite" "pre-theater player", with an
"elegant" outdoor deck that brings down the house.

	FOOD	DECOR	SERVICE	COST

Soto ●🍵🈂 *Japanese* — 27 | 19 | 19 | $86

W Village | 357 Sixth Ave. (bet. 4th St. & Washington Pl.) | 212-414-3088
"True sushi lovers unite" in their praise of Sotohiro Kosugi's "out-of-this-world" West Village Japanese, where "sublime" raw fish and "innovative" hot appetizers "reign supreme"; the "amazing" experience leaves diners in "an oasis of calm" – at least until the bill comes.

South Fin Grill *Seafood/Steak* — 19 | 23 | 16 | $50

Staten Island | 300 Father Capodanno Blvd. (Sand Ln.) | 718-447-7679 | www.southfingrill.com
"Surf's up" at this "solid" Staten Island steak-and-seafooder sporting "gorgeous" boardwalk views of the ocean and Verrazano Bridge; service is merely "adequate", but the staff "doesn't rush you", and really it's all about the "terrific location" and ambiance recalling "South Beach's glory days."

South Gate *American* — 24 | 25 | 23 | $71

W 50s | Jumeirah Essex Hse. | 154 Central Park S. (bet. 6th & 7th Aves.) | 212-484-5120 | www.154southgate.com
Kerry Heffernan's "sophisticated" cooking lives up to the "beautiful, modern" surroundings at this "surprisingly under-the-radar" Central Park South New American; its "delightful" food, "glam" setting and "impeccable" service – not to mention "high prices" – sweep surveyors "off their feet."

🆕 South Houston ● *Southern* — - | - | - | M

SoHo | 331 W. Broadway (Grand St.) | 212-431-0131 | www.southhoustonnyc.com
Bringing some Southern comfort to SoHo's Restaurant Row, this new arrival dishes out Dixie specialties like buttermilk fried chicken, washed down with unusual tap brews; lots of windows give the stripped-down digs an airy feel, while a wall-length chalkboard acts as a canvas for aspiring artists.

🅩 Sparks Steak House 🈂 *Steak* — 25 | 19 | 23 | $81

E 40s | 210 E. 46th St. (bet. 2nd & 3rd Aves.) | 212-687-4855 | www.sparkssteakhouse.com
This "venerable" Midtown "slab shop" keeps "devoted" carnivores "in heaven" with "buttery" chops, "excellent" sides and "unbeatable" wines; the "attitudinal" "men's club" service isn't "for the faint of heart" or the frugal, but to connoisseurs it's a "winning experience" that's hard to top.

Spice *Thai* — 20 | 15 | 17 | $26

Chelsea | 199 Eighth Ave. (bet. 19th & 20th Sts.) | 212-989-1116
🆕 **Chelsea** | 236 Eighth Ave. (22nd St.) | 212-620-4585
E 70s | 1411 Second Ave. (bet. 73rd & 74th Sts.) | 212-988-5348
E Village | 104 Second Ave. (6th St.) | 212-533-8900
E Village | 77 E. 10th St. (4th Ave.) | 212-388-9006
G Village | 39 E. 13th St. (bet. B'way & University Pl.) | 212-982-3758
www.spicethainyc.com
With six locations and counting, this "affordable" local chain doles out "generous portions" of Thai "basics" to "students", "budget"-watchers and seekers of a "quick meal"; the decor is "spare" and service can be "rushed", but then there's always "takeout or delivery."

| | FOOD | DECOR | SERVICE | COST |

⊠ Spice Market ● *Asian* | 23 | 27 | 21 | $61 |

Meatpacking | 403 W. 13th St. (9th Ave.) | 212-675-2322 |
www.jean-georges.com

A "must if you are visiting and a staple if you live here", Jean-Georges Vongerichten's "phenomenal" Meatpacking "homage" to "Southeast Asian street food" is a duplex "stunner" done up in "transporting", "movie set"-worthy "exotica"; "fab" family-style plates and "potent" cocktails ferried by an "impressive" staff make it a "wonderful" place for a "special occasion" – especially in the "private nooks" downstairs.

Spicy & Tasty ⊟ *Chinese* | 23 | 9 | 12 | $25 |

Flushing | 39-07 Prince St. (39th Ave.) | Queens | 718-359-1601

If you "can take the heat" head for this "terrific" Flushing Chinese that "lives up to its name" with "exciting", "hot" Sichuan dishes; you'll find "no celebs, no bar scene, no decor" and a staff with "limited English" – but that's fine for a "taste adventure" at very "doable" prices.

Spiga *Italian* | 23 | 18 | 21 | $49 |

W 80s | 200 W. 84th St. (bet. Amsterdam Ave. & B'way) | 212-362-5500 |
www.spiganyc.com

"Perfect" for "date night", this UWS Italian is beloved for its "heart-warming" yet "refined" fare delivered by a "polished" staff; it's true this "neighborhood hangout" is "not fancy", but most are happy to "leave the big names behind" and go.

Spigolo *Italian* | 25 | 16 | 21 | $62 |

E 80s | 1561 Second Ave. (81st St.) | 212-744-1100

It's amazing that such "outstanding food" comes out of "such a small kitchen" at Scott and Heather Fratangelo's UES Italian "jewel"; it's "not cheap" and usually "hard to get into" (easier when "outdoor seating" is open), but the "culinary achievements" and "knowledgeable" service are "worth the effort."

Spitzer's Corner ● *American* | 20 | 18 | 17 | $29 |

LES | 101 Rivington St. (Ludlow St.) | 212-228-0027 |
www.spitzerscorner.com

This "casual" LES gastropub's affordable "comfort" fare is plenty "tasty", but its "exotic specialty brews" steal the show; on weekends, "rowdy" crowds (think "grown-up frat" boys) pack into the "communal tables", overlooking iffy service and "dim" digs.

NEW Spot *Dessert* | ∇ 23 | 20 | 22 | $17 |

E Village | 13 St. Marks Pl. (bet. 2nd & 3rd Aves.) | 212-677-5670 |
www.spotdessertbar.com

Though "easy to miss", this East Village dessert bar is hailed by hipster sweet tooths for its "creative" blend of American and Asian ingredients orchestrated by maestro Pichet Ong; serving as a "welcome alternative" to the ubiquitous cupcake, its puddings, cookies and ice cream come in "inventive flavors."

Spotted Pig ● *European* | 23 | 19 | 18 | $48 |

W Village | 314 W. 11th St. (Greenwich St.) | 212-620-0393 |
www.thespottedpig.com

You can count on "spotting a celeb" – as well as a "killer wait" – at this West Village "experience" where April Bloomfield's "fantastic" Modern

Euro "pub grub" ("oh, that gnudi") inspires "A-list" "pig-outs"; it's a "scene" "on steroids", presided over by a "smiling" but "weary" staff – thankfully it's "relaxing" at lunch.

S.P.Q.R. *Italian*　　　　　　　　　20 | 20 | 20 | $51

Little Italy | 133 Mulberry St. (bet. Grand & Hester Sts.) |
212-925-3120

Pasta-loving peeps give this wood-paneled Little Italy vet kudos for its "surprisingly good" Southern Italian classics served by "charming" waiters; it's "roomier" and more "elegant" than "most" on Mulberry, a plus for "large parties", so never mind if the prices "have gone up."

Spunto *Pizza*　　　　　　　▽ 21 | 13 | 17 | $23

W Village | 65 Carmine St. (7th Ave. S.) | 212-242-1200 |
www.spuntothincrust.com

A Gruppo/Posto/Vezzo sibling, this Village "pizza joint" "stands out" from the crowd with "fantastic" pies boasting "delicious sauce" and "cracker-thin crust"; the service and brick-lined decor "aren't anything to write home about", but the lunch-special "steals" are.

Square Meal *American*　　　　　　24 | 17 | 22 | $51

E 90s | 30 E. 92nd St. (bet. 5th & Madison Aves.) | 212-860-9872 |
www.squaremealnyc.com

Proof that it's hip to be square, this "aptly named", BYO-friendly Carnegie Hill American supplies "outstanding, imaginative meals" based on "whatever's in season"; a "caring staff" and "cheerful room" where "grown-ups" can talk are two more reasons this "gem" – "square-cut, of course" – sparkles.

⊠ Sripraphai *✑ Thai*　　　　　　26 | 13 | 16 | $27

Woodside | 64-13 39th Ave. (bet. 64th & 65th Sts.) | Queens |
718-899-9999 | www.sripraphairestaurant.com

"No gimmicks", just "Thai-no-mite" cooking is the deal at this "cheap", cash-only Woodside "hot spot", where the "authentic", "divine" flavors are "unwavering" – and once again rated top-in-the-genre in NYC; it may be "the best reason to discover the 7 train", but "go early" or plan to "take a number and wait."

Stage Deli ◑ *Deli*　　　　　　20 | 10 | 14 | $30

W 50s | 834 Seventh Ave. (bet. 53rd & 54th Sts.) | 212-245-7850 |
www.stagedeli.com

Maybe this Midtown "landmark" is "not as famous as the Carnegie Deli", but "fressers" tout its sandwiches "on steroids" and other "old-fashioned Jewish" specialties as a "special treat"; tourist "masses" seeking a "quintessential NYC" experience find the decor and "gruff" staff not unlike the eats: "seasoned, sassy and salty."

Stamatis ◑ *Greek*　　　　　　21 | 12 | 17 | $34

Astoria | 29-09 23rd Ave. (bet. 29th & 31st Sts.) | Queens |
718-932-8596

Seemingly "everyone speaks Greek" at this "down-to-earth" Astoria taverna, where diners "can see the chefs hard at work" cooking "fresh, delicious", "like-in-Athens" staples; the "updated" decor is now a bit "brighter", but it's still the "solid", "well-priced" dishes that elicit "*opas!*" here.

Stand *Burgers* | 19 | 14 | 15 | $24 |

G Village | 24 E. 12th St. (bet. 5th Ave. & University Pl.) | 212-488-5900 | www.standburger.com

Though this "trendy" Villager serves a "supreme" burger, it's the "divine" shakes – "alcoholic" as well as "imaginative" unspiked flavors like "toasted marshmallow" – that win it a standing ovation; "affordable" bites "without the wait" balance out "blah service" and "loud music."

☑ Standard Grill *American* | 21 | 22 | 19 | $56 |

Meatpacking | Standard Hotel | 848 Washington St. (bet. Little W. 12th & 13th Sts.) | 212-645-4100 | www.thestandardgrill.com

"Anything but standard", this "much-hyped" Meatpacking American "under the High Line" serves first-rate basics in a "scene" "extraordinaire" brimming with the "beautiful" and "famous"; whether in the sidewalk seats, the "noisy" cafe or "cool" main dining room, expect "commotion", as well as – once you "get by the beasts at the door" – "friendly" service from "plaid getup"–clad staffers; scoring a rez is a "hassle" for mere mortals, but "keep trying."

NEW St. Anselm *American* | - | - | - | M |

Williamsburg | 355 Metropolitan Ave. (Havemeyer St.) | Brooklyn | 718-384-5054

Fette Sau's Joe Carroll brings yet more meat to Williamsburg with this arrival offering "satisfying" fancy hot dogs (try the Newark Style), burgers, sausages and even a 'Nasty Bits' offal menu; the highlight of its minimalist space is the garden shared with neighbor Spuyten Duyvil.

Stanton Social *Eclectic* | 23 | 22 | 20 | $52 |

LES | 99 Stanton St. (bet. Ludlow & Orchard Sts.) | 212-995-0099 | www.thestantonsocial.com

"Awesome" "tapas-style" plates and "cool" "loungey" decor attract "hip" things to this "high-energy" LES Eclectic; those nibbles "add up", but "charming" service and "delicious drinks" help the tabs go down easier.

STK *Steak* | 23 | 24 | 20 | $74 |

Meatpacking | 26 Little W. 12th St. (bet. 9th Ave. & Washington St.) | 646-624-2444 | www.stkhouse.com

"Scenesters" gorge on "delish" slabs at this Meatpacking steakhouse, which forgoes the typical clubby decor for a "sleek" "lounge" look with "cool music"; some say it's "more sizzle" than substance, but the "glamour" satisfies most, "as long as the boss is paying."

Stone Park Café *American* | 25 | 20 | 22 | $49 |

Park Slope | 324 Fifth Ave. (3rd St.) | Brooklyn | 718-369-0082 | www.stoneparkcafe.com

"Classy but not stuffy", this "Manhattan-worthy" Park Sloper is "perfect for a special night out", thanks to its "lovely", "imaginative" New American cuisine and "knowledgeable" staff; its "pleasant" space gets "a little noisy", but "the price is right", and "brunch is a winner" too.

☑ Strip House *Steak* | 25 | 23 | 23 | $77 |

G Village | 13 E. 12th St. (bet. 5th Ave. & University Pl.) | 212-328-0000 | www.striphouse.com

"Truly memorable steaks" and sides come with a "cheeky" backdrop at the Glaziers' "bordello-inspired" Villager featuring "burlesque queen"

| | FOOD | DECOR | SERVICE | COST |

pinups and scarlet "flocked wallpaper"; maybe this "carnivore's delight" isn't "for your grandpa", but everyone else "looks good in the red light."

NEW Strong Place ● *American*
| | - | - | - | M |

Cobble Hill | 270 Court St. (bet. Butler & Douglass Sts.) | Brooklyn | 718-522-0913

Bustling from the get-go, this midpriced Cobble Hill arrival from the Bocca Lupo folks boasts a mighty brew list and wide-ranging American gastropub eats; exposed brick, warm wood and workman-style cage lights lend the space a faint industrial feel, yet a cozy vibe prevails.

Sueños M *Mexican*
| | 24 | 19 | 21 | $47 |

Chelsea | 311 W. 17th St. (bet. 8th & 9th Aves.) | 212-243-1333 | www.suenosnyc.com

At her "dreamy" Chelsea "gem", "talented" chef Sue Torres matches "bold flavors" with "phenomenal drinks", proving that "gourmet Mexican is not an oxymoron"; it's "pricier" than your local taqueria, but fans are "never disappointed" by the "ever-changing menu" and "attentive service."

Z Sugiyama ●ⓏM *Japanese*
| | 26 | 19 | 24 | $96 |

W 50s | 251 W. 55th St. (bet. B'way & 8th Ave.) | 212-956-0670 | www.sugiyama-nyc.com

"Stunning" kaiseki repasts rank up there with "Tokyo's best" at this Midtown Japanese, where "charming" chef-owner Nao Sugiyama "never steers you wrong" with his "seasonal" extravaganzas in which "each course is a joy unto itself"; it'll cost you (prix fixe–only options start at $51), and as for the "unimpressive" decor, that just "keeps it from being snooty."

Sunburnt Cow ● *Australian*
| | ▽ 18 | 15 | 18 | $24 |

E Village | 137 Ave. C (bet. 8th & 9th Sts.) | 212-529-0005
Sunburnt Calf ● *Australian*
NEW W 70s | 226 W. 79th St. (bet. Amsterdam Ave. & B'way) | 646-823-9255
www.thesunburntcow.com

For "divey Australian" "fun", revelers turn to this "lively, loud" East Villager and its UWS offshoot known for "two-hour" happy hours and "all-you-can-drink brunch"; an "efficient" staff presides over the "shenanigans", and oh, the low-cost "bar food" is "surprisingly good" too.

Superfine M *Mediterranean*
| | 20 | 20 | 18 | $32 |

Dumbo | 126 Front St. (bet. Jay & Pearl Sts.) | Brooklyn | 718-243-9005

A "happy, relaxed clientele" touts this "funky" Dumbo Mediterranean as much for its "cool Brooklyn vibe" and lively "bar scene" as for its "reasonably priced" "seasonal" eats; maybe service is on the "slow" side, but where else will you find a "pool table" and "rockin'" "blue-grass" brunch?

Supper ●≠ *Italian*
| | 24 | 19 | 19 | $39 |

E Village | 156 E. Second St. (bet. Aves. A & B) | 212-477-7600 | www.supperrestaurant.com

What with the "flavorful" pastas and "low prices", this "fantastic", "cash-only" East Village Italian is "always bustling", despite a "no-rez" policy that spells "long waits"; "rustic fare" this "delicious" is "hard to beat", so "go hungry", grab a "communal table" and "leave happy."

Menus, photos, voting and more – free at ZAGAT.com

	FOOD	DECOR	SERVICE	COST

Surya *Indian* — 22 | 17 | 21 | $38

W Village | 302 Bleecker St. (bet. Grove St. & 7th Ave. S.) | 212-807-7770 | www.suryany.com

"High-quality" Indian fare and "friendly" service have made this somewhat "upscale" yet modestly priced Villager a local "favorite"; the "comfortable" interior is augmented with "wonderful garden" seating in summer, while the bar's "exotic cocktails" are a year-round draw.

SushiAnn 🈂 *Japanese* — 25 | 18 | 21 | $65

E 50s | 38 E. 51st St. (bet. Madison & Park Aves.) | 212-755-1780 | www.sushiann.com

"Clients direct from Tokyo" mix "business meetings" with pleasure at this "reliable" Midtown Japanese, where the "excellent", "straightforward" sushi is paired with "doting service"; the "austere", "corporate" setting comes "with prices to match."

Sushiden *Japanese* — 25 | 17 | 22 | $61

E 40s | 19 E. 49th St. (bet. 5th & Madison Aves.) | 212-758-2700
W 40s | 123 W. 49th St. (bet. 6th & 7th Aves.) | 212-398-2800 🈂
www.sushiden.com

"Soothing" and "trustworthy", this Midtown duo provides the "freshest" sushi served by a "patient" kimono-clad staff in "sanctuary"-like settings; it's "pricey", but the "chefs take care of you", and the extensive menu of cooked dishes is "top-notch" too.

SushiSamba ◗ *Brazilian/Japanese* — 22 | 20 | 18 | $50

Flatiron | 245 Park Ave. S. (bet. 19th & 20th Sts.) | 212-475-9377
W Village | 87 Seventh Ave. S. (Barrow St.) | 212-691-7885
www.sushisamba.com

"Who would have thought" Japanese and Brazilian cuisines "would mix", but these "vibrant", slightly "pricey" twins have a "flair" for fabricating "fusion" fare; they can be almost "too trendy" (read: "crowded and noisy"), but sushi with cocktails "doesn't get more fun", especially on the Village location's "happening rooftop."

🄩 Sushi Seki ◗🈂 *Japanese* — 26 | 13 | 20 | $73

E 60s | 1143 First Ave. (bet. 62nd & 63rd Sts.) | 212-371-0238
At this "outstanding" Eastsider, wise "gourmets" "spend the money" and go for the "unforgettable" omakase, allowing "master" chef Seki to "do his thing"; despite "drab" digs, there's "nothing like" "pristine" sushi "available after midnight" (served until 2:30 AM).

Sushi Sen-nin *Japanese* — 25 | 17 | 20 | $56

Murray Hill | 30 E. 33rd St. (bet. Madison Ave. & Park Ave. S.) |
212-889-2208 | www.sushisennin.com

Those who know about this semi-"secret" Murray Hill Japanese "nirvana" and its "excellent" fish find it "hard to eat sushi anywhere else"; despite "lofty pricing" and kinda "kitschy" decor, given the "excellent" service and overall "quality" it's worth seeking out its "odd location."

🄩 Sushi Yasuda 🈂 *Japanese* — 28 | 21 | 24 | $84

E 40s | 204 E. 43rd St. (bet. 2nd & 3rd Aves.) | 212-972-1001 |
www.sushiyasuda.com

"Reservations are mandatory" at this "minimalist" sushi "standard-bearer" near Grand Central, where "Yasuda-san" rewards "adventurousness" at the bar with "masterful delivery" of "flawless" fish, including "unusual varieties", "without gimmicks"; this "level of bliss" costs "bucks", but it's "cheaper than a flight to Tokyo", and the $23 dinner prix fixe is a super "bargain."

Sushi Zen 🗷 Japanese

25 | 21 | 22 | $69

W 40s | 108 W. 44th St. (bet. B'way & 6th Ave.) | 212-302-0707 | www.sushizen-ny.com

This Theater District Japanese turns out "exquisite", "fascinating creations" in a "small, tightly packed" yet "pleasant" room; a meal here is "like a massage" – and costs nearly as much – but the "exceptional" fish and "impeccable" service ensure it's "worth every yen."

Suteishi Japanese

∇ 22 | 21 | 23 | $41

Seaport | 24 Peck Slip (Front St.) | 212-766-2344 | www.suteishi.com

A "great pick" in the South Street Seaport area, this "charming" Japanese offers "upscale sushi" and cooked dishes at low-for-the-genre prices via a "knowledgeable" staff; the appeal of its "ultramodern" space increases "in warm weather" when there's "outdoor seating."

Sweetiepie 🅼 American/Dessert

∇ 15 | 24 | 18 | $31

W Village | 19 Greenwich Ave. (bet. Christopher & W. 10th Sts.) | 212-337-3333 | www.sweetiepierestaurant.com

A "mecca for little girls" and "mothers who lunch", this Village American's "pinkalicious" decor (including the coveted "birdcage booth") outshines its "upscale kiddie" fare and "basic" sweets; it's like a "tea party on steroids" when the "showers and tween birthdays" crank up, but to "cute"-seekers it's always a "fun treat."

Sweet Melissa Dessert/Sandwiches

20 | 16 | 15 | $20

Cobble Hill | 276 Court St. (bet. Butler & Douglass Sts.) | Brooklyn | 718-855-3410

Park Slope | 175 Seventh Ave. (bet. 1st & 2nd Sts.) | Brooklyn | 718-502-9153

www.sweetmelissapatisserie.com

"High tea" has never been so "delicious" as at these "cheery" Cobble Hill–Park Slope patisseries, where "garden seating" augments "cozy" interiors; locals overlook "uneven" service and "pricey-for-what-it-is" rates and just "gorge" on the "perfect sweet treats" or "solid" lunch.

Sweetwater ● American

∇ 23 | 20 | 20 | $44

Williamsburg | 105 N. Sixth St. (bet. Berry St. & Wythe Ave.) | Brooklyn | 718-963-0608 | www.sweetwaterny.com

The New American menu at this "comfy" Williamsburg bistro is "small", but from the "must-try" hamburger to the moules frites, it offers "excellent", "affordable" dishes considered "worth coming back to"; the garden and "adorable" staff sweeten the deal.

Swifty's ● American

18 | 18 | 21 | $68

E 70s | 1007 Lexington Ave. (bet. 72nd & 73rd Sts.) | 212-535-6000 | www.swiftysny.com

"Civilized" "elegance" rules the day at this UES "Wasp sanctum", where the "elite" congregate between visits to the Vineyard and Palm Beach to down "martinis" with "ok" "country-club fare"; "everyone" in the "society" set "seems to enjoy themselves", but they go "to see and be seen" and only secondarily "for the food."

	FOOD	DECOR	SERVICE	COST

Sylvia's *Soul Food*
19 | **13** | **18** | **$35**

Harlem | 328 Lenox Ave. (bet. 126th & 127th Sts.) | 212-996-0660 | www.sylviassoulfood.com

They don't call this soul food "institution" (circa 1962) the "queen of Harlem" for nothing – it still "satisfies" with "finger-lickin'" Southern comfort fare, especially at "fantastic" Sunday gospel brunch; it packs "a lot of history", but some say it "would taste better without the tourists."

Szechuan Gourmet *Chinese*
22 | **11** | **15** | **$28**

Garment District | 21 W. 39th St. (bet. 5th & 6th Aves.) | 212-921-0233 | www.szechuangourmetnyc.com

W 50s | 242 W. 56th St. (bet. B'way & 8th Ave.) | 212-265-2226 | www.szechuangourmet56.com

Flushing | 135-15 37th Ave. (bet. Main & Prince Sts.) | Queens | 718-888-9388

"Blow-your-doors-off" "fiery" Sichuan cuisine that's "more authentic than anything this side of Shanghai" accounts for the "long lines" at this "divey" trio; prices are more than "reasonable", and if the service is "indifferent", at least it's plenty "efficient."

NEW Taberna *Spanish*
– | **-** | **-** | **M**

W 80s | 429 Amsterdam Ave. (bet. 80th & 81st Sts.) | 917-388-3500

Step in and feel far from the sports bars that line this new Spaniard's UWS block, thanks to its moody interior featuring heraldic shields and swords, wine casks and candlelight; the menu of modern tapas is from a former Tía Pol chef, paired with mostly Iberian wines.

Z Tabla *Indian*
25 | **25** | **24** | **$67**

Flatiron | 11 Madison Ave. (24th St.) | 212-889-0667 | www.tablany.com

Chef Floyd Cardoz's "bewitching touch with spices" is evident in his "magical blend of Indian and American" cuisines at this "polished" Madison Square Park perennial; a "gracious team" and "posh" bi-level setting complete the "knockout" experience, whether in the "lively" downstairs or "gorgeous" second floor – and best of all, the prices have gotten slightly "gentler" since a "retooling" unified the menus.

Table d'Hôte *French*
20 | **15** | **19** | **$47**

E 90s | 44 E. 92nd St. (bet. Madison & Park Aves.) | 212-348-8125

"Cute as a button", this "unassuming" Carnegie Hill bistro is a "sure bet" for "solid", "simple" French fare – if you're "svelte" enough to fit into its "Lilliputian" digs; relatively "reasonable" rates and convenience to the 92nd Street Y have most declaring it "worth" the squeeze.

Taboon *Mediterranean/Mideastern*
24 | **20** | **21** | **$54**

W 50s | 773 10th Ave. (52nd St.) | 212-713-0271

"Sumptuous" takes on Med-Mideastern, including "divine" bread, keep this "casual" Hell's Kitchen "gem" "jammed", despite being "so far west" you're practically "in another time zone"; "professional yet warm" staffers and relatively "affordable" tabs boost the "party atmosphere."

Taci's Beyti *Mediterranean/Turkish*
24 | **11** | **18** | **$30**

Midwood | 1955 Coney Island Ave. (bet. Ave. P & Kings Hwy.) | Brooklyn | 718-627-5750

"Top-notch" Turkish fare is the lure at this BYO Midwood mecca, but not the "spartan" setting equipped with "heavy-duty fluorescent lights";

"summoning a waiter can be a project" too when it gets "mobbed", but who cares when you "dine like a pasha and pay like a pauper."

Tacos Matamoros *Mexican* ▽ 25 | 9 | 17 | $16

Sunset Park | 4508 Fifth Ave. (bet. 45th & 46th Sts.) | Brooklyn | 718-871-7627

"So authentic you need a translator", this "standout" Sunset Park Mexican offers its "amazing" tacos and such at "recession-friendly" rates that get even better when you factor in the "BYO policy"; there's "little ambience" unless you count "bad telenovelas on the TV" – but never mind because "it's all about the *comida*" here.

Taco Taco *Mexican* 21 | 13 | 17 | $26

E 80s | 1726 Second Ave. (bet. 89th & 90th Sts.) | 212-289-8226

Mexican "home-cookin'" includes "excellent margaritas" to wash down the "superior tacos" and "guacamole made tableside" at this "tiny" Yorkville "*favorita*"; the "colorful" decor's on the "tacky" side and service a bit "relaxed", but "reasonable" tabs ensure its "tables are always full."

Taïm ⊘ *Israeli* 26 | 8 | 17 | $14

W Village | 222 Waverly Pl. (bet. Perry & W. 11th Sts.) | 212-691-1287 | www.taimfalafel.com

"Terrifyingly addictive" veggie Israeli fare – notably "stylish", "heavenly falafel" and "out-of-this-world" garlic fries – means this "value"-oriented, garbanzo-size West Villager is always "packed"; service is "fast", but most "do takeout to avoid the inevitable elbows" in its four-seater space.

Taj Tribeca *Indian* ▽ 22 | 15 | 19 | $29

Financial District | 18 Murray St. (bet. B'way & Church St.) | 212-608-5555 | www.tajtribeca.com

This Indian "standout" on the TriBeCa–Financial District border skews upscale with its pedigreed chefs (ex Tamarind, Earthen Oven) and serene, waterfall-enhanced interior; the "first-rate" menu emphasizes tandoori dishes, while the $13.95 lunch buffet guarantees a "lively" midday scene.

Takahachi *Japanese* 24 | 16 | 22 | $40

E Village | 85 Ave. A (bet. 5th & 6th Sts.) | 212-505-6524 ☽
TriBeCa | 145 Duane St. (bet. Church St. & W. B'way) | 212-571-1830
www.takahachi.net

"Dependable sushi" and "tasty" daily specials come by way of a "personable" staff at these "relaxed" Japanese "workhorses"; maybe they "don't distinguish themselves on decor", but "reasonable" prices and "excellent quality" ensure they "pack in the crowds every night."

NEW Takashi Ⓜ *Japanese* - | - | - | M

W Village | 456 Hudson St. (Barrow St.) | 212-414-2929

Yakiniku, or grill-your-own BBQ, is the specialty of this bustling new Village Japanese, where the walls are painted with cheerful grilling instructions and the hoods over the grills lend a sci-fi feel; the moderately priced menu includes standard grillables like rib-eye and short ribs, plus some more outré cuts (fourth stomach or tongue sinew, we're looking at you).

	FOOD	DECOR	SERVICE	COST

Takesushi *Japanese*   ▽ 24 | 13 | 21 | $52
E 50s | 1026 Second Ave. (54th St.) | 212-355-3557

"Asian ladies who lunch" are among the "varied clientele" at this "calm" Japanese Midtowner, where the sushi is "so fresh" you almost "taste the sea"; the "simple" setting is warmed by "courteous" service, and though dinner's "not cheap", the "lunch specials" are a "value."

Taksim *Turkish*   21 | 11 | 17 | $29
E 50s | 1030 Second Ave. (bet. 54th & 55th Sts.) | 212-421-3004 | www.taksimnyc.com

"Recently renovated", this "trusted" Midtown Turk "feels fancier", but its "terrific" "traditional" fare still comes in "plentiful", "budget"-priced portions, delivered by "dedicated" staffers; though it's gotten "much more comfortable", some tilt to "takeout."

☑ Tamarind ● *Indian*   26 | 23 | 23 | $56
Flatiron | 41-43 E. 22nd St. (bet. B'way & Park Ave. S.) | 212-674-7400
NEW **TriBeCa** | 99 Hudson St. (bet. Franklin & Harrison Sts.) | 212-775-9000
www.tamarinde22.com

"See what fine Indian dining is all about" at this "classy" Flatironer and its new, "even lovelier" TriBeCa offshoot with a wider menu, both of which offer "exquisite" cuisine served with "haute style" in "elegant" environs; such "luxury" helps you "tolerate the tab", though frugalistas opt for the $24 prix fixe lunch – or the original's casual Tea Room adjunct.

Tang Pavilion *Chinese*   22 | 17 | 19 | $38
W 50s | 65 W. 55th St. (bet. 5th & 6th Aves.) | 212-956-6888 | www.tangpavilionnyc.com

"Fresh" Shanghainese fare keeps this "old-school", "white-tablecloth" Chinese a Midtown staple; the "tranquil" atmosphere and "efficient" "tuxedoed" service make it "ideal for a business lunch" or pre-"City Center", or anytime you seek "quality" "without spending a fortune."

☑ Tanoreen Ⓜ *Mediterranean/Mideastern* 27 | 18 | 22 | $36
Bay Ridge | 7523 Third Ave. (76th St.) | Brooklyn | 718-748-5600 | www.tanoreen.com

"There aren't enough superlatives" to describe the "fabulous" Med-Mideastern fare at this "lively" Bay Ridge "must-try", where "magic" chef-owner Rawia Bishara's "hospitality" is matched by an "eager-to-please" staff; "attractive" new digs mean "no more banging elbows", while "low prices" keep the far-flung convinced it's "worth the drive."

NEW Tanuki Tavern ● *Japanese*   ▽ 19 | 18 | 17 | $52
Meatpacking | Gansevoort Hotel | 18 Ninth Ave. (enter on 13th St., bet. Hudson St. & 9th Ave.) | 212-660-6766 | www.chinagrillmgt.com

Replacing Ono in the Gansevoort Hotel, this Meatpacking duplex from Jeffrey Chodorow offers "tasty" Japanese izakaya grub and sushi in a "fun" hot-pink space that looks like Barbie's Dream House as envisioned by Hello Kitty; just keep in mind that those small plates add up fast.

☑ Tao ● *Asian*   21 | 26 | 19 | $59
E 50s | 42 E. 58th St. (bet. Madison & Park Aves.) | 212-888-2288 | www.taorestaurant.com

"A big Buddha overlooks" the "fun scene" at this Midtown Pan-Asian, a kind of "dining theater" starring the "young and beautiful", with "pulse-pounding music" and "pricey" grub that – though "impersonally" served – is "surprisingly good"; no wonder "tourists and city folk alike" register "memorable experiences" here.

Tarallucci e Vino *Italian* | 21 | 18 | 16 | $37 |

E Village | 163 First Ave. (10th St.) | 212-388-1190
Flatiron | 15 E. 18th St. (bet. B'way & 5th Ave.) | 212-228-5400
www.tarallucievino.net

"Make it past the front counter laden with baked goods" at this affordable Flatiron Italian, and you'll find "tasty small plates and interesting wines" enjoyed by an "expat" crowd in "laid-back" "modern-rustic" environs; "fantastic" pastries, panini and coffee are the mainstays at the counter-service East Village original.

Tartine ⊘ *French* | 21 | 13 | 18 | $32 |

W Village | 253 W. 11th St. (4th St.) | 212-229-2611

It's near-"microscopic", but this "quaint", cash-only West Village vet remains a "neighborhood favorite", thanks to its "wonderful" French bistro eats, "reliable" service and "reasonable" prices abetted by a BYO policy; "the only downside": "be prepared to wait out in the elements" for your table.

NEW Tartinery ● *Sandwiches* | - | - | - | M |

NoLita | 209 Mulberry St. (Spring St.) | 212-300-5838 |
www.tartinery.com

At this chic NoLita newcomer specializing in the namesake open-faced French sandwiches, it's all about the bread: sourdough imported from Paris' renowned Poilâne; the "hip" space features a bar and open kitchen on the ground floor and a downstairs dining room complete with a live tree and double-sided fireplace.

Taste *American* | 22 | 18 | 22 | $52 |

E 80s | 1413 Third Ave. (80th St.) | 212-717-9798 | www.elizabar.com

A "wonderful" "self-serve cafe" by day, this "undiscovered" Upper East Side American "chameleon" from Eli Zabar "transforms itself" into a "welcoming" restaurant with "delightful" service and a "solid wine list" at dinner; whatever the hour, expect the freshest possible "seasonal" "comfort" fare "for gastronomes" in "pleasant", "quiet" environs – in sum, go!

Tasty Hand-Pulled Noodles ⊘ *Noodle Shop* | ∇ 22 | 6 | 14 | $14 |

Chinatown | 1 Doyers St. (Bowery) | 212-791-1817

"Flavorful" noodle soups and "delicious" dumplings for "cheap" are the thing at this "tiny", "hard-to-find" Chinatowner; overlook the "funky" digs and "get a table" where you can "watch the chefs pulling the dough" in the open kitchen – what "a treat."

Tatiana ● *Russian* | ∇ 21 | 19 | 16 | $55 |

Brighton Bch | 3152 Brighton 6th St. (Brightwater Ct.) | Brooklyn | 718-891-5151 | www.tatianarestaurant.com

It's "Russia by the sea" at this Brighton Beach bastion dispensing "huge", pricey portions of borscht, pierogi and such; its ornate interior is host to a floor show sure to take your mind off the "Cold War service", but many prefer "a table overlooking the boardwalk and ocean."

	FOOD	DECOR	SERVICE	COST

NEW Taureau *Fondue*
– | – | – | E

E Village | 127 E. Seventh St. (bet. Ave. A & 1st Ave.) | 212-228-2222 |
www.taureaunyc.com

From La Sirène's well-loved owner comes this petite, pricey BYO East
Villager specializing in fondue, including cheese, meat and chocolate
versions; it's a ready-made date place, with plush banquettes and
French music enhancing the sensuous experience; P.S. two people required per pot, priced per person.

Taverna Kyclades *Greek/Seafood*
26 | 12 | 18 | $36

Astoria | 33-07 Ditmars Blvd. (bet. 33rd & 35th Sts.) | Queens |
718-545-8666 | www.tavernakyclades.com

There's "always a full house" at this "hectic" Astoria Greek famed for
"fantastic", "fresh" seafood at "value" rates, served "wham-bam" by a
"jovial" staff; yes, it's "decor-challenged" and the waits for a table can
be "insane", but for most it's "totally worth it."

T-Bar Steak & Lounge *Steak*
21 | 19 | 20 | $56

E 70s | 1278 Third Ave. (bet. 73rd & 74th Sts.) | 212-772-0404 |
www.tbarnyc.com

Sometimes it seems like the "whole UES" is gathered at Tony Fortuna's
"tony" American, supping on "satisfying steaks" ably delivered;
"lively" "cougars and panthers" kick up a "deafening" din at the "hopping" bar, but the quieter, "cozy" back area is deemed "date"-worthy.

Tea & Sympathy *British*
19 | 18 | 18 | $29

W Village | 108 Greenwich Ave. (bet. 12th & 13th Sts.) | 212-807-8329 |
www.teaandsympathynewyork.com

A "British haven" in the Village, this "delightful" teahouse dishes up
"spotted dick" and other "tastes of Britannia" in "tiny", "quaint" digs like
"nana's house"; it's "cramped", and waits can be "long", but once the
"quirky" staff pours you "a spot of afternoon tea", "you'll feel civilized."

Ⓩ Telepan *American*
26 | 21 | 25 | $71

W 60s | 72 W. 69th St. (bet. Columbus Ave. & CPW) | 212-580-4300 |
www.telepan-ny.com

To experience the "glories of fresh, locally grown food" "artfully prepared", hit "farm-to-table pioneer" Bill Telepan's "brilliant" UWS New
American; its prix fixe options suit "varied budgets", the "refined",
"monotone" decor strikes most as "calming" and service is "prompt and
helpful", making it an all-around "favorite to fortify" pre–Lincoln Center.

Telly's Taverna ❶ *Greek/Seafood*
23 | 14 | 19 | $39

Astoria | 28-13 23rd Ave. (bet. 28th & 29th Sts.) | Queens |
718-728-9056 | www.tellystaverna.com

The "freshest grilled fish" and other "won't-break-the-bank" Greek
classics served by a "warm" crew have kept finatics "coming for
decades" to this "friendly" Astoria taverna; the "simple", "noisy" milieu
makes the roomy garden especially attractive in fair weather.

10 Downing ❶ *American*
20 | 20 | 19 | $51

W Village | 10 Downing St. (6th Ave.) | 212-255-0300 |
www.10downingnyc.com

Never mind the "cheeky" moniker, this "stylish" West Villager draws
"carefree" types with its "imaginative" New American plates and "ex-

uberant" mood; the "bright", "big-windowed" space and "eclectic" artwork are "definitely not a downer", though the "cacophony" can be "nerve-frazzling."

Tenzan *Japanese*   22 | 16 | 19 | $35

E 50s | 988 Second Ave. (bet. 52nd & 53rd Sts.) | 212-980-5900 ◐
E 80s | 1714 Second Ave. (89th St.) | 212-369-3600
W 70s | 285 Columbus Ave. (73rd St.) | 212-580-7300 ◐
Bensonhurst | 7116 18th Ave. (71st St.) | Brooklyn | 718-621-3238
www.tenzanrestaurants.com

"Fresh", "no-nonsense" sushi nets schools of cross-borough fans for this "quality" Japanese quartet boasting a fine "fish-to-rice ratio" in its "creative rolls"; even those who "marvel at how low the bill is" say the decor is "on the neon side" – maybe it's "better for takeout."

Teodora *Italian*   21 | 16 | 20 | $50

E 50s | 141 E. 57th St. (bet. Lexington & 3rd Aves.) | 212-826-7101 | www.teodorarestaurant.com

Something of a "sleeper in a prime location", this "calm", "comfortable" Midtown Northern Italian can be counted on for "nice welcomes" as well as "excellent housemade pastas"; it's "somewhat pricey", but what's the value of "having a conversation without the din"?

⧉ Terrace in the Sky Ⓜ *French/Mediterranean*   22 | 25 | 22 | $67

W 100s | 400 W. 119th St. (bet. Amsterdam Ave. & Morningside Dr.) | 212-666-9490 | www.terraceinthesky.com

"Spectacular" "skyline views" on all sides and "harp music in the background" set the tone at this "elegant" Morningside Heights penthouse, a "special-occasion" standby where the French-Med fare's pretty "terrific" too; "unobtrusive" service seals the "romantic" mood – and takes the edge off the "mortgage payment–size" tab; P.S. it's "great for private parties."

Terrazza Toscana *Italian*   ▽ 21 | 20 | 20 | $39

W 50s | 742 Ninth Ave. (50th St.) | 212-315-9191 | www.terrazzatoscana.com

Showgoers applaud this "gracious" Theater District option that plies a "well-priced" Tuscan menu abetted by a 400-label wine list; its "attractive", ornate interior is outfitted with wrought iron and chandeliers, while it lives up to its name with a "lovely" rooftop terrace.

Terroir ◐ *Italian*   ▽ 24 | 22 | 25 | E

E Village | 413 E. 12th St. (bet. Ave. A & 1st Ave)
NEW **TriBeCa** | 24 Harrison St. (bet. Greenwich & Hudson Sts.) | 212-625-9463
www.wineisterroir.com

Oenophiles are all over these "fantastic" wine bars (siblings to Hearth) whose "tasty" Italian small bites are matched with an "extensive", "interesting" list of vintages and ferried by an "eager" team; the "cozy" original is "small, small, small", but the new TriBeCa branch is roomier.

NEW **Testaccio** ◐ *Italian*   ▽ 22 | 22 | 19 | $46

LIC | 47-30 Vernon Blvd. (47th Rd.) | Queens | 718-937-2900 | www.testacciony.com

A new source of "culinary sophistication" in "the wilds" of Long Island City, this "chic", upscale Italian offers "authentic Roman cuisine" in *"bellissima"* multilevel environs with "cool" rustic-contemporary style; now if they would just "ramp up the service", things would be even more "comfortable."

Tevere | *Italian* ▽ 24 | 19 | 22 | $63

E 80s | 155 E. 84th St. (bet. Lexington & 3rd Aves.) | 212-744-0210 | www.teverenyc.com

"You don't have to be" orthodox to enjoy the "excellent" Roman specialties that are "as good as kosher gets" at this "pleasant", "pretty" UES Italian; a "polite" staff strives to keep the mood "quiet and intimate" for those "prepared to spend."

Thai Pavilion | *Thai* ▽ 25 | 18 | 23 | $26

Astoria | 23-92 21st St. (bet. 23rd Terrace & 24th Ave.) | Queens | 718-274-2088
Astoria | 37-10 30th Ave. (37th St.) | Queens | 718-777-5546
www.thaipavilionny.com

"Excellent Thai cooking" – both "classics" and some "unusual, delicious" specials – keeps Astorians coming back to these "unpretentious" Thais; "helpful, charming" service and "unbelievably cheap" tabs make "so-so" decor easy to overlook.

Thalassa ⊠ *Greek/Seafood* 23 | 25 | 23 | $62

TriBeCa | 179 Franklin St. (bet. Greenwich & Hudson Sts.) | 212-941-7661 | www.thalassanyc.com

"Succulent" seafood "delicately prepared" and "served with style" is the deal at this "transporting" TriBeCa Greek, whose "nautical" "loft-like space" may be the next best thing to boarding "a yacht on the Mediterranean"; it "touches all the senses", so Aristotle Onassis types muse "who cares if it's pricey?"

Thalia ● *American* 20 | 20 | 19 | $49

W 50s | 828 Eighth Ave. (50th St.) | 212-399-4444 | www.restaurantthalia.com

A longtime "pre-theater go-to", this "pretty" Hell's Kitchen New American offers its "interesting" range of dishes at "fair"-for-the-area prices, snappily supplied by an "efficient" crew; the "bustling" vibe verges on "frenetic" at "curtain time", but otherwise it's an "enjoyable" "hang."

NEW This Little Piggy ▽ 23 | 10 | 17 | $13
Had Roast Beef ⊟ *Sandwiches*

E Village | 149 First Ave. (bet. 9th & 10th Sts.) | 212-253-1500

As the name suggests, this cash-only East Villager from the Artichoke Basille folks specializes in roast beef sandwiches; it's teeny (eight seats) and no-frills, but the goods are so "huge, delicious" and "cheap", most sing 'wee wee wee' all the way home.

NEW Thistle Hill Tavern | *American* - | - | - | M

Park Slope | 441 Seventh Ave. (15th St.) | Brooklyn | 347-599-1262 | www.thistlehillbrooklyn.com

This laid-back new tavern feels a bit more Williamsburg than Park Slope with its old-time aesthetic (lots of salvaged wood, tin ceilings) and emphasis on retro cocktails; its locavore-friendly New American small plates are from an 'inoteca vet, and priced low enough to keep the locals coming.

Thomas Beisl ● *Austrian* — 16 | 16 | 16 | $39

Fort Greene | 25 Lafayette Ave. (Ashland Pl.) | Brooklyn | 718-222-5800
Get your "Wiener schnitzel" fix at this "little bit of Mitteleuropa" in Fort Greene, whose "sweet" staff dispenses "hearty", well-priced Austrian fare, plus "wonderful" wines and beer; even those who'd prefer "more quality and less quantity" can't fault the *gemütlich* feel and "prime location" by BAM.

Tía Pol *Spanish* — 25 | 15 | 19 | $41

Chelsea | 205 10th Ave. (bet. 22nd & 23rd Sts.) | 212-675-8805 | www.tiapol.com
The "Lionel Messi of NY tapas", this Chelsea Spaniard has fans of its "authentic", "*supremo*" bites chanting "so many choices, so little time"; it's a "shoebox", so expect a "wait", a "squeeze" and possibly "sticker shock" (those morsels "add up quickly") – but it's "worth it" for a "memorable meal."

Tierras Colombianas ⊘ *Colombian* — ▽ 21 | 13 | 17 | $24

Astoria | 33-01 Broadway (33rd St.) | Queens | 718-956-3012
"Soulful", "stick-to-your-ribs" Colombian fare ensures this "dinerlike", cash-only Astorian remains a local "standby"; "warm" "hospitality" takes the chill off the "fluorescent-lit", "bare-bones" digs, while low prices and "humongous portions" ensure you'll "leave with a full stomach and plenty left in your wallet."

Tiffin Wallah *Indian* — 23 | 13 | 18 | $20

Murray Hill | 127 E. 28th St. (bet. Lexington & Park Aves.) | 212-685-7301 | www.tiffinwallah.us
"Fantastic" Southern Indian "street food" that's "vegetarian and kosher to boot" is the deal at this "friendly", "unassuming" Curry Hill standout; the "minimalist" aesthetic extends to the "cheap" tab, which gets even better during weekday buffet lunch ("the best $7 you'll ever spend").

Tio Pepe ● *Mexican/Spanish* — 19 | 15 | 18 | $37

W Village | 168 W. Fourth St. (bet. Cornelia & Jones Sts.) | 212-242-9338 | www.tiopepenyc.com
"Dependable", "plentiful" Spanish-Mexican fare has kept this Village "old-timer" "busy" for 40 years; the "uninspired" find "nothing to *escriba casa* about", but they are outvoted by those who like the "friendly" "hospitality", "lovely back garden room" and "bargain" $12 brunch.

NEW Tipsy Parson *Southern* — 18 | 18 | 18 | $46

Chelsea | 156 Ninth Ave. (bet. 19th & 20th Sts.) | 212-620-4545 | www.tipsyparson.com
Named after a booze-soaked dessert, this "charming" Chelsea newcomer from the owners of Little Giant specializes in "fancy" Southern comfort fare; "caring" service and "homey" "grandma's-kitchen" decor – not to mention "inventive julep slushies" – distract from any start-up "kinks."

Toby's Public House ⊘ *Pizza* — ▽ 25 | 16 | 21 | $28

Greenwood Heights | 686 Sixth Ave. (21st St.) | Brooklyn | 718-788-1186 | www.tobyspublichouse.com
"Superior" wood-oven pizzas and a "boatload of beer choices" make this "casual", affordable pub a popular "stop off" in Brooklyn's bur-

	FOOD	DECOR	SERVICE	COST

geoning Greenwood Heights; the decor's unremarkable, but never mind – most are watching "the game on one of the big screens" anyway.

☑ Tocqueville ☒ *American/French* — 25 | 24 | 25 | $76

Union Sq | 1 E. 15th St. (bet. 5th Ave. & Union Sq. W.) | 212-647-1515 | www.tocquevillerestaurant.com

"Gracious", "low-key" staffers "make you feel special" at this "calm", "classy" Union Square "oasis", where "grown-ups" "luxuriate" in "stunning chandeliered" quarters while quietly "raving about" Marco Moreira's "scrumptious" and "imaginative" French–New American cuisine; it's a "special splurge" rated "worth every penny" – and there's always the "steal" of a $24 lunch prix fixe.

Toledo ☒ *Spanish* — ▽ 24 | 20 | 24 | $56

Murray Hill | 6 E. 36th St. (bet. 5th & Madison Aves.) | 212-696-5036 | www.toledorestaurant.com

It may seem that this "grand old" Murray Hill Spaniard is "off everyone's radar", yet those who've discovered it say its "diverse", "enjoyable" eats are "well prepared" and the service is "swell"; it's a bit "pricey", but the "handsome" setting makes it a solid "business-lunch" pick.

Toloache *Mexican* — 23 | 18 | 20 | $46

W 50s | 251 W. 50th St. (bet. B'way & 8th Ave.) | 212-581-1818 | www.toloachenyc.com

Touted as a Theater District "find", this "sophisticated" Nuevo Mexicano's "palate-pleasing" cuisine is conveyed by an "eager" crew; fueling its duplex space's "boisterous" mood is an "enormous" tequila list (over 150) – which helps take the sting out of "lotsa-peso" tabs.

Tommaso *Italian* — 24 | 19 | 22 | $51

Dyker Heights | 1464 86th St. (bet. Bay 8th St. & 15th Ave.) | Brooklyn | 718-236-9883 | www.tommasoinbrooklyn.com

It's "been around forever" but this "festive" Dyker Heights vet still hits the high notes with "old-time Italian" favorites, sauced with "operatic serenades" from chef-owner Thomas Verdillo; "Brooklyn prices" and an "outstanding wine cellar" seal a deal that's "satisfying in every way."

☑ Tomoe Sushi *Japanese* — 26 | 8 | 16 | $44

G Village | 172 Thompson St. (bet. Bleecker & Houston Sts.) | 212-777-9346

"Fat slices" of "velvety, succulent" fish are the hallmark of this "tiny" "Tokyo"-esque sushi specialist in the Village; long known as a "jewel in the rough", it balances "crowded, dumpy" digs and "ridiculous waits" with "quality" rolls at "value" prices – "the lines outside" "tell it all."

Tom's ⊖ *Diner* — 21 | 17 | 24 | $17

Prospect Heights | 782 Washington Ave. (Sterling Pl.) | Brooklyn | 718-636-9738

"Everything a diner should be", this Prospect Heights "old reliable" has been dishing up "inspired pancakes" and other "marvelous" comfort classics in "gaudy", "Woody Allen movie"-worthy digs since the 1930s; "congenial" service and "cheap" tabs lead to "good vibes" – not to mention "huge lines."

Tony's Di Napoli *Italian* — 20 | 15 | 19 | $39

E 80s | 1606 Second Ave. (83rd St.) | 212-861-8686

(continued)

(continued)

Tony's Di Napoli

W 40s | 147 W. 43rd St. (bet. B'way & 6th Ave.) | 212-221-0100 ◑
www.tonysnyc.com

"Big platters" of "garlic-laden red-sauce" basics have the "crowds" "loosening their belts" for "family-style" feasts at these "cheerful", "Carmine's"-like Italians; "price-is-right" tabs ensure they're "terrific for large groups", but given the "cacophony", "forget conversation."

Topaz Thai *Thai* | 21 | 11 | 16 | $30 |

W 50s | 127 W. 56th St. (bet. 6th & 7th Aves.) | 212-957-8020
Located "near everything", this "tiny" Thai "in the shadow of Carnegie Hall" dishes up "delicious", "well-spiced" eats to those prepared to "endure the wait" in "zero-atmosphere" digs; sweetening the deal are "total bargain" rates and servers who are "friendly" even as "they rush you out."

NEW Torrisi Italian Specialties *Italian*   ▽ 27 | 15 | 22 | $46 |

NoLita | 250 Mulberry St. (bet. Prince & Spring Sts.) | 212-965-0955 |
www.piginahat.com

By day, this "wonderful" NoLita nook is an Italian deli/sandwich shop with a twist: everything's made exclusively from quality domestic ingredients; come evening, it rolls out a "value"-priced ($45) five-course dinner, featuring "creative" flavors and techniques reflective of its young chef-owners' credentials (ex Café Boulud, Del Posto); too bad the no-rez policy and 18-seat capacity spell "awful waits."

Tortilleria Nixtamal ⊄ *Mexican*   ▽ 25 | 12 | 20 | $13 |

Corona | 104-05 47th Ave. (bet. 104th & 108th Sts.) | Queens |
718-699-2434 | www.tortillerianixtamal.com

What may be the city's only "housemade masa" is the secret behind the "out-of-this-world" "fresh" tortillas and tamales tendered at this "warm, gracious" Corona Mexican; the colorful space is "tiny" and the menu "limited", but all agree such "terrific value" is "worth a schlep."

Tosca Café ◑ *Italian* | 21 | 21 | 18 | $35 |

Bronx | 4038 E. Tremont Ave. (bet. Miles & Sampson Aves.) | 718-239-3300 |
www.toscanyc.com

"Crowds" convene to "see and be seen" at this "clubby" Throgs Neck standout, whose broad menu of "consistently good" Italian eats stretches to sushi ("who'd have thunk?"); the "cool" setup includes a "nice rooftop", and as for the "slow" service, it "isn't a problem" if you're there to "relax."

Totonno's Pizzeria Napolitano *Pizza* | 21 | 10 | 15 | $24 |

E 80s | 1544 Second Ave. (bet. 80th & 81st Sts.) | 212-327-2800
Murray Hill | 462 Second Ave. (26th St.) | 212-213-8800
Coney Island | 1524 Neptune Ave. (bet. W. 15th & 16th Sts.) |
Brooklyn | 718-372-8606 Ⓜ⊄
www.totonnos.com

Most agree the original 1920s-era Coney Island "mecca of pizza" is the best, but all three of these pie palaces turn out "terrific thin-crust" babies "like no other"; when you're "world renowned", "dumpy" decor "absolutely doesn't matter", ditto "no-nonsense service."

	FOOD	DECOR	SERVICE	COST

NEW Totto Ramen ⊘ *Noodle Shop* — | — | — | I

W 50s | 366 W. 52nd St. (bet. 8th & 9th Aves.) | 212-582-0052 |
www.tottoramen.com
Arrive early if you want to nab one of the 20 counter seats at this tiny,
bare-bones new Hell's Kitchen ramen joint; a sibling to Soba Totto and
Yakitori Totto, it presents a brief, affordable lineup that features organic ramen and celebrates the pig.

Tournesol *French* 24 | 15 | 19 | $42

LIC | 50-12 Vernon Blvd. (bet. 50th & 51st Aves.) | Queens |
718-472-4355 | www.tournesolnyc.com
An LIC "diamond in the rough", this "delightful" French bistro
"dynamo" has long supplied "first-rate" country French fare to a "gentrifying neighborhood"; service is "amiable" and tabs a "bargain", so
really "the only complaint" is "tables thisclose."

Tra Da Noi Ⓜ *Italian* ▽ 22 | 15 | 20 | $38

Bronx | 622 E. 187th St. (bet. Belmont & Hughes Sts.) | 718-295-1784
It's "nothing much from the outside", but "those who know" say this
"informal", family-run Arthur Avenue–area Italian is worth searching out
for "huge plates" of "simple" but "high-quality" eats "reminiscent of
homemade"; "reasonable rates" and solid service seal the deal.

NEW Traif ⓿Ⓜ *Eclectic* — | — | — | M

Williamsburg | 229 S. Fourth St. (bet. Havemeyer & Roebling Sts.) |
Brooklyn | 347-844-9578 | www.traifny.com
"Drive your rabbi nuts" by visiting this newcomer on the edge of
Hasidic Williamsburg specializing in unkosher delicacies (namely
pork and shellfish) ordered from an Eclectic small-plates menu; its
long space, complete with a curved bar and stone patio, is already
packed – keep those bacon doughnuts coming.

Trattoria Cinque *Italian* ▽ 22 | 22 | 22 | $47

TriBeCa | 363 Greenwich St. (bet. Franklin & Harrison Sts.) | 212-965-0555 |
www.trattoriacinquenyc.com
From the Alfredo of Rome folks, this "energetic" TriBeCa Italian demonstrates the "virtue of doing a few things well" by offering just five
"enticing" midpriced options for each course, plus "delicious" pizzas;
the "gorgeous" space is "massive", but a "super-friendly" staff helps
keep the vibe "comfortable."

Trattoria Dell'Arte ⓿ *Italian* 21 | 20 | 21 | $59

W 50s | 900 Seventh Ave. (bet. 56th & 57th Sts.) | 212-245-9800 |
www.trattoriadellarte.com
A Midtown "celebrity haven" with "Carnegie Hall in its backyard", this
"hopping" Northern Italian is famed for "fabulous" antipasti, "to-die-
for" thin pizzas and "whimsical" decor with "plaster body parts
emerging from the wall"; service is "with a smile", and the tabs are
"not outrageous" given the "exciting" "scene."

Ⓩ Trattoria L'incontro Ⓜ *Italian* 27 | 19 | 25 | $56

Astoria | 21-76 31st St. (Ditmars Blvd.) | Queens | 718-721-3532 |
www.trattorialincontro.com
There's "always something new" and "off-the-charts delicious" at this
"buzzy" Astoria Italian, where the servers reciting the "mile-long list

of specials" are a "floor show", and chef-owner Rocco Sacramone "makes time to greet customers" too; borough boosters stack it against "anything Manhattan has to offer"; P.S. the next-door wine bar is "a must while waiting for your table."

Trattoria Pesce & Pasta *Italian/Seafood*   18 | 14 | 18 | $37

E 50s | 1079 First Ave. (59th St.) | 212-888-7884
W 90s | 625 Columbus Ave. (bet. 90th & 91st Sts.) | 212-579-7970
W Village | 262 Bleecker St. (bet. 6th Ave. & 7th Ave. S.) |
212-645-2993 | www.pesce-pasta.com ◕

So long as you "like garlic", you'll enjoy the "wonderful choice" of fish, "fresh pastas" and "fine antipasti" at this "pleasant" trio of "neighborhood" Italians; "frumpy" they may be, but you'll "feel welcome", and the tab "won't break the bank."

Trattoria Romana *Italian*   24 | 17 | 23 | $47

Staten Island | 1476 Hylan Blvd. (Benton Ave.) | 718-980-3113 |
www.trattoriaromana.com

"Staten Island's dining elite" gathers at this "appealing" Dongan Hills trattoria for the "ultimate" in "traditional" Italian "comfort food" dished up in "plentiful" supply; service is "friendly and attentive", leaving "tight tables" and "waits" at prime times as "the only downside."

Trattoria Toscana *Italian*   24 | 15 | 23 | $46

W Village | 64 Carmine St. (bet. Bedford St. & 7th Ave. S.) | 212-675-8736

"Marvelous" Tuscan cuisine and "old-world" ambiance make this "relaxed" West Village Italian a "neighborhood standout"; with the "delightful" owner overseeing its "personal" service, getting "treated like family" is the norm – as are tabs that "meet your budget."

Trattoria Trecolori *Italian*   21 | 18 | 22 | $41

W 40s | 254 W. 47th St. (bet. B'way & 8th Ave.) | 212-997-4540 |
www.trattoriatrecolori.com

The "gracious" staff "knows how to handle the crowds" at this "lively" Theater District Italian, whose "red-sauce" repasts are rated a "terrific choice" "pre- or post-show"; the "festive" space is "surprisingly cozy", and "gentle" prices please the "value-centric."

NEW Travertine ◕ *Mediterranean*   ▽ 22 | 24 | 20 | $64

NoLita | 19 Kenmare St. (bet. Bowery & Elizabeth St.) | 212-966-1810 |
www.travertinenyc.com

Set in a sleek, "sexy" space with a "cool bar", this "trendy" new NoLita Med-Italian offers "delish" dishes and cocktails; start-up snags include service that runs from "top-notch" to "nonchalant", and the tabs are serious, but most don't notice when the "downtown vibe" turns "loungey" (complete with "thudding music").

Tre Dici ⊠ *Italian*   21 | 18 | 20 | $54

Chelsea | 128 W. 26th St. (bet. 6th & 7th Aves.) | 212-243-8183

Tre Dici Steak ⊠ *Steak*

Chelsea | 128 W. 26th St., 2nd fl. (bet. 6th & 7th Aves.) | 212-243-2085
www.tredicinyc.com

On "a sleepy street in Chelsea", this "oasis" delivers "tasty" Italian fare "with ingenuity" in "modern", street-level digs, while "well-prepared" beef comes in "bordello"-like quarters in the upstairs steakhouse; either way, a "sexy" vibe and "genial" staff make it a "perfect date" pick.

	FOOD	DECOR	SERVICE	COST

NEW Tre Otto *Italian* ▽ 21 | 17 | 20 | $39

E 90s | 1408 Madison Ave. (bet. 97th & 98th Sts.) | 212-860-8880 | www.treotto.com

A "most welcome" addition to Carnegie Hill, this "tiny" trattoria plies "diverse", midpriced Italiana, including "terrific pastas" and "elegant" thin-crust pizzas; feeling "more downtown than UES", its narrow, brick-walled room is lined with black leather banquettes and augmented with a garden.

Trestle on Tenth *American* 20 | 17 | 19 | $47

Chelsea | 242 10th Ave. (24th St.) | 212-645-5659 | www.trestleontenth.com

The food's "Swiss accent" provides a "delicious" "change" from the same-old at this "smart" Chelsea New American, which also stands out with "outstanding" housemade charcuterie and an "intriguing wine list"; it's "worth a stop after the High Line", especially in the "lovely garden."

Z Tribeca Grill ● *American* 22 | 21 | 21 | $59

TriBeCa | 375 Greenwich St. (Franklin St.) | 212-941-3900 | www.tribecagrill.com

"After all these years", this "still-happening" New American from Drew Nieporent and Robert De Niro remains a TriBeCa "champ", where a "smiling" crew ferries "food that's always up to snuff" and wines from "one of NY's best lists"; it's "casual, dressy – anything goes", and the "people-watching is a 10", but "just expect to pay a little."

Triomphe *French* 23 | 21 | 22 | $72

W 40s | Iroquois Hotel | 49 W. 44th St. (bet. 5th & 6th Aves.) | 212-453-4233 | www.triompheny.com

A "relaxing" "retreat" located "steps from the Theater District", this "romantic" Midtown "hideaway" is all "cozy elegance" with its "sophisticated", "scrumptious" French cuisine, "value-laden wine list" and "pampering", "unstuffy" service; naturally, it all "comes at a price."

Tsampa ● *Tibetan* ▽ 21 | 17 | 18 | $27

E Village | 212 E. Ninth St. (bet. 2nd & 3rd Aves.) | 212-614-3226

"Who knew Tibetans ate so well?" marvel novices impressed by this "calm" East Villager whose "exotic" dishes include lots of "vegetarian options"; tabs are "cheap", and a "gentle" staff adds to the "tranquil" ambiance you'd expect in a place with a "Buddhist shrine in back."

Tse Yang *Chinese* 24 | 24 | 24 | $64

E 50s | 34 E. 51st St. (bet. Madison & Park Aves.) | 212-688-5447 | www.tseyangnyc.com

"High-end" Chinese cuisine comes in a "gorgeous" setting replete with "bronze murals and colorful aquariums" at this "quiet" East Midtowner known for its "perfect Peking duck"; the "elegant" environs and "superb" service befit a "money-is-no-object" "power-lunch" venue – though the three-course prix fixe is a "bargain."

Tulcingo del Valle ⊅ *Mexican* ▽ 24 | 8 | 18 | $20

W 40s | 665 10th Ave. (bet. 46th & 47th Sts.) | 212-262-5510 | www.tulcingorestaurant.com

A pilgrimage to this Hell's Kitchen "hole-in-the-wall" yields "wonderful", "savory" Puebla-style "Mexican home cooking" that's as "authen-

| | FOOD | DECOR | SERVICE | COST |

tic as it comes"; such "unusual and extensive" offerings easily "outweigh" the "nondescript coffee-shop decor", as do the "low prices" and "warm" service.

Turkish Cuisine ● *Turkish* | 20 | 14 | 18 | $35 |

W 40s | 631 Ninth Ave. (bet. 44th & 45th Sts.) | 212-397-9650 | www.turkishcuisinenyc.com

"Distinctive Turkish dishes" and "helpful" staffers who ensure you're "well fed before your curtain" make this "tiny" Hell's Kitchen standby "perfect pre-theater"; surveyors debate whether the interior's "cute or tacky", but no one finds fault with the "pleasant" garden or the prices.

Turkish Grill *Turkish* | 24 | 19 | 21 | $31 |

Sunnyside | 42-03 Queens Blvd. (42nd St.) | Queens | 718-392-3838

Recently "refurbished", this "pleasing" Sunnyside Turk now sports the "sleek look" of a "winner" to go with its "outstanding" eats (the meze in particular "shine"); it's generally "crowded", and its "inexpensive" rates and "deal" of a prix fixe lunch are part of the reason.

❷ Turkish Kitchen *Turkish* | 22 | 18 | 19 | $42 |

Murray Hill | 386 Third Ave. (bet. 27th & 28th Sts.) | 212-679-6633 | www.turkishkitchen.com

You could "make a meal" of the "heavenly" meze at this "popular" Murray Hill Turk that "merits a detour" for its "piquant", "real-deal" cuisine; add "cheerful", "informed waiters", "dramatic" red decor and "approachable" prices (especially the lunch prix fixe), and "no wonder it's so busy."

Turks & Frogs *Turkish* | 18 | 19 | 19 | $40 |

TriBeCa | 458 Greenwich St. (bet. Desbrosses & Watts Sts.) | 212-966-4774
W Village | 323 W. 11th St. (bet. Greenwich & Washington Sts.) | 212-691-8875
www.turksandfrogs.com

"Lovely, low-lit", "antiques"-abetted decor makes for a "sensual" vibe at this "romantic" TriBeCa Turk whose "tasty" specialties come via a "polite" staff; the wine-bar Village original has the same "cool" vibe, but limits its menu to "delicious meze."

Turkuaz *Turkish* | 20 | 19 | 19 | $38 |

W 100s | 2637 Broadway (100th St.) | 212-665-9541 | www.turkuazrestaurant.com

Visit "the exotic Mideast" via this "enticing" UWS Turk that turns out a "smashing variety" of dishes, particularly at the "bargain" Sunday brunch (a "trencherman's paradise"); a "tented" "harem"-worthy room, "costumed waiters" and weekend belly dancing round out the "transporting" experience.

Tuscany Grill *Italian* | 24 | 19 | 23 | $46 |

Bay Ridge | 8620 Third Ave. (bet. 86th & 87th Sts.) | Brooklyn | 718-921-5633

"Outta sight" Tuscan fare at "reasonable" rates keeps this "tiny" "Bay Ridge jewel" "full"; friendly servers and a "homey", "feel-good" vibe cement its standing as a reliable "date place" and "comfortable" hangout", though a few wish its "crowded" quarters were just a bit "bigger."

	FOOD	DECOR	SERVICE	COST

12th St. Bar & Grill *American* `20` `19` `20` `$38`

Park Slope | 1123 Eighth Ave. (12th St.) | Brooklyn | 718-965-9526 |
www.12thstreetbarandgrill.com

Park Slopers praise the "consistent quality" at this "low-key", "grown-up" "neighborhood staple", a "cozy go-to" for "tasty", "inexpensive" New American fare served by "friendly" folks; its around-the-corner bar offers the same chow in "publike" environs.

12 Chairs *American/Mideastern* `19` `14` `18` `$27`

SoHo | 56 MacDougal St. (bet. Houston & Prince Sts.) | 212-254-8640

"Affordable" tabs and a "mellow" atmosphere make this "informal", "classically SoHo" cafe inviting to "younger people" ready to pull up a chair for "decent" American-Mideastern eats; however, the space is "small as expected" and the service "über-relaxed."

Z 21 Club Z *American* `22` `24` `24` `$73`

W 50s | 21 W. 52nd St. (bet. 5th & 6th Aves.) | 212-582-7200 |
www.21club.com

Once a "1920s speakeasy", this Midtown "icon" only "gets better with age" according to "establishment" types digging into "American classics" like its "legendary" $30 burger; from the "knickknacks hanging from the ceiling" to the "black-tied" waiters and the "de rigueur" dress code (jackets required), it's an "irreplaceable" part of NY where "time really seems to stand still"; P.S. the $24 lunch prix fixe is one of NYC's best buys, and for party-givers, there are swell private rooms upstairs.

26 Seats M *French* `22` `16` `19` `$40`

E Village | 168 Ave. B (bet. 10th & 11th Sts.) | 212-677-4787 |
www.26seatsonb.com

This "unpretentious" East Villager turns out "*très good*" French fare in a "quaint" space that's "as cramped as it is charming"; "affordable" tabs make it "worth squeezing in" – even though "none of the 26 seats is all that comfortable."

Two Boots *Pizza* `18` `10` `14` `$15`

E 40s | Grand Central | lower level (42nd St. & Vanderbilt Ave.) |
212-557-7992 | www.twoboots.com
E 80s | 1617 Second Ave. (84th St.) | 212-734-0317 |
www.twoboots.com ☽
E Village | 42 Ave. A (3rd St.) | 212-254-1919 |
www.twoboots.com ☽
NoHo | 74 Bleecker St. (B'way) | 212-777-1033 | www.twoboots.com ☽
W 40s | 625 Ninth Ave. (bet. 44th & 45th Sts.) | 212-956-2668 |
www.twoboots.com ☽
NEW **W 90s** | 2547 Broadway (bet. 95th & 96th Sts.) | 212-280-2668 |
www.twoboots.com ☽
W Village | 201 W. 11th St. (7th Ave. S.) | 212-633-9096 |
www.twoboots.com ☽
Park Slope | 514 Second St. (bet. 7th & 8th Aves.) | Brooklyn |
718-499-3253 | www.twobootsbrooklyn.com

"Not your ordinary" pizza purveyor, this "quirky" chain proffers "change-of-pace" pies with "crispy" cornmeal crusts, "zesty", "ragin' Cajun flavors" and "clever names"; basic but "funky" digs suit those "with kids in tow", particularly at the separately owned Park Sloper that's usually "swarming with families."

	FOOD	DECOR	SERVICE	COST

202 Cafe *Mediterranean*

19 | 19 | 17 | $36

Chelsea | Chelsea Mkt. | 75 Ninth Ave. (bet. 15th & 16th Sts.) | 646-638-1173

Shoppers who "can't afford the Nicole Farhi merchandise" in her Chelsea Market boutique "admire it over brunch" at this "spiffy" eatery "nestled among colorful clothes"; though the "well-crafted", "modestly priced" Med menu draws applause, the "sluggish" service needs a makeover.

2 West *American*

21 | 22 | 22 | $60

Financial District | Ritz-Carlton Battery Park | 2 West St. (Battery Pl.) | 917-790-2525 | www.ritzcarlton.com

After a recent shift to a New American menu, this former steakhouse in the "remote" Ritz-Carlton Battery Park remains "convenient" for biz diners and "hotel guests" with a taste for modern decor and "attentive service"; while "expensive", it's a "solid" option "if you're in the area."

Txikito Ⓜ *Spanish*

24 | 16 | 20 | $45

Chelsea | 240 Ninth Ave. (bet. 24th & 25th Sts.) | 212-242-4730 | www.txikitonyc.com

"Top-of-the-line tapas" are the reason this "tiny", "stylish" Chelsea Basque is known as a "foodie heaven" where each dish "you can't pronounce" is a "new adventure"; an "upbeat" staff works the recently expanded digs, so the only downside of the "wonderful evening" is that "costs can mount" fast.

Umberto's Clam House *Italian/Seafood*

19 | 14 | 17 | $40

Little Italy | 386 Broome St. (Mulberry St.) | 212-343-2053 | www.umbertosclamhouse.com
Bronx | 2356 Arthur Ave. (186th St.) | 718-220-2526 | www.umbertosclamhousebronx.com

As famous for its *"Goodfellas* atmosphere" as for its "special" "spicy tomato sauce", this Little Italy "institution" and its brother in the Bronx offer "plentiful portions" of "righteous", "basic" Italian; "brusque" service doesn't put off the "tourists" or anyone seeking "late-night pasta."

Umi Nom Ⓢ *Filipino/Thai*

∇ 24 | 21 | 22 | $32

Clinton Hill | 433 DeKalb Ave. (Classon Ave.) | Brooklyn | 718-789-8806 | www.uminom.com

"Adventurous specials" "truly shine" at this "stylish" Clinton Hill Filipino-Thai rated just "as satisfying" as its "older LES sibling", Kuma Inn; the staff "bounces along to the hipster soundtrack" and portions are "pretty big" for small plates, while the prices are sized "just right."

Uncle Jack's Steakhouse *Steak*

22 | 19 | 21 | $70

Garment District | 440 Ninth Ave. (bet. 34th & 35th Sts.) | 212-244-0005
W 50s | 44 W. 56th St. (bet. 5th & 6th Aves.) | 212-245-1550
Bayside | 39-40 Bell Blvd. (40th Ave.) | Queens | 718-229-1100 | www.unclejacks.com

These "stately old-school" "boys' clubs" dispense some "fine cow" along with "fabulous martinis", making for "enjoyable meals" that "stack up well" against the competition; however, wallet-watchers consider them "expense account-only", because those "well-mannered", "white-glove" waiters will bring you a "big bill."

Uncle Nick's *Greek*

FOOD	DECOR	SERVICE	COST
21	13	18	$35

Chelsea | 382 Eighth Ave. (29th St.) | 212-609-0500
W 50s | 747 Ninth Ave. (bet. 50th & 51st Sts.) | 212-245-7992
www.unclenicksgreekrestaurant.com

"Unadorned but delectable" grilled fish and other "solid" Greek specialties keep these "affordable", "no-frills" tavernas "bustling"; to avoid Hell's Kitchen's "crowded", "ho-hum" setting, try the garden or adjacent ouzaria – or hit the less-"squished" Chelsea branch.

Union Smith Café *American*

FOOD	DECOR	SERVICE	COST
20	18	19	$44

Carroll Gardens | 305 Smith St. (Union St.) | Brooklyn | 718-643-3293

"Excellent for brunch" (served daily) and "solid" pub grub, this "pleasant", "diner"-like Carroll Gardens New American has become a local "standby"; the "generous" drinks are "always good", as is the opportunity to "chill" and "people-watch" on the patio.

⚡ Union Square Cafe *American*

FOOD	DECOR	SERVICE	COST
26	23	26	$70

Union Sq | 21 E. 16th St. (bet. 5th Ave. & Union Sq. W.) | 212-243-4020 | www.unionsquarecafe.com

"Year in, year out", Danny Meyer's "ultrapopular" Union Square "paragon" "lives up to its top-notch reputation" for "superior" New American cooking based on "fresh produce from the Greenmarket", delivered by a "polished", "never-snooty" staff in "civilized", "understated" digs; prices are "high-end", but considering that it's a "class act from start to finish", you'll leave thinking it's "worth every cent."

Ushiwakamaru ⚡ *Japanese*

FOOD	DECOR	SERVICE	COST
27	18	22	$88

G Village | 136 W. Houston St. (bet. MacDougal & Sullivan Sts.) | 212-228-4181

"Discriminating" sushi lovers get a "thrill" at this Village "hidden gem", where the chef is "an artist" and his omakase offerings are "super-fresh" and "from near and far"; it's "not high-end looking" and sure "not cheap" either, but "who cares" – the "quality-to-value ratio" is unbeatable.

Uskudar *Turkish*

FOOD	DECOR	SERVICE	COST
21	12	20	$37

E 70s | 1405 Second Ave. (bet. 73rd & 74th Sts.) | 212-988-4046 | www.uskudarnyc.com

"Blink and you've passed" this "under-the-radar" Upper Eastsider serving "perfectly seasoned", "predictably good" Turkish "delights" in "minuscule" digs; there's "no glamour here", just "doting" service "with a smile" and the satisfaction that you'll "get your money's worth."

Utsav *Indian*

FOOD	DECOR	SERVICE	COST
21	20	20	$41

W 40s | 1185 Sixth Ave., 2nd fl. (bet. 46th & 47th Sts.) | 212-575-2525 | www.utsavny.com

Fans of "flavorful" Indian fare are as "happy as puffed-up papadums" at this "serene" Midtowner, whose "elegant" surroundings and "thoughtful" service make for a "marvelous pre-theater" pick; prices are "fair" in general, but the lunch buffet is an "exceptional bargain."

Uva ⚫ *Italian*

FOOD	DECOR	SERVICE	COST
21	21	20	$41

E 70s | 1486 Second Ave. (bet. 77th & 78th Sts.) | 212-472-4552 | www.uvawinebar.com

"Young metrosexuals flirt with each other" at this "intimate" UES "hot spot"–cum–"date place", while an "attentive" crew delivers "interesting" Italian small plates and "wonderful wines"; when the "Downtown vibe" inside gets "too loud", turn to the "super-cute garden."

	FOOD	DECOR	SERVICE	COST

Uvarara ◨ Italian
▽ 26 | 25 | 23 | $34

Middle Village | 79-28 Metropolitan Ave. (bet. 79th & 80th Sts.) | Queens | 718-894-0052 | www.uvararany.com

A "standout" in a zone boasting "tons of Italian" eateries, this "little" family-run Middle Village "gem" serves "exceptional regional fare" with "many wines" from The Boot to match; its "beautiful", "vaulted-ceiling" space and "warm" service ensure you'll "want to linger."

Vai Mediterranean
21 | 16 | 17 | $45

W 70s | 225 W. 77th St. (bet. Amsterdam Ave. & B'way) | 212-362-4500 | www.vairestaurant.com

"Scrumptious" Med eats and "well-chosen wines" draw a "fun" crowd to this "cute", "friendly" UWS "date place"; expect the "shoulder-to-shoulder" crowd to kick up some "noise" in its "little" space.

◨ Valbella ◨ Italian
25 | 25 | 25 | $78

Meatpacking | 421 W. 13th St. (bet. 9th Ave. & Washington St.) | 212-645-7777 | www.valbellany.com

With its "sumptuous" Northern Italian cuisine matched with "stellar" wines, "beautiful" space and "above-and-beyond" service, this "memorable" Meatpacking "experience" is deemed a "special place for special occasions"; its "stunning" spiral staircase leads to the "private wine rooms", but it's the "$$$ prices" that may have you a bit "breathless."

NEW Vandaag Danish/Dutch
- | - | - | E

E Village | 103 Second Ave. (6th St.) | 212-253-0470 | www.vandaagnyc.com

Bringing rare-in-NYC Northern European flavors to a neighborhood always looking for the next thing, this pricey new East Villager features Dutch-Danish cuisine by an ex-Corton chef and a drinks list showcasing the region's spirits and beers; the modernist interior features a picture window looking onto bustling Second Avenue.

NEW Vanderbilt, The ◉ American
21 | 22 | 20 | $43

Prospect Heights | 570 Vanderbilt Ave. (Bergen St.) | Brooklyn | 718-623-0570 | www.thevanderbiltnyc.com

On Prospect Heights' burgeoning "Vanderbilt strip", Saul Bolton's "handsome, sleek" new "hangout" plies "flavorful", "upscale" American small plates and "crazy-good cocktails"; it's a "hot", "young"-skewing "scene" overseen by a "pro" staff, but beware: those "tasty" bites "add up."

V&T ◉ Italian/Pizza
18 | 10 | 14 | $25

W 100s | 1024 Amsterdam Ave. (bet. 110th & 111th Sts.) | 212-666-8051 | www.vtpizzeriarestaurant.com

"Same red gravy, same grumpy waiters" – this Columbia-area "checkered-tablecloth" Italian "hasn't changed" since "grandma was a kid"; it turns out "the best" pizzas and other "homestyle" eats "for the money", so naturally "locals" and "hungry" students "love it."

Vanessa's Dumpling House Chinese
22 | 7 | 11 | $13

E Village | 220 E. 14th St. (bet. 2nd & 3rd Aves.) | 212-529-1329
LES | 118A Eldridge St. (bet. Broome & Grand Sts.) | 212-625-8008

"Ridiculously good" dumplings for "ridiculously low" prices says it all about this East Village–LES Chinese duo where "addicted" fans are tempted to "order everything" on the menu; given "nonexistent" decor and "no place to sit and eat", most go the "takeout" route.

NEW Vapiano ❶ *Italian*   - | - | - | I

G Village | 113 University Pl. (13th St.) | 212-777-9477 | www.vapiano.com

A display of potted herbs and a live olive tree cast a verdant note at this Village link of a German-based Italian fast-food chain vending pastas, pizzas and panini; the cafeteria-style service, communal tables and stylish bar are already filling up with young types who like that its electronic chip-card payment system makes splitting the small tabs a cinch.

Vatan Ⓜ *Indian*   23 | 21 | 22 | $40

Murray Hill | 409 Third Ave. (29th St.) | 212-689-5666 | www.vatanny.com

There's "no menu" to decipher when you settle into the "exotic" "fairy-tale-village" setting of this Murray Hill Indian vegetarian, just a "remarkable", "limitless" spread for $31, presided over by "lovely" staffers; it's a perfect "way to explore" India without flying.

Veloce Pizzeria ❶ *Pizza*   ▽ 20 | 14 | 16 | $28

E Village | 103 First Ave. (bet. 6th & 7th Sts.) | 212-777-6677 | www.velocepizzeria.com

"Serious pizzavores" go for the "delicate, delicious" Sicilian square pies with "purist toppings" "conjured up" by chef Sara Jenkins (of Porchetta fame) at this "stylish"-for-the-genre East Villager; the general feel is "wine bar", with "approachable" pricing balancing the sometimes-"indifferent" service.

Veniero's ❶ *Dessert*   24 | 14 | 15 | $17

E Village | 342 E. 11th St. (bet. 1st & 2nd Aves.) | 212-674-7070 | www.venierospastry.com

"In a class by itself", this East Village Italian "pastry palace" has been the reigning "king of cannoli" since 1894; just "expect to wait" before savoring one of the "zillion" "morsels" amid its "old-world charm", because this "diet buster" and "tourist" favorite is "always crowded."

ⓩ Veritas *American*   26 | 22 | 25 | $111

Flatiron | 43 E. 20th St. (bet. B'way & Park Ave. S.) | 212-353-3700 | www.veritas-nyc.com

What this "fancy" Flatiron New American is "famed" for is its "amazing wine list", but its "superb" vintages "don't overshadow" the "dazzling" cooking and the "excellent" service from a "white-glove" staff; factor in "quiet", "intimate" environs, and overall it's a "brilliant" experience – of course you may have to "knock over a bank" to pay the $85 prix fixe–only tab; P.S. it's closed for renovations.

Vermicelli *Vietnamese*   19 | 14 | 17 | $30

E 70s | 1492 Second Ave. (bet. 77th & 78th Sts.) | 212-288-8868 | www.vermicellirestaurant.com

Despite the "surprising" name, this "popular" UES "standby" specializes in "tasty", "varied" Vietnamese fare, offered in "generous portions"; the service is "congenial", while the "low" prices get even better at lunch, when the "bargain specials" are "cheaper than eating at home."

	FOOD	DECOR	SERVICE	COST

Veselka ◑ *Ukrainian* — 19 | 12 | 15 | $23

E Village | 144 Second Ave. (9th St.) | 212-228-9682
E Village | First Park | 75 E. First St. (1st Ave.) | 347-907-3317 ⊄
www.veselka.com

East Village "gentrification stopped at the doorstep" of this "timeless" Ukrainian "institution" dishing up "hearty", "soul-warming" grub "on the cheap" 24/7; loyalists maintain its "lack of decor and service is its charm", but others looking to avoid all that hit the First Street kiosk.

Vespa *Italian* — 19 | 19 | 18 | $44

E 80s | 1625 Second Ave. (bet. 84th & 85th Sts.) | 212-472-2050 |
www.vesparestaurant.us

"Tasty vittles", Italian-style, come in a "darling" (read: "small") package at this "friendly", "reasonably priced" Upper Eastsider with a "cool scooter motif" and an "aim-to-please" staff; it's a year-round "safe bet" with a "lovely" garden that's a "summertime hot spot."

Vesta *Italian* — ▽ 24 | 18 | 23 | $34

Astoria | 21-02 30th Ave. (21st St.) | Queens | 718-545-5550 |
www.vestavino.com

Considered among the "besta" in an "off-the-beaten-track" corner of Astoria, this "neighborhood treasure" serves up pizzas and other "fantastic" "Greenmarket"-oriented Italian cuisine and "amazing wines" at "fair prices"; the "tight" casual quarters are "jumping" at prime times, but the staff "handles things well."

Vezzo *Pizza* — 23 | 15 | 17 | $27

Murray Hill | 178 Lexington Ave. (31st St.) | 212-839-8300 |
www.vezzothincrust.com

"Flat, crispy and delicious" with "toppings for every taste" sums up the "fancy", thin-crust "gourmet pizzas" plied by this "pub"-like Murray Hill Italian; it's "small" and "loud" with "so-so decor and service", but that doesn't deter the "crowds."

Via Emilia ⊠⊄ *Italian* — 23 | 16 | 20 | $40

Flatiron | 47 E. 21st St. (bet. B'way & Park Ave. S.) | 212-505-3072 |
www.viaemilia.us

"Not your run-of-the-mill Italian", this "quirky" Flatiron "gem" focuses on "extraordinary" specialties from Emilia-Romagna, dispensing "fresh-made pastas" along with its "famous Lambrusco" wines; other pluses are "friendly" welcomes and "affordable" prices; P.S. "bring cash" – it takes "no plastic."

Viand *Coffee Shop* — 17 | 8 | 17 | $23

E 60s | 673 Madison Ave. (bet. 61st & 62nd Sts.) | 212-751-6622 ⊄
E 70s | 1011 Madison Ave. (78th St.) | 212-249-8250
E 80s | 300 E. 86th St. (2nd Ave.) | 212-879-9425 ◑
Viand Cafe ◑ *Coffee Shop*
W 70s | 2130 Broadway (75th St.) | 212-877-2888 |
www.viandnyc.com

These "dependable" coffee shops maintain a "cult following" (including "Mayor Bloomberg") thanks to their "world-class turkey sandwiches" and "endless menu" of diner "basics" that "get the job done"; they have "zero ambiance", but never mind – "snappy" service means "you're outta there in no time."

	FOOD	DECOR	SERVICE	COST

Via Quadronno *Italian* | 21 | 15 | 17 | $42

E 70s | 25 E. 73rd St. (bet. 5th & Madison Aves.) | 212-650-9880

Via Quadronno Cafe 🖾 *Italian*

E 50s | GM Bldg. | 767 Fifth Ave. (59th St.) | 212-421-5300
www.viaquadronno.com

"Fabulous panini and even better people-watching" await those willing to "shoehorn" themselves in with the "hordes" of "Euro jet-setters" at this "cute", "socialite-friendly" UES Milanese; "distracted" service and "expensive" tabs are part of the package; P.S. the Fifth Avenue offshoot is takeout only.

ViceVersa 🖾 *Italian* | 22 | 21 | 22 | $52

W 50s | 325 W. 51st St. (bet. 8th & 9th Aves.) | 212-399-9291 | www.viceversarestaurant.com

This "welcoming" Theater District Italian "chestnut" "hits all the right notes": "wonderful" food, "engaging" service and a "sleek, sophisticated" setting with "delightful" garden; it's on the "pricey" side, but "outstanding" prix fixe deals mean even wallet-watchers "leave happy."

Vico *Italian* | 20 | 14 | 19 | $69

E 90s | 1302 Madison Ave. (bet. 92nd & 93rd Sts.) | 212-876-2222

Looking "like a neighborhood" joint but acting "like a grande dame", this "quaint" Carnegie Hill Italian offers "simple, expertly prepared" eats to its "well-heeled" regulars but "can be gruff" with strangers; first-timers may be "shocked when the bill arrives" (it's "pricey"), but loyalists leave chanting "veni vidi Vico!"

Victor's Cafe ● *Cuban* | 22 | 20 | 21 | $51

W 50s | 236 W. 52nd St. (bet. B'way & 8th Ave.) | 212-586-7714 | www.victorscafe.com

"Luscious" Cuban cuisine and a touch of "mojito madness" fuel the "festive" "old Havana" mood at this "vibrant", "venerable" Theater District "mainstay"; other pluses: the "cheerful" staff "takes good care of you" and one can manage the tab "without an expense account."

Vida 🖾Ⓜ *Eclectic* | ▽ 23 | 20 | 25 | $37

Staten Island | 381 Van Duzer St. (bet. Beach & Wright Sts.) | 718-720-1501

An "ebullient" owner contributes to the "inviting" mood at this colorful Staten Island "hangout", where the "multicultural" Eclectic eats run from Mexico to Morocco and suit "vegans" and omnivores alike; "personalized attention" and affordable tabs round out the appeal.

View, The Ⓜ *American* | 17 | 25 | 18 | $90

W 40s | Marriott Marquis Hotel | 1535 Broadway, 47th fl. (bet. 45th & 46th Sts.) | 212-704-8880 | www.nymarriottmarquis.com

"Out-of-towners" gravitate to this "rotating" New American atop the Times Square Marriott to gaze out on "panoramic" views of Manhattan and beyond; the "premium-priced" prix fixe fare is just "so-so", so the "better bet" may be the "cheaper" "lounge buffet" that's one flight below.

Villa Berulia *Italian* | 22 | 19 | 25 | $56

Murray Hill | 107 E. 34th St. (bet. Lexington & Park Aves.) | 212-689-1970 | www.villaberulia.com

Even first-timers "feel at home" at this "hospitable" Northern Italian "old faithful" that's among "Murray Hill's winningest" thanks to its "well-priced", "darn-good" fare, a staff that's "courteous without being fawning" and "lovely, quiet" room; no surprise, it's "filled every night with regulars."

NEW Village Tart ● *Dessert* ▽ 20 | 21 | 21 | $30

NoLita | 86 Kenmare St. (Mulberry St.) | 212-226-4980 | www.villagetart.com
"Beautiful" gilded mirrors, tile floors and marble-topped tables give this "charming" new NoLita bakery/wine bar the look of an "old-world" European cafe; "divine" tarts are among the affordable bistro-ish offerings, and there's also a case full of "delicious" confections.

Villa Mosconi ☒ *Italian* 23 | 16 | 23 | $47

G Village | 69 MacDougal St. (bet. Bleecker & Houston Sts.) | 212-673-0390 | www.villamosconi.com
Specializing in "the same fantastic dishes for more than 30 years", this "traditional" family-run Village Italian is like a "time machine – in the best sense"; "good prices", "tasteful" decor and "patient" servers "make you feel like *la famiglia.*"

Vincent's ● *Italian* 21 | 13 | 17 | $38

Little Italy | 119 Mott St. (Hester St.) | 212-226-8133 | www.originalvincents.com
"Authentic" as all get out, this circa-1904 Little Italy "survivor" is famed for its "trademark hot sauce" and "tried-and-true" standards; sure, the decor is "dated" and the "servers won't coddle you", but it's an "experience" for "tourists and locals" alike.

Vinegar Hill House *American* 25 | 19 | 20 | $46

Vinegar Hill | 72 Hudson Ave. (bet. Front & Water Sts.) | Brooklyn | 718-522-1018 | www.vinegarhillhouse.com
"Exceptional" New American cooking awaits "intrepid" travelers to this "quintessentially cool" outpost in Brooklyn's "forgotten" Vinegar Hill neighborhood; "funky" salvaged decor, a "quaint backyard", "personable" service and "modest prices" seal its standing as a "hipster magnet", so expect a "wait" at the "crowded" bar.

Virgil's Real Barbecue ● *BBQ* 20 | 14 | 17 | $36

W 40s | 152 W. 44th St. (bet. B'way & 6th Ave.) | 212-921-9494 | www.virgilsbbq.com
"Ooo-wee, that's down-home!" squeal fans of the "lip-smacking" BBQ and sides at this "big, brassy" Times Square ribhouse where portions are "humongous" and prices "reasonable (for the area)"; despite "low-level service", "tourists" and locals alike "stuff themselves silly" here.

Vivolo ☒ *Italian* 21 | 19 | 21 | $50

E 70s | 140 E. 74th St. (bet. Lexington & Park Aves.) | 212-737-3533

Cucina Vivolo ☒ *Italian*

E 70s | 138 E. 74th St. (bet. Lexington & Park Aves.) | 212-717-4700 www.vivolonyc.com
Occupying two floors of a "classy" UES townhouse since 1977, this "civilized" Italian attracts "diners of a certain age" with its "traditional" cooking, fireplaces and "dark-paneled", "conversation-friendly" setting; its "informal" adjacent cafe is more of a "bargain" and open for breakfast.

	FOOD	DECOR	SERVICE	COST

Vynl ◑ *American/Thai* 　17 | 18 | 17 | $27

Chelsea | 102 Eighth Ave. (15th St.) | 212-400-2118
W 50s | 754 Ninth Ave. (51st St.) | 212-974-2003
www.vynl-nyc.com

"Kitsch" is the thing at this American-Thai diner duo offering "comfort foods" from "mac 'n' cheese to pad Thai" in "fun" "LP-themed" digs; apart from "cute waiters" and "rock 'n' roll bathrooms", it's "nothing fancy", but "low prices" pack in a "young crowd."

Wa Jeal *Chinese* 　25 | 15 | 19 | $30

E 80s | 1588 Second Ave. (bet. 82nd & 83rd Sts.) | 212-396-3339 |
www.wajealrestaurant.com

"Yorkville residents mourning the loss of Wu Liang Ye" are delighted to find some of "the same crew" cooking "10-alarm" "super-fresh" Sichuan fare at this relative newcomer; "reasonable" rates and "attentive" service are other pluses, but the setting suggests "takeout."

Waldy's Wood Fired Pizza *Pizza* 　21 | 10 | 16 | $18

Chelsea | 800 Sixth Ave. (bet. 27th & 28th Sts.) | 212-213-5042 |
www.waldyspizza.com

At Waldy Malouf's "nondescript little" Chelsea pizzeria, the "brilliant thin-crust pizzas" come with their "exotic" toppings ready for a "cut-your-own herb garnish"; the staff "aims to please", but "reliable delivery" and takeout are more appealing because of the "limited seating."

Walker's ◑ *Pub Food* 　18 | 13 | 17 | $32

TriBeCa | 16 N. Moore St. (Varick St.) | 212-941-0142

"Skip the fancy stuff" at this "popular", "lively" TriBeCa "watering hole" and tuck into its "solid" "straightforward" pub grub dished up in "friendly" fashion; factor in "cheap" tabs, and all agree "every neighborhood needs" a "comfy" "hangout" like this one.

NEW Wall & Water *American* 　∇ 21 | 23 | 21 | $51

Financial District | Andaz Wall Street Hotel | 75 Wall St. (Water St.) |
212-699-1700 | www.wallandwaterny.com

The FiDi gets a new "power"-dining place with this "high-end" New American arrival in the Andaz Hotel, where the "exquisite" Rockwell-designed decor features a swooping, "J.P. Morgan–worthy" staircase and a display kitchen; the "pricey" three-meal-a-day offerings showcase Hudson Valley ingredients that would please "the fussiest locavore."

Z Wallsé *Austrian* 　26 | 22 | 24 | $72

W Village | 344 W. 11th St. (Washington St.) | 212-352-2300 |
www.kg-ny.com

"Austrian haute cuisine" is no "oxymoron" at Kurt Gutenbrunner's "elegant" West Village "jewel", where he "reinvents" schnitzel and other "favorites" as "superb" "delicacies"; "pristine" service and a "tranquil" setting with artwork by Julian Schnabel add to the "transcending" experience – for those who "can afford it."

Walter Foods ◑ *American* 　∇ 23 | 22 | 23 | $46

Williamsburg | 253 Grand St. (Roebling St.) | Brooklyn | 718-387-8783 |
www.walterfoods.com

Epitomizing Williamsburg "cool", this saloon-style New American is deemed a "perfect neighborhood restaurant" thanks to its "sneaky" cocktails, "fantastically fresh" raw bar and "delicious" "comfort" fare served by "nice hipsters with bow ties"; the "beautiful" garden and "lively vibe" are bonuses.

Wasabi Lobby ● *Japanese* — 21 | 14 | 18 | $34

E 80s | 1584 Second Ave. (82nd St.) | 212-988-8882 | www.wasabilobbynyc.com

"Ok, it's a silly name", but this UES Japanese is "serious" about its "beautifully prepared", "imaginative" sushi; the atmosphere may be "generic", but "courteous, quick" service and prices that are "low for the quality" have most declaring it a "winner."

Watawa *Japanese* — ▽ 25 | 19 | 23 | $28

Astoria | 33-10 Ditmars Blvd. (bet. 33rd & 35th Sts.) | Queens | 718-545-9596

"Fresh", "wow"-worthy sushi makes this "unpretentious" Astoria Japanese a "go-to" for locals who "savor" its "versatile menu", "accommodating" service and gentle prices; "since it's small", it's often "packed", i.e. expect "waits on weekends."

Water Club *American* — 21 | 25 | 22 | $66

Murray Hill | East River & 30th St. (enter on 23rd St.) | 212-683-3333 | www.thewaterclub.com

"Dynamite" waterfront views "mesmerize" diners at this "elegant", "nautically decorated" American on a moored East River barge that creates a "truly romantic" "mini-vacation" feel; if this weren't enough, "polite" staffers and "terrific" eats ensure it's "worth the crazy $$$" – and there's always the "amazing" $39 brunch buffet; P.S. it's a "great party venue."

☑ Water's Edge ☒ *American/Seafood* — 20 | 25 | 22 | $66

LIC | East River & 44th Dr. (Vernon Blvd.) | Queens | 718-482-0033 | www.watersedgenyc.com

"Magnificent views" of the Midtown skyline, a "luxurious" atmosphere and "imaginative" New American seafood "graciously served" mean this "classy" LIC stalwart is just the thing for a "big night out"; sure, it costs "major bucks", but the water taxi ride from Manhattan is free and "adds a touch of enchantment" to an already "terribly romantic" evening.

Watty & Meg *American* — 20 | 21 | 19 | $40

Cobble Hill | 248 Court St. (Kane St.) | Brooklyn | 718-643-0007 | www.wattyandmeg.com

"Warm and welcoming", this "lovely" Cobble Hill American "puts a smile on your face" with "tasty" Southern-accented fare served in a "cozy", "dark-wood" setting that exudes "nice energy"; to some it's "slightly overpriced", with "too many strollers", but the nightly specials "can't be beat."

☑ Waverly Inn ● *American* — 20 | 22 | 20 | $77

W Village | 16 Bank St. (Waverly Pl.) | 917-828-1154

"Celebrities" and "socialites" congregate at this "exclusive" West Village "scene", where being a "friend of owner Graydon Carter" ("Mr. Vanity Fair") is the entree to a "buzzy" evening of "style" and "good" American "home cooking"; it recently started serving brunch, and now that it actually takes phone reservations, "getting in" is no longer such a "hassle."

| | FOOD | DECOR | SERVICE | COST |

WD-50 ●◐Ⓜ *American/Eclectic*   `25` `19` `24` `$89`

LES | 50 Clinton St. (bet. Rivington & Stanton Sts.) | 212-477-2900 |
www.wd-50.com

"Paradise" for "serious foodies", this "unassuming LES storefront" is
the scene of chef Wylie Dufresne's "culinary chemistry" experiments,
resulting in "mind-bending" New American–Eclectic cuisine with "surprises in every bite"; the "wowed" find the "astronomical" prices "totally worth it", but the unwowed find the "bizarre combos" "better as
concepts than on the plate."

West Bank Cafe *American*   `19` `16` `19` `$44`

W 40s | Manhattan Plaza | 407 W. 42nd St. (bet. 9th & 10th Aves.) |
212-695-6909 | www.westbankcafe.com

This "bustling" Hell's Kitchen "old reliable" matches "satisfying",
"inexpensive"-for-the-area New American eats with "competent" service, getting theatergoers "well fed" and "to the show on time"; the
decor's "about zilch", unless you count the occasional "Broadway
star" grabbing an "after-show drink."

Westville *American*   `22` `12` `17` `$26`

NEW Chelsea | 246 W. 18th St. (bet. 7th & 8th Aves.) | 212-924-2223
W Village | 210 W. 10th St. (bet. Bleecker & W. 4th Sts.) | 212-741-7971

Westville East *American*

E Village | 173 Ave. A (11th St.) | 212-677-2033
www.westvillenyc.com

Ingredients go "from greenmarket to plate with little interference" at
these "relaxed" cross-Village Americans (with a Chelsea offshoot that
opened post-Survey); they serve "wonderful", "super-cheap" fare satisfying vegetarians and omnivores alike, thus there's "always a line."

White Slab Palace ●◐ *Scandinavian*   ▽ `18` `22` `18` `$40`

LES | 77 Delancey St. (Allen St.) | 212-334-0913

Rapidly gentrifying Allen Street is home to this "unexpected"
Scandinavian offering Nordic noshes to Lower Eastsiders in need of a
cheap feed; the "beautiful", amply windowed corner setting feels like
an old saloon, done up with taxidermy and distressed wood.

Whole Foods Café *Eclectic*   `19` `10` `11` `$18`

LES | 95 E. Houston St., 2nd fl. (bet. Bowery & Chrystie St.) | 212-420-1320
TriBeCa | 270 Greenwich St., 2nd fl. (bet. Murray & Warren Sts.) |
212-349-6555
Union Sq | 4 Union Sq. S. (bet. B'way & University Pl.) | 212-673-5388
W 60s | Time Warner Ctr. | 10 Columbus Circle, downstairs (60th St.
at B'way) | 212-823-9600
www.wholefoods.com

For "grab and go" or a "tasty" on-premises "gobbledown", you can't
match the "fantastic" "smorgasbord" of "multi-ethnic, hot and cold"
eats at these self-serve, in-supermarket emporiums; they're "a zoo",
but that's "due to their popularity."

Whym *American*   `20` `17` `20` `$40`

W 50s | 889 Ninth Ave. (bet. 57th & 58th Sts.) | 212-315-0088 |
www.whymnyc.com

"Whymsical" indeed, this Hell's Kitchen "go-to" delivers "fancied-up"
American "comfort food" at the "right price" in "modern" digs manned

by a "good-natured" crew; it's "an easy choice" pre- or post-theater,
but gets "noisy" thanks to those "young things carbo-loading."

'Wichcraft *Sandwiches* 20 | 11 | 15 | $17

Chelsea | 269 11th Ave. (bet. 27th & 28th Sts.) | 212-780-0577
E 40s | 245 Park Ave. (47th St.) | 212-780-0577
E 40s | 555 Fifth Ave. (46th St.) | 212-780-0577
Flatiron | 11 E. 20th St. (bet. B'way & 5th Ave.) | 212-780-0577
G Village | 60 E. Eighth St. (Mercer St.) | 212-780-0577
SoHo | Equinox | 568 Broadway (Prince St.) | 212-780-0577
TriBeCa | 397 Greenwich St. (Beach St.) | 212-780-0577
W 40s | 11 W. 40th St. (6th Ave.) | 212-780-0577
W 50s | 1 Rockefeller Plaza (49th St., bet. 5th & 6th Aves.) | 212-780-0577
NEW **W 60s** | David Rubenstein Atrium at Lincoln Ctr. | 61 W. 62nd St.
(bet. B'way & Columbus Ave.) | 212-780-0577
www.wichcraftnyc.com
Additional locations throughout the NY area

"Happifying", "seriously good" sandwiches in "original" "variations"
made with "first-rate ingredients" have most "bewitched" at Tom
Colicchio's chainlet; it's a bit "pricey" and peak-time waits can be "ex-
cruciating", but it's been "energizing cubicle-dwellers" for years.

Wild Ginger Pan-Asian Vegan Café *Asian* 22 | 18 | 20 | $26

Little Italy | 380 Broome St. (Mott St.) | 212-966-1883 |
www.wildgingervegan.com
Cobble Hill | 112 Smith St. (bet. Dean & Pacific Sts.) | Brooklyn |
718-858-3880
Williamsburg | 212 Bedford Ave. (bet. 5th & 6th Sts.) | Brooklyn |
718-218-8828

"Truly delicious" vegetarian fare at this "inexpensive" Pan-Asian trio
comes with "enough surprises to satisfy the adventurous" and sufficient "subtleties" for even "non-vegans to love"; the "minimalist" digs
have a "peaceful" vibe abetted by "polite" service; P.S. the Little Italy
branch is separately owned.

Wildwood Barbeque *BBQ* 18 | 16 | 18 | $36

Flatiron | 225 Park Ave. S. (bet. 18th & 19th Sts.) | 212-533-2500 |
www.brguestrestaurants.com

Think "upscale frat party" with "respectable" – "for NYC", anyway –
"down-home BBQ", and you've got Stephen Hanson's "huge", "festive"
Flatironer, where "boisterous MBAs" gather to "watch the game"; rustic
digs, "reasonable" rates and "tenderfoot" service complete the picture.

Wo Hop ●⌿ *Chinese* 21 | 5 | 13 | $20

Chinatown | 17 Mott St., downstairs (Canal St.) | 212-267-2536

"Dependable as the sunrise", this "iconic" C-town Cantonese has been
"around forever", slinging "good old-fashioned" "Americanized Chinese"
eats at "bargain" rates "all night long"; fans endure "waits", "dungeon-
like" digs and "stone-faced" service – it's a "true NYC experience."

Ⓩ Wolfgang's Steakhouse *Steak* 25 | 21 | 21 | $77

NEW **E 50s** | 200 E. 54th St. (3rd Ave.) | 212-588-9653
Murray Hill | 4 Park Ave. (33rd St.) | 212-889-3369
TriBeCa | 409 Greenwich St. (bet. Beach & Hubert Sts.) | 212-925-0350
www.wolfgangssteakhouse.com

For "superb", "high-priced" slabs of beef, try these Peter Luger
"knockoff" steakhouses manned by "gruff" but "competent" waiters;

they "pack the suits in", resulting in a "rushed", "crowded" "noisefest", yet for most they're "really worth going to" all the same.

Wollensky's Grill ● *Steak*

| 23 | 17 | 21 | $59 |

E 40s | 201 E. 49th St. (3rd Ave.) | 212-753-0444 |
www.smithandwollensky.com

"More user-friendly" than Smith & Wollensky, this "lively", "less-costly" steakhouse "offshoot" offers the "same quality meat" and "all the best parts of the mother ship" "without the hoopla" or "crotchety" staff; it's "terrific" for those "feeling carnivorous" late at night, as closing time is 2 AM and the burgers are as good as it gets.

Wondee Siam *Thai*

| 21 | 9 | 16 | $24 |

W 40s | 641 10th Ave. (bet. 45th & 46th Sts.) | 212-245-4601 |
www.wondeesiam3.com
W 50s | 792 Ninth Ave. (bet. 52nd & 53rd Sts.) | 212-459-9057 ⊘
W 50s | 813 Ninth Ave. (bet. 53rd & 54th Sts.) | 917-286-1726 |
www.wondeesiam2.com
W 100s | 969 Amsterdam Ave. (bet. 107th & 108th Sts.) | 212-531-1788 |
www.wondeesiamv.com

A "treat" for those who "love Thai food", this "bare-bones" West Side quartet offers the "real-deal" "flavorful" eats you'd find "in Bangkok"; the storefront spaces are "not the prettiest", and service can be "brusque", but the rates are "rock-bottom."

WonJo ● *Korean*

| 20 | 12 | 15 | $34 |

Garment District | 23 W. 32nd St. (bet. B'way & 5th Ave.) | 212-695-5815 |
www.wonjo32.com

Night owls craving "delicious Korean barbecue" tout this "loud, smoky" Garment District standby as a "can't-go-wrong" option for tableside grilling 24/7; "newly decorated" digs, "attentive" service and affordable tabs keep the place "packed."

Woo Lae Oak *Korean*

| 22 | 22 | 20 | $52 |

SoHo | 148 Mercer St. (bet. Houston & Prince Sts.) | 212-925-8200 |
www.woolaeoaksoho.com

"Cook-for-yourself Korean barbecue" goes "upscale" at this "sleek" SoHo standout, where the "gorgeous waiters" are "almost as hot as the grill"; it's more "trendy than authentic" and costs "a bit extra" than K-town, but who cares? – it's "darn good."

NEW Wright, The *American*

| ▽ 21 | 24 | 21 | $56 |

E 80s | Guggenheim Museum | 1071 Fifth Ave. (88th St.) | 212-427-5690 |
www.thewrightrestaurant.com

With "beautiful", "modernist", white-on-white decor, this "cool" newcomer to the Guggenheim Museum – named after the building's architect, Frank Lloyd Wright – offers "inventive" New American cuisine ferried by a "competent" crew; it's open for dinner, but it's more of a "lunch place" given the "cafeteria-style" setup with counter seating.

Wu Liang Ye *Chinese*

| 23 | 11 | 15 | $34 |

W 40s | 36 W. 48th St. (bet. 5th & 6th Aves.) | 212-398-2308
Now the "sole survivor" of a onetime trio, this Rock Center–area Chinese is still setting "mouths on fire" with its "rich, savory", "real Sichuan" fare; "surly staffers" and "dingy digs" are offset by "low prices" and a "convenient location" for theatergoers.

Xi'an Famous Foods *Chinese*

	FOOD	DECOR	SERVICE	COST
	-	-	-	I

NEW Chinatown | 88 E. Broadway (Forsyth St.) | 212-786-2068
NEW E Village | 81 St. Marks Pl. (1st Ave.) | 212-786-2068
NEW Flushing | Flushing Mall | 133-31 39th Ave. (bet. College Point Blvd. & Prince St.) | Queens | 212-786-2068
Flushing | Golden Shopping Mall | 41-28 Main St., downstairs (41st Rd.) | Queens | 212-786-2068
www.xianfoods.com

With a cult following in Flushing, this mini-chain recently added two Manhattan outposts where lines are forming for its bargain fare from the namesake capital of China's Shaanxi Province; if you don't like eating from Styrofoam plates in small, spartan spaces, you'd better get it to go.

NEW Xiao Ye *Chinese*

	FOOD	DECOR	SERVICE	COST
	-	-	-	M

LES | 198 Orchard St. (Houston St.) | 212-777-7733

This Lower East Side sliver from BaoHaus' Eddie Huang specializes in pork-heavy Taiwanese street food made from top-quality ingredients; the neon paint splattered on its black walls feels more arty-NYC than Taipei, likewise the irreverent names of its affordable dishes – Concubine Cucumbers, Kim Jong's Ill Noodles, etc. – which have its hipster clientele chuckling.

X.O. *Chinese*

	FOOD	DECOR	SERVICE	COST
	20	8	12	$20

Chinatown | 96 Walker St. (bet. Centre & Lafayette Sts.) | 212-343-8339
Little Italy | 148 Hester St. (bet. Bowery & Elizabeth St.) | 212-965-8645 ☒

There are so "many choices" at these Hong Kong–style dim sum specialists in Chinatown and Little Italy that ditherers get "dizzy" deciding which "tasty" tidbits to try; they're "nothing fancy" and service is strictly "throw-it-on-the-table", but "dirt-cheap" prices compensate.

Yakitori Totto ● *Japanese*

	FOOD	DECOR	SERVICE	COST
	24	15	18	$46

W 50s | 251 W. 55th St., 2nd fl. (bet. B'way & 8th Ave.) | 212-245-4555 | www.tottonyc.com

"Not your run-of-the-mill Japanese", this little Midtown yakitori joint turns meats, veggies and "every chicken part imaginable" into "divine" "morsels on skewers", all "grilled in front of you"; the seating's "tight", and if you "keep ordering" the check's "not cheap", yet there's "always a line" to get in.

Yama ☒ *Japanese*

	FOOD	DECOR	SERVICE	COST
	24	14	18	$42

E 40s | 308 E. 49th St. (bet. 1st & 2nd Aves.) | 212-355-3370
Gramercy | 122 E. 17th St. (Irving Pl.) | 212-475-0969
W Village | 38-40 Carmine St. (bet. Bedford & Bleecker Sts.) | 212-989-9330
www.yamarestaurant.com

"For those who think size matters", the "gargantuan" slices of "ultra-fresh", "top-grade" sushi at this "modest" Japanese trio far outweigh the "basic" service and "crush" in its "crowded" spaces; for such a "steal", enthusiasts "get there early" or survive "lines out the door."

Yerba Buena *Pan-Latin*

	FOOD	DECOR	SERVICE	COST
	23	19	21	$47

E Village | 23 Ave. A (bet. Houston & 2nd Sts.) | 212-529-2919
W Village | 1 Perry St. (Greenwich Ave.) | 212-620-0808 ●
www.ybnyc.com

East and West Villagers find their "taste buds doing a tango" over the "inspired" *comida* at Julian Medina's "exciting" "upscale" Pan-Latins;

they're a "hip scene" with "old Havana" ambiance, "solicitous" service and "killer" cocktails to take your mind off the "squeeze."

	FOOD	DECOR	SERVICE	COST

York Grill *American*
21 | 19 | 22 | $49

E 80s | 1690 York Ave. (bet. 88th & 89th Sts.) | 212-772-0261
"Leisurely" dining lives on at this "classy" Yorkville New American, a "trusted neighbor" with a "loyal following"; maybe the "pretty" digs could use some "pep" and the bill strikes some as "pricey", but the "caring" staff makes you "feel like a regular right away."

Yuca Bar ● *Pan-Latin*
23 | 15 | 17 | $31

E Village | 111 Ave. A (7th St.) | 212-982-9533 | www.yucabarnyc.com
A "good-time place" full of "young" things "talking up a storm", this "reasonable" East Village Pan-Latin mixes "flavorful" "standards" with "potent" drinks to create a "spirited" brew; tables are "tight" but a "coveted" "open-window seat" is perfect to witness the world go by.

Yuka *Japanese*
20 | 11 | 17 | $30

E 80s | 1557 Second Ave. (bet. 80th & 81st Sts.) | 212-772-9675
"Don't expect anything fancy" at this "busy" Yorkville Japanese where the "fresh" all-you-can-eat sushi costs just $21 a head; the space is "pretty bare" and "not for lingering", so simply "close your eyes" and savor the savings.

Yura on Madison *Sandwiches*
21 | 12 | 14 | $22

E 90s | 1292 Madison Ave. (92nd St.) | 212-860-1598 | www.yuraonmadison.com
"Everything looks delicious" and "prepared just so" at this "bustling" Carnegie Hill "corner cafe" where "private school kids and their moms" come to "snack" on "wonderful" sandwiches and other "tasty" bites; since its "informal" space has only a "few small tables", many get it to go.

Yuva *Indian*
23 | 18 | 21 | $40

E 50s | 230 E. 58th St. (bet. 2nd & 3rd Aves.) | 212-339-0090 | www.yuvanyc.com
They're "not shy about spicing" at this "upscale" East Midtown Indian where the "traditional" fare is made with the "freshest everything" and "charming" waiters add to the "memorable" experience; it's "priced well" too, especially the "bargain" $14 buffet lunch.

Zabar's Cafe *Deli*
20 | 7 | 12 | $19

W 80s | 2245 Broadway (80th St.) | 212-787-2000 | www.zabars.com
"You come, you nosh, you leave" – or read the paper – at this "zippy" UWS "icon" dispensing bagels, lox and other "top-quality" deli "treats" at "rock-bottom" rates; it's famously "chaotic" with decor that's "virtually nil" – and "don't expect smiles", either – but it's practically "mandatory" before noon.

Zaitzeff *Burgers*
20 | 12 | 15 | $20

E Village | 18 Ave. B (bet. 2nd & 3rd Sts.) | 212-477-7137 ●
Financial District | 72 Nassau St. (John St.) | 212-571-7272
www.zaitzeffnyc.com
"Quintessential American" favorites – "fabulous", "juicy" burgers – are made with Kobe beef, turkey and other "quality ingredients" and paired with "out-of-this-world" fries at this "low-key" Downtown duo;

naturally, it's "more costly" than the usual "fast-food dreck", but the "crowds" happily pay up; P.S. a Midtown outpost at 711 Second Avenue is in the works.

Zarela *Mexican*

FOOD	DECOR	SERVICE	COST
22	16	18	$44

E 50s | 953 Second Ave. (bet. 50th & 51st Sts.) | 212-644-6740 | www.zarela.com

It's "always a party" at Zarela Martinez's "colorful" East Midtown eatery whose *"mucho bueno"* "real Mexican" dishes go down well with "downright dangerous margaritas"; its "young" patrons kick up a "mad" "bar scene", but if you want to talk "it's quieter upstairs."

Zaytoons *Mideastern*

20	13	17	$21

Carroll Gardens | 283 Smith St. (Sackett St.) | Brooklyn | 718-875-1880
Fort Greene | 472 Myrtle Ave. (bet. Hall St. & Washington Ave.) | Brooklyn | 718-623-5522
Prospect Heights | 594 Vanderbilt Ave. (St. Marks Ave.) | Brooklyn | 718-230-3200
www.zaytoonsrestaurant.com

For "high-quality" Middle Eastern fare, stay tooned to this Brooklyn trio, which trades in portions "big enough for leftovers" dished up by a "casual" crew; you may have to "fight for a table", but "there's no ouch in the bill", especially in Carroll Gardens and Fort Greene, which are BYO.

Za Za *Italian*

20	16	20	$41

E 60s | 1207 First Ave. (bet. 65th & 66th Sts.) | 212-772-9997 | www.zazanyc.com

"All in all, a nice place" with a "cozy" "neighborhood feel", this "consistent" East Side Florentine offers "delicious pastas" at "moderate" rates; add a "delightful" staff and a "lovely" "little back garden", and the "ambience is fine" too.

Zebú Grill *Brazilian*

21	16	19	$42

E 90s | 305 E. 92nd St. (bet. 1st & 2nd Aves.) | 212-426-7500 | www.zebugrill.com

Upper Eastsiders in search of "something a little different" hit this "relaxed" Brazilian specializing in "interesting", "flavorful" churrasco; "congenial" service and "a couple of their caipirinhas" confirm that this somewhat "hidden away" spot is "worth repeat visits."

Ze Café *French/Italian*

22	24	22	$53

E 50s | 398 E. 52nd St. (bet. FDR Dr. & 1st Ave.) | 212-758-1944 | www.zecafe.com

A "hit" with the Sutton Place set, this "charmer" owned by floral designer Zezé and housed in his former shop offers a menu of "delicious" French-Italian fare; "glorious" flower-and-topiary-filled environs and a "welcoming" staff offset high prices for "tiny portions."

NEW Zengo *Pan-Latin*

∇ 24	25	24	$50

E 40s | 622 Third Ave. (40th St.) | 212-808-8110 | www.richardsandoval.com

Chef Richard Sandoval "takes risks" with the "excellent" Pan-Latin fusion fare at this "sophisticated" arrival to the "culinary wasteland" east of Grand Central; a zealous staff mans the "beautiful, airy" space (formerly Wild Salmon), while "fancy drinks" and the basement Biblioteca pouring a "library of tequilas" suggest this will be a "winner."

	FOOD	DECOR	SERVICE	COST

Zenkichi Ⓜ *Japanese*
25 | 26 | 25 | $60

Williamsburg | 77 N. Sixth St. (Wythe Ave.) | Brooklyn | 718-388-8985 | www.zenkichi.com

Once "you find it", get ready for a "Japanese fantasy" at Williamsburg's "dimly lit" izakaya "den" serving "heavenly" small plates and sake in a "chic, sexy" triplex with "curtained-off tables" and "impeccable" service via staffers summoned at the "press of a button"; naturally, such "otherworldly" experiences are "expensive"; P.S. a next-door oyster and sake bar is in the works.

Zen Palate ● *Vegetarian*
19 | 15 | 18 | $31

NEW Gramercy | 115 E. 18th St. (bet. Irving Pl. & Park Ave. S.) | 212-387-8885

W 40s | 663 Ninth Ave. (46th St.) | 212-582-1669
www.zenpalate.com

"Imaginative" veggie fare that "makes you forget" about meat is the hallmark of this BYO Hell's Kitchen "granddaddy"; "daring", "wholesome" eats at "modest prices" account for the "tight tables"; P.S. a Gramercy branch opened post-Survey, and another on the UWS is in the works at 239 West 105th Street.

Zero Otto Nove Ⓜ *Pizza*
25 | 22 | 21 | $40

Bronx | 2357 Arthur Ave. (186th St.) | 718-220-1027 | www.roberto089.com

A "stellar sibling" to Arthur Avenue's popular Roberto, this "relaxed" Bronx pizzeria turns out "fantastic" pies and "Napoletana specials"; "fair" prices, "pro" service and trompe l'oeil murals that make "you feel transported to an Italian piazza" are other reasons it's "worth" the trek.

Zerza ● *Moroccan*
▽ 22 | 17 | 19 | $37

E Village | 308 E. Sixth St. (bet. 1st & 2nd Aves.) | 212-529-8250 | www.zerza.com

"Hidden" on Sixth Street's Indian strip, this "tiny little" East Village Moroccan delivers "delectable" tagines and such in a "long, narrow", bi-level space done up with "lamps and tiled tables"; "reasonable" rates and "friendly" service are two more reasons it's worth the zearch.

Zest Ⓜ *American*
▽ 25 | 24 | 22 | $49

Staten Island | 977 Bay St. (Willow Ave.) | 718-390-8477 | www.zestsiny.com

"Excellent" French-accented New American cooking, a "luxe" setting and staffers "falling over themselves" to please make this a "classy" "oasis" in Staten Island's otherwise underserved Rosebank area; although a tad "pricey", it's "romantic" – especially the "magical garden."

Zeytin *Turkish*
18 | 16 | 16 | $41

W 80s | 519 Columbus Ave. (85th St.) | 212-579-1145 | www.zeytinny.com

"All the usual suspects" "and then some" grace the menu of "tasty" fare at this UWS Turk; an atmosphere "calm" enough for "schmoozing" and "decent prices" are pluses, but sometimes "slow" service means it's best if you're "not in a hurry."

Zoma *Ethiopian*
▽ 25 | 21 | 20 | $30

Harlem | 2084 Frederick Douglass Blvd. (bet. 112th & 113th Sts.) | 212-662-0620 | www.zomanyc.com

This "chic" yet "inexpensive" Ethiopian on a Harlem "budding Restaurant Row" offers "enticing" stews and other traditional dishes scooped up

 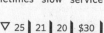

with "perfect injera" bread; factor in "soothing", "modern" decor, "courteous" service and a "cool bar", and it's a "must-try" "adventure."

Zum Schneider ⊄ German
20	17	17	$30

E Village | 107 Ave. C (7th St.) | 212-598-1098 | www.zumschneider.com
It's "Oktoberfest year-round" at this "exuberant" East Village German where "throngs of college kids" in the mood for a "blowout" nosh on "filling", "cheap" fare and chug "giant mugs" of "fantastic beer"; it really "oompahs" when "packed", so "bring earplugs."

Zum Stammtisch German
23	19	21	$39

Glendale | 69-46 Myrtle Ave. (bet. 69th Pl. & 70th St.) | Queens | 718-386-3014 | www.zumstammtisch.com
"Prepare to loosen your belt" at this Glendale German standby doling out "hearty" "classics" in "portions that would feed a long-shoreman"; "friendly frauleins in Bavarian dress" toting steins of "outstanding beer" bolster the "kitschy" "Black Forest" feel – with "fair" prices, it's all *"wunderbar."*

Zuni ● American
20	15	21	$36

W 40s | 598 Ninth Ave. (43rd St.) | 212-765-7626 | www.zuniny.com
"One of Hell's Kitchen's best-kept secrets", this "quiet" New American is "usually easy to get into" despite its "enjoyable eats" and "price-is-right" rates; "considerate" service and a "jazzy", "congenial" vibe mean it's "a good choice" for either "pre-theater or a leisurely dinner."

Zutto Japanese
21	17	19	$37

TriBeCa | 77 Hudson St. (Harrison St.) | 212-233-3287
"Definitely recommended" by "TriBeCa denizens", this "out-of-the-way" Japanese stalwart offers "quality" sushi and cooked dishes at "budget"-friendly rates; maybe the "homey" interior could use a "face-lift", but it's "inviting" enough that most don't seem to mind.

Zuzu Ramen Ⓜ⊄ Noodle Shop
∇ 21	16	19	$22

Park Slope | 173 Fourth Ave. (Degraw St.) | Brooklyn | 718-398-9898 | www.zuzuramen.com
A "noodle-muncher's dream", this "inexpensive", under-the-radar West Park Sloper "feeds the soul" with "seriously good" ramen soups, including the namesake version showcasing "tender, fatty" pork-belly *charshu*; the "small" sleek space and its "high stools" have some saying "better for takeout."

INDEXES

LOCATION MAPS

Cuisines

Includes names, locations and Food ratings.

AFGHAN

Afghan Kebab | multi. — 20

AFRICAN

Abistro | Ft Greene — 24
Ponty Bistro | Gramercy — 23

AMERICAN

🄾 NEW ABC Kitchen | Flatiron — 24
NEW Abe/Arthur | Meatpacking — 22
Alchemy | Park Slope — 19
Algonquin | W 40s — 18
Alias | LES — 22
Alice's Tea | multi. — 19
Angus McIndoe | W 40s — 16
Annisa | W Vill — 28
Apiary | E Vill — 23
Applewood | Park Slope — 25
🄾 Asiate | W 60s — 24
Aspen Social | W 40s — 18
🄾 Aureole | W 40s — 26
Back Forty | E Vill — 22
Bar Americain | W 50s — 23
NEW Bar Henry | G Vill — 19
Barmarché | NoLita — 21
Battery Gdns. | Financial — 17
Beacon | W 50s — 22
NEW Benchmark | Park Slope — –
Bistro Ten 18 | W 100s — 19
Black Duck | Murray Hill — 21
Black Whale | Bronx — 20
NEW BLT B&G | Financial — –
BLT Market | W 50s — 22
🄾 Blue Hill | G Vill — 27
🄾 Blue Ribbon | multi. — 25
Blue Ribbon Bakery | W Vill — 24
Boathouse | E 70s — 18
Bobo | W Vill — 21
Bouchon Bakery | W 60s — 24
Braeburn | W Vill — 21
NEW Bread/Butter | Bklyn Hts — 18
Bridge Cafe | Financial — 22
Brooklyn Diner | multi. — 17
Brown Café | LES — 22
Bruckner B&G | Bronx — 19
Bryant Park | W 40s — 18
Bubba Gump | W 40s — 14
Bubby's | multi. — 18
Burger Shoppe | Financial — 21
Butter | E Vill — 22
Buttermilk | Carroll Gdns — 24
Cafe Cluny | W Vill — 21

NEW Café Colette | W'burg — –
Cafe S.F.A. | E 40s — 18
Cafeteria | Chelsea — 19
CamaJe | G Vill — 22
Caviar Russe | E 50s — 25
Chadwick's | Bay Ridge — 23
Chestnut | Carroll Gdns — 23
Cibo | E 40s — 21
Clinton St. Baking | LES — 24
Coffee Shop | Union Sq — 15
NEW Colicchio/Sons | Chelsea — 23
Commerce | W Vill — 23
Community Food | W 100s — 22
🄾 Compass | W 70s — 22
Cookshop | Chelsea — 22
Cornelia St. Cafe | W Vill — 19
Corner Bistro | W Vill — 22
Craft | Flatiron — 25
Craftbar | Flatiron — 23
🄾 Cru | G Vill — 25
Cupping Rm. | SoHo — 18
David Burke Townhse. | E 60s — 24
Delicatessen | NoLita — 19
Diner | W'burg — 22
🄾 Dovetail | W 70s — 26
Dressler | W'burg — 25
Duane Park | TriBeCa — 21
DuMont | W'burg — 23
Dylan Prime | TriBeCa — 24
NEW East Side Social | E 50s — 17
E.A.T. | E 80s — 20
Eatery | W 50s — 20
EJ's Luncheon. | multi. — 16
Elaine's | E 80s — 14
NEW El Ay Si | LIC — –
Essex | LES — 18
Fairway Cafe | multi. — 18
Farm/Adderley | Ditmas Pk — 24
Five Leaves | Greenpt — 25
5 9th | Meatpacking — 19
5 Points | NoHo — 22
Flatbush Farm | Park Slope — 21
44 & X/44½ | W 40s — 21
🄾 Four Seasons | E 50s — 26
Fred's at Barneys | E 60s — 21
Freemans | LES — 21
Friend/Farmer | Gramercy — 19
Fulton | E 70s — 21
Gen. Greene | Ft Greene — 20
🄾 Gilt | E 50s — 24
Giorgio's | Flatiron — 21

Glass House | **W 40s**	21
Good | **W Vill**	19
Good Enough/Eat | **W 80s**	20
Ⓩ Gotham B&G | **G Vill**	27
Ⓩ Gramercy Tavern | **Flatiron**	28
Greenhouse | **Bay Ridge**	19
Ⓩ Grocery | **Carroll Gdns**	26
Harrison | **TriBeCa**	24
Hearth | **E Vill**	24
Heartland | **multi.**	14
NEW Henry Public | **Cobble Hill**	17
Henry's End | **Bklyn Hts**	24
NEW Highpoint | **Chelsea**	-
Hillstone | **multi.**	21
HK | **Garment**	18
Home | **W Vill**	22
Hope & Anchor | **Red Hook**	19
Hotel Griffou | **G Vill**	19
House | **Gramercy**	22
NEW Hudson Eatery | **W 50s**	-
NEW Hudson Hall | **W 50s**	-
Hudson River | **Harlem**	21
Hundred Acres | **SoHo**	19
Ici | **Ft Greene**	22
Inside Park | **E 50s**	17
Isabella's | **W 70s**	20
Jackson Hole | **multi.**	17
Jack Horse | **Bklyn Hts**	22
James | **Prospect Hts**	24
Jane | **G Vill**	21
Jimmy's | **E Vill**	22
Joe Allen | **W 40s**	17
JoeDoe | **E Vill**	23
Josephina | **W 60s**	18
Joseph Leonard | **W Vill**	22
NEW Kenmare | **L Italy**	21
Kings' Carriage | **E 80s**	23
Kingswood | **W Vill**	19
Klee Brass. | **Chelsea**	19
Knickerbocker | **G Vill**	20
Lady Mendl's | **Gramercy**	21
NEW Lambs Club | **Financial**	-
Landmark Tavern | **W 40s**	18
NEW Lion | **G Vill**	-
Little Giant | **LES**	23
Little Owl | **W Vill**	25
NEW Macbar | **SoHo**	19
Mama's Food | **E Vill**	20
Marc Forgione | **TriBeCa**	24
NEW Mark | **E 70s**	24
Market Table | **W Vill**	23
Marlow/Sons | **W'burg**	24
Ⓩ Mas | **W Vill**	27
Angelo/Maxie's | **Flatiron**	21
Melba's | **Harlem**	25

Mercer Kitchen | **SoHo**	22
Metrazur | **E 40s**	21
Ⓩ Modern | **W 50s**	26
Mojo | **Harlem**	21
Momofuku Ko | **E Vill**	27
Momofuku Noodle | **E Vill**	24
Momofuku Ssäm | **E Vill**	25
Ⓩ Monkey Bar | **E 50s**	17
Morgan | **Murray Hill**	20
Morrell Wine | **W 40s**	19
NEW M. Wells | **LIC**	-
New Leaf | **Wash. Hts**	21
NoHo Star | **NoHo**	17
Norma's | **W 50s**	25
NEW Northern Spy | **E Vill**	23
North Sq. | **G Vill**	23
No. 7 | **Ft Greene**	23
Oak Room | **W 50s**	20
Oceana | **W 40s**	23
Odeon | **TriBeCa**	20
Ⓩ One if By Land | **W Vill**	24
101 | **Bay Ridge**	20
Orchard | **LES**	23
Ⓩ Ouest | **W 80s**	24
Palm Court | **W 50s**	-
Ⓩ Park Avenue ... | **E 60s**	25
Patroon | **E 40s**	22
NEW Patty/Bun | **G Vill**	20
NEW Peels | **E Vill**	-
Penelope | **Murray Hill**	22
NEW Penny Farthing | **E Vill**	-
Perilla | **W Vill**	26
Perry St. | **W Vill**	25
Ⓩ Per Se | **W 60s**	28
Pershing Sq. | **E 40s**	15
Philip Marie | **W Vill**	20
Place | **W Vill**	21
Popover Cafe | **W 80s**	19
Prime Meat | **Carroll Gdns**	24
NEW Print | **W 40s**	25
Prune | **E Vill**	24
Quaint | **Sunnyside**	25
Quality Meats | **W 50s**	24
Rachel's American | **W 40s**	17
NEW Recette | **W Vill**	24
Recipe | **W 80s**	22
Red Cat | **Chelsea**	24
Redeye Grill | **W 50s**	20
Redhead | **E Vill**	22
Ⓩ Regency | **E 60s**	19
Riingo | **E 40s**	21
Ⓩ River Café | **Dumbo**	26
Riverview | **LIC**	20
NEW Robert | **W 50s**	19
Rock Ctr. | **W 50s**	18

Roebling | **W'burg**	19
Rose Water | **Park Slope**	25
🆕 Rothschild's | **Boerum Hill**	-
Rouge Tomate | **E 60s**	23
Rye | **W'burg**	23
Salt | **multi.**	23
Sarabeth's | **multi.**	20
🇿 Saul | **Boerum Hill**	26
Savoy | **SoHo**	24
Schnipper´s | **W 40s**	19
Shorty's.32 | **SoHo**	21
S'MAC | **E Vill**	21
Smith | **E Vill**	19
South Gate | **W 50s**	24
Spitzer's | **LES**	20
Square Meal | **E 90s**	24
🇿 Standard Grill | **Meatpacking**	21
🆕 St. Anselm | **W'burg**	-
Stone Park | **Park Slope**	25
🆕 Strong Pl. | **Cobble Hill**	-
Sweetiepie | **W Vill**	15
Sweetwater | **W'burg**	23
Swifty's | **E 70s**	18
Taste | **E 80s**	22
T-Bar Steak | **E 70s**	21
🇿 Telepan | **W 60s**	26
10 Downing | **W Vill**	20
Thalia | **W 50s**	20
🆕 Thistle Hill | **Park Slope**	-
🇿 Tocqueville | **Union Sq**	25
Trestle on 10th | **Chelsea**	20
🇿 Tribeca Grill | **TriBeCa**	22
12th St. B&G | **Park Slope**	20
12 Chairs | **SoHo**	19
🇿 21 Club | **W 50s**	22
2 West | **Financial**	21
Union Smith | **Carroll Gdns**	20
🇿 Union Sq. Cafe | **Union Sq**	26
🆕 Vanderbilt | **Prospect Hts**	21
🇿 Veritas | **Flatiron**	26
View | **W 40s**	17
Vinegar Hill Hse. | **Vinegar Hill**	25
Vynl | **multi.**	17
Walker's | **TriBeCa**	18
🆕 Wall/Water | **Financial**	21
Walter Foods | **W'burg**	23
Water Club | **Murray Hill**	21
🇿 Water's Edge | **LIC**	20
Watty/Meg | **Cobble Hill**	20
🇿 Waverly Inn | **W Vill**	20
WD-50 | **LES**	25
West Bank | **W 40s**	19
Westville | **multi.**	22
Whym | **W 50s**	20
🆕 Wright | **E 80s**	21

York Grill | **E 80s**	21
Zest | **SI**	25
Zuni | **W 40s**	20

ARGENTINEAN

Azul Bistro | **LES**	20
Buenos Aires | **E Vill**	23
Chimichurri Grill | **W 40s**	23
El Almacén | **W'burg**	24
Libertador | **E 80s**	21
Mundo | **Astoria**	22
Nina's Argentin. | **E 90s**	23
Novecento | **SoHo**	23
Sosa Borella | **W 50s**	19

ASIAN

Abigael's | **Garment**	20
Aja | **E 50s**	20
Ajna Bar | **Meatpacking**	20
Amber | **multi.**	19
Aquamarine | **Murray Hill**	21
Asia de Cuba | **Murray Hill**	23
🇿 Asiate | **W 60s**	24
🆕 Betel | **W Vill**	25
🇿 Buddakan | **Chelsea**	24
Cafe Asean | **W Vill**	21
🇿 China Grill | **W 50s**	22
Chinese Mirch | **Murray Hill**	20
Citrus B&G | **W 70s**	19
Double Crown | **NoHo**	20
🆕 Fatty 'Cue | **W'burg**	23
🆕 Fatty Fish | **E 60s**	22
JJ's Asian Fusion | **Astoria**	24
Pranna | **Murray Hill**	20
🆕 Purple Yam | **Ditmas Pk**	23
🆕 Qi | **Union Sq**	22
Ruby Foo's | **W 40s**	19
🇿 Spice Market | **Meatpacking**	23
🇿 Tao | **E 50s**	21
Wild Ginger | **multi.**	22
🆕 Zengo | **E 40s**	24

AUSTRALIAN

Bondi Rd. | **LES**	17
Five Leaves | **Greenpt**	25
Kingswood | **W Vill**	19
Sheep Sta. | **Park Slope**	18
Sunburnt Cow/Calf | **multi.**	18

AUSTRIAN

Blaue Gans | **TriBeCa**	22
Café Katja | **LES**	24
Café Sabarsky | **E 80s**	23
Cafe Steinhof | **Park Slope**	20
Mont Blanc | **W 40s**	21
🇿 Seasonal | **W 50s**	25

Thomas Beisl	**Ft Greene**	16
Z Wallsé	**W Vill**	26

BAKERIES

Amy's Bread	**multi.**	24
Blue Ribbon Bakery	**W Vill**	24
Bouchon Bakery	**W 60s**	24
City Bakery	**Flatiron**	22
Clinton St. Baking	**LES**	24
NEW Eataly	**Flatiron**	-
Ferrara	**L Italy**	23
La Bergamote	**multi.**	24
Le Pain Q.	**multi.**	18
Momofuku Bakery	**multi.**	22
Once Upon a Tart	**SoHo**	21
Provence/Boite	**Carroll Gdns**	20
NEW Village Tart	**NoLita**	20

BARBECUE

Blue Smoke	**multi.**	21
Brother Jimmy's	**multi.**	16
Daisy May's	**W 40s**	22
Dallas BBQ	**multi.**	15
Dinosaur BBQ	**Harlem**	22
NEW Fatty 'Cue	**W'burg**	23
Z Fette Sau	**W'burg**	25
Hill Country	**Flatiron**	22
Rack & Soul	**W 100s**	21
RUB BBQ	**Chelsea**	21
Smoke Joint	**Ft Greene**	22
Virgil's BBQ	**W 40s**	20
Wildwood BBQ	**Flatiron**	18

BELGIAN

B. Café	**multi.**	21
BXL	**multi.**	19
Le Pain Q.	**multi.**	18
Markt	**Flatiron**	19
Petite Abeille	**multi.**	18
Resto	**Murray Hill**	21

BRAZILIAN

Churrascaria	**multi.**	23
Circus	**E 60s**	21
Coffee Shop	**Union Sq**	15
Malagueta	**Astoria**	25
SushiSamba	**multi.**	22
Zebú Grill	**E 90s**	21

BRITISH

Z NEW Breslin	**Chelsea**	21
ChipShop	**multi.**	19
NEW Rabbit in Moon	**G Vill**	-
Tea & Sympathy	**W Vill**	19

BURGERS

Back Forty	**E Vill**	22
BareBurger	**Astoria**	23

Big Nick's	**W 70s**	18
NEW Bill's Bar	**Meatpacking**	20
Black Iron	**E Vill**	20
BLT Burger	**G Vill**	21
Brgr	**multi.**	19
Burger Heaven	**multi.**	16
Burger Joint/Le Parker	**W 50s**	24
Burger Shoppe	**Financial**	21
Corner Bistro	**W Vill**	22
Z DB Bistro Moderne	**W 40s**	25
DuMont	**W'burg**	23
Five Guys	**multi.**	20
5 Napkin Burger	**multi.**	21
Goodburger	**multi.**	17
NEW Henry Public	**Cobble Hill**	17
Island Burgers	**W 50s**	21
Jackson Hole	**multi.**	17
J.G. Melon	**E 70s**	21
Z Minetta	**G Vill**	24
NEW Patty/Bun	**G Vill**	20
P.J. Clarke's	**multi.**	17
Pop Burger	**multi.**	18
Rare B&G	**multi.**	21
Sandwich Planet	**Garment**	22
Schnipper's	**W 40s**	19
Shake Shack	**multi.**	23
67 Burger	**Ft Greene**	21
Stand	**G Vill**	19
NEW St. Anselm	**W'burg**	-
Zaitzeff	**multi.**	20

BURMESE

Mingala Burmese	**E 70s**	21

CAJUN/CREOLE

Bayou	**SI**	23
Bourbon St. Café	**Bayside**	17
Delta Grill	**W 40s**	19
Great Jones Cafe	**NoHo**	20
Mara's	**E Vill**	22
NEW Rothschild's	**Boerum Hill**	-

CALIFORNIAN

Z Michael's	**W 50s**	21

CAMBODIAN

Num Pang	**G Vill**	26

CARIBBEAN

(See also Cuban, Dominican, Jamaican, Puerto Rican)

Don Pedro's	**E 90s**	22
Ivo & Lulu	**SoHo**	19
NEW Kaz An Nou	**Prospect Hts**	-
Mo-Bay	**Harlem**	21

CAVIAR

Caviar Russe | **E 50s**	25
Mari Vanna | **Flatiron**	20
Petrossian | **W 50s**	23
Russian Tea | **W 50s**	19

CHEESESTEAKS

Carl's Steaks | **multi.**	20
99 Mi. to Philly | **E Vill**	19
Shorty's | **W 40s**	24

CHICKEN

Bon Chon | **multi.**	20
Coco Roco | **multi.**	19
El Malecon | **multi.**	22
Flor/Mayo | **multi.**	20
Kyochon | **multi.**	20
Mancora | **E Vill**	21
Pies-n-Thighs | **W'burg**	23
Pio Pio | **multi.**	22
Rack & Soul | **W 100s**	21

CHILEAN

Pomaire | **W 40s**	20

CHINESE

(* dim sum specialist)

Amazing 66 | **Chinatown**	22
Au Mandarin | **Financial**	20
NEW BaoHaus | **LES**	-
Big Wong | **Chinatown**	22
Bo-Ky | **multi.**	22
Café Evergreen* | **E 60s**	19
Chef Ho's | **E 80s**	21
Chiam | **E 40s**	22
China Chalet | **multi.**	18
Chinatown Brass.* | **NoHo**	22
Z Chin Chin | **E 40s**	23
Congee | **LES**	21
Dim Sum Go Go | **Chinatown**	20
Dumpling Man | **E Vill**	20
East Manor* | **Flushing**	19
Empire Szechuan | **multi.**	16
Excellent Dumpling* | **Chinatown**	20
Flor/Mayo | **multi.**	20
Fuleen | **Chinatown**	22
Golden Unicorn* | **Chinatown**	21
Grand Sichuan | **multi.**	22
Jing Fong* | **Chinatown**	19
Joe's Shanghai | **multi.**	22
Joe's | **Chinatown**	20
NEW Lychee Hse.* | **E 50s**	25
Macao Trading | **TriBeCa**	18
Mandarin Court* | **Chinatown**	20
Mee Noodle | **multi.**	17
Mr. Chow | **multi.**	22

Mr. K's | **E 50s**	23
M Shanghai/Noodle* | **W'burg**	21
New Hawaii Sea | **Bronx**	22
Nice Green Bo | **Chinatown**	23
NoHo Star | **NoHo**	17
Ollie's | **multi.**	16
Z Oriental Gdn.* | **Chinatown**	24
Pacificana* | **Sunset Pk**	25
Peking Duck | **multi.**	23
Philippe | **E 60s**	23
Phoenix Gdn. | **E 40s**	24
Pig Heaven | **E 80s**	20
Ping's Sea.* | **multi.**	22
Red Egg* | **L Italy**	21
Shang | **LES**	21
Shanghai Café | **L Italy**	21
Shanghai Cuisine | **Chinatown**	22
Shanghai Pavilion | **E 70s**	21
Shun Lee Cafe* | **W 60s**	21
Z Shun Lee Palace | **E 50s**	24
Shun Lee West | **W 60s**	22
Spicy & Tasty | **Flushing**	23
Szechuan Gourmet | **multi.**	22
Tang Pavilion | **W 50s**	22
Tasty Hand-Pulled | **Chinatown**	22
Tse Yang | **E 50s**	24
Vanessa's Dumpling | **multi.**	22
Wa Jeal | **E 80s**	25
Wo Hop | **Chinatown**	21
Wu Liang Ye | **W 40s**	23
Xi'an | **multi.**	-
NEW Xiao Ye | **LES**	-
X.O.* | **multi.**	20

COFFEEHOUSES

Ferrara | **L Italy**	23
French Roast | **multi.**	17
Le Pain Q. | **multi.**	18
Omonia | **multi.**	20
Once Upon a Tart | **SoHo**	21
Yura on Madison | **E 90s**	21

COFFEE SHOPS/ DINERS

Brooklyn Diner | **multi.**	17
Burger Heaven | **multi.**	16
Diner | **W'burg**	22
Edison | **W 40s**	15
EJ's Luncheon. | **multi.**	16
Hope & Anchor | **Red Hook**	19
Junior's | **multi.**	17
La Taza de Oro | **Chelsea**	21
NEW M. Wells | **LIC**	-
Schnipper's | **W 40s**	19
Tom's | **Prospect Hts**	21
Viand | **multi.**	17

COLOMBIAN

Tierras | **Astoria**	21

CONTINENTAL

Battery Gdns. | **Financial**	17
Cebu | **Bay Ridge**	22
Cole's Dock | **SI**	18
Jack's Lux. | **E Vill**	27
Lake Club | **SI**	23
Petrossian | **W 50s**	23
Russian Samovar | **W 50s**	20
Russian Tea | **W 50s**	19
Sardi's | **W 40s**	17

CUBAN

Amor Cubano | **Harlem**	22
Asia de Cuba | **Murray Hill**	23
Cafecito | **E Vill**	22
Cafe Con Leche | **multi.**	18
Café Habana/Outpost | **multi.**	22
Cuba | **G Vill**	22
Cubana Café | **multi.**	20
Havana Alma | **W Vill**	21
Havana Central | **multi.**	18
Son Cubano | **Meatpacking**	21
Victor's Cafe | **W 50s**	22

DANISH

NEW Vandaag | **E Vill**	-

DELIS

Artie's Deli | **W 80s**	18
Z Barney Greengrass | **W 80s**	24
Ben's Best | **Rego Pk**	23
Ben's Kosher | **multi.**	19
Z Carnegie Deli | **W 50s**	22
Ess-a-Bagel | **multi.**	23
Z Katz's Deli | **LES**	24
Lenny's | **E 50s**	17
Leo's Latticini | **Corona**	26
Liebman's | **Bronx**	22
NEW Mile End | **Boerum Hill**	25
Mill Basin Deli | **Mill Basin**	22
Pastrami Queen | **E 70s**	20
Sarge's Deli | **Murray Hill**	20
2nd Ave Deli | **Murray Hill**	22
Stage Deli | **W 50s**	20
NEW Torrisi | **NoLita**	27
Zabar's Cafe | **W 80s**	20

DESSERT

Amy's Bread | **multi.**	24
Bouchon Bakery | **W 60s**	24
Café Sabarsky | **E 80s**	23
ChikaLicious | **E Vill**	25
Chocolate Room | **multi.**	24
Ferrara | **L Italy**	23

Junior's | **multi.**	17
Kyotofu | **W 40s**	23
La Bergamote | **multi.**	24
Lady Mendl's | **Gramercy**	21
L&B Spumoni | **Bensonhurst**	24
Max Brenner | **G Vill**	20
Momofuku Bakery | **multi.**	22
Omonia | **multi.**	20
Sant Ambroeus | **multi.**	21
Serendipity 3 | **E 60s**	19
NEW Spot | **E Vill**	23
Sweetiepie | **W Vill**	15
Sweet Melissa | **multi.**	20
Veniero's | **E Vill**	24
NEW Village Tart | **NoLita**	20

DOMINICAN

Cafe Con Leche | **multi.**	18
El Malecon | **multi.**	22
Mamajuana | **Inwood**	20

DUTCH

NEW Vandaag | **E Vill**	-

EASTERN EUROPEAN

Sammy's | **LES**	20

ECLECTIC

Abigael's | **Garment**	20
Carol's | **SI**	26
NEW Collective | **Meatpacking**	21
NEW Crosby Bar | **SoHo**	19
Double Crown | **NoHo**	20
Elizabeth | **NoLita**	18
Good Fork | **Red Hook**	25
Graffiti | **E Vill**	25
Harry's Cafe/Steak | **Financial**	23
Josie's | **multi.**	19
Lake Club | **SI**	23
Nook | **W 50s**	22
NEW Plaza Food Hall | **W 50s**	22
Z Public | **NoLita**	24
Rice | **multi.**	19
Schiller's | **LES**	19
Sojourn | **E 70s**	22
Stanton Social | **LES**	23
NEW Traif | **W'burg**	-
Vida | **SI**	23
WD-50 | **LES**	25
Whole Foods | **multi.**	19

EGYPTIAN

Kabab Café | **Astoria**	25

ETHIOPIAN

Awash | **multi.**	21
Ghenet | **Park Slope**	23

CUISINES

Meskerem	**multi.**	22
Queen of Sheba	**W 40s**	23
Zoma	**Harlem**	25

EUROPEAN

August	**W Vill**	22
Belcourt	**E Vill**	19
Danny Brown	**Forest Hills**	26
Don Pedro's	**E 90s**	22
Employees Only	**W Vill**	20
Klee Brass.	**Chelsea**	19
NEW Le Caprice	**E 60s**	17
Radegast	**W'burg**	18
Spotted Pig	**W Vill**	23

FILIPINO

Kuma Inn	**LES**	25
Umi Nom	**Clinton Hill**	24

FONDUE

Mont Blanc	**W 40s**	21
NEW Taureau	**E Vill**	-

FRENCH

Z Adour	**E 50s**	26
Allegretti	**Flatiron**	23
Bagatelle	**Meatpacking**	18
Barbès	**Murray Hill**	19
Bistro 33	**Astoria**	20
Bouchon Bakery	**W 60s**	24
Z Bouley	**TriBeCa**	27
Breeze	**W 40s**	22
Brick Cafe	**Astoria**	22
Z Café Boulud	**E 70s**	27
Café du Soleil	**W 100s**	19
Cafe Gitane	**multi.**	20
Café Henri	**multi.**	20
Z Carlyle	**E 70s**	23
Chez Lucienne	**Harlem**	22
Z Corton	**TriBeCa**	26
Z Cru	**G Vill**	25
Danal	**G Vill**	20
Z Daniel	**E 60s**	28
Z Degustation	**E Vill**	27
Elephant	**E Vill**	21
Z Eleven Madison	**Flatiron**	28
Geisha	**E 60s**	23
Gordon Ramsay	**W 50s**	23
Ici	**Ft Greene**	22
Indochine	**E Vill**	21
Ivo & Lulu	**SoHo**	19
Jack's Lux.	**E Vill**	27
Z Jean Georges	**W 60s**	28
Z Jean Georges Noug.	**W 60s**	27
Jolie	**Boerum Hill**	21
NEW Kaz An Nou	**Prospect Hts**	-

La Baraka	**Little Neck**	21
La Bergamote	**multi.**	24
La Boîte en Bois	**W 60s**	22
Z La Grenouille	**E 50s**	28
Z L'Atelier/Robuchon	**E 50s**	27
Z Le Bernardin	**W 50s**	29
Z Le Cirque	**E 50s**	24
L'Ecole	**SoHo**	24
Le Colonial	**E 50s**	21
Le Marais	**W 40s**	22
Le Perigord	**E 50s**	25
Le Pescadeux	**SoHo**	23
Le Rivage	**W 40s**	20
NEW Má Pêche	**W 50s**	22
Maze	**W 50s**	22
Mercer Kitchen	**SoHo**	22
Z Modern	**W 50s**	26
Nizza	**W 40s**	20
Once Upon a Tart	**SoHo**	21
Pascalou	**E 90s**	21
Z Per Se	**W 60s**	28
Petrossian	**W 50s**	23
Z Picholine	**W 60s**	27
Ponty Bistro	**Gramercy**	23
718	**Astoria**	22
Z SHO Shaun Hergatt	**Financial**	26
NEW Tartinery	**NoLita**	-
Z Terrace in Sky	**W 100s**	22
Z Tocqueville	**Union Sq**	25
Triomphe	**W 40s**	23
26 Seats	**E Vill**	22
Ze Café	**E 50s**	22

FRENCH (BISTRO)

Almond	**Flatiron**	19
Alouette	**W 90s**	21
A.O.C.	**multi.**	19
Bacchus	**Boerum Hill**	21
Bar Boulud	**W 60s**	23
NEW Bar Henry	**G Vill**	19
Belleville	**Park Slope**	18
Benoit	**W 50s**	20
Bistro Cassis	**W 70s**	20
Bistro Chat Noir	**E 60s**	19
Bistro Citron	**W 80s**	19
Bistro Les Amis	**SoHo**	21
Bistro 61	**E 60s**	19
NEW Bistro Vendôme	**E 50s**	21
Bliss Bistro	**Sunnyside**	21
Cafe Cluny	**W Vill**	21
Cafe Joul	**E 50s**	18
Cafe Loup	**W Vill**	19
Cafe Luluc	**Cobble Hill**	20
Z Cafe Luxembourg	**W 70s**	20
Cafe Un Deux	**W 40s**	17

CamaJe	**G Vill**	22
Capsouto Frères	**TriBeCa**	24
Chez Jacqueline	**G Vill**	20
Chez Josephine	**W 40s**	20
Chez Napoléon	**W 50s**	21
Chez Oskar	**Ft Greene**	19
Cornelia St. Cafe	**W Vill**	19
Z DB Bistro Moderne	**W 40s**	25
Demarchelier	**E 80s**	18
Deux Amis	**E 50s**	19
Félix	**SoHo**	17
Flea Mkt. Cafe	**E Vill**	19
French Roast	**multi.**	17
Gascogne	**Chelsea**	21
Jean Claude	**SoHo**	22
JoJo	**E 60s**	25
Jubilee	**E 50s**	23
Jules	**E Vill**	20
La Bonne Soupe	**W 50s**	18
La Lunchonette	**Chelsea**	21
La Mangeoire	**E 50s**	20
La Mirabelle	**W 80s**	23
Landmarc	**multi.**	20
La Petite Aub.	**Murray Hill**	21
La Ripaille	**W Vill**	20
La Sirène	**SoHo**	22
Le Barricou	**W'burg**	21
Le Bilboquet	**E 60s**	23
Le Charlot	**E 60s**	21
Le Gigot	**W Vill**	24
Le Jardin	**NoLita**	20
Le Magnifique	**E 70s**	20
Le Monde	**W 100s**	17
NEW Le Parisien	**Murray Hill**	-
Les Halles	**multi.**	20
Le Singe Vert	**Chelsea**	18
L'Express	**Flatiron**	18
NEW Lina Frey	**LES**	-
Lucien	**E Vill**	22
Lucky Strike	**SoHo**	17
Z Minetta	**G Vill**	24
Nice Matin	**W 70s**	20
Odeon	**TriBeCa**	20
Paradou	**Meatpacking**	21
Pastis	**Meatpacking**	21
Picnic	**W 100s**	20
Provence/Boite	**Carroll Gdns**	20
Quatorze Bis	**E 70s**	21
Quercy	**Cobble Hill**	21
Raoul's	**SoHo**	23
Sweetwater	**W'burg**	23
Table d'Hôte	**E 90s**	20
Tartine	**W Vill**	21
Tournesol	**LIC**	24

FRENCH (BRASSERIE)

Z Artisanal	**Murray Hill**	23
Z Balthazar	**SoHo**	23
Bar Breton	**Chelsea**	19
Brasserie	**E 50s**	20
Brasserie Cognac	**W 50s**	19
Brasserie 8½	**W 50s**	22
Brasserie Julien	**E 80s**	18
Brass. Ruhlmann	**W 50s**	19
Café d'Alsace	**E 80s**	21
NEW Ça Va	**W 40s**	-
Cercle Rouge	**TriBeCa**	19
Z DBGB	**E Vill**	22
Jacques	**multi.**	19
L'Absinthe	**E 60s**	22
Maison	**W 50s**	19
Marseille	**W 40s**	20
Orsay	**E 70s**	18
Pigalle	**W 40s**	17
NEW Plein Sud	**TriBeCa**	18
Rue 57	**W 50s**	18
Serge	**Murray Hill**	20

GASTROPUB

Alchemy	Amer.	**Park Slope**	19
Kingswood	Australian	**W Vill**	19
NEW Penny Farthing	Amer.	**E Vill**	-
NEW Rabbit in Moon	British	**G Vill**	-
Resto	Belgian	**Murray Hill**	21
Spitzer's	Amer.	**LES**	20
Spotted Pig	Euro.	**W Vill**	23
NEW Strong Pl.	Amer.	**Cobble Hill**	-

GERMAN

Blaue Gans	**TriBeCa**	22
Hallo Berlin	**W 40s**	18
Heidelberg	**E 80s**	20
Killmeyer	**SI**	20
Nurnberger	**SI**	21
Rolf's	**Gramercy**	14
Zum Schneider	**E Vill**	20
Zum Stammtisch	**Glendale**	23

GREEK

Aegean Cove	**Astoria**	24
Agnanti	**multi.**	23
Ammos	**E 40s**	22
Anthos	**W 50s**	24
Avra	**E 40s**	25
Cafe Bar	**Astoria**	20
Cávo	**Astoria**	20
Dafni Greek	**W 40s**	20

Eliá | **Bay Ridge**	26
Elias Corner | **Astoria**	23
NEW Estiatorio Rafina | **Murray Hill**	-
Ethos | **multi.**	21
Greek Kitchen | **W 50s**	19
Ithaka | **E 80s**	22
Kefi | **W 80s**	22
Kellari Tav./Parea | **multi.**	22
NEW Kouzina/Trata | **E 70s**	-
Meltemi | **E 70s**	-
Z Milos | **W 50s**	27
Molyvos | **W 50s**	23
Omonia | **multi.**	20
Periyali | **Flatiron**	24
Persephone | **E 60s**	21
Philoxenia | **Astoria**	21
Pylos | **E Vill**	25
Snack | **SoHo**	22
Snack Taverna | **W Vill**	22
Stamatis | **Astoria**	21
Taverna Kyclades | **Astoria**	26
Telly's Taverna | **Astoria**	23
Thalassa | **TriBeCa**	23
Uncle Nick's | **multi.**	21

HEALTH FOOD

(See also Vegetarian)

Energy Kitchen | **multi.**	17
NEW Qi | **Union Sq**	22

HOT DOGS

Bark Hot Dogs | **Park Slope**	21
Gray's Papaya | **multi.**	20
Shake Shack | **multi.**	23
NEW St. Anselm | **W'burg**	-

ICE CREAM PARLORS

L&B Spumoni | **Bensonhurst**	24
Serendipity 3 | **E 60s**	19

INDIAN

Amma | **E 50s**	25
At Vermilion | **E 40s**	20
Baluchi's | **multi.**	18
Banjara | **E Vill**	22
Bay Leaf | **W 50s**	21
Bombay Palace | **W 50s**	19
Bombay Talkie | **Chelsea**	20
Brick Ln. Curry | **multi.**	21
Bukhara Grill | **E 40s**	23
Chennai Gdn. | **Murray Hill**	21
Chola | **E 50s**	24
Curry Leaf | **Murray Hill**	18
Darbar | **multi.**	21
Dawat | **E 50s**	23
Delhi Palace | **Jackson Hts**	21

Z Dévi | **Flatiron**	23
Dhaba | **Murray Hill**	23
Earthen Oven | **W 70s**	20
Hampton Chutney | **multi.**	20
Haveli | **E Vill**	21
Indus Valley | **W 100s**	23
Jackson Diner | **Jackson Hts**	22
Jewel of India | **W 40s**	20
Kati Roll | **multi.**	21
NEW Masala Times | **G Vill**	-
Mint | **E 50s**	22
Mughlai | **W 70s**	20
Nirvana | **Murray Hill**	23
Pongal | **Murray Hill**	22
Salaam Bombay | **TriBeCa**	22
Sapphire | **W 60s**	21
Saravanaas | **Murray Hill**	25
Surya | **W Vill**	22
Z Tabla | **Flatiron**	25
Taj Tribeca | **Financial**	22
Z Tamarind | **multi.**	26
Tiffin Wallah | **Murray Hill**	23
Utsav | **W 40s**	21
Vatan | **Murray Hill**	23
Yuva | **E 50s**	23

IRISH

Landmark Tavern | **W 40s**	18
Molly's | **Gramercy**	20
Neary's | **E 50s**	18

ISRAELI

Azuri Cafe | **W 50s**	25
Hummus Pl. | **multi.**	22
Miriam | **Park Slope**	22
Taïm | **W Vill**	26

ITALIAN

(N=Northern; S=Southern)

Abboccato | **W 50s**	21
Z Acappella | **N** | **TriBeCa**	25
Accademia/Vino | **multi.**	19
Acqua | **S** | **W 90s**	19
Alberto | **N** | **Forest Hills**	23
Z Al Di La | **N** | **Park Slope**	27
Alfredo/Rome | **S** | **W 40s**	19
Alloro | **E 70s**	24
Z Alto | **N** | **E 50s**	26
Amorina | **Prospect Hts**	25
Anella | **Greenpt**	26
Angelina's | **SI**	22
Angelo's/Mulberry | **S** | **L Italy**	23
Angelo's Pizza | **multi.**	20
Ann & Tony's | **Bronx**	20
Antica Venezia | **W Vill**	22
Antonucci | **E 80s**	22

Aperitivo | **E 40s**	21
Ápizz | **LES**	24
Areo | **Bay Ridge**	24
Armani Rist. | N | **E 50s**	19
Arno | N | **Garment**	19
Aroma | **NoHo**	23
Arté | N | **G Vill**	18
Arté Café | **W 70s**	18
Arturo's | **G Vill**	21
Aurora | **multi.**	24
Z A Voce | **multi.**	24
Z Babbo | **G Vill**	27
Bamonte's | **W'burg**	23
Baraonda | **E 70s**	19
Z Barbetta | N | **W 40s**	20
Barbone | **E Vill**	24
Barbuto | **W Vill**	23
Barolo | **SoHo**	19
Barosa | **Rego Pk**	22
Bar Pitti | **G Vill**	22
Bar Stuzz. | S | **multi.**	20
Bar Tano | **Park Slope**	21
Bar Toto | **Park Slope**	21
Bar Vetro | **E 50s**	22
Basilica | **W 40s**	20
Basso56 | S | **W 50s**	23
Basta Pasta | **Flatiron**	23
Becco | **W 40s**	23
Beccofino | **Bronx**	20
Bella Blu | N | **E 70s**	21
Bella Via | **LIC**	23
Bello | **W 50s**	21
Bettola | **W 70s**	20
Bianca | N | **NoHo**	24
Bice | N | **E 50s**	21
NEW Bino | **Carroll Gdns**	–
Bocca | S | **Flatiron**	23
Bocca di Bacco | N | **W 50s**	22
Bocca Lupo | **Cobble Hill**	24
Bocelli | **SI**	25
Bond 45 | **W 40s**	19
Bottega/Vino | **E 50s**	22
Bottino | N | **Chelsea**	20
Bravo Gianni | N | **E 60s**	22
Bread | **TriBeCa**	20
Bricco | **multi.**	19
Brick Cafe | N | **Astoria**	22
Brio | **E 60s**	20
Brioso | **SI**	25
NEW Broken Eng. | **Cobble Hill**	–
Cacio e Pepe | S | **E Vill**	21
Cacio e Vino | S | **E Vill**	22
Cafe Fiorello | **W 60s**	20
Caffe Cielo | **W 50s**	20
Caffe Grazie | **E 80s**	20

Campagnola | **E 70s**	24
Canaletto | N | **E 60s**	21
Cara Mia | **W 40s**	21
Caravaggio | **E 70s**	23
Carmine's | S | **multi.**	20
NEW Casa Lever | **E 50s**	23
Celeste | S | **W 80s**	24
Cellini | N | **E 50s**	22
Centolire | N | **E 80s**	21
Centro Vinoteca | **W Vill**	21
'Cesca | S | **W 70s**	23
Ciaobella | **E 80s**	20
Cibo | N | **E 40s**	21
Cipriani Dolci | **E 40s**	20
Cipriani D'twn | **SoHo**	22
Z Convivio | S | **E 40s**	26
Coppola's | **multi.**	20
NEW Corsino | **W Vill**	20
Covo | **Harlem**	22
Crispo | N | **W Vill**	23
Cucina/Pesce | **E Vill**	19
Da Andrea | N | **G Vill**	22
Da Ciro | **Murray Hill**	22
Da Nico | **L Italy**	22
Da Noi | N | **SI**	23
Da Silvano | N | **G Vill**	21
Da Tommaso | N | **W 50s**	21
Da Umberto | N | **Chelsea**	25
Dean's | **multi.**	18
Defonte's | **multi.**	22
DeGrezia | **E 50s**	24
Dell'anima | **W Vill**	25
Z Del Posto | **Chelsea**	26
Dominick's | **Bronx**	23
Don Peppe | **Ozone Pk**	26
Due | N | **E 70s**	21
NEW East Side Social | **E 50s**	17
NEW Eataly | **Flatiron**	–
Ecco | **TriBeCa**	22
Elaine's | **E 80s**	14
Z Elio's | **E 80s**	24
Emporio | **NoLita**	21
Enoteca Maria | **SI**	23
Enzo's | **Bronx**	23
Erminia | S | **E 80s**	25
Z Esca | S | **W 40s**	25
Etcetera Etcetera | **W 40s**	21
Fabio Piccolo | **E 40s**	22
Falai | **multi.**	25
F & J Pine | **Bronx**	22
NEW Faustina | **E Vill**	23
Felice | **E 60s**	21
Felidia | **E 50s**	26
Filippo's | **SI**	25
F.illi Ponte | **TriBeCa**	22

Fiorentino's | S | **Gravesend**	21
Fiorini | S | **E 50s**	22
Firenze | N | **E 80s**	20
Forlini's | N | **Chinatown**	20
Fornino | **Park Slope**	23
Fragole | **Carroll Gdns**	24
Frank | **E Vill**	24
Frankies | **multi.**	24
Franny's | **Prospect Hts**	24
Fratelli | **Bronx**	21
Fred's at Barneys | N | **E 60s**	21
Fresco | N | **multi.**	22
Gabriel's | N | **W 60s**	22
Gargiulo's | S | **Coney Is**	22
Gemma | **E Vill**	20
Gennaro | **W 90s**	24
Gigino | **multi.**	21
Giorgione | **SoHo**	24
Giovanni | N | **E 80s**	23
Girasole | **E 80s**	23
Gnocco | N | **E Vill**	24
Gottino | **W Vill**	22
Grace's Tratt. | **E 70s**	18
Gradisca | **W Vill**	23
Grand Tier | **W 60s**	20
Grifone | N | **E 40s**	23
Grotta Azzurra | S | **L Italy**	17
Gusto | **W Vill**	23
Harry Cipriani | N | **E 50s**	21
Harry's Italian | **Financial**	21
Hearth | N | **E Vill**	24
NEW Hello Pasta | **multi.**	–
I Coppi | N | **E Vill**	22
Il Bagatto | **E Vill**	24
Il Bambino | **Astoria**	24
Il Bastardo | N | **Chelsea**	18
Z Il Buco | **NoHo**	26
Il Cantinori | N | **G Vill**	23
Il Corallo | **SoHo**	22
Il Cortile | **L Italy**	23
Il Gattopardo | S | **W 50s**	25
Il Giglio | N | **TriBeCa**	25
NEW Il Matto | **TriBeCa**	–
Il Mattone | **TriBeCa**	21
Z Il Mulino | **G Vill**	27
Il Postino | **E 40s**	23
Il Punto | **Garment**	21
Il Riccio | S | **E 70s**	22
Z Il Tinello | N | **W 50s**	25
'Ino | **W Vill**	24
'Inoteca | **multi.**	22
Insieme | **W 50s**	23
I Sodi | **W Vill**	25
Italianissimo | **E 80s**	24
I Tre Merli | N | **multi.**	19

I Trulli | **Murray Hill**	23
Joe & Pat's | **SI**	23
John's/12th St. | **E Vill**	21
La Carbonara | S | **W Vill**	19
NEW La Gazzetta | **Meatpacking**	–
La Masseria | S | **W 40s**	22
L&B Spumoni | **Bensonhurst**	24
Lanza | S | **E Vill**	18
La Pizza Fresca | **Flatiron**	23
L'Artusi | **W Vill**	24
Lattanzi | S | **W 40s**	22
Lavagna | **E Vill**	23
La Villa Pizzeria | **multi.**	21
Leo's Latticini | **Corona**	26
Le Zie 2000 | N | **Chelsea**	22
Lil' Frankie | **E Vill**	23
NEW Lincoln | **W 60s**	–
Lisca | N | **W 90s**	20
Locale | **Astoria**	21
Locanda Verde | **TriBeCa**	24
Locanda Vini | N | **Clinton Hill**	27
Lorenzo's | **SI**	23
Lunetta | **Boerum Hill**	22
Z Lupa | S | **G Vill**	25
Lusardi's | N | **E 70s**	24
Luzzo's/Ovest | S | **multi.**	22
Macelleria | N | **Meatpacking**	22
Madison's | **Bronx**	22
NEW Maialino | S | **Gramercy**	25
Malatesta | N | **W Vill**	24
Manducatis | **LIC**	23
NEW Mappamondo | **W Vill**	–
NEW Marcony | **Murray Hill**	22
Z Marea | **W 50s**	27
Maria Pia | **W 50s**	20
Marinella | **W Vill**	23
Mario's | S | **Bronx**	21
Maruzzella | N | **E 70s**	23
Matilda | N | **E Vill**	23
Max | **multi.**	21
Max SoHa/Caffe | **W 100s**	20
Mediterraneo | N | **E 60s**	20
Mezzaluna/Pizza | **E 70s**	20
Mezzogiorno | N | **SoHo**	21
Mia Dona | **E 50s**	20
Miranda | **W'burg**	23
Montebello | N | **E 50s**	24
Montenapo | N | **W 40s**	21
Morandi | **W Vill**	22
Nanni | N | **E 40s**	25
Naples 45 | S | **E 40s**	17
Natsumi | **W 50s**	24
Nello | N | **E 60s**	18
Nicola's | **E 80s**	22
Nino's | N | **multi.**	20

Nizza	W 40s	20	Rughetta	S	E 80s	22
Nocello	N	W 50s	21	Sac's Place	Astoria	23
Noodle Pudding	Bklyn Hts	24	NEW Salumè	SoHo	-
Nove	SI	25	Salumeria Rosi	N	W 70s	24
Novitá	N	Gramercy	24	Salute!	Murray Hill	19
One 83	N	E 80s	19	Sambuca	S	W 70s	20
101	Bay Ridge	20	Sandro's	S	E 80s	24
Orso	N	W 40s	22	☑ San Pletro	S	E 50s	25
Osso Buco	E 90s	19	Sant Ambroeus	N	multi.	21
Osteria al Doge	N	W 40s	20	Sapori D'Ischia	S	Woodside	23
Osteria del Circo	N	W 50s	22	Savoia	Carroll Gdns	20
Osteria Laguna	E 40s	19	Scaletta	N	W 70s	21
Otto	G Vill	22	☑ Scalinatella	E 60s	24
Padre Figlio	E 40s	22	☑ Scalini Fedeli	N	TriBeCa	27
Palma	S	W Vill	22	Scalino	Park Slope	24
Paola's	E 90s	22	Scarlatto	N	W 40s	20
Pappardella	W 70s	20	☑ Scarpetta	Chelsea	26
Park Side	Corona	24	Scottadito	N	Park Slope	21
Parma	N	E 70s	22	NEW SD26	Murray Hill	22
Pasquale's	Bronx	21	Serafina	multi.	19
Patricia's	Bronx	22	Sette	S	Park Slope	20
Patsy's	S	W 50s	22	Sette Mezzo	E 70s	22
Peasant	NoLita	24	Sfoglia	N	E 90s	23
Pellegrino's	L Italy	23	Shelly's Tratt.	W 50s	20
Pepe	multi.	21	☑ Sistina	N	E 80s	26
Pepolino	N	TriBeCa	25	Sorella	LES	24
Perbacco	E Vill	23	Sosa Borella	W 50s	19
Per Lei	E 70s	21	Spiga	W 80s	23
Petaluma	E 70s	17	Spigolo	E 80s	25
☑ Piano Due	W 50s	24	S.P.Q.R.	S	L Italy	20
Piccola Venezia	Astoria	25	Supper	N	E Vill	24
Piccolo Angolo	W Vill	25	Tarallucci	multi.	21
Pietrasanta	W 40s	18	Teodora	N	E 50s	21
Pietro's	E 40s	24	Terrazza Toscana	N	W 50s	21
Pinocchio	E 90s	22	Terroir	multi.	24
Pisticci	S	W 100s	23	NEW Testaccio	S	LIC	22
Pó	W Vill	24	Tevere	S	E 80s	24
Pomodoro Rosso	W 70s	21	Tommaso	Dyker Hts	24
Ponticello	N	Astoria	24	Tony's Di Napoli	S	multi.	20
Porchetta	E Vill	23	NEW Torrisi	NoLita	27
Portofino	N	Bronx	21	Tosca Café	Bronx	21
Positano	S	L Italy	23	Tra Da Noi	Bronx	22
Primola	E 60s	23	Trattoria Cinque	TriBeCa	22
Provini	Park Slope	22	Tratt. Dell'Arte	N	W 50s	21
Puttanesca	W 50s	19	☑ Tratt. L'incontro	Astoria	27
NEW Quattro Gastro.	N	SoHo	21	Tratt. Pesce	multi.	18
Quattro Gatti	E 80s	21	Tratt. Romana	SI	24
Queen	Bklyn Hts	24	Trattoria Toscana	N	W Vill	24
Rao's	S	Harlem	22	Trattoria Trecolori	W 40s	21
Remi	W 50s	23	NEW Travertine	NoLita	22
Re Sette	W 40s	19	Tre Dici/Steak	Chelsea	21
Risotteria	W Vill	22	NEW Tre Otto	E 90s	21
☑ Roberto	Bronx	27	Tuscany Grill	N	Bay Ridge	24
Rocco	N	G Vill	21	Umberto's	multi.	19
Rossini's	N	Murray Hill	24	Uva	E 70s	21

Uvarara	**Middle Vill**	26
☑ Valbella	N	**Meatpacking**	25
V&T	**W 100s**	18
NEW Vapiano	**G Vill**	–
Veniero's	**E Vill**	24
Vespa	**E 80s**	19
Vesta	**Astoria**	24
Vezzo	**Murray Hill**	23
Via Emilia	N	**Flatiron**	23
Via Quadronno	N	**multi.**	21
ViceVersa	**W 50s**	22
Vico	**E 90s**	20
Villa Berulia	N	**Murray Hill**	22
Villa Mosconi	**G Vill**	23
Vincent's	**L Italy**	21
Vivolo/Cucina	**E 70s**	21
Za Za	N	**E 60s**	20
Ze Café	**E 50s**	22
Zero Otto	S	**Bronx**	25

JAMAICAN

Negril	**G Vill**	21

JAPANESE

(* sushi specialist)

Aburiya Kinnosuke	**E 40s**	25
Aki*	**W Vill**	25
Arirang Hibachi	**multi.**	19
Bistro 33	**Astoria**	20
Blue Ginger*	**Chelsea**	22
☑ Blue Ribbon Sushi*	**multi.**	26
Blue Ribbon Sushi B&G*	**W 50s**	24
☑ Bond St.*	**NoHo**	25
Donguri	**E 80s**	27
EN Japanese	**W Vill**	24
15 East*	**Union Sq**	25
Fushimi*	**multi.**	23
☑ Gari/Sushi*	**multi.**	27
Geido*	**Prospect Hts**	24
Geisha	**E 60s**	23
Greenwich Grill/Sushi Azabu*	**TriBeCa**	25
Gyu-Kaku	**multi.**	21
Haru*	**multi.**	20
Hasaki*	**E Vill**	24
Hatsuhana*	**E 40s**	25
Hibino*	**Cobble Hill**	25
NEW Hide-Chan	**E 50s**	–
Inakaya	**W 40s**	19
Ippudo	**E Vill**	25
Ise*	**multi.**	21
Japonais	**Gramercy**	20
Japonica*	**G Vill**	24
☑ Jewel Bako*	**E Vill**	26
Kajitsu	**E Vill**	27
Kanoyama*	**E Vill**	26

Katsu-Hama	**multi.**	21
Ki Sushi*	**Boerum Hill**	26
Koi*	**W 40s**	23
Kuruma Zushi*	**E 40s**	26
Kyotofu	**W 40s**	23
Kyo Ya	**E Vill**	26
☑ Masa/Bar Masa*	**W 60s**	27
Matsugen	**TriBeCa**	23
☑ Matsuri*	**Chelsea**	22
☑ Megu	**multi.**	24
Menchanko-tei	**multi.**	20
Minca	**E Vill**	21
Mishima*	**Murray Hill**	24
Mizu Sushi*	**Flatiron**	24
Momoya*	**multi.**	22
Monster Sushi*	**multi.**	18
☑ Morimoto	**Chelsea**	25
Natsumi*	**W 50s**	24
New Hawaii Sea*	**Bronx**	22
Ninja	**TriBeCa**	17
Nippon*	**E 50s**	21
☑ Nobu*	**multi.**	26
Omen	**SoHo**	24
Osaka*	**Cobble Hill**	22
Poke*	**E 80s**	25
Rai Rai Ken	**E Vill**	22
NEW Ramen Kuidouraku	**multi.**	–
Ramen Setagaya	**multi.**	18
NEW Robataya	**E Vill**	23
Rosanjin	**TriBeCa**	27
Sakagura	**E 40s**	24
☑ Sasabune*	**E 70s**	29
Seo*	**E 40s**	21
Shabu-Shabu 70*	**E 70s**	22
Shabu-Tatsu	**E Vill**	20
SobaKoh	**E Vill**	24
Soba Nippon	**W 50s**	23
Soba Totto	**E 40s**	21
Soba-ya	**E Vill**	24
Soto*	**W Vill**	27
☑ Sugiyama	**W 50s**	26
SushiAnn*	**E 50s**	25
Sushiden*	**multi.**	25
SushiSamba*	**multi.**	22
☑ Sushi Seki*	**E 60s**	26
Sushi Sen-nin*	**Murray Hill**	25
☑ Sushi Yasuda*	**E 40s**	28
Sushi Zen*	**W 40s**	25
Suteishi*	**Seaport**	22
Takahachi*	**multi.**	24
NEW Takashi	**W Vill**	–
Takesushi*	**E 50s**	24
NEW Tanuki*	**Meatpacking**	19
Tenzan*	**multi.**	22
☑ Tomoe Sushi*	**G Vill**	26

NEW Totto Ramen	W 50s	–
Ushiwakamaru*	G Vill	27
Wasabi Lobby*	E 80s	21
Watawa*	Astoria	25
Yakitori Totto	W 50s	24
Yama*	multi.	24
Yuka*	E 80s	20
Zenkichi	W'burg	25
Zutto*	TriBeCa	21
Zuzu Ramen	Park Slope	21

JEWISH

Artie's Deli	W 80s	18
Z Barney Greengrass	W 80s	24
Ben's Best	Rego Pk	23
Ben's Kosher	multi.	19
Z Carnegie Deli	W 50s	22
Edison	W 40s	15
Z Katz's Deli	LES	24
Lattanzi	W 40s	22
Liebman's	Bronx	22
NEW Mile End	Boerum Hill	25
Mill Basin Deli	Mill Basin	22
Pastrami Queen	E 70s	20
Sammy's	LES	20
Sarge's Deli	Murray Hill	20
2nd Ave Deli	Murray Hill	22
Stage Deli	W 50s	20

KOREAN

(* barbecue specialist)

Bann	W 50s	22
Bon Chon	multi.	20
Cho Dang Gol	Garment	23
NEW Chom Chom	W 50s	–
Do Hwa*	W Vill	21
Gahm Mi Oak	Garment	20
Z HanGawi	Murray Hill	24
Kang Suh*	Garment	22
Kum Gang San*	multi.	21
Kyochon	multi.	20
Madangsui*	Garment	23
Mandoo Bar	Garment	20
Moim	Park Slope	23
WonJo*	Garment	20
Woo Lae Oak*	SoHo	22

KOSHER/ KOSHER-STYLE

Abigael's	Garment	20
Azuri Cafe	W 50s	25
Ben's Best	Rego Pk	23
Ben's Kosher	multi.	19
Caravan/Dreams	E Vill	22
Chennai Gdn.	Murray Hill	21
Hummus Pl.	multi.	22

Le Marais	W 40s	22
Liebman's	Bronx	22
Mike's Bistro	W 70s	26
Mill Basin Deli	Mill Basin	22
Pastrami Queen	E 70s	20
Pongal	Murray Hill	22
Prime Grill	E 40s	22
2nd Ave Deli	Murray Hill	22
Solo	E 50s	26
Tevere	E 80s	24
Tiffin Wallah	Murray Hill	23

LEBANESE

Al Bustan	E 50s	19
Ilili	Chelsea	24
Naya	E 50s	23

MALAYSIAN

Fatty Crab	multi.	20
Laut	Union Sq	23
Nyonya	multi.	21
Sentosa	Flushing	23

MEDITERRANEAN

Alta	G Vill	24
Amaranth	E 60s	20
NEW Balaboosta	NoLita	–
Barbounia	Flatiron	21
Beast	Prospect Hts	21
Bello Sguardo	W 70s	20
NEW B.E.S.	Chelsea	–
Bodrum	W 80s	20
Cafe Bar	Astoria	20
Cafe Centro	E 40s	20
Café du Soleil	W 100s	19
Cafe Ronda	W 70s	20
City Winery	SoHo	16
Z Conviv. Osteria	Park Slope	26
Danal	G Vill	20
Dee's	Forest Hills	21
Dervish	W 40s	19
Epices/Traiteur	W 70s	21
Extra Virgin	W Vill	21
Fig & Olive	multi.	20
5 Points	NoHo	22
Greenwich Grill/Sushi Azabu	TriBeCa	25
Z Il Buco	NoHo	26
Isabella's	W 70s	20
NEW Kenmare	L Italy	21
Little Owl	W Vill	25
NEW L'Ybane	W 40s	–
Mangia	multi.	20
Marseille	W 40s	20
Miriam	Park Slope	22
Nanoosh	multi.	19

Nice Matin | **W 70s**	20
Nick & Toni | **W 60s**	19
Olea | **Ft Greene**	23
Olives | **Union Sq**	23
Palma | **W Vill**	22
Park | **Chelsea**	17
Pera | **E 40s**	21
Peri Ela | **E 90s**	19
ⓩ Picholine | **W 60s**	27
Place | **W Vill**	21
ᴺᴱᵂ Pop Art Bar | **E 60s**	–
Red Cat | **Chelsea**	24
Sahara | **Gravesend**	22
Savoy | **SoHo**	24
Sel de Mer | **W'burg**	24
Sezz Medi' | **W 100s**	20
Solo | **E 50s**	26
Superfine | **Dumbo**	20
Taboon | **W 50s**	24
ⓩ Tanoreen | **Bay Ridge**	27
ⓩ Terrace in Sky | **W 100s**	22
ᴺᴱᵂ Travertine | **NoLita**	22
202 Cafe | **Chelsea**	19
Vai | **W 70s**	21

MEXICAN

Alma | **Carroll Gdns**	21
Barrio | **Park Slope**	17
Blockhead Burrito | **multi.**	16
Cabrito | **W Vill**	17
Café Frida | **multi.**	20
Café Habana/Outpost | **multi.**	22
Calexico | **Carroll Gdns**	25
ⓩᴺᴱᵂ Cascabel | **E 80s**	25
Centrico | **TriBeCa**	20
Crema | **Chelsea**	23
Dos Caminos | **multi.**	20
ᴺᴱᵂ Dos Toros | **E Vill**	24
El Parador Cafe | **Murray Hill**	22
El Paso Taqueria | **multi.**	23
Fonda | **Park Slope**	24
Gabriela's | **W 90s**	18
ᴺᴱᵂ Hecho en Dumbo | **NoHo**	25
Hell's Kitchen | **W 40s**	23
Itzocan | **multi.**	22
La Esquina | **L Italy**	22
La Palapa | **multi.**	20
La Superior | **W'burg**	24
La Taqueria/Rachel | **Park Slope**	20
Lime Jungle | **W 50s**	–
ᴺᴱᵂ Los Feliz | **LES**	20
Mamá Mexico | **multi.**	19
Matilda | **E Vill**	23
Maya | **E 60s**	24
Maz Mezcal | **E 80s**	20

Mercadito | **multi.**	23
Mesa Coyoacan | **W'burg**	24
Mexicana Mama | **multi.**	23
Mexican Radio | **NoLita**	20
Molé | **multi.**	25
ᴺᴱᵂ Mxco | **E 70s**	18
Noche Mex. | **W 100s**	22
ᴺᴱᵂ Ofrenda | **W Vill**	25
Pampano | **E 40s**	24
Rocking Horse | **Chelsea**	20
Rosa Mexicano | **multi.**	22
Sinigual | **E 40s**	21
Sueños | **Chelsea**	24
Tacos Matamoros | **Sunset Pk**	25
Taco Taco | **E 80s**	21
Tio Pepe | **W Vill**	19
Toloache | **W 50s**	23
Tortilleria Nixtamal | **Corona**	25
Tulcingo del Valle | **W 40s**	24
Zarela | **E 50s**	22

MIDDLE EASTERN

ᴺᴱᵂ Balaboosta | **NoLita**	–
Chickpea | **multi.**	19
Gazala Place | **multi.**	23
Maoz Veg. | **multi.**	21
Mimi's Hummus | **Ditmas Pk**	25
Moustache | **multi.**	21
Taboon | **W 50s**	24
ⓩ Tanoreen | **Bay Ridge**	27
12 Chairs | **SoHo**	19
Zaytoons | **multi.**	20

MOROCCAN

Barbès | **Murray Hill**	19
Cafe Gitane | **multi.**	20
Cafe Mogador | **E Vill**	22
Zerza | **E Vill**	22

NEW ENGLAND

Ed's Lobster | **NoLita**	23
Mermaid | **multi.**	21
ⓩ Pearl Oyster | **W Vill**	26

NOODLE SHOPS

Bao Noodles | **Gramercy**	19
Bôi | **W 40s**	20
Bo-Ky | **multi.**	22
Donguri | **E 80s**	27
Great NY Noodle | **Chinatown**	22
ᴺᴱᵂ Hide-Chan | **E 50s**	–
Ippudo | **E Vill**	25
Matsugen | **TriBeCa**	23
Mee Noodle | **multi.**	17
Menchanko-tei | **multi.**	20
Minca | **E Vill**	21
Momofuku Noodle | **E Vill**	24

M Shanghai/Noodle	**W'burg**	21
Noodle Bar	**multi.**	20
Pho Bang	**multi.**	20
Pho Viet Huong	**Chinatown**	22
Rai Rai Ken	**E Vill**	22
NEW Ramen Kuidouraku	**multi.**	-
Ramen Setagaya	**multi.**	18
Republic	**Union Sq**	18
SobaKoh	**E Vill**	24
Soba Nippon	**W 50s**	23
Soba Totto	**E 40s**	21
Soba-ya	**E Vill**	24
Tasty Hand-Pulled	**Chinatown**	22
NEW Totto Ramen	**W 50s**	-
Zuzu Ramen	**Park Slope**	21

NORTH AFRICAN

Nomad	**E Vill**	21

NUEVO LATINO

At Vermilion	**E 40s**	20
Cabana	**multi.**	21
Calle Ocho	**W 80s**	21
Citrus B&G	**W 70s**	19
Luz	**Ft Greene**	24
Mamajuana	**Inwood**	20

PAN-LATIN

A Casa Fox	**LES**	20
Agua Dulce	**W 50s**	22
Boca Chica	**E Vill**	21
Bogota	**Park Slope**	23
Macondo	**LES**	23
Miranda	**W'burg**	23
NEW Nuela	**Flatiron**	-
Palo Santo	**Park Slope**	25
Rayuela	**LES**	23
Yerba Buena	**multi.**	23
Yuca Bar	**E Vill**	23
NEW Zengo	**E 40s**	24

PERSIAN

Persepolis	**E 70s**	21
Ravagh	**multi.**	21
Shalezeh	**E 80s**	21

PERUVIAN

NEW Bar Paya	**E Vill**	-
Chimu	**W'burg**	25
Coco Roco	**multi.**	19
Flor/Mayo	**multi.**	20
Mancora	**E Vill**	21
Z Nobu	**multi.**	26
Pio Pio	**multi.**	22

PIZZA

Acqua	**W 90s**	19
Adrienne's	**Financial**	24
Amorina	**Prospect Hts**	25
Anella	**Greenpt**	26
Angelo's Pizza	**multi.**	20
Aperitivo	**E 40s**	21
Ápizz	**LES**	24
Artichoke Basille	**E Vill**	23
Arturo's	**G Vill**	21
Bella Blu	**E 70s**	21
Bella Via	**LIC**	23
Bettola	**W 70s**	20
Big Nick's	**W 70s**	18
Bricco	**multi.**	19
Brio	**E 60s**	20
Cacio e Vino	**E Vill**	22
Cafe Fiorello	**W 60s**	20
NEW Campo/Fiori	**Park Slope**	-
Co.	**Chelsea**	22
Coals	**Bronx**	23
Covo	**Harlem**	22
Da Ciro	**Murray Hill**	22
Dean's	**multi.**	10
Dee's	**Forest Hills**	21
Denino	**SI**	26
Z Di Fara	**Midwood**	27
NEW Eataly	**Flatiron**	-
Fornino	**multi.**	23
Franny's	**Prospect Hts**	24
Gigino	**multi.**	21
Grimaldi's	**multi.**	24
Gruppo	**E Vill**	24
Harry's Italian	**Financial**	21
Il Mattone	**TriBeCa**	21
Joe & Pat's	**SI**	23
Joe's Pizza	**multi.**	23
Z John's Pizzeria	**multi.**	22
Keste Pizza	**W Vill**	25
L&B Spumoni	**Bensonhurst**	24
La Pizza Fresca	**Flatiron**	23
La Villa Pizzeria	**multi.**	21
Lazzara's	**multi.**	21
Lil' Frankie	**E Vill**	23
Lombardi's	**NoLita**	23
Lucali	**Carroll Gdns**	26
Luzzo's/Ovest	**multi.**	22
Mediterraneo	**E 60s**	20
Mezzaluna/Pizza	**multi.**	20
Motorino	**multi.**	24
Naples 45	**E 40s**	17
Nick's	**multi.**	23
Nina's Argentin.	**E 90s**	23
Nino's	**E 40s**	20
No. 28	**multi.**	23
NEW Olio	**W Vill**	-
Otto	**G Vill**	22
Patsy's Pizzeria	**multi.**	20

Pintaile's Pizza | **multi.**	21
Pizza 33 | **multi.**	19
Posto | **Gramercy**	24
NEW Pulino's | **NoLita**	19
Rizzo's Pizza | **Astoria**	23
Roberta's | **Bushwick**	23
Sac's Place | **Astoria**	23
Savoia | **Carroll Gdns**	20
Sezz Medi' | **W 100s**	20
Spunto | **W Vill**	21
Toby's Public | **Greenwood Hts**	25
Totonno Pizza | **multi.**	21
Two Boots | **multi.**	18
V&T | **W 100s**	18
Veloce Pizzeria | **E Vill**	20
Vesta | **Astoria**	24
Vezzo | **Murray Hill**	23
Waldy's Pizza | **Chelsea**	21
Zero Otto | **Bronx**	25

POLYNESIAN

NEW Hurricane Club | **Flatiron**	–

PORTUGUESE

Aldea | **Flatiron**	25
Macao Trading | **TriBeCa**	18

PUB FOOD

Elephant & Castle | **W Vill**	18
Heartland | **multi.**	14
NEW Henry Public | **Cobble Hill**	17
J.G. Melon | **E 70s**	21
Landmark Tavern | **W 40s**	18
Neary's | **E 50s**	18
Pete's Tavern | **Gramercy**	16
P.J. Clarke's | **multi.**	17
Sheep Sta. | **Park Slope**	18
Smith | **E Vill**	19
Union Smith | **Carroll Gdns**	20
Walker's | **TriBeCa**	18

PUERTO RICAN

La Taza de Oro | **Chelsea**	21
Sazon | **TriBeCa**	23
Sofrito | **E 50s**	22

RUSSIAN

∅ FireBird | **W 40s**	20
Mari Vanna | **Flatiron**	20
Russian Samovar | **W 50s**	20
Russian Tea | **W 50s**	19
Tatiana | **Brighton Bch**	21

SANDWICHES

Amy's Bread | **multi.**	24
Baoguette | **multi.**	21
∅ Barney Greengrass | **W 80s**	24

Bôi | **multi.**	20
Bouchon Bakery | **W 60s**	24
Bread | **NoLita**	20
Brennan | **Sheepshead**	21
Così | **multi.**	16
Defonte's | **multi.**	22
Dishes | **multi.**	21
DuMont | **W'burg**	23
E.A.T. | **E 80s**	20
Ess-a-Bagel | **multi.**	23
Hale/Hearty | **multi.**	19
Hanco's | **multi.**	21
Il Bambino | **Astoria**	24
∅ Katz's Deli | **LES**	24
Lenny's | **multi.**	17
Mangia | **multi.**	20
NEW Meatball Shop | **LES**	22
Nicky's | **multi.**	21
NEW No. 7 Sub | **Chelsea**	23
Olive's | **SoHo**	22
Pastrami Queen | **E 70s**	20
Peanut Butter Co. | **G Vill**	19
Porchetta | **E Vill**	23
Press 195 | **multi.**	21
Pret A Manger | **multi.**	18
Roll-n-Roaster | **Sheepshead**	21
NEW Saltie | **W'burg**	25
NEW Salumè | **SoHo**	–
Sandwich Planet | **Garment**	22
Sarge's Deli | **Murray Hill**	20
2nd Ave Deli | **Murray Hill**	22
sNice | **multi.**	20
Stage Deli | **W 50s**	20
Sweet Melissa | **multi.**	20
NEW Tartinery | **NoLita**	–
NEW This Little Piggy | **E Vill**	23
NEW Torrisi | **NoLita**	27
'Wichcraft | **multi.**	20
Yura on Madison | **E 90s**	21
Zabar's Cafe | **W 80s**	20
Zaitzeff | **multi.**	20

SCANDINAVIAN

AQ Kafé | **W 50s**	20
∅ Aquavit | **E 50s**	25
Smorgas Chef | **multi.**	19
White Slab | **LES**	18

SEAFOOD

Ammos | **E 40s**	22
∅ Aquagrill | **SoHo**	26
Atlantic Grill | **E 70s**	23
Avra | **E 40s**	25
Black Duck | **Murray Hill**	21
∅ BLT Fish | **Flatiron**	24
Blue Fin | **W 40s**	22

Blue Water	**Union Sq**	23
Bocelli	**SI**	25
Brooklyn Fish	**Park Slope**	23
Bubba Gump	**W 40s**	14
NEW Choptank	**W Vill**	17
City Crab	**Flatiron**	19
City Hall	**TriBeCa**	21
City Is. Lobster	**Bronx**	19
City Lobster	**W 40s**	19
Cole's Dock	**SI**	18
Cowgirl	**Seaport**	16
Cucina/Pesce	**E Vill**	19
Ditch Plains	**W Vill**	18
Docks Oyster	**E 40s**	19
NEW Ed's Chowder	**W 60s**	19
Ed's Lobster	**NoLita**	23
Elias Corner	**Astoria**	23
Esca	**W 40s**	25
NEW Estiatorio Rafina	**Murray Hill**	–
Fish	**W Vill**	21
Fishtail	**E 60s**	23
Flex Mussels	**E 80s**	23
Francisco's	**Chelsea**	22
Fuleen	**Chinatown**	22
Fulton	**E 70s**	21
Hudson River	**Harlem**	21
Ithaka	**E 80s**	22
Jack's Lux.	**E Vill**	27
Kellari Tav./Parea	**multi.**	22
Le Bernardin	**W 50s**	29
Le Pescadeux	**SoHo**	23
Lobster Box	**Bronx**	18
London Lennie	**Rego Pk**	22
NEW Luke's Lobster	**multi.**	–
Lure Fishbar	**SoHo**	23
Marea	**W 50s**	27
Marina Cafe	**SI**	20
Mary's Fish	**W Vill**	25
McCormick/Schmick	**W 50s**	20
Mermaid	**multi.**	21
Milos	**W 50s**	27
Oceana	**W 40s**	23
Ocean Grill	**W 70s**	24
Oriental Gdn.	**Chinatown**	24
Oyster Bar	**E 40s**	22
Pampano	**E 40s**	24
Parlor Steak	**E 90s**	22
Pearl Oyster	**W Vill**	26
Pearl Room	**Bay Ridge**	22
Periyali	**Flatiron**	24
Petite Crev.	**Carroll Gdns**	24
Ping's Sea.	**multi.**	22
Portofino	**Bronx**	21
Redeye Grill	**W 50s**	20

Sammy's Fishbox	**Bronx**	20
Sea Grill	**W 40s**	24
Sel de Mer	**W'burg**	24
Shelly's Tratt.	**W 50s**	20
South Fin	**SI**	19
Taverna Kyclades	**Astoria**	26
Telly's Taverna	**Astoria**	23
Thalassa	**TriBeCa**	23
Tratt. Pesce	**multi.**	18
Umberto's	**multi.**	19
Water's Edge	**LIC**	20

SERBIAN

Kafana	**E Vill**	24

SINGAPOREAN

Laut	**Union Sq**	23

SMALL PLATES

(See also Spanish tapas specialist)

Alta	Med.	**G Vill**	24
Bar Breton	French	**Chelsea**	19
NEW Bar Paya	Peruvian	**E Vill**	–
Bar Stuzz.	Italian	**multi.**	20
Beast	Med.	**Prospect Hts**	21
Bello Sguardo	Med.	**W 70s**	20
Beyoglu	Turkish	**E 80s**	22
Bocca Lupo	Italian	**Cobble Hill**	24
Centro Vinoteca	Italian	**W Vill**	21
NEW Chom Chom	Korean	**W 50s**	–
City Winery	Med.	**SoHo**	16
NEW Corsino	Italian	**W Vill**	20
Degustation	French/Spanish	**E Vill**	27
EN Japanese	Japanese	**W Vill**	24
Enoteca Maria	Italian	**SI**	23
Fig & Olive	Med.	**multi.**	20
Frankies	Italian	**multi.**	24
Gen. Greene	Amer.	**Ft Greene**	20
Gottino	Italian	**W Vill**	22
Graffiti	Eclectic	**E Vill**	25
NEW Hudson Hall	Amer.	**W 50s**	–
Ilili	Lebanese	**Chelsea**	24
'Inoteca	Italian	**multi.**	22
Jimmy's	Amer.	**E Vill**	22
Kuma Inn	Asian	**LES**	25
L'Atelier/Robuchon	French	**E 50s**	27
Lunetta	Italian	**Boerum Hill**	22
Macao Trading	Chinese/Portuguese	**TriBeCa**	18
Macondo	Pan-Latin	**LES**	23
Marlow/Sons	Amer.	**W'burg**	24
Maze	French	**W 50s**	22
Mercadito	Mex.	**multi.**	23

Nizza	French/Italian	**W 40s**	20
NEW Nuela	Pan-Latin	**Flatiron**	-
Olea	Med.	**Ft Greene**	23
Prime Meat	Amer.	**Carroll Gdns**	24
Rayuela	Pan-Latin	**LES**	23
NEW Recette	Amer.	**W Vill**	24
NEW Robataya	Japanese	**E Vill**	23
Sakagura	Japanese	**E 40s**	24
Salumeria Rosi	Italian	**W 70s**	24
Sojourn	Eclectic	**E 70s**	22
Sorella	Italian	**LES**	24
Stanton Social	Eclectic	**LES**	23
NEW Tanuki	Japanese	**Meatpacking**	19
Tarallucci	Italian	**multi.**	21
Terroir	Italian	**multi.**	24
NEW Thistle Hill	Amer.	**Park Slope**	-
NEW Traif	Eclectic	**W'burg**	-
Turks/Frogs	Turkish	**W Vill**	18
Umi Nom	Asian	**Clinton Hill**	24
Uva	Italian	**E 70s**	21
NEW Vanderbilt	Amer.	**Prospect Hts**	21
Zenkichi	Japanese	**W'burg**	25

SOUL FOOD

Amy Ruth's	**Harlem**	20
Londel's	**Harlem**	20
Miss Mamie/Maude	**Harlem**	20
Mo-Bay	**Harlem**	21
Pies-n-Thighs	**W'burg**	23
Rack & Soul	**W 100s**	21
Sylvia's	**Harlem**	19

SOUP

Hale/Hearty	**multi.**	19
La Bonne Soupe	**W 50s**	18

SOUTH AFRICAN

Braai	**W 50s**	21
Madiba	**Ft Greene**	22

SOUTH AMERICAN

(See also Argentinean, Brazilian, Chilean, Colombian, Peruvian, Venezuelan)

Cafe Ronda	**W 70s**	20
Empanada Mama	**W 50s**	22

SOUTHERN

Amy Ruth's	**Harlem**	20
Bourbon St. Café	**Bayside**	17
B. Smith's	**W 40s**	19
Char No. 4	**Cobble Hill**	22
NEW Choptank	**W Vill**	17
NEW Commodore	**W'burg**	-
Egg	**W'burg**	23
Kitchenette	**multi.**	19
Londel's	**Harlem**	20
Miss Mamie/Maude	**Harlem**	20
Peaches	**Bed-Stuy**	22
Pink Tea Cup	**W Vill**	-
Rack & Soul	**W 100s**	21
NEW Seersucker	**Carroll Gdns**	-
NEW South Houston	**SoHo**	-
Sylvia's	**Harlem**	19
NEW Tipsy Parson	**Chelsea**	18

SOUTHWESTERN

Agave	**W Vill**	18
Canyon Rd.	**E 70s**	20
Cilantro	**multi.**	17
Cowgirl	**multi.**	16
Los Dos Molinos	**Gramercy**	21
Z Mesa Grill	**Flatiron**	23

SPANISH

(* tapas specialist)

Boqueria*	**multi.**	22
Cafe Español	**multi.**	20
Casa Mono*	**Gramercy**	26
Z Degustation	**E Vill**	27
El Charro	**W Vill**	22
El Faro*	**W Vill**	22
El Pote	**Murray Hill**	22
El Quijote	**Chelsea**	21
El Quinto Pino*	**Chelsea**	21
Euzkadi*	**E Vill**	20
Flor/Sol*	**TriBeCa**	20
Francisco's	**Chelsea**	22
La Fonda/Sol	**E 40s**	22
La Paella*	**E Vill**	20
Las Ramblas*	**W Vill**	24
Mercat*	**NoHo**	20
Nomad*	**E Vill**	21
Pipa*	**Flatiron**	22
Real Madrid	**SI**	22
Sala*	**multi.**	22
Sevilla	**W Vill**	22
Socarrat*	**Chelsea**	24
Solera*	**E 50s**	21
NEW Taberna*	**W 80s**	-
Tía Pol*	**Chelsea**	25
Tio Pepe	**W Vill**	19
Toledo	**Murray Hill**	24
Txikito*	**Chelsea**	24

STEAKHOUSES

Aged	**multi.**	17
A.J. Maxwell's	**W 40s**	22
Angelo/Maxie's	**Flatiron**	21
Arirang Hibachi	**multi.**	19

Austin's Steak | **Bay Ridge**	22
Azul Bistro | **LES**	20
Ben & Jack's | **multi.**	23
Ben Benson's | **W 50s**	24
NEW Benchmark | **Park Slope**	–
Benjamin Steak | **E 40s**	25
BLT Prime | **Gramercy**	25
🔒 BLT Steak | **E 50s**	25
Bobby Van's | **multi.**	22
Buenos Aires | **E Vill**	23
Bull & Bear | **E 40s**	21
Capital Grille | **multi.**	24
Chimichurri Grill | **W 40s**	23
Christos | **Astoria**	23
Churrascaria | **multi.**	23
Circus | **E 60s**	21
City Hall | **TriBeCa**	21
🔒 Del Frisco's | **W 40s**	25
Delmonico's | **Financial**	23
Dylan Prime | **TriBeCa**	24
Embers | **Bay Ridge**	21
Erawan | **Bayside**	23
Fairway Cafe | **W 70s**	18
Frankie/Johnnie | **multi.**	23
Gallagher's | **W 50s**	21
Harry's Cafe/Steak | **Financial**	23
Il Bastardo | **Chelsea**	18
Jake's | **Bronx**	24
🔒 Keens | **Garment**	25
Le Marais | **W 40s**	22
Le Relais/Venise | **E 50s**	20
Les Halles | **multi.**	20
Macelleria | **Meatpacking**	22
Maloney/Porcelli | **E 50s**	23
MarkJoseph | **Financial**	24
Michael Jordan | **E 40s**	21
Morton's | **multi.**	24
Nick & Stef | **Garment**	21
Novecento | **SoHo**	23
NYY Steak | **Bronx**	21
Old Homestead | **Meatpacking**	24
Outback | **multi.**	15
Padre Figlio | **E 40s**	22
🔒 Palm | **multi.**	24
Parlor Steak | **E 90s**	22
🔒 Peter Luger | **W'burg**	27
Pietro's | **E 40s**	24
Porter House | **W 60s**	24
Post House | **E 60s**	24
Prime Grill | **E 40s**	22
Primehouse | **Murray Hill**	24
Prime Meat | **Carroll Gdns**	24
Quality Meats | **W 50s**	24
Ricardo | **Harlem**	22
Rothmann's | **E 50s**	23

Ruth's Chris | **W 50s**	24
Shula's | **W 40s**	20
🔒 Smith/Wollensky | **E 40s**	24
South Fin | **SI**	19
🔒 Sparks | **E 40s**	25
STK | **Meatpacking**	23
🔒 Strip House | **G Vill**	25
T-Bar Steak | **E 70s**	21
Tre Dici/Steak | **Chelsea**	21
Uncle Jack's | **multi.**	22
🔒 Wolfgang's | **multi.**	25
Wollensky's | **E 40s**	23

SWISS

Café Select | **SoHo**	19
Mont Blanc | **W 40s**	21

TEAROOMS

Alice's Tea | **multi.**	19
Lady Mendl's | **Gramercy**	21
Roebling | **W'burg**	19
Sweet Melissa | **multi.**	20
Tea & Sympathy | **W Vill**	19

TEX-MEX

Mary Ann's | **multi.**	15

THAI

Bann Thai | **Forest Hills**	19
Breeze | **W 40s**	22
Elephant | **E Vill**	21
Erawan | **Bayside**	23
Holy Basil | **E Vill**	21
Jaiya Thai | **Murray Hill**	22
Joya | **Cobble Hill**	23
Kittichai | **SoHo**	23
Klong | **E Vill**	20
Kuma Inn | **LES**	25
Land | **multi.**	22
Lantern | **multi.**	19
Laut | **Union Sq**	23
Lemongrass | **multi.**	17
Long Tan | **Park Slope**	20
Pam Real Thai | **W 40s**	23
Peep | **SoHo**	20
Pongsri Thai | **multi.**	20
Pukk | **E Vill**	21
Q Thai Bistro | **Forest Hills**	20
Room Service | **multi.**	21
Royal Siam | **Chelsea**	20
Sala Thai | **E 80s**	21
Sea | **multi.**	21
Siam Inn | **W 50s**	21
Siam Sq. | **Bronx**	23
Song | **Park Slope**	23
Sookk | **W 100s**	21

Spice | **multi.** 20
☑ Sripraphai | **Woodside** 26
Thai Pavilion | **Astoria** 25
Topaz Thai | **W 50s** 21
Umi Nom | **Clinton Hill** 24
Vynl | **multi.** 17
Wondee Siam | **multi.** 21

TIBETAN

Tsampa | **E Vill** 21

TUNISIAN

Epices/Traiteur | **W 70s** 21

TURKISH

Akdeniz | **W 40s** 21
A La Turka | **E 70s** 18
Ali Baba | **multi.** 21
Bereket | **LES** 19
Beyoglu | **E 80s** 22
Bodrum | **W 80s** 20
Hanci | **W 50s** 22
Limon | **Murray Hill** 24
Mundo | **Astoria** 22
Pasha | **W 70s** 20
Pera | **E 40s** 21
Peri Ela | **E 90s** 19
Sahara | **Gravesend** 22
Sahara's Turkish | **Gramercy** 22
Sip Sak | **E 40s** 20
Taci's Beyti | **Midwood** 24
Taksim | **E 50s** 21
Turkish Cuisine | **W 40s** 20
Turkish Grill | **Sunnyside** 24
☑ Turkish Kitchen | **Murray Hill** 22
Turks/Frogs | **multi.** 18
Turkuaz | **W 100s** 20
Uskudar | **E 70s** 21
Zeytin | **W 80s** 18

UKRAINIAN

Veselka | **E Vill** 19

VEGETARIAN

(* vegan)
Angelica Kit.* | **E Vill** 21
Blossom* | **multi.** 22

Candle Cafe* | **E 70s** 23
Candle 79* | **E 70s** 24
Caravan/Dreams* | **E Vill** 22
Chennai Gdn. | **Murray Hill** 21
Counter* | **E Vill** 21
Dirt Candy | **E Vill** 27
Gobo* | **multi.** 22
☑ HanGawi | **Murray Hill** 24
Hummus Pl. | **multi.** 22
Kajitsu | **E Vill** 27
Maoz Veg. | **multi.** 21
Peacefood Café* | **W 80s** 21
Pongal | **Murray Hill** 22
Pukk | **E Vill** 21
Pure Food/Wine* | **Gramercy** 23
Quantum Leap | **multi.** 20
Saravanaas | **Murray Hill** 25
sNice | **multi.** 20
Taïm | **W Vill** 26
Tiffin Wallah | **Murray Hill** 23
Vatan | **Murray Hill** 23
Wild Ginger* | **multi.** 22
Zen Palate | **multi.** 19

VENEZUELAN

Arepas Café | **Astoria** 24
Caracas | **multi.** 24

VIETNAMESE

Baoguette | **multi.** 21
Bao Noodles | **Gramercy** 19
Bôi | **multi.** 20
Bo-Ky | **multi.** 22
Hanco's | **multi.** 21
Indochine | **E Vill** 21
Le Colonial | **E 50s** 21
NEW Má Pêche | **W 50s** 22
Nam | **TriBeCa** 22
Nha Trang | **Chinatown** 22
Nicky's | **multi.** 21
☑ Omai | **Chelsea** 23
Pho Bang | **multi.** 20
Pho Viet Huong | **Chinatown** 22
Saigon Grill | **multi.** 21
Vermicelli | **E 70s** 19

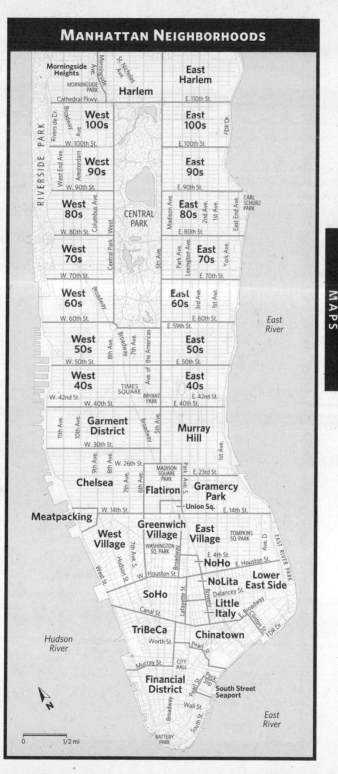

MANHATTAN NEIGHBORHOODS

Morningside
Heights

MORNINGSIDE
PARK

Cathedral Pkwy.

Harlem

**East
Harlem**

E. 110th St.

**West
100s**

W. 100th St.

**East
100s**

E. 100th St.

**West
90s**

W. 90th St.

**East
90s**

E. 90th St.

RIVERSIDE PARK

**West
80s**

W. 80th St.

**CENTRAL
PARK**

**East
80s**

E. 80th St.

CARL
SCHURZ
PARK

**West
70s**

W. 70th St.

**East
70s**

E. 70th St.

**West
60s**

W. 60th St.

**East
60s**

E. 59th St.

E. 60th St.

*East
River*

**West
50s**

W. 50th St.

**East
50s**

E. 50th St.

**West
40s**

W. 42nd St.

W. 40th St.

TIMES
SQUARE

BRYANT
PARK

**East
40s**

E. 42nd St.

E. 40th St.

**Garment
District**

W. 30th St.

**Murray
Hill**

Chelsea

W. 26th St.

MADISON
SQUARE
PARK

E. 23rd St.

Flatiron

**Gramercy
Park**

W. 14th St.

Union Sq.

E. 14th St.

Meatpacking

**West
Village**

**Greenwich
Village**

WASHINGTON
SQ. PARK

**East
Village**

TOMPKINS
SQ. PARK

E. 4th St.

NoHo

E. Houston St.

W. Houston St.

NoLita

**Lower
East
Side**

Delancey St.

SoHo

Canal St.

**Little
Italy**

TriBeCa

Worth St.

Chinatown

*Hudson
River*

Murray St.

CITY
HALL

**Financial
District**

**South Street
Seaport**

Wall St.

BATTERY
PARK

*East
River*

N

0   1/2 mi

MAPS

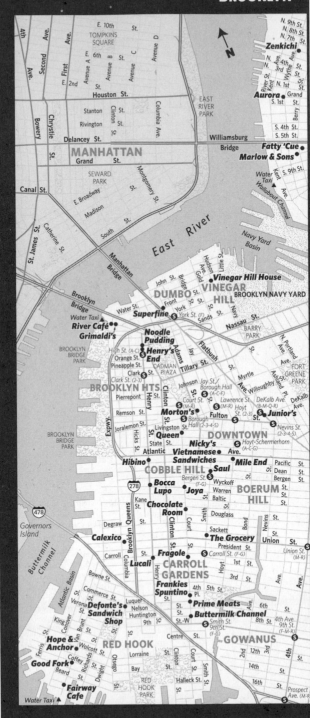

4th Ave.

Second Ave.

First Ave.

E. 10th St.
TOMPKINS
SQUARE
6th St.

Avenue A
Avenue B
Avenue C
Avenue D

Houston St.

Chrystie St.
Bowery

Stanton St.
Rivington St.
Clinton St.
Columbia Ave.

Delancey St.

MANHATTAN

Grand St.

SEWARD
PARK

Canal St.

E. Broadway

Madison St.

Montgomery St.

South St.

N. 9th St.
N. 8th St.
N. 7th St.

Zenkichi

N. Ave. 4th
3rd Wythe St.
River St. Kent

Aurora
S. 1st St.
Grand

Berry

S. 4th St.
S. 5th St.

Williamsburg
Bridge

Fatty 'Cue
Marlow & Sons

Water Kent
Taxi Ave. 9th St.
Wallabout Channel

East River

Navy Yard
Basin

BROOKLYN NAVY YARD

St. James St.

Catherine St.

Manhattan
Bridge

Brooklyn
Bridge

John St.
Bridge St.
Gold St.
Little St.
Hudson Ave.

Vinegar Hill House

DUMBO
Front St.
York St.

**VINEGAR
HILL**

Water St.

Nassau St.

Navy St.

BARRY
PARK

Water Taxi
River Café
Grimaldi's

Superfine
York St. (F)
Sands St.

Flatbush Ave.

N. Portland
N. Oxford
Ashland Pl.

FORT
GREENE
PARK

BROOKLYN
BRIDGE
PARK

Clark St. (2-3)

High St. (A-C)

**Noodle
Pudding**

**Henry's
End**

Orange St.
Pineapple St.
Clark St.

CADMAN
PLAZA

Adams St.
Jay St.
Tillary St.

Myrtle Ave.
Willoughby Ave.

DeKalb Ave.

FORT
GREENE

BROOKLYN HTS

Pierrepont St.

Johnson St.

Jay St./
Borough Hall
(A-C-F)

Court St.
(M-R)

Lawrence St.

DeKalb Ave.
(B-M-Q-R)

Henry St.
Clinton St.

Remsen St.

Morton's

Fulton St.

Hoyt St. (2-3)

Junior's

Nevins St.

Joralemon St.

Livingston St.

Borough
Hall
(2-3-4-5)

Hoyt St.

Queen

DOWNTOWN

Hoyt-Schermerhorn
(A-C-G)

Hicks St.

State St.

Nicky's

Atlantic Ave.

**Vietnamese
Sandwiches**

BROOKLYN
BRIDGE
PARK

Expwy

Hibino

COBBLE HILL

Saul

Mile End

Pacific St.
Dean St.
Bergen St.

Bergen St.
(F-G)

Wyckoff St.
Warren St.
Baltic St.

**BOERUM
HILL**

278

**Bocca
Lupo**

Joya

**Chocolate
Room**

Kane St.

Douglass St.

Queens St.

Clinton St.

Court St.

Smith St.

Bond St.

Nevins St.

478

Governors
Island

Degraw St.

Calexico

Carroll St.

Sackett St.

President St.

The Grocery

Union St.

Union St.
(M-R)

Buttermilk
Channel

Bowne St.

Columbia St.

Lucali

Fragole

Carroll St. (F-G)

**CARROLL
GARDENS**

3rd St.

Hoyt St.

Commerce St.

Luquer St.
Nelson St.
Huntington St.

**Frankies
Spuntino**

4th 5th St.
Pl.

4th Ave.

6th St.

Atlantic Basin

Verona St.

**Defonte's
Sandwich
Shop**

9th St.

Henry St.

St.-W

Prime Meats
Buttermilk Channel

Smith St.
9th St.
(F-G)

8th St.
9th St.
(F-M-R)

King St.

Conover St.

Van Brunt St.

Centre St.

GOWANUS

**Hope &
Anchor**

Ferris St.

Wolcott St.

RED HOOK

Lorraine St.

Clinton St.

Court St.

Smith St.

9th 12th 3rd
2nd

Good Fork

Coffey St.
Richards St.
Dwight St.

Beard St.

Otsego St.

Bay St.

14th St.

4th

**Fairway
Cafe**

Water Taxi

RED
HOOK
PARK

Halleck St.

16th St.

Prospect
Ave. (M-R)

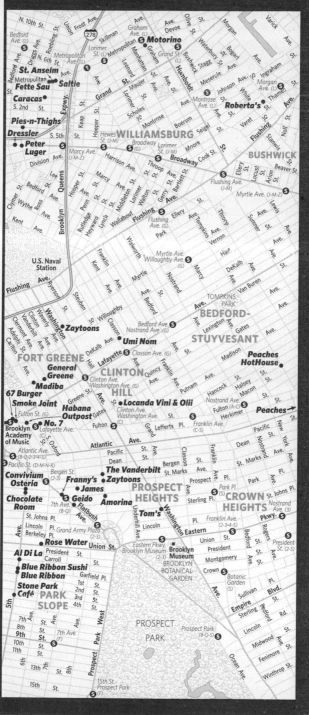

MAPS

Locations

Includes names, street locations and Food ratings. Abbreviations key:
(a=Avenue, s=Street, e.g. 1a/116s=First Ave. at 116th St.;
3a/82-83s=Third Ave. between 82nd & 83rd Sts.)

Manhattan

CHELSEA

(26th to 30th Sts., west of 5th;
14th to 26th Sts., west of 6th)

Amy's Bread | 9a/15-16s	24
Bar Breton | 5a/28-29s	19
NEW B.E.S. | 22s/10-11a	-
Blossom | 9a/21-22s	22
Blue Ginger | 8a/15-16s	22
Bombay Talkie | 9a/21-22s	20
Bottino | 10a/24-25s	20
Z NEW Breslin | 29s/Bway-5a	21
Brgr | 7a/26-27s	19
Z Buddakan | 9a/15-16s	24
Cafeteria | 7a/17s	19
Co. | 9a/24s	22
NEW Colicchio/Sons | 10a/15-16s	23
Cookshop | 10a/20s	22
Crema | 17s/6-7a	23
Dallas BBQ | 8a/23s	15
Da Umberto | 17s/6-7a	25
Z Del Posto | 10a/15-16s	26
El Quijote | 23s/7-8a	21
El Quinto Pino | 24s/9-10a	21
Energy Kitchen | 17s/8-9a	17
Francisco's | 23s/6-7a	22
Gascogne | 8a/17-18s	21
Grand Sichuan | 9a/24s	22
Hale/Hearty | 9a/15-16s	19
NEW Highpoint | 7a/22-23s	-
Il Bastardo | 7a/21-22s	18
Ilili | 5a/27-28s	24
Klee Brass. | 9a/22-23s	19
La Bergamote | 9a/20s	24
La Lunchonette | 10a/18s	21
La Taza de Oro | 8a/14-15s	21
Le Singe Vert | 7a/19-20s	18
Le Zie 2000 | 7a/20-21s	22
Luzzo's/Ovest | 27s/10-11a	22
Mary Ann's | 8a/16s	15
Z Matsuri | 16s/9a	22
Momoya | 7a/21s	22
Monster Sushi | 23s/6-7a	18
Z Morimoto | 10a/15-16s	25
NEW No. 7 Sub | Bway/28-29s	23
Z Omai | 9a/19-20s	23
Park | 10a/17-18s	17

Patsy's Pizzeria | 23s/8-9a	20
Pepe | 10a/24-25s	21
Pizza 33 | 23s/8a	19
Pongsri Thai | 23s/6-7a	20
Rare B&G | 26s/6-7a	21
Red Cat | 10a/23-24s	24
Rocking Horse | 8a/19-20s	20
Room Service | 8a/18-19s	21
Royal Siam | 8a/22-23s	20
RUB BBQ | 23s/7-8a	21
Sarabeth's | 9a/15-16s	20
Z Scarpetta | 14s/8-9a	26
Socarrat | 19s/7-8a	24
Spice | multi.	20
Sueños | 17s/8-9a	24
Tía Pol | 10a/22-23s	25
NEW Tipsy Parson | 9a/19-20s	18
Tre Dici/Steak | 26s/6-7a	21
Trestle on 10th | 10a/24s	20
202 Cafe | 9a/15-16s	19
Txikito | 9a/24-25s	24
Uncle Nick's | 8a/29s	21
Vynl | 8a/15s	17
Waldy's Pizza | 6a/27-28s	21
Westville | 18s/7-8a	22
'Wichcraft | 11a/27-28s	20

CHINATOWN

(Canal to Pearl Sts., east of B'way)

Amazing 66 | Mott/Canal	22
Big Wong | Mott/Canal	22
Bo-Ky | Bayard/Mott	22
Dim Sum Go Go | E Bway/Chatham	20
Excellent Dumpling | Lafayette/Canal	20
Forlini's | Baxter/Walker	20
Fuleen | Division/Bowery	22
Golden Unicorn | E Bway/Catherine	21
Grand Sichuan | Canal/Chrystie	22
Great NY Noodle | Bowery/Bayard	22
Jing Fong | Elizabeth/Canal	19
Joe's Shanghai | Pell/Bowery	22
Joe's | Pell/Doyers	20
Mandarin Court | Mott/Canal	20
Nha Trang | multi.	22
Nice Green Bo | Bayard/Elizabeth	23
Z Oriental Gdn. | Elizabeth/Canal	24

Peking Duck | *Mott/Mosco-Pell* | 23
Pho Viet Huong | *Mulberry/Canal* | 22
Ping's Sea. | *Mott/Chatham-Pell* | 22
Pongsri Thai | *Bayard/Baxter* | 20
Shanghai Cuisine | *Bayard/Mulberry* | 22
Tasty Hand-Pulled | *Doyers/Bowery* | 22
Wo Hop | *Mott/Canal* | 21
Xi'an | *E Bway/Forsyth* | -
X.O. | *Walker/Centre-Lafayette* | 20

EAST 40s

Aburiya Kinnosuke | *45s/2-3a* | 25
Ali Baba | *2a/46s* | 21
Ammos | *Vanderbilt/44-45s* | 22
Aperitivo | *3a/48s* | 21
At Vermilion | *Lex/46s* | 20
Avra | *48s/Lex-3a* | 25
Ben & Jack's | *44s/2-3a* | 23
Benjamin Steak | *41s/Mad-Park* | 25
Bobby Van's | *Park/46s* | 22
Bôi | *multi.* | 20
Brother Jimmy's | *42s/Vanderbilt* | 16
Bukhara Grill | *49s/2-3a* | 23
Bull & Bear | *Park/49s* | 21
Burger Heaven | *multi.* | 16
Cafe Centro | *Park/45s* | 20
Cafe S.F.A. | *5a/49-50s* | 18
Capital Grille | *42s/Lex-3a* | 24
Chiam | *48s/Lex-3a* | 22
Ⓩ Chin Chin | *49s/2-3a* | 23
Cibo | *2a/41s* | 21
Cipriani Dolci | *42s/Vanderbilt* | 20
Ⓩ Convivio | *42s/1-2a* | 26
Così | *45s/Mad-Vanderbilt* | 16
Darbar | *46s/Lex-3a* | 21
Dean's | *2a/42-43s* | 18
Dishes | *multi.* | 21
Docks Oyster | *3a/40s* | 19
Energy Kitchen | *41s/2a* | 17
Fabio Piccolo | *44s/2-3a* | 22
Five Guys | *3a/43-44s* | 20
Goodburger | *2a/42s* | 17
Grifone | *46s/2-3a* | 23
Gyu-Kaku | *3a/49-50s* | 21
Hale/Hearty | *multi.* | 19
Haru | *Park/48s* | 20
Hatsuhana | *multi.* | 25
ⓃⒺⓌ Hello Pasta | *3a/44-45s* | -
Il Postino | *49s/1-2a* | 23
Ise | *49s/Lex-3a* | 21
Junior's | *42s/Vanderbilt* | 17
Katsu-Hama | *47s/5a-Mad* | 21
Kuruma Zushi | *47s/5a-Mad* | 26

La Fonda/Sol | *Park/44s* | 22
Mamá Mexico | *49s/2-3a* | 19
Mangia | *48s/5a-Mad* | 20
Mee Noodle | *2a/49s* | 17
Ⓩ Megu | *1a/47s* | 24
Menchanko-tei | *45s/Lex-3a* | 20
Metrazur | *42s/Vanderbilt* | 21
Michael Jordan | *43s/Vanderbilt* | 21
Morton's | *5a/45s* | 24
Nanni | *46s/Lex-3a* | 25
Naples 45 | *Park/45s* | 17
Nino's | *2a/47-48s* | 20
Osteria Laguna | *42s/2-3a* | 19
Ⓩ Oyster Bar | *42s/Vanderbilt* | 22
Padre Figlio | *44s/1-2a* | 22
Ⓩ Palm | *2a/44-45s* | 24
Pampano | *49s/2-3a* | 24
Patroon | *46s/Lex-3a* | 22
Pepe | *42s/Vanderbilt* | 21
Pera | *Mad/41-42s* | 21
Pershing Sq. | *42s/Park* | 15
Phoenix Gdn. | *40s/2-3a* | 24
Pietro's | *43s/2-3a* | 24
Pret A Manger | *multi.* | 18
Prime Grill | *49s/Mad-Park* | 22
Riingo | *45s/2-3a* | 21
Sakagura | *43s/2-3a* | 24
Seo | *49s/2-3a* | 21
Sinigual | *3a/41s* | 21
Sip Sak | *2a/49-50s* | 20
Ⓩ Smith/Wollensky | *3a/49s* | 24
Soba Totto | *43s/2-3a* | 21
Ⓩ Sparks | *46s/2-3a* | 25
Sushiden | *49s/5a-Mad* | 25
Ⓩ Sushi Yasuda | *43s/2-3a* | 28
Two Boots | *42s/Vanderbilt* | 18
'Wichcraft | *multi.* | 20
Wollensky's | *49s/3a* | 23
Yama | *49s/1-2a* | 24
ⓃⒺⓌ Zengo | *3a/40s* | 24

EAST 50s

Ⓩ Adour | *55s/5a-Mad* | 26
Aja | *1a/58s* | 20
Al Bustan | *53s/1-2a* | 19
Ⓩ Alto | *53s/5a-Mad* | 26
Amma | *51s/2-3a* | 25
Angelo's Pizza | *2a/55s* | 20
Ⓩ Aquavit | *55s/Mad-Park* | 25
Armani Rist. | *5a/56s* | 19
Baluchi's | *53s/2-3a* | 18
Bar Vetro | *58s/2-3a* | 22
Bice | *54s/5a-Mad* | 21
ⓃⒺⓌ Bistro Vendôme | *58s/1a-Sutton* | 21

Blockhead Burrito | 2a/50-51s	16
🄩 BLT Steak | 57s/Lex-Park	25
Bobby Van's | 54s/Lex-Park	22
Bottega/Vino | 59s/5a-Mad	22
Brasserie | 53s/Lex-Park	20
Brick Ln. Curry | 53s/2-3a	21
Burger Heaven | multi.	16
BXL | 51s/2-3a	19
Cafe Joul | 1a/58-59s	18
NEW Casa Lever | 53s/Mad-Park	23
Caviar Russe | Mad/54-55s	25
Cellini | 54s/Mad-Park	22
Chola | 58s/2-3a	24
Così | 56s/Mad-Park	16
Darbar | 55s/Lex-3a	21
Dawat | 58s/2-3a	23
DeGrezia | 50s/2-3a	24
Deux Amis | 51s/1-2a	19
Dishes | Park/54s	21
Dos Caminos | 3a/50-51s	20
NEW East Side Social | 51s/2-3a	17
Energy Kitchen | 2a/57-58s	17
Ess-a-Bagel | 3a/50-51s	23
Ethos | 1a/51s	21
Felidia | 58s/2-3a	26
Fig & Olive | 52s/5a-Mad	20
Fiorini | 56s/2-3a	22
🄩 Four Seasons | 52s/Lex-Park	26
Fresco | 52s/Mad-Park	22
🄩 Gilt | Mad/50-51s	24
Goodburger | Lex/54s	17
Grand Sichuan | 2a/55-56s	22
Harry Cipriani | 5a/59-60s	21
NEW Hello Pasta | Lex/54-55s	-
NEW Hide-Chan | 52s/2-3a	-
Hillstone | 3a/54s	21
Inside Park | Park/50s	17
Jubilee | 54s/1-2a	23
🄩 La Grenouille | 52s/5a-Mad	28
La Mangeoire | 2a/53-54s	20
🄩 L'Atelier/Robuchon | 57s/Mad	27
🄩 Le Cirque | 58s/Lex-3a	24
Le Colonial | 57s/Lex-3a	21
Lenny's | 2a/54s	17
Le Perigord | 52s/FDR-1a	25
Le Relais/Venise | Lex/52s	20
NEW Lychee Hse. | 55s/Lex-3a	25
Maloney/Porcelli | 50s/Mad-Park	23
Mia Dona | 58s/2-3a	20
Mint | 50s/Lex-3a	22
🄩 Monkey Bar | 54s/Mad	17
Montebello | 56s/Lex-Park	24
Mr. Chow | 57s/1-2a	22

Mr. K's | Lex/51s	23
Naya | 2a/55-56s	23
Neary's | 57s/1a	18
Nino's | 58s/2-3a	20
Nippon | 52s/Lex-3a	21
Outback | 56s/2-3a	15
Peking Duck | 53s/2-3a	23
P.J. Clarke's | 3a/55s	17
Pop Burger | 58s/5a-Mad	18
Pret A Manger | multi.	18
Rosa Mexicano | 1a/58s	22
Rothmann's | 54s/5a-Mad	23
🄩 San Pietro | 54s/5a-Mad	25
Serafina | 58s/Mad-Park	19
🄩 Shun Lee Palace | 55s/Lex-3a	24
Sofrito | 57s/1a-Sutton	22
Solera | 53s/2-3a	21
Solo | Mad/55-56s	26
SushiAnn | 51s/Mad-Park	25
Takesushi | 2a/54s	24
Taksim | 2a/54-55s	21
🄩 Tao | 58s/Mad-Park	22
Tenzan | 2a/52-53s	22
Teodora | 57s/Lex-3a	21
Tratt. Pesce | 1a/59s	18
Tse Yang | 51s/Mad-Park	24
Via Quadronno | 5a/59s	21
🄩 Wolfgang's | 54s/3a	25
Yuva | 58s/2-3a	23
Zarela | 2a/50-51s	22
Ze Café | 52s/FDR-1a	22

EAST 60s

Accademia/Vino | 3a/63-64s	19
Alice's Tea | 64s/Lex	19
Amaranth | 62s/5a-Mad	20
Bistro Chat Noir | 66s/5a-Mad	19
Bistro 61 | 1a/61s	19
Bravo Gianni | 63s/2-3a	22
Brgr | 3a/60-61s	19
Brio | 61s/Lex	20
Burger Heaven | Lex/62s	16
Cabana | 3a/60-61s	21
Café Evergreen | 1a/69-70s	19
Canaletto | 60s/2-3a	21
Circus | 61s/Lex-Park	21
🄩 Daniel | 65s/Mad-Park	28
David Burke Townhse. | 61s/Lex	24
NEW Fatty Fish | 64s/1a-York	22
Felice | 1a/64s	21
Fig & Olive | Lex/62-63s	20
Fishtail | 62s/Lex-Park	23
Fred's at Barneys | Mad/60s	21
Geisha | 61s/Mad-Park	23
Hale/Hearty | Lex/64-65s	19

Jackson Hole | 64s/2-3a 17

🄴 John's Pizzeria | 64s/1a-York 22

JoJo | 64s/Lex-3a 25

L'Absinthe | 67s/2-3a 22

Le Bilboquet | 63s/Mad-Park 23

NEW Le Caprice | 61s/5a 17

Le Charlot | 69s/Mad-Park 21

Lenny's | 1a/68s 17

Le Pain Q. | Lex/63-64s 18

Maya | 1a/64-65s 24

Mediterraneo | 2a/66s 20

Nanoosh | 1a/68-69s 19

Nello | Mad/62-63s 18

🄴 Park Avenue ... | 63s/Lex 25

Patsy's Pizzeria | multi. 20

Persephone | 60s/Lex 21

Philippe | 60s/Mad-Park 23

NEW Pop Art Bar | 62s/1-2a -

Post House | 63s/Mad-Park 24

Primola | 2a/64-65s 23

Ravagh | 1a/66-67s 21

🄴 Regency | Park/61s 19

Rouge Tomate | 60s/5a 23

🄴 Scalinatella | 61s/3a 24

Serafina | 61s/Mad-Park 19

Serendipity 3 | 60s/2-3a 19

🄴 Sushi Seki | 1a/62-63s 26

Viand | Mad/61-62s 17

Za Za | 1a/65-66s 20

EAST 70s

Afghan Kebab | 2a/70-71s 20

A La Turka | 2a/74s 18

Alloro | 77s/1-2a 24

Atlantic Grill | 3a/76-77s 23

Baraonda | 2a/75s 19

B. Café | 75s/2-3a 21

Bella Blu | Lex/70-71s 21

Boathouse | Central Pk/72s 18

Brother Jimmy's | 2a/77-78s 16

🄴 Café Boulud | 76s/5a-Mad 27

Campagnola | 1a/73-74s 24

Candle Cafe | 3a/74-75s 23

Candle 79 | 79s/Lex-3a 24

Canyon Rd. | 1a/76-77s 20

Caravaggio | 74s/5a-Mad 23

🄴 Carlyle | 76s/Mad 23

Cilantro | 1a/71s 17

Dallas BBQ | 3a/72-73s 15

Due | 3a/79-80s 21

EJ's Luncheon. | 3a/73s 16

Fulton | 75s/2-3a 21

🄴 Gari/Sushi | 78s/1a-York 27

Grace's Tratt. | 71s/2-3a 18

Haru | 3a/76s 20

Il Riccio | 79s/Lex-3a 22

J.G. Melon | 3a/74s 21

NEW Kouzina/Trata | 2a/70-71s -

Le Magnifique | Lex/73s 20

Lenny's | 2a/77s 17

Le Pain Q. | 77s/2-3a 18

Lusardi's | 2a/77-78s 24

NEW Mark | 77s/5a-Mad 24

Maruzzella | 1a/77-78s 23

Meltemi | York/78-79s -

Mezzaluna/Pizza | 3a/74-75s 20

Mingala Burmese | 2a/72-73s 21

NEW Mxco | 2a/78s 18

Nino's | 1a/72-73s 20

Orsay | Lex/75s 18

Parma | 3a/79-80s 22

Pastrami Queen | Lex/78-79s 20

Per Lei | 2a/71s 21

Persepolis | 2a/73-74s 21

Petaluma | 1a/73s 17

Quatorze Bis | 79s/1-2a 21

Sant Ambroeus | Mad/77-78s 21

🄴 Sasabune | 73s/1a-York 29

Serafina | Mad/79s 19

Sette Mezzo | Lex/70-71s 22

Shabu-Shabu 70 | 70s/1-2a 22

Shanghai Pavilion | 3a/78-79s 21

Sojourn | 79s/2-3a 22

Spice | 2a/73-74s 20

Swifty's | Lex/72-73s 18

T-Bar Steak | 3a/73-74s 21

Uskudar | 2a/73-74s 21

Uva | 2a/77-78s 21

Vermicelli | 2a/77-78s 19

Viand | Mad/78s 17

Via Quadronno | 73s/5a-Mad 21

Vivolo/Cucina | 74s/Lex-Park 21

EAST 80s

Alice's Tea | 81s/2-3a 19

Amber | 3a/80s 19

Antonucci | 81s/Lex-3a 22

Baluchi's | 2a/89-90s 18

Beyoglu | 3a/81s 22

Blockhead Burrito | 2a/81-82s 16

Brasserie Julien | 3a/80-81s 18

Burger Heaven | 3a/86-87s 16

Café d'Alsace | 2a/88s 21

Café Sabarsky | 5a/86s 23

Caffe Grazie | 84s/5a-Mad 20

🄴NEW Cascabel | 2a/80-81s 25

Centolire | Mad/85-86s 21

Chef Ho's | 2a/89-90s 21

Ciaobella | 2a/85s 20

Cilantro | 2a/88-89s 17

Demarchelier | 86s/Mad-Park	18
Donguri | 83s/1-2a	27
E.A.T. | Mad/80-81s	20
Elaine's | 2a/88-89s	14
☑ Elio's | 2a/84-85s	24
Energy Kitchen | 2a/84-85s	17
Erminia | 83s/2-3a	25
Firenze | 2a/82-83s	20
Flex Mussels | 82s/Lex-3a	23
Giovanni | 83s/5a-Mad	23
Girasole | 82s/Lex-3a	23
Gobo | 3a/81s	22
Heidelberg | 2a/85-86s	20
Italianissimo | 84s/1-2a	24
Ithaka | 86s/1-2a	22
Jackson Hole | 2a/83-84s	17
Jacques | 85s/2-3a	19
Kings' Carriage | 82s/2-3a	23
Land | 2a/81-82s	22
Le Pain Q. | Mad/84-85s	18
Libertador | 2a/89s	21
NEW Luke's Lobster | 81s/2-3a	25
Maz Mezcal | 86s/1-2a	20
Nicola's | 84s/Lex-3a	22
One 83 | 1a/83-84s	19
Pig Heaven | 2a/80-81s	20
Pintaile's Pizza | York/83-84s	21
Poke | 85s/1-2a	25
Quattro Gatti | 81s/2-3a	21
Rughetta | 85s/1-2a	22
Sala Thai | 2a/89-90s	21
Sandro's | 81s/1-2a	24
Shake Shack | 86s/Lex-3a	23
Shalezeh | 3a/80-81s	21
☑ Sistina | 2a/80-81s	26
Spigolo | 2a/81s	25
Taco Taco | 2a/89-90s	21
Taste | 3a/80s	22
Tenzan | 2a/89s	22
Tevere | 84s/Lex-3a	24
Tony's Di Napoli | 2a/83s	20
Totonno Pizza | 2a/80-81s	21
Two Boots | 2a/84s	18
Vespa | 2a/84-85s	19
Viand | 86s/2a	17
Wa Jeal | 2a/82-83s	25
Wasabi Lobby | 2a/82s	21
NEW Wright | 5a/88s	21
York Grill | York/88-89s	21
Yuka | 2a/80-81s	20

EAST 90s & 100s

(90th to 110th Sts.)

Brother Jimmy's | 3a/92s	16
Don Pedro's | 2a/96s	22
El Paso Taqueria | multi.	23

Itzocan | Lex/101s	22
Jackson Hole | Mad/91s	17
Moustache | Lex/102s	21
Nick's | 2a/94s	23
Nina's Argentin. | 2a/91s	23
Osso Buco | 3a/93s	19
Paola's | Mad/92s	22
Parlor Steak | 3a/90s	22
Pascalou | Mad/92-93s	21
Peri Ela | Lex/90-91s	19
Pinocchio | 1a/90-91s	22
Pintaile's Pizza | 91s/5a-Mad	21
Pio Pio | 1a/90-91s	22
Sarabeth's | Mad/92-93s	20
Sfoglia | Lex/92s	23
Square Meal | 92s/5a-Mad	24
Table d'Hôte | 92s/Mad-Park	20
NEW Tre Otto | Mad/97-98s	21
Vico | Mad/92-93s	20
Yura on Madison | Mad/92s	21
Zebú Grill | 92s/1-2a	21

EAST VILLAGE

(14th to Houston Sts., east of B'way, excluding NoHo)

Angelica Kit. | 12s/1-2a	21
Apiary | 3a/10-11s	23
Artichoke Basille | 14s/1-2a	23
Awash | 6s/1-2a	21
Back Forty | Ave B/11-12s	22
Banjara | 1a/6s	22
Baoguette | St Marks/2a	21
Barbone | Ave B/11-12s	24
NEW Bar Paya | 2a/3-4s	-
Belcourt | 4s/2a	19
Black Iron | 5s/Aves A-B	20
Boca Chica | 1a/1s	21
Bon Chon | St Marks/2-3a	20
Brick Ln. Curry | 6s/1-2a	21
Buenos Aires | 6s/Aves A-B	23
Butter | Lafayette/Astor-4s	22
Cacio e Pepe | 2a/11-12s	21
Cacio e Vino | 2a/4-5s	22
Cafecito | Ave C/11-12s	22
Cafe Mogador | St Marks/Ave A	22
Caracas | multi.	24
Caravan/Dreams | 6s/1a	22
Chickpea | 14s/2-3a	19
ChikaLicious | 10s/1-2a	25
Counter | 1a/6-7s	21
Cucina/Pesce | 4s/Bowery-2a	19
Dallas BBQ | 2a/St Marks	15
☑ DBGB | Bowery/Houston	22
☑ Degustation | 5s/2-3a	27
Dirt Candy | 9s/Ave A-1a	27
NEW Dos Toros | 4a/13s	24

Menus, photos, voting and more – free at ZAGAT.com

Dumpling Man	*St Marks/Ave A*	20
Elephant	*1s/1-2a*	21
Euzkadi	*4s/1-2a*	20
NEW Faustina	*Cooper/5-6a*	23
Flea Mkt. Cafe	*Ave A/9s*	19
Frank	*2a/5-6s*	24
Gemma	*Bowery/2-3s*	20
Gnocco	*10s/Aves A-B*	24
Graffiti	*10s/1-2a*	25
Grand Sichuan	*St Marks/2-3a*	22
Gruppo	*Ave B/11-12s*	24
Gyu-Kaku	*Cooper/Astor-4s*	21
Hasaki	*9s/2-3a*	24
Haveli	*2a/5-6s*	21
Hearth	*12s/1a*	24
Holy Basil	*2a/9-10s*	21
Hummus Pl.	*St Marks/Ave A*	22
I Coppi	*9s/Ave A-1a*	22
Il Bagatto	*2s/Aves A-B*	24
Indochine	*Lafayette/Astor-4s*	21
Ippudo	*4a/9-10s*	25
Itzocan	*9s/Ave A-1a*	22
Jack's Lux.	*2a/5-6s*	27
Z Jewel Bako	*5s/2-3a*	26
Jimmy's	*7s/2-3a*	22
JoeDoe	*1s/1-2a*	23
John's/12th St.	*12s/2a*	21
Jules	*St Marks/1-2a*	20
Kafana	*Ave C/7-8s*	24
Kajitsu	*9s/Ave A-1a*	27
Kanoyama	*2a/11s*	26
Klong	*St Marks/2-3a*	20
Kyo Ya	*7s/1a*	26
Lanza	*1a/10-11s*	18
La Paella	*9s/2-3a*	20
La Palapa	*St Marks/1-2a*	20
Lavagna	*5s/Aves A-B*	23
Lil' Frankie	*1a/1-2s*	23
Lucien	*1a/1s*	22
NEW Luke's Lobster	*7s/Ave A-1a*	25
Luzzo's/Ovest	*1a/12-13s*	22
Mama's Food	*3s/Aves A-B*	20
Mancora	*1a/6s*	21
Mara's	*6s/1-2a*	22
Mary Ann's	*2a/5s*	15
Matilda	*11s/Aves B-C*	23
Max	*Ave B/3-4s*	21
Mercadito	*multi.*	23
Mermaid	*2a/5-6s*	21
Minca	*5s/Aves A-B*	21
Momofuku Bakery	*2a/13s*	22
Momofuku Ko	*1a/10s*	27
Momofuku Noodle	*1a/10s*	24
Momofuku Ssäm	*2a/13s*	25

Motorino	*12s/1-2a*	24
Moustache	*10s/Ave A-1a*	21
Nicky's	*2s/Ave A*	21
99 Mi. to Philly	*3a/12-13s*	19
Nomad	*2a/4s*	21
NEW Northern Spy	*12s/Aves A-B*	23
No. 28	*2a/11s*	23
NEW Peels	*Bowery/2s*	-
NEW Penny Farthing	*3a/13s*	-
Perbacco	*4s/Aves A-B*	23
Porchetta	*7s/Ave A-1a*	23
Prune	*1s/1-2a*	24
Pukk	*1a/4-5s*	21
Pylos	*7s/Ave A-1a*	25
Quantum Leap	*1a/12-13s*	20
Rai Rai Ken	*10s/1-2a*	22
NEW Ramen Kuidouraku	*1a/9s-St Marks*	-
Ramen Setagaya	*St Marks/2-3a*	18
Redhead	*13s/1-2a*	22
NEW Robataya	*9s/2-3a*	23
Shabu-Tatsu	*10s/1-2a*	20
S'MAC	*12s/1-2a*	21
Smith	*3a/10-11s*	19
SobaKoh	*5s/1-2a*	24
Soba-ya	*9s/2-3a*	24
Spice	*multi.*	20
NEW Spot	*St Marks/2-3s*	23
Sunburnt Cow/Calf	*Ave C/8-9s*	18
Supper	*2s/Aves A-B*	24
Takahachi	*Ave A/5-6s*	24
Tarallucci	*1a/10s*	21
NEW Taureau	*7s/Ave A-1a*	-
Terroir	*12s/Ave A-1a*	24
NEW This Little Piggy	*1a/9-10s*	23
Tsampa	*9s/2-3a*	21
26 Seats	*Ave B/10-11s*	22
Two Boots	*Ave A/3s*	18
NEW Vandaag	*2a/6s*	-
Vanessa's Dumpling	*14s/2-3a*	22
Veloce Pizzeria	*1a/6-7s*	20
Veniero's	*11s/1-2A*	24
Veselka	*multi.*	19
Westville	*Ave A/11s*	22
Xi'an	*St Marks/1a*	-
Yerba Buena	*Ave A/Houston*	23
Yuca Bar	*Ave A/7s*	23
Zaitzeff	*Ave B/2-3s*	20
Zerza	*6s/1-2A*	22
Zum Schneider	*Ave C/7s*	20

FINANCIAL DISTRICT

(South of Murray St.)

Adrienne's	*Pearl/Coenties*	24
Au Mandarin	*Vesey/West*	20

Baoguette | *Maiden/Bway* — 21
Battery Gdns. | *Battery Pk* — 17
Blockhead Burrito | *North/Vesey* — 16
NEW BLT B&G | *Wash/Albany* — -
Bobby Van's | *Broad/Exchange* — 22
Bon Chon | *John/Cliff* — 20
Bridge Cafe | *Water/Dover* — 22
Burger Shoppe | *Water/Broad* — 21
Capital Grille | *Bway/Nassau-Pine* — 24
China Chalet | *Bway/Exchange* — 18
Così | *Vesey/West* — 16
Delmonico's | *Beaver/William* — 23
Energy Kitchen | *Nassau/Fulton* — 17
Fresco | *Pearl/Hanover* — 22
Gigino | *Battery/West* — 21
Goodburger | *Maiden/Pearl* — 17
Hale/Hearty | *Broad/Beaver* — 19
Harry's Cafe/Steak | *multi.* — 23
Harry's Italian | *Gold/Maiden* — 21
Haru | *Wall/Beaver-Pearl* — 20
Ise | *Pine/Pearl-William* — 21
NEW Lambs Club | *44s/6-7a* — -
Lemongrass | *William/Maiden* — 17
Lenny's | *John/Cliff-Pearl* — 17
Les Halles | *John/Bway-Nassau* — 20
MarkJoseph | *Water/Peck* — 24
P.J. Clarke's | *World Fin/Vesey* — 17
Pret A Manger | *Broad/Beaver* — 18
Z SHO Shaun Hergatt | *Broad/Exchange* — 26
Smorgas Chef | *Stone/William* — 19
Taj Tribeca | *Murray/Bway-Church* — 22
2 West | *West/Battery* — 21
NEW Wall/Water | *Wall/Water* — 21
Zaitzeff | *Nassau/John* — 20

FLATIRON

(14th to 26th Sts., 6th Ave. to
Park Ave. S., excluding Union Sq.)

Z NEW ABC Kitchen | *18s/Bway-Park* — 24
Aldea | *17s/5-6a* — 25
Allegretti | *22s/5-6a* — 23
Almond | *22s/Bway-Park* — 19
Angelo/Maxie's | *Park/19s* — 21
Z A Voce | *Mad/26s* — 24
Barbounia | *Park/20s* — 21
Bar Stuzz. | *Bway/21-22s* — 20
Basta Pasta | *17s/5-6a* — 23
Z BLT Fish | *17s/5-6a* — 24
Bocca | *19s/Bway-Park* — 23
Boqueria | *19s/5-6a* — 22
Chickpea | *6a/21-22s* — 19
City Bakery | *18s/5-6a* — 22
City Crab | *Park/19s* — 19
Così | *6a/22-23s* — 16

Craft | *19s/Bway-Park* — 25
Craftbar | *Bway/19-20s* — 23
Z Dévi | *18s/Bway-5a* — 23
NEW Eataly | *5a/23-24s* — -
Z Eleven Madison | *Mad/24s* — 28
Energy Kitchen | *23s/5-6a* — 17
Giorgio's | *21s/Bway-Park* — 21
Goodburger | *Bway/17-18s* — 17
Z Gramercy Tavern | *20s/Bway* — 28
Haru | *Park/18s* — 20
Hill Country | *26s/Bway-6a* — 22
NEW Hurricane Club | *Park/26s* — -
Kellari Tav./Parea | *20s/Bway* — 22
La Pizza Fresca | *20s/Bway-Park* — 23
Lenny's | *23s/5-6a* — 17
Le Pain Q. | *19s/Bway-Park* — 18
L'Express | *Park/20s* — 18
Mangia | *23s/5-6a* — 20
Mari Vanna | *20s/Bway-Park* — 20
Markt | *6a/21s* — 19
Z Mesa Grill | *5a/15-16s* — 23
Mizu Sushi | *20s/Bway-Park* — 24
NEW Nuela | *24s/Bway-6a* — -
Outback | *23s/5-6a* — 15
Periyali | *20s/5-6a* — 24
Pètite Abeille | *17s/5-6a* — 18
Pipa | *19s/Bway-Park* — 22
Rosa Mexicano | *18s/Bway* — 22
Sala | *19s/5-6a* — 22
Shake Shack | *23s/Mad* — 23
SushiSamba | *Park/19-20s* — 22
Z Tabla | *Mad/24s* — 25
Z Tamarind | *22s/Bway-Park* — 26
Tarallucci | *18s/Bway-5a* — 21
Z Veritas | *20s/Bway-Park* — 26
Via Emilia | *21s/Bway-Park* — 23
'Wichcraft | *20s/Bway-5a* — 20
Wildwood BBQ | *Park/18-19s* — 18

GARMENT DISTRICT

(30th to 40th Sts., west of 5th)

Abigael's | *Bway/38-39s* — 20
Arno | *38s/Bway-7a* — 19
Ben's Kosher | *38s/7-8a* — 19
Bon Chon | *38s/7-8a* — 20
Brother Jimmy's | *8a/31s* — 16
Cho Dang Gol | *35s/5-6a* — 23
Frankie/Johnnie | *37s/5-6a* — 23
Gahm Mi Oak | *32s/Bway-5a* — 20
Gray's Papaya | *8a/37s* — 20
Hale/Hearty | *7a/35s* — 19
Heartland | *5a/34s* — 14
HK | *9a/39s* — 18
Il Punto | *9a/38s* — 21
Kang Suh | *Bway/32s* — 22

Kati Roll | 39s/5-6a 21
🄩 Keens | 36s/5-6a 25
Kum Gang San | 32s/Bway-5a 21
Lazzara's | 38s/7-8a 21
Madangsui | 35s/6a 23
Mandoo Bar | 32s/Bway-5a 20
Nick & Stef | 33s/7-8a 21
Pret A Manger | 7a/38 39s 18
Sandwich Planet | 9a/39s 22
Sarabeth's | 5a/38-39s 20
Szechuan Gourmet | 39s/5-6a 22
Uncle Jack's | 9a/34-35s 22
WonJo | 32s/Bway-5A 20

GRAMERCY PARK

(14th to 23rd Sts., east of Park Ave. S.)

Bao Noodles | 2a/22-23s 19
BLT Prime | 22s/Lex-Park 25
Brother Jimmy's | 16s/Irving 16
Casa Mono | Irving/17s 26
Defonte's | 3a/21s 22
Ess-a-Bagel | 1a/21s 23
Friend/Farmer | Irving/18-19s 19
House | 17s/Irving-Park 22
Japonais | 18s/Irving-Park 20
Lady Mendl's | Irving/17-18s 21
Lantern | 2a/18s 19
Los Dos Molinos | 21
    18s/Irving-Park
NEW Maialino | Lex/21s 25
Molly's | 3a/22-23s 20
Novitá | 22s/Lex-Park 24
Pete's Tavern | 18s/Irving 16
Petite Abeille | 20s/1a 18
Ponty Bistro | 3a/18-19s 23
Posto | 2a/18s 24
Pure Food/Wine | Irving/17s 23
Rolf's | 3a/22s 14
Sahara's Turkish | 2a/28-29s 22
Yama | 17s/Irving 24
Zen Palate | 18s/Irving-Park 19

GREENWICH VILLAGE

(Houston to 14th Sts., west of
B'way, east of 6th Ave.)

Alta | 10s/5-6a 24
Amber | 6a/9-10s 19
Arté | 9s/5a-Uni 18
Arturo's | Houston/Thompson 21
🄩 Babbo | Waverly/MacDougal 27
NEW Bar Henry | 19
    Houston/La Guardia
Bar Pitti | 6a/Blkr-Houston 22
BLT Burger | 6a/11-12s 21
🄩 Blue Hill | Wash pl/MacDougal 27
Cafe Español | Blkr/MacDougal 20

CamaJe | MacDougal/Blkr 22
Chez Jacqueline | 20
    MacDougal/Blkr
Così | multi. 16
🄩 Cru | 5a/9-10s 25
Cuba | Thompson/Blkr-3s 22
Cubana Café | Thompson/Prince 20
Da Andrea | 13s/5-6a 22
Danal | 5a/12-13s 20
Da Silvano | 6a/Blkr 21
Five Guys | La Guardia/Blkr 20
French Roast | 11s/5-6a 17
🄩 Gotham B&G | 12s/5a-Uni 27
Gray's Papaya | 6a/8s 20
Hotel Griffou | 9s/5-6a 19
Hummus Pl. | MacDougal/Blkr 22
Il Cantinori | 10s/Bway-Uni 23
🄩 Il Mulino | 3s/Sullivan 27
Jane | Houston/La Guardia 21
Japonica | Uni/12s 24
Kati Roll | MacDougal/Blkr-3s 21
Knickerbocker | Uni/9s 20
Lenny's | 6a/9s 17
Le Pain Q. | multi. 18
NEW Lion | 9s/5-6a -
🄩 Lupa | Thompson/Blkr 25
Maoz Veg. | 8s/Bway-Uni 21
NEW Masala Times | Blkr/6a -
Max Brenner | Bway/13-14s 20
Mermaid | MacDougal/Blkr 21
Meskerem | MacDougal/Blkr-3s 22
Mexicana Mama | 12s/Bway 23
Mezzaluna/Pizza | 20
    Houston/MacDougal
🄩 Minetta | MacDougal/Blkr-3s 24
Nanoosh | Uni/12-13s 19
Negril | 3s/La Guardia 21
North Sq. | Waverly/MacDougal 23
Num Pang | 12s/5a-Uni 26
Otto | 8s/5a-Uni 22
Patsy's Pizzeria | Uni/10-11s 20
NEW Patty/Bun | 20
    8s/MacDougal-6s
Peanut Butter Co. | Sullivan/3s 19
Pizza 33 | 6a/14s 19
Quantum Leap | Thompson/3s 20
NEW Rabbit in Moon | 8s/5-6a -
Rocco | Thompson/Houston 21
Saigon Grill | Uni/11-12s 21
Spice | 13s/Bway-Uni 20
Stand | 12s/5a-Uni 19
🄩 Strip House | 12s/5a-Uni 25
🄩 Tomoe Sushi | Thompson/Blkr 26
Ushiwakamaru | 27
    Houston/MacDougal
NEW Vapiano | Uni/13s -

Villa Mosconi | *MacDougal/Blkr* 23
'Wichcraft | *8s/Mercer* 20

HARLEM/ EAST HARLEM

(110th to 155th Sts., excluding Columbia U. area)

Amor Cubano | *3a/111s* 22
Amy Ruth's | *116s/Lenox-7a* 20
Chez Lucienne | *Lenox/125-126s* 22
Covo | *135s/12a* 22
Dinosaur BBQ | *131s/12a* 22
El Paso Taqueria | *116s/3a* 23
Hudson River | *133s/12a* 21
Kitchenette | *Amst/122-123s* 19
Londel's | *Douglass/139-140s* 20
Melba's | *114s/Douglass* 25
Miss Mamie/Maude | *multi.* 20
Mo-Bay | *125s/Sa-Lenox* 21
Mojo | *Nicholas/119s* 21
Patsy's Pizzeria | *1a/117-118s* 20
Rao's | *114s/Pleasant* 22
Ricardo | *2A/110-1s* 22
Sylvia's | *Lenox/126-127s* 19
Zoma | *Douglass/112-113s* 25

LITTLE ITALY

(Canal to Kenmare Sts., Bowery to Lafayette St.)

Angelo's/Mulberry | *Mulberry/Grand* 23
Bo-Ky | *Grand/Elizabeth* 22
Da Nico | *Mulberry/Broome* 22
Ferrara | *Grand/Mott-Mulberry* 23
Grotta Azzurra | *Mulberry/Broome* 17
Il Cortile | *Mulberry/Canal* 23
NEW Kenmare | *Kenmare/Lafayette* 21
La Esquina | *Kenmare/Cleveland* 22
Nyonya | *Grand/Mott-Mulberry* 21
Pellegrino's | *Mulberry/Grand* 23
Pho Bang | *Mott/Broome-Grand* 20
Positano | *Mulberry/Canal* 23
Red Egg | *Centre/Howard* 21
Shanghai Café | *Mott/Canal* 21
S.P.Q.R. | *Mulberry/Grand* 20
Umberto's | *Broome/Mulberry* 19
Vincent's | *Mott/Hester* 21
Wild Ginger | *Broome/Mott* 22
X.O. | *Hester/Bowery-Elizabeth* 20

LOWER EAST SIDE

(Houston to Canal Sts., east of Bowery)

A Casa Fox | *Orchard/Stanton* 20
Alias | *Clinton/Riv* 22
Ápizz | *Eldridge/Riv-Stanton* 24
Azul Bistro | *Stanton/Suffolk* 20
NEW BaoHaus | *Riv/Norfolk* -
Bereket | *Houston/Orchard* 19
Bondi Rd. | *Riv/Clinton-Suffolk* 17
Brown Café | *Hester/Essex* 22
Café Katja | *Orchard/Broome* 24
Clinton St. Baking | *Clinton/Houston* 24
Congee | *multi.* 21
Essex | *Essex/Riv* 18
Falai | *multi.* 25
Frankies | *Clinton/Houston* 24
Freemans | *Riv/Bowery-Chrystie* 21
'Inoteca | *Riv/Ludlow* 22
Z Katz's Deli | *Houston/Ludlow* 24
Kuma Inn | *Ludlow/Delancey* 25
NEW Lina Frey | *Houston/Ludlow* -
Little Giant | *Orchard/Broome* 23
NEW Los Feliz | *Ludlow/Delancey* 20
Macondo | *Houston/Allen* 23
NEW Meatball Shop | *Stanton/Allen* 22
Molé | *Allen/Houston* 25
Noodle Bar | *Orchard/Stanton* 20
Orchard | *Orchard/Riv* 23
NEW Ramen Kuidouraku | *Ludlow/Delancey* -
Rayuela | *Allen/Riv-Stanton* 23
Salt | *Clinton/Houston* 23
Sammy's | *Chrystie/Delancey* 20
Schiller's | *Riv/Norfolk* 19
Shang | *Orchard/Houston* 21
Sorella | *Allen/Broome* 24
Spitzer's | *Riv/Ludlow* 20
Stanton Social | *Stanton/Ludlow* 23
Vanessa's Dumpling | *Eldridge/Broome* 22
WD-50 | *Clinton/Riv-Stanton* 25
White Slab | *Delancey/Allen* 18
Whole Foods | *Houston/Bowery* 19
NEW Xiao Ye | *Orchard/Houston* -

MEATPACKING

(Gansevoort to 15th Sts., west of 9th Ave.)

NEW Abe/Arthur | *14s/Wash* 22
Ajna Bar | *Little W 12s/9a* 20
Bagatelle | *13s/9a-Wash* 18
NEW Bill's Bar | *9a/13s* 20
NEW Collective | *Little W 12s/9a* 21
Dos Caminos | *Hudson/14s* 20
Fig & Olive | *13s/9a-Wash* 20
5 9th | *9a/Gansevoort* 19
NEW La Gazzetta | *Gansevoort/Greenwich s* -

Macelleria | Gansevoort/Greenwich s — 22

Old Homestead | 9a/14-15s — 24

Paradou | Little W 12s/Greenwich s — 21

Pastis | 9a/Little W 12s — 21

Pop Burger | 9a/14-15s — 18

Sea | Wash/Little W 12s — 21

Son Cubano | 14s/9a-Wash — 21

🗹 Spice Market | 13s/9a — 23

🗹 Standard Grill | Wash/Little W 12s — 21

STK | Little W 12s/9a-Wash — 23

🆕 Tanuki | 9a/13s — 19

🗹 Valbella | 13s/9a-Wash — 25

MURRAY HILL

(26th to 40th Sts., east of 5th; 23rd to 26th Sts., east of Park Ave. S.)

Ali Baba | 34s/2-3a — 21

Amber | 3a/27-28s — 19

Aquamarine | 2a/38-39s — 21

🗹 Artisanal | 32s/Mad-Park — 23

Asia de Cuba | Mad/37-38s — 23

Baluchi's | 3a/24-25s — 18

Baoguette | Lex/25-26s — 21

Barbès | 36s/5a-Mad — 19

Ben & Jack's | 5a/28-29s — 23

Black Duck | 28s/Lex-Park — 21

Blockhead Burrito | 3a/33-34s — 16

Blue Smoke | 27s/Lex-Park — 21

Bon Chon | 5a/32-3s — 20

Brother Jimmy's | Lex/31s — 16

Carl's Steaks | 3a/34s — 20

Chennai Gdn. | 27s/Park — 21

Chinese Mirch | Lex/28s — 20

Coppola's | 3a/27-28s — 20

Così | Park/31s — 16

Curry Leaf | Lex/27s — 18

Da Ciro | Lex/33-34s — 22

Dhaba | Lex/27-28s — 23

Dos Caminos | Park/26-27s — 20

El Parador Cafe | 34s/1-2a — 22

El Pote | 2a/38-39s — 22

🆕 Estiatorio Rafina | 1a/37s — —

Ethos | 3a/33-34s — 21

Grand Sichuan | Lex/33-34s — 22

🗹 HanGawi | 32s/5a-Mad — 24

Hillstone | Park/27s — 21

'Inoteca | 3a/24s — 22

I Trulli | 27s/Lex-Park — 23

Jackson Hole | 3a/35s — 17

Jaiya Thai | 3a/28s — 22

Josie's | 3a/37s — 19

Kyochon | 5a/32-33s — 20

La Petite Aub. | Lex/27-28s — 21

Lemongrass | 34s/Lex-3a — 17

🆕 Le Parisien | 33s/Lex-3a — —

Les Halles | Park/28-29s — 20

Limon | 24s/2-3a — 24

🆕 Marcony | Lex/31-32s — 22

Mee Noodle | 2a/30-31s — 17

Mishima | Lex/30-31s — 24

Morgan | Mad/36-37s — 20

Nanoosh | Mad/33-34s — 19

Nirvana | Lex/39-40s — 23

Patsy's Pizzeria | 3a/34-35s — 20

Penelope | Lex/30s — 22

Pio Pio | 34s/2-3a — 22

Pizza 33 | 3a/33s — 19

Pongal | Lex/27-28s — 22

Pranna | Mad/28-29s — 20

Primehouse | Park/27s — 24

Rare B&G | Lex/37s — 21

Ravagh | 30s/5a-Mad — 21

Resto | 29s/Lex-Park — 21

Rossini's | 38s/Lex-Park — 24

Salute! | Mad/39s — 19

Saravanaas | Lex/26s — 25

Sarge's Deli | 3a/36-37s — 20

🆕 SD26 | 26s/5a-Mad — 22

2nd Ave Deli | 33s/Lex-3a — 22

Serge | Mad/32-33s — 20

Smorgas Chef | Park/37-38s — 19

Sushi Sen-nin | 33s/Mad — 25

Tiffin Wallah | 28s/Lex-Park — 23

Toledo | 36s/5a-Mad — 24

Totonno Pizza | 2a/26s — 21

🗹 Turkish Kitchen | 3a/27-28s — 22

Vatan | 3a/29s — 23

Vezzo | Lex/31s — 23

Villa Berulia | 34s/Lex-Park — 22

Water Club | E River/23s — 21

🗹 Wolfgang's | Park/33s — 25

NOHO

(Houston to 4th Sts., Bowery to B'way)

Aroma | 4s/Bowery-Lafayette — 23

Bianca | Blkr/Bowery-Elizabeth — 24

🗹 Bond St. | Bond/Bway-Lafayette — 25

Chinatown Brass. | Lafayette/Gr Jones — 22

Double Crown | Bowery/Blkr — 20

5 Points | Gr Jones/Bowery — 22

Great Jones Cafe | Gr Jones/Bowery — 20

🆕 Hecho en Dumbo | Bowery/4s-Gr Jones — 25

🗹 Il Buco | Bond/Bowery-Lafayette — 26

Mercat | Bond/Bowery-Lafayette — 20

NoHo Star | Lafayette/Blkr — 17

Rice | Elizabeth/Blkr-Houston — 19

Sala | *Bowery/Gr Jones* 22
Two Boots | *Blkr/Bway* 18

NOLITA

(Houston to Kenmare Sts.,
Bowery to Lafayette St.)

NEW Balaboosta | –
Mulberry/Prince
Barmarché | *Spring/Elizabeth* 21
Bread | *Spring/Elizabeth-Mott* 20
Cafe Gitane | *Mott/Prince* 20
Café Habana/Outpost | 22
Prince/Elizabeth
Delicatessen | *Prince/Lafayette* 19
Ed's Lobster | *Lafayette/Spring* 23
Elizabeth | *Elizabeth/Houston* 18
Emporio | *Mott/Prince* 21
Jacques | *Prince/Elizabeth-Mott* 19
Le Jardin | *Cleveland/Kenmare* 20
Lombardi's | *Spring/Mott* 23
Mexican Radio | 20
Cleveland/Kenmare
Peasant | *Elizabeth/Prince* 24
Z Public | *Elizabeth/Prince* 24
NEW Pulino's | *Bowery/Houston* 19
NEW Tartinery | *Mulberry/Spring* –
NEW Torrisi | *Mulberry/Prince* 27
NEW Travertine | 22
Kenmare/Bowery
NEW Village Tart | 20
Kenmare/Mulberry

SOHO

(Canal to Houston Sts.,
west of Lafayette St.)

Z Aquagrill | *Spring/6a* 26
Aurora | *Broome/Thompson* 24
Z Balthazar | *Spring/Bway* 23
Baluchi's | *Spring/Sullivan* 18
Barolo | *W Bway/Broome-Spring* 19
Bistro Les Amis | *Spring/Thompson* 21
Z Blue Ribbon | *Sullivan/Prince* 25
Z Blue Ribbon Sushi | 26
Sullivan/Prince
Boqueria | *Spring/Thompson* 22
Café Select | *Lafayette/Broome* 19
Cipriani D'twn | *W Bway/Broome* 22
City Winery | *Varick/Vandam* 16
NEW Crosby Bar | 19
Crosby/Prince-Spring
Cupping Rm. | 18
W. Bway/Broome
Dos Caminos | *W Bway/Houston* 20
Falai | *Lafayette/Prince* 25
Félix | *W Bway/Grand* 17
Giorgione | *Spring/Greenwich s* 24
Hampton Chutney | 20
Prince/Crosby

Hundred Acres | 19
MacDougal/Prince
Il Corallo | *Prince/Sullivan* 22
I Tre Merli | *W Bway/Houston* 19
Ivo & Lulu | *Broome/6a-Varick* 19
Jean Claude | *Sullivan/Houston* 22
Kittichai | *Thompson/Broome* 23
La Sirène | *Broome/Varick* 22
L'Ecole | *Bway/Grand* 24
Le Pain Q. | *Grand/Greene* 18
Le Pescadeux | *Thompson/Prince* 23
Lucky Strike | *Grand/W Bway* 17
Lure Fishbar | *Mercer/Prince* 23
NEW Macbar | *Prince/Lafayette* 19
Mercer Kitchen | *Prince/Mercer* 22
Mezzogiorno | *Spring/Sullivan* 21
No. 28 | *Spring/Sullivan* 23
Novecento | *W Bway/Broome* 23
Olive's | *Prince/Greene* 22
Omen | *Thompson/Prince* 24
Once Upon a Tart | 21
Sullivan/Houston
Peep | *Prince/Sullivan* 20
Pepe | *Sullivan/Houston* 21
NEW Quattro Gastro. | 21
Spring/6a-Varick
Raoul's | *Prince/Sullivan* 23
Salt | *MacDougal/Prince* 23
NEW Salumè | *W Bway/Grand* –
Savoy | *Prince/Crosby* 24
Shorty's.32 | *Prince/MacDougal* 21
Snack | *Thompson/Prince* 22
sNice | *Sullivan/Houston* 20
NEW South Houston | –
W Bway/Grand
12 Chairs | *MacDougal/Prince* 19
'Wichcraft | *Bway/Prince* 20
Woo Lae Oak | *Mercer/Houston* 22

SOUTH STREET SEAPORT

Cabana | *South/Fulton* 21
Cowgirl | *Front/Dover* 16
Heartland | *South/Fulton* 14
Suteishi | *Peck/Front* 22

TRIBECA

(Canal to Murray Sts.,
west of B'way)

Z Acappella | *Hudson/Chambers* 25
Baluchi's | *Greenwich s/Warren* 18
Bar Stuzz. | *Church/Lispenard* 20
Blaue Gans | *Duane/Church* 22
Bon Chon | *Chambers/Church* 20
Z Bouley | *Duane/Hudson* 27
Bread | *Church/Walker* 20
Bubby's | *Hudson/N Moore* 18

Capsouto Frères | *Wash/Watts* 24
Carl's Steaks | *Chambers/Bway* 20
Centrico | *W Bway/Franklin* 20
Cercle Rouge | *W Bway/N Moore* 19
Churrascaria | *W Bway/Franklin* 23
City Hall | *Duane/Church* 21
🛛 Corton | *W Bway/Walker* 26
Dean's | *Greenwich s/Harrison* 18
Duane Park | *Duane/Hudson* 21
Dylan Prime | *Laight/Greenwich s* 24
Ecco | *Chambers/Church* 22
F.illi Ponte | *Desbrosses/Wash* 22
Flor/Sol | *Greenwich s/Franklin* 20
Gigino | *Greenwich s/Duane* 21
Greenwich Grill/Sushi Azabu | 25
  Greenwich s/Laight
Harrison | *Greenwich s/Harrison* 24
Il Giglio | *Warren/Greenwich s* 25
NEW Il Matto | *Church/White* -
Il Mattone | *Greenwich s/Hubert* 21
Kitchenette | 19
  Chambers/Greenwich s
Landmarc | *W Bway/Leonard* 20
Locanda Verde | 24
  Greenwich s/N Moore
Macao Trading | 18
  Church/Lispenard
Marc Forgione | 24
  Reade/Greenwich s
Mary Ann's | 15
  Greenwich s/Harrison
Matsugen | *Church/Leonard* 23
Max | *Duane/Greenwich s* 21
🛛 Megu | 24
  Thomas/Church-W Bway
Mr. Chow | *Hudson/N Moore* 22
Nam | *Reade/W Bway* 22
Ninja | *Hudson/Duane-Reade* 17
🛛 Nobu | *multi.* 26
Odeon | *W Bway/Duane* 20
🛛 Palm | *West/Chambers* 24
Pepolino | *W Bway/Canal* 25
Petite Abeille | *W Bway/Duane* 18
NEW Plein Sud | 18
  W Bway/Chambers
Rosanjin | *Duane/Church* 27
Salaam Bombay | 22
  Greenwich s/Duane-Reade
Sazon | *Reade/Church* 23
🛛 Scalini Fedeli | 27
  Duane/Greenwich s
Takahachi | *Duane/Church* 24
🛛 Tamarind | *Hudson/Franklin* 26
Terroir | *Harrison/Lispenard* 24
Thalassa | *Franklin/Greenwich s* 23
Trattoria Cinque | 22
  Greenwich s/Franklin

🛛 Tribeca Grill | 22
  Greenwich s/Franklin
Turks/Frogs | 18
  Greenwich s/Desbrosses
Walker's | *N Moore/Varick* 18
Whole Foods | 19
  Greenwich s/Murray
'Wichcraft | *Greenwich s/Beach* 20
🛛 Wolfgang's | 25
  Greenwich s/Beach
Zutto | *Hudson/Harrison* 21

UNION SQUARE

(14th to 17th Sts., 5th Ave. to
Union Sq. E.)

🛛 Blue Water | *Union sq/16s* 23
Coffee Shop | *Union sq/16s* 15
15 East | *15s/5a-Union sq* 25
Havana Central | *17s/Bway-5a* 18
Heartland | *Union sq/16-17s* 14
Laut | *17s/Bway-5a* 23
Maoz Vog. | *Union sq/16-17s* 21
Olives | *Park/17s* 23
NEW Qi | *14s/5-6a* 22
Republic | *Union sq/16-17s* 18
🛛 Tocqueville | *15s/5a-Union sq* 25
🛛 Union Sq. Cafe | *16s/5a* 26
Whole Foods | *Union sq/Bway* 19

WASHINGTON HTS./ INWOOD

(North of W. 155th St.)

Dallas BBQ | *Bway/165-166s* 15
El Malecon | *Bway/175s* 22
Empire Szechuan | *Bway/170s* 16
Mamajuana | *Dyckman/Payson* 20
New Leaf | *Corbin/190s* 21

WEST 40s

A.J. Maxwell's | *48s/5-6a* 22
Akdeniz | *46s/5-6a* 21
Alfredo/Rome | *49s/5-6a* 19
Algonquin | *44s/5-6a* 18
Amy's Bread | *9a/46-47s* 24
Angus McIndoe | *44s/Bway-8a* 16
Aspen Social | *47s/6-7a* 18
🛛 Aureole | *42s/Bway-6a* 26
🛛 Barbetta | *46s/8-9a* 20
Basilica | *9a/46-47s* 20
Becco | *46s/8-9a* 23
Blue Fin | *Bway/47s* 22
Bôi | *40s/7-8a* 20
Bond 45 | *45s/6-7a* 19
Breeze | *9a/45-46s* 22
Bricco | *42s/11-12a* 19
Brooklyn Diner | *43s/Bway-6a* 17
Bryant Park | *40s/5-6a* 18

B. Smith's	46s/8-9a	19
Bubba Gump	Bway/43-44s	14
BXL	43s/Bway-6a	19
Cafe Un Deux	44s/Bway-6a	17
Cara Mia	9a/45-46s	21
Carmine's	44s/Bway-8a	20
NEW Ça Va	44s/8a	–
Chez Josephine	42s/9-10a	20
Chimichurri Grill	9a/43-44s	23
Churrascaria	49s/8-9a	23
City Lobster	49s/6a	19
Così	42s/5-6a	16
Dafni Greek	42s/8-9a	20
Daisy May's	11a/46s	22
Dallas BBQ	42s/7-8a	15
Z DB Bistro Moderne	44s/5a	25
Z Del Frisco's	6a/48-49s	25
Delta Grill	9a/48s	19
Dervish	47s/6-7a	19
Edison	47s/Bway-8a	15
Energy Kitchen	47s/9-10a	17
Z Esca	43s/9a	25
Etcetera Etcetera	44s/8-9a	21
Z FireBird	46s/8-9a	20
Five Guys	48s/5-6a	20
5 Napkin Burger	9a/45s	21
44 & X/44½	multi.	21
Frankie/Johnnie	45s/Bway-8a	23
Z Gari/Sushi	46s/8-9a	27
Gazala Place	9a/48-49s	23
Glass House	47s/Bway-8a	21
Goodburger	45s/5-6a	17
Grand Sichuan	46s/8-9a	22
Hale/Hearty	multi.	19
Hallo Berlin	10a/44-45s	18
Haru	43s/Bway-8a	20
Havana Central	46s/6-7a	18
Heartland	multi.	14
Hell's Kitchen	9a/46-47s	23
Inakaya	40s/7-8a	19
Jewel of India	44s/5-6a	20
Joe Allen	46s/8-9a	17
Z John's Pizzeria	44s/Bway	22
Junior's	45s/Bway-8a	17
Kellari Tav./Parea	44s/5-6a	22
Koi	40s/5-6a	23
Kyotofu	9a/48-49s	23
La Masseria	48s/Bway-8a	22
Landmark Tavern	11a/46s	18
Lattanzi	46s/8-9a	22
Lazzara's	9a/43-44s	21
Le Marais	46s/6-7a	22
Lenny's	multi.	17
Le Rivage	46s/8-9a	20
NEW L'Ybane	8a/44-45s	–

Maoz Veg.	40s/7a	21
Marseille	9a/44s	20
Meskerem	47s/9-10a	22
Monster Sushi	46s/5-6a	18
Mont Blanc	48s/8-9a	21
Montenapo	41s/7-8a	21
Morrell Wine	49s/5-6a	19
Nizza	9a/44-45s	20
Oceana	49s/6-7a	23
Ollie's	42s/9-10a	16
Orso	46s/8-9a	22
Osteria al Doge	44s/Bway-6a	20
Pam Real Thai	multi.	23
Pietrasanta	9a/47s	18
Pigalle	8a/48s	17
Pio Pio	10a/43-44s	22
Pomaire	46s/8-9a	20
Pongsri Thai	48s/Bway-8a	20
Pret A Manger	multi.	18
NEW Print	11a/47-48s	25
Queen of Sheba	10a/45-46s	23
Rachel's American	9a/43-4s	17
Re Sette	45s/5-6a	19
Room Service	9a/47-48s	21
Ruby Foo's	Bway/49s	19
Sardi's	44s/Bway-8a	17
Scarlatto	47s/Bway-8a	20
Schnipper's	8a/41s	19
Sea Grill	49s/5-6a	24
Serafina	49s/Bway-8a	19
Shake Shack	44s/8a	23
Shorty's	9a/41-42s	24
Shula's	43s/Bway-8a	20
Sushiden	49s/6-7a	25
Sushi Zen	44s/Bway-6a	25
Tony's Di Napoli	43s/Bway-6a	20
Trattoria Trecolori	47s/Bway	21
Triomphe	44s/5-6a	23
Tulcingo del Valle	10a/46-47s	24
Turkish Cuisine	9a/44-45s	20
Two Boots	9a/44-45s	18
Utsav	6a/46-47s	21
View	Bway/45-46s	17
Virgil's BBQ	44s/Bway-6a	20
West Bank	42s/9-10a	19
'Wichcraft	40s/6a	20
Wondee Siam	10a/45-46s	21
Wu Liang Ye	48s/5-6a	23
Zen Palate	9a/46s	19
Zuni	9a/43s	20

WEST 50s

Abboccato	55s/6-7a	21
Afghan Kebab	9a/51-52s	20
Agua Dulce	9a/53-54s	22

Angelo's Pizza	*multi.*	20	La Bonne Soupe	*55s/5-6a*	18
Anthos	*52s/5-6a*	24	⬛ Le Bernardin	*51s/6-7a*	29
AQ Kafé	*Bway/CPS-58s*	20	Le Pain Q.	*7a/58s*	18
Azuri Cafe	*51s/9-10a*	25	Lime Jungle	*multi.*	-
Baluchi's	*56s/Bway-8a*	18	Maison	*Bway/53s*	19
Bann	*50s/8-9a*	22	Mangia	*57s/5-6a*	20
Bar Americain	*52s/6-7a*	23	NEW Má Pêche	*56s/5-6a*	22
Basso56	*56s/Bway-8a*	23	⬛ Marea	*CPS/Bway-7a*	27
Bay Leaf	*56s/5-6a*	21	Maria Pia	*51s/8-9a*	20
Beacon	*56s/5-6a*	22	Maze	*54s/6-7a*	22
Bello	*9a/56s*	21	McCormick/Schmick	*52s/6a*	20
Ben Benson's	*52s/6-7a*	24	Mee Noodle	*9a/53s*	17
Benoit	*55s/5-6a*	20	⬛ Michael's	*55s/5-6a*	21
Blockhead Burrito	*50s/8-9a*	16	⬛ Milos	*55s/6-7a*	27
BLT Market	*6a/CPS*	22	⬛ Modern	*53s/5-6a*	26
Blue Ribbon Sushi B&G	*58s/8a*	24	Molyvos	*7a/55-56s*	23
Bobby Van's	*50s/6-7a*	22	Momofuku Bakery	*56s/5-6a*	22
Bocca di Bacco	*9a/54-55s*	22	Natsumi	*50s/Bway-8a*	24
Bombay Palace	*52s/5-6a*	19	Nino's	*58s/6-7a*	20
Braai	*51s/8-9a*	21	⬛ Nobu	*57s/5-6a*	26
Brasserie Cognac	*Bway/55s*	19	Nocello	*55s/Bway-8a*	21
Brasserie 8½	*57s/5-6a*	22	Nook	*9a/50-51s*	22
Brass. Ruhlmann	*50s/5-6a*	19	Norma's	*56s/6-7a*	25
Bricco	*56s/8-9a*	19	Oak Room	*CPS/5-6a*	20
Brooklyn Diner	*57s/Bway-7a*	17	Osteria del Circo	*55s/6-7a*	22
Burger Joint/Le Parker	*56s/6-7a*	24	⬛ Palm	*50s/Bway-8a*	24
Caffe Cielo	*8a/52-53s*	20	Palm Court	*5a/59s*	-
Capital Grille	*51s/6-7a*	24	Patsy's	*56s/Bway-8a*	22
⬛ Carnegie Deli	*7a/55s*	22	Petrossian	*58s/7a*	23
Chez Napoléon	*50s/8-9a*	21	⬛ Piano Due	*51s/6-7a*	24
⬛ China Grill	*53s/5-6a*	22	NEW Plaza Food Hall	*59s/5a*	22
NEW Chom Chom	*56s/5-6a*	-	Pret A Manger	*multi.*	18
Così	*Bway/50s*	16	Puttanesca	*9a/56s*	19
Da Tommaso	*8a/53-54s*	21	Quality Meats	*58s/5-6a*	24
Eatery	*9a/53s*	20	Redeye Grill	*7a/56s*	20
Empanada Mama	*9a/51-52s*	22	Remi	*53s/6-7a*	23
Five Guys	*55s/5-6a*	20	NEW Robert	*Bway/8a*	19
Gallagher's	*52s/Bway-8a*	21	Rock Ctr.	*50s/5-6a*	18
Goodburger	*8a/57-58s*	17	Rue 57	*57s/6a*	18
Gordon Ramsay	*54s/6-7a*	23	Russian Samovar	*52s/Bway*	20
Greek Kitchen	*10a/58s*	19	Russian Tea	*57s/6-7a*	19
Hale/Hearty	*56s/5-6a*	19	Ruth's Chris	*51s/6-7a*	24
Hanci	*10a/56-57s*	22	Sarabeth's	*CPS/5-6a*	20
Heartland	*6a/51s*	14	⬛ Seasonal	*58s/6-7a*	25
NEW Hudson Eatery	*57s/11a-West*	-	Serafina	*55s/Bway*	19
NEW Hudson Hall	*58s/8-9a*	-	Shelly's Tratt.	*57s/5-6a*	20
Il Gattopardo	*54s/5-6a*	25	Siam Inn	*51s/Bway-8a*	21
⬛ Il Tinello	*56s/5-6a*	25	Soba Nippon	*52s/5-6a*	23
Insieme	*7a/50-51s*	23	Sosa Borella	*8a/50s*	19
Ise	*56s/5-6a*	21	South Gate	*CPS/6-7a*	24
Island Burgers	*9a/51-52s*	21	Stage Deli	*7a/53-54s*	20
Joe's Shanghai	*56s/5-6a*	22	⬛ Sugiyama	*55s/Bway-8a*	26
Katsu-Hama	*55s/5-6a*	21	Szechuan Gourmet	*56s/8a*	22
La Bergamote	*52s/10-11a*	24	Taboon	*10a/52s*	24

Tang Pavilion	55s/5-6a	22
Terrazza Toscana	9a/50s	21
Thalia	8a/50s	20
Toloache	50s/Bway-8a	23
Topaz Thai	56s/6-7a	21
NEW Totto Ramen	52s/8-9a	-
Tratt. Dell'Arte	7a/56-57s	21
☒ 21 Club	52s/5-6a	22
Uncle Jack's	56s/5-6a	22
Uncle Nick's	9a/50-51s	21
ViceVersa	51s/8-9a	22
Victor's Cafe	52s/Bway-8a	22
Vynl	9a/51s	17
Whym	9a/57-58s	20
'Wichcraft	Rock plz/49s	20
Wondee Siam	multi.	21
Yakitori Totto	55s/Bway-8a	24

WEST 60s

☒ Asiate	60s/Bway	24
☒ A Voce	60s/Bway	24
Bar Boulud	Bway/63-64s	23
Bouchon Bakery	60s/Bway	24
Cafe Fiorello	Bway/63-64s	20
NEW Ed's Chowder	63s/Bway-Colum	19
Empire Szechuan	Colum/68s	16
Gabriel's	60s/Bway-Colum	22
Grand Tier	Lincoln Ctr/63-65s	20
☒ Jean Georges	CPW/60-61s	28
☒ Jean Georges Noug.	CPW/60-61s	27
Josephina	Bway/63-64s	18
La Boîte en Bois	68s/Colum	22
Landmarc	60s/Bway	20
Le Pain Q.	65s/Bway-CPW	18
NEW Lincoln	65s/Bway	-
☒ Masa/Bar Masa	60s/Bway	27
Nanoosh	Bway/68-69s	19
Nick & Toni	67s/Bway	19
Ollie's	Bway/67-68s	16
☒ Per Se	60s/Bway	28
☒ Picholine	64s/Bway-CPW	27
P.J. Clarke's	63s/Colum	17
Porter House	60s/Bway	24
Rosa Mexicano	Colum/62s	22
Sapphire	Bway/60-61s	21
Shun Lee Cafe	65s/Colum	21
Shun Lee West	65s/Colum	22
☒ Telepan	69s/Colum	26
Whole Foods	60s/Bway	19
'Wichcraft	62s/Bway-Colum	20

WEST 70s

Alice's Tea	73s/Amst	19
Amber	Colum/70s	19

Arté Café	73s/Amst-Colum	18
Bello Sguardo	Amst/79-80s	20
Bettola	Amst/79-80s	20
Big Nick's	multi.	18
Bistro Cassis	Colum/70-71s	20
Café Frida	Colum/77-78s	20
☒ Cafe Luxembourg	70s/Amst	20
Cafe Ronda	Colum/71-72s	20
'Cesca	75s/Amst	23
Citrus B&G	Amst/75s	19
☒ Compass	70s/Amst-W End	22
Coppola's	79s/Amst-Bway	20
Così	Bway/77-78s	16
Dallas BBQ	72s/Colum-CPW	15
☒ Dovetail	77s/Colum	26
Earthen Oven	72s/Colum-CPW	20
Epices/Traiteur	70s/Colum	21
Fairway Cafe	Bway/74s	18
Fatty Crab	Bway/77s	20
☒ Gari/Sushi	Colum/77-78s	27
Gazala Place	Colum/78s	23
Gray's Papaya	Bway/72s	20
Hummus Pl.	Amst/74-75s	22
Isabella's	Colum/77s	20
Josie's	Amst/74s	19
Lenny's	Colum/74s	17
Le Pain Q.	72s/Colum-CPW	18
Maoz Veg.	Amst/70-71s	21
Mike's Bistro	72s/Bway-W End	26
Mughlai	Colum/75s	20
Nice Matin	79s/Amst	20
Ocean Grill	Colum/78-79s	24
Pappardella	Colum/75s	20
Pasha	71s/Colum-CPW	20
Patsy's Pizzeria	74s/Colum	20
Pomodoro Rosso	Colum/70s	21
Salumeria Rosi	Amst/73-74s	24
Sambuca	72s/Colum-CPW	20
Scaletta	77s/Colum-CPW	21
Shake Shack	Colum/77s	23
Sunburnt Cow/Calf	79s/Amst-Bway	18
Tenzan	Colum/73s	22
Vai	77s/Amst-Bway	21
Viand	Bway/75s	17

WEST 80s

Accademia/Vino	Bway/89-90s	19
Aged	Bway/88s	17
Artie's Deli	Bway/82-83s	18
☒ Barney Greengrass	Amst/86s	24
B. Café	Amst/87-88s	21
Bistro Citron	Colum/82-83s	19
Blossom	Colum/82-83s	22
Bodrum	Amst/88-89s	20

Brother Jimmy's | *Amst/80-81s* [16]
Cafe Con Leche | *Amst/80-81s* [18]
Calle Ocho | *Colum/81-82s* [21]
Celeste | *Amst/84-85s* [24]
Cilantro | *Colum/83-84s* [17]
Dean's | *85s/Amst-Bway* [18]
EJ's Luncheon. | *Amst/81-82s* [16]
5 Napkin Burger | *Bway/84s* [21]
Flor/Mayo | *Amst/83-84s* [20]
French Roast | *Bway/85s* [17]
Good Enough/Eat | *Amst/83s* [20]
Hampton Chutney | *Amst/82s* [20]
Haru | *Amst/80-81s* [20]
Jackson Hole | *Colum/85s* [17]
Kefi | *Colum/84-85s* [22]
La Mirabelle | *86s/Amst-Colum* [23]
Land | *Amst/81-82s* [22]
Lenny's | *Colum/84-5s* [17]
Mermaid | *Amst/87-88s* [21]
Momoya | *Amst/80-81s* [22]
Ollie's | *Bway/89-90s* [16]
🆉 Ouest | *Bway/83-84s* [24]
Peacefood Café | *Amst/82a* [21]
Popover Cafe | *Amst/86-87s* [19]
Recipe | *Amst/81-82s* [22]
Sarabeth's | *Amst/80-81s* [20]
Spiga | *84s/Amst-Bway* [23]
🆕 Taberna | *Amst/80-81s* [-]
Zabar's Cafe | *Bway/80s* [20]
Zeytin | *Col./85s* [18]

WEST 90s

Acqua | *Amst/95s* [19]
Alouette | *Bway/97-98s* [21]
Cafe Con Leche | *Amst/95-96s* [18]
Café Frida | *Amst/97-98s* [20]
Carmine's | *Bway/90-91s* [20]
El Malecon | *Amst/97-98s* [22]
Gabriela's | *Colum/93-94s* [18]
Gennaro | *Amst/92-93s* [24]
Hummus Pl. | *Bway/98-99s* [22]
Lisca | *Amst/92-93s* [20]
Pio Pio | *Amst/94s* [22]
Saigon Grill | *Amst/90s* [21]
Tratt. Pesce | *Colum/90-91s* [18]
Two Boots | *Bway/95-96s* [18]

WEST 100s

(See also Harlem/East Harlem)
Awash | *Amst/106-107s* [21]
Bistro Ten 18 | *Amst/110s* [19]
Blockhead Burrito | *Amst/106s* [16]
Café du Soleil | *Bway/104s* [19]
Community Food | [22]
    Bway/112-113s
Empire Szechuan | *Bway/100s* [16]

Flor/Mayo | *Bway/100-101s* [20]
Havana Central | *Bway/113s* [18]
Indus Valley | *Bway/100s* [23]
Le Monde | *Bway/112-113s* [17]
Mamá Mexico | *Bway/102s* [19]
Maoz Veg. | *Bway/110-111s* [21]
Max SoHa/Caffe | *multi.* [20]
Noche Mex. | *Amst/101-102s* [22]
Ollie's | *Bway/116s* [16]
Picnic | *Bway/101s* [20]
Pisticci | *La Salle/Bway* [23]
Rack & Soul | *109s/Bway* [21]
Sezz Medi' | *Amst/122s* [20]
Sookk | *Bway/102-103s* [21]
🆉 Terrace in Sky | *119s/Amst* [22]
Turkuaz | *Bway/100s* [20]
V&T | *Amst/110-111s* [18]
Wondee Siam | *Amst/107-108s* [21]

WEST VILLAGE

(Houston to 14th Sts., west of 6th Ave.,
excluding Meatpacking District)
Agave | *7a/Charles-10s* [18]
Aki | *4s/Barrow-Jones* [25]
Amy's Bread | *Blkr/Leroy* [24]
Annisa | *Barrow/7a-4s* [28]
Antica Venezia | *West/10s* [22]
A.O.C. | *Blkr/Grove* [19]
August | *Blkr/Charles-10s* [22]
Baoguette | *Christopher/Bedford* [21]
Barbuto | *Wash/Jane-12s* [23]
🆕 Betel | *Grove/Blkr-7a* [25]
Blue Ribbon Bakery | [24]
    Downing/Bedford
Bobo | *10s/7a* [21]
Braeburn | *Perry/Greenwich s* [21]
Cabrito | *Carmine/Bedford-Blkr* [17]
Cafe Asean | *10s/6a* [21]
Cafe Cluny | *12s/4s* [21]
Cafe Español | [20]
    Carmine/Bedford-7a
Cafe Gitane | *Jane/West* [20]
Café Henri | *Bedford/Downing* [20]
Cafe Loup | *13s/6-7a* [19]
Centro Vinoteca | *7a/Barrow* [21]
🆕 Choptank | *Blkr/Grove-7a* [17]
Commerce | *Commerce/Barrow* [23]
Cornelia St. Cafe | *Cornelia/4s* [19]
Corner Bistro | *4s/Jane* [22]
🆕 Corsino | *Hudson/Horatio* [20]
Cowgirl | *Hudson/10s* [16]
Crispo | *14s/7-8a* [23]
Dell'anima | *8a/Jane* [25]
Ditch Plains | *Bedford/Downing* [18]
Do Hwa | *Carmine/Bedford* [21]
El Charro | *Charles/Greenwich a* [22]

Elephant & Castle | *Greenwich a/Perry*	18
El Faro | *Greenwich s/Horatio*	22
Empire Szechuan | *7a/Perry-11s*	16
Employees Only | *Hudson/Christopher*	20
Energy Kitchen | *Christopher/7a*	17
EN Japanese | *Hudson/Leroy*	24
Extra Virgin | *4s/Perry*	21
Fatty Crab | *Hudson/Gansevoort*	20
Fish | *Blkr/Jones*	21
Five Guys | *Blkr/7a*	20
Gobo | *6a/8s-Waverly*	22
Good | *Greenwich a/Bank-12s*	19
Gottino | *Greenwich a/Charles*	22
Gradisca | *13s/6-7a*	23
Grand Sichuan | *7a/Carmine*	22
Gusto | *Greenwich a/Perry*	23
Havana Alma | *Christopher/Bedford*	21
Home | *Cornelia/Blkr-4s*	22
Hummus Pl. | *7a/Barrow*	22
'Ino | *Bedford/Downing-6a*	24
I Sodi | *Christopher/Blkr*	25
I Tre Merli | *10s/4s*	19
Joe's Pizza | *Carmine/Blkr-6a*	23
☑ John's Pizzeria | *Blkr/6-7a*	22
Joseph Leonard | *Waverly/Grove*	22
Keste Pizza | *Blkr/Cornelia*	25
Kingswood | *10s/6a*	19
La Carbonara | *14s/7-8a*	19
La Palapa | *6a/Wash pl-4s*	20
La Ripaille | *Hudson/Bethune*	20
L'Artusi | *10s/Blkr*	24
Las Ramblas | *4s/Cornelia-Jones*	24
Le Gigot | *Cornelia/Blkr-4s*	24
Little Owl | *Bedford/Grove*	25
Malatesta | *Wash/Christopher*	24
NEW Mappamondo | *8a/Blkr-12s*	–
Marinella | *Carmine/Bedford*	23
Market Table | *Carmine/Bedford*	23
Mary's Fish | *Charles/4s*	25
☑ Mas | *Downing/Bedford*	27
Mercadito | *7a/Blkr-Grove*	23
Mexicana Mama | *Hudson/Charles*	23
Molé | *Jane/Hudson*	25
Morandi | *Waverly/Charles*	22
Moustache | *Bedford/Grove*	21
Noodle Bar | *Carmine/Bedford*	20
No. 28 | *Carmine/Bedford-Blkr*	23
NEW Ofrenda | *7a/Christopher*	25
NEW Olio | *Greenwich a/Christopher*	–
☑ One if by Land | *Barrow/7a*	24
Palma | *Cornelia/Blkr-4s*	22
☑ Pearl Oyster | *Cornelia/Blkr*	26
Pepe | *Hudson/Perry-11s*	21
Perilla | *Jones/Blkr-4s*	26
Perry St. | *Perry/West*	25
Petite Abeille | *Hudson/Barrow*	18
Philip Marie | *Hudson/11s*	20
Piccolo Angolo | *Hudson/Jane*	25
Pink Tea Cup | *7a/Barrow-Grove*	–
Place | *4s/Bank-12s*	21
Pó | *Cornelia/Blkr-4s*	24
NEW Recette | *12s/Greenwich s*	24
Risotteria | *Blkr/Morton*	22
Sant Ambroeus | *4s/Perry*	21
Sevilla | *Charles/4s*	22
Smorgas Chef | *12s/4s*	19
Snack Taverna | *Bedford/Morton*	22
sNice | *8a/Horatio-Jane*	20
Soto | *6a/Wash-4s*	27
Spotted Pig | *11s/Greenwich s*	23
Spunto | *Carmine/7a*	21
Surya | *Blkr/Grove-7a*	22
SushiSamba | *7a/Barrow*	22
Sweetiepie | *Greenwich a/10s*	15
Taïm | *Waverky/11s-Perry*	26
NEW Takashi | *Hudson/Barrow*	–
Tartine | *11s/4s*	21
Tea & Sympathy | *Greenwich a/12-13s*	19
10 Downing | *Downing/6a*	20
Tio Pepe | *4s/Cornelia-Jones*	19
Tratt. Pesce | *Blkr/6-7a*	18
Trattoria Toscana | *Carmine/Bedford-7a*	24
Turks/Frogs | *11s/Greenwich s-Wash*	18
Two Boots | *11s/7a*	18
☑ Wallsé | *11s/Wash*	26
☑ Waverly Inn | *Bank/Waverly*	20
Westville | *10s/Blkr-4s*	22
Yama | *Carmine/Bedford-Blkr*	24
Yerba Buena | *Perry/Greenwich a*	23

Bronx

Ann & Tony's | *Arthur/187-188s*	20
Beccofino | *Mosholu/Fieldston*	20
Black Whale | *City Is/Hawkins*	20
Bruckner B&G | *Bruckner/3a*	19
City Is. Lobster | *Bridge/City Is*	19
Coals | *Eastchester/Morris Pk*	23
Dallas BBQ | *Fordham/Deegan*	15
Dominick's | *Arthur/Crescent*	23
El Malecon | *Bway/231s*	22
Enzo's | *multi.*	23
F & J Pine | *Bronxdale/Matthews*	22
Fratelli | *Eastchester/Mace*	21

Jake's | *Bway/242s* | 24
Liebman's | *235s/Johnson* | 22
Lobster Box | *City Is/Belden* | 18
Madison's | *Riverdale/259s* | 22
Mario's | *Arthur/184-186s* | 21
New Hawaii Sea | | 22
  Williamsbridge/Raymond
NYY Steak | *161s/River* | 21
Pasquale's | *Arthur/Crescent* | 21
Patricia's | *multi.* | 22
Pio Pio | *Cypress/138-139s* | 22
Portofino | *City Is/Cross* | 21
Z Roberto | *Crescent/Hughes* | 27
Sammy's Fishbox | | 20
  City Is/Rochelle
Siam Sq. | *Kappock/Henry* | 23
Tosca Café | *Tremont/Miles* | 21
Tra Da Noi | *187s/Belmont* | 22
Umberto's | *Arthur/186s* | 19
Zero Otto | *Arthur/186s* | 25

Brooklyn

BAY RIDGE

Agnanti | *5a/78s* | 23
Areo | *3a/84-85s* | 24
Arirang Hibachi | *4a/88-89s* | 19
Austin's Steak | *5a/90s* | 22
Cebu | *3a/88s* | 22
Chadwick's | *3a/89s* | 23
Eliá | *3a/86-87s* | 26
Embers | *3a/95-96s* | 21
Five Guys | *5a/85-86s* | 20
Fushimi | *4a/93-94s* | 23
Greenhouse | *3a/77-78s* | 19
Omonia | *3a/76-77s* | 20
101 | *4a/101s* | 20
Pearl Room | *3a/82s* | 22
Z Tanoreen | *3a/76s* | 27
Tuscany Grill | *3a/86-87s* | 24

BEDFORD-STUYVESANT

Peaches | *multi.* | 22

BENSONHURST

L&B Spumoni | *86s/10-11s* | 24
Nyonya | *86s/23-24a* | 21
Tenzan | *18a/71s* | 22

BOERUM HILL

Bacchus | *Atlantic/Bond-Nevins* | 21
Hanco's | *Bergen/Hoyt-Smith* | 21
Jolie | *Atlantic/Hoyt-Smith* | 21
Ki Sushi | *Smith/Dean-Pacific* | 26
Lunetta | *Smith/Dean-Pacific* | 22

NEW Mile End | | 25
  Hoyt/Atlantic-Pacific
Nicky's | *Atlantic/Hoyt-Smith* | 21
NEW Rothschild's | | –
  Atlantic/Bond-Nevins
Z Saul | *Smith/Bergen-Dean* | 26

BRIGHTON BEACH

Tatiana | *Brighton 6s/Brightwater* | 21

BROOKLYN HEIGHTS

NEW Bread/Butter | | 18
  Henry/Cranberry
ChipShop | *Atlantic/Henry* | 19
Five Guys | *Montague/Clinton* | 20
Hale/Hearty | *Court/Remsen* | 19
Henry's End | *Henry/Cranberry* | 24
Jack Horse | *Hicks/Cranberry* | 22
Lantern | *Montague/Henry* | 19
Noodle Pudding | | 24
  Henry/Cranberry
Queen | *Court/Livingston* | 24

BUSHWICK

Roberta's | *Moore/Bogart* | 23

CARROLL GARDENS

Alma | *Columbia/Degraw* | 21
NEW Bino | *Smith/Degraw* | –
Buttermilk | *Court/Huntington* | 24
Calexico | *Union/Hicks* | 25
Chestnut | *Smith/Degraw-Sackett* | 23
Cubana Café | *Smith/Degraw* | 20
Fragole | *Court/1pl* | 24
Frankies | *Court/4pl* | 24
Z Grocery | *Smith/Sackett* | 26
Lucali | *Henry/Carroll-1pl* | 26
Petite Crev. | *Union/Hicks* | 24
Prime Meat | *Court/Luquer* | 24
Provence/Boite | *Smith/Degraw* | 20
Savoia | *Smith/Degraw-Sackett* | 20
NEW Seersucker | *Smith/Carroll* | –
Union Smith | *Smith/Union* | 20
Zaytoons | *Smith/Sackett* | 20

CLINTON HILL

Locanda Vini | *Gates/Cambridge* | 27
Umi Nom | *DeKalb/Classon* | 24

COBBLE HILL

Bocca Lupo | *Henry/Warren* | 24
NEW Broken Eng. | | –
  Bergen/Court-Smith
Cafe Luluc | *Smith/Baltic* | 20
Char No. 4 | *Smith/Baltic* | 22
Chocolate Room | *Court/Butler* | 24
Coco Roco | *Smith/Bergen-Dean* | 19

NEW Henry Public | *Henry/Atlantic* — 17

Hibino | *Henry/Pacific* — 25

Joya | *Court/Warren* — 23

Lemongrass | *Court/Dean* — 17

Osaka | *Court/Butler* — 22

Quercy | *Court/Baltic-Kane* — 21

NEW Strong Pl. | *Court/Butler* — –

Sweet Melissa | *Court/Butler* — 20

Watty/Meg | *Court/Kane* — 20

Wild Ginger | *Smith/Dean-Pacific* — 22

CONEY ISLAND

Gargiulo's | *15s/Mermaid-Surf* — 22

Totonno Pizza | *Neptune/15-16s* — 21

DITMAS PARK

Farm/Adderley | *Cortelyou/Stratford* — 24

Mimi's Hummus | *Cortelyou/Westminster* — 25

NEW Purple Yam | *Cortelyou/Argyle* — 23

DOWNTOWN BROOKLYN

Dallas BBQ | *Livingston/Hoyt* — 15

Junior's | *Flatbush/DeKalb* — 17

Morton's | *Adams/Tillary* — 24

DUMBO

Bubby's | *Main/Plymouth-Water* — 18

Grimaldi's | *Old Fulton/Front* — 24

Rice | *Wash/Front-York* — 19

Z River Café | *Water/Furman* — 26

Superfine | *Front/Jay-Pearl* — 20

DYKER HEIGHTS

Outback | *86s/15a* — 15

Tommaso | *86s/Bay 8s-15a* — 24

FORT GREENE

Abistro | *Carlton/Myrtle* — 24

Café Habana/Outpost | *Fulton/Portland* — 22

Chez Oskar | *DeKalb/Adelphi* — 19

Gen. Greene | *DeKalb/Clermont* — 20

Ici | *DeKalb/Clermont* — 22

Luz | *Vanderbilt/Myrtle* — 24

Madiba | *DeKalb/Carlton* — 22

No. 7 | *Greene/Fulton* — 23

Olea | *Lafayette/Adelphi* — 23

Rice | *DeKalb/Cumberland* — 19

67 Burger | *Lafayette/Fulton* — 21

Smoke Joint | *Elliott/Lafayette* — 22

Thomas Beisl | *Lafayette/Ashland* — 16

Zaytoons | *Myrtle/Hall-Wash* — 20

GRAVESEND

Fiorentino's | *Ave U/McDonald* — 21

Sahara | *Coney Is/Aves T-U* — 22

GREENPOINT

Anella | *Franklin/Green* — 26

Five Leaves | *Bedford/Lorimer* — 25

GREENWOOD HEIGHTS

Toby's Public | *6a/21s* — 25

MIDWOOD

Z Di Fara | *Ave J/15s* — 27

Joe's Pizza | *Kings/16s* — 23

Taci's Beyti | *Coney Is/Ave P* — 24

MILL BASIN

La Villa Pizzeria | *Ave U/66-67s* — 21

Mill Basin Deli | *Ave T/59s* — 22

PARK SLOPE

Alchemy | *5a/Bergen-St Marks* — 19

Z Al Di La | *5a/Carroll* — 27

A.O.C. | *5a/Garfield* — 19

Applewood | *11s/7-8a* — 25

Baluchi's | *5a/2-3s* — 18

Bark Hot Dogs | *Bergen/5-6a* — 21

Barrio | *7a/3s* — 17

Bar Tano | *3a/9s* — 21

Bar Toto | *11s/6a* — 21

Belleville | *5s/5a* — 18

NEW Benchmark | *2s/4-5a* — –

Z Blue Ribbon | *5a/1s-Garfield* — 25

Z Blue Ribbon Sushi | *5a/1s* — 26

Bogota | *5a/Lincoln-St Johns* — 23

Brooklyn Fish | *5a/Degraw* — 23

Cafe Steinhof | *7a/14s* — 20

NEW Campo/Fiori | *5a/Berkley* — –

ChipShop | *5a/6-7s* — 19

Chocolate Room | *5a/Propsect* — 24

Coco Roco | *5a/6-7s* — 19

Z Conviv. Osteria | *5a/Bergen* — 26

Cubana Café | *6a/St Marks* — 20

Five Guys | *7a/6-7s* — 20

Flatbush Farm | *St Marks/Flatbush* — 21

Fonda | *7a/14-15s* — 24

Fornino | *5a/Carroll-Garfield* — 23

Ghenet | *Douglass/4-5a* — 23

Hanco's | *7a/10s* — 21

Joe's Pizza | *7a/Carroll-Garfield* — 23

La Taqueria/Rachel | *multi.* — 20

La Villa Pizzeria | *5a/1s-Garfield* — 21

Lemongrass | *7a/Berkeley* — 17

Long Tan | *5a/Berkeley-Union* — 20

Miriam | *5a/Prospect* — 22

Moim | *Garfield/7-8a* — 23
Palo Santo | *Union/4-5a* — 25
Press 195 | *5a/Berkeley-Union* — 21
Provini | *8a/13s* — 22
Rose Water | *Union/6a* — 25
Scalino | *7a/10s* — 24
Scottadito | *Union/6-7a* — 21
Sette | *7a/3s* — 20
Sheep Sta. | *4a/Douglass* — 18
sNice | *5a/2-3s* — 20
Song | *5a/1-2s* — 23
Stone Park | *5a/3s* — 25
Sweet Melissa | *7a/1-2s* — 20
NEW Thistle Hill | *7a/15s* — -
12th St. B&G | *8a/12s* — 20
Two Boots | *2s/7-8a* — 18
Zuzu Ramen | *4a/Degraw* — 21

PROSPECT HEIGHTS

Amorina | *Vanderbilt/Prospect* — 25
Beast | *Bergen/Vanderbilt* — 21
Franny's | *Flatbush/Prospect* — 24
Geido | *Flatbush/7a* — 24
James | *Carlton/St Marks* — 24
NEW Kaz An Nou |
  6a/Bergen-Dean — -
Tom's | *Wash/Sterling* — 21
NEW Vanderbilt |
  Vanderbilt/Bergen — 21
Zaytoons | *Vanderbilt/St Marks* — 20

RED HOOK

Defonte's | *Columbia/Luquer* — 22
Fairway Cafe | *Van Brunt/Reed* — 18
Good Fork | *Van Brunt/Coffey* — 25
Hope & Anchor |
  Van Brunt/Wolcott — 19

SHEEPSHEAD BAY

Brennan | *Nostrand/Ave U* — 21
Roll-n-Roaster | *Emmons/29s* — 21

SUNSET PARK

Nyonya | *8a/54s* — 21
Pacificana | *55s/8a* — 25
Tacos Matamoros | *5a/45-46s* — 25

VINEGAR HILL

Vinegar Hill Hse. | *Hudson/Front* — 25

WILLIAMSBURG

Aurora | *Grand/Wythe* — 24
Bamonte's | *Withers/Lorimer* — 23
NEW Café Colette | *Berry/N 9s* — -
Caracas | *Grand/Havemeyer* — 24
Chimu | *Union/Meeker* — 25

NEW Commodore |
  Metro/Havemeyer — -
Diner | *Bway/Berry* — 22
Dressler | *Bway/Bedford-Driggs* — 25
DuMont | *multi.* — 23
Egg | *N 5s/Bedford-Berry* — 23
El Almacén | *Driggs/N 6-7s* — 24
NEW Fatty 'Cue | *S 6s/Berry* — 23
Z Fette Sau | *Metro/Havemeyer* — 25
Fornino | *Bedford/6-7s* — 23
La Superior | *Berry/S 2-3s* — 24
Le Barricou | *Grand/Lorimer* — 21
Marlow/Sons | *Bway/Berry* — 24
Mesa Coyoacan |
  Graham/Skillman — 24
Miranda | *Berry/N 9s* — 23
Motorino | *Graham/Devoe* — 24
M Shanghai/Noodle | *multi.* — 21
Z Peter Luger | *Bway/Driggs* — 27
Pies-n-Thighs | *4s/Driggs* — 23
Radegast | *N 3s/Berry* — 18
Roebling | *Roebling/Metro* — 19
Rye | *S 1s/Havemeyer* — 23
NEW Saltie | *Metro/Havemeyer* — 25
Sea | *N 6s/Berry* — 21
Sel de Mer | *Graham/Skillman* — 24
NEW St. Anselm |
  Metro/Havemeyer — -
Sweetwater | *N 6s/Berry-Wythe* — 23
NEW Traif | *S 4s/Havemeyer* — -
Walter Foods | *Grand/Roebling* — 23
Wild Ginger | *Bedford/5-6s* — 22
Zenkichi | *N 6s/Wythe* — 25

Queens

ASTORIA

Aegean Cove | *Steinway/20a* — 24
Afghan Kebab | *Steinway/28a* — 20
Agnanti | *Ditmars/19s* — 23
Arepas Café | *36a/34s* — 24
BareBurger | *31a/34s* — 23
Bistro 33 | *Ditmars/21s* — 20
Brick Cafe | *33s/31a* — 22
Cafe Bar | *36s/34a* — 20
Cávo | *31a/42-43s* — 20
Christos | *23a/41s* — 23
Elias Corner | *31s/24a* — 23
5 Napkin Burger | *36s/35u* — 21
Il Bambino | *31a/34-35s* — 24
JJ's Asian Fusion | *31a/37-38s* — 24
Kabab Café | *Steinway/25a* — 25
Locale | *34a/33s* — 21
Malagueta | *36a/28s* — 25
Mundo | *Bway/32s* — 22
Omonia | *Bway/33s* — 20

Philoxenia	*34a/32-33s*	21
Piccola Venezia	*28a/42s*	25
Ponticello	*Bway/46-47s*	24
Rizzo's Pizza	*Steinway/30-31a*	23
Sac's Place	*Bway/29s*	23
718	*Ditmars/35s*	22
Stamatis	*23a/29-31s*	21
Taverna Kyclades	*Ditmars/35s*	26
Telly's Taverna	*23a/28-29s*	23
Thai Pavilion	*multi.*	25
Tierras	*Bway/33s*	21
☑ Tratt. L'incontro	*31s/Ditmars*	27
Vesta	*30a/21s*	24
Watawa	*Ditmars/35s*	25

BAYSIDE

Ben's Kosher	*26a/211s*	19
Bon Chon	*Bell/45dr-45r*	20
Bourbon St. Café	*Bell/40-41a*	17
Erawan	*multi.*	23
Jackson Hole	*Bell/35a*	17
Kyochon	*Springfield/Horace*	20
Outback	*Bell/26a*	15
Press 195	*Bell/40-41a*	21
Uncle Jack's	*Bell/40a*	22

COLLEGE POINT

Five Guys	*14a/132s*	20

CORONA

Leo's Latticini	*104s/46a*	26
Park Side	*Corona/51a*	24
Tortilleria Nixtamal	*47a/104-108s*	25

DOUGLASTON

Grimaldi's	*61a/244s*	24

ELMHURST

Outback	*Queens/56a*	15
Pho Bang	*Bway/Elmhurst*	20
Ping's Sea.	*Queens/Goldsmith*	22

FLUSHING

Blue Smoke	*126s/Roosevelt*	21
East Manor	*Kissena/Kalmia*	19
Joe's Shanghai	*37a/Main*	22
Kum Gang San	*Northern/Bowne*	21
Kyochon	*Northern/156s*	20
Pho Bang	*Kissena/Main*	20
Ramen Setagaya	*Prince/37a*	18
Sentosa	*Prince/39a*	23
Shake Shack	*126s/Roosevelt*	23
Spicy & Tasty	*Prince/39a*	23
Szechuan Gourmet	*37a/Main*	22
Xi'an	*multi.*	-

FOREST HILLS

Aged	*70r/Austin*	17
Alberto	*Metro/69-70a*	23
Baluchi's	*Queens/76a-76r*	18
Bann Thai	*Austin/Yellowstone*	19
Cabana	*70r/Austin-Queens*	21
Danny Brown	*Metro/71dr*	26
Dee's	*Metro/74a*	21
Nick's	*Ascan/Austin*	23
Q Thai Bistro	*Ascan/Austin*	20

GLENDALE

Five Guys	*Woodhaven/74a*	20
Zum Stammtisch	*Myrtle/69pl*	23

HOWARD BEACH

La Villa Pizzeria	*153a/82s*	21

JACKSON HEIGHTS

Afghan Kebab	*37a/74-75s*	20
Delhi Palace	*74s/37a-37r*	21
Jackson Diner	*74s/Roosevelt*	22
Jackson Hole	*Astoria/70s*	17
Pio Pio	*Northern/84-85s*	22

JAMAICA

Bobby Van's	*American Airlines*	22

LITTLE NECK

La Baraka	*Northern/Little Neck*	21

LONG ISLAND CITY

Bella Via	*Vernon/48a*	23
Café Henri	*50a/Jackson*	20
NEW El Ay Si	*Vernon/47r-48a*	-
Manducatis	*Jackson/47a*	23
NEW M. Wells	*49a/21s*	-
Riverview	*50a/E River-49a*	20
NEW Testaccio	*Vernon/47r*	22
Tournesol	*Vernon/50-51a*	24
☑ Water's Edge	*E River/44dr*	20

MIDDLE VILLAGE

Uvarara	*Metro/79-80s*	26

OZONE PARK

Don Peppe	*Lefferts/135-149a*	26

REGO PARK

Barosa	*Woodhaven/62r*	22
Ben's Best	*Queens/63r*	23
Grand Sichuan	*Queens/66r*	22
London Lennie	*Woodhaven/Fleet*	22
Pio Pio	*Woodhaven/62r*	22

SUNNYSIDE

Bliss Bistro | *Skillman/46s* <u>21</u>
Quaint | *Skillman/46-47s* <u>25</u>
Turkish Grill | *Queens/42s* <u>24</u>

WOODSIDE

Sapori D'Ischia | *37a/56s* <u>23</u>
☒ Sripraphai | *39a/64-65s* <u>26</u>

Staten Island

Angelina's | *Ellis/Arthur Kill* <u>22</u>
Arirang Hibachi | *Nelson/Locust* <u>19</u>
Bayou | *Bay/Chestnut* <u>23</u>
Bocelli | *Hylan/Old Town Parkinson* <u>25</u>
Brioso | *New Dorp/9s* <u>25</u>
Carol's | *Richmond/Four Corners* <u>26</u>
China Chalet | *Amboy/Armstrong* <u>18</u>
Cole's Dock | *Cleveland/Hylan* <u>18</u>

Da Noi | *multi.* <u>23</u>
Denino | *Port Richmond/Hooker* <u>26</u>
Enoteca Maria | *Hyatt/Central* <u>23</u>
Filippo's | *Richmond/Buel* <u>25</u>
Fushimi | *Richmond/Lincoln* <u>23</u>
Joe & Pat's | *Victory/Manor* <u>23</u>
Killmeyer | *Arthur Kill/Sharrotts* <u>20</u>
Lake Club | *Clove/Victory* <u>23</u>
Lorenzo's | *South/Lois* <u>23</u>
Marina Cafe | *Mansion/Hillside* <u>20</u>
Nove | *Richmond/Amboy* <u>25</u>
Nurnberger | *Castleton/Davis* <u>21</u>
Outback | *Marsh/Platinum* <u>15</u>
Real Madrid | *Forest/Union* <u>22</u>
South Fin | *Capodanno/Sand* <u>19</u>
Tratt. Romana | *Hylan/Benton* <u>24</u>
Vida | *Van Duzer/Beach* <u>23</u>
Zest | *Bay/Willow* <u>25</u>

LOCATIONS

Special Features

Listings cover the best in each category and include names, locations and Food ratings. Multi-location restaurants' features may vary by branch.

BREAKFAST

(See also Hotel Dining)

AQ Kafé	**W 50s**	20
☑ Balthazar	**SoHo**	23
☑ Barney Greengrass	**W 80s**	24
BLT Market	**W 50s**	22
Brasserie	**E 50s**	20
☑NEW Breslin	**Chelsea**	21
Brooklyn Diner	**multi.**	17
Bubby's	**TriBeCa**	18
Cafe Con Leche	**W 80s**	18
☑ Cafe Luxembourg	**W 70s**	20
Cafe Mogador	**E Vill**	22
Café Sabarsky	**E 80s**	23
☑ Carnegie Deli	**W 50s**	22
NEW Ça Va	**W 40s**	-
City Bakery	**Flatiron**	22
City Hall	**TriBeCa**	21
Clinton St. Baking	**LES**	24
Cupping Rm.	**SoHo**	18
E.A.T.	**E 80s**	20
Egg	**W'burg**	23
EJ's Luncheon.	**multi.**	16
Good Enough/Eat	**W 80s**	20
HK	**Garment**	18
☑ Jean Georges Noug.	**W 60s**	27
Joseph Leonard	**W Vill**	22
☑ Katz's Deli	**LES**	24
Kitchenette	**multi.**	19
NEW Lambs Club	**Financial**	-
Landmarc	**W 60s**	20
Le Pain Q.	**multi.**	18
NEW Lina Frey	**LES**	-
Locanda Verde	**TriBeCa**	24
NEW Maialino	**Gramercy**	25
☑ Michael's	**W 50s**	21
Morandi	**W Vill**	22
NEW M. Wells	**LIC**	-
Naples 45	**E 40s**	17
Nice Matin	**W 70s**	20
NoHo Star	**NoHo**	17
Norma's	**W 50s**	25
NEW Northern Spy	**E Vill**	23
Pastis	**Meatpacking**	21
NEW Peels	**E Vill**	-
Penelope	**Murray Hill**	22
Pershing Sq.	**E 40s**	15
Popover Cafe	**W 80s**	19
Prime Meat	**Carroll Gdns**	24
Rue 57	**W 50s**	18

Sant Ambroeus	**multi.**	21
Sarabeth's	**multi.**	20
☑ Standard Grill	**Meatpacking**	21
Tartine	**W Vill**	21
NEW Tartinery	**NoLita**	-
Taste	**E 80s**	22
Veselka	**E Vill**	19

BRUNCH

Alias	**LES**	22
Amy Ruth's	**Harlem**	20
A.O.C.	**W Vill**	19
Applewood	**Park Slope**	25
☑ Aquagrill	**SoHo**	26
☑ Aquavit	**E 50s**	25
☑ Artisanal	**Murray Hill**	23
Atlantic Grill	**E 70s**	23
Back Forty	**E Vill**	22
Bagatelle	**Meatpacking**	18
NEW Balaboosta	**NoLita**	-
☑ Balthazar	**SoHo**	23
Beacon	**W 50s**	22
Beast	**Prospect Hts**	21
Belcourt	**E Vill**	19
Black Whale	**Bronx**	20
Blue Ribbon Bakery	**W Vill**	24
☑ Blue Water	**Union Sq**	23
Bocca Lupo	**Cobble Hill**	24
Bondi Rd.	**LES**	17
Braeburn	**W Vill**	21
Brasserie 8½	**W 50s**	22
NEW Broken Eng.	**Cobble Hill**	-
Bubby's	**multi.**	18
Cafe Cluny	**W Vill**	21
Cafe Loup	**W Vill**	19
Cafe Luluc	**Cobble Hill**	20
☑ Cafe Luxembourg	**W 70s**	20
Cafe Mogador	**E Vill**	22
Cafe Ronda	**W 70s**	20
Cafeteria	**Chelsea**	19
Caffe Cielo	**W 50s**	20
Calle Ocho	**W 80s**	21
Capsouto Frères	**TriBeCa**	24
☑ Carlyle	**E 70s**	23
Carmine's	**W 40s**	20
Cebu	**Bay Ridge**	22
Celeste	**W 80s**	24
City Winery	**SoHo**	16
Clinton St. Baking	**LES**	24
NEW Colicchio/Sons	**Chelsea**	23

Community Food | **W 100s**	22
Cookshop | **Chelsea**	22
Cornelia St. Cafe | **W Vill**	19
Danal | **G Vill**	20
Danny Brown | **Forest Hills**	26
David Burke Townhse. | **E 60s**	24
Dell'anima | **W Vill**	25
Delta Grill | **W 40s**	19
Diner | **W'burg**	22
E.A.T. | **E 80s**	20
Eatery | **W 50s**	20
NEW Ed's Chowder | **W 60s**	19
Elephant & Castle | **W Vill**	18
Employees Only | **W Vill**	20
Essex | **LES**	18
Extra Virgin | **W Vill**	21
Fatty Crab | **multi.**	20
NEW Faustina | **E Vill**	23
Félix | **SoHo**	17
5 Points | **NoHo**	22
Friend/Farmer | **Gramercy**	19
Good | **W Vill**	19
Good Enough/Eat | **W 80s**	20
Great Jones Cafe | **NoHo**	20
HK | **Garment**	18
Home | **W Vill**	22
Hope & Anchor | **Red Hook**	19
Hundred Acres | **SoHo**	19
Isabella's | **W 70s**	20
Jane | **G Vill**	21
JoeDoe | **E Vill**	23
JoJo | **E 60s**	25
Kitchenette | **multi.**	19
NEW Le Caprice | **E 60s**	17
Le Gigot | **W Vill**	24
Les Halles | **multi.**	20
L'Express | **Flatiron**	18
Little Giant | **LES**	23
Locale | **Astoria**	21
NEW Los Feliz | **LES**	20
NEW Mark | **E 70s**	24
Mercadito | **multi.**	23
Z Mesa Grill | **Flatiron**	23
Z Minetta | **G Vill**	24
Miriam | **Park Slope**	22
Miss Mamie/Maude | **Harlem**	20
Nice Matin | **W 70s**	20
Norma's | **W 50s**	25
No. 7 | **Ft Greene**	23
Oceana | **W 40s**	23
Ocean Grill | **W 70s**	24
Odeon | **TriBeCa**	20
NEW Ofrenda | **W Vill**	25
Olea | **Ft Greene**	23
Z Ouest | **W 80s**	24

Paradou | **Meatpacking**	21
Pastis | **Meatpacking**	21
Penelope | **Murray Hill**	22
Petrossian | **W 50s**	23
Pietrasanta | **W 40s**	18
Pipa | **Flatiron**	22
NEW Plein Sud | **TriBeCa**	18
NEW Pop Art Bar | **E 60s**	-
Popover Cafe | **W 80s**	19
Prune | **E Vill**	24
Z Public | **NoLita**	24
NEW Pulino's | **NoLita**	19
Z River Café | **Dumbo**	26
Rose Water | **Park Slope**	25
NEW Rothschild's | **Boerum Hill**	-
Sarabeth's | **multi.**	20
Schiller's | **LES**	19
NEW Seersucker | **Carroll Gdns**	-
718 | **Astoria**	22
NEW South Houston | **SoHo**	-
Spotted Pig | **W Vill**	23
Square Meal | **E 90s**	24
Stanton Social | **LES**	23
Stone Park | **Park Slope**	25
Sylvia's | **Harlem**	19
Tartine | **W Vill**	21
Taste | **E 80s**	22
Z Telepan | **W 60s**	26
NEW Thistle Hill | **Park Slope**	-
NEW Tipsy Parson | **Chelsea**	18
Tom's | **Prospect Hts**	21
NEW Travertine | **NoLita**	22
Z Tribeca Grill | **TriBeCa**	22
Z Turkish Kitchen | **Murray Hill**	22
202 Cafe | **Chelsea**	19
NEW Vanderbilt | **Prospect Hts**	21
Z Wallsé | **W Vill**	26
Water Club | **Murray Hill**	21
Z Waverly Inn | **W Vill**	20

BUFFET

Z Aquavit | **E 50s**	25
Bay Leaf | **W 50s**	21
Black Whale | **Bronx**	20
Bombay Palace | **W 50s**	19
Brasserie 8½ | **W 50s**	22
Brick Ln. Curry | **E Vill**	21
Bukhara Grill | **E 40s**	23
Z Carlyle | **E 70s**	23
Chennai Gdn. | **Murray Hill**	21
Chola | **E 50s**	24
Darbar | **multi.**	21
Delhi Palace | **Jackson Hts**	21
Dhaba | **Murray Hill**	23
Earthen Oven | **W 70s**	20

East Manor	**Flushing**	19
Indus Valley	**W 100s**	23
Jackson Diner	**Jackson Hts**	22
Jewel of India	**W 40s**	20
La Baraka	**Little Neck**	21
Lake Club	**SI**	23
Londel's	**Harlem**	20
Lorenzo's	**SI**	23
Mamajuana	**Inwood**	20
Mari Vanna	**Flatiron**	20
Nirvana	**Murray Hill**	23
☑ One if by Land	**W Vill**	24
Palm Court	**W 50s**	-
Salaam Bombay	**TriBeCa**	22
Sapphire	**W 60s**	21
South Fin	**SI**	19
South Gate	**W 50s**	24
Taj Tribeca	**Financial**	22
Taste	**E 80s**	22
Tiffin Wallah	**Murray Hill**	23
Tosca Café	**Bronx**	21
☑ Turkish Kitchen	**Murray Hill**	22
Turkuaz	**W 100s**	20
2 West	**Financial**	21
Utsav	**W 40s**	21
Water Club	**Murray Hill**	21
Yuva	**E 50s**	23

BYO

Abistro	**Ft Greene**	24
Afghan Kebab	**multi.**	20
Amy Ruth's	**Harlem**	20
Angelica Kit.	**E Vill**	21
Baluchi's	**multi.**	18
Fatty Fish	**E 60s**	22
Gazala Place	**W 70s**	23
Ivo & Lulu	**SoHo**	19
Kabab Café	**Astoria**	25
NEW Kaz An Nou	**Prospect Hts**	-
Kuma Inn	**LES**	25
La Sirène	**SoHo**	22
Limon	**Murray Hill**	24
Little Giant	**LES**	23
Lucali	**Carroll Gdns**	26
Mama's Food	**E Vill**	20
Mee Noodle	**E 40s**	17
Mezzaluna/Pizza	**G Vill**	20
Mimi's Hummus	**Ditmas Pk**	25
Noodle Bar	**LES**	20
Nook	**W 50s**	22
Peking Duck	**Chinatown**	23
Petite Crev.	**Carroll Gdns**	24
Phoenix Gdn.	**E 40s**	24
Poke	**E 80s**	25
NEW Ramen Kuidouraku	**LES**	-

Square Meal	**E 90s**	24
Szechuan Gourmet	**W 50s**	22
Taci's Beyti	**Midwood**	24
Tacos Matamoros	**Sunset Pk**	25
Taj Tribeca	**Financial**	22
Tartine	**W Vill**	21
Square Meal	**E 90s**	24
NEW Taureau	**E Vill**	-
Tea & Sympathy	**W Vill**	19
Wondee Siam	**multi.**	21
Zaytoons	**multi.**	20
Zen Palate	**W 40s**	19

CELEBRATIONS

(Special prix fixe meals offered at major holidays)

☑ Adour	**E 50s**	26
Allegretti	**Flatiron**	23
☑ Aureole	**W 40s**	26
Beacon	**W 50s**	22
☑ BLT Fish	**Flatiron**	24
BLT Prime	**Gramercy**	25
☑ Blue Hill	**G Vill**	27
Bond 45	**W 40s**	19
☑ Bouley	**TriBeCa**	27
Braeburn	**W Vill**	21
'Cesca	**W 70s**	23
☑ Cru	**G Vill**	25
☑ Daniel	**E 60s**	28
Duane Park	**TriBeCa**	21
☑ FireBird	**W 40s**	20
☑ Four Seasons	**E 50s**	26
Fresco	**E 50s**	22
Gallagher's	**W 50s**	21
☑ Gotham B&G	**G Vill**	27
Home	**W Vill**	22
☑ La Grenouille	**E 50s**	28
NEW Lambs Club	**Financial**	-
☑ Le Bernardin	**W 50s**	29
☑ Le Cirque	**E 50s**	24
NEW Maialino	**Gramercy**	25
Marc Forgione	**TriBeCa**	24
☑ Marea	**W 50s**	27
☑ Mas	**W Vill**	27
Mercer Kitchen	**SoHo**	22
☑ Minetta	**G Vill**	24
☑ Modern	**W 50s**	26
Molyvos	**W 50s**	23
Oak Room	**W 50s**	20
Olives	**Union Sq**	23
☑ One if by Land	**W Vill**	24
☑ Ouest	**W 80s**	24
☑ Palm	**multi.**	24
☑ Park Avenue ...	**E 60s**	25
☑ Peter Luger	**W'burg**	27
Petrossian	**W 50s**	23

Raoul's | **SoHo**	23
Redeye Grill | **W 50s**	20
🅩 River Café | **Dumbo**	26
Rock Ctr. | **W 50s**	18
🅩 Scarpetta | **Chelsea**	26
Sea Grill | **W 40s**	24
🅩 SHO Shaun Hergatt | **Financial**	26
🅩 Terrace in Sky | **W 100s**	22
Tratt. Dell'Arte | **W 50s**	21
View | **W 40s**	17
Water Club | **Murray Hill**	21
🅩 Water's Edge | **LIC**	20

CELEBRITY CHEFS

Dan Barber
| 🅩 Blue Hill \| **G Vill** | 27 |

Lidia Bastianich
🅩 Del Posto | **Chelsea**	26
NEW Eataly | **Flatiron**	-
Felidia | **E 50s**	26

Mario Batali
🅩 Babbo | **G Vill**	27
Casa Mono | **Gramercy**	26
🅩 Del Posto | **Chelsea**	26
NEW Eataly | **Flatiron**	-
🅩 Esca | **W 40s**	25
🅩 Lupa | **G Vill**	25
Otto | **G Vill**	22

Jonathan Benno
| NEW Lincoln \| **W 60s** | - |

April Bloomfield
| 🅩 NEW Breslin \| **Chelsea** | 21 |
| Spotted Pig \| **W Vill** | 23 |

Saul Bolton
| 🅩 Saul \| **Boerum Hill** | 26 |
| NEW Vanderbilt \| **Prospect Hts** | 21 |

David Bouley
| 🅩 Bouley \| **TriBeCa** | 27 |

Daniel Boulud
Bar Boulud | **W 60s**	23
🅩 Café Boulud | **E 70s**	27
🅩 Daniel | **E 60s**	28
🅩 DB Bistro Moderne | **W 40s**	25
🅩 DBGB | **E Vill**	22

Antoine Bouterin
| Le Perigord \| **E 50s** | 25 |

Jimmy Bradley
| Harrison \| **TriBeCa** | 24 |
| Red Cat \| **Chelsea** | 24 |

Terrance Brennan
| 🅩 Artisanal \| **Murray Hill** | 23 |
| 🅩 Picholine \| **W 60s** | 27 |

Scott Bryan
| Apiary \| **E Vill** | 23 |

David Burke
| David Burke Townhse. \| **E 60s** | 24 |
| Fishtail \| **E 60s** | 23 |

Marco Canora
| Hearth \| **E Vill** | 24 |
| Terroir \| **multi.** | 24 |

Floyd Cardoz
| 🅩 Tabla \| **Flatiron** | 25 |

Andrew Carmellini
| Locanda Verde \| **TriBeCa** | 24 |

Michael Cetrulo
| 🅩 Piano Due \| **W 50s** | 24 |
| 🅩 Scalini Fedeli \| **TriBeCa** | 27 |

David Chang
NEW Má Pêche | **W 50s**	22
Momofuku Bakery | **E Vill**	22
Momofuku Ko | **E Vill**	27
Momofuku Noodle | **E Vill**	24
Momofuku Ssäm | **E Vill**	25

Rebecca Charles
| 🅩 Pearl Oyster \| **W Vill** | 26 |

Tom Colicchio
NEW Colicchio/Sons | **Chelsea**	23
Craft | **Flatiron**	25
Craftbar | **Flatiron**	23
'Wichcraft | **multi.**	20

Scott Conant
| NEW Faustina \| **E Vill** | 23 |
| 🅩 Scarpetta \| **Chelsea** | 26 |

Josh de Chellis
| La Fonda/Sol \| **E 40s** | 22 |

Christian Delouvrier
| La Mangeoire \| **E 50s** | 20 |

John DeLucie
| NEW Lion \| **G Vill** | - |

Alain Ducasse
| 🅩 Adour \| **E 50s** | 26 |
| Benoit \| **W 50s** | 20 |

Wylie Dufresne
| WD-50 \| **LES** | 25 |

Todd English
NEW Ça Va | **W 40s**	-
Olives | **Union Sq**	23
NEW Plaza Food Hall | **W 50s**	22

Sandro Fioriti
| Sandro's \| **E 80s** | 24 |

Bobby Flay
| Bar Americain \| **W 50s** | 23 |
| 🅩 Mesa Grill \| **Flatiron** | 23 |

Kurt Gutenbrunner
Blaue Gans | **TriBeCa**	22
Café Sabarsky | **E 80s**	23
🅩 Wallsé | **W Vill**	26

Gabrielle Hamilton	
Prune | **E Vill**	24
Kerry Heffernan	
South Gate | **W 50s**	24
Shaun Hergatt	
Z SHO Shaun Hergatt | **Financial**	26
Peter Hoffman	
Back Forty | **E Vill**	22
Savoy | **SoHo**	24
Daniel Humm	
Z Eleven Madison | **Flatiron**	28
Michael Huynh	
Baoguette | **multi.**	21
Sara Jenkins	
Porchetta | **E Vill**	23
Veloce Pizzeria | **E Vill**	20
Thomas Keller	
Bouchon Bakery | **W 60s**	24
Z Per Se | **W 60s**	28
Matthew Kenney	
NEW Bar Paya | **E Vill**	—
Gabriel Kreuther	
Z Modern | **W 50s**	26
Susur Lee	
Shang | **LES**	21
Paul Liebrandt	
Z Corton | **TriBeCa**	26
Anita Lo	
Annisa | **W Vill**	28
Michael Lomonaco	
Porter House | **W 60s**	24
Pino Luongo	
Centolire | **E 80s**	21
Waldy Malouf	
Beacon | **W 50s**	22
Waldy's Pizza | **Chelsea**	21
Zarela Martinez	
Zarela | **E 50s**	22
Nobu Matsuhisa	
Z Nobu | **multi.**	26
Marco Moreira	
15 East | **Union Sq**	25
Z Tocqueville | **Union Sq**	25
Masaharu Morimoto	
Z Morimoto | **Chelsea**	25
Tadashi Ono	
Z Matsuri | **Chelsea**	22
Charlie Palmer	
Z Aureole | **W 40s**	26
Metrazur | **E 40s**	21
David Pasternack	
Z Esca | **W 40s**	25
Zak Pelaccio	
Fatty Crab | **multi.**	20
NEW Fatty 'Cue | **W'burg**	23

Alfred Portale	
Z Gotham B&G | **G Vill**	27
Michael Psilakis	
Kefi | **W 80s**	22
Mary Redding	
Brooklyn Fish | **Park Slope**	23
Mary's Fish | **W Vill**	25
Eric Ripert	
Z Le Bernardin | **W 50s**	29
Missy Robbins	
Z A Voce | **multi.**	24
Joël Robuchon	
Z L'Atelier/Robuchon | **E 50s**	27
Richard Sandoval	
Pampano | **E 40s**	24
NEW Zengo | **E 40s**	24
Suvir Saran	
Z Dévi | **Flatiron**	23
Gari Sugio	
Z Gari/Sushi | **multi.**	27
Nao Sugiyama	
Z Sugiyama | **W 50s**	26
Masayoshi Takayama	
Z Masa/Bar Masa | **W 60s**	27
Bill Telepan	
Z Telepan | **W 60s**	26
Sue Torres	
Sueños | **Chelsea**	24
Laurent Tourondel	
BLT Market | **W 50s**	22
Tom Valenti	
Z Ouest | **W 80s**	24
Jean-Georges Vongerichten	
Z NEW ABC Kitchen | **Flatiron**	24
Z Jean Georges | **W 60s**	28
JoJo | **E 60s**	25
NEW Mark | **E 70s**	24
Matsugen | **TriBeCa**	23
Mercer Kitchen | **SoHo**	22
Perry St. | **W Vill**	25
Z Spice Market | **Meatpacking**	23
Jonathan Waxman	
Barbuto | **W Vill**	23
Michael White	
Z Alto | **E 50s**	26
Z Convivio | **E 40s**	26
Z Marea | **W 50s**	27
Naomichi Yasuda	
Z Sushi Yasuda | **E 40s**	28
Geoffrey Zakarian	
NEW Lambs Club | **Financial**	—
Galen Zamarra	
Z Mas | **W Vill**	27

CHEESE SPECIALISTS

🛾 Adour | E 50s	26
🛾 Artisanal | Murray Hill	23
🛾 Babbo | G Vill	27
Bar Boulud | W 60s	23
Celeste | W 80s	24
Craft | Flatiron	25
🛾 Daniel | E 60s	28
NEW Eataly | Flatiron	-
🛾 Eleven Madison | Flatiron	28
Gordon Ramsay | W 50s	23
🛾 Gramercy Tavern | Flatiron	20
'Inoteca | multi.	22
🛾 Jean Georges | W 60s	28
🛾 La Grenouille | E 50s	28
NEW Maialino | Gramercy	25
🛾 Modern | W 50s	26
Otto | G Vill	22
🛾 Per Se | W 60s	28
🛾 Picholine | W 60s	27
NEW Plaza Food Hall | W 50s	22
Terroir | multi.	24

CHEF'S TABLE

Abigael's | Garment	20
🛾 Acappella | TriBeCa	25
Aldea | Flatiron	25
🛾 Aquavit | E 50s	25
Avra | E 40s	25
Bar Boulud | W 60s	23
Barbuto | W Vill	23
Café Select | SoHo	19
Gordon Ramsay | W 50s	23
Hearth | E Vill	24
House | Gramercy	22
🛾 Il Buco | NoHo	26
Kyo Ya | E Vill	26
Maloney/Porcelli | E 50s	23
🛾 Megu | TriBeCa	24
Mercadito | E Vill	23
Montenapo | W 40s	21
Oceana | W 40s	23
Olives | Union Sq	23
Palma | W Vill	22
🛾 Park Avenue ... | E 60s	25
Patroon | E 40s	22
Remi | W 50s	23
NEW SD26 | Murray Hill	22
🛾 Smith/Wollensky | E 40s	24
Sojourn | E 70s	22
Solo | E 50s	26
Tosca Café | Bronx	21
🛾 Valbella | Meatpacking	25
NEW Wall/Water | Financial	21
Yuva | E 50s	23

CHILD-FRIENDLY

(*children's menu available)

Alice's Tea* | W 70s	19
Amorina* | Prospect Hts	25
Amy Ruth's | Harlem	20
Arirang Hibachi* | multi.	19
Artie's Deli* | W 80s	18
Bamonte's | W'burg	23
Barrio* | Park Slope	17
Bar Tano | Park Slope	21
Bar Toto | Park Slope	21
Beacon* | W 50s	22
Belleville* | Park Slope	18
BLT Burger* | G Vill	21
🛾 Blue Ribbon* | multi.	25
Blue Smoke* | Murray Hill	21
Boathouse* | E 70s	18
Bocca Lupo* | Cobble Hill	24
Brennan | Sheepshead	21
Brooklyn Fish* | Park Slope	23
Bubba Gump* | W 40s	14
Bubby's* | multi.	18
Buttermilk* | Carroll Gdns	24
Café Habana/Outpost | Ft Greene	22
Cafe Un Deux* | W 40s	17
Carmine's* | W 40s	20
ChipShop* | multi.	19
Cowgirl* | W Vill	16
Dallas BBQ | multi.	15
🛾 DBGB* | E Vill	22
Dean's | multi.	18
EJ's Luncheon.* | multi.	16
NEW El Ay Si* | LIC	-
Farm/Adderley* | Ditmas Pk	24
Fatty Crab* | multi.	20
Friend/Farmer* | Gramercy	19
Gabriela's* | W 90s	18
Gargiulo's | Coney Is	22
Good Enough/Eat* | W 80s	20
Jackson Hole* | multi.	17
Joe & Pat's | SI	23
Junior's* | multi.	17
Klee Brass.* | Chelsea	19
L&B Spumoni* | Bensonhurst	24
Landmarc* | multi.	20
La Villa Pizzeria | multi.	21
London Lennie* | Rego Pk	22
Max* | multi.	21
Max Brenner* | G Vill	20
Miss Mamie/Maude* | Harlem	20
Nick's | multi.	23
Ninja* | TriBeCa	17
Noodle Pudding | Bklyn Hts	24
Osso Buco | E 90s	19

Otto	**G Vill**	22
Peanut Butter Co.	**G Vill**	19
Petite Abeille*	**multi.**	18
Pig Heaven	**E 80s**	20
NEW Pulino's*	**NoLita**	19
Rack & Soul*	**W 100s**	21
Riverview*	**LIC**	20
Rock Ctr.*	**W 50s**	18
Ruby Foo's*	**W 40s**	19
Sambuca*	**W 70s**	20
Sarabeth's	**multi.**	20
Serendipity 3	**E 60s**	19
Shake Shack	**multi.**	23
Sweetiepie*	**W Vill**	15
Sylvia's*	**Harlem**	20
Tony's Di Napoli	**multi.**	20
Two Boots*	**multi.**	18
View*	**W 40s**	17
Virgil's BBQ*	**W 40s**	20
Whole Foods	**multi.**	19
Zero Otto	**Bronx**	25
Zum Stammtisch*	**Glendale**	23

COMMUTER OASES

Grand Central
Ammos	**E 40s**	22
Bobby Van's	**E 40s**	22
Brother Jimmy's	**E 40s**	16
Burger Heaven	**E 40s**	16
Cafe Centro	**E 40s**	20
Capital Grille	**E 40s**	24
Cipriani Dolci	**E 40s**	20
Dishes	**E 40s**	21
Docks Oyster	**E 40s**	19
Hale/Hearty	**E 40s**	19
Hatsuhana	**E 40s**	25
Junior's	**E 40s**	17
La Fonda/Sol	**E 40s**	22
Menchanko-tei	**E 40s**	20
Metrazur	**E 40s**	21
Michael Jordan	**E 40s**	21
Morton's	**E 40s**	24
Nanni	**E 40s**	25
☑ Oyster Bar	**E 40s**	22
Patroon	**E 40s**	22
Pepe	**E 40s**	21
Pershing Sq.	**E 40s**	15
☑ Sushi Yasuda	**E 40s**	28
Two Boots	**E 40s**	18

Penn Station
Gray's Papaya	**Garment**	20
Nick & Stef	**Garment**	21
Uncle Jack's	**Garment**	22

Port Authority
Angus McIndoe	**W 40s**	16
Chez Josephine	**W 40s**	20

Chimichurri Grill	**W 40s**	23
Dallas BBQ	**W 40s**	15
☑ Esca	**W 40s**	25
Etcetera Etcetera	**W 40s**	21
Heartland	**W 40s**	14
HK	**Garment**	18
☑ John's Pizzeria	**W 40s**	22
NEW L'Ybane	**W 40s**	-
Marseille	**W 40s**	20
Montenapo	**W 40s**	21
Rachel's American	**W 40s**	17
Schnipper´s	**W 40s**	19
Shorty's	**W 40s**	24
Shula's	**W 40s**	20
West Bank	**W 40s**	19

ENTERTAINMENT

(Call for days and times
of performances)
Blue Fin	jazz	**W 40s**	22
Blue Smoke	jazz	**Murray Hill**	21
☑ Blue Water	jazz	**Union Sq**	23
Cafe Steinhof	varies	**Park Slope**	20
Cávo	dancing	**Astoria**	20
Chez Josephine	piano	**W 40s**	20
Cornelia St. Cafe	varies	**W Vill**	19
Delta Grill	live music	**W 40s**	19
Flor/Sol	flamenco dance	**TriBeCa**	20
Jules	jazz	**E Vill**	20
Knickerbocker	jazz	**G Vill**	20
La Lunchonette	varies	**Chelsea**	21
Londel's	jazz	**Harlem**	20
☑ River Café	piano	**Dumbo**	26
Sofrito	dancing	**E 50s**	22
Son Cubano	dancing	**Meatpacking**	21
Sylvia's	varies	**Harlem**	19
Tommaso	piano & vocalist	**Dyker Hts**	24
Walker's	jazz	**TriBeCa**	18

FIREPLACES

A Casa Fox	**LES**	20
Aegean Cove	**Astoria**	24
Alberto	**Forest Hills**	23
Ali Baba	**E 40s**	21
Allegretti	**Flatiron**	23
Alta	**G Vill**	24
Antica Venezia	**W Vill**	22
Applewood	**Park Slope**	25
Arté	**G Vill**	18
Battery Gdns.	**Financial**	17
Benjamin Steak	**E 40s**	25
Bistro Ten 18	**W 100s**	19
Black Duck	**Murray Hill**	21
Boathouse	**E 70s**	18

Bouley | **TriBeCa**	27
Bourbon St. Café | **Bayside**	17
Bruckner B&G | **Bronx**	19
Cebu | **Bay Ridge**	22
Christos | **Astoria**	23
Cornelia St. Cafe | **W Vill**	19
Cucina/Pesce | **E Vill**	19
Dee's | **Forest Hills**	21
Delta Grill | **W 40s**	19
Elizabeth | **NoLita**	18
Employees Only | **W Vill**	20
F & J Pine | **Bronx**	22
Z FireBird | **W 40s**	20
5 9th | **Meatpacking**	19
Frankie/Johnnie | **Garment**	23
Friend/Farmer | **Gramercy**	19
Geisha | **E 60s**	23
Giorgione | **SoHo**	24
Glass House | **W 40s**	21
Greenhouse | **Bay Ridge**	19
Ilouse | **Gramercy**	22
Ici | **Ft Greene**	22
I Trulli | **Murray Hill**	23
Z Keens | **Garment**	25
Lady Mendl's | **Gramercy**	21
Lake Club | **SI**	23
NEW Lambs Club | **Financial**	-
La Ripaille | **W Vill**	20
Lattanzi | **W 40s**	22
Le Barricou | **W'burg**	21
Lobster Box | **Bronx**	18
Lorenzo's | **SI**	23
Manducatis | **LIC**	23
Molly's | **Gramercy**	20
Nino's | **E 50s**	20
Nurnberger | **SI**	21
Z One if by Land | **W Vill**	24
Park | **Chelsea**	17
Pearl Room | **Bay Ridge**	22
Z Per Se | **W 60s**	28
Piccola Venezia | **Astoria**	25
Place | **W Vill**	21
Z Public | **NoLita**	24
Quality Meats | **W 50s**	24
NEW Rabbit in Moon | **G Vill**	-
Sac's Place | **Astoria**	23
Savoy | **SoHo**	24
Scottadito | **Park Slope**	21
Sheep Sta. | **Park Slope**	18
South Gate | **W 50s**	24
STK | **Meatpacking**	23
NEW Tartinery | **NoLita**	-
Telly's Taverna | **Astoria**	23
Z Terrace in Sky | **W 100s**	22
Tosca Café | **Bronx**	21

Trattoria Cinque | **TriBeCa**	22
Triomphe | **W 40s**	23
Z 21 Club | **W 50s**	22
Vivolo/Cucina | **E 70s**	21
Water Club | **Murray Hill**	21
Z Water's Edge | **LIC**	20
Z Waverly Inn | **W Vill**	20
WD-50 | **LES**	25

GREEN/LOCAL/ ORGANIC

(Places specializing in organic, local ingredients)

Z NEW ABC Kitchen | **Flatiron**	24
Aldea | **Flatiron**	25
Amy's Bread | **multi.**	24
Angelica Kit. | **E Vill**	21
Applewood | **Park Slope**	25
Aroma | **NoHo**	23
Z Aureole | **W 40s**	26
Aurora | **multi.**	24
Z Babbo | **G Vill**	27
Back Forty | **E Vill**	22
Z Barbetta | **W 40s**	20
Bar Boulud | **W 60s**	23
Barbuto | **W Vill**	23
Bark Hot Dogs | **Park Slope**	21
Belcourt | **E Vill**	19
Blossom | **Chelsea**	22
BLT Market | **W 50s**	22
Z Blue Hill | **G Vill**	27
Brown Café | **LES**	22
Buttermilk | **Carroll Gdns**	24
Café Habana/Outpost | **Ft Greene**	22
Candle Cafe | **E 70s**	23
Candle 79 | **E 70s**	24
Caravan/Dreams | **E Vill**	22
Chennai Gdn. | **Murray Hill**	21
Chestnut | **Carroll Gdns**	23
City Bakery | **Flatiron**	22
Clinton St. Baking | **LES**	24
Community Food | **W 100s**	22
Cookshop | **Chelsea**	22
Counter | **E Vill**	21
Craft | **Flatiron**	25
Z Degustation | **E Vill**	27
Dell'anima | **W Vill**	25
Dirt Candy | **E Vill**	27
Z Dovetail | **W 70s**	26
NEW Eataly | **Flatiron**	-
Egg | **W'burg**	23
Z Eleven Madison | **Flatiron**	28
Z Esca | **W 40s**	25
Falai | **LES**	25
Farm/Adderley | **Ditmas Pk**	24
Z Fette Sau | **W'burg**	25

SPECIAL FEATURES

Flatbush Farm | **Park Slope** 21
Fornino | **W'burg** 23
Frankies | **multi.** 24
Franny's | **Prospect Hts** 24
Gen. Greene | **Ft Greene** 20
Gobo | **multi.** 22
Good Enough/Eat | **W 80s** 20
Good Fork | **Red Hook** 25
🆉 Gotham B&G | **G Vill** 27
🆉 Gramercy Tavern | **Flatiron** 28
🆉 Grocery | **Carroll Gdns** 26
Harrison | **TriBeCa** 24
Hearth | **E Vill** 24
Home | **W Vill** 22
Hundred Acres | **SoHo** 19
Ici | **Ft Greene** 22
🆉 Il Buco | **NoHo** 26
Isabella's | **W 70s** 20
James | **Prospect Hts** 24
🆉 Jewel Bako | **E Vill** 26
Jimmy's | **E Vill** 22
Josephina | **W 60s** 18
Josie's | **multi.** 19
L'Artusi | **W Vill** 24
Le Pain Q. | **Flatiron** 18
🆕 Lincoln | **W 60s** -
Little Giant | **LES** 23
Locanda Verde | **TriBeCa** 24
Marc Forgione | **TriBeCa** 24
Market Table | **W Vill** 23
Marlow/Sons | **W'burg** 24
🆉 Mas | **W Vill** 27
New Leaf | **Wash. Hts** 21
🆕 Northern Spy | **E Vill** 23
Palo Santo | **Park Slope** 25
Peaches | **Bed-Stuy** 22
🆉 Per Se | **W 60s** 28
Picnic | **W 100s** 20
🆕 Print | **W 40s** 25
Pure Food/Wine | **Gramercy** 23
Quaint | **Sunnyside** 25
Recipe | **W 80s** 22
Rose Water | **Park Slope** 25
Rouge Tomate | **E 60s** 23
🆉 Saul | **Boerum Hill** 26
Savoy | **SoHo** 24
🆕 Seersucker | **Carroll Gdns** -
Sfoglia | **E 90s** 23
🆉 Telepan | **W 60s** 26
🆕 Tipsy Parson | **Chelsea** 18
🆉 Tocqueville | **Union Sq** 25
🆉 Union Sq. Cafe | **Union Sq** 26
🆕 Vanderbilt | **Prospect Hts** 21
Vesta | **Astoria** 24
🆕 Wall/Water | **Financial** 21

Whole Foods | **multi.** 19
Zen Palate | **W 40s** 19

HISTORIC PLACES

(Year opened; * building)

1767 | One if by Land* | **W Vill** 24
1794 | Bridge Cafe* | **Financial** 22
1864 | Pete's Tavern | **Gramercy** 16
1868 | Landmark Tavern* | **W 40s** 18
1868 | Old Homestead | **Meatpacking** 24
1884 | P.J. Clarke's | **E 50s** 17
1885 | Keens | **Garment** 25
1887 | Peter Luger | **W'burg** 27
1888 | Katz's Deli | **LES** 24
1890 | Walker's* | **TriBeCa** 18
1892 | Ferrara | **L Italy** 23
1894 | Veniero's | **E Vill** 24
1896 | Rao's | **Harlem** 22
1900 | Bamonte's | **W'burg** 23
1902 | Algonquin | **W 40s** 18
1902 | Angelo's/Mulberry | **L Italy** 23
1904 | Lanza | **E Vill** 18
1904 | Vincent's | **L Italy** 21
1906 | Barbetta | **W 40s** 20
1907 | Gargiulo's | **Coney Is** 22
1907 | Oak Room | **W 50s** 20
1908 | Barney Greengrass | **W 80s** 24
1908 | John's/12th St. | **E Vill** 21
1910 | Wolfgang's* | **Murray Hill** 25
1913 | Oyster Bar | **E 40s** 22
1919 | Mario's | **Bronx** 21
1920 | Leo's Latticini | **Corona** 26
1920 | Waverly Inn | **W Vill** 20
1921 | Sardi's | **W 40s** 17
1922 | Defonte's | **Red Hook** 22
1922 | Rocco | **G Vill** 21
1922 | Tosca Café | **Bronx** 21
1924 | Totonno Pizza | **Coney Is** 21
1925 | El Charro | **W Vill** 22
1926 | Frankie/Johnnie | **W 40s** 23
1926 | Palm | **E 40s** 24
1927 | Ann & Tony's | **Bronx** 20
1927 | Diner* | **W'burg** 22
1927 | El Faro | **W Vill** 22
1927 | Gallagher's | **W 50s** 21
1929 | Eleven Madison* | **Flatiron** 28
1929 | John's Pizzeria | **W Vill** 22
1929 | Russian Tea | **W 50s** 19
1929 | 21 Club | **W 50s** 22
1930 | Carlyle | **E 70s** 23
1930 | El Quijote | **Chelsea** 21
1933 | Patsy's Pizzeria | **Harlem** 20
1936 | Monkey Bar | **E 50s** 17
1936 | Tom's | **Prospect Hts** 21
1937 | Carnegie Deli | **W 50s** 22

1937 | Denino | **SI**	26	Chatwal Hotel	
1937 | Minetta | **G Vill**	24	**NEW** Lambs Club | **Financial**	–
1937 | Stage Deli | **W 50s**	20	City Club Hotel	
1938 | Brennan | **Sheepshead**	21	**Z** DB Bistro Moderne | **W 40s**	25
1938 | Heidelberg | **E 80s**	20	Cooper Square Hotel	
1938 | Wo Hop | **Chinatown**	21	**NEW** Faustina | **E Vill**	23
1939 | L&B Spumoni | **Bensonhurst**	24	Crosby Street Hotel	
1941 | Commerce | **W Vill**	23	**NEW** Crosby Bar | **SoHo**	19
1941 | Sevilla | **W Vill**	22	Dream Hotel	
1943 | Forlini's | **Chinatown**	20	Serafina | **W 50s**	19
1944 | Patsy's | **W 50s**	22	Dylan Hotel	
1945 | Ben's Best | **Rego Pk**	23	Benjamin Steak | **E 40s**	25
1945 | V&T | **W 100s**	18	Edison Hotel	
1946 | Lobster Box | **Bronx**	18	Edison | **W 40s**	15
1950 | Junior's | **Downtown Bklyn**	17	Elysée Hotel	
1953 | Liebman's | **Bronx**	22	**Z** Monkey Bar | **E 50s**	17
1954 | Serendipity 3 | **E 60s**	19	Empire Hotel	
1954 | Veselka | **E Vill**	19	**NEW** Ed's Chowder | **W 60s**	19
1957 | Arturo's | **G Vill**	21	Fashion 26 Hotel	
1957 | La Taza de Oro | **Chelsea**	21	Rare B&G | **Chelsea**	21
1958 | Queen | **Bklyn Hts**	24	Four Seasons Hotel	
1959 | Brasserie | **E 50s**	20	**Z** L'Atelier/Robuchon | **E 50s**	27
1959 | El Parador Cafe | **Murray Hill**	22		
1959 | Four Seasons | **E 50s**	26	Gansevoort Hotel	
1959 | London Lennie | **Rego Pk**	22	**NEW** Tanuki | **Meatpacking**	19
1959 | Rizzo's Pizza | **Astoria**	23	Gramercy Park Hotel	
1960 | Bull & Bear | **E 40s**	21	**NEW** Maialino | **Gramercy**	25
1960 | Chez Napoléon | **W 50s**	21	Greenwich Hotel	
1960 | Joe & Pat's | **SI**	23	Locanda Verde | **TriBeCa**	24
1960 | Molly's | **Gramercy**	20	Hilton Garden Inn	
1961 | Corner Bistro | **W Vill**	22	Pigalle | **W 40s**	17

HOTEL DINING

Ace Hotel		Hudson Hotel	
Z NEW Breslin | **Chelsea**	21	**NEW** Hudson Hall | **W 50s**	–
NEW No. 7 Sub | **Chelsea**	23	Ink48 Hotel	
Alex Hotel		**NEW** Print | **W 40s**	25
Riingo | **E 40s**	21	Inn at Irving Pl.	
Algonquin Hotel		Lady Mendl's | **Gramercy**	21
Algonquin | **W 40s**	18	InterContinental NY Times Sq.	
Amsterdam Court Hotel		**NEW** Ça Va | **W 40s**	–
Natsumi | **W 50s**	24	Shake Shack | **W 40s**	23
Andaz Wall Street Hotel		Iroquois Hotel	
NEW Wall/Water | **Financial**	21	Triomphe | **W 40s**	23
Blakely Hotel		Jane Hotel	
Abboccato | **W 50s**	21	Cafe Gitane | **W Vill**	20
Bowery Hotel		Jumeirah Essex Hse.	
Gemma | **E Vill**	20	South Gate | **W 50s**	24
Bryant Park Hotel		Le Parker Meridien	
Koi | **W 40s**	23	Burger Joint/Le Parker | **W 50s**	24
Carlyle Hotel		Norma's | **W 50s**	25
Z Carlyle | **E 70s**	23	Loews Regency Hotel	
Chambers Hotel		**Z** Regency | **E 60s**	19
NEW Má Pêche | **W 50s**	22	London NYC Hotel	
Momofuku Bakery | **W 50s**	22	Gordon Ramsay | **W 50s**	23
		Maze | **W 50s**	22

Lowell Hotel
Post House | **E 60s** _24_

Mandarin Oriental Hotel
Ⓩ Asiate | **W 60s** _24_

Maritime Hotel
Ⓩ Matsuri | **Chelsea** _22_

Mark Hotel
NEW Mark | **E 70s** _24_

Marriott Marquis Hotel
View | **W 40s** _17_

Mercer Hotel
Mercer Kitchen | **SoHo** _22_

Michelangelo Hotel
Insieme | **W 50s** _23_

Morgans Hotel
Asia de Cuba | **Murray Hill** _23_

NY Marriott Brooklyn
Morton's | **Downtown Bklyn** _24_

NY Palace Hotel
Ⓩ Gilt | **E 50s** _24_

Park South Hotel
Black Duck | **Murray Hill** _21_

Pierre Hotel
NEW Le Caprice | **E 60s** _17_

Plaza Hotel
Oak Room | **W 50s** _20_
Palm Court | **W 50s** _-_
NEW Plaza Food Hall | **W 50s** _22_

Pod Hotel
NEW East Side Social | **E 50s** _17_

Ritz-Carlton Battery Park
2 West | **Financial** _21_

Ritz-Carlton Central Park
BLT Market | **W 50s** _22_

San Carlos Hotel
Mint | **E 50s** _22_

Shelburne Murray Hill Hotel
Rare B&G | **Murray Hill** _21_

Sherry-Netherland Hotel
Harry Cipriani | **E 50s** _21_

6 Columbus Hotel
Blue Ribbon Sushi B&G | **W 50s** _24_

60 Thompson
Kittichai | **SoHo** _23_

Smyth Hotel
NEW Plein Sud | **TriBeCa** _18_

Standard Hotel
Ⓩ Standard Grill | **Meatpacking** _21_

Stay Hotel
Aspen Social | **W 40s** _18_

St. Regis Hotel
Ⓩ Adour | **E 50s** _26_

Surrey Hotel
Ⓩ Café Boulud | **E 70s** _27_

Thompson LES Hotel
Shang | **LES** _21_

Time Hotel
Serafina | **W 40s** _19_

Trump Int'l Hotel
Ⓩ Jean Georges | **W 60s** _28_
Ⓩ Jean Georges Noug. | **W 60s** _27_

Trump SoHo Hotel
NEW Quattro Gastro. | **SoHo** _21_

Waldorf-Astoria
Bull & Bear | **E 40s** _21_

Wales Hotel
Paola's | **E 90s** _22_

Washington Square Hotel
North Sq. | **G Vill** _23_

Westin Times Sq. Hotel
Shula's | **W 40s** _20_

W Hotel Downtown
NEW BLT B&G | **Financial** _-_

W Hotel Times Sq.
Blue Fin | **W 40s** _22_

W Hotel Union Sq.
Olives | **Union Sq** _23_

JACKET REQUIRED

Ⓩ Carlyle | **E 70s** _23_
Ⓩ Daniel | **E 60s** _28_
Ⓩ Four Seasons | **E 50s** _26_
Ⓩ Jean Georges | **W 60s** _28_
Ⓩ La Grenouille | **E 50s** _28_
Ⓩ Le Bernardin | **W 50s** _29_
Ⓩ Le Cirque | **E 50s** _24_
Le Perigord | **E 50s** _25_
Ⓩ Modern | **W 50s** _26_
Ⓩ Per Se | **W 60s** _28_
Ⓩ River Café | **Dumbo** _26_
Ⓩ 21 Club | **W 50s** _22_

JURY DUTY

(Near Foley Sq.)
Ⓩ Acappella | **TriBeCa** _25_
Big Wong | **Chinatown** _22_
Blaue Gans | **TriBeCa** _22_
Bo-Ky | **Chinatown** _22_
Ⓩ Bouley | **TriBeCa** _27_
Bread | **TriBeCa** _20_
Carl's Steaks | **TriBeCa** _20_
Centrico | **TriBeCa** _20_
City Hall | **TriBeCa** _21_
Dim Sum Go Go | **Chinatown** _20_
Ecco | **TriBeCa** _22_
Excellent Dumpling | **Chinatown** _20_
Forlini's | **Chinatown** _20_
Fuleen | **Chinatown** _22_
Golden Unicorn | **Chinatown** _21_
Great NY Noodle | **Chinatown** _22_

Jing Fong | **Chinatown** | 19
Joe's | **Chinatown** | 20
Mandarin Court | **Chinatown** | 20
Nam | **TriBeCa** | 22
Nha Trang | **Chinatown** | 22
Nice Green Bo | **Chinatown** | 23
Odeon | **TriBeCa** | 20
🆉 Oriental Gdn. | **Chinatown** | 24
Peking Duck | **Chinatown** | 23
Petite Abeille | **TriBeCa** | 18
Pho Viet Huong | **Chinatown** | 22
Ping's Sea. | **Chinatown** | 22
Pongsri Thai | **Chinatown** | 20
Red Egg | **L Italy** | 21
Shanghai Cuisine | **Chinatown** | 22
Takahachi | **TriBeCa** | 24
Wo Hop | **Chinatown** | 21

LATE DINING

(Weekday closing hour)

Agua Dulce | 3:30 AM | **W 50s** | 22
Artichoke Basille | 3 AM | **E Vill** | 23
Arturo's | 1 AM | **G Vill** | 21
Baraonda | 1 AM | **E 70s** | 19
NEW Bar Paya | varies | **E Vill** | –
Bereket | 24 hrs. | **LES** | 19
Big Nick's | varies | **W 70s** | 18
🆉 Blue Ribbon | varies | **SoHo** | 25
🆉 Blue Ribbon Sushi | varies | **SoHo** | 26
Blue Ribbon Sushi B&G | 2 AM | **W 50s** | 24
Bocca di Bacco | 2 AM | **W 50s** | 22
Bon Chon | varies | **multi.** | 20
Brennan | 1 AM | **Sheepshead** | 21
Bubby's | 24 hrs. | **TriBeCa** | 18
Cafeteria | 24 hrs. | **Chelsea** | 19
Caffe Cielo | 1 AM | **W 50s** | 20
🆉 Carnegie Deli | 3:30 AM | **W 50s** | 22
Cebu | 3 AM | **Bay Ridge** | 22
Chickpea | varies | **Flatiron** | 19
Coffee Shop | varies | **Union Sq** | 15
NEW Collective | varies | **Meatpacking** | 21
Corner Bistro | 3:30 AM | **W Vill** | 22
NEW Corsino | 2 AM | **W Vill** | 20
Dell'anima | 2 AM | **W Vill** | 25
Ditch Plains | 2 AM | **W Vill** | 18
DuMont | 2 AM | **W'burg** | 23
Elaine's | 2 AM | **E 80s** | 14
Elizabeth | 2 AM | **NoLita** | 18
El Malecon | varies | **Wash. Hts** | 22
Empanada Mama | 1 AM | **W 50s** | 22
Empire Szechuan | varies | **multi.** | 16
Employees Only | 3:30 AM | **W Vill** | 20

Frank | 1 AM | **E Vill** | 24
French Roast | 24 hrs. | **multi.** | 17
Fuleen | 2:30 AM | **Chinatown** | 22
Gahm Mi Oak | 24 hrs. | **Garment** | 20
Gottino | 2 AM | **W Vill** | 22
Gray's Papaya | 24 hrs. | **multi.** | 20
Great NY Noodle | 4 AM | **Chinatown** | 22
NEW Henry Public | 1 AM | **Cobble Hill** | 17
NEW Hide-Chan | 2 AM | **E 50s** | –
HK | 1 AM | **Garment** | 18
'Ino | 2 AM | **W Vill** | 24
'Inoteca | 3 AM | **multi.** | 22
I Tre Merli | varies | **W Vill** | 19
Jackson Hole | varies | **multi.** | 17
J.G. Melon | 2:30 AM | **E 70s** | 21
Joe's Pizza | 5 AM | **W Vill** | 23
Joseph Leonard | 2 AM | **W Vill** | 22
Kang Suh | 24 hrs. | **Garment** | 22
Kati Roll | varies | **G Vill** | 21
NEW Kenmare | 1 AM | **L Italy** | 21
Knickerbocker | 1 AM | **G Vill** | 20
Kum Gang San | 24 hrs. | **multi.** | 21
Kyochon | 2 AM | **Murray Hill** | 20
La Esquina | 2 AM | **L Italy** | 22
NEW La Gazzetta | 1:30 AM | **Meatpacking** | –
Landmarc | 2 AM | **multi.** | 20
L'Express | 24 hrs. | **Flatiron** | 18
Lil' Frankie | 2 AM | **E Vill** | 23
Lime Jungle | 1 AM | **W 50s** | –
NEW Los Feliz | 2 AM | **LES** | 20
Lucky Strike | varies | **SoHo** | 17
NEW L'Ybane | 2 AM | **W 40s** | –
Macao Trading | 4 AM | **TriBeCa** | 18
Maison | 24 hrs. | **W 50s** | 19
Mari Vanna | 1 AM | **Flatiron** | 20
NEW Mark | 1 AM | **E 70s** | 24
NEW Masala Times | 3 AM | **G Vill** | –
Max SoHa/Caffe | varies | **W 100s** | 20
NEW Meatball Shop | varies | **LES** | 22
🆉 Minetta | 2 AM | **G Vill** | 24
M Shanghai/Noodle | 6 AM | **W'burg** | 21
99 Mi. to Philly | 1 AM | **E Vill** | 19
Ollie's | varies | **W 100s** | 16
Omonia | 4 AM | **multi.** | 20
Park | 1 AM | **Chelsea** | 17
Pastis | varies | **Meatpacking** | 21
Pink Tea Cup | 2 AM | **W Vill** | –
P.J. Clarke's | varies | **multi.** | 17
Pop Burger | varies | **multi.** | 18

SPECIAL FEATURES

Prime Meat | 2 AM | **Carroll Gdns**	24
NEW Pulino's | 2 AM | **NoLita**	19
Redhead | 1 AM | **E Vill**	22
Roll-n-Roaster | 1 AM | **Sheepshead**	21
Sahara | 2 AM | **Gravesend**	22
Sammy's Fishbox | 2 AM | **Bronx**	20
Sarge's Deli | 24 hrs. | **Murray Hill**	20
Shorty's | varies | **W 40s**	24
Sorella | 2 AM | **LES**	24
NEW South Houston | 2 AM | **SoHo**	–
Spotted Pig | 2 AM | **W Vill**	23
Stage Deli | 2 AM | **W 50s**	20
Stanton Social | 3 AM | **LES**	23
SushiSamba | varies | **multi.**	22
Z Sushi Seki | 2:30 AM | **E 60s**	26
Tacos Matamoros | 1 AM | **Sunset Pk**	25
Tatiana | 1 AM | **Brighton Bch**	21
Terroir | varies | **E Vill**	24
NEW This Little Piggy | 5 AM | **E Vill**	23
Tio Pepe | 1 AM | **W Vill**	19
Tosca Café | 1 AM | **Bronx**	21
NEW Traif | 2 AM | **W'burg**	–
NEW Travertine | 1 AM | **NoLita**	22
Two Boots | varies | **multi.**	18
Umberto's | 4 AM | **L Italy**	19
Uva | 2 AM | **E 70s**	21
Veloce Pizzeria | 1 AM | **E Vill**	20
Veselka | varies | **E Vill**	19
Viand | varies | **multi.**	17
Vincent's | 1:30 AM | **L Italy**	21
Walker's | 1 AM | **TriBeCa**	18
Walter Foods | varies | **W'burg**	23
Wollensky's | 2 AM | **E 40s**	23
WonJo | 24 hrs. | **Garment**	20
NEW Xiao Ye | 2 AM | **LES**	–

MEET FOR A DRINK

(Most top hotels, bars and
the following standouts)

Ajna Bar | **Meatpacking**	20
Algonquin | **W 40s**	18
Amaranth | **E 60s**	20
Z Artisanal | **Murray Hill**	23
Atlantic Grill | **E 70s**	23
Aurora | **W'burg**	24
Z Balthazar | **SoHo**	23
Bar Boulud | **W 60s**	23
Barbounia | **Flatiron**	21
NEW Betel | **W Vill**	25
Blue Fin | **W 40s**	22
Z Blue Water | **Union Sq**	23
Z Bond St. | **NoHo**	25

Boqueria | **Flatiron**	22
Brick Cafe | **Astoria**	22
Bryant Park | **W 40s**	18
Z Buddakan | **Chelsea**	24
Bull & Bear | **E 40s**	21
Z Cafe Luxembourg | **W 70s**	20
Cafe Steinhof | **Park Slope**	20
Centro Vinoteca | **W Vill**	21
City Hall | **TriBeCa**	21
City Winery | **SoHo**	16
NEW Colicchio/Sons | **Chelsea**	23
Z Compass | **W 70s**	22
Z Daniel | **E 60s**	28
Z Del Frisco's | **W 40s**	25
Demarchelier | **E 80s**	18
Dos Caminos | **multi.**	20
Double Crown | **NoHo**	20
Dressler | **W'burg**	25
Employees Only | **W Vill**	20
Five Leaves | **Greenpt**	25
Flatbush Farm | **Park Slope**	21
Z Four Seasons | **E 50s**	26
Freemans | **LES**	21
Geisha | **E 60s**	23
Glass House | **W 40s**	21
Z Gotham B&G | **G Vill**	27
Z Gramercy Tavern | **Flatiron**	28
Harry's Cafe/Steak | **Financial**	23
Hillstone | **multi.**	21
HK | **Garment**	18
Hotel Griffou | **G Vill**	19
House | **Gramercy**	22
Hudson River | **Harlem**	21
'Inoteca | **LES**	22
Z Jean Georges | **W 60s**	28
J.G. Melon | **E 70s**	21
Z Keens | **Garment**	25
Kellari Tav./Parea | **W 40s**	22
Koi | **W 40s**	23
La Fonda/Sol | **E 40s**	22
Landmarc | **W 60s**	20
Z Le Cirque | **E 50s**	24
Le Colonial | **E 50s**	21
Lucky Strike | **SoHo**	17
Macao Trading | **TriBeCa**	18
Maloney/Porcelli | **E 50s**	23
Mari Vanna | **Flatiron**	20
NEW Mark | **E 70s**	24
Markt | **Flatiron**	19
Z Masa/Bar Masa | **W 60s**	27
Z Matsuri | **Chelsea**	22
Maze | **W 50s**	22
Michael Jordan | **E 40s**	21
Z Modern | **W 50s**	26
Z Monkey Bar | **E 50s**	17

Montenapo | **W 40s**	21	Colicchio/Sons | **Chelsea**	23
🅉 Morimoto | **Chelsea**	25	Collective | **Meatpacking**	21
M Shanghai/Noodle | **W'burg**	21	Commodore | **W'burg**	-
Natsumi | **W 50s**	24	Corsino | **W Vill**	20
🅉 Nobu | **W 50s**	26	Crosby Bar | **SoHo**	19
Odeon | **TriBeCa**	20	Dos Toros | **E Vill**	24
Orsay | **E 70s**	18	East Side Social | **E 50s**	17
🅉 Ouest | **W 80s**	24	Eataly | **Flatiron**	-
Park | **Chelsea**	17	Ed's Chowder | **W 60s**	19
Pastis | **Meatpacking**	21	El Ay Si | **LIC**	-
Patroon | **E 40s**	22	Estiatorio Rafina | **Murray Hill**	-
Pera | **E 40s**	21	Fatty 'Cue | **W'burg**	23
🅉 Piano Due | **W 50s**	24	Fatty Fish | **E 60s**	22
Pies-n-Thighs | **W'burg**	23	Faustina | **E Vill**	23
P.J. Clarke's | **multi.**	17	Hecho en Dumbo | **NoHo**	25
Pop Burger | **E 50s**	18	Hello Pasta | **multi.**	-
Quaint | **Sunnyside**	25	Henry Public | **Cobble Hill**	17
Rayuela | **LES**	23	Hide-Chan | **E 50s**	-
Sala | **NoHo**	22	Highpoint | **Chelsea**	-
🆕 SD26 | **Murray Hill**	22	Hudson Eatery | **W 50s**	-
South Gate | **W 50s**	24	Hudson Hall | **W 50s**	-
🅉 Spice Market | **Meatpacking**	23	Hurricane Club | **Flatiron**	-
🅉 Standard Grill | **Meatpacking**	21	Il Matto | **TriBeCa**	-
Stanton Social | **LES**	23	Kaz An Nou | **Prospect Hts**	-
STK | **Meatpacking**	23	Kenmare | **L Italy**	21
Stone Park | **Park Slope**	25	Kouzina/Trata | **E 70s**	-
🅉 Tao | **E 50s**	21	La Gazzetta | **Meatpacking**	-
Tio Pepe | **W Vill**	19	Lambs Club | **Financial**	-
White Slab | **LES**	18	Le Caprice | **E 60s**	17
Wollensky's | **E 40s**	23	Le Parisien | **Murray Hill**	-
		Lina Frey | **LES**	-

NEWCOMERS (123)

		Lincoln | **W 60s**	-
🅉 ABC Kitchen | **Flatiron**	24	Lion | **G Vill**	-
Abe/Arthur | **Meatpacking**	22	Los Feliz | **LES**	20
Balaboosta | **NoLita**	-	Luke's Lobster | **multi.**	25
BaoHaus | **LES**	-	L'Ybane | **W 40s**	-
Bar Henry | **G Vill**	19	Lychee Hse. | **E 50s**	25
Bar Paya | **E Vill**	-	Macbar | **SoHo**	19
Benchmark | **Park Slope**	-	Maialino | **Gramercy**	25
B.E.S. | **Chelsea**	-	Má Pêche | **W 50s**	22
Betel | **W Vill**	25	Mappamondo | **W Vill**	-
Bill's Bar | **Meatpacking**	20	Marcony | **Murray Hill**	22
Bino | **Carroll Gdns**	-	Mark | **E 70s**	24
Bistro Vendôme | **E 50s**	21	Masala Times | **G Vill**	-
BLT B&G | **Financial**	-	Meatball Shop | **LES**	22
Bread/Butter | **Bklyn Hts**	18	Mile End | **Boerum Hill**	25
🅉 Bréslin | **Chelsea**	21	M. Wells | **LIC**	-
Broken Eng. | **Cobble Hill**	-	Mxco | **E 70s**	18
Café Colette | **W'burg**	-	Northern Spy | **E Vill**	23
Campo/Fiori | **Park Slope**	-	No. 7 Sub | **Chelsea**	23
Casa Lever | **E 50s**	23	Nuela | **Flatiron**	-
🅉 Cascabel | **E 80s**	25	Ofrenda | **W Vill**	25
Ça Va | **W 40s**	-	Olio | **W Vill**	-
Chom Chom | **W 50s**	-	Patty/Bun | **G Vill**	20
Choptank | **W Vill**	17	Peels | **E Vill**	-

Penny Farthing | **E Vill**	–
Plaza Food Hall | **W 50s**	22
Plein Sud | **TriBeCa**	18
Pop Art Bar | **E 60s**	–
Print | **W 40s**	25
Pulino's | **NoLita**	19
Purple Yam | **Ditmas Pk**	23
Qi | **Union Sq**	22
Quattro Gastro. | **SoHo**	21
Rabbit in Moon | **G Vill**	–
Ramen Kuidouraku | **multi.**	–
Recette | **W Vill**	24
Robataya | **E Vill**	23
Robert | **W 50s**	19
Rothschild's | **Boerum Hill**	–
Saltie | **W'burg**	25
Salumè | **SoHo**	–
SD26 | **Murray Hill**	22
Seersucker | **Carroll Gdns**	–
South Houston | **SoHo**	–
Spot | **E Vill**	23
St. Anselm | **W'burg**	–
Strong Pl. | **Cobble Hill**	–
Taberna | **W 80s**	–
Takashi | **W Vill**	–
Tanuki | **Meatpacking**	19
Tartinery | **NoLita**	–
Taureau | **E Vill**	–
Testaccio | **LIC**	22
This Little Piggy | **E Vill**	23
Thistle Hill | **Park Slope**	–
Tipsy Parson | **Chelsea**	18
Torrisi | **NoLita**	27
Totto Ramen | **W 50s**	–
Traif | **W'burg**	–
Travertine | **NoLita**	22
Tre Otto | **E 90s**	21
Vandaag | **E Vill**	–
Vanderbilt | **Prospect Hts**	21
Vapiano | **G Vill**	–
Village Tart | **NoLita**	20
Wall/Water | **Financial**	21
Wright | **E 80s**	21
Xiao Ye | **LES**	–
Zengo | **E 40s**	24

NEWCOMERS ON TAP

(keep posted at ZAGAT.com)

Ai Fiori | *Italian* | **Garment**
Baorito | *Asian/Mex.* | **Gramercy**
Bar Basque | *Basque* | **Chelsea**
Beauty & Essex | *Amer.* | **LES**
Bell Book & Candle | *Amer.* | **W Vill**
Brushstroke | *Japanese* | **TriBeCa**
Chinito | *Asian/Mex.* | **LES**
Ciano | *Italian* | **Flatiron**

Donatella | *Pizza* | **Chelsea**	
Essbar | *Austrian* | **E Vill**	
Fedora | *Amer.* | **G Vill**	
Fish Tag | *Med./Seafood* | **W 70s**	
FoodParc | *Eclectic* | **Chelsea**	
FPB | *Bakery* | **G Vill**	
Highliner | *Amer.* | **Chelsea**	
Hill Country Chicken | *Ch.* | **Flatiron**	
Imperial No. 9 | *Seafood* | **SoHo**	
J&S Food Hall | *Amer.* | **NoLita**	
Jeffrey's | *Amer.* | **W Vill**	
John Dory | *Seafood* | **Chelsea**	
Kin Shop | *Thai* | **W Vill**	
Lani Kai | *Polynesian* | **SoHo**	
La Petite Maison | *French* | **W 50s**	
Lincoln | *Amer.* | **W 60s**	
Mary Queen of Scots | *Scot.* | **LES**	
Mehtaphor | *Amer.* | **TriBeCa**	
MexiQ | *Mex.* | **Astoria**	
Millesime | *Seafood* | **Murray Hill**	
MPD | *Amer.* | **Meatpacking**	
National | *Amer.* | **E 50s**	
Neely's Pig Parlor | *BBQ* | **E 60s**	
Niko | *Japanese* | **SoHo**	
Osteria Morini | *Italian* | **SoHo**	
Porsena | *Italian* | **E Vill**	
Redfarm | *Amer./Asian* | **W Vill**	
Red Rooster | *Amer.* | **Harlem**	
Riverpark | *Amer.* | **Murray Hill**	
Spritzenhaus | *Gastro.* | **Greenpt**	
Tribeca Canvas | *Amer./Japanese* | **TriBeCa**	
Tulsi | *Indian* | **E 40s**	
Valentino's on Green | *It.* | **Bayside**	
Villa Pacri | *Italian* | **Meatpacking**	

NOTEWORTHY CLOSINGS (90)

Allen & Delancey
Anselmo's Pizza
Arqua
Bar Artisanal
BarBao
Bar Blanc Bistro
Bellavitae
Beppe
Bistro du Nord
Bizaare Avenue Cafe
Borgo Antico
Bouley Upstairs
Bussaco
Butcher Bay
Cafe Colonial
Cafe de Bruxelles
Cascina
Chanterelle

Civetta
Cosette
Country
Cortina
Craftsteak
Cube 63
Da Filippo
Eighty One
Empire Diner
Etats-Unis
Fat Hippo
Five Front
Flying Cow
Gavroche
Gonzo
Gus & Gabriel
Gus' Place
Harbour
Hudson Cafeteria
Inagiku
Irving Mill
Kai
Kampuchea
Kitchen Club
Knife + Fork
La Rural
Le Boeuf à la Mode
Leela Lounge
Le Petit Marche
Le Refuge
Los Dados
Lucy Browne's
Lusso
Métisse
Metro Marche
Mott
Neo Sushi
Niche
Olana
Onda
1 Dominick
O'Neals'
Opus
Pamplona
Perle
Permanent Brunch
Planethailand 212
Pomme de Terre
Prem-on Thai
Primavera
Relish
River Room
Roberto Passon
Rock-n-Sake
Safran

SavorNY
Sharz Cafe & Wine Bar
Sonia Rose
Sweet Emily's
Table 8
Tailor
Talay
Tavern on the Green
Trata
Triangolo
Turquoise
Vento
Vong
West Branch
Yuki Sushi
Zoë
Zorzi

OUTDOOR DINING

(G=garden; P=patio; R=Rooftop;
S=sidewalk; T=terrace)

Alma | R | **Carroll Gdns**	21
Anella | P | **Greenpt**	26
A.O.C. | G | **W Vill**	19
☑ Aquagrill | T | **SoHo**	26
Aurora | G | **W'burg**	24
Avra | P | **E 40s**	25
Bacchus | G | **Boerum Hill**	21
☑ Barbetta | G | **W 40s**	20
Barolo | G | **SoHo**	19
Bar Pitti | S | **G Vill**	22
Barrio | P | **Park Slope**	17
Battery Gdns. | G, P, T | **Financial**	17
Bistro 33 | S | **Astoria**	20
☑ Blue Water | T | **Union Sq**	23
Boathouse | P | **E 70s**	18
Bobo | T | **W Vill**	21
Bogota | P | **Park Slope**	23
Bottino | G | **Chelsea**	20
Brass. Ruhlmann | P | **W 50s**	19
Bryant Park | G, R | **W 40s**	18
Cabana | T | **Seaport**	21
Cacio e Pepe | G, S | **E Vill**	21
Cafe Centro | S | **E 40s**	20
Cafe Fiorello | S | **W 60s**	20
Cávo | G, P | **Astoria**	20
Chimu | P | **W'burg**	25
Coffee Shop | S | **Union Sq**	15
☑ Convivio | P | **E 40s**	26
☑ Conviv. Osteria | G | **Park Slope**	26
Da Nico | G, S | **L Italy**	22
Da Silvano | S | **G Vill**	21
Employees Only | G | **W Vill**	20
☑ Esca | P | **W 40s**	25
Farm/Adderley | G | **Ditmas Pk**	24

SPECIAL FEATURES

POWER LUNCH

PRIVATE ROOMS/PARTIES

(Capacity figures following name are approximate; call venue for details)

NEW Casa Lever	20	E 50s	23
Cellini	100	E 50s	22
Centolire	30	E 80s	21
City Hall	110	TriBeCa	21
City Winery	18	SoHo	16
☑ Compass	44	W 70s	22
Craft	40	Flatiron	25
☑ Daniel	90	E 60s	28
☑ Del Frisco's	80	W 40s	25
Delmonico's	70	Financial	23
☑ Del Posto	200	Chelsea	26
☑ Eleven Madison	50	Flatiron	28
EN Japanese	25	W Vill	24
Felidia	45	E 50s	26
F.illi Ponte	120	TriBeCa	22
☑ FireBird	250	W 40s	20
☑ Four Seasons	300	E 50s	26
Fresco	45	E 50s	22
Gabriel's	36	W 60s	22
Geisha	25	E 60s	23
☑ Gramercy Tavern	22	Flatiron	28
Harry's Cafe/Steak	80	Financial	23
NEW Hurricane Club	80	Flatiron	-
☑ Il Buco	25	NoHo	26
Il Cortile	120	L Italy	23
Ilili	42	Chelsea	24
'Inoteca	30	LES	22
☑ Jean Georges	35	W 60s	28
☑ Keens	85	Garment	25
☑ La Grenouille	70	E 50s	28
Landmark Tavern	50	W 40s	18
☑ Le Bernardin	80	W 50s	29
☑ Le Cirque	90	E 50s	24
Le Perigord	35	E 50s	25
Le Zie 2000	22	Chelsea	22
NEW Lincoln	16	W 60s	-
Maloney/Porcelli	110	E 50s	23
☑ Matsuri	56	Chelsea	22
☑ Megu	50	TriBeCa	24
☑ Michael's	75	W 50s	21
☑ Milos	24	W 50s	27
☑ Modern	64	W 50s	26
Mr. Chow	35	E 50s	22
Mr. K's	50	E 50s	23
☑ Nobu	40, 50	multi.	26
Oceana	80	W 40s	23
Park	170	Chelsea	17
Parlor Steak	50	E 90s	22
Patroon	60	E 40s	22
Periyali	45	Flatiron	24
☑ Per Se	65	W 60s	28
☑ Picholine	22	W 60s	27
Raoul's	35	SoHo	23

Redeye Grill	75	W 50s	20
Remi	80	W 50s	23
Re Sette	40	W 40s	19
Riingo	35	E 40s	21
☑ River Café	100	Dumbo	26
Rock Ctr.	30	W 50s	18
Sambuca	150	W 70s	20
☑ Shun Lee Palace	30	E 50s	24
Solo	26	E 50s	26
☑ Sparks	250	E 40s	25
☑ Spice Market	30	Meatpacking	23
☑ Tao	26	E 50s	21
☑ Terrace in Sky	80	W 100s	22
Thalassa	120	TriBeCa	22
☑ Tocqueville	30	Union Sq	25
☑ Tribeca Grill	350	TriBeCa	22
☑ 21 Club	200	W 50s	22
☑ Valbella	80	Meatpacking	25
Water Club	210	Murray Hill	21

QUIET CONVERSATION

☑ Adour	E 50s	26
Allegretti	Flatiron	23
☑ Alto	E 50s	26
Aroma	NoHo	23
☑ Asiate	W 60s	24
☑ Aureole	W 40s	26
Giovanni	E 80s	23
Il Gattopardo	W 50s	25
☑ Jean Georges	W 60s	28
Kings' Carriage	E 80s	23
Kyotofu	W 40s	23
☑ La Grenouille	E 50s	28
Le Barricou	W'burg	21
☑ Le Bernardin	W 50s	29
☑ Marea	W 50s	27
☑ Masa/Bar Masa	W 60s	27
Mr. K's	E 50s	23
North Sq.	G Vill	23
Oak Room	W 50s	20
Palm Court	W 50s	-
☑ Per Se	W 60s	28
Petite Crev.	Carroll Gdns	24
Petrossian	W 50s	23
☑ Picholine	W 60s	27
Provence/Boite	Carroll Gdns	20
Rosanjin	TriBeCa	27
Seo	E 40s	21
Sfoglia	E 90s	23
Square Meal	E 90s	24
☑ Terrace in Sky	W 100s	22
☑ Tocqueville	Union Sq	25
Tsampa	E Vill	21
12 Chairs	SoHo	19

Ze Café | **E 50s** 22
Zenkichi | **W'burg** 25

RAW BARS

Ammos | **E 40s** 22
🅉 Aquagrill | **SoHo** 26
Arté | **G Vill** 18
Atlantic Grill | **E 70s** 23
🅉 Balthazar | **SoHo** 23
Bar Americain | **W 50s** 23
🅉 BLT Fish | **Flatiron** 24
🅉 Blue Ribbon | **multi.** 25
🅉 Blue Water | **Union Sq** 23
Bondi Rd. | **LES** 17
Brasserie Cognac | **W 50s** 19
NEW Broken Eng. | **Cobble Hill** –
NEW Choptank | **W Vill** 17
City Crab | **Flatiron** 19
City Hall | **TriBeCa** 21
City Lobster | **W 40s** 19
Docks Oyster | **E 40s** 19
NEW Ed's Chowder | **W 60s** 19
Ed's Lobster | **NoLita** 23
🅉 Esca | **W 40s** 25
NEW Faustina | **E Vill** 23
Fig & Olive | **multi.** 20
Fish | **W Vill** 21
Fishtail | **E 60s** 23
Flex Mussels | **E 80s** 23
Flor/Sol | **TriBeCa** 20
Giorgione | **SoHo** 24
Jack's Lux. | **E Vill** 27
London Lennie | **Rego Pk** 22
Lure Fishbar | **SoHo** 23
🅉 Marea | **W 50s** 27
NEW Mark | **E 70s** 24
Marlow/Sons | **W'burg** 24
Mercer Kitchen | **SoHo** 22
Mermaid | **E Vill** 21
Nove | **SI** 25
Oceana | **W 40s** 23
Ocean Grill | **W 70s** 24
Olea | **Ft Greene** 23
🅉 Oyster Bar | **E 40s** 22
Parlor Steak | **E 90s** 22
🅉 Pearl Oyster | **W Vill** 26
Pearl Room | **Bay Ridge** 22
P.J. Clarke's | **multi.** 17
NEW Plaza Food Hall | **W 50s** 22
Primehouse | **Murray Hill** 24
Riverview | **LIC** 20
Shelly's Tratt. | **W 50s** 20
South Fin | **SI** 19
🅉 Standard Grill | **Meatpacking** 21
NEW Strong Pl. | **Cobble Hill** –

Thalia | **W 50s** 20
Tosca Café | **Bronx** 21
🅉 21 Club | **W 50s** 22
Umberto's | **multi.** 19
Uncle Jack's | **multi.** 22
Walter Foods | **W'burg** 23

ROMANTIC PLACES

Algonquin | **W 40s** 18
Alma | **Carroll Gdns** 21
Alta | **G Vill** 24
🅉 Asiate | **W 60s** 24
August | **W Vill** 22
🅉 Aureole | **W 40s** 26
🅉 Balthazar | **SoHo** 23
🅉 Barbetta | **W 40s** 20
Barolo | **SoHo** 19
Battery Gdns. | **Financial** 17
🅉 Blue Hill | **G Vill** 27
Blue Ribbon Bakery | **W Vill** 24
Boathouse | **E 70s** 18
Bottino | **Chelsea** 20
🅉 Bouley | **TriBeCa** 27
CamaJe | **G Vill** 22
Capsouto Frères | **TriBeCa** 24
Caviar Russe | **E 50s** 25
Chez Josephine | **W 40s** 20
🅉 Conviv. Osteria | **Park Slope** 26
🅉 Daniel | **E 60s** 28
David Burke Townhse. | **E 60s** 24
🅉 Del Posto | **Chelsea** 26
Dressler | **W'burg** 25
Duane Park | **TriBeCa** 21
🅉 Eleven Madison | **Flatiron** 28
Erminia | **E 80s** 25
🅉 FireBird | **W 40s** 20
Firenze | **E 80s** 20
Flor/Sol | **TriBeCa** 20
🅉 Four Seasons | **E 50s** 26
Frankies | **LES** 24
Gascogne | **Chelsea** 21
Gigino | **Financial** 21
House | **Gramercy** 22
I Coppi | **E Vill** 22
🅉 Il Buco | **NoHo** 26
I Trulli | **Murray Hill** 23
Jack's Lux. | **E Vill** 27
James | **Prospect Hts** 24
JoJo | **E 60s** 25
Jolie | **Boerum Hill** 21
Kings' Carriage | **E 80s** 23
Kyotofu | **W 40s** 23
L'Absinthe | **E 60s** 22
Lady Mendl's | **Gramercy** 21
🅉 La Grenouille | **E 50s** 28

La Mangeoire | E 50s	20
NEW Lambs Club | Financial	-
La Ripaille | W Vill	20
Le Gigot | W Vill	24
Maria Pia | W 50s	20
Mari Vanna | Flatiron	20
Z Mas | W Vill	27
Mr. K's | E 50s	23
Nino's | E 70s	20
Olea | Ft Greene	23
Z One if by Land | W Vill	24
Pam Real Thai | W 40s	23
Paola's | E 90s	22
Pasha | W 70s	20
Periyali | Flatiron	24
Petrossian | W 50s	23
Philip Marie | W Vill	20
Z Piano Due | W 50s	24
Piccola Venezia | Astoria	25
Pinocchio | E 90s	22
Place | W Vill	21
Quercy | Cobble Hill	21
Raoul's | SoHo	23
Z River Café | Dumbo	26
Riverview | LIC	20
Rye | W'burg	23
Z Saul | Boerum Hill	26
Savoy | SoHo	24
Z Scalini Fedeli | TriBeCa	27
Z Sistina | E 80s	26
Z Spice Market | Meatpacking	23
NEW Taureau | E Vill	-
Teodora | E 50s	21
Z Terrace in Sky | W 100s	22
Z Tocqueville | Union Sq	25
Tre Dici/Steak | Chelsea	21
Uva | E 70s	21
View | W 40s	17
Z Wallsé | W Vill	26
Water Club | Murray Hill	21
Z Water's Edge | LIC	20
Zenkichi | W'burg	25

SENIOR APPEAL

Arté | G Vill	18
Artie's Deli | W 80s	18
Z Aureole | W 40s	26
Bamonte's | W'burg	23
Z Barbetta | W 40s	20
Z Barney Greengrass | W 80s	24
Bravo Gianni | E 60s	22
Campagnola | E 70s	24
Capsouto Frères | TriBeCa	24
Chadwick's | Bay Ridge	23
Chez Napoléon | W 50s	21

Dawat | E 50s	23
DeGrezia | E 50s	24
Z Del Posto | Chelsea	26
Due | E 70s	21
Elaine's | E 80s	14
Embers | Bay Ridge	21
Felidia | E 50s	26
Fiorini | E 50s	22
Gallagher's | W 50s	21
Giovanni | E 80s	23
Grifone | E 40s	23
Z Il Tinello | W 50s	25
Z Jean Georges | W 60s	28
Jubilee | E 50s	23
La Bonne Soupe | W 50s	18
Z La Grenouille | E 50s	28
La Mangeoire | E 50s	20
La Mirabelle | W 80s	23
Lanza | E Vill	18
La Petite Aub. | Murray Hill	21
Lattanzi | W 40s	22
NEW Le Caprice | E 60s	17
Z Le Cirque | E 50s	24
Le Marais | W 40s	22
Le Perigord | E 50s	25
Lusardi's | E 70s	24
NEW Mark | E 70s	24
Mr. K's | E 50s	23
Nicola's | E 80s	22
Nippon | E 50s	21
Oak Room | W 50s	20
Palm Court | W 50s	-
Pastrami Queen | E 70s	20
Z Piano Due | W 50s	24
Piccola Venezia | Astoria	25
Pietro's | E 40s	24
Ponticello | Astoria	24
Primola | E 60s	23
Quatorze Bis | E 70s	21
Quattro Gatti | E 80s	21
Rao's | Harlem	22
Z River Café | Dumbo	26
Rossini's | Murray Hill	24
Rughetta | E 80s	22
Russian Tea | W 50s	19
Z San Pietro | E 50s	25
Sardi's | W 40s	17
Z Saul | Boerum Hill	26
Scaletta | W 70s	21
Shun Lee West | W 60s	22
12 Chairs | SoHo	19

SINGLES SCENES

NEW Abe/Arthur | Meatpacking	22
Ajna Bar | Meatpacking	20

SPECIAL FEATURES

Angelo/Maxie's | **Flatiron**	21
Asia de Cuba | **Murray Hill**	23
Aspen Social | **W 40s**	18
Atlantic Grill | **E 70s**	23
Bagatelle | **Meatpacking**	18
Baraonda | **E 70s**	19
Barrio | **Park Slope**	17
🆕 Betel | **W Vill**	25
🆕 Bill's Bar | **Meatpacking**	20
ⓩ Blue Ribbon | **multi.**	25
ⓩ Blue Water | **Union Sq**	23
Bobo | **W Vill**	21
Boca Chica | **E Vill**	21
ⓩ🆕 Breslin | **Chelsea**	21
Brother Jimmy's | **multi.**	16
Bryant Park | **W 40s**	18
ⓩ Buddakan | **Chelsea**	24
Butter | **E Vill**	22
Cabana | **multi.**	21
Café Select | **SoHo**	19
Canyon Rd. | **E 70s**	20
Chinatown Brass. | **NoHo**	22
Citrus B&G | **W 70s**	19
Coffee Shop | **Union Sq**	15
ⓩ DBGB | **E Vill**	22
ⓩ Del Frisco's | **W 40s**	25
Delicatessen | **NoLita**	19
Dos Caminos | **multi.**	20
Double Crown | **NoHo**	20
Elephant | **E Vill**	21
Employees Only | **W Vill**	20
Félix | **SoHo**	17
Freemans | **LES**	21
Heartland | **multi.**	14
Hillstone | **multi.**	21
Hotel Griffou | **G Vill**	19
🆕 Hurricane Club | **Flatiron**	-
'Inoteca | **LES**	22
Joya | **Cobble Hill**	23
🆕 Kenmare | **L Italy**	21
Kingswood | **W Vill**	19
Koi | **W 40s**	23
La Esquina | **L Italy**	22
🆕 Lion | **G Vill**	-
Lure Fishbar | **SoHo**	23
Macao Trading | **TriBeCa**	18
Otto | **G Vill**	22
Pastis | **Meatpacking**	21
🆕 Peels | **E Vill**	-
Peep | **SoHo**	20
Pete's Tavern | **Gramercy**	16
🆕 Pulino's | **NoLita**	19
Schiller's | **LES**	19
Smith | **E Vill**	19
ⓩ Spice Market | **Meatpacking**	23

ⓩ Standard Grill | **Meatpacking**	21
Stanton Social | **LES**	23
STK | **Meatpacking**	23
SushiSamba | **multi.**	22
🆕 Tanuki | **Meatpacking**	19
ⓩ Tao | **E 50s**	21
Walter Foods | **W'burg**	23
Zarela | **E 50s**	22

SLEEPERS
(Fine food, but little known)

Anella | **Greenpt**	26
Arepas Café | **Astoria**	24
Café Katja | **LES**	24
Chimu | **W'burg**	25
Coals | **Bronx**	23
El Almacén | **W'burg**	24
Filippo's | **SI**	25
Ghenet | **Park Slope**	23
Greenwich Grill/Sushi Azabu | **TriBeCa**	25
Hibino | **Cobble Hill**	25
Il Bambino | **Astoria**	24
JJ's Asian Fusion | **Astoria**	24
Kabab Café | **Astoria**	25
Kafana | **E Vill**	24
Ki Sushi | **Boerum Hill**	26
Kuruma Zushi | **E 40s**	26
Le Pescadeux | **SoHo**	23
Limon | **Murray Hill**	24
Lorenzo's | **SI**	23
Luz | **Ft Greene**	24
Madangsui | **Garment**	23
Malagueta | **Astoria**	25
Matilda | **E Vill**	23
Melba's | **Harlem**	25
Mesa Coyoacan | **W'burg**	24
Miranda | **W'burg**	23
Nina's Argentin. | **E 90s**	23
Nirvana | **Murray Hill**	23
Palo Santo | **Park Slope**	25
Petite Crev. | **Carroll Gdns**	24
Ponty Bistro | **Gramercy**	23
Quaint | **Sunnyside**	25
Scalino | **Park Slope**	24
Sel de Mer | **W'burg**	24
Sentosa | **Flushing**	23
SobaKoh | **E Vill**	24
Sorella | **LES**	24
Sweetwater | **W'burg**	23
Toledo | **Murray Hill**	24
Tortilleria Nixtamal | **Corona**	25
Tulcingo del Valle | **W 40s**	24
Umi Nom | **Clinton Hill**	24
Vesta | **Astoria**	24

Zest | **SI**	25
Zoma | **Harlem**	25

SUNDAY BEST BETS

(See also Hotel Dining)

☑ Aquagrill | **SoHo**	26
☑ Aquavit | **E 50s**	25
☑ Artisanal | **Murray Hill**	23
☑ Balthazar | **SoHo**	23
Bar Americain | **W 50s**	23
☑ Blue Hill | **G Vill**	27
☑ Blue Ribbon | **SoHo**	25
☑ Blue Water | **Union Sq**	23
☑ Bouley | **TriBeCa**	27
Chez Oskar | **Ft Greene**	19
David Burke Townhse. | **E 60s**	24
Demarchelier | **E 80s**	18
5 Points | **NoHo**	22
☑ Gotham B&G | **G Vill**	27
☑ Gramercy Tavern | **Flatiron**	28
Lucky Strike | **SoHo**	17
☑ Lupa | **G Vill**	25
☑ Mesa Grill | **Flatiron**	23
Odeon | **TriBeCa**	20
☑ Ouest | **W 80s**	24
☑ Peter Luger | **W'burg**	27
Piccolo Angolo | **W Vill**	25
☑ Picholine | **W 60s**	27
Pomaire | **W 40s**	20
Prune | **E Vill**	24
☑ River Café | **Dumbo**	26
Solo | **E 50s**	26
Tratt. Dell'Arte | **W 50s**	21
☑ Tribeca Grill | **TriBeCa**	22
☑ Union Sq. Cafe | **Union Sq**	26
Water Club | **Murray Hill**	21

TEA SERVICE

Abigael's | **Garment**	20
Alice's Tea | **multi.**	19
☑ Asiate | **W 60s**	24
Cafe S.F.A. | **E 40s**	18
🆕 Crosby Bar | **SoHo**	19
Duane Park | **TriBeCa**	21
Kings' Carriage | **E 80s**	23
Lady Mendl's | **Gramercy**	21
Morgan | **Murray Hill**	20
North Sq. | **G Vill**	23
Palm Court | **W 50s**	-
🆕 Robert | **W 50s**	19
Russian Tea | **W 50s**	19
Sant Ambroeus | **multi.**	21
Sarabeth's | **multi.**	20
Sweet Melissa | **multi.**	20
☑ Tamarind | **Flatiron**	26
Tea & Sympathy | **W Vill**	19

🆕 Travertine | **NoLita**	22
Uncle Jack's | **multi.**	22

THEME RESTAURANTS

Braai | **W 50s**	21
Bubba Gump | **W 40s**	14
Cowgirl | **W Vill**	16
🆕 Hurricane Club | **Flatiron**	-
Ninja | **TriBeCa**	17
Ruby Foo's | **W 40s**	19

TRANSPORTING EXPERIENCES

Ajna Bar | **Meatpacking**	20
☑ Asiate | **W 60s**	24
☑ Balthazar | **SoHo**	23
Boathouse | **E 70s**	18
☑ Buddakan | **Chelsea**	24
Chez Josephine | **W 40s**	20
Double Crown | **NoHo**	20
☑ FireBird | **W 40s**	20
☑ Il Buco | **NoHo**	26
Ilili | **Chelsea**	24
☑ Keens | **Garment**	25
☑ La Grenouille | **E 50s**	28
🆕 Lambs Club | **Financial**	-
Le Colonial | **E 50s**	21
Mari Vanna | **Flatiron**	20
☑ Masa/Bar Masa | **W 60s**	27
☑ Matsuri | **Chelsea**	22
☑ Megu | **TriBeCa**	24
☑ Monkey Bar | **E 50s**	17
Ninja | **TriBeCa**	17
☑ One if by Land | **W Vill**	24
☑ Per Se | **W 60s**	28
🆕 Qi | **Union Sq**	22
Rao's | **Harlem**	22
☑ Spice Market | **Meatpacking**	23
☑ Tao | **E 50s**	21
Vatan | **Murray Hill**	23
☑ Water's Edge | **LIC**	20

VIEWS

Alma | **Carroll Gdns**	21
Angelina's | **SI**	22
Antica Venezia | **W Vill**	22
☑ Asiate | **W 60s**	24
☑ A Voce | **W 60s**	24
Battery Gdns. | **Financial**	17
Boathouse | **E 70s**	18
Bouchon Bakery | **W 60s**	24
Bryant Park | **W 40s**	18
Bubby's | **Dumbo**	18
Cabana | **Seaport**	21
Cafe S.F.A. | **E 40s**	18
Cipriani Dolci | **E 40s**	20

City Is. Lobster | **Bronx** | _19_
Cole's Dock | **SI** | _18_
Fairway Cafe | **Red Hook** | _18_
F.illi Ponte | **TriBeCa** | _22_
Gigino | **Financial** | _21_
Heartland | **Seaport** | _14_
Hudson River | **Harlem** | _21_
Lake Club | **SI** | _23_
Landmarc | **W 60s** | _20_
NEW Lincoln | **W 60s** | _-_
Lobster Box | **Bronx** | _18_
Marina Cafe | **SI** | _20_
Metrazur | **E 40s** | _21_
Michael Jordan | **E 40s** | _21_
🔼 Modern | **W 50s** | _26_
🔼 Per Se | **W 60s** | _28_
P.J. Clarke's | **Financial** | _17_
Porter House | **W 60s** | _24_
Portofino | **Bronx** | _21_
🔼 River Café | **Dumbo** | _26_
Riverview | **LIC** | _20_
NEW Robert | **W 50s** | _19_
Rock Ctr. | **W 50s** | _18_
Sea Grill | **W 40s** | _24_
South Fin | **SI** | _19_
Suteishi | **Seaport** | _22_
🔼 Terrace in Sky | **W 100s** | _22_
2 West | **Financial** | _21_
View | **W 40s** | _17_
Water Club | **Murray Hill** | _21_
🔼 Water's Edge | **LIC** | _20_

VISITORS ON EXPENSE ACCOUNT

🔼 Adour | **E 50s** | _26_
Anthos | **W 50s** | _24_
🔼 Aureole | **W 40s** | _26_
🔼 Babbo | **G Vill** | _27_
🔼 Bouley | **TriBeCa** | _27_
🔼 Café Boulud | **E 70s** | _27_
NEW Colicchio/Sons | **Chelsea** | _23_
🔼 Corton | **TriBeCa** | _26_
Craft | **Flatiron** | _25_
🔼 Daniel | **E 60s** | _28_
🔼 Del Frisco's | **W 40s** | _25_
🔼 Del Posto | **Chelsea** | _26_
🔼 Eleven Madison | **Flatiron** | _28_
🔼 Four Seasons | **E 50s** | _26_
🔼 Gari/Sushi | **W 40s** | _27_
Gordon Ramsay | **W 50s** | _23_
🔼 Gramercy Tavern | **Flatiron** | _28_
🔼 Il Mulino | **G Vill** | _27_
🔼 Jean Georges | **W 60s** | _28_
🔼 Keens | **Garment** | _25_
Kuruma Zushi | **E 40s** | _26_
🔼 La Grenouille | **E 50s** | _28_

NEW Lambs Club | **Financial** | _-_
🔼 Le Bernardin | **W 50s** | _29_
🔼 Le Cirque | **E 50s** | _24_
🔼 Marea | **W 50s** | _27_
🔼 Masa/Bar Masa | **W 60s** | _27_
🔼 Milos | **W 50s** | _27_
🔼 Modern | **W 50s** | _26_
Montebello | **E 50s** | _24_
🔼 Nobu | **multi.** | _26_
🔼 Palm | **multi.** | _24_
🔼 Per Se | **W 60s** | _28_
🔼 Peter Luger | **W'burg** | _27_
🔼 Picholine | **W 60s** | _27_
🔼 River Café | **Dumbo** | _26_
🔼 Scarpetta | **Chelsea** | _26_
🔼 SHO Shaun Hergatt | **Financial** | _26_
🔼 Spice Market | **Meatpacking** | _23_
🔼 Sushi Yasuda | **E 40s** | _28_
🔼 Union Sq. Cafe | **Union Sq** | _26_
🔼 Veritas | **Flatiron** | _26_

WATERSIDE

Angelina's | **SI** | _22_
Battery Gdns. | **Financial** | _17_
Boathouse | **E 70s** | _18_
Bubby's | **Dumbo** | _18_
Cabana | **Seaport** | _21_
City Is. Lobster | **Bronx** | _19_
Cole's Dock | **SI** | _18_
Gigino | **Financial** | _21_
Lake Club | **SI** | _23_
London Lennie | **Rego Pk** | _22_
Marina Cafe | **SI** | _20_
Portofino | **Bronx** | _21_
🔼 River Café | **Dumbo** | _26_
Riverview | **LIC** | _20_
South Fin | **SI** | _19_
Tatiana | **Brighton Bch** | _21_
Water Club | **Murray Hill** | _21_
🔼 Water's Edge | **LIC** | _20_

WINNING WINE LISTS

Accademia/Vino | **multi.** | _19_
🔼 Adour | **E 50s** | _26_
Aldea | **Flatiron** | _25_
Allegretti | **Flatiron** | _23_
Alta | **G Vill** | _24_
🔼 Alto | **E 50s** | _26_
Annisa | **W Vill** | _28_
Anthos | **W 50s** | _24_
🔼 Artisanal | **Murray Hill** | _23_
🔼 Asiate | **W 60s** | _24_
🔼 Aureole | **W 40s** | _26_
🔼 A Voce | **Flatiron** | _24_
🔼 Babbo | **G Vill** | _27_

Bacchus | **Boerum Hill**	21	
Z Balthazar | **SoHo**	23	
Z Barbetta | **W 40s**	20	
Bar Boulud | **W 60s**	23	
Barolo | **SoHo**	19	
Becco | **W 40s**	23	
Benoit | **W 50s**	20	
Z BLT Fish | **Flatiron**	24	
BLT Market | **W 50s**	22	
BLT Prime | **Gramercy**	25	
Z BLT Steak | **E 50s**	25	
Blue Fin | **W 40s**	22	
Z Blue Hill | **G Vill**	27	
Bobby Van's | **multi.**	22	
Bottega/Vino | **E 50s**	22	
Z Bouley | **TriBeCa**	27	
Braeburn | **W Vill**	21	
Z Café Boulud | **E 70s**	27	
Café d'Alsace | **E 80s**	21	
Café Select | **SoHo**	19	
Capital Grille | **E 40s**	24	
Casa Mono | **Gramercy**	26	
'Cesca | **W 70s**	23	
City Hall | **TriBeCa**	21	
City Winery | **SoHo**	16	
Z Compass | **W 70s**	22	
Counter | **E Vill**	21	
Craft | **Flatiron**	25	
Z Cru | **G Vill**	25	
Z Daniel | **E 60s**	28	
David Burke Townhse. | **E 60s**	24	
Z DB Bistro Moderne | **W 40s**	25	
Z Del Frisco's | **W 40s**	25	
Dell'anima | **W Vill**	25	
Delmonico's | **Financial**	23	
Z Del Posto | **Chelsea**	26	
NEW Eataly | **Flatiron**	-	
Z Eleven Madison | **Flatiron**	28	
Z Esca | **W 40s**	25	
Felidia | **E 50s**	26	
Z Gilt | **E 50s**	24	
Z Gotham B&G | **G Vill**	27	
Z Gramercy Tavern | **Flatiron**	28	
Harry's Cafe/Steak | **Financial**	23	
Hearth | **E Vill**	24	
Z Il Buco | **NoHo**	26	
'Ino | **W Vill**	24	
'Inoteca | **LES**	22	
I Trulli | **Murray Hill**	23	
Z Jean Georges | **W 60s**	28	
Landmarc | **multi.**	20	
La Pizza Fresca | **Flatiron**	23	
Z Le Bernardin | **W 50s**	29	

Le Charlot | **E 60s**	21	
Z Le Cirque | **E 50s**	24	
Z Lupa | **G Vill**	25	
NEW Maialino | **Gramercy**	25	
Z Marea | **W 50s**	27	
Z Mas | **W Vill**	27	
Z Megu | **TriBeCa**	24	
Z Michael's | **W 50s**	21	
Z Milos | **W 50s**	27	
Z Modern | **W 50s**	26	
Morrell Wine | **W 40s**	19	
Motorino | **multi.**	24	
Nice Matin | **W 70s**	20	
Oceana | **W 40s**	23	
Otto | **G Vill**	22	
Z Ouest | **W 80s**	24	
Z Per Se | **W 60s**	28	
Z Picholine | **W 60s**	27	
Pomaire | **W 40s**	20	
Porter House | **W 60s**	24	
Post House | **E 60s**	24	
Primehouse | **Murray Hill**	24	
Raoul's | **SoHo**	23	
Z River Café | **Dumbo**	26	
Rothmann's | **E 50s**	23	
Rouge Tomate | **E 60s**	23	
Salumeria Rosi | **W 70s**	24	
Z San Pietro | **E 50s**	25	
Z Scalini Fedeli | **TriBeCa**	27	
Z Scarpetta | **Chelsea**	26	
NEW SD26 | **Murray Hill**	22	
Z SHO Shaun Hergatt | **Financial**	26	
Z Smith/Wollensky | **E 40s**	24	
Solera | **E 50s**	21	
Z Sparks | **E 40s**	25	
Z Tabla | **Flatiron**	25	
Z Telepan | **W 60s**	26	
Terrazza Toscana | **W 50s**	21	
Terroir | **multi.**	24	
Thalassa | **TriBeCa**	23	
Tía Pol | **Chelsea**	25	
Tommaso | **Dyker Hts**	24	
Trestle on 10th | **Chelsea**	20	
Z Tribeca Grill | **TriBeCa**	22	
Tse Yang | **E 50s**	24	
Z 21 Club | **W 50s**	22	
Txikito | **Chelsea**	24	
Z Union Sq. Cafe | **Union Sq**	26	
Uva | **E 70s**	21	
Z Valbella | **Meatpacking**	25	
Z Veritas | **Flatiron**	26	
Z Wallsé | **W Vill**	26	
Z Water's Edge | **LIC**	20	

SPECIAL FEATURES

Wine Vintage Chart

This chart is based on our 0 to 30 scale. The ratings (by U. of South Carolina law professor **Howard Stravitz**) reflect vintage quality and the wine's readiness to drink. A dash means the wine is past its peak or too young to rate. Loire ratings are for dry whites.

Whites	95	96	97	98	99	00	01	02	03	04	05	06	07	08	09
France:															
Alsace	24	23	23	25	23	25	26	23	21	24	25	24	26	25	25
Burgundy	27	26	22	21	24	24	24	27	23	26	27	25	26	25	25
Loire Valley	-	-	-	-	-	-	-	26	21	23	27	23	24	24	26
Champagne	26	27	24	23	25	24	21	26	21	-	-	-	-	-	-
Sauternes	21	23	25	23	24	24	29	24	26	21	26	24	27	25	27
California:															
Chardonnay	-	-	-	-	22	21	25	26	22	26	29	24	27	25	-
Sauvignon Blanc	-	-	-	-	-	-	-	-	-	26	25	27	25	24	25
Austria:															
Grüner V./Riesl.	22	-	25	22	25	21	22	25	26	25	24	26	25	23	27
Germany:	21	26	21	22	24	20	29	25	26	27	28	25	27	25	25

Reds	95	96	97	98	99	00	01	02	03	04	05	06	07	08	09
France:															
Bordeaux	26	25	23	25	24	29	26	24	26	25	28	24	23	25	27
Burgundy	26	27	25	24	27	22	24	27	25	23	28	25	25	24	26
Rhône	26	22	23	27	26	27	26	-	26	25	27	25	26	23	26
Beaujolais	-	-	-	-	-	-	-	-	-	-	27	24	25	23	27
California:															
Cab./Merlot	27	25	28	23	25	-	27	26	25	24	26	23	26	23	25
Pinot Noir	-	-	-	-	-	-	25	26	25	26	24	23	27	25	24
Zinfandel	-	-	-	-	-	-	25	23	27	22	24	21	21	25	23
Oregon:															
Pinot Noir	-	-	-	-	-	-	-	26	24	26	25	24	23	27	25
Italy:															
Tuscany	25	24	29	24	27	24	27	-	25	27	26	26	25	24	-
Piedmont	21	27	26	25	26	28	27	-	24	27	26	25	26	26	-
Spain:															
Rioja	26	24	25	-	25	24	28	-	23	27	26	24	24	-	26
Ribera del Duero/ Priorat	26	27	25	24	25	24	27	-	24	27	26	24	26	-	-
Australia:															
Shiraz/Cab.	24	26	25	28	24	24	27	27	25	26	27	25	23	-	-
Chile:	-	-	-	-	25	23	26	24	25	24	27	25	24	26	-
Argentina:															
Malbec	-	-	-	-	-	-	-	-	-	25	26	27	25	24	-

Most Popular Restaurants

Map coordinates follow each name. Sections A–H lie south of 34th Street (see adjacent map). Sections I–P lie north of 34th Street (see reverse side of map).

1 Gramercy Tavern (B-4)

2 Le Bernardin (O-3)

3 Eleven Madison Park (B-4)

4 Peter Luger Steak House (E-7)

5 Union Square Cafe (B-4)

6 Babbo (C-3)

7 Daniel (M-4)

8 Gotham Bar & Grill (C-4)

9 Balthazar (E-4)

10 Jean Georges (N-3)

11 Bouley (F-4)

12 Nobu (F-3, N-4)

13 Per Se (N-3)

14 Becco (O-3)

15 Café Boulud (L-4)

16 Atlantic Grill (L-5, N-3)

17 Blue Water Grill (B-4)

18 Aureole (P-4)

19 Modern (O-4)

20 Del Posto (C-2)

21 Artisanal (A-4)

22 Aquagrill (E-3)

23 La Grenouille (O-4)

74 Four Seasons (O-5)

25 Blue Hill (D-3)

26 Il Mulino (D-4)

27 Rosa Mexicano (B-4, N-3, N-6)

28 Del Frisco's (O-4)

29 A Voce (B-4, N-3)

30 Palm (F-3, O-3, P-5)

31 Aquavit (N-4)

32 5 Napkin Burger (K-2, N-7, P-3)

33 21 Club (O-4)

34 Bar Americain (O-3)

35 Shake Shack (B-4, K-5, L-2, P-3, P-7)

36 Felidia (N-5)

37 Buddakan (C-2)

38 Carmine's (K-2, P-3)

39 Convivio (P-6)

40 Bar Boulud (N-3)

41 Blue Smoke (A-4, P-7)

42 Katz's Delicatessen (D-5)

43 River Café (G-6)

44 Marea (N-3)

45 Spice Market (C-2)

46 Sushi Yasuda (P-5)

47 Telepan (M-3)

48 Tabla (B-4)

49 One if by Land, Two if by Sea (D-3)

50 BLT Steak (N-5)

ZAGATMAP

Manhattan Subway Map